PENGUIN ACADEMICS

THE SPIRIT OF SOCIOLOGY

A READER

SECOND EDITION

Ron Matson

Wichita State University

PEARSON
and

Boston   New York   San Francisco
Mexico City   Montreal   Toronto   London   Madrid   Munich   Paris
Hong Kong   Singapore   Tokyo   Cape Town   Sydney

Executive Editor: Jeff Lasser
Series Editorial Assistant: Lauren Houlihan
Senior Marketing Manager: Kelly May
Production Supervisor: Karen Mason
Editorial-Production Service: GGS Book Services
Composition and Prepress Buyer: Linda Cox
Manufacturing Buyer: Debbie Rossi
Cover Administrator: Linda Knowles
Electronic Composition: GGS Book Services
Interior Design: Penguin Academics

For related titles and support materials, visit our online catalog at
www.ablongman.com.

ISBN 13: 978-0-205-52464-8
ISBN 10:   0-205-52464-8

Library of Congress Cataloging-in-Publication Data

The spirit of sociology: a reader / [edited by] Ron Matson.—2nd ed.
    p. cm.
    Includes bibliographical references.
    ISBN 978-0-205-52464-8 (pbk.)
1. Sociology. 2. Applied sociology. 3. United States—Social conditions—1980-
I. Matson, Ronald R. (Ronald Robert)

    HM585.S67 2008
    301—dc22

                                                        2007017854

Printed in the United States of America

10 9 8 7 6 5   11 10

*It is with deep gratitude that I dedicate this volume
to my parents, Ed and Grace Matson, and
my aunt and uncle, Lucy and D. Wayne George.
They taught me, unselfishly, the joy of learning and teaching.*

contents

PART 2   The Organization of Society   65

It is interesting that parent messages about racial pride positively affect peer self-esteem, but school self-esteem was negatively affected. We all might wonder how, as children, our socialization experiences affected our self-concepts and identities.

This is a classic example of opportunistic research that allows for the examination of the age-old controversy of "nature versus nurture." Davis writes about two young girls who were isolated from social interaction as they developed. Their lack of physical, social, and intellectual development gives ample evidence regarding the importance of socialization over genetics.

Sociologists are not immune to the influences of social class, any more than others. Morris and Grimes give us a glimpse of how working-class sociologists must deal with the inherent contradictions of upward mobility when they become professionals. Can the readers look back and see how their childhood, class-based socialization experiences have affected them?

In a personal and readable account, Lemert is able to show us how we develop a sociological imagination. Specifically, the discussion and review of Durkheim and Mills give us a way to see and understand social structure, the macro-level variables that have such a dramatic impact on our personal lives.

Chambliss uses exceptional qualitative skills to investigate the relationship between social class and boys' participation in gangs. The intricate combination of observational data with theory bridges the gap between the structural world and the interpersonal world, and this gives all of us a lesson on how we might connect these two sets of social variables.

The interactions between married couples are an excellent place to see how structure affects behavior. Rubin uses rich text from interviews and therapy sessions to demonstrate the gender-structure effects on marriage relationships. The paradox of this "approach-avoidance dance" will raise important questions for all of us as we deal with cross-gender relations.

sane people and how they are defined by the context of the institution and the treatment staff. Isn't it ironic that only the mental patients knew the "visitors" were sane?

PART 3 Social Inequalities 227

disaster for certain species is being created by the human elements in the systems, and overpopulation, at base, is the cause of a great portion of this global disaster.

introduction and author's note to the second edition

In preparing a second edition to a reader in sociology, I have been struck with how rapidly things change and how quickly society begins to unfold in different directions. September 11, 2001, and the consequences of this single event, put into motion thousands of daily changes in the lives of millions of people around the globe. On the turn of one dramatic event, the world was changed, and the ramifications of the "War on Terrorism" are now being woven into all of our lives. Katrina, the violent hurricane which hit New Orleans on September 29, 2005, brought personal despair in the hardest hit neighborhoods and political upheaval at the national level—those of us watching have learned lessons about social class, race, power, corruption, and compassion. In the last three years since the first edition was being prepared, political winds have changed dramatically and new faces appear in the most important places in the U.S. government. Perhaps it is our involvement in Iraq, in addition to the terrorism and the tsunami in southeast Asia, that have made me much more aware of being a global citizen in a smaller and more interconnected world. The new readings chosen for this second edition reflect this awareness and change.

My first focus while preparing the manuscript for this book has been the teaching possibilities of an introductory reader for sociology. It is my fervent wish that professors and students will find the selections and introductions to each section stimulating and educational. My second focus has been the diversity of sociology itself. Trying to bring a fair and balanced presentation of sociology is a daunting but rewarding task. I have come to a deepened appreciation for what it is we all do as students and teachers in a discipline that has such a broad application to life.

Conceptually, this volume centers around 3 central ideas to create and organize 45 readings in 15 topic areas or three readings per topic. First, readings were chosen to demonstrate the quantitative or theoretical ideas representative of the dominant scientific ethos of sociology. Second, readings were chosen to illustrate the qualitative approach to understanding social life, which is so much a part of both the historical and contemporary settings of sociology. Third, readings were selected to look at what sociologists do with their degrees in sociology—something very applied, something biographical, that enables students to see what sociology is through the people who *do sociology*. In this last regard, students will be exposed to the applications of an education in sociology beyond the theory and research done by Ph.D.'s in academic settings. This organization is designed to give the users of the book a more "complete" look at sociology as a science and as a career.

The spirit of sociology is an idea that embraces many qualities used to examine a "discipline." A discipline, as defined in the dictionary (Webster 1986, 360), is "a subject that is taught; a field of study." Disciplines have disciples, "a convinced adherent of a school . . . " (p. 360), and sociology educates sociologists who become adherents of the discipline's tenents and spread the "word" in practice and in education. The "spirit" of sociology would capture the "animating or vital principle," it would present the "feeling, quality, or disposition," and "general intent or real meaning" (p. 1137) of our discipline. Importantly, many sociologists who are the disciples of our discipline have an "enthusiastic loyalty" (p. 1137)—where enthusiasm itself translates literally to "filled with the spirit." I believe there is for many who wear the mantle of sociology a strong commitment to our discipline and our work, a passion that shows itself in the research and teaching and practice of sociology.

Welcome to the passionate exploration of a field of study, one where people often care deeply about their research, their ideas, and their clients. This author shares their excitement and hopes to bring such energy to the volume you have in your hands. Dispassionate science often languishes in objectivity and cold numbers that help with our research and publications, but in the background of these products are people, very alive people, who search for understanding and justice with an intense desire to make the world a better place for everyone. And, as you will see in many pages that follow, the world needs as much help as it can get to become a more humane and just place for all its inhabitants.

Acknowledgments (First Edition)

This has been a project that included the work and support of many people. Nikki Mooers and Jenni Osborne were my able Graduate Teaching Assistants and they worked selflessly when I needed their energy and skill.

The people at Allyn & Bacon–Longman were extremely helpful, and I want to thank Andrea Christie, Sara Owen, and, mostly, Executive Editor Jeff Lasser. Jeffrey Teachout, my most able and trusted assistant on the project, devoted himself to the details of permissions and paperwork—without complaint or error—and this collection is as much his as anyone's. Finally, I want to thank my family, especially Linda, who is more understanding than I deserve.

As I spoke and wrote about the collection, the ownership pronoun was always "we" and not "I," and at the end of more than a year of planning and editing and writing, *we* did it!

Acknowledgments (Second Edition)

Doing a second edition brought me into connections with new and supportive persons along the way. Holly Fussell worked with speed and a most positive attitude by retrieving materials and copying. To her for her work skills and spirit, I am grateful.

Once again, the people at Allyn & Bacon–Longman have handled me with kid gloves when a sledge hammer might have been more appropriate. For all the patience and connections this past year, I say thanks. Jeff Lasser deserves special acknowledgment for his management of and attention to this project, and Lauren Houlihan provided sparks of enthusiasm at the perfect moments.

Writing and editing can produce isolation, separation, and preoccupation. Linda, my wife and partner, was involved, patient, and completely understanding. For that, and more, I am eternally devoted.

PART ONE

The Sociological Perspective

Introduction
to the Discipline

"The first wisdom of sociology is that things are not as they seem."

—Peter Berger, *Invitation to Sociology*

IF WHAT PETER BERGER SAYS ABOUT SOCIOLOGY IS TRUE, then the discipline of sociology can aid students in discovering what is real about society and social life. If "things are not what they seem" on the surface, then what are things like "really"? This idea suggests that most of us live in a world that we don't understand. If we are not questioning what we see on the surface of society, the things that seem real to us in our daily lives may actually be illusions. The goal of sociology, therefore, and of this first topic, is to aid students in the development of the sociological perspective, or as C. Wright Mills writes, "the sociological imagination."

"The promise of sociology" is to illuminate the social world so that people can understand it and help themselves to a life lived with greater efficacy, a greater ability to understand and control their lives. Some people believe that since they live in society and are surviving, they understand it. Sociologists assert that most people do not understand society any more than they understand the physiology of their own bodies. Who among us could explain the intricate interactions between the digestive and cardiovascular systems, which are so much a part of our physical selves? If we could understand life by being close to it or living

3

in it, then what would be the purpose of education in any subject? Most of us have a long way to go to appreciate fully the social lives we lead.

Please enter into the study of sociology, these preliminary steps in developing a sociological perspective, with an openness to learn. Most of us are very inquisitive about other people—we love to watch them in shopping malls, listen to their conversations in restaurants, and often see ourselves in their actions. It is this curiosity, this openness, that will aid all of us in coming to the sociological perspective. It is important to note that this process of developing and using a sociological imagination has the power to transform the world as we know it and transform our personal lives in the process. To see the social world as it really is, rather than as it appears, is a gift that will last a lifetime—a gift that will benefit the learner in any social situation.

Society, in all of its complexity, has multiple layers. Much like an onion, what we see on the surface tells us little about what lies beneath. Once peeled and cut, the onion can provide delicious flavor and tears. In much the same way, society holds for us these paradoxical opposites—it nurtures us and frees us to attain full potential as human beings while it creates a prison of rules to follow that take away our ability to be free at all. Living creatively inside this paradox will take all the understanding we can attain, and it will also require that we continue to learn and be adaptive as the society around us changes at an ever-faster pace. Having a sociological imagination will truly be a gift that comes from the discipline of sociology, but a gift we give ourselves through increasing awareness about society and our personal lives.

In this first topic articles by Peter Berger, C. Wright Mills, and W. Richard Stephens offer the first glimpse of the discipline of sociology. Peter Berger writes an invitation to study sociology that presents our discipline as one with exciting possibilities. He invites all of us to a discipline where people are benefited if they have a curiosity about things social. C. Wright Mills writes that the sociological imagination must be informed by seeing the connection between our personal lives (biography) and larger social structures (history) that greatly affect us. In this selection we will see that personal *troubles* and social *issues* are closely related, and understanding the relationship will illuminate part of the social world many of us have never seen before. Finally, W. Richard Stephens presents what it means to have a career in sociology and what we might do to "make the most of our first class in sociology." He will give us five important ideas to guide us through an Introduction to Sociology course with the intent of pushing us toward a life with increased relevance and meaning.

PETER BERGER

Invitation to Sociology

We would say then that the sociologist (that is, the one we would really like to invite to our game) is a person intensively, endlessly, shamelessly interested in the doings of men. His natural habitat is all the human gathering places of the world, wherever men* come together. The sociologist may be interested in many other things. But his consuming interest remains in the world of men, their institutions, their history, their passions. And since he is interested in men, nothing that men do can be altogether tedious for him. He will naturally be interested in the events that engage men's ultimate beliefs, their moments of tragedy and grandeur and ecstasy. But he will also be fascinated by the commonplace, the everyday. He will know reverence, but this reverence will not prevent him from wanting to see and to understand. He may sometimes feel revulsion or contempt. But this also will not deter him from wanting to have his questions answered. The sociologist, in his quest for understanding, moves through the world of men without respect for the usual lines of demarcation. Nobility and degradation, power and obscurity, intelligence and folly—these are equally *interesting* to him, however unequal they may be in his personal values or tastes. Thus his questions may lead him to all possible levels of society, the best and the least known places, the most respected and the most despised. And, if he is a good sociologist, he will find himself in all these places because his own questions have so taken possession of him that he has little choice but to seek for answers.

It would be possible to say the same things in a lower key. We could say that the sociologist, but for the grace of his academic title, is

*[To be understood as people or persons.]

the man who must listen to gossip despite himself, who is tempted to look through keyholes, to read other people's mail, to open closed cabinets. Before some otherwise unoccupied psychologist sets out now to construct an aptitude test for sociologists on the basis of sublimated *voyeurism*, let us quickly say that we are speaking merely by way of analogy. Perhaps some little boys consumed with curiosity to watch their maiden aunts in the bathroom later become inveterate sociologists. This is quite uninteresting. What interests us is the curiosity that grips any sociologist in front of a closed door behind which there are human voices. If he is a good sociologist, he will want to open that door, to understand these voices. Behind each closed door he will anticipate some new facet of human life not yet perceived and understood.

The sociologist will occupy himself with matters that others regard as too sacred or as too distasteful for dispassionate investigation. He will find rewarding the company of priests or of prostitutes, depending not on his personal preferences but on the questions he happens to be asking at the moment. He will also concern himself with matters that others may find much too boring. He will be interested in the human interaction that goes with warfare or with great intellectual discoveries, but also in the relations between people employed in a restaurant or between a group of little girls playing with their dolls. His main focus of attention is not the ultimate significance of what men do, but the action in itself, as another example of the infinite richness of human conduct. So much for the image of our playmate.

In these journeys through the world of men the sociologist will inevitably encounter other professional Peeping Toms. Sometimes these will resent his presence, feeling that he is poaching on their preserves. In some places the sociologist will meet up with the economist, in others with the political scientist, in yet others with the psychologist or the ethnologist. Yet chances are that the questions that have brought him to these same places are different from the ones that propelled his fellow trespassers. The sociologist's questions always remain essentially the same: "What are people doing with each other here?" "What are their relationships to each other?" "How are these relationships organized in institutions?" "What are the collective ideas that move men and institutions?" In trying to answer these questions in specific instances, the sociologist will, of course, have to deal with economic or political matters, but he will do so in a way rather different from that of the economist or the political scientist. The scene that he contemplates is the same human scene that these other scientists concern themselves with. But the sociologist's angle of vision is different. When this is understood, it becomes clear that it makes little sense to try to stake out a special enclave within which the sociologist will carry on business in his own right. Like Wesley the sociologist will have to confess that his parish is the world. But unlike some latter-day Wesleyans he will gladly share this parish with others. There is, however, one traveler whose path the sociologist will cross more often than anyone else's on his journeys. This is the historian. Indeed, as soon as the sociologist turns from the present to the past, his preoccupations are very hard indeed to distinguish from those of the historian . . . the sociological journey will be much impoverished unless it is punctuated frequently by conversation with that other particular traveler.

Any intellectual activity derives excitement from the moment it becomes a trail of discovery. In some fields of learning this is the discovery of worlds previously unthought and unthinkable. This is the excitement of the astronomer or of the nuclear physicist on the antipodal boundaries of the realities that man is capable of conceiving. But it can also be the excitement of bacteriology or geology. In a different way it can be the excitement of the linguist discovering new realms of human expression or of the anthropologist exploring human customs in faraway countries. In such discovery, when undertaken with passion, a widening of awareness, sometimes a veritable transformation of consciousness, occurs. The universe turns out to be much more wonder full than one had ever dreamed. The excitement of sociology is usually of a different sort. Sometimes, it is true, the sociologist penetrates into worlds that had previously been quite unknown to him—for instance, the world of crime, or the world of some bizarre religious sect, or the world fashioned by the exclusive concerns of some group such as medical specialists or military leaders or advertising executives. However, much of the time the sociologist moves in sectors of experience that are familiar to him and to most people in his society. He investigates communities, institutions and activities that one can read about every day in the newspapers. Yet there is another excitement of discovery beckoning in his investigations. It is not the excitement of coming upon the totally unfamiliar, but rather the excitement of finding the familiar becoming transformed in its meaning. The fascination of sociology lies in the fact that its perspective makes us see in a new light the very world in which we have lived all our lives. This also constitutes a transformation of consciousness. Moreover, this transformation is more relevant existentially than that of many other intellectual disciplines, because it is more difficult to segregate in some special compartment of the mind. The astronomer does not live in the remote galaxies, and the nuclear physicist can, outside his laboratory, eat and laugh and marry and vote without thinking about the insides of the atom. The geologist looks at rocks only at appropriate times, and the linguist speaks English with his wife. The sociologist lives in society, on the job and off it. His own life, inevitably, is part of his subject matter. Men being what they are, sociologists too manage to segregate their professional insights from their everyday affairs. But it is a rather difficult feat to perform in good faith.

The sociologist moves in the common world of men, close to what most of them would call real. The categories he employs in his analyses are only refinements of the categories by which other men live—power, class, status, race, ethnicity. As a result, there is a deceptive simplicity and obviousness about some sociological investigations. One reads them, nods at the familiar scene, remarks that one has heard all this before and don't people have better things to do than to waste their time on truisms—until one is suddenly brought up against an insight that radically questions everything one had previously assumed about this familiar scene. This is the point at which one begins to sense the excitement of sociology.

Let us take a specific example. Imagine a sociology class in a Southern college where almost all the students are white Southerners. Imagine a lecture on the subject of the racial system of the South. The lecturer is talking here of matters that have been familiar to his students from the time of their infancy. Indeed, it may be that they are much more familiar with the minutiae of this system than he is. They are quite bored as a result. It seems to them that he is only using more pretentious words to describe what they already know. Thus he may use the term "caste," one commonly used now by American sociologists to describe the Southern racial system. But in explaining the term he shifts to traditional Hindu society, to make it clearer. He then goes on to analyze the magical beliefs inherent in caste tabus, the social dynamics of *commensalism* and *connubium*, the economic interests concealed within the system, the way in which religious beliefs relate to the tabus, the effects of the caste system upon the industrial development of the society and vice versa—all in India. But suddenly India is not very far away at all. The lecture then goes back to its Southern theme. The familiar now seems not quite so familiar anymore. Questions are raised that are new, perhaps raised angrily, but raised all the same. And at least some of the students have begun to understand that there are functions involved in this business of race that they have not read about in the newspapers (at least not those in their hometowns) and that their parents have not told them—partly, at least, because neither the newspapers nor the parents knew about them.

It can be said that the first wisdom of sociology is this—things are not what they seem. This too is a deceptively simple statement. It ceases to be simple after a while. Social reality turns out to have many layers of meaning. The discovery of each new layer changes the perception of the whole.

Anthropologists use the term "culture shock" to describe the impact of a totally new culture upon a newcomer. In an extreme instance such shock will be experienced by the Western explorer who is told, halfway through dinner, that he is eating the nice old lady he had been chatting with the previous day—a shock with predictable physiological if not moral consequences. Most explorers no longer encounter cannibalism in their travels today. However, the first encounters with polygamy or with puberty rites or even with the way some nations drive their automobiles can be quite a shock to an American visitor. With the shock may go not only disapproval or disgust but a sense of excitement that things can *really* be that different from what they are at home. To some extent, at least, this is the excitement of any first travel abroad. The experience of sociological discovery could be described as "culture shock" minus geographical displacement. In other words, the sociologist travels at home—with shocking results. He is unlikely to find that he is eating a nice old lady for dinner. But the discovery, for instance, that his own church has considerable money invested in the missile industry or that a few blocks from his home there are people who engage in cultic orgies may not be drastically different in emotional impact. Yet we would not want to imply that sociological discoveries are always or even usually outrageous to moral sentiment. Not at all. What they have in common with exploration in distant lands, however, is the sudden illumination of new and unsuspected facets of human existence in society. This is the excitement and . . . the humanistic justification of sociology.

People who like to avoid shocking discoveries, who prefer to believe that society is just what they were taught in Sunday School, who like the safety of the rules and the maxims of what Alfred Schuetz has called the "world-taken-for-granted," should stay away from sociology. People who feel no temptation before closed doors, who have no curiosity about human beings, who are content to admire scenery without wondering about the people who live in those houses on the other side of that river, should probably also stay away from sociology. They will find it unpleasant or, at any rate, unrewarding. People who are interested in human beings only if they can change, convert or reform them should also be warned, for they will find sociology much less useful than they hoped. And people whose interest is mainly in their own conceptual constructions will do just as well to turn to the study of little white mice. Sociology will be satisfying, in the long run, only to those who can think of nothing more entrancing than to watch men and to understand things human.

It may now be clear that we have, albeit deliberately, understated the case in the title of this chapter. To be sure, sociology is an individual pastime in the sense that it interests some men and bores others. Some like to observe human beings, others to experiment with mice. The world is big enough to hold all kinds and there is no logical priority for one interest as against another. But the word "pastime" is weak in describing what we mean. Sociology is more like a passion. The sociological perspective is more like a demon that possesses one, that drives one compellingly, again and again, to the questions that are its own. An introduction to sociology is, therefore, an invitation to a very special kind of passion.

STUDY QUESTIONS

1. What personal qualities does Berger argue will make for a good sociologist?
2. Why might we be shocked as sociology reveals its understanding of the world?

C. WRIGHT MILLS

The Sociological Imagination

Nowadays men often feel that their private lives are a series of traps. They sense that within their everyday worlds, they cannot overcome their troubles, and in this feeling, they are often quite correct: What ordinary men are directly aware of and what they try to do are bounded by the private orbits in which they live; their visions and their powers are limited to the close-up scenes of job, family, neighborhood; in other milieux, they move vicariously and remain spectators. And the more aware they become, however vaguely, of ambitions and of threats which transcend their immediate locales, the more trapped they seem to feel.

Underlying this sense of being trapped are seemingly impersonal changes in the very structure of continent-wide societies. The facts of contemporary history are also facts about the success and the failure of individual men and women. When a society is industrialized, a peasant becomes a worker; a feudal lord is liquidated or becomes a business-man. When classes rise or fall, a man is employed or unemployed; when the rate of investment goes up or down, a man takes new heart or goes broke. When wars happen, an insurance salesman becomes a rocket launcher; a store clerk, a radar man; a wife lives alone; a child grows up without a father. Neither the life of an individual nor the his-tory of a society can be understood without understanding both.

Yet men do not usually define the troubles they endure in terms of historical change and institutional contradiction. The well-being they enjoy, they do not usually impute to the big ups and downs of the societies in which they live. Seldom aware of the intricate connection between the patterns of their own lives and the course of world history, ordinary men do not usually know what this connection means for the kinds of men they are becoming and for the kinds of history-making in which they might take part. They do not possess the quality of mind essential to grasp the interplay of man and society, of biography and history, of self and world. They cannot cope with their personal troubles in such ways as to control the structural transformations that usually lie behind them.

Surely it is no wonder. In what period have so many men been so totally exposed at so fast a pace to such earthquakes of change? That Americans have not known such catastrophic changes as have the men and women of other societies is due to historical facts that are now quickly becoming "merely history." The history that now affects every man is world history. Within this scene and this period, in the course of a single generation, one sixth of mankind is transformed from all that is feudal and backward into all that is modern, advanced, and fearful. Political colonies are freed; new and less visible forms of imperialism installed. Revolutions occur; men feel the intimate grip of new kinds of authority. Totalitarian societies rise, and are smashed to bits—or succeed fabulously. After two centuries of ascendancy, capitalism is shown up as only one way to make society into an industrial apparatus. After two centuries of hope, even formal democracy is restricted to a quite small portion of mankind. Everywhere in the underdeveloped world, ancient ways of life are broken up and vague expectations become urgent demands. Everywhere in the overdeveloped world, the means of authority and of violence become total in scope and bureaucratic in form. Humanity itself now lies before us, the super-nation at either pole concentrating its most co-ordinated and massive efforts upon the preparation of World War Three.

The very shaping of history now outpaces the ability of men to orient themselves in accordance with cherished values. And which values? Even when they do not panic, men often sense that older ways of feeling and thinking have collapsed and that newer beginnings are ambiguous to the point of moral stasis. Is it any wonder that ordinary men feel they cannot cope with the larger worlds with which they are so suddenly confronted? That they cannot understand the meaning of their epoch for their own lives? That—in defense of selfhood—they become morally insensible, trying to remain altogether private men? Is it any wonder that they come to be possessed by a sense of the trap?

It is not only information that they need—in this Age of Fact, information often dominates their attention and overwhelms their capacities to assimilate it. It is not only the skills of reason that they need—although their struggles to acquire these often exhaust their limited moral energy.

What they need, and what they feel they need, is a quality of mind that will help them to use information and to develop reason in order to achieve lucid summations of what is going on in the world and of what may be happening within themselves. It is this quality, I am going to contend, that journalists and scholars, artists and publics, scientists and editors are coming to expect of what may be called the sociological imagination.

1

The sociological imagination enables its possessor to understand the larger historical scene in terms of its meaning for the inner life and the external career of a variety of individuals. It enables him to take into account how individuals, in the welter of their daily experience, often become falsely conscious of their social positions. Within that welter, the framework of modern society is sought, and within that framework the psychologies of a variety of men and women are formulated. By such means the personal uneasiness of individuals is focused upon explicit troubles and the indifference of publics is transformed into involvement with public issues.

The first fruit of this imagination—and the first lesson of the social science that embodies it—is the idea that the individual can understand his own experience and gauge his own fate only by locating himself within his period, that he can know his own chances in life only by becoming aware of those of all individuals in his circumstances. In many ways it is a terrible lesson; in many ways a magnificent one. We do not know the limits of man's capacities for supreme effort or willing degradation, for agony or glee, for pleasurable brutality or the sweetness of reason. But in our time we have come to know that the limits of "human nature" are frighteningly broad. We have come to know that every individual lives, from one generation to the next, in some society; that he lives out a biography, and that he lives it out within some historical sequence. By the fact of his living he contributes, however minutely, to the shaping of this society and to the course of its history, even as he is made by society and by its historical push and shove.

The sociological imagination enables us to grasp history and biography and the relations between the two within society. That is its task and its promise. To recognize this task and this promise is the mark of the classic social analyst. It is characteristic of Herbert Spencer—turgid, polysyllabic, comprehensive; of E. A. Ross—graceful, muckraking, upright; of Auguste Comte and Emile Durkheim; of the intricate and subtle Karl Mannheim. It is the quality of all that is intellectually excellent in Karl Marx; it is the clue to Thorstein Veblen's brilliant and ironic insight, to Joseph Schumpeter's many-sided constructions of reality; it is the basis of the psychological sweep of W. E. H. Lecky no less than of the profundity and clarity of Max Weber. And it is the signal of what is best in contemporary studies of man and society.

No social study that does not come back to the problems of biography, of history and of their intersections within a society has completed its intellectual journey. Whatever the specific problems of the classic social analysts, however limited or however broad the features of social reality they have examined, those who have been imaginatively aware of the promise of their work have consistently asked three sorts of questions:

(1)   What is the structure of this particular society as a whole? What are its essential components, and how are they related to one another? How does it differ from other varieties of social order? Within it, what is the meaning of any particular feature for its continuance and for its change?

(2)   Where does this society stand in human history? What are the mechanics by which it is changing? What is its place within and its meaning for the development of humanity as a whole? How does any particular feature we are examining affect, and how is it affected by, the historical period in which it moves? And this period—what are its essential features? How does it differ from other periods? What are its characteristic ways of history-making?

(3)   What varieties of men and women now prevail in this society and in this period? And what varieties are coming to prevail? In what ways are they selected and formed, liberated and repressed, made sensitive and blunted? What kinds of "human nature" are revealed in the conduct and character we observe in this society in this period? And what is the meaning for "human nature" of each and every feature of the society we are examining?

Whether the point of interest is a great power state or a minor literary mood, a family, a prison, a creed—these are the kinds of questions the best social analysts have asked. They are the intellectual pivots of classic studies of man in society—and they are the questions inevitably raised by any mind possessing the sociological imagination. For that imagination is the capacity to shift from one perspective to another—from the political to the psychological; from examination of a single family to comparative assessment of the national budgets of the world; from the theological school to the military establishment; from considerations of an oil industry to studies of contemporary poetry. It is the capacity to range from the most impersonal and remote transformations to the most intimate features of the human self—and to see the relations between the two. Back of its use there is always the urge to know the social and historical meaning of the individual in the society and in the period in which he has his quality and his being.

That, in brief, is why it is by means of the sociological imagination that men now hope to grasp what is going on in the world, and to understand what is happening in themselves as minute points of the intersections of biography and history within society. In large part, contemporary man's self-conscious view of himself as at least an outsider, if not a permanent stranger, rests upon an absorbed realization of social relativity and of the transformative power of history. The sociological imagination is the most fruitful form of this self-consciousness. By its use men whose mentalities have swept only a series of limited orbits often come to feel as if suddenly awakened in a house with which they had only supposed themselves to be familiar. Correctly or incorrectly, they often come to feel that they can now provide themselves with adequate summations, cohesive assessments, comprehensive orientations. Older decisions that once appeared sound now seem to them products of a mind unaccountably dense. Their capacity for astonishment is made lively again. They acquire a new way of thinking, they experience a transvaluation of values: in a word, by their reflection and by their sensibility, they realize the cultural meaning of the social sciences.

2

Perhaps the most fruitful distinction with which the sociological imagination works is between "the personal troubles of milieu" and "the public issues of social structure." This distinction is an essential tool of the sociological imagination and a feature of all classic work in social science.

Troubles occur within the character of the individual and within the range of his immediate relations with others; they have to do with his self and with those limited areas of social life of which he is directly and personally aware. Accordingly, the statement and the resolution of troubles properly lie within the individual as a biographical entity and within the scope of his immediate milieu—the social setting that is directly open to his personal experience and to some extent his willful activity. A trouble is a private matter: values cherished by an individual are felt by him to be threatened.

Issues have to do with matters that transcend these local environments of the individual and the range of his inner life. They have to do with the organization of many such milieux into the institutions of an historical society as a whole, with the ways in which various milieux overlap and interpenetrate to form the larger structure of social and historical life. An issue is a public matter: some value cherished by publics is felt to be threatened. Often there is a debate about what that value really is and about what it is that really threatens it.

This debate is often without focus if only because it is the very nature of an issue, unlike even widespread trouble, that it cannot very well be defined in terms of the immediate and everyday environments of ordinary men. An issue, in fact, often involves a crisis in institutional arrangements, and often too it involves what Marxists call "contradictions" or "antagonisms."

In these terms, consider unemployment. When, in a city of 100,000, only one man is unemployed, that is his personal trouble, and for its relief we properly look to the character of the man, his skills, and his immediate opportunities. But when in a nation of 50 million employees, 15 million men are unemployed, that is an issue, and we may not hope to find its solution within the range of opportunities open to any one individual. The very structure of opportunities has collapsed. Both the correct statement of the problem and the range of possible solutions require us to consider the economic and political institutions of the society, and not merely the personal situation and character of a scatter of individuals.

Consider war. The personal problem of war, when it occurs, may be how to survive it or how to die in it with honor; how to make money out of it; how to climb into the higher safety of the military apparatus; or how to contribute to the war's termination. In short, according to one's values, to find a set of milieux and within it to survive the war or make one's death in it meaningful. But the structural issues of war have to do with its causes; with what types of men it throws up into command; with its effects upon economic and political, family and religious institutions, with the unorganized irresponsibility of a world of nation-states.

Consider marriage. Inside a marriage a man and a woman may experience personal troubles, but when the divorce rate during the first four years of marriage is 250 out of every 1,000 attempts, this is an indication of a structural issue having to do with the institutions of marriage and the family and other institutions that bear upon them.

Or consider the metropolis—the horrible, beautiful, ugly, magnificent sprawl of the great city. For many upper-class people, the personal solution to "the problem of the city" is to have an apartment with private garage under it in the heart of the city, and forty miles out, a house by Henry Hill, garden by Garrett Eckbo, on a hundred acres of private land. In these two controlled environments—with a small staff at each end and a private helicopter connection—most people could solve many of the problems of personal milieux caused by the facts of the city. But all this, however splendid, does not solve the public issues that the structural fact of the city poses. What should be done with this wonderful monstrosity? Break it all up into scattered units, combining residence and work? Refurbish it as it stands? Or, after evacuation, dynamite it and build new cities according to new plans in new places? What should those plans be? And who is to decide and to accomplish whatever choice is made? These are structural issues; to confront them and to solve them requires us to consider political and economic issues that affect innumerable milieux.

Insofar as an economy is so arranged that slumps occur, the problem of unemployment becomes incapable of personal solution. Insofar as war is inherent in the nation-state system and in the uneven industrialization of the world, the ordinary individual in his restricted milieu will be powerless—with or without psychiatric aid—to solve the troubles this system or lack of system imposes upon him. Insofar as the family as an institution turns women into darling little slaves and men into their chief providers and unweaned dependents, the problem of a satisfactory marriage remains incapable of purely private solution. Insofar as the overdeveloped megalopolis and the overdeveloped automobile are built-in features of the overdeveloped society, the issues of urban living will not be solved by personal ingenuity and private wealth.

What we experience in various and specific milieux, I have noted, is often caused by structural changes. Accordingly, to understand the changes of many personal milieux we are required to look beyond them. And the number and variety of such structural changes increase as the institutions within which we live become more embracing and more intricately connected with one another. To be aware of the idea of social structure and to use it with sensibility is to be capable of tracing such linkages among a great variety of milieux. To be able to do that is to possess the sociological imagination.

3

What are the major issues for publics and the key troubles of private individuals in our time? To formulate issues and troubles, we must ask what values are cherished yet threatened, and what values are cherished and supported, by the characterizing trends of our period. In the case both of threat and of support we must ask what salient contradictions of structure may be involved.

When people cherish some set of values and do not feel any threat to them, they experience *well-being*. When they cherish values but *do* feel them to be threatened, they experience a crisis—either as a personal trouble or as a public issue. And if all their values seem involved, they feel the total threat of panic.

But suppose people are neither aware of any cherished values nor experience any threat? That is the experience of *indifference*, which, if it seems to involve all their values, becomes apathy. Suppose, finally, they are unaware of any cherished values, but still are very much aware of a threat? That is the experience of *uneasiness*, of anxiety, which, if it is total enough, becomes a deadly unspecified malaise.

Ours is a time of uneasiness and indifference—not yet formulated in such ways as to permit the work of reason and the play of sensibility. Instead of troubles—defined in terms of values and threats—there is often the misery of vague uneasiness; instead of explicit issues there is often merely the beat feeling that all is somehow not right. Neither the values threatened nor whatever threatens them has been stated; in short, they have not been carried to the point of decision. Much less have they been formulated as problems of social science.

In the 'thirties there was little doubt—except among certain deluded business circles—that there was an economic issue which was also a pack of personal troubles. In these arguments about "the crisis of capitalism," the formulations of Marx and the many unacknowledged re-formulations of his work probably set the leading terms of the issue, and some men came to understand their personal troubles in these terms. The values threatened were plain to see and cherished by all; the structural contradictions that threatened them also seemed plain. Both were widely and deeply experienced. It was a political age.

But the values threatened in the era after World War Two are often neither widely acknowledged as values nor widely felt to be threatened. Much private uneasiness goes unformulated; much public malaise and many decisions of enormous structural relevance never become public issues. For those who accept such inherited values as reason and freedom, it is the uneasiness itself that is the trouble; it is the indifference itself that is the issue. And it is this condition, of uneasiness and indifference, that is the signal feature of our period.

All this is so striking that it is often interpreted by observers as a shift in the very kinds of problems that need now to be formulated. We are frequently told that the problems of our decade, or even the crises of our period, have shifted from the external realm of economics and now have to do with the quality of individual life—in fact with the question of whether there is soon going to be anything that can properly be called individual life. Not child labor but comic books, not poverty but mass leisure, are at the center of concern. Many great public issues as well as many private troubles are described in terms of "the psychiatric"—often, it seems, in a pathetic attempt to avoid the large issues and problems of modern society. Often this statement seems to rest upon a provincial narrowing of interest to the Western societies, or even to the United States—thus ignoring two-thirds of mankind often, too, it arbitrarily divorces the individual life from the larger institutions within which that life is enacted, and which on occasion bear upon it more grievously than do the intimate environments of childhood.

Problems of leisure, for example, cannot even be stated without considering problems of work. Family troubles over comic books cannot be formulated as problems without considering the plight of the contemporary family in its new relations with the newer institutions of the social structure. Neither leisure nor its debilitating uses can be understood as problems without recognition of the extent to which malaise and indifference now form the social and personal climate of contemporary American society. In this climate, no problems of "the private life" can be stated and solved without recognition of the crisis of ambition that is part of the very career of men at work in the incorporated economy.

It is true, as psychoanalysts continually point out, that people do often have "the increasing sense of being moved by obscure forces within themselves which they are unable to define." But it is *not* true, as

Ernest Jones asserted, that "man's chief enemy and danger is his own unruly nature and the dark forces pent up within him." On the contrary: "Man's chief danger" today lies in the unruly forces of contemporary society itself, with its alienating methods of production, its enveloping techniques of political domination, its international anarchy—in a word, its pervasive transformations of the very "nature" of man and the conditions and aims of his life.

It is now the social scientist's foremost political and intellectual task—for here the two coincide—to make clear the elements of contemporary uneasiness and indifference. It is the central demand made upon him by other cultural workmen—by physical scientists and artists, by the intellectual community in general. It is because of this task and these demands, I believe, that the social sciences are becoming the common denominator of our cultural period, and the sociological imagination our most needed quality of mind.

STUDY QUESTIONS

1. How would you explain the relationship between "troubles" and "issues"?
2. What do you think Mills means when he says, "Ours is a time of uneasiness and indifference"?

W. RICHARD STEPHENS, Jr.

Careers in Sociology

Step #1: "Why am I in Sociology Anyway?"

If you are like most students, sociology is a new and somewhat strange discipline to be studying. It is new in that few students entering college have even heard of it, and even fewer intend to major in it. It is strange in that there is virtually no topic which sociology does not touch and therefore it is difficult to see where the discipline is distinct from others. It is probably also the case that you are reading this book, and therefore taking this course because the degree you are interested in requires it. Or, it is part of the general education requirements for all students at your college. In other words, you *have* to take this course. Have you wondered why?

The answer lies in the fact that sociology is such a topically broad discipline. If there is a central focus it is the issues, problems, trials, and triumphs of people trying to get along with each other; in other words, human relationships. So, the discipline has something to say to people trying to get along in a structure called a family, or members of a team, or neighbors, or employees trying to figure out work relations. The point is, sociology is relevant wherever human relations are at work. It follows then, that an improved understanding of human relations should translate into better conduct of those relations. There are exceptions, of course, such as the manipulation of those relations for the benefit of some while at the expense of others. But the general point remains, sociology provides insights which are applicable to a wide array of human circumstances. . . .

Over the course of a semester most students will have one or both of the following experiences.

The first experience is that you will identify personally with one or more of the topics explored. You will see clearly what the discipline has to say about some aspect of human relations because you have actually experienced the phenomenon in question. For example, Emile Durkheim used the term *anomie* to describe the effects of radical social change on people. He was writing about the effects of mass migration from the countryside to the city in early 20th century France. On the surface such ideas seem remote, but in class they become real as the concept is applied to our own experiences. In the case of students, nearly all experience some degree of anomie when they first encounter college or, for that matter, when they are "clueless" as to the reason they have to take sociology! The point is, the sociological concept does apply to your life. On a more topical level you have experienced sociologically relevant phenomena such as family, socialization, peer pressure, intergenerational relations, being hired and/or fired, death, crime and deviance, religion, commercials, prejudice, etc., etc., etc. Only if you have not experienced such phenomena is sociology irrelevant to you.

The second experience is that most students will take a genuine interest in at least one of the topics covered. It could be the role of women in big business, the changing demographic face of America, the impact of new technologies on work, family life, and leisure, or issues such as universal health care and social security for the aged. Related to this last point, my introductory students participate in a one-hour a week elder visitation program. In this program students are paired with senior citizens from all over town and they simply visit. Most students groan, excessively, about this assignment prior to engaging in it. However, most report that the experience was a valuable one by the time the semester is completed. Often, students continue visiting their new friend after the course is completed. They found that something they had not really considered, intergenerational relations, really was interesting. The point here is, you will most likely find *something* interesting to the point that study of it is no longer a chore, but becomes an aspect of study and life you actually like or enjoy.

Now, take the two experiences, coming across something you have personally experienced and discovering something of special interest, and combine them. The result, while not necessarily an epiphany..., it is nonetheless potentially significant. Your level of interest in sociology, or at least some topic within the field has been raised. Evidence of this comes from friends and often family who notice a difference in the way their friend or child (you) now sees and talks about the world. Some will say that now you use "big" words! This will most likely happen to you. As this happens you then begin to raise questions about yourself and your place in the scheme of things. This is natural, it is to be expected, and it is an indicator of maturity. You are becoming more conscious of what is happening to and around you. You are now in a position to be an active participant in your and other people's lives, rather than being primarily acted upon by others. We call this empowerment.

Step #2: "OK, I'm Interested, But is There a Future for Me in Sociology?"

It is the *extremely* rare student who comes out of high school with their mind made up to study sociology in college. The number is something like 3 out of every 10,000 (Howery, 1985). Yikes! If it were not for the requirements most colleges impose on students you would find a lot of academic sociologists roaming the streets. . . .

What I am suggesting, is it could happen to you; you could choose to major in sociology. It has happened to others. The question is, how should you respond? What type of questions should you ask? How does one go about pursuing sociology as a major? Is there a future in sociology? This choice, making sociology your major, or part of a double major, is a critical choice, and should not be made lightly. . . .

In my experience once the typical student decides on sociology there develops a sense of energy and anticipation about the future. But the future is as much on the collective minds of parents as it is on the mind of the son or daughter. At some point the student tells Mom and Dad what their interests are and what their decision is. And, Mom and Dad do what good parents should do; they test the decision. Recently I had lunch with a parent of [a] junior sociology major who is interested in a career in criminal justice. This parent and I have had several in-depth discussions about his son. At one point the father said, "The bottom line is, will my son be able to get a job when he graduates? By that time we will have spent $60,000 on his education. That's quite an investment. We want to make sure he has a future." Such sentiment is valid and is to be expected. . . .

Now back to the question regarding the future. The short answer is, yes, there is a future. And it is a future which is bright and growing brighter as time passes. It is bright because people with vision have begun to take the central and universal ideas of sociology and have begun looking for ways to put them into action. This effort in itself is neither new nor unique. Many other disciplines have been doing this for decades or centuries. Some have been doing this for years, but with tools and concepts derived from sociology. Marketing experts, political pollsters, etc., have been employing basic survey research techniques and statistical procedures developed over time in sociology for very practical purposes. It is also the case that sociology has developed and given birth to whole new disciplines such as criminal justice/criminology, gerontology, women's studies, black studies, demography, and social work. Each of these has put the discipline to work in very specific ways. Now sociology as a discipline, and sociologists as a profession are asserting their collective strengths. And, we find that more and more these strengths are finding expression and applications outside the classroom. . . .

In 1988 the U.S. Office of Personal Management established a position-classification standard for sociology. This means that the federal government officially recognizes the specific contributions which sociology can make. The standard for "Sociology GS-184" begins with the following statement:

> This series includes positions which involve professional work requiring a knowledge of sociology and sociological methods specifically related to the establishment, validation, interpretation, and application of knowledge about social processes. Sociologists study specialized areas such as: changes in the character, size, distribution, and composition of the population: social mechanisms for enforcing compliance with widely accepted norms and for controlling deviance; social phenomena having to do with human health and disease; the structure and operation of organizations; and the complex interrelationship of the individual and society.
>
> Sociologists are concerned primarily with the study of patterns of group and organizational behavior, social interaction, and social situations in which interaction occurs. The emphasis is on the patterns of behavior that are characteristic of social groups, organizations, institutions, and nations. Some sociologists perform sociological research, others apply sociological principles and findings, and some perform a combination of both kinds of work.

Based on this standard five specializations are recommended, including demography, law and social control, medical sociology, organizational analysis, and social psychology. In addition the standard advises prospective applicants that sociology is appropriate education for work in other areas such as but not limited to:

GS-020	Community Planning Series
GS-101	Social Work Series
GS-131	International Relations Series
GS-135	Foreign Agricultural Affairs Series
GS-140	Manpower Research and Analysis Series
GS-142	Manpower Development Series
GS-160	Civil Rights Analysis Series
GS-185	Social Work Series
GS-230	Employee Relations Series
GS-685	Public Health Program Specialist Series
GS-696	Consumer Safety Series
GS-1150	Industrial Specialist Series

The prospects have further brightened to the point where over the last ten years new associations of sociologists who work primarily in non-academic settings have been established and are flourishing. These would include organizations such as:

The Society for Applied Sociology
The Sociological Practice Association
The Chicago Sociological Practice Association
The District of Columbia Sociological Society
The Sociologists in Business
The Sociological Practice Section of the American Sociological Association

What follows is a partial listing of non-academic settings where sociologists are currently employed, compiled from the directories of the associations just referenced (Stephens, 1994):

Where Sociological Practitioners Work:

A.C. Neilsen
American Bar Association
American Express
American International Group
American Medical
   Association
Argone National Laboratory
Army Research Institute

AT&T
Atari
Avon Products Inc.
Boys Town Center
CBS, Inc.
Citibank, N.A.
City of Chicago Department
   of Housing

Cleveland Clinic
Equitable Life
Federation of Protestant
Churches
Financial News Network
G.S. Searle Laboratories
General Accounting Office
General Electric
General Foods
General Motors Research
Laboratories
Hughes Aircraft Co.
Hutchings Psychiatric Center
Illinois Criminal Justice
Authority
Internal Revenue Service
KMPG Peat Marwick
Litigation Sciences, Inc.
Mayatech Corporation
NASA
National Analysts
National Institutes of Health
NBC
New York Business Group on
Health
New York City Fire
Department
New York City Human
Resources Administration
Rand Corporation
Rockefeller Foundation
Rubbermaid Inc.
Saint Vincents Hospital
Sears, Roebuck, & Co.
Standard and Poor
The Equitable
The Gallup Organization
The Public Health
Foundation
The Vanderveer Group
U.S. Bureau of the Census
U.S. Department of
Agriculture
U.S. Department of Energy
U.S. Department of
Health and Human
Services
Wells Fargo Bank
Xerox
Young & Rubican

As you can see, there is great variety to the job settings. There is similar variety to non-academic job titles, as evidenced by the GS-184 series standard. But how do you translate the potential of a discipline like sociology into an actual career? The parent with the $60,000 invested in his son appreciates potential, but how can his son go from degree to job? Does one just look for "sociologist wanted" job ads? Is graduate school necessary? Even if a job is available and you take it, can you make a living? . . .

Step #3: "What Will I Achieve?"

. . . The goal is not to make you into a professional sociologist per se. It is to pass on to you significant skills and perspectives, and a legacy which makes you a thoughtful, and therefore an empowered, person.

Whatever career dreams you have, consider the following. Your work options can be divided broadly into two categories, or worlds. One is the world of people. The other is the world of things. Now examine your interests and your dreams. Do you see these as focused primarily on people, or is your focus primarily on technical matters, things? My brother used to say that he was going into medicine so that he could deal with concrete issues, exact answers. He could not stand the ambiguity of any of the other "philosophies." Now he has been a practicing rural family physician for nearly 10 years. When asked about concrete issues he admits that nearly all of what he does is a matter of judgement. His position in the community and his reputation are as much a part of his profession as knowing how to deliver babies. The point is, you must think hard and creatively to come up with a career that does not bring you into close contact with others. The argument could be made that on this basis there is no career that cannot be profited by a sociological perspective. This is not to say that sociology should therefore be your degree of choice. But it does suggest that there is a significant contribution sociology can make to any career. . . .

Step #4: "Now . . . What Do I Do Next?"

. . . You are beginning! So, in what ways can you begin? Let's start by noting three common elements among the CP's [character profiles of employed sociologists].

First, the CP's evidenced an increasingly common development in modern careers: they are characterized by change. If you do not expect change in your work life then you will most certainly be left "holding the short end" when it comes to career development. In fact, the idea of a career developing implies change. The difference now is that the changes to be expected are generally more radical than in the past. Look back at the CP's and you will see frequent career turns and shifts. These occur within and across job categories. This means both advancement within a job type and organization, as well as movement from one type of work to another. Besides job changes, CP subjects are primed for life changes. The fact is, our lives are made complicated by the presence of others. Because of this we can expect circumstances, especially our relations to others, to be always in some state of flux. As some CP subjects suggested, ten years ago the issues were not AIDS, sexual harassment, diversity in the workplace, a world turned upside-down by the collapse of the Soviet Union, an aging population, foreign economic competition, etc. The sociologist, because of his/her ability to see the "big picture," is in a favorable position to see, or anticipate these trends in their early stages.

A second common element among CP's is a commitment to education and continued learning. In fact, the CP's evidence great diversity, and therefore breadth of perspective, in degrees earned. Bachelor level degrees were earned in fields such as biology, education, nuclear engineering and physics, history, chemistry, and business, as well as sociology. Advanced degrees were earned in fields such as law, criminal justice, business, and communications. Besides, formal degrees, many CP subjects have taken advantage of seminars and professional associations in order to stay on top of their professions. The point is, sociology is a discipline which promotes continuation of the learning process, both in perspective and practice.

The third element in common is what I call opportunism. Because sociologists combine both an anticipation of change with an orientation and an ability to learn, opportunism is produced. For many of us, an opportunity is something which simply happens. However, an appropriate orientation can produce opportunities. There are three important steps to producing opportunities. These are 1) actively looking for opportunities, 2) recognizing opportunities when they appear, and 3) taking advantage of opportunities once they are recognized. For example, networking is one way in which opportunities are produced. We all have networks but the question is whether the network is actively operated. If you understand the concept you can employ it; if not, then opportunities are limited. . . .

The three elements in common among the CP's, understanding change, pursuing education, and being opportunistic, are only part of the story. Other characteristics possessed by those with successful careers include personal traits such as perseverance and a willingness to work hard. . . .

The reason for reviewing these characteristics is to emphasize that your career is the result of a set of *conscious choices* and *actions*. The better your insights and information about the circumstances you are in, the better your choices and subsequent actions will serve your interests. But this is likely only when you begin the process of taking responsibility for your own future. If you recall, . . . I told you about a parent who was concerned about the career prospects of their son's $60,000 college education. The problem is, dollars invested and career development do not smoothly correlate; that is, one does not automatically translate into the other. You must put yourself in a position where you can exercise opportunism. . . . But how is this done?

Step #5: The Objective is Relevance

. . . It has not been my intent to talk you into making sociology your academic major or your career. I do believe, however, that sociology can significantly enhance any career you choose. . . . But more than this, take what you learn from the classroom . . . to your life outside the classroom. Be aggressive about it. Ask questions. See what others who have gone before you have experienced. Ask your professor to bring alumni to class. Write to the ASA and begin researching the careers of other sociologists. Ask the questions you have written in the margins. Challenge the common assumptions. Expect change. Learn about your world. Be opportunistic. Your future is not a simple statistical function of chance. It is a function of conscious choice and intentional action. Therefore, look for the opportunities, see the opportunities, and seize the opportunities.

Ultimately the objective is relevance. You want yourself, your life, your work and career to be meaningful, to make a difference. . . . And that is the beauty of the discipline. It can be relevant regardless of the circumstance. However, you must be prepared, you must be responsible, you must articulate some values around which your future can be focused. Mere activity is meaningless. A job for a job's sake will not take you far. But through this course . . . you have begun a process of consciously choosing and producing a life characterized by relevance and meaning.

REFERENCES

Carla Howery. "Teaching High School Sociology." ASA Footnotes, p. 13, no. 4. 1985.
W. Richard Stephens, Jr., from "What Now? The Relevance of Sociology to Your Life and Career," in Using Sociology (2nd ed.), Roger A. Straus, Editor. General Hall, Inc., 1994.

STUDY QUESTIONS

1. What are some of the typical jobs sociologists do with their degree?
2. What are the prospects for "income" and for "meaning" with a career in sociology, according to Stephens?

Sociology as a Science

ALL SCIENCES FOLLOW SIMILAR METHODS AND BRING evidence to bear on important questions within the domain of each discipline. Physics and chemistry, biology and psychology, anthropology and sociology, all have more in common as sciences than might first appear. The questions posed by each discipline belong to a comprehensive worldview, or paradigm, that houses all the theories that connect the important concepts and ideas used to explain each discipline's portion of the cosmos. These theories guide scientific investigations by pointing to important questions that must still be answered, or at least examined. Research applies scientific methods to collect and analyze information (data) that bring evidence to bear on the important theoretical questions. Science, with all its flaws and uncertainties, is the best set of ideas and practices known to understand the empirical (measurable, material) world.

Sociology has its place in the sciences and is one with its own domain and its own theories and methods. Social life, for sociology, has come to be understood at the macro (large worldview of social structures and institutions) and micro (small worldview of face-to-face, interpersonal associations) levels. We need theories and research methods to aid in the discovery of each set of influences on human behavior. One theory, one set of data, and one approach to looking at the world will not suffice. Multiple theories, multiple research methods, and many applications of our discipline will be needed to comprehend the complexity of the social world. This topic of the text and, indeed, each reading within the following topics, will speak to the diverse world of sociology.

Theories are explanations that tell us about the social world. They tell us why things occur, in what sequence they happen, and so on. Theories are like maps, and just as we need different maps to get us from place to place (road maps, hiking trail maps), we need different theories to help us understand the different terrains of social life. Typically, for introductory students in sociology, three theoretical perspectives are presented. Functionalism and conflict theories aid in the understanding of the macro or structural world, that is, gender, social class. Symbolic interaction theory focuses on the interpersonal world and explains face-to-face interaction and, therefore, examines the micro-social world of peer groups, coworkers, and so on.

In this reader, you will see examples of quantitative, qualitative, and participant observation research. Much of sociological research depends on surveys that ask people to complete written questionnaires or answer interview questions. Sometimes large national data sets are used to answer questions about educational attainment, social inequality, or health issues, and these approaches use quantitative data to look at the social world. An example of such a large-scale survey is the U.S. Census, and many sociologists use these data to answer their research questions. Qualitative research might use informal interviews and observations for its data. The qualitative approach gives us in-depth looks at social processes among smaller samples of people. Sociology is a science that depends on different theories and multiple research methods to capture and understand social life.

The readings in this section will show how theories, styles of research, and the practice of sociology all come together to create the discipline we are now studying. Paul Colomy's clearly written reading will introduce the three major theoretical perspectives most commonly used in sociology to explain the social world. Functionalism, conflict, and symbolic interaction theories likely will become ordinary ideas to the new students of sociology. Elliot Liebow's fine ethnography of homeless women illustrates how a master of this research tradition uses qualitative sociology to give a poignant view of life among homeless women. Finally, the reading by Allan J. Kimmell takes us through the value and ethical issues in doing applied research. Several pieces of research, perhaps the most controversial pieces ever done, are examined to illustrate the ethical complications of applied scholarship.

PAUL COLOMY

Three Sociological Perspectives

When conducting research, sociologists typically draw on one or more perspectives. Sociological perspectives provide very general ways of conceptualizing the social world and its basic elements. A perspective consists of a set of fairly abstract assumptions about the nature of human action and the character of social organization. Each perspective can be likened to a spotlight that brightly illuminates select aspects of behavior and social relations while leaving other areas shrouded in darkness. Because a single perspective supplies only a partial or one-sided view, a comprehensive understanding of social life requires becoming familiar with several different perspectives.

Sociology contains a large number of distinct perspectives, and they can be divided into two broad categories: micro and macro. In very general terms, micro perspectives are oriented toward small time and small space, while macro perspectives are oriented toward big time and big space (Collins 1981). That is, micro perspectives are usually concerned with the conduct of individuals and small groups as it unfolds in relatively small spatial contexts and over short durations of time. Macro perspectives, on the other hand, focus on larger entities—not individuals and small groups, but institutions, entire societies, and even the global system—and on how these entities emerge, maintain themselves, and change over decades, centuries, and millennia. The following section outlines one micro perspective (symbolic interactionism) and two macro perspectives (functionalism and the conflict approach).

Symbolic Interactionism

Symbolic interactionism's intellectual roots reside in pragmatism, a philosophical tradition developed by such prominent, early twentieth-century American thinkers as John Dewey, William James, George Herbert Mead, and Charles Peirce. The sociological implications of pragmatism were articulated by several innovative sociologists, including Robert Park, W. I. Thomas, Herbert Blumer, Everett Hughes, and Erving Goffman, who taught or studied at the University of Chicago between 1910 and 1960. Because it originated at the University of Chicago, symbolic interactionism is sometimes referred to as the Chicago School.

Symbolic interactionism is based on five core ideas. First, it assumes that human beings act in terms of the meanings they assign to objects in their environment. (Interactionists define the term object very broadly to include material things, events, symbols, actions, and other people and groups.) Using slightly different terminology to make the same point, interactionists maintain that people's conduct is power-fully influenced by their definition of the situation. This assumption can be clarified by contrasting it to a rudimentary model of social action advanced by a psychological perspective known as behaviorism. The behaviorist approach characterizes conduct as a response to objective stimuli, and suggests that human behavior resembles a series of stimulus-response chains:

$$stimulus \longrightarrow response.$$

Rejecting the notion that individuals respond directly to an objective stimulus, interactionists insist that people interpret, or assign meanings to, the stimulus before they act:

$$stimulus \longrightarrow interpretation \longrightarrow response.$$

Athletes' reactions to coaches' criticisms, for instance, depend largely on whether they interpret that criticism as a constructive attempt to improve their play or as a malicious attack on their character.

Even when a definition of the situation is demonstrably false, it can still exert a powerful effect on behavior. As W. I. Thomas once said, "A situation defined as real is real in its consequences." Many adults, for example, perceive Halloween as filled with potential danger, and believe that their young children are vulnerable to sadistic strangers dispensing drug-tainted candy or apples laced with razor blades. The belief that such acts of Halloween sadism are widespread is, in fact, an urban legend with virtually no factual basis (Best and Horiuchi 1985). Nevertheless, millions of parents are convinced that the threat is genuine and, acting in terms of their definition of the situation, continue to inspect their children's treats for signs of tampering.

Symbolic interactionism's second assumption asserts that social action typically involves making a series of adjustments and readjustments as an individual's interpretation of the situation changes. Interactionists reject the notion that behavior is the unmediated product of a variable or cause. Instead, they view action as something that is continually being built up, modified, re-directed, and transformed (Blumer 1969). People's initial definition of the situation is always subject to change, and as they redefine the situation their conduct changes accordingly. Effective teachers, for example, routinely interpret students' comments, facial expressions, and other gestures to determine whether the subject matter is being communicated clearly. They rely on this feedback to define and redefine the unfolding classroom situation and to make corresponding adjustments in their presentations. When students look confused, they may introduce a familiar example; if students' attention should wander, the instructors may call on them; and if students are visibly upset, they may ask to meet privately with them after class.

Third, interactionists assume that the meanings imputed to an object are socially constructed (Berger and Luckmann 1966). Meanings do not, in other words, simply reflect a quality or essence built into the very nature of an object. Other than its size and color, the cloth used to make handkerchiefs is virtually identical to that used to produce American flags. Though handkerchiefs and flags are sewn from the same physical material, the meanings attached to these two objects differ in dramatic ways. Rather than being intrinsic to an object, then, meanings are attributed to it by individuals, groups, and communities.

Elaborating this logic, some interactionists treat the self as an object whose meanings are socially constructed. In other words, the kind of person you assume yourself to be, and that others take you to be, mirror the meanings that individuals and groups have assigned to you. If, from a young age, family members, friends, and teachers have said you were "brilliant" and have acted toward you in a manner consistent with that characterization, then one assumption you are likely to make about yourself—one meaning that you are likely to assign to yourself—is that you are a highly intelligent person.

Fourth, symbolic interactionism holds that in modern, heterogeneous societies, different groups often assign divergent meanings to the "same" object. Contemporary societies contain a wide variety of groups (e.g., occupational, religious, age-based, racial and ethnic groups). Since group members interact and communicate frequently with one another, they tend to develop a common "universe of discourse" (Mead 1934) or shared meanings about the objects comprising their social world. Not surprisingly, discrepancies are likely to arise between the distinctive systems of meanings devised by different groups. Parents and adolescents, for instance, commonly attach opposing meanings to curfews, underage drinking, and body piercing.

Discrepant meanings can be a significant source of social conflict, with rival groups mobilizing to insure that their definition of the situation is officially acknowledged and enforced by the larger society. A classic interactionist study discovered that Prohibition was largely a battle over the meanings assigned to drinking (Gusfield 1963). In the early twentieth century, small-town, middle-class WASPS (white, Anglo-Saxon, Protestants) regarded drinking as sinful, while the working-class and largely Catholic immigrants from Southeastern Europe who settled in the nation's largest cities viewed drinking as an integral part of everyday life. More adept at organizing and lobbying politicians, the small-town Protestants succeeded in inscribing their interpretation into law: the Eighteenth Amendment, approved by Congress in 1919, outlawed (at least for a time) the manufacture and sale of alcoholic liquors.

Fifth, established meanings are always subject to transformation, and interactionists maintain that the emergence and diffusion of novel definitions of reality are a critically important feature of social change. At any given time, the meanings attached to some objects and practices are so entrenched that they appear natural and beyond question. Behavior that deviates sharply from these prescribed meanings is regarded as threatening, immoral, and even a little crazy. Interactionists examine how social movements, broad cultural shifts, and/or deviant individuals and groups sometimes challenge long-standing meanings and replace them with alternative conceptions of reality. From an interactionist perspective, one of the most significant consequences of the feminist movement is its redefinition of what it means to be a woman. A generation or two ago, it was simply assumed, particularly by members of the middle class and by women as well as men, that a woman's "proper place" was in the home taking care of her household, husband,

and children. In the late 1960s and throughout the 1970s, feminists questioned this assumption and ushered in a strikingly different conception of women, one that affirmed a woman's right to work outside the home and to be treated as an equal, in every respect, to her male colleagues. Today, feminism's once novel and radical definition of reality has been institutionalized, and the earlier view, which at the time was widely accepted and regarded as obvious and commonsensical, has now been redefined as an arbitrary infringement on women's freedom.

Functionalism

Functionalism is a macro perspective that examines the creation, maintenance, and alteration of durable social practices, institutions, and entire societies. Emile Durkheim, a great French sociologist who published several provocative books between 1890 and 1915, is often regarded as the classic founder of functionalism. This approach was articulated most forcefully, however, during the twenty-five years between 1945 and 1970 by a group of American sociologists, most of whom were trained at Harvard or Columbia. Key figures in this group include Robert Bellah, Robert Merton, Wilbert Moore, Talcott Parsons, Neil Smelser, and Robin Williams.

Functionalism assumes, first, that societies can be likened to problem-solving entities. If a society is to persist, functionalists argue, it must address a large (but not infinite) number of problems in a reasonably satisfactory way. (Functionalists sometimes refer to these problems as requirements, functions, prerequisites, or functional prerequisites.) An enduring society must, for example, socialize its youngest members, distribute food and other goods and services, and devise mechanisms to control deviance and contain conflict. If a society does not satisfactorily address these (and other) problems, it will experience considerable strain, and if its failure to address these problems continues, it will collapse.

Extending the metaphor that likens societies to problem-solving entities, functionalism portrays persisting practices and institutions as answers or solutions to the kinds of problems mentioned above. Customary practices and institutions are established to meet the problems every society must confront. Families and schools, for instance, are institutions that arise to answer the problem of socializing and educating the young; free markets, on the other hand, are created to address the problem of producing and distributing goods and services, while police and prisons are mechanisms for controlling deviance and containing conflict.

Second, functionalists assume that during the course of human history societies have developed many different answers to basic needs. This assumption can be termed the principle of institutional alternatives. In traditional societies, for instance, the extended family had sole responsibility for supporting dependents, whether they be very young or very old. In many modern societies, however, insurance policies, pensions, social security, and welfare programs share responsibility for the problem of caring for dependents. From a functionalist perspective, these programs are institutional alternatives to the extended family.

The principle of institutional alternatives implies that any single functional prerequisite can be met in many different ways. Many functionalists argue, however, that in an attempt to address prerequisites more efficiently and more effectively, modern societies have increasingly replaced multi-functional institutions with more specialized ones (Parsons 1977). Two hundred years ago, the family was a multi-functional institution in that it assumed primary responsibility for many different tasks, such as economic production, procreation, socialization, care for the infirm elderly, and social control. Today, however, many of these problems have been delegated to specialized institutions. Economic production, for instance, is no longer addressed by the family but by business enterprises located (for the most part) outside the home, while the control of deviance is a problem for specialized social control agents like the police and criminal courts. The family, too, has become a more specialized institution, one whose primary tasks include procreation, socialization of the very young, and emotional support for family members.

Third, functionalism presumes that the particular practices and institutions that arise in response to one problem have crucial repercussions for the practices and institutions devised to address other problems. A society, in other words, can be viewed as a system of practices and institutions. The notion that persisting practices or institutions are part of a larger system has led some functionalists to develop a distinctive protocol for studying the inter-relations between different parts of social systems. Referred to as functional analysis (Merton 1968), this method examines the effects a practice or institution has on other institutions and on the larger society. These effects or consequences assume four principal forms. Manifest functions refer to the consequences or objectives an institution explicitly attempts to achieve. Universities, for instance, are designed to impart knowledge and skills that will enable students to become productive workers and thoughtful citizens. Latent functions, on the other hand, identify effects that typically go unnoticed by the general public and frequently appear unrelated or starkly incompatible with an institution's (or the larger society's) explicit objectives. For example, while many citizens routinely denounce crime, functionalists argue that it—or, more specifically, the condemnation crime provokes—has the important latent function of clearly defining and affirming a community's normative boundaries (i.e., its sense of right and wrong). Prisons, too, have a latent function: by serving as "schools of crime," they insure that many ex-prisoners will commit new crimes which, in turn, will elicit still more community outrage and additional affirmation of a society's moral code.

In addition to being either manifest or latent, the functions served by a practice or institution can be positive or negative. Positive functions are evident when an institution facilitates the operation of other institutions and/or contributes to the overall stability and effectiveness of the larger society. In this vein, Davis and Moore (1945) hypothesize that attaching unequal financial and social rewards to different occupations has the positive effect of attracting the most talented and qualified individuals to a society's most "functionally important" positions. Negative consequences, which are sometimes called dysfunctions, occur when a practice or institution impedes the operation of other institutions and/or produces instability. For example, the "soft money" donated by corporations and other large contributors to political campaigns fosters the perception that contemporary politics is corrupt and convinces many citizens that their votes "don't count." That perception, moreover, is partially responsible for shockingly low rates of voter turnout.

Fourth, functionalism suggests that in contemporary societies containing scores of specialized institutions and hundreds of heterogenous sub-groups, societal integration is a recurring but manageable problem. In modern social orders, societal integration is achieved in two primary ways. First, specialized integrative institutions and processes—e.g., religious ceremonies, athletic contests, media events, and nationally celebrated holidays—heighten cohesion among people who otherwise share little in common. Second, consensus or agreement on such core values as individualism, freedom, achievement, and equal opportunity also serves to integrate complex societies. Incorporated into different institutions and internalized by individuals (during the course of their early socialization), shared values enable the diverse components of a large, differentiated society to co-exist and bond rather than dissolve into chronic chaos or a "war of all against all." According to one prominent functionalist, the relative stability of American society over the last two hundred years (the Civil War being a glaring exception) is largely attributable to the continuing consensus on the values of achievement and liberty (Lipset 1979).

Fifth, functionalism asserts that deviance and conflict arise from social strains, or contradictions within an institution or between institutions. That is, the primary source of contention and crime are inconsistencies inherent in the social system itself. In an influential essay, Robert Merton (1938) contends that in American society everyone, regardless of his or her station in life, is encouraged to pursue the American Dream. At the same time, however, the institutional means (e.g., a quality education and well-connected friends or acquaintances on the job market) for attaining success are not equally distributed: middle- and upper-class people are, in general, much more likely to have access to these institutional means than are working-class people. Confronted with this contradiction between a cultural goal (i.e., success) and the institutional means (e.g., a quality education) to achieve it, some individuals and groups will turn to crime (e.g., selling drugs). Note that in Merton's terms, crime often involves using "innovative," illegal means to realize a cultural goal prized both by criminals and law-abiding citizens. Under certain conditions, the same contradiction between cultural goals and institutional means can prompt widespread rebellion, with various groups replacing established cultural goals and the standard, institutional means with radically different values and means.

The Conflict Perspective

Like functionalism, the conflict perspective is a macrosociological approach that examines the emergence, persistence, and transformation of long-standing practices, institutions, and societies. Karl Marx, whose work first appeared in the mid-nineteenth century, is usually credited with crystallizing the key principles of this approach. Max Weber, an early twentieth-century German sociologist, is also recognized as a founding figure of conflict sociology. Leading contemporary conflict theorists include William Chambliss, Randall Collins, Ralf Dahrendorf, William Domhoff, and C. Wright Mills.

The conflict perspective rejects the functionalist notion that societies can be accurately portrayed as problem-solving entities. It also disputes the complementary idea that long-standing practices and institutions represent reasonably satisfactory answers to problems and as such contribute to a society's general welfare. Conflict sociologists embrace a very different orienting assumption: societies are arenas in which groups with fundamentally antagonistic interests struggle against one another. Different theorists within this tradition differ in terms of which particular groups and struggles they emphasize. Marx, for instance, highlights the conflicts between social classes, while Weber focuses on competing status groups (e.g., racial, ethnic, religious, age-based, etc.) and Dahrendorf and Collins draw attention to the battles between those who have authority and those subject to that authority. Despite disagreements about which groups and struggles are most important, all conflict sociologists believe that the interests that divide groups (whether classes, status groups, and so on) are built into the very fabric of a social order; these opposing interests are not readily negotiated, compromised, or resolved, nor can they be wished away or papered-over.

Second, conflicts among classes, status groups, and between those exercising authority and those subject to it supply the energy and the motivation for constructing and maintaining (as well as challenging and transforming) practices and institutions. Platt's (1977) well-known study of the origins of the juvenile court, for example, contends that this institution was created (in 1899) by social and economic elites and was employed to target and control the children of working-class immigrants residing in large cities. Conflict sociologists argue that today the nation's newly constructed maximum security prisons are, in practice, reserved predominantly for young, minority males raised in inner-city areas where good jobs are scarce (Chambliss 1999). On the other hand, white-collar, middle-class criminals, if they receive a prison sentence at all, are rarely housed in these types of facilities.

Third, the conflict perspective characterizes ongoing practices and institutions as structures of domination that promote the interests of a relatively powerful, superordinate group while subverting the interests of relatively powerless, subordinate groups, even though the latter are usually much larger, numerically, than the powerful elites. Consequently, this perspective's orienting question is: which group's interests are served by a specific practice or institution? Kozol's (1991) investigation of how public schools are funded found that schools located in well-to-do suburban areas receive substantially more support than inner-city schools, which often lack textbooks, desks, and even serviceable plumbing. Far from enabling students from economically disadvantaged backgrounds to compete fairly on a level playing field, the current school system simply reflects and reproduces existing class inequalities.

Fourth, the conflict perspective reconceptualizes what functionalism terms values as ideologies. The primary purpose of an ideology is to protect and promote the distinctive interests of a particular class (or status or authority group). This legitimating purpose is best served when the ideology is presented in universal terms; when its ideas are stated as if they apply to everyone equally. According to the conflict approach, achievement and equal opportunity are most accurately viewed not as widely shared values but as a dominant ideology that operates to preserve (and reproduce) existing systems of inequality. In essence, the ideology of achievement and equal opportunity asserts that individuals and groups with great wealth, prestige, and power are rightfully entitled to these rewards because they have sacrificed, worked hard, and/or displayed exceptional talent. This ideology also explains why many people have few or none of these rewards: they are lazy, unwilling to make the sacrifices necessary for success, and/or lack the requisite talent. This ideology justifies the unequal distribution of social rewards by referring to individuals' character and moral virtues (or lack thereof). At the same time, it draws attention away from the structural inequities that largely explain why members of some groups are much more likely to "succeed" than are members of other groups.

Fifth, the conflict approach holds that significant social change usually reflects the efforts of groups mobilizing to advance their collective interests, often at the expense of other groups' interests. In this regard, proponents of conflict sociology question the functionalist claim that the substantial financial rewards enjoyed by physicians are due to the fact that medical doctors perform tasks that are, objectively, of great functional importance to society. Physicians' impressive incomes are more persuasively explained, conflict sociologists contend, with the observation that the American medical profession has established, in effect, a monopoly on the provision of health care (Starr 1982). Prior to 1850, this monopoly did not exist, and physicians were poorly paid and given little esteem. After the Civil War, however, doctors began to organize in earnest, and by the late nineteenth century they secured legislation prohibiting other groups and individuals from providing health care. The exclusion of competitors paved the way for a remarkable surge in doctors' income and a parallel rise in their prestige.

REFERENCES

Berger, Peter and Thomas Luckmann. 1966. *The Social Construction of Reality*. New York: Doubleday.

Best, Joel and Gerald Horiuchi. 1985. "The Razor Blade in the Apple: The Social Construction of Urban Legends." *Social Problems* 32: 488–499.

Blumer, Herbert. 1969. *Symbolic Interactionism*. Englewood Cliffs: Prentice-Hall.

Chambliss, William J. 1999. *Power, Politics, and Crime*. Boulder: Westview Press.

Collins, Randall. 1981. "On the Microfoundations of Macrosociology." *American Journal of Sociology* 86: 984–1014.

Davis, Kingsley and Wilbert E. Moore. 1945. "Some Principles of Stratification." *American Sociological Review* 10: 242–249.

Gusfield, Joseph R. 1963. *Symbolic Crusade*. Urbana: University of Illinois Press.

Kozol, Jonathan. 1991. *Savage Inequalities*. New York: HarperCollins.

Lipset, Seymour M. 1979. *The First New Nation*. New York: W. W. Norton.

Mead, George H. 1934. *Mind, Self and Society*. Edited by Charles W. Morris. Chicago: University of Chicago Press.

Merton, Robert K. 1938. "Social Structure and Anomie." *American Societal Review* 3: 672–682.

———. 1968. *Social Theory and Social Structure*. Enlarged edition. New York: Free Press.

Parsons, Talcott. 1977. *The Evolution of Society*. Edited and with an Introduction by Jackson Toby. Englewood Cliffs: Prentice-Hall.

Platt, Anthony M. 1977. *The Child Savers*. 2nd edition. Chicago: University of Chicago Press.

Starr, Paul. 1982. *The Social Transformation of American Medicine*. Cambridge: Harvard University Press.

STUDY QUESTIONS

1. Distinguish the main qualities of symbolic interaction, functionalism, and conflict theories.
2. What are the main terms you can identify that belong to each of the three theoretical perspectives? Make a list of each.

ELLIOT LIEBOW

Tell Them Who I Am
The Lives of Homeless Women

This is a participant observer study of single, homeless women in emergency shelters in a small city just outside Washington, D.C. In participant observation, the researcher tries to participate as fully as possible in the life of the people being studied. Of course, there are obvious and severe limits to how well a man with a home and family can put himself in the place of homeless women. One simply goes where they go, gets to know them over time as best one can, and tries very hard to see the world from their perspective.

It is often said that, in participant observation studies, the researcher is the research instrument. So is it here. Everything reported about the women in this study has been selected by me and filtered through me, so it is important that I tell you something about myself and my prejudices as well as how this study came about. Indeed, I feel obliged to tell you more than is seemly and more than you may want to know, but these are things that the women themselves knew about me and that had an important if unknown influence on my relationship with them.

In a real sense, I backed into this study, which took shape, more or less, as I went along. In 1984, I learned that I had cancer and a very limited life expectancy. I did not want to spend my last months on the 12th floor of a government office building, so at 58 I retired on disability from my job of 20-some years as an anthropologist with the National Institute of Mental Health.

I looked well, felt well, and had a lot of time on my hands, so I became a volunteer at a soup kitchen that had recently opened. I worked there one night a week. In the early part of the evening, I helped serve food or just sat around with the men and women who had come there, usually eating with them. In case of trouble, I tried to keep the peace. Later I went upstairs to "the counselor's office," where I met with people who needed assistance in getting shelter for the night. For the next hour or so, I called around to the various shelters in the county or in downtown Washington, D.C., trying to locate and reserve sleeping space for the men and women who needed it.

I enjoyed the work and the people at the soup kitchen, but this was only one night a week, so I became a volunteer at The Refuge, an emergency shelter for homeless women. This, too, was one night a week, from 6:30 to 10:00, and involved sleeping overnight twice a month. I picked this shelter because I had visited there briefly the year before and liked the feel of it. Here, along with three other volunteers, my job was to help prepare the food (usually just heat the main dishes and make a salad); help serve the food; distribute towels, soap, and other sundries on request; socialize with the women; keep order; and keep a daily log that included the names of all the women present and their time of arrival.

Almost immediately, I found myself enjoying the company of the women. I was awed by the enormous effort that most of them made to secure the most elementary necessities and decencies of life that the rest of us take for granted. And I was especially struck by their sense of humor, so at odds with any self-pity—the ability to step back and laugh at oneself, however wryly. One evening, soon after I started working at the shelter, several of us remained at the table to talk after finishing dinner. Pauline turned to me and said, in a stage whisper, making sure that Hilda would hear her, "Hilda has a Ph.D."

Hilda laughed. "No," she said, "I don't have a Ph.D., but I do have a bachelor's degree in biology." She paused, then began again. "You know," she said, "all my life I wanted to be an MD and now, at the age of 54, I finally made it. I'm a Manic Depressive."

Seduced by the courage and the humor of the women, and by the pleasure of their company, I started going to the shelter four and sometimes five days a week. (For the first two years, I also kept my one-night-a-week job with the soup kitchen.) Probably because it was something I was trained to do, or perhaps out of plain habit, I decided to take notes.

"Listen," I said at the dinner table one evening, after getting permission to do a study from the shelter director. "I want your permission to take notes. I want to go home at night and write down what I can remember about the things you say and do. Maybe I'll write a book about homeless women."

Most of the dozen or so women there nodded their heads or simply shrugged. All except Regina. Her acceptance was conditional. "Only if you promise not to publish before I do," she said. Believing that neither one of us, for different reasons, would ever publish anything in the future, I readily agreed.[1] . . .

It is difficult to be precise about how I was perceived by the women. I am 6′1″ and weigh about 175 pounds. I had a lot of white hair but was otherwise nondescript. I dressed casually, often in corduroy pants, shirt, and cardigan. The fact that I was Jewish did not seem to matter much one way or another so far as I could tell.

Most of the women probably liked having me around. Male companionship was generally in short supply and the women often made a fuss about the few male volunteers. I would guess that there were as many women who actively sought me out as there were women who avoided me. The fact that I had written a book that was available at the library (three or four women took the trouble to read it) enhanced my legitimacy in their eyes.[2]

Principally, I think, the women saw me as an important resource. I had money and a car, and by undertaking to write a book, I had made it my business to be with them. I routinely lent out $2, $5, $10 or even $20 on request to the handful who asked. I told them I had set aside a certain amount as a revolving fund and I could only keep lending money if they kept returning it. This worked fairly well.

There were a few women, of course, who would never be in a position to return the money, and this made for a problem. It would have been patronizing simply to make a gift of the money; they wanted to be borrowers, not beggars, and I was just as eager as they to avoid a demeaning panhandler/donor relationship. But I did not want them to be embarrassed or to avoid me simply because they couldn't repay a loan, nor did I want to shut them off from borrowing more. My solution was to reassure these women I had no immediate need for the money and could wait indefinitely for repayment.

Some of the women would perhaps characterize me as a friend, but I am not certain how deep or steadfast this sense of friendship might be. One day, Regina and I were talking about her upcoming trial about two months away. I had already agreed to accompany her to the courtroom and serve as an advisor, but Regina wanted further reassurance.

"You will be there, won't you?" she said.

As a way of noting the profundity that nothing in life is certain, I said, jokingly, "It's not up to me, it's up to The Man Upstairs."

"Well," she said, "if you die before the trial, you will ask one of your friends to help me, won't you?" I looked hard at her to see if she was joking, too. She wasn't. She was simply putting first things first.

One or two of the women did say something like "If you weren't married, would you give me a run for my money?" Neither "yes" nor "no" was a suitable response, but it usually sufficed for me to say (and mean), "I think you are a very nice person."

I tried to make myself available for driving people to Social Services, a job interview, a clinic or hospital, a cemetery, to someone's house, to another shelter, to help them move their belongings, or on other personal errands. With my consent, several women used my name as a personal reference for jobs or housing, and a few used my home as a mailing address for income tax refunds or other business.

Several of the women got to know my two daughters, both of whom came to The Refuge a few evenings each during the winters. One daughter was engaged to be married and her fiancé also came a few times. These visits helped strengthen my ties to those women who knew my daughters by face and name. They could ask me how my wife, Harriet, or Elisabeth and Jessica and Eric were doing, and my subsequent participation in discussions about family or child-rearing was much more personal and immediate as a result.

It is difficult to exaggerate the importance of this kind of familiarity. It is essential, I believe, in this kind of study—a participant observer kind of study—that relationships be as symmetrical as possible, that there be a quid pro quo; the women needed to know as much about me as I knew about them.

My association with the women was most intense during the winter of 1984–85, all of 1986, much of 1987, and the winter of 1987–88. Thereafter, I slackened off, partly for health reasons and partly because I had already collected more notes than I knew what to do with.[3] I continued to go to the shelters intermittently, and several of the women called me regularly at home. It was also at this time that I started playing around with the notes to see how I might eventually make sense of them.

In general, I have tried to avoid labeling any of the women as "mentally ill," "alcoholic," "drug addicted," or any other characterization that is commonly used to describe—or, worse, to explain—the homeless person. Judgments such as these are almost always made against a background of homelessness. If the same person were seen in another setting, the judgment might be altogether different. Like you, I know people who drink, people who do drugs, and bosses who have tantrums and treat their subordinates like dirt. They all have good jobs. Were they to become homeless, some of them would surely also become "alcoholics," "addicts," or "mentally ill." Similarly, if some of the homeless women who are now so labeled were to be magically transported to a more usual and acceptable setting, some of them—not all, of course—would shed their labels and take their places with the rest of us somewhere on the spectrum of normality.

The reader may be puzzled by the short shrift given here to mental illness. This was no oversight. I have no training as a mental health professional so it is not always clear to me who is mentally ill and who is not. There were always some women who acted crazy or whom most considered crazy, and the women themselves often agreed with the public at large that many homeless people are mentally ill.

From the beginning, however, I paid little attention to mental illness, partly because I had difficulty recognizing it, and partly for other reasons. Sometimes mental illness seemed to be a "now-you-see-it, now-you-don't" phenomenon; some of the women were fine when their public assistance checks arrived, but became increasingly "symptomatic" as the month progressed and their money (security?) diminished, coming full circle when the next check arrived.[4] Others had good or bad days or weeks but with no obvious pattern or periodicity, although one woman linked her down period to her menstrual cycle. With a little patience on my part, almost all the women with mental or emotional problems were eventually and repeatedly accessible. Even on "bad" days, perhaps especially on "bad" days, these women sometimes said things that seemed to come, uncensored, from the depths of their emotional lives.

It seems to me that those women who may have been mentally ill (or alcoholic or drug addicted) by one or another standard were homeless for exactly the same proximal reason that everyone else was homeless: they had no place to live. Similarly, their greatest need of the moment was the same as everyone else's: to be assured of a safe, warm place to sleep at night, one or more hot meals a day, and the presence, if not the companionship, of fellow human beings. Given this perspective and my purposes, which and how many of the women were mentally ill was not a critical issue.

Whatever one's view of mental illness, it is probably true that the more one gets to know about a person, the easier it is to put oneself in that person's place or to understand his or her viewpoint, and the less reason one has for thinking of that person or treating that person as mentally ill.[5]

This perspective—indeed, participant observation itself—raises the age-old problem of whether anyone can understand another or put oneself in another's place. Many thoughtful people believe that a sane person cannot know what it is to be crazy, that a white man cannot understand a black man, a Jew cannot see through the eyes of a Christian, a man through the eyes of a woman, and so forth in both directions. In an important sense, of course, and to a degree, this is certainly true; in another sense, and to a degree, it is surely false, because the logical extension of such a view is that no one can know another, that only John Jones can know John Jones, in which case social life would be impossible.[6]

I do not mean that a man with a home and family can see and feel the world as homeless women see and feel it. I do mean, however, that it is reasonable and useful to try to do so. Trying to put oneself in the place of the other lies at the heart of the social contract and of social life itself.

In the early months, I sometimes tried to get Betty or one of the other women to see things as I saw them. One night Betty waited half an hour in back of the library for a bus that never came. She was convinced this was deliberate and personal abuse on the part of the Metro system. Metro was out to get her, she said. "But how did Metro know you were waiting for a bus at that time?" I asked. Betty shook her head in pity of me. "Well for Christ's sake, Elliot, I was there on the street, right there in public, in the open! How could they not see me waiting for that damn bus?"

Fairly quickly, I learned not to argue with Betty but simply to relax and marvel at her end-of-the-month ingenuity. ("End-of-the-month" because that's when her public assistance money ran out and when she was most bitter at the way the world was treating her. At that time, a $10 or $20 loan could dramatically reduce or even eliminate her paranoid thoughts.) Once, when her food stamps had not come, even two days after Judy had received hers, Betty dryly observed that this was further proof that Richman County was trying to rid itself of homeless women. "They give Judy Tootie her food stamps so she'll eat herself to death [Judy weighed 300 pounds]. They won't give me mine so I'll starve to death." She got no argument from me. I had learned to go with the flow.

Sometimes I annoyed or even angered some of the women. When Louise told me that some of the women were following her around all day and harassing her, I asked her why they did these things. "You're just like the state's attorney," she said, "always asking for reasons. Whenever I tell him that someone assaulted me, he always asks me why they did it. People with criminal minds don't need a reason to do something. That's what makes them criminals."

I think of Betty and Louise and many of the other women as friends. As a friend, I owe them friendship. Perhaps I also owe them something because I have so much and they have so little, but I do not feel under any special obligation to them as research subjects. Indeed, I do not think of them as "research subjects." Since they knew what I was trying to do and allowed me to do it, they could just as well be considered collaborators in what might fairly be seen as a cooperative enterprise.

NOTES

1. Let the record show that now, some seven-plus years later, I have her permission to go ahead.
2. *Tally's Corner: A Study of Negro Streetcorner Men.*
3. For the same reason, I stopped taking life histories. After the women had known me for a few months, I took about 20 life histories on tape, often at the request of the women themselves and over a period of two years or so. Some of these lasted several hours over two or three sessions and I found myself accumulating more information than I could handle.
4. Many schizophrenics are completely lucid for long periods of time, and their thoughts and behavior are completely indistinguishable from those of normals. Even Bleuler . . . asserted that there were certain very important cognitive processes . . . that were frequently identical among schizophrenics and normals. *In many important respects, then, an insane person may be completely sane* (emphasis added). Morris Rosenberg, "A Symbolic Interactionist View of Psychosis," *Journal of Health and Social Behavior*, 25, no. 3 (September 1984), p. 291.
5. In a symbolic interactionist view, "insanity is not a matter of . . . impaired functioning or social maladjustment. . . . It is unequivocally an interactional concept that is distinguished by an *observer's* inability to take the role of the actor" (emphasis in original). Rosenberg, "A Symbolic Interactionist View," p. 291.
6. Those who romanticize history and heroes are especially likely to close their minds to the possibility of people "understanding" one another. Allan Bloom, who does not let his brilliance get in the way of drawing wrong conclusions, is one such person. After separating "thinkers" from "doers," he argues that the thinker cannot understand the doer, then proceeds to a spectacular nonsequitur: "Does one not have to be akin to Caesar to understand him? To say that one does not have to be Caesar to understand him is equivalent to saying that one does not have to be anything to understand everything." *The Closing of the American Mind*, p. 303.

STUDY QUESTIONS

1. What sort of personal relationships did Liebow have with the members of his study sample?
2. How are Liebow's relationships both helpful and harmful to his research?

ALLAN J. KIMMELL

Ethics and Values in Applied Social Research

The ethical issues encountered in applied social research are subtle and complex, raising difficult moral dilemmas that, at least on a superficial level, appear unresolvable. These dilemmas often require the researcher to strike a delicate balance between the scientific requirements of methodology and the human rights and values potentially threatened by the research. As such, the underlying guiding research principle is to proceed both ethically and without threatening the validity of the research endeavor insofar as possible. It thus is essential that investigators continually ask how they can conduct themselves ethically and still make progress through sound and generalizable research. In subsequent chapters, current ethical standards and regulations will be reviewed, and their implications as guiding mechanisms will be discussed in the context of dilemmas encountered in actual research cases. . . .

The Goals of Basic and Applied Science

While sharing certain fundamental principles of research, social scientists may choose to direct their scientific activity from a "pure" or "applied" orientation. The basic distinction—albeit an oversimplified one—underlying this dichotomy is that "pure" science remains unchallenged by practical, concrete social problems and issues while "applied" research is essentially atheoretical in nature (Pepitone, 1981). Individuals who limit their scientific activity to purely theoretical work unrelated in any apparent way to real-world problems are typically referred to as "basic" researchers. Basic researchers hold that the proper course of science is the objective study and ultimate solution of basic scientific questions, regardless of whether their solutions have practical applications.

Around the turn of the twentieth century, social science research first became largely guided by a mechanistic paradigm or conceptual scheme borrowed—not by accident—from the experimental approach of the natural sciences. Since that time, basic researchers typically have viewed themselves as value-free "technicians," maintaining an active role in the discovery of truth but a passive role in determining the societal use of their findings (Rosnow, 1981). The assumption underlying this position of scientific nonresponsibility was (and still is, to a large extent) that although research findings can be used for good or bad ends, knowledge is ethically neutral. Working from this value-free tradition, basic researchers generally agree that their work is objective and morally neutral (as implied by the labels "pure" and "basic"), since their goal is the disinterested and impersonal pursuit of scientific knowledge for its own sake.

Some critics of the basic science tradition maintain that pure research is not value free since, in their view, it is immoral *not* to use the knowledge we have from theoretical research to attempt to reduce real-life social problems (e.g., Baumrin, 1970; Weber, 1949). But other critics of the supposed moral neutrality of basic science (e.g., Giddens, 1976, 1979; Smith, 1978) have argued the reverse point by claiming that, in fact, there *have* been past abuses in applications of "pure knowledge" (such as splitting the atom and Hiroshima, in vitro fertilization and test tube babies, and the like). Further, critics contend that basic research often entails the use of unethical procedures for obtaining knowledge (as when human subjects are harmed during a theoretical study), and they point out the potential destructiveness of some knowledge for personal and social life, such as the undermining of character and social customs (Luria, 1976; Smith, 1978). Thus when one considers the basic scientist's "right to know" within a larger social perspective, it is apparent that such a right—which is an implicit assumption within the pure science framework—can conflict with the obligation to do no harm (Steininger, Newell, & Garcia, 1984). . . .

Many individuals within the scientific community would argue that research ethics become increasingly important as the results of investigations acquire policy, professional, and personal implications outside the social science professions. However, this is not meant to imply that one can avoid responsibility for knowledge produced by restricting his or her scientific activity to a basic science approach. Conversely, the view that only applied research is ethical because of its assumed potential for social benefits is a short-sighted one, since some of the greatest break-throughs in science have come about through basic theoretical research. For example, chemistry did not advance as a science until chemists shifted away from an applied end (the creation of gold) to a concern for understanding chemistry at a theoretical level (Diener & Crandall, 1978).

When the dichotomy between pure and applied science is more closely evaluated, moral distinctions tend to blur. There are those who currently maintain that the "pure" versus "applied" distinction is a misconception and should be rejected (Georgoudi & Rosnow, 1985; Pepitone, 1981). According to this argument, because applied research often leads to theoretical understanding, and theoretical advances permit practical applications, the two types of research may not be as different as they initially appear. Theory does not arise in a social vacuum apart from concrete events that gave impetus to it (Sarason, 1981), and, conversely, theories of social behavior must withstand tests of practical application within concrete social settings in order to become established within the scientific community (Georgoudi & Rosnow, 1985). Consistent with this view, social psychologist Kurt Lewin (1947) advanced the idea that theoretical advances and the understanding of social problems are interdependent. Lewin proposed an "action research" that centered on studying things by changing them and observing the effects of the change. In Lewin's view, it is possible to be a scientific researcher who is, at the same time, concerned with the potential application of one's findings. Social scientists can hardly be expected to obtain a complete understanding of such social phenomena as leadership, political and economic behavior, and interpersonal relations without the observation of individuals within their sociocultural context (Pepitone, 1981). . . .

Preventive Intervention: An Illustrative Example of Applied Social Research

The primary goal of an "action-oriented" science is to accumulate facts and principles for immediate application to social problems and for the betterment of the human condition. Applied social researchers conduct their studies in the hope that they yield results that have significant potential value in the formulation or improvement of programs intended to help solve a wide range of social problems (Rivlin & Timpane, 1975).

Social scientists who apply their science in real-life settings where people live and work are inevitably acting on morally relevant decisions about what should be changed and why (Reynolds, 1979). Values enter into applied social investigations at various levels of the research process: with the decision that there is a problem, definition of the problem in terms of its presumed cause and potential solutions, and identification and selection of individuals for research participation and targeted change (Fischer, 1980; Warwick & Kelman, 1973). . . .

Values play an important role in prevention intervention studies because the research represents an attempt to prevent mental health patterns the scientist believes are potentially damaging to others. . . . Research suggests that answers to ethical questions may depend as much on one's view of science and one's general ethical philosophy as they depend on the current state of scientific research (e.g., Schlenker & Forsyth, 1977).

Case Studies in Social Research Ethics

. . . What follows below are four briefcase studies that serve to illustrate unanticipated ethical dilemmas that might emerge during the social research process: (1) Project Camelot, a political science research project that focused on the determinants of revolution in Latin American nations and that was quickly condemned as a counterinsurgency effort; (2) the Cambridge-Somerville Youth Study, a secondary prevention program aimed at delinquent youths, in which all reasonable steps were taken to protect research participants, but that nevertheless resulted in unanticipated negative consequences; (3) the "Springdale" study, a sociological investigation of a small town in upstate New York, which demonstrates how serious infractions of the right to privacy can arise from the publication of research findings that fail to disguise the identities of individual participants; and (4) the "tearoom trade" study of homosexual behavior in public restrooms, which raised questions about the extent to which disguised research practices can be used to study the ongoing behavior of unsuspecting participants.

Project Camelot

The results of social research are often perceived to be useful to those who seek either to justify change or to retard it. As a result, powerful control elements of society, such as the administrative sector of the social system that supports these research efforts, recognize the potential usefulness of research concerning social structure and change. Project Camelot is considered by many social scientists to be a clear example of a project that could have generated knowledge that, in the wrong hands, might have provided a potential for dramatic misuse (Levin, 1981; Reynolds, 1979). Sponsored by the U.S. Department of Defense, the $6 million project focused on the determinants of revolution in various Latin American countries.

The impetus for Project Camelot came from the office of the Army's Chief of Research and Development, and the project subsequently was carried out by the Special Operations Research Office of the American University, Washington, D.C., which was under contract with the Army to conduct "research in the social and behavior science fields in support of the Army's mission" (in *Behavioral Sciences and the National Security*, 1965, p. 192). Project Camelot was described in an Army fact sheet as a "social science project on preconditions of internal conflict, and on effects of indigenous governmental actions—easing, exacerbating or resolving—on these preconditions" (statement by Senator J. W. Fulbright on Department of Defense Research in Foreign Policy Matters, *Congressional Record*, August 25, 1965, p. 20906). The objectives of the investigation, according to Irving Louis Horowitz's (1967, p. vi) detailed account of the project, were "to devise procedures for assessing the potential for internal war within national societies" and "to identify with increased degrees of confidence those actions which a government might take to relieve conditions which are assessed as giving rise to potential for internal war." If successful, the project would have resulted in a systematic description of the events that preceded, occurred during, and followed either a peaceful or violent change in government.

In essence, Project Camelot was predicated on the assumption that with increased knowledge of the problem of counterinsurgency, the Army could effectively cope with the problem when it developed in other nations. The project was officially initiated in December 1964 (shortly after the United States had sent Marines to the Dominican Republic) when a project director was appointed and a number of social scientists (including sociologists, political scientists, economists, and a psychologist) were recruited to serve as consultants. The consultants were to provide technical support, mostly on a temporary basis, or to maintain longer-term responsibility for aspects of the research design. The actual investigation was to involve surveys and other field studies in various Latin American countries, and ultimately elsewhere in the world.

Project Camelot was very quickly condemned by social scientists who viewed it as an attempt by the Department of Defense to intervene in the internal affairs of Latin American countries by sponsoring research designed to reduce the likelihood of revolution. Under pressure from several fronts, Secretary of Defense Robert McNamara canceled the study on June 8, 1965, prior to initiation of the actual fieldwork within the targeted countries. The demise of Project Camelot has been traced to adverse reaction that arose in Chile, following certain informal efforts to establish working relations with Chilean social scientists (Horowitz, 1967). The project was brought to the attention of Chilean intellectuals and, subsequently, to certain members of the Chilean Senate and various left-wing elements in that country, who reacted with a number of charges against the U.S. government and its researchers. The controversy eventually led to a presidential communication instructing the U.S. State Department to review all federally funded investigations involving cross-societal research activities potentially affecting foreign policy.

The controversy surrounding Project Camelot demonstrates the drawbacks of social research conducted under the sponsorship of organizations, such as the Army, whose primary function is that of control. It is difficult to say whether the project would have met with similar attacks had it been carried out by social researchers with a sufficient degree of autonomy from the government. Due to the source of financial support, there was considerable suspicion that the knowledge developed from the investigation would be used to help prevent changes in existing governments, and though the actual objectives and intended use of findings were never publicly specified, the suspicions and ensuing political controversy created enough international hostility to cause termination of the project (Beals, 1969; Reynolds, 1979). Outside social science circles, Project Camelot had the overall effect of calling into question the legitimacy of social science research in general, including several other research projects in South America that were stopped as a result (Glazer, 1972).

The debate over the appropriateness of Project Camelot raged on for several years after its termination, and the political and ethical reactions to the study reflect the vastly different views that social scientists hold about such issues (Sjoberg, 1967). Whereas some social scientists accepted the objectives of the American government and the military as legitimate, others clearly challenged the goals of the project's sponsors and their failure to consider the positive aspects of revolution. For example, Glazer (1972, p. 39) explained his condemnation of the project on three counts: "for simply assuming that the U.S. military has a legitimate role in dealing with social problems of other countries, for asserting that this country's foreign policy was a major factor in determining the site of research, and for implying that internal war is always the greatest threat to a population's well-being."

The major ethical problem encountered in Project Camelot (and many other similar investigations) was the inability of the researchers to acquire knowledge while achieving a sufficient amount of autonomy from controlling governmental units. According to Sjoberg (1967), this type of problem intensifies as the social sciences play an increasingly larger role in governmental and other large-scale organization activities. Since Project Camelot, other similar cases have come to light (such as those involving the CIA's sponsorship of research), revealing that the project was not an isolated case. As social scientists attempt to orient their research in the direction of broader human concerns while accepting support from specific social organizations, major ethical and political dilemmas, such as those characterized by Project Camelot, will continue to arise.

The Cambridge-Somerville Youth Study

The Cambridge-Somerville Youth Study serves as a strong reminder of the need to conduct evaluated pilot studies in order to assess the potentially damaging effects of treatments, and to take precautionary measures to guard against them. In 1939, Richard Clark Cabot, a social philosopher and physician, began an experimental childhood treatment program intended to prevent delinquency among boys (aged 5 to 13) in Boston. The subsequent research program became known as the Cambridge-Somerville Youth Study (Powers & Witmer, 1951), and is notable because of its truly experimental nature and the random assignment of more than 500 research participants. Although methodologically the Cambridge-Sommerville stands as an exemplary example of a large-scale, long-term social experiment, it apparently is one in which the treatment under study unexpectedly hurt more than it helped.

Cabot's research involved 506 boys, half of whom were judged as "difficult" or delinquency prone, while the remainder were judged as "average." An equal number of individuals from each group were randomly assigned to a preventively oriented counseling program during which they received tutoring, medical assistance, and friendly advice for approximately five years. The other subjects were randomly assigned to a no-treatment control group.

More than thirty years later, in 1975 and 1976, Joan McCord and her research team conducted an evaluation of the Cambridge-Somerville Study in an attempt to assess its long-term effects. Through the use of official records and personal contacts, McCord (1978) obtained information about the early study's long-term effects on the life experiences of 95% of the original participants. The evaluation compared men who had been in the treatment group with "matched mates" from the control group. Although subjective judgments of the program's value by those who received its services were found by McCord to be generally favorable, the objective criteria presented a quite different and disturbing picture. None of the comparisons between the treatment and control groups showed that the prevention program had improved the lives of those in the treatment group; in fact, the only significant differences favored those who had *not* experienced the intervention. Treated subjects were more likely than controls to evidence signs of alcoholism and serious mental illness, died at a younger age, suffered from more stress-related diseases, tended to be employed in lower-prestige occupations, and were more likely to commit second crimes.

As a plausible interpretation of the unintended effects of the Cambridge-Somerville Project, McCord suggested that a dependency upon agency assistance might have developed among treated subjects, and that these individuals then experienced resentment when the outside assistance was no longer available. McCord also conjectured that the treatment program may have created in treated subjects high expectations that led to feelings of deprivation in subsequent experiences, or perhaps increased the likelihood that they misperceived themselves as in need of help in order to justify receiving the program's services.

Whatever the explanation for the study's outcome, McCord's follow-up revealed not only that the Cambridge-Somerville Project apparently failed to achieve one of its basic goals in preventing treated subjects from committing crimes, but also seems to have produced negative side effects no doubt unanticipated by Cabot and members of the research team who implemented the program. Equally distressing is that such findings in social research are hardly unique. Other prevention programs that increased dysfunctional risk have been reported by Fo and O'Donnell (1975) and Gersten, Langner, and Simcha-Fagan (1979). Lorion (1984) has pointed to the effects of widespread adoption of open classrooms for learning disabled children, and swine flu vaccinations for the elderly, as representative additional examples of the unintended consequences of social intervention strategies. It should be noted, however, that when a widely accepted, ongoing intervention produces the negative effects and evaluation research uncovers these effects, the research may be viewed as having served as a positive moral force. In such cases, the research will have uncovered the negative effects of a treatment that was both common and thought to be positive.

The "Springdale" Case. Whereas ethics in social research frequently involves the deliberate attempt to affect phenomena through direct manipulations, a substantial amount of research in the social sciences instead focuses on descriptions of natural processes. Social science research at the descriptive level is characterized by procedures that emphasize the direct observation of specific individuals or a social system, and the intensive review of natural behaviors and events. Such an approach is commonly employed by anthropologists, sociologists, and psychologists who are allowed access to a social setting and an opportunity to talk to participants in an attempt to discover and describe important social processes and cultural structures of a group. These investigations are often undertaken with the full knowledge of the individuals involved, and, unlike experimental and other types of research, the investigations are more likely to be merely exploratory, resulting in descriptions that tend to be discursive and anecdotal (Reynolds, 1979).

Serious infractions of the right to privacy and anonymity can arise from the publication of research findings that expose community institutions or unique individuals to public scrutiny. As a consequence, the ethical issues associated with descriptive field studies of social structure, group or community activity, and the like, tend to arise in the reporting or publishing phase rather than during the data-collection stage, as is more typical of experimental investigations (Levin, 1981). The descriptive field study of a small town in upstate New York (Vidich & Bensman, 1958) clearly illustrates how the impact of indirect effects occurring after the research is completed may be substantially greater than that of direct effects that occur during data collection. In their book *Small Town in Mass Society: Class,*

Power and Religion in a Rural Community, Vidich and Bensman describe the political and social life of a community identified by the fictitious name "Springdale," based on Vidich's observations while living there for two and one-half years. The book was intended to "explore the foundations of social life in a community which lacks the power to control the institutions that regulate and determine its existence" (Vidich & Bensman, 1958, p. vii).

Before the Springdale project was begun, the town's residents were assured by the research staff that no individuals would be identified in printed reports, and, in fact, a code of ethics was specifically devised for the project. The stated purpose of the code was to safeguard "the integrity and welfare of research participants" through the protection of their privacy and anonymity, and by assuring that the data collected would remain confidential (Bell & Bronfenbrenner, 1959). However, when a manuscript of Vidich and Bensman's book was reviewed prior to its publication there was some concern that, while individuals within the book were given fictitious names, certain persons were identifiable within Springdale and described in ways that would be damaging to them (Johnson, 1982). This assessment turned out to be all too prophetic. Publication of the study embarrassed members of the town, who recognized and strongly objected to the descriptions of various members of their community, including its leaders, despite the attempt to disguise their identities.

Springdale residents no doubt felt that the researchers' promise of anonymity had been betrayed. The tone of the book, which has been characterized as condescending and patronizing, also came into question, as did the causal attribution of attitudes and motives to the various members of the community (Reynolds, 1979). For example, one passage in the book reads as follows:

> *The people of Springdale are unwilling to recognize the defeat of their values, their personal impotence in the face of larger events, and many failures in their ways of life. By techniques of self-avoidance and self-deception, they strive to avoid facing issues that, if recognized, would threaten the total fabric of their personal and social existence. Instead of facing the issues, they make compromises and modify their behavior in some cases, and reaffirm their traditional patterns in other cases. (p. 314)*

The citizens of Springdale reacted to publication of the book by publicly lampooning the researchers in a Fourth of July parade, and by refusing further cooperation with any social scientists whatsoever, thereby negating the possibility of replication and long-term follow-up.

The ethical question raised by the Springdale affair, and one often associated with the publication of fieldwork, is "To what extent is the author of a community study obligated to pursue the anonymity of the people of the community studied?" (Johnson, 1982). When research participants can recognize themselves in embarrassing or uncomplimentary descriptions in print, resulting negative effects might include a reduction in their self-esteem and loss of confidence in the scientific process. At the same time, their claim that the portrayal of their social structure is misleading calls into question the accuracy of the report, and inevitably reduces confidence in the descriptions contained within it. Ironically, their antagonism to social research, resulting from their earlier experience, precludes any follow-up study to resolve the problem of accuracy.

The "Tearoom Trade" Study

Many ethical issues involved in the conduct of social research concern the use of deception, whether it is employed in experimental studies in which a treatment is administered to a group of unsuspecting subjects, or in less controlled research where respondents are secretly observed or asked disguised questions. While the use of deception in social research poses a number of ethical issues, perhaps the most serious consequence is that certain forms of deception often invade the privacy of research participants by violating their right to choose the circumstances and extent to which their opinions, beliefs, and behaviors are revealed or withheld from others (Ruebhausen & Brim, 1966). The violation of subjects' right to privacy is a likely outcome of participant observation research in which an investigator assumes a disguised role.

The case of sociologist Laud Humphreys's "tearoom trade" study perhaps best illustrates the ethical problems that can emerge in disguised research in public settings. As a doctoral candidate in sociology at Washington University, Humphreys became a participant-observer in a number of homosexual acts occurring in "tearooms"—public restrooms where homosexuals engaged in sexual activity. He assumed the role of tearoom "watchqueen" by serving as a lookout with the responsibility to warn of approaching strangers in exchange for the right to observe the homosexual activity.

Humphreys sought to learn about the lifestyles and motives of the men who congregated in the tearooms, but who otherwise seemed to lead normal heterosexual lives as accepted members of their communities. By obtaining the confidence of some of the men he observed, Humphreys revealed to them his role as a scientist and was able to convince them to talk openly about their lives. Upon learning that these men were among the better educated of the tearoom participants, Humphreys sought to obtain a more representative sample by tracing the registration numbers of subjects' automobiles to determine their home addresses. A year later, Humphreys altered his appearance and, claiming to be a health service interviewer, questioned his subjects at home.

The findings of Humphreys's research revealed that only a small percentage of his subjects were members of the gay community. Many of the subjects studied were married men who did not think of themselves as either homosexual or bisexual, but whose marriages were marked with tension. As might be expected, publication of the tearoom trade study (Humphreys, 1970) was met by strong reactions by both critics and supporters alike. The research was applauded by members of the gay community and some social scientists for shedding light on a little-known segment of our society, and for dispelling stereotypes and myths. Others, however, accused Humphreys of failing to protect his subjects' right to privacy, increasing their vulnerability to police detection, and deceiving his subjects about his true identity. Some faculty members at Washington University were so outraged by the research methods employed that they demanded (unsuccessfully) that Humphreys's doctoral degree be revoked.

A number of ethical questions were raised by the tearoom trade study, including whether a researcher is justified in acting contrary to the best interests of subjects in attempts to obtain valuable knowledge, to what extent deception is justified by the importance of an investigation, how one might go about studying illegal behavior in scientifically valid and ethically justifiable ways, and so on (see Sieber, 1982b). In this example, the conflict between the interests of scientists in obtaining knowledge and the interests of society in the protection of privacy and other rights is readily apparent.

Summary

The case studies described in this chapter reveal the complex nature of social science research. The ethical issues they raise often provide impediments to scientific progress oriented toward the betterment of the human social condition; they need not, however, result in exasperation among social researchers. Reviewing case studies of ethical dilemmas compels one to contemplate how such problems arise, and to consider potential solutions that do not seriously impair either the validity of an investigation or the respect for its participants (Sieber, 1982b).

REFERENCES

Baumrin, B. H. (1970). The immorality of irrelevance: The social role of science. In F. F. Korten, S. W. Cook, & J. I. Lacey (Eds.), *Psychology and the problems of society*. Washington, DC: APA.

Beals, R. L. (1969). *Politics of social change*. Chicago: Aldine.

Bell, E. H., & Bronfenbrenner, U. (1959). Freedom and responsibility in research: Comments. *Human Organization, 18,* 49–52.

Diener, E., & Crandall, R. (1978). *Ethics in social and behavioral research*. Chicago: University of Chicago Press.

Fo, W. S., & O'Donnell, C. R. (1975). The buddy system: Effects of community intervention on delinquent offenses. Behavior *Therapy, 6,* 522–524.

Georgoudi, M., & Rosnow, R. L. (1985). Notes toward a contextualist understanding of social psychology. *Personality and Social Psychology Bulletin, 11,* 5–22.

Gersten, J. C, Langner, T. S., & Simcha-Fagan, O. (1979). Developmental patterns of types of behavioral disturbance and secondary prevention. *International Journal of Mental Health, 7,* 132–149.

Giddens, A. (1976). *New rules of sociological method*. London: Hutchinson.

Giddens, A. (1979). *Central problems in social theory*. London: Macmillan.

Glazer, M. (1972). *The research adventure*. New York: Random House.

Horowitz, I. L. (1967). *The rise and fall of Project Camelot*. Cambridge: MIT Press.

Humphreys, L. (1970). *Tearoom trade*. Chicago: Aldine.

Johnson, C. G. (1982). Risks in the publication of fieldwork. In J. E. Sieber (Ed.), *The ethics of social research: Fieldwork, regulation, and publication*. New York: Springer-Verlag.

Lewin, K. (1947). Group decision and social change. In T. M. Newcomb & E. L. Hartley (Eds.), *Readings in social psychology*. New York: Holt.

Luria, S. E. (1976). Biological aspects of ethical principles. *Journal of Medicine and Philosophy, 1,* 332–336.

McCord, J. (1978). A thirty-year follow-up of treatment effects. *American Psychologist, 33,* 284–289.

Pepitone, A. (1981). Lessons from the history of social psychology. *American Psychologist, 36,* 972–985.

Powers, E., & Witmer, H. (1951). *An experiment in the prevention of delinquency: The Cambridge-Somerville youth study*. New York: Columbia University Press.

Reynolds, P. D. (1979). *Ethical dilemmas and social science research*. San Francisco: Jossey-Bass.

Rivlin, A. M., & Timpane, P. M. (Eds.). (1975). *Ethical and legal issues of social experimentation*. Washington, DC: Brookings Institution.

Rosnow, R. L. (1981). *Paradigms in transition: The methodology of social inquiry*. New York: Oxford University Press.

Ruebhausen, O. M., & Brim, O. G., Jr. (1966). Privacy and behavioral research. *American Psychologist, 21,* 423–437.

Sarason, S. B. (1981). *Psychology misdirected*. New York: Free Press.

Schlenker, B. R., & Forsyth, D. R. (1977). On the ethics of psychological research. *Journal of Experimental Social Psychology, 13,* 369–396.

Sieber, J. E. (1982b). Ethical dilemmas in social research. In J. E. Sieber (Ed.), *The ethics of social research: Surveys and experiments*. New York: Springer-Verlag.

Sjoberg, G. (1967). Project Camelot: Selected reactions and personal reflections. In G. Sjoberg (Ed.), *Ethics, politics, and social research*. Cambridge, MA: Schenkman.

Smith, D. H. (1978). Scientific knowledge and forbidden truths—are there things we should not know? *Hastings Center Report, 8,* 30–35.

Steininger, M., Newell, J. D., & Garcia, L. T. (1984). *Ethical issues in psychology.* Homewood, IL: Dorsey.

Vidich, A. J., & Bensman, J. (1958). *Small town in mass society: Class, power, and religion in a rural community.* Princeton, NJ: Princeton University Press.

Warwick, D. P., & Kelman, H. C. (1973). Ethical issues in social intervention. In G. Zaltman (Ed.), *Processes and phenomena of social change.* New York: John Wiley.

Weber, M. (1949). *The methodology of the social sciences* (Trans. and eds. E. A. Shils & H. A. Finch). New York: Free Press.

STUDY QUESTIONS

1. Identify the distinctions the author makes between "basic" and "applied" research.

2. Examine each of the four applied studies reviewed in this article and write out one value or ethical issue that arose in each.

PART TWO

The Organization of Society

TOPIC 3

Culture

It HAS BEEN SAID THAT CULTURE IS TO PEOPLE AS WATER is to fish—it is the last thing we would recognize about our social environment, unless we are outside this milieu. As the fish might be gasping for air, persons might be gasping for social sustenance, for a commonly understood way to act and communicate with others. As long as people grow up inside a society and culture and learn all the values, norms (rules), behaviors and language as they age, the culture will come to be viewed as "only natural," as something "taken for granted." In this circumstance, we are acculturated and the culture is understood as something we do each day that requires no conscious thought, no real decisions, just "doing what comes naturally." Clearly, if we were to wake up tomorrow and be in another culture where we did not know the values, norms and language, we would quickly come to appreciate how much we depend on culture and how much culture shapes our lives.

Kendall (2004, p. 43) defines culture as "the knowledge, language, values, customs, and material objects that are passed from person to person and from one generation to the next in a human group or society." According to this definition, culture is the repository of accumulated knowledge, of the language spoken by the members of the culture, of the values and beliefs and customs—even material objects—which we inherit socially from previous generations. Where would we be without culture? How would we communicate? What rules would need to be followed to keep order and create patterns in the society? Stop and think about all the assumptions people make regarding customs of meeting one another, of rules to guide moving traffic, or of social activities centering around a meal. As long as the assumptions are commonly shared, we can anticipate what will happen next, what others will do in response to us and us to them. Without the cultural guides, these everyday occurrences might come to a standstill—moments of silence filled with awkward feelings, traffic that is grid-locked, and continual embarrassment over missed cues to act or speak. Appreciating culture as an elemental, organizing principle of social life brings us closer to an important dimension of the sociological imagination.

Culture is the crucible of social life. Each of us is born out of it, and each of us lives our social lives through it. The values, beliefs, norms, and customs tell us what we can and cannot do, think, and how we are to behave. Culture is a paradox—both prison and playground. As a prison we are tied by the many rules that tell us we must go to school, work, meeting our obligations to our family, and so on. As a playground, culture is the medium through which we develop our social and physical skills, the vehicle for our self-actualization and development. Learning to live a balanced and happy life inside the paradox of culture will require a lifetime of effort and learning.

Topic 3: Culture includes readings from Barry Glassner, "The Culture of Fear," Horace Miner, "Body Ritual among the Nacerima," and Mitch Albom's discussion with Morrie Schwartz entitled "We Talk About Our Culture." From Glassner we will learn that popular media (popular culture) creates a sort of sentiment among the population that creates fear. He adds that the media might be using information that is more inflammatory than accurate. In the piece by Miner, we are taking a look at a most unusual culture in which people have equally unusual habits. I wonder how an anthropologist, in search of objectivity, might describe our own society. In the last reading, Morrie Schwartz, a Brandeis sociologist, is dying while the entire world is getting his final lessons, and one of his students writes to tell the narrative in a popular book, *Tuesdays with Morrie*. Morrie gives us some thought-provoking insights about culture in this brief but emotional excerpt. How might we go about "creating our own culture"?

BARRY GLASSNER

The Culture of Fear
Why Americans Fear the Wrong Things

Why are so many fears in the air, and so many of them unfounded? Why, as crime rates plunged throughout the 1990s, did two-thirds of Americans believe they were soaring? How did it come about that by mid-decade 62 percent of us described ourselves as "truly desperate" about crime—almost twice as many as in the late 1980s, when crime rates were higher? Why, on a survey in 1997, when the crime rate had already fallen for a half dozen consecutive years, did more than half of us disagree with the statement "This country is finally beginning to make some progress in solving the crime problem"?[1]

In the late 1990s the number of drug users had decreased by half compared to a decade earlier; almost two-thirds of high school seniors had never used any illegal drugs, even marijuana. So why did a majority of adults rank drug abuse as the greatest danger to America's youth? Why did nine out of ten believe the drug problem is out of control, and only one in six believe the country was making progress?[2]

Give us a happy ending and we write a new disaster story. In the late 1990s the unemployment rate was below 5 percent for the first time in a quarter century. People who had been pounding the pavement for years could finally get work. Yet pundits warned of imminent economic disaster. They predicted inflation would take off, just as they had a few years earlier—also erroneously—when the unemployment rate dipped below 6 percent.[3]

We compound our worries beyond all reason. Life expectancy in the United States has doubled during the twentieth century. We are better able to cure and control diseases than any other civilization in history. Yet we hear that phenomenal numbers of us are dreadfully ill. In 1996 Bob Garfield, a magazine writer, reviewed articles about serious diseases published over the course of a year in the *Washington Post*, the *New York Times*, and *USA Today*. He learned that, in addition to 59 million Americans with heart disease, 53 million with migraines, 25 million with osteoporosis, 16 million with obesity, and 3 million with cancer, many Americans suffer from more obscure ailments such as temporomandibular joint disorders (10 million) and brain injuries (2 million). Adding up the estimates, Garfield determined that 543 million Americans are seriously sick—a shocking number in a nation of 266 million inhabitants. "Either as a society we are doomed, or someone is seriously double-dipping," he suggested.[4]

Garfield appears to have underestimated one category of patients: for psychiatric ailments his figure was 53 million. Yet when Jim Windolf, an editor of the *New York Observer*, collated estimates for maladies ranging from borderline personality disorder (10 million) and sex addiction (11 million) to less well-known conditions such as restless leg syndrome (12 million) he came up with a figure of 152 million. "But give the experts a little time," he advised. "With another new quantifiable disorder or two, everybody in the country will be officially nuts."[5]

Indeed, Windolf omitted from his estimates new-fashioned afflictions that have yet to make it into the *Diagnostic and Statistical Manual of Mental Disorders* of the American Psychiatric Association: ailments such as road rage, which afflicts more than half of Americans, according to a psychologist's testimony before a congressional hearing in 1997.[6] . . .

Killer Kids

When we are not worrying about deadly diseases we worry about homicidal strangers. Every few months for the past several years it seems we discover a new category of people to fear: government thugs in Waco, sadistic cops on Los Angeles freeways and in Brooklyn police stations, mass-murdering youths in small towns all over the country. A single anomalous event can provide us with multiple groups of people to fear. After the 1995 explosion at the federal building in Oklahoma City first we panicked about Arabs. "Knowing that the car bomb indicates Middle Eastern terrorists at work, it's safe to assume that their goal is to promote free-floating fear and a measure of anarchy, thereby disrupting American life," a *New York Post* editorial asserted. "Whatever we are doing to destroy Mideast terrorism, the chief terrorist threat against Americans, has not been working," wrote A. M. Rosenthal in the *New York Times.*[7]

When it turned out that the bombers were young white guys from middle America, two more groups instantly became spooky: right-wing radio talk show hosts who criticize the government—depicted by President Bill Clinton as "purveyors of hatred and division"—and members of militias. No group of disgruntled men was too ragtag not to warrant big, prophetic news stories.[8]. . .

The more things improve the more pessimistic we become. Violence-related deaths at the nation's schools dropped to a record low during the 1996–97 academic year (19 deaths out of 54 million children), and only one in ten public schools reported *any* serious crime. Yet *Time* and *U.S. News & World Report* both ran headlines in 1996 referring to "Teenage Time Bombs." In a nation of "Children Without Souls" (another *Time* headline that year), "America's beleaguered cities are about to be victimized by a paradigm shattering wave of ultraviolent, morally vacuous young people some call 'the superpredators,'" William Bennett, the former Secretary of Education, and John DiIulio, a criminologist, forecast in a book published in 1996.[9]

Instead of the arrival of superpredators, violence by urban youths continued to decline. So we went looking elsewhere for proof that heinous behavior by young people was "becoming increasingly more commonplace in America" (CNN). After a sixteen-year-old in Pearl, Mississippi, and a fourteen-year-old in West Paducah, Kentucky, went on shooting sprees in late 1997, killing five of their classmates and wounding twelve others, these isolated incidents were taken as evidence of "an epidemic of seemingly depraved adolescent murderers" (Geraldo Rivera). Three months later in March 1998 all sense of proportion vanished after two boys ages eleven and thirteen killed four students and a teacher in Jonesboro, Arkansas. No longer, we learned in *Time*, was it "unusual for kids to get back at the world with live ammunition." When a child psychologist on NBC's "Today" show advised parents to reassure their children that shootings at schools are rare, reporter Ann Curry corrected him. "But this is the fourth case since October," she said.[10]

Over the next couple of months young people failed to accommodate the trend hawkers. None committed mass murder. Fear of killer kids remained very much in the air nonetheless. In stories on topics such as school safety and childhood trauma, reporters recapitulated the gory details of the killings. And the news media made a point of reporting every incident in which a child was caught at school with a gun or making a death threat. In May, when a fifteen-year-old in Springfield, Oregon, did open fire in a cafeteria filled with students, killing two and wounding twenty-three others, the event felt like a continuation of a "disturbing trend" (*New York Times*). The day after the shooting, on National Public Radio's "All Things Considered," the criminologist Vincent Schiraldi tried to explain that the recent string of incidents did not constitute a trend, that youth homicide rates had declined by 30 percent in recent years, and more than three times as many people were killed by lightning than by violence at schools. But the show's host, Robert Siegel, interrupted him. "You're saying these are just anomalous events?" he asked, audibly peeved. The criminologist reiterated that *anomalous* is precisely the right word to describe the events, and he called it "a grave mistake" to imagine otherwise. . . .

Roosevelt Was Wrong

We had better learn to doubt our inflated fears before they destroy us. Valid fears have their place; they cue us to danger. False and overdrawn fears only cause hardship. . . .

I do not contend, as did President Roosevelt in 1933, that "the only thing we have to fear is fear itself." My point is that we often fear the wrong things. In the 1990s middle-income and poorer Americans should have worried about unemployment insurance, which covered a smaller share of workers than twenty years earlier. Many of us have had friends or family out of work during economic downturns or as a result of corporate restructuring. Living in a nation with one of the largest income gaps of any industrialized country, where the bottom 40 percent of the population is worse off financially than their counterparts two decades earlier, we might also have worried about income inequality. Or poverty. During the mid- and late 1990s 5 million elderly Americans had no food in their homes, more than 20 million people used emergency food programs each year, and one in five children lived in poverty—more than a quarter million of them homeless. All told, a larger proportion of Americans were poor than three decades earlier.[11]

One of the paradoxes of a culture of fear is that serious problems remain widely ignored even though they give rise to precisely the dangers that the populace most abhors. Poverty, for example, correlates strongly with child abuse, crime, and drug abuse. Income inequality is also associated with adverse outcomes for society as a whole. The larger the gap between rich and poor in a society, the higher its overall death rates from heart disease, cancer, and murder. Some social scientists argue that extreme inequality also threatens political stability in a nation such as the United States, where we think of ourselves not as "haves and have nots" but as "haves and will haves." "Unlike the citizens of most other nations, Americans have always been united less by a shared past than by the shared dreams of a better future. If we lose that common future," the Brandeis University economist Robert Reich has suggested, "we lose the glue that holds our nation together."[12]

The combination of extreme inequality and poverty can prove explosive. In an insightful article in *U.S. News & World Report* in 1997 about militia groups reporters Mike Tharp and William Holstein noted that people's motivations for joining these groups are as much economic as ideological. The journalists argued that the disappearance of military and blue-collar jobs, along with the decline of family farming, created the conditions under which a new breed of protest groups flourished. "What distinguishes these antigovernment groups from, say, traditional conservatives who mistrust government is that their anger is fueled by direct threats to their livelihood, and they carry guns," Tharp and Holstein wrote.[13]

That last phrase alludes to a danger that by any rational calculation deserves top billing on Americans' lists of fears. So gun crazed is this nation that Burger King had to order a Baltimore franchise to stop giving away coupons from a local sporting goods store for free boxes of bullets with the purchase of guns. We have more guns *stolen* from their owners—about 300,000 annually—than many countries have gun owners. In Great Britain, Australia, and Japan, where gun ownership is severely restricted, no more than a few dozen people are killed each year by handguns. In the United States, where private citizens own a quarter-billion guns, around 15,000 people are killed, 18,000 commit suicide, and another 1,500 die accidentally from firearms. American children are twelve times more [likely] to die from gun injuries than are youngsters in other industrialized nations.[14]

Yet even after tragedies that could not have occurred except for the availability of guns, their significance is either played down or missed altogether. Had the youngsters in the celebrated schoolyard shootings of 1997–98 not had access to guns, some or all of the people they killed would be alive today. Without their firepower those boys lacked the strength, courage, and skill to commit multiple murders. Nevertheless newspapers ran editorials with titles such as "It's Not Guns, It's Killer Kids" (*Fort Worth Star-Telegram*) and "Guns Aren't the Problem" (*New York Post*), and journalists, politicians, and pundits blathered on endlessly about every imaginable cause of youthful rage, from "the psychology of violence in the South" to satanism to fights on "Jerry Springer" and simulated shooting in Nintendo games.[15]. . .

In Praise of Journalists

Any analysis of the culture of fear that ignored the news media would be patently incomplete, and of the several institutions most culpable for creating and sustaining scares the news media are arguably first among equals. They are also the most promising candidates for positive change. Yet by the same token critiques such as Stolberg's presage a crucial shortcoming in arguments that blame the media. Reporters not only spread fears, they also debunk them and criticize one another for spooking the public. A wide array of groups, including businesses, advocacy organizations, religious sects, and political parties, promote and profit from scares. News organizations are distinguished from other fear-mongering groups because they sometimes bite the scare that feeds them.

A group that raises money for research into a particular disease is not likely to negate concerns about that disease. A company that sells alarm systems is not about to call attention to the fact that crime is down. News organizations, on the other hand, periodically allay the very fears they arouse to lure audiences. Some newspapers that ran stories about child murderers, rather than treat every incident as evidence of a shocking trend, affirmed the opposite. After the schoolyard shooting in Kentucky the *New York Times* ran a sidebar alongside its feature story with the headline "Despite Recent Carnage, School Violence Is Not on Rise." Following the Jonesboro killings they ran a similar piece, this time on a recently released study showing the rarity of violent crimes in schools.[16]

Several major newspapers parted from the pack in other ways. *USA Today* and the *Washington Post*, for instance, made sure their readers knew that what should worry them is the availability of guns. *USA Today* ran news stories explaining that easy access to guns in homes accounted for increases in the number of juvenile arrests for homicide in rural areas during the 1990s. While other news outlets were respectfully quoting the mother of the thirteen-year-old Jonesboro shooter, who said she did not regret having encouraged her son to learn to fire a gun ("it's like anything else, there's some people that can drink a beer, and not become an alcoholic"), *USA Today* ran an op-ed piece proposing legal parameters for gun ownership akin to those for the use of alcohol and motor vehicles. And the paper published its own editorial in support of laws that require gun owners to lock their guns or keep them in locked containers. Adopted at that time by only fifteen states, the laws had reduced the number of deaths among children in those states by 23 percent.[17]

Morality and Marketing

Why do news organizations and their audiences find themselves drawn to one hazard rather than another?...

In the first half of the 1990s U.S. cities spent at least $10 billion to purge asbestos from public schools, even though removing asbestos from buildings posed a greater health hazard than leaving it in place. At a time when about one-third of the nation's schools were in need of extensive repairs the money might have been spent to renovate dilapidated buildings. But hazards posed by seeping asbestos are morally repugnant. A product that was supposed to protect children from fires might be giving them cancer. By directing our worries and dollars at asbestos we express outrage at technology and industry run afoul.[18]...

Within public discourse fears proliferate through a process of exchange. It is from crosscurrents of scares and counterscares that the culture of fear swells ever larger. Even as feminists disparage large classes of men, they themselves are a staple of fear mongering by conservatives. To hear conservatives tell it, feminists are not only "anti-child and anti-family" (Arianna Huffington) but through women's studies programs on college campuses they have fomented an "anti-science and anti-reason movement" (Christina Hoff Sommers).[19]

Conservatives also like to spread fears about liberals, who respond in kind. Among other pet scares, they accuse liberals of creating "children without consciences" by keeping prayer out of schools—to which liberals rejoin with warnings that right-wing extremists intend to turn youngsters into Christian soldiers.[20]

Samuel Taylor Coleridge was right when he claimed, "In politics, what begins in fear usually ends up in folly." Political activists are more inclined, though, to heed an observation from Richard Nixon: "People react to fear, not love. They don't teach that in Sunday school, but it's true." That principle, which guided the late president's political strategy throughout his career, is the sine qua non of contemporary political campaigning. Marketers of products and services ranging from car alarms to TV news programs have taken it to heart as well.[21]

The short answer to why Americans harbor so many misbegotten fears is that immense power and money await those who tap into our moral insecurities and supply us with symbolic substitutes.

NOTES

1. Crime data here and throughout are from reports of the Bureau of Justice Statistics unless otherwise noted. Fear of crime: Esther Madriz, *Nothing Bad Happens to Good Girls* (Berkeley: University of California Press, 1997), ch. 1; Richard Morin, "As Crime Rate Falls, Fears Persist," *Washington Post* National Edition, 16 June 1997, p. 35; David Whitman, "Believing the Good News," *U.S. News & World Report*, 5 January 1998, pp. 45–46.

2. Eva Bertram, Morris Blachman et al., *Drug War Politics* (Berkeley: University of California Press, 1996), p. 10; Mike Males, *Scapegoat Generation* (Monroe, ME: Common Courage Press, 1996), ch. 6; Karen Peterson, "Survey: Teen Drug Use Declines," *USA Today*, 19 June 1998, p. A6; Robert Blendon and John Young, "The Public and the War on Illicit Drugs," *Journal of the American Medical Association* 279 (18 March 1998): 827–32. In presenting these statistics and others I am aware of a seeming paradox: I criticize the abuse of statistics by fearmongering politicians, journalists, and others but hand down precise-sounding numbers myself. Yet to eschew all estimates because some are used inappropriately or do not withstand scrutiny would be as foolhardy as ignoring all medical advice because some doctors are quacks. Readers can be assured I have interrogated the statistics presented here as factual. As notes throughout the book make clear, I have tried to rely on research that appears in peer-reviewed scholarly journals. Where this was not possible or sufficient, I traced numbers back to their sources, investigated the research methodology utilized to produce them, or conducted searches of the popular and scientific literature for critical commentaries and conflicting findings.

3. Bob Herbert, "Bogeyman Economics," *New York Times*, 4 April 1997, p. A15; Doug Henwood, "Alarming Drop in Unemployment," *Extra*, September 1994, pp. 16–17; Christopher Shea, "Low Inflation and Low Unemployment Spur Economists to Debate 'Natural Rate' Theory," *Chronicle of Higher Education*, 24 October 1997, p. A13.

4. Bob Garfield, "Maladies by the Millions," *USA Today*, 16 December 1996, p. A15.

5. Jim Windolf, "A Nation of Nuts," *Wall Street Journal*, 22 October 1997, p. A22.

6. Andrew Ferguson, "Road Rage," *Time*, 12 January 1998, pp. 64–68; Joe Sharkey, "You're Not Bad, You're Sick. It's in the Book," *New York Times*, 28 September 1997, pp. N1, 5.

7. Jim Naureckas, "The Jihad That Wasn't," *Extra*, July 1995, pp. 6–10, 20 (contains quotes). See also Edward Said, "A Devil Theory of Islam," *Nation*, 12 August 1996, pp. 28–32.

8. Lewis Lapham, "Seen but Not Heard," *Harper's*, July 1995, pp. 29–36 (contains Clinton quote). See also Robin Wright and Ronald Ostrow, "Illusion of Immunity Is Shattered," *Los Angeles*

Times, 20 April 1995, pp. Al, 18; Jack Germond and Jules Witcover, "Making the Angry White Males Angrier," column syndicated by Tribune Media Services, May 1995; and articles by James Bennet and Michael Janofsky in the *New York Times*, May 1995.

9. Statistics from "Violence and Discipline Problems in U.S. Public Schools: 1996–97," National Center on Education Statistics, U.S. Department of Education, Washington, DC, March 1998; CNN, "Early Prime," 2 December 1997; and Tamar Lewin, "Despite Recent Carnage, School Violence Is Not on Rise," *New York Times*, 3 December 1997, p. A14. Headlines: *Time*, 15 January 1996; *U.S. News & World Report*, 25 March 1996; Margaret Carlson, "Children Without Souls," *Time*, 2 December 1996, p. 70; William J. Bennett, John J. DiIulio, and John Walters, *Body Count* (New York: Simon & Schuster, 1996).

10. CNN, "Talkback Live," 2 December 1997; CNN, "The Geraldo Rivera Show," 11 December 1997; Richard Lacayo, "Toward the Root of Evil," *Time*, 6 April 1998, pp. 38–39; NBC, "Today," 25 March 1998. See also Rick Bragg, "Forgiveness, After 3 Die in Shootings in Kentucky," *New York Times*, 3 December 1997, p. A14; Maureen Downey, "Kids and Violence," 28 March 1998, *Atlanta Journal and Constitution*, p. A12.

11. "The State of America's Children," report by the Children's Defense Fund, Washington, DC, March 1998; "Blocks to Their Future," report by the National Law Center on Homelessness and Poverty, Washington, DC, September 1997; reports released in 1998 from the National Center for Children in Poverty, Columbia University, New York; Douglas Massey, "The Age of Extremes," *Demography* 33 (1996): 395–412; Trudy Lieberman, "Hunger in America," *Nation*, 30 March 1998, pp. 11–16; David Lynch, "Rich Poor World," *USA Today*, 20 September 1996, p. B1; Richard Wolf, "Good Economy Hasn't Helped the Poor," *USA Today*, 10 March 1998, p. A3; Robert Reich, "Broken Faith," *Nation*, 16 February 1998, pp. 11–17.

12. Inequality and mortality studies: Bruce Kennedy et al., "Income Distribution and Mortality," *British Medical Journal* 312 (1996): 1004–7; Ichiro Kawachi and Bruce Kennedy, "The Relationship of Income Inequality to Mortality," *Social Science and Medicine* 45 (1997): 1121–27. See also Barbara Chasin, *Inequality and Violence in the United States* (Atlantic Highlands, NJ: Humanities Press, 1997). Political stability: John Sloan, "The Reagan Presidency, Growing Inequality, and the American Dream," *Policy Studies Journal* 25 (1997): 371–86 (contains Reich quotes and "will haves" phrase). On both topics see also Philippe Bourgois, *In Search of Respect: Selling Crack in El Barrio* (Cambridge: Cambridge University Press, 1996); William J. Wilson, *When Work Disappears* (New York, Knopf, 1996); Richard Gelles, "Family Violence," *Annual Review of Sociology* 11 (1985): 347–67; Sheldon Danziger and Peter Gottschalk, *America Unequal* (Cambridge, MA: Harvard University Press, 1995); Claude Fischer et al., *Inequality by Design* (Princeton, NJ: Princeton University Press, 1996).

13. Mike Tharp and William Holstein, "Mainstreaming the Militia," *U.S. News & World Report*, 21 April 1997, pp. 24–37.

14. Burger King: "Notebooks," *New Republic*, 29 April 1996, p. 8. Statistics from the FBI's Uniform Crime Reports, Centers for Disease Control reports, and Timothy Egan, "Oregon Freeman Goes to Court," *New York Times*, 23 May 1998, pp. A1, 8.

15. Bill Thompson, "It's Not Guns, It's Killer Kids," *Fort Worth Star-Telegram*, 31 March 1998, p. 14; "Guns Aren't the Problem," *New York Post*, 30 March 1998 (from *Post* Web site); "Arkansas Gov. Assails 'Culture of Violence,' " Reuters, 25 March 1998; Bo Emerson, "Violence Feeds 'Redneck,' Gun-Toting Image," *Atlanta Journal and Constitution*, 29 March 1998, p. A8; Nadya Labi, "The Hunter and the Choir Boy," *Time*, 6 April 1998, pp. 28–37; Lacayo, "Toward the Root of Evil."

16. Lewin, "More Victims and Less Sense"; Tamar Lewin, "Study Finds No Big Rise in Public-School Crimes," *New York Times*, 25 March 1998, p. A18.

17. "Licensing Can Protect," *USA Today*, 7 April 1998, p. A11; Jonathan Kellerman, "Few Surprises When It Comes to Violence," *USA Today*, 27 March 1998, p. A13; Gary Fields, "Juvenile Homicide Arrest Rate on Rise in Rural USA," *USA Today*, 26 March 1998, p. A11; Karen Peterson and Glenn O'Neal, "Society More Violent, So Are Its Children," *USA Today*, 25 March 1998, p. A3; Scott Bowles, "Armed, Alienated and Adolescent," *USA Today*, 26 March 1998, p. A9. Similar suggestions about guns appear in Jonathan Alter, "Harnessing the Hysteria," *Newsweek*, 6 April 1998, p. 27.

18. Mary Douglas and Aaron Wildavsky, *Risk and Culture* (Berkeley: University of California Press, 1982), see esp. pp. 6–9; Mary Douglas, *Risk and Blame* (London: Routledge, 1992). See also Mary Douglas, *Purity and Danger* (New York: Praeger, 1966). Asbestos and schools: Peter Cary, "The

Asbestos Panic Attack," *U.S. News & World Report*, 20 February 1995, pp. 61–64; Children's Defense Fund, "State of America's Children."

19. CNN, "Crossfire," 27 August 1995 (contains Huffington quote); Ruth Conniff, "Warning: Feminism Is Hazardous to Your Health," *Progressive*, April 1997, pp. 33–36 (contains Sommers quote). See also Susan Faludi, *Backlash* (New York: Crown, 1991); Deborah Rhode, "Media Images, Feminist Issues," *Signs* 20 (1995): 685–710; Paula Span, "Did Feminists Forget the Most Crucial Issues?" *Los Angeles Times*, 28 November 1996, p. E8.

20. See Katha Pollitt, "Subject to Debate," *Nation*, 26 December 1994, p. 788, and idem, 20 November 1995, p. 600.

21. Henry Nelson Coleridge, ed., *Specimens of the Table Talk of the Late Samuel Taylor Coleridge* (London: J. Murray, 1935), entry for 5 October 1930. Nixon quote cited in William Safire, *Before the Fall* (New York: Doubleday, 1975), Prologue.

STUDY QUESTIONS

1. What are the reasons given by Glassner that Americans are "afraid of the wrong things"?

2. Based on Glassner's analysis, what is the role of sociology in dispelling a culture of fear?

HORACE MINER

Body Ritual among the Nacirema

The anthropologist has become so familiar with the diversity of ways in which different peoples behave in similar situations that he is not apt to be surprised by even the most exotic customs. In fact, if all of the logically possible combinations of behavior have not been found somewhere in the world, he is apt to suspect that they must be present in some yet undescribed tribe. This point has, in fact, been expressed with respect to clan organization by Murdock (1949:71). In this light, the magical beliefs and practices of the Nacirema present such unusual aspects that it seems desirable to describe them as an example of the extremes to which human behavior can go.

Professor Linton first brought the ritual of the Nacirema to the attention of anthropologists twenty years ago (1936:326), but the culture of this people is still very poorly understood. They are a North American group living in the territory between the Canadian Cree, the Yaqui and Tarahumare of Mexico, and the Carib and Arawak of the Antilles. Little is known of their origin, although tradition states that they came from the east. According to Nacirema mythology, their nation was originated by a culture hero, Notgnihsaw, who is otherwise known for two great feats of strength—the throwing of a piece of wampum across the river Pa-To-Mac and the chopping down of a cherry tree in which the Spirit of Truth resided.

Nacirema culture is characterized by a highly developed market economy which has evolved in a rich natural habitat. While much of the people's time is devoted to economic pursuits, a large part of the fruits of these labors and a considerable portion of the day are spent in ritual activity. The focus of this activity is the human body, the appearance and health of which loom as a dominant concern in the ethos of the people. While such a concern is certainly not unusual, its ceremonial aspects and associated philosophy are unique.

The fundamental belief underlying the whole system appears to be that the human body is ugly and that its natural tendency is to debility and disease. Incarcerated in such a body, man's only hope is to avert these characteristics through the use of the powerful influences of ritual and ceremony. Every household has one or more shrines devoted to this purpose. The more powerful individuals in the society have several shrines in their houses and, in fact, the opulence of a house is often referred to in terms of the number of such ritual centers it possesses. Most houses are of wattle and daub construction, but the shrine rooms of the more wealthy are walled with stone. Poorer families imitate the rich by applying pottery plaques to their shrine walls.

While each family has at least one such shrine, the rituals associated with it are not family ceremonies but are private and secret. The rites are normally only discussed with children, and then only during the period when they are being initiated into these mysteries. I was able, however, to establish sufficient rapport with the natives to examine these shrines and to have the rituals described to me.

The focal point of the shrine is a box or chest which is built into the wall. In this chest are kept the many charms and magical potions without which no native believes he could live. These preparations are secured from a variety of specialized practitioners. The most powerful of these are the medicine men, whose assistance must be rewarded with substantial gifts. However, the medicine men do not provide the curative potions for their clients, but decide what the ingredients should be and then write them down in an ancient and secret language. This writing is understood only by the medicine men and by the herbalists who, for another gift, provide the required charm.

The charm is not disposed of after it has served its purpose, but is placed in the charm-box of the household shrine. As these magical materials are specific for certain ills, and the real or imagined maladies of the people are many, the charm-box is usually full to overflowing. The magical packets are so numerous that people forget what their purposes were and fear to use them again. While the natives are very vague on this point, we can only assume that the idea in retaining all the old magical materials is that their presence in the charm-box, before which the body rituals are conducted, will in some way protect the worshipper.

Beneath the charm-box is a small font. Each day every member of the family, in succession, enters the shrine room, bows his head before the charm-box, mingles different sorts of holy water in the font, and proceeds with a brief rite of ablution. The holy waters are secured from the Water Temple of the community, where the priests conduct elaborate ceremonies to make the liquid ritually pure.

In the hierarchy of magical practitioners, and below the medicine men in prestige, are specialists whose designation is best translated "holy-mouth-men." The Nacirema have an almost pathological horror of and fascination with the mouth, the condition of which is believed to have a supernatural influence on all social relationships. Were it not for the rituals of the mouth, they believe that their teeth would fall out, their gums bleed, their jaws shrink, their friends desert them, and their lovers reject them. They also believe that a strong relationship exists between oral and moral characteristics. For example, there is a ritual ablution of the mouth for children which is supposed to improve their moral fiber.

The daily body ritual performed by everyone includes a mouth-rite. Despite the fact that these people are so punctilious about care of the mouth, this rite involves a practice which strikes the uninitiated stranger as revolting. It was reported to me that the ritual consists of inserting a small bundle of hog hairs into the mouth, along with certain magical powders, and then moving the bundle in a highly formalized series of gestures.

In addition to the private mouth-rite, the people seek out a holy-mouth-man once or twice a year. These practitioners have an impressive set of paraphernalia, consisting of a variety of augers, awls, probes, and prods. The use of these objects in the exorcism of the evils of the mouth involves almost unbelievable ritual torture of the client. The holy-mouth-man opens the client's mouth and, using the above mentioned tools, enlarges any holes which decay may have created in the teeth. Magical materials are put into these holes. If there are no naturally occurring holes in the teeth, large sections of one or more teeth are gouged out so that the supernatural substance can be applied. In the client's view, the purpose of these ministrations is to arrest decay and to draw friends. The extremely sacred and traditional character of the rite is evident in the fact that the natives return to the holy-mouth-men year after year, despite the fact that their teeth continue to decay.

It is to be hoped that, when a thorough study of the Nacirema is made, there will be careful inquiry into the personality structure of these people. One has but to watch the gleam in the eye of a holy-mouth-man, as he jabs an awl into an exposed nerve, to suspect that a certain amount of sadism is involved. If this can be established, a very interesting pattern emerges, for most of the population shows definite masochistic tendencies. It was to these that Professor Linton referred in discussing a distinctive part of the daily body ritual which is performed only by men. This part of the rite involves scraping and lacerating the surface of the face with a sharp instrument. Special women's rites are performed only four times during each lunar month, but what they lack in frequency is made up in barbarity. As part of this ceremony, women bake their heads in small ovens for about an hour. The theoretically interesting point is that what seems to be a preponderantly masochistic people have developed sadistic specialists.

The medicine men have an imposing temple, or *latipso*, in every community of any size. The more elaborate ceremonies required to treat very sick patients can only be performed at this temple. These ceremonies involve not only the thaumaturge but a permanent group of vestal maidens who move sedately about the temple chambers in distinctive costume and headdress.

The *latipso* ceremonies are so harsh that it is phenomenal that a fair proportion of the really sick natives who enter the temple ever recover. Small children whose indoctrination is still incomplete have been known to resist attempts to take them to the temple because "that is where you go to die." Despite this fact, sick adults are not only willing but eager to undergo the protracted ritual purification, if they can afford to do so. No matter how ill the supplicant or how grave the emergency, the guardians of many temples will not admit a client if he cannot give a rich gift to the custodian. Even after one has gained admission and survived the ceremonies, the guardians will not permit the neophyte to leave until he makes still another gift.

The supplicant entering the temple is first stripped of all his or her clothes. In every-day life the Nacirema avoids exposure of his body and its natural functions. Bathing and excretory acts are performed only in the secrecy of the household shrine, where they are ritualized as part of the body-rites. Psychological shock results from the fact that body secrecy is suddenly lost upon entry into the *latipso*. A man, whose own wife has never seen him in an excretory act, suddenly finds himself naked and assisted by a vestal maiden while he performs his natural functions into a sacred vessel. This sort of ceremonial treatment is necessitated by the fact that the excreta are used by a diviner to ascertain the course and nature of the client's sickness. Female clients, on the other hand, find their naked bodies are subjected to the scrutiny, manipulation and prodding of the medicine men.

Few supplicants in the temple are well enough to do anything but lie on their hard beds. The daily ceremonies, like the rites of the holy-mouth-men, involve discomfort and torture. With ritual precision, the vestals awaken their miserable charges each dawn and roll them about on their beds of pain while performing ablutions, in the formal movements of which the maidens are highly trained. At other times they insert magic wands in the supplicant's mouth or force him to eat substances which are supposed to be healing. From time to time the medicine men come to their clients and jab magically treated needles into their flesh. The fact that these temple ceremonies may not cure, and may even kill the neophyte, in no way decreases the people's faith in the medicine men.

There remains one other kind of practitioner, known as a "listener." This witch-doctor has the power to exorcise the devils that lodge in the heads of people who have been bewitched. The Nacirema believe that parents bewitch their own children. Mothers are particularly suspected of putting a curse on children while teaching them the secret body rituals. The counter-magic of the witch-doctor is unusual in its lack of ritual. The patient simply tells the "listener" all his troubles and fears, beginning with the earliest difficulties he can remember. The memory displayed by the Nacirema in these exorcism sessions is truly remarkable. It is not uncommon for the patient to bemoan the rejection he felt upon being weaned as a babe, and a few individuals even see their troubles going back to the traumatic effects of their own birth.

In conclusion, mention must be made of certain practices which have their base in native esthetics but which depend upon the pervasive aversion to the natural body and its functions. There are ritual fasts to make fat people thin and ceremonial feasts to make thin people fat. Still other rites are used to make women's breasts larger if they are small, and smaller if they are large. General dissatisfaction with breast shape is symbolized in the fact that the ideal form is virtually outside the range of human variation. A few women afflicted with almost inhuman hypermammary development are so idolized that they make a handsome living by simply going from village to village and permitting the natives to stare at them for a fee.

Reference has already been made to the fact that excretory functions are ritualized, routinized, and relegated to secrecy. Natural reproductive functions are similarly distorted. Intercourse is taboo as a topic and scheduled as an act. Efforts are made to avoid pregnancy by the use of magical materials or by limiting intercourse to certain phases of the moon. Conception is actually very infrequent. When pregnant, women dress so as to hide their condition. Parturition takes place in secret, without friends or relatives to assist, and the majority of women do not nurse their infants.

Our review of the ritual life of the Nacirema has certainly shown them to be a magic-ridden people. It is hard to understand how they have managed to exist so long under the burdens which they have imposed upon themselves. But even such exotic customs as these take on real meaning when they are viewed with the insight provided by Malinowski when he wrote (1948:70):

> Looking from far and above, from our high places of safety in the developed civilization, it is easy to see all the crudity and irrelevance of magic. But without its power and guidance early man could not have mastered his practical difficulties as he has done, nor could man have advanced to the higher stages of civilization.

REFERENCES

Linton, Ralph
  1936 The Study of Man. New York, D. Appleton-Century Co.
Malinowski, Bronislaw
  1948 Magic, Science, and Religion. Glencoe, The Free Press.
Murdock, George P.
  1949 Social Structure. New York, The Macmillan Co.

STUDY QUESTIONS

1. Why would such a group have the rituals described by Miner?
2. Who are the Nacirema? Can you say for sure?

MITCH ALBOM

We Talk About Our Culture

"Hit him harder."

I slapped Morrie's back.

"Harder."

I slapped him again.

"Near his shoulders . . . now down lower."

Morrie, dressed in pajama bottoms, lay in bed on his side, his head flush against the pillow, his mouth open. The physical therapist was showing me how to bang loose the poison in his lungs—which he needed done regularly now, to keep it from solidifying, to keep him breathing.

"I. . . always knew. . . you wanted. . . to hit me. . ." Morrie gasped.

Yeah, I joked as I rapped my fist against the alabaster skin of his back. This is for that B you gave me sophomore year! *Whack!*

We all laughed, a nervous laughter that comes when the devil is within earshot. It would have been cute, this little scene, were it not what we all knew it was, the final calisthenics before death. Morrie's disease was now dangerously close to his surrender spot, his lungs. He had been predicting he would die from choking, and I could not imagine a more terrible way to go. Sometimes he would close his eyes and try to draw the air up into his mouth and nostrils, and it seemed as if he were trying to lift an anchor.

Outside, it was jacket weather, early October, the leaves clumped in piles on the lawns around West Newton. Morrie's physical therapist had come earlier in the day, and I usually excused myself when nurses or specialists had business with him. But as the weeks passed and our time ran down, I was increasingly less self-conscious about the physical embarrassment. I wanted to be there. I wanted to observe everything. This was not like me, but then, neither were a lot of things that had happened these last few months in Morrie's house.

So I watched the therapist work on Morrie in the bed, pounding the back of his ribs, asking if he could feel the congestion loosening within him. And when she took a break, she asked if I wanted to try it. I said yes. Morrie, his face on the pillow, gave a little smile.

"Not too hard," he said. "I'm an old man."

I drummed on his back and sides, moving around, as she instructed. I hated the idea of Morrie's lying in bed under any circumstances (his last aphorism, "When you're in bed, you're dead," rang in my ears), and curled on his side, he was so small, so withered, it was more a boy's body than a man's. I saw the paleness of his skin, the stray white hairs, the way his arms hung limp and helpless. I thought about how much time we spend trying to shape our bodies, lifting weights, crunching sit-ups, and in the end, nature takes it away from us anyhow. Beneath my fingers, I felt the loose flesh around Morrie's bones, and I thumped him hard, as instructed. The truth is, I was pounding on his back when I wanted to be hitting the walls. . . .

Morrie believed in the inherent good of people. But he also saw what they could become.

"People are only mean when they're threatened," he said later that day, "and that's what our culture does. That's what our economy does. Even people who have jobs in our economy are threatened, because they worry about losing them. And when you get threatened, you start looking out only for yourself. You start making money a god. It is all part of this culture."

He exhaled. "Which is why I don't buy into it."

I nodded at him and squeezed his hand. We held hands regularly now. This was another change for me. Things that before would have made me embarrassed or squeamish were now routinely handled. The catheter bag, connected to the tube inside him and filled with greenish waste fluid, lay by my foot near the leg of his chair. A few months earlier, it might have disgusted me; it was inconsequential now. So was the smell of the room after Morrie had used the commode. He did not have the luxury of moving from place to place, of closing a bathroom door behind him, spraying some air freshener when he left. There was his bed, there was his chair, and that was his life. If my life were squeezed into such a thimble, I doubt I could make it smell any better.

"Here's what I mean by building your own little subculture," Morrie said. "I don't mean you disregard every rule of your community. I don't go around naked, for example. I don't run through red lights. The little things, I can obey. But the big things—how we think, what we value—those you must choose yourself. You can't let anyone—or any society—determine those for you.

"Take my condition. The things I am supposed to be embarrassed about now—not being able to walk, not being able to wipe my ass, waking up some mornings wanting to cry—there is nothing innately embarrassing or shaming about them.

"It's the same for women not being thin enough, or men not being rich enough. It's just what our culture would have you believe. Don't believe it."

I asked Morrie why he hadn't moved somewhere else when he was younger.

"Where?"

I don't know. South America. New Guinea. Someplace not as selfish as America.

"Every society has its own problems," Morrie said, lifting his eyebrows, the closest he could come to a shrug. "The way to do it, I think, isn't to run away. You have to work at creating your own culture.

"Look, no matter where you live, the biggest defect we human beings have is our shortsightedness. We don't see what we could be. We should be looking at our potential, stretching ourselves into everything we can become. But if you're surrounded by people who say 'I want mine now,' you end up with a few people with everything and a military to keep the poor ones from rising up and stealing it."

Morrie looked over my shoulder to the far window. Sometimes you could hear a passing truck or a whip of the wind. He gazed for a moment at his neighbors' houses, then continued.

"The problem, Mitch, is that we don't believe we are as much alike as we are. Whites and blacks, Catholics and Protestants, men and women. If we saw each other as more alike, we might be very eager to join in one big human family in this world, and to care about that family the way we care about our own.

"But believe me, when you are dying, you see it is true. We all have the same beginning—birth—and we all have the same end—death. So how different can we be?

"Invest in the human family. Invest in people. Build a little community of those you love and who love you."

He squeezed my hand gently. I squeezed back harder. And like that carnival contest where you bang a hammer and watch the disk rise up the pole, I could almost see my body heat rise up Morrie's chest and neck into his cheeks and eyes. He smiled.

"In the beginning of life, when we are infants, we need others to survive, right? And at the end of life, when you get like me, you need others to survive, right?"

His voice dropped to a whisper. "But here's the secret: in between, we need others as well."

STUDY QUESTIONS

1. In following Morrie's advice, how would one go about "creating his or her own culture"?
2. What point is Morrie making about similarity between people? Why is this important in culture?

TOPIC 4

Socialization

A BABY BORN INTO SOCIAL LIFE WILL UNDERGO A MOST remarkable transformation in the first few years. From a crying, random, moving, stretching baby, this child will soon learn to sit and crawl and walk and talk and think and react to others in patterned and predictable ways. In the span of a few months, the child will learn to think for itself, express itself, and develop some very sophisticated physical, intellectual, and social skills. By age four or five, this child will be able to leave the home and effectively operate at school, with other children at play, as well as in many other social settings. Amazing!! How does this happen?

Sociology, along with the other sciences, knows this is much more than a biological process. Socialization is the process whereby persons develop the skills to operate effectively in social life. Families are a large contributor to socialization, for it is through these early moments in our lives that we come to develop the physical and intellectual abilities that will carry us for decades to come. But as our world grows, the influence of other adults, peers, schools, and neighborhoods impinge on us and affect our socialization as well. It is through this process of socialization that we must learn to become both an individual and a member of a community, and it is through this process of socialization that what exists outside us in society will become part of our personal makeup as unique human beings.

The debate over the relative contributions of biology and social experience—*nature* and *nurture*—has been raging for nearly two centuries. Sometimes we are more ready to listen to the genetic arguments, sometimes to the social science arguments. In fact, both sets of variables affect who we are as adult human beings, but we work to refine the information in ways that make our models more accurate and more complete. For example, is our *gendered* behavior more from our genetic makeup or our social experiences? There is evidence on both sides, but the social sciences stress the data that show we are mostly human, and socialized, because of our associations with other people.

Importantly, socialization will continue for the entirety of our lives. We will be socialized in school settings, we will be socialized during our employment, and we will move to different communities and learn the social habits and patterns of this new environment as well. This socialization process enables us to learn and be effective in the new roles we adopt; at the same time, it alters our self-concepts and identities. As social beings we are in a constant state of flux as we change and adapt to the altered social circumstances life presents. If we are able to make these changes with skill and ease, we will increase measurably the equanimity in our lives. We can learn from sociology, and from understanding the process of socialization, some very important and valuable information.

The three articles for this topic, Socialization, include first, by Madonna Constantine and Sha'kema Blackmon, a study about the racial socialization experiences of "Black Adolescents." This quantitative research article shows the relationship of certain social events to the students' self-esteem. It also raises interesting questions for African-American parents and educators regarding conformity to dominant cultural norms. Second, a very important article by Kingsley Davis illustrates how the "extreme isolation" of two girls underscores the fact that children require human contact and social interaction to develop beyond the most rudimentary levels. Indeed, our humanness depends on social contact. This is case study research in the descriptive tradition. Finally, Joan Morris and Michael Grimes give us an insider's view of working class sociologists who become Ph.D.s. The contradictions inherent in jumping from one class to another can uncover problems that are both professional and personal. This is yet another glimpse of sociology from the inside and encourages readers to wonder about the contradiction potential in their own biographies.

MADONNA G. CONSTANTINE AND
SHA'KEMA M. BLACKMON

Black Adolescents' Racial Socialization Experiences

Their Relations to Home, School, and Peer Self-Esteem

Many researchers have theorized that racism and discrimination act as developmental mediators in the lives of Black Americans across their life spans (e.g., Comer, 1989; Duncan, 1993; Fischer & Shaw, 1999; Gougis, 1986; Spencer, Swanson, & Cunningham, 1991). Among Black adolescents, in particular, developing and maintaining a healthy racial identity can be daunting in the context of current turbulent race relations in the United States (Stevenson, Reed, Bodison, & Bishop, 1997). The task of healthy racial identity development may be especially challenging for Black adolescents because they must negotiate mainstream, minority, and Black cultural and community experiences (Boykin, 1986; Boykin & Toms, 1985; Thornton, 1997). Mainstream experiences represent experiences related to the dominant culture of the United States, minority experiences may represent political and social injustices associated with being a numerical and social minority in the United States, and Black cultural and community experiences represent experiences within the African American community (Boykin, 1986; Boykin & Toms, 1985; Thornton, 1997)...

The link between self-esteem and academic performance among Black American adolescents may be related to how they process achievement experiences at school and in other areas of their lives. According to van Laar (2000), African American students may make two kinds of attributions about their experiences. The first type, internal attributions, cause individuals to internalize negative stigma and self-blame for lowered academic performance. In contrast, external attributions lead individuals to direct blame away from themselves and assign blame to structural barriers such as racism and discrimination (Crocker & Major, 1989; Crocker & Quinn, 1998). Thus, Black adolescents who make external attributions related to their academic performance may selectively devalue the importance of school and academic achievement in the overall context of their lives (Crocker & Quinn, 1998). Such attributions may be a primary reason that Black youth disengage their self-esteem from academically related outcomes in grade school through college (Hare, 1985; Major, Spencer, Schmader, Wolfe, & Crocker, 1998; Osbourne, 1995). Further, many Black adolescents may derive a positive sense of self from their families and peers who may encourage them to derive their self-esteem from achievements outside of the academic realm. . . .

Not only may racial socialization messages be linked to Black adolescents' self-esteem at a global level, but they may also be related to these youths' self-esteem in specific areas of their lives. Because sense of self among Black American youth is complex and because the examination of global self-esteem may not provide a clear understanding of the experiences of Black adolescents, it seems important to explore specific self-esteem domains (i.e., home, school, and peer) in this population of individuals. For example, although many Black American adolescents' general sense of self is not significantly affected by lowered performance in school (e.g., Schmader et al., 2001; van Laar, 2000, 2001), it is possible that these students may have differing self-perceptions across home, school, and peer milieus (McAdoo, 1985; Smith, Walker, Fields, Brookins, & Seay, 1999).

Hence, the primary goal of this study was to examine the relationship between parental racial socialization messages and area-specific self-esteem (i.e., home, school, and peer) among Black American adolescents. Based on previous literature in the areas of academic achievement, self-esteem, and racial socialization, we hypothesized that racial socialization messages would be significantly predictive of Black adolescents' area-specific self-esteem.

Method

Participants and Procedure

The participants consisted of 115 middle-school (6th, 7th, and 8th grade) students attending a predominantly Black parochial school in the northeast region of the United States. These students were asked to participate in an anonymous study examining their personal attitudes and experiences. They completed a survey packet consisting of the Teenager Experiences of Racial Socialization Scale (TERS) (Stevenson, Cameron, Herrero-Taylor, & Davis, 2001), the Hare General and Area-Specific Self-Esteem Scale (HGASSES) (Hare, 1996), and a brief demographic questionnaire. Informed consent was obtained from both students and their parents prior to students' participation in the study, and no incentives were provided for their participation. However, students, parents, teachers, and administrators were told that they would be given the study's results at their request. Because the surveys were administered and completed during specific class times, the return rate of surveys was high (i.e., 100%). . . .

Instrument

. . . *HGASSES*. The HGASSES (Hare, 1996) is a 30-item, 4-point, Likert-type instrument (1 = *strongly disagree* to 4 = *strongly agree*) that assesses both general self-esteem and area-specific self-esteem in the home, school, and peer domains. These domains correspond to the three HGASSES subscales, each of which consists of 10 items. The general self-esteem score is derived by computing the three subscales. . . .

Results

Table 1 provides the means and standard deviations for the study's variables, along with the interscale correlations. Prior to conducting the main analysis, a series of multivariate analyses of variance ($p = .05$) was computed to determine whether students differed by sex and ethnicity with regard to the study's variables. Results revealed no statistically significant interaction, Pillai's Trace $= .18$, $F(16, 204) =1.26$, $p > .05$; or main effect differences by sex, Pillai's Trace $= .12$, $F(8, 101) = 1.70$, $p > .05$; or ethnicity, Pillai's Trace $= .12$, $F(16, 204) = 0.79$, $p > .05$. Hence, sex and ethnicity were not included as independent variables in the main analysis.

TABLE 4.1   Means, Standard Deviations, and Intercorrelations of the Study's Variables

Variable	M	SD	1	2	3	4	5	6	7	8
Teenager Experience of Racial Socialization Scale (Stevenson, Cameron, Herrero-Taylor, & Davis, 2001)										
1. Cultural coping with antagonism subscale	24.93	5.70	—	.67***	.57***	.69***	.39***	.16	-.03	-.04
2. Cultural pride reinforcement subscale	22.94	3.20		—	.49***	.71***	.26***	.26***	.08	.20*
3. Cultural appreciation of legacy subscale	12.74	2.97			—	.64***	.35***	.24***	.04	.09
4. Cultural alertness to discrimination subscale	10.49	2.92				—	.36***	.05	-.05	-.03
5. Cultural endorsement of the mainstream subscale	7.71	1.87					—	-.09	-.31**	-.10
Hare General and Area-Specific Self-Esteem Scale (Hare, 1996)										
6. Home self-esteem subscale	33.92	5.06						—	.45***	.36***
7. School self-esteem subscale	30.41	3.93							—	.41***
8. Peer self-esteem subscale	30.20	4.29								—

$*p < .05.$ $**p < .01.$ $***p < .001.$

To examine the study's hypothesis, a multivariate multiple regression analysis was performed. This analytic procedure was chosen to control for the possible intercorrelations between the predictor and criterion variables (Haase & Ellis, 1987; Lunneborg & Abbot, 1983; Stevens, 1986). A multivariate multiple regression analysis can accommodate multiple predictor and multiple criterion variables, all of which are continuously distributed, from which follow-up tests can determine the unique contribution of each predictor variable on each criterion variable (Lutz & Eckert, 1994). In our study, the predictor variables were the five subscales of the TERS (i.e., cultural coping with antagonism, cultural pride reinforcement, cultural appreciation of legacy, cultural alertness to discrimination, and cultural endorsement of the mainstream). The criterion variables were the three subscales of the HGASSES (i.e., home, school, and peer self-esteem).

Results revealed that the overall proportion of variance in Black adolescents' home, school, and peer self-esteem accounted for by the five TERS subscales was statistically significant. . . . Results of [univariate] analyses revealed that the five TERS subscales accounted for significant variance in Black American youths' home self-esteem, . . . school self-esteem, . . . and peer self-esteem. . . .

Follow-up analyses were then conducted to examine the unique contribution of each of the predictor variables on the criterion variables. Results of these analyses indicated that greater cultural pride reinforcement socialization messages were related to higher peer self-esteem in Black American adolescents. . . . Conversely, higher cultural endorsement of the mainstream racial socialization messages were found to be associated with lower school self-esteem in Black youth. . . .

Discussion

The purpose of this study was to examine the relationship between parental racial socialization messages and area-specific self-esteem in Black American youth. Results revealed that cultural pride reinforcement socialization messages were positively correlated with Black adolescents' peer self-esteem. This finding may suggest that some of the racial values and practices taught by many Black American parents or caregivers are expressed and validated within Black adolescents' peer groups. Conversely, it is possible that Black youths' peer groups may reinforce their cultural pride socialization messages. Nonetheless, the potentially interdependent roles of parents and peers with regard to providing positive racial group messages seem crucial to the social success of many Black youths, and the ways in which these roles affect each other may provide Black adolescents with the skills to develop healthy self-perceptions and means for coping with racial discrimination and prejudice (Johnson, 1988). Hence, home and peer milieus that support the development of Black American youths' positive self-esteem may equip them to face a sometimes unfriendly and hostile world outside of these safe havens.

The finding that higher cultural endorsement of the mainstream racial socialization messages were negatively associated with school self-esteem may suggest that adopting more Eurocentric cultural values and behaviors (i.e., the "acting White" assumption) could serve as a detriment to Black students' academic self-efficacy in the context of predominantly Black school settings. . . . Hence, it is not surprising that some Black parents may choose to place their children in predominantly Black or Afrocentric school environments to (a) expose them to certain aspects of their culture in the context of educational settings, (b) affirm and reinforce some race-related practices and competencies with which they entered school, and (c) insulate them from racism until they have developed their own effective coping mechanisms.

In light of the aforementioned finding, it is also plausible to consider that Black adolescents who are exposed to greater cultural endorsement of the mainstream racial socialization messages may feel more comfortable in predominantly White school environments because their values may be more congruent with students matriculating in these settings. However, regardless of educational environment, the adoption of largely White cultural values or behaviors may be detrimental to some Black adolescents' self-esteem and racial identity development because it may promote the misconception that Black is inferior to White. It is also possible that this finding may be related, in part, to the ways that self-esteem generally develops among Black American youth in schools and in other institutions that may mirror cultural values associated with the dominant culture in the United States. For example, according to Crocker and Quinn (1998), Black Americans' self-esteem may be protected by directing blame away from themselves and assigning blame to structural barriers such as racism and discrimination and by devaluing domains and areas in which some members of their racial or ethnic group do not perform well historically (e.g., academics). Thus, Black American students who endorse mainstream values and behaviors, regardless of their educational setting, may evidence lower school self-esteem because they are unable or unwilling to consider the possibility that racism or discrimination could be contributing to their suboptimal academic functioning in the context of some school environments. . . .

Future investigations should continue examining racial socialization experiences and self-esteem in Black American adolescents from multiple research paradigms. For example, there is a need for longitudinal studies with Black American youth and their families to understand the specific strategies that parents may use to impart racial socialization messages and experiences to their children. Moreover, it may be important for future researchers to investigate how Black children and adolescents may process racial socialization messages in the context of home, school, and peer situations. Finally, future investigators may wish to explore how racial socialization messages may mediate the relationship between experiences of chronic racial discrimination and the development of psychological distress in African American youth.

REFERENCES

Boykin, A. W. (1986). The triple quandary and the schooling of Afro-American children. In U. Neiseser (Ed.), *The school achievement of minority children: New perspectives* (pp. 57–92). London: Lawrence Erlbaum.

Boykin, A. W., & Toms, F. D. (1985). Black child socialization. In H. P. McAdoo & J. L. McAdoo (Eds.), *Black children: Social, educational, and parental environments* (pp. 33–51). London: Sage.

Comer, J. P. (1989). Racism and the education of young children. *Teachers College Record, 90*(3), 352–361.

Crocker, J., & Major, B. (1989). Social stigma and self-esteem: The self-protective properties of stigma. *Psychological Review, 96*, 608–630.

Crocker, J., & Quinn, D. (1998). Racism and self-esteem. In J. L. Eberhardt & S. T. Fiske (Eds.), *Confronting racism: The problem and the response* (pp. 169–233). London: Sage.

Duncan, G. (1993). Racism as a developmental mediator. *Educational Forum, 57*, 360–370.

Fischer, A. R., & Shaw, C. M. (1999). African Americans' mental health and perceptions of racist discrimination: The moderating effects of racial socialization experiences and self-esteem. *Journal of Counseling Psychology, 46*, 395–407.

Gougis, R. A. (1986). The effects of prejudice and stress on the academic performance of Black Americans. In U. Neiseser (Ed.), *The school achievement of minority children* (pp. 145–158). Hillsdale, NJ: Lawrence Erlbaum.

Haase, R. F., & Ellis, M. V. (1987). Multivariate analysis of variance. *Journal of Counseling Psychology, 34*, 404–413.

Hare, B. R. (1985). No place to run, no place to hide: Comparative status and future prospects of Black boys. In M. B. Spencer, G. K. Brookins, & W. R. Allen (Eds.), *Beginnings: The social and affective development of Black children* (pp. 201–214). Hillsdale, NJ: Lawrence Erlbaum.

Hare, B. R. (1996). The HARE General and Area-Specific (School, Peer and Home) Self-Esteem Scale. In R. L. Jones (Ed.), *Handbook of tests and measurements for Black populations* (Vol. 1, pp. 199–206). Richmond, CA: Cobb & Henry.

Johnson, D. J. (1988). Racial socialization strategies of parents in three Black private schools. In D. T. Slaughter & D. J. Johnson (Eds.), *Visible now: Blacks in private schools* (pp. 251–267). New York: Greenwood.

Lunneborg, C. E., & Abbott, R. D. (1983). *Elementary multivariate analysis for the behavioral sciences.* New York: North-Holland.

Lutz, J. G., & Eckert, T. L. (1994). The relationship between canonical correlation analysis and multivariate multiple regression. *Educational and Psychological Measurement, 54*, 666–675.

Major, B., Spencer, S., Schmader, T, Wolfe, C., & Crocker, J. (1998). Coping with negative stereotypes about intellectual performance: The role of psychological disengagement. *Personality & Social Psychology, 24*, 34–50.

McAdoo, H. P. (1985). Racial attitudes and self-concept of young Black children over time. In H. P. McAdoo & J. L. McAdoo (Eds.), *Black children: Social, educational, and parental environments* (pp. 213–242). London: Sage.

Osbourne, J. W. (1995). Academics, self-esteem, and race: A look at the underlying assumptions of the disidentification hypothesis. *Personal and Social Psychology Bulletin, 21*, 449–455.

Schmader, T., Major, B., & Gramzow, R. H. (2001). Coping with ethnic stereotypes in the academic domain: Perceived injustice and psychological disengagement. *Journal of Social Issues, 57*, 93–111.

Smith, E. P., Walker, K., Fields, L., Brookins, C. C., & Seay, R. (1999). Ethnic identity and its relationship to self-esteem, perceived efficacy and prosocial attitudes in early adolescence. *Journal of Adolescence, 22*, 867–880.

Spencer, M. B., Swanson, D. P., & Cunningham, M. (1991). Ethnicity, ethnic identity, and competence formation: Adolescent transition and cultural transformation. *Journal of Negro Education, 60*, 366–387.

Stevens, J. (1986). *Applied multivariate statistics for the social sciences.* Hillsdale, NJ: Lawrence Erlbaum.

Stevenson, H. C., Cameron, R., Herrero-Taylor, T., & Davis, G. Y. (2001). *Development of the Teenage Experience of Racial Socialization Scale: Correlates of race-related socialization frequency from the perspective of Black youth.* Unpublished manuscript.

Stevenson, H. C., Reed, J., Bodison, P., & Bishop, A. (1997). Racism stress management: Racial socialization beliefs and the experience of depression and anger in African American youth. *Youth & Society, 29*, 197–222.

Thornton, M. C. (1997). Strategies of racial socialization among Black parents: Mainstream, minority, and cultural messages. In R. J. Taylor, J. S. Jackson, & L. M. Chatters (Eds.), *Family life in Black America* (pp. 201–215). Thousand Oaks, CA: Sage.

van Laar, C. (2000). The paradox of low academic achievement but high self-esteem in African American students. *Educational Psychology Review, 12*, 33–61.

van Laar, C. (2001). Declining optimism in ethnic minority students: The role of attributions and self-esteem. In F. Salili, C. Chiu, & Y. Hong (Eds.), *Student motivation: The culture and context of learning* (pp. 79–104). New York: Kluwer Academic/Plenum.

STUDY QUESTIONS

1. What are the relationships between self-esteem at school and the racial pride messages given by parents?

2. What cultural messages might you give your children so they have positive self-esteem and perform well in the school setting?

KINGSLEY DAVIS

Extreme Isolation

Early in 1940 there appeared in this *Journal* an account of a girl called Anna.[1] She had been deprived of normal contact and had received a minimum of human care for almost the whole of her first six years of life. At that time observations were not complete and the report had a tentative character. Now, however, the girl is dead, and, with more information available,[2] it is possible to give a fuller and more definitive description of the case from a sociological point of view.

Anna's death, caused by hemorrhagic jaundice, occurred on August 6, 1942. Having been born on March 1 or 6,[3] 1932, she was approximately ten and a half years of age when she died. The previous report covered her development up to the age of almost eight years; the present one recapitulates the earlier period on the basis of new evidence and then covers the last two and a half years of her life.

Early History

The first few days and weeks of Anna's life were complicated by frequent changes of domicile. It will be recalled that she was an illegitimate child, the second such child born to her mother, and that her grandfather, a widowed farmer in whose house her mother lived, strongly disapproved of this new evidence of the mother's indiscretion. This fact led to the baby's being shifted about.

Two weeks after being born in a nurse's private home, Anna was brought to the family farm, but the grandfather's antagonism was so great that she was shortly taken to the house of one of her mother's friends. At this time a local minister became interested in her and took her to his house with an idea of possible adoption. He decided against adoption, however, when he discovered that she had vaginitis. The infant was then taken to a children's home in the nearest large city. This agency found that at the age of only three weeks she was already in a miserable condition, being "terribly galled and otherwise in very bad shape." It did not regard her as a likely subject for adoption but took her in for a while anyway, hoping to benefit her. After Anna had spent nearly eight weeks in this place, the agency notified her mother to come to get her. The mother responded by sending a man and his wife to the children's home with a view to their adopting Anna, but they made such a poor impression on the agency that permission was refused. Later the mother came herself and took the child out of the home and then gave her to this couple. It was in the home of this pair that a social worker found the girl a short time thereafter. The social worker went to the mother's home and pleaded with Anna's grandfather to allow the mother to bring the child home. In spite of threats, he refused. The child, by then more than four months old, was next taken to another children's home in a near-by town. A medical examination at this time revealed that she had impetigo, vaginitis, umbilical hernia, and a skin rash.

Anna remained in this second children's home for nearly three weeks, at the end of which time she was transferred to a private foster-home. Since, however, the grandfather would not, and the mother could not, pay for the child's care, she was finally taken back as a last resort to the grandfather's house (at the age of five and a half months). There she remained, kept on the second floor in an attic-like room because her mother hesitated to incur the grandfather's wrath by bringing her downstairs.

The mother, a sturdy woman weighing about 180 pounds, did a man's work on the farm. She engaged in heavy work such as milking cows and tending hogs and had little time for her children. Sometimes she went out at night, in which case Anna was left entirely without attention. Ordinarily, it seems, Anna received only enough care to keep her barely alive. She appears to have been seldom moved from one position to another. Her clothing and bedding were filthy. She apparently had no instruction, no friendly attention.

It is little wonder that, when finally found and removed from the room in the grandfather's house at the age of nearly six years, the child could not talk, walk, or do anything that showed intelligence. She was in an extremely emaciated and undernourished condition, with skeleton-like legs and a bloated abdomen. She had been fed on virtually nothing except cow's milk during the years under her mother's care.

Anna's condition when found, and her subsequent improvement, have been described in the previous report. It now remains to say what happened to her after that.

Later History

In 1939, nearly two years after being discovered, Anna had progressed, as previously reported, to the point where she could walk, understand simple commands, feed herself, achieve some neatness, remember people, etc. But she still did not speak, and, though she was much more like a normal infant of something over one year of age in mentality, she was far from normal for her age.

On August 30, 1939, she was taken to a private home for retarded children, leaving the county home where she had been for more than a year and a half. In her new setting she made some further progress, but not a great deal. In a report of an examination made November 6 of the same year, the head of the institution pictured the child as follows:

> Anna walks about aimlessly, makes periodic rhythmic motions of her hands, and, at intervals, makes gutteral and sucking noises. She regards her hands as if she had seen them for the first time. It was impossible to hold her attention for more than a few seconds at a time—not because of distraction due to external stimuli but because of her inability to concentrate. She ignored the task in hand to gaze vacantly about the room. Speech is entirely lacking. Numerous unsuccessful attempts have been made with her in the hope of developing initial sounds. I do not believe that this failure is due to negativism or deafness but that she is not sufficiently developed to accept speech at this time. . . . The prognosis is not favorable. . . .

More than five months later, on April 25, 1940, a clinical psychologist, the late Professor Francis N. Maxfield, examined Anna and reported the following: large for her age; hearing "entirely normal"; vision apparently normal; able to climb stairs; speech in the "babbling stage" and "promise for developing intelligible speech later seems to be good." He said further that "on the Merrill-Palmer scale she made a mental score of 19 months. On the Vineland social maturity scale she made a score of 23 months."[4]

Professor Maxfield very sensibly pointed out that prognosis is difficult in such cases of isolation. "It is very difficult to take scores on tests standardized under average conditions of environment and experience," he wrote, "and interpret them in a case where environment and experience have been so unusual." With this warning he gave it as his opinion at that time that Anna would eventually "attain an adult mental level of six or seven years."[5]

The school for retarded children, on July 1, 1941, reported that Anna had reached 46 inches in height and weighed 60 pounds. She could bounce and catch a ball and was said to conform to group socialization, though as a follower rather than a leader. Toilet habits were firmly established. Food habits were normal, except that she still used a spoon as her sole implement. She could dress herself except for fastening her clothes. Most remarkable of all, she had finally begun to develop speech. She was characterized as being at about the two-year level in this regard. She could call attendants by name and bring in one when she was asked to. She had a few complete sentences to express her wants. The report concluded that there was nothing peculiar about her, except that she was feeble-minded—"probably congenital in type."[6]

A final report from the school, made on June 22, 1942, and evidently the last report before the girl's death, pictured only a slight advance over that given above. It said that Anna could follow directions, string beads, identify a few colors, build with blocks, and differentiate between attractive and unattractive pictures. She had a good sense of rhythm and loved a doll. She talked mainly in phrases but would repeat words and try to carry on a conversation. She was clean about clothing. She habitually washed her hands and brushed her teeth. She would try to help other children. She walked well and could run fairly well, though clumsily. Although easily excited, she had a pleasant disposition.

Interpretation

Such was Anna's condition just before her death. It may seem as if she had not made much progress, but one must remember the condition in which she had been found. One must recall that she had no glimmering of speech, absolutely, no ability to walk, no sense of gesture, not the least capacity to feed herself even when the food was put in front of her, and no comprehension of cleanliness. She was so apathetic that it was hard to tell whether or not she could hear. And all this at the age of nearly six years. Compared with this condition, her capacities at the time of her death seem striking indeed, though they do not amount to much more than a two-and-a-half year mental level. One conclusion therefore seems safe, namely, that her isolation prevented a considerable amount of mental development that was undoubtedly part of her capacity. Just what her original capacity was, of course, is hard to say; but her development after her period of confinement (including the ability to walk and run, to play, dress, fit into a social situation, and, above all, to speak) shows that she had at least this much capacity—capacity that never could have been realized in her original condition of isolation.

A further question is this: What would she have been like if she had received a normal upbringing from the moment of birth? A definitive answer would have been impossible in any case, but even an approximate answer is made difficult by her early death. If one assumes, as was tentatively surmised in the previous report, that it is "almost impossible for any child to learn to speak, think, and act like a normal person after a long period of early isolation," it seems likely that Anna might have had a normal or near-normal capacity, genetically speaking. On the other hand, it was pointed out that Anna represented "a marginal case [because] she was discovered before she had reached six years of age," an age "young enough to allow for some plasticity."[7] While admitting, then, that Anna's isolation *may* have been the major cause (and was certainly a minor cause) of her lack of rapid mental progress during the four and a half years following her rescue from neglect, it is necessary to entertain the hypothesis that she was congenitally deficient.

In connection with this hypothesis, one suggestive though by no means conclusive circumstance needs consideration, namely, the mentality of Anna's forebears. Information on this subject is easier to obtain, as one might guess, on the mother's than on the father's side. Anna's maternal grandmother, for example, is said to have been college educated and wished to have her children receive a good education, but her husband, Anna's stern grandfather, apparently a shrewd, hard-driving, calculating farmowner, was so penurious that her ambitions in this direction were thwarted. Under the circumstances her daughter (Anna's mother) managed, despite having to do hard work on the farm, to complete the eighth grade in a country school. Even so, however, the daughter was evidently not very smart. "A schoolmate of [Anna's mother] stated that she was retarded in school work; was very gullible at this age; and that her morals even at this time were discussed by other students." Two tests administered to her on March 4, 1938, when she was thirty-two years of age, showed that she was mentally deficient. On the Stanford Revision of the Binet-Simon Scale her performance was equivalent to that of a child of eight years, giving her an I.Q. of 50 and indicating mental deficiency of "middle-grade moron type."[8]

As to the identity of Anna's father, the most persistent theory holds that he was an old man about seventy-four years of age at the time of the girl's birth. If he was the one, there is no indication of mental or other biological deficiency, whatever one may think of his morals. However, someone else may actually have been the father.

To sum up: Anna's heredity is the kind that *might* have given rise to innate mental deficiency, though not necessarily.

Comparison with Another Case

Perhaps more to the point than speculations about Anna's ancestry would be a case for comparison. If a child could be discovered who had been isolated about the same length of time as Anna but had achieved a much quicker recovery and a greater mental development, it would be a stronger indication that Anna was deficient to start with.

Such a case does exist. It is the case of a girl found at about the same time as Anna and under strikingly similar circumstances. . . .

Born apparently one month later than Anna, the girl in question, who has been given the pseudonym Isabelle, was discovered in November, 1938, nine months after the discovery of Anna. At the time she was found she was approximately six and a half years of age. Like Anna, she was an illegitimate child and had been kept in seclusion for that reason. Her mother was a deaf-mute, having become so at the age of two, and it appears that she and Isabelle had spent most of their time together in a dark room shut off from the rest of the mother's family. As a result Isabelle had no chance to develop speech; when she communicated with her mother, it was by means of gestures. Lack of sunshine and inadequacy of diet had caused Isabelle to become rachitic. Her legs in particular were affected; they "were so bowed that as she stood erect the soles of her shoes came nearly flat together, and she got about with a skittering gait."[9] Her behavior toward strangers, especially men, was almost that of a wild animal, manifesting much fear and hostility. In lieu of speech she made only a strange croaking sound. In many ways she acted like an infant. "She was apparently utterly unaware of relationships of any kind. When presented with a ball for the first time, she held it in the palm of her hand, then reached out and stroked my face with it. Such behavior is comparable to that of a child of six months."[10] At first it was even hard to tell whether or not she could hear, so unused were her senses. Many of her actions resembled those of deaf children.

It is small wonder that, once it was established that she could hear, specialists working with her believed her to be feeble-minded. . . . "The general impression was that she was wholly uneducable and that any attempt to teach her to speak, after so long a period of silence, would meet with failure."[11]

In spite of this interpretation, the individuals in charge of Isabelle launched a systematic and skilful program of training. It seemed hopeless at first. The approach had to be through pantomime and dramatization, suitable to an infant. It required one week of intensive effort before she even made her first attempt at vocalization. Gradually she began to respond, however, and, after the first hurdles had at last been overcome, a curious thing happened. She went through the usual stages of learning characteristic of the years from one to six not only in proper succession but far more rapidly than normal. In a little over two months after her first vocalization she was putting sentences together. Nine months after that she could identify words and sentences on the printed page, could write well, could add to ten, and could retell a story after hearing it. Seven months beyond this point she had a vocabulary of 1,500–2,000 words and was asking complicated questions. Starting from an educational level of between one and three years (depending on what aspect one considers), she had reached a normal level by the time she was eight and a half years old. In short, she covered in two years the stages of learning that ordinarily require six.[12] Or, to put it another way, her I.Q. trebled in a year and a half.[13] The speed with which she reached the normal level of mental development seems analogous to the recovery of body weight in a growing child after an illness, the recovery being achieved by an extra fast rate of growth for a period after the illness until normal weight for the given age is again attained.

When the writer saw Isabelle a year and a half after her discovery, she gave him the impression of being a very bright, cheerful, energetic little girl. She spoke well, walked and ran without trouble, and sang with gusto and accuracy. Today she is over fourteen years old and has passed the sixth grade in a public school. Her teachers say that she participates in all school activities as normally as other children. Though older than her classmates, she has fortunately not physically matured too far beyond their level.[14]

Clearly the story of Isabelle's development is different from that of Anna's. In both cases there was an exceedingly low, or rather blank, intellectual level to begin with. In both cases it seemed that the girl might be congenitally feeble minded. In both a considerably higher level was reached later on. But the Ohio girl achieved a normal mentality within two years, whereas Anna was still marked inadequate at the end of four and a half years. This difference in achievement may suggest that Anna had less initial capacity. But an alternative hypothesis is possible.

One should remember that Anna never received the prolonged and expert attention that Isabelle received. The result of such attention, in the case of the Ohio girl, was to give her speech at an early stage, and her subsequent rapid development seems to have been a consequence of that. "Until Isabelle's speech and language development, she had all the characteristics of a feeble-minded child." Had Anna, who, from the standpoint of psychometric tests and early history, closely resembled this girl at the start, been given a mastery of speech at an earlier point by intensive training, her subsequent development might have been much more rapid.[15]

The hypothesis that Anna began with a sharply inferior mental capacity is therefore not established. Even if she were deficient to start with, we have no way of knowing how much so. Under ordinary conditions she might have been a dull normal or, like her mother, a moron. Even after the blight of her isolation, if she had lived to maturity, she might have finally reached virtually the full level of her capacity, whatever it may have been. That her isolation did have a profound effect upon her mentality, there can be no doubt. This is proved by the substantial degree of change during the four and a half years following her rescue.

Consideration of Isabelle's case serves to show, as Anna's case does not clearly show, that isolation up to the age of six, with failure to acquire any form of speech and hence failure to grasp nearly the whole world of cultural meaning, does not preclude the subsequent acquisition of these. Indeed, there seems to be a process of accelerated recovery in which the child goes through the mental stages at a more rapid rate than would be the case in normal development. Just what would be the maximum age at which a person could remain isolated and still retain the capacity for full cultural acquisition is hard to say. Almost certainly it would not be as high as age fifteen; it might possibly be as low as age ten. Undoubtedly various individuals would differ considerably as to the exact age.

Anna's is not an ideal case for showing the effects of extreme isolation, partly because she was possibly deficient to begin with, partly because she did not receive the best training available, and partly because she did not live long enough. Nevertheless, her case is instructive when placed in the record with numerous other cases of extreme isolation. This and the previous article about her are meant to place her in the record. It is to be hoped that other cases will be described in the scientific literature as they are discovered (as unfortunately they will be), for only in these rare cases of extreme isolation is it possible "to observe *concretely separated* two factors in the development of human personality which are always otherwise only analytically separated, the biogenic and the sociogenic factors."[16]

NOTES

1. Kingsley Davis, "Extreme Social Isolation of a Child," *American Journal of Sociology*, XLV (January, 1940), 554–65.
2. Sincere appreciation is due to the officials in the Department of Welfare, Commonwealth of Pennsylvania, for their kind co-operation in making available the records concerning Anna and discussing the case frankly with the writer. Helen C. Hubbell, Florentine Hackbusch, and Eleanor Meckelnburg were particularly helpful, as was Fanny L. Matchette. Without their aid neither of the reports on Anna could have been written.
3. The records are not clear as to which day.
4. Letter to one of the state officials in charge of the case.
5. *Ibid.*
6. Progress report of the school.
7. Davis, *op. cit.*, p. 564.
8. The facts set forth here as to Anna's ancestry are taken chiefly from a report of mental tests administered to Anna's mother by psychologists at a state hospital where she was taken for this purpose after the discovery of Anna's seclusion. This excellent report was not available to the writer when the previous paper on Anna was published.
9. Maxfield, unpublished manuscript cited above.
10. Mason, *op. cit.*, p. 299.
11. Mason, *op. cit.*, p. 299.
12. *Ibid.*, pp. 300–304.
13. Maxfield, unpublished manuscript.
14. Based on a personal letter from Dr. Mason to the writer, May 13, 1946.
15. This point is suggested in a personal letter from Dr. Mason to the writer, October 22, 1946.
16. Singh and Zingg, *op. cit.*, pp. xxi–xxii, in a foreword by the writer.

STUDY QUESTIONS

1. Based on the research evidence in this article, how would you answer the nature versus nurture question?
2. What was the outcome for the two girls once they were found and educated?

JOAN M. MORRIS AND MICHAEL D. GRIMES

Contradictions in the Childhood Socialization of Sociologists from the Working Class

Early socialization within a class culture has important and long-lasting effects. Therefore, when individuals are socialized within a working-class family environment, they can expect to experience "culture shock" when they achieve upward mobility that takes them out of their class-of-origin and into the foreign terrain of middle-class culture. And, to the extent that gender and race or ethnicity manifest themselves in ways that are distinctively class-oriented, the effects of this "shock" are magnified for women, for people of color, and for the members of ethnic minorities. The focus of this paper is on the childhood socialization of a group of sociologists from working-class backgrounds— a group of people who have, by most standards, "made something" of themselves, but not necessarily in the ways their parents intended. In fact, for many of them, their successes have been accomplished in spite of what their parents taught them about what it means to be successful; their successes have also sometimes come at the expense of the approval and acceptance of their families and childhood peers.

... The focus of this paper is on the childhood socialization of a group of sociologists from working-class backgrounds—a group of people who have, by most standards, "made something" of themselves, but not necessarily in the ways their parents intended. In fact, as will be demonstrated below, for many of them, their successes have been accomplished in spite of what they were taught about what it means to be successful during their childhoods; their successes have also sometimes come at the expense of the approval and acceptance of their families and childhood peers. The data for the paper come from a larger study that addresses events throughout the life courses and careers of a group of forty-five sociologists from working-class backgrounds. Each participant who volunteered to be part of the study was asked to contribute three things: responses to a set of open-ended questions; responses to a questionnaire; and a curriculum vitae.

The major thesis of this paper is that early socialization within a class culture has deep and abiding effects. More specifically, when individuals are socialized within a working-class family environment, they can expect to experience "culture shock" when they achieve upward mobility that takes them out of their class-of-origin and into the foreign terrain of middle-class culture. And, to the extent that gender and race or ethnicity manifest themselves in ways that are distinctively class-oriented, the effects of this "shock" are magnified for women, for people of color, and for the members of ethnic minorities. The present analysis focuses its attention on the impacts of early socialization within working-class culture, how these experiences have influenced the careers of academics from working-class backgrounds, and the unique effects that result for women and for the members of racial and ethnic minorities from working-class backgrounds.

Learning What "Feels Right"

The first and most enduring exposure to culture occurs during childhood socialization. A number of analysts have concluded that the class location of parents is one of the most important influences on the socialization experiences of children (Kohn and Schooler 1983; Bourdieu 1984, 1986; Coleman 1990; Lareau 1989) because the parents' class location is directly linked to the nature of the resources that a family possesses and makes available to its children.

Parents may pass a variety of resources down to their children, including a range of explicit but also implicit goods, not the least of which is the cultural knowledge associated with their social class. Wright defines social class as based on three dimensions, each a type of power that is indicative of where one stands in the class structure. The three (property, skills/credentials, and organizational control) combine to produce a class system in which the hierarchy is defined according to power over oneself and others (see Wright 1985). The working-class, in Wright's model, have least power over the three dimensions, i.e., they do not own the means of production; they possess few credentials; and they have little decision-making power over their work or the work of others. Kohn and Schooler (1983) and others have found that the power relations present in one's job carry over into the home. Families who command few of the resources valued in the work world cannot help also including a sense of powerlessness in the resources they pass down to their children.

Bourdieu (1984, 1986) refers to family resources as the total volume of "capital" available for expropriation by a child. He argues that capital assumes three forms: economic, cultural, and social. Economic capital refers to material wealth or economic power, a form of capital "which is immediately or directly convertible into money and may be institutionalized in the form of property rights" (Bourdieu 1986:243). Cultural capital refers to a broad range of knowledge about the world within which an individual lives. This form of capital is important because it is "convertible, in certain situations, into economic capital and may be institutionalized in the form of educational qualifications" (Bourdieu 1986:243). Social capital refers to the network of social connections (a social network) that can be effectively mobilized by the family for its use. It too can be converted into economic capital under certain circumstances. Bourdieu argues that social classes can be placed on a continuum (or a set of continua) according to the level of economic or material wealth it controls, the cultural capital it possesses, and the potential benefits of its social contacts.

Bourdieu devotes most of his attention to cultural capital because he sees it as essential to the utilization of the other two forms and because of its central role in the intergenerational reproduction of social class. He argues that cultural capital may be manifested in three different ways: the embodied state, the objectified state, and institutionalized state (Bourdieu 1986:254).

The "embodied state" of cultural capital refers to the most fundamental state, that which is linked to the body. It is "external wealth converted into an integral part of the person, into a habitus . . . " (1986:245). All forms of communication in the presentation-of-self are included here, e.g., ways of speaking (vocabulary and accent), manners, posture or poise, etc. This form of capital, since it is embodied within individuals, cannot (like money or property) be transmitted by gift, bequest, purchase or exchange. This form of capital is, above all, an investment of time. . . .

Bourdieu's second type of cultural capital, objectified capital, exists in the form of material objects such as writings, paintings, etc., and as such, has some properties that are only defined in relationship to cultural capital in its embodied form. That is, the material objects can only be appreciated by those with *embodied* culture. . . .

Bourdieu's third type, the "institutionalized state" of cultural capital, is best exemplified by the academic credential. Similar to cultural capital in its embodied state, the institutionalized form of cultural capital has the same biological limits as its bearer (i.e., it can't be bequeathed, it applies only to the bearer). Cultural capital in its institutionalized state, unlike the embodied form, is more manifest. In its institutionalized form, it takes on the character of a conventional, constant, legally guaranteed value. Holding a credential means there is official recognition that one meets certain qualifications, has achieved a particular level of competence. . . .

While the participants in our study obviously possess the necessary credentials for high levels of institutionalized cultural capital, we found evidence of a lack of exposure to both "embodied" and "objectified" cultural capital. For example, we asked them to describe the cultural environment in their homes while growing up. Based on their responses, we developed a coding scheme that contained a total of eighteen indicators of cultural activities. This list included such things as: (the presence of) books, newspapers, magazines in the home; listening to music (and the type of music); visits to museums and libraries; attending movies; going to plays and concerts; taking music or dance lessons; television viewing, etc. Following Bourdieu's (1984) distinction between "high" and "low" cultural activities, we then selected a sub-set of these activities that served as a kind of index of "high" culture. This group of activities included such things as listening to classical music, taking music/dance lessons, visits to museums, attending plays and concerts, and engaging in intellectual discussions with parents or older siblings.

Our results show that a full two-thirds of our respondents had experienced *none* of these activities during their childhoods. Only two out of ten had experienced one of them; and no respondent had experienced more than three of them. In terms of gender, female respondents were no more likely to have experienced these activities than were our male respondents (though the one respondent who experienced three of them was a woman). Without identical data on this subject from a group of academics from middle-class backgrounds with which to compare findings, it is difficult to place them in a meaningful context. What we can say, however, is that these data contrast sharply with the levels of exposure to "high" culture enjoyed by our own children and those of most of our colleagues. They are also consistent with Bourdieu's (1984) conclusion that the exposure to "high" culture is directly related to the family's position in the class structure. . . .

As the work of Bourdieu, Coleman, and others makes clear, socialization in working-class homes is, in many ways, different from socialization in middle-class or upper middle-class homes. This goes beyond the level of material consumption (economic capital) the family is able to enjoy. In comparison to middle-class children, working-class children are taught a different set of values and are, themselves, valued differently. As has been well established (Kohn and Schooler 1983; Coleman 1990; Parcel and Menaghan 1994), the socialization of working-class children is heavily influenced by the occupational experiences of their parents. Parents tend to re-create components of their work environments at home; e.g., when parents work in jobs that provide little opportunity for autonomy and independent thought, they are likely to encourage their children to conform rather than to think independently. Despite the fact that most parents stress "independence" in their children, it is what they mean by it that differs. While middle-class parents may be more interested in creativity and self-determination, the primary concern of working-class parents is that their children be able to support themselves, i.e., to do a "day's work for a day's pay" and to avoid appearing weak by asking for help. To the extent that a high level of conformity is required in most working-class jobs, "independence" may come to mean just the opposite of what middle-class parents expect. In making comparisons such as these it is necessary to recognize that the differences between class cultures means there is also a lack of agreement on meanings and values—differences that may be masked by the use of similar language. . . .

Economic Capital

The U.S. working-class is a heterogeneous group in its range of material circumstances and our respondents' childhood homes were not exceptional in that regard. About one-third of respondents reported no material deprivation during their childhoods (16 respondents); another third reported they did feel a sense of material deprivation as children (15 respondents); and the remainder fell between these two extremes, reporting various experiences of relative deprivation.

The following examples are typical of those who commented on their recognition of socioeconomic differences and their disadvantaged status.

"I became aware of income differences (which is not to say class differences) around the fifth grade. Another child in my class asked me why I wore the same thing to school every day."

"I felt materially deprived after my father died. As the years after went by we became poorer and poorer. By high school, I was wearing old (my mother's) clothes, my middle brother would complain about not being able to buy new clothes. My older brother and mother would fight constantly about his giving more money to the household. The meals became smaller, but always attractively prepared."

The example below describes the sense of relative deprivation that one woman remembered feeling when she compared herself to her childhood peers.

"I was quite aware of the fact that other Jewish families often went on summer vacations . . . we never did. My father had overtime, a concept unknown to my friends, their fathers worked 9 to 5. Also, when I was in elementary school and my mother went back to work, I had to go to summer day camp. I could not go to the day camp associated with the Jewish Community Center (JCC), but had to go to Girl Scouts Camp, because it cost less. . . . We only got one present on Hanukkah, not eight. I had hand-me-down clothes, not full priced clothing from department stores."

Cultural Capital

The participants in this study provided a wealth of evidence in support of Bourdieu's statement that cultural capital is "determinant in the reproduction of social structure" (1986:254). Yet, the fact that they have failed to reproduce the class structure within which they were raised raises an important point. Cultural capital is based on values, knowledge, and meaning. The autobiographical accounts provided by our respondents show how the social structure is reinforced and usually reproduced, often in subtle, nonobvious ways by the transmission of working-class culture. Parental encouragement and expectations are perhaps the most influential, but interaction with others is also important. . . .

Encouragement and Expectations

The majority of respondents to our study reported that their parents encouraged them in their early educations. This is consistent with Laureau's (1989) findings that both working-class and middle-class parents prepare their children for school. The main difference, however, is that working-class parents tend to leave education to the "professionals" (teachers, guidance counselors, etc.) while middle-class parents stay more involved with their children's education throughout their school years. Working-class parents often see education as the route to a better job. One respondent wrote:

> "My parents were both committed to our gaining an education so we could have 'sit-down' jobs performing 'clean' work."

To many, however, parental encouragement to "do well" in school meant to follow the rules, keep out of trouble, etc. To many working-class parents, a "good" report card was equivalent to a satisfactory evaluation at work. Getting good grades was an outward sign that you were able to fit into a system and accomplish what was expected. One respondent referred to his father's efforts to teach him "industrial discipline" in the following way:

> "He explained that I would always have a 'boss,' and that I would have to obey authority without question or reason."

And in a similar vein, a respondent talks about her parents' concern that she "do well" in school:

> "... this urgent need for conformity could be attributed in part to the working-class attitudes toward work. For the types of work that everyone did and that I was expected to do when I was grown, it was very necessary that one develop the 'proper' attitude toward authority."

Education was perhaps more important in minority families. Several African American respondents commented on their families' exceptional encouragement of education—encouragement at a level that was somewhat unusual for white working-class children. For example:

> "My parents, grandparents and other relatives encouraged me during the years of my early education. My maternal grandmother, with whom I spent a great deal of time when I was very young, remembered the days when it was illegal to teach blacks to read. Therefore, she was

able to impress upon us the value of education. My parents were always supportive as well."

"I was an only child and the center of a great deal of attention and favor. I was sheltered from the streets, continually watched and not allowed to play with many of the kids in the neighborhood and was sent back to the South during the summer, a not uncommon pattern of Black Southerners. In many ways, my mother and our family always had high expectations for behavior since it was one of the ways to separate us from 'low class' people."

Pursuit of the "American Dream"

Respondents often gave accounts of parental support that were couched in the ideology of the dominant culture—the idea that one's achievements are only limited by individual ability, willingness to work, etc. In the case of childhood socialization into the working-class, this ideology is inherently contradictory. That is, the belief that individuals can "make something of themselves," and in fact, that *anyone* can make *anything* of themselves that they wish, suggests an open system, a meritocracy. However, any system within which merit would determine success would have to be based on equal access to resources, information being the most important. Working-class kids simply do not "see" the same career opportunities that middle-class kids see. Part of this is due to limited information about what is available and what the requirements are for seeking it. But some, and perhaps this is the larger issue, is due to limited aspirations. The following is a good example:

"... Being a white, working class male in a stable household made me secure and comfortable. I believed in the 'American Dream' which meant that I could do or be almost anything I wanted. That I didn't aspire to be a professional or manager was like not thinking that I could fly, it wasn't a possibility. I figured I was going to do some type of blue-collar work, get married, have children, and own my own house."

All children develop their career aspirations within a class-specific culture. The fact that proportionately fewer children attend college at each lower level of the socioeconomic hierarchy is no accident—and it is not entirely due to affordability factors. One of the major places in which the class system is institutionalized is the family. The family's location in the class system, in turn, determines the location and content of early educational experiences, and has a huge effect on the make-up and orientation of peer groups. Values, expectations, and aspirations are formed and reinforced through interaction with family, friends, and teachers. Thus the social-psychological effects of early socialization have deep and enduring effects on individuals' lives. The following examples illustrate some of this.

> "... I was never encouraged to think about college (by teachers) and I was even discouraged from attending college by family and friends. Their attitudes had been developed by class background. The impact was that I got a terribly late start in completing my first college class (age 24).
>
> "None of my teachers were influential in directing my path towards higher education before I dropped out of school. In fact, just the opposite. In the 9th grade, we were tested with a battery of tests. My homeroom teacher, an English teacher whom I was crazy about, informed my mother that I was a B student and was not college material. This was ironic because two years later, while I was pregnant, I undertook testing by (a federal agency ... my mother made me do it) and they told me that I was almost a genius. I remember her words as we were leaving the building ... she looked at my stomach and said, 'some genius.' "

Inherent Contradictions in Parental Encouragement

Most respondents reported that their parents were interested in seeing their children "do better" than they had done. These interests were usually stated in general terms such as the following:

> "Both my parents had strong upwardly mobile ambitions for themselves, but especially for their children; they strove always to 'get ahead' to improve their economic condition and achieve some mobility."

Such generalized "encouragement" constitutes another contradiction to a common theme in these essays. This is something David Halle reported in his 1984 book, *America's Working Man*, the definition of manual work as the only real work, with intellectual or managerial work dismissed as not really work at all. By this definition, nonmanual workers are shamming, getting by, often not knowing what they are doing, and existing at the expense of the real workers. In response to a question concerning their parents' feelings about their work and its relative status and importance in society, the respondents repeatedly echoed this theme. One respondent said his father made a distinction between himself and those at higher levels of the socioeconomic hierarchy by referring to himself as ". . . someone who actually works for a living." Another referred to his father's "canned phrases," most of which he has forgotten but which implied that the "working man was always getting the shaft." Other examples follow.

". . . he was hostile to the 'big shots' who worked in the plant office. . . "

". . . she felt that her work was very necessary—what would all those middle-class and rich women do without people like my mother to alter and mend their clothing?—was her line. She frequently compared herself invidiously to her customers, commented that they didn't know how to thread a needle."

"Both parents felt their work was important. My dad believed the working man did the real work while managers and engineers/ architects did not generally know what they were doing."

"My father would boast about how smart he was and how stupid his bosses were, I think to elevate the importance of his job."

Social Capital

Bourdieu's third form of capital is social capital, the potential to mobilize resources to one's advantage through social ties. The clearest case of a shortage of social capital expressed by our respondents concerned access to higher education. Academics from working-class backgrounds often lack the information they need to achieve upward mobility, but this is, in large part, due to their limited access to a network of social ties with people who know the answers to their questions. For the members of working-class families who achieve mobility into professional positions, not only is it unclear how to map out a career path, but the options themselves are often as hidden as the means for finding out how to learn about them. The autobiographical essays written for this study contain numerous examples of individuals' uncertainty about the answers to important questions, but more than that, they convey the retrospective recognition that they were as ignorant about the appropriate questions to be asked as they were of whom to ask them. One respondent gave the following account of her entry into college:

"It is at this point that I became aware that both my economic and social origins provided a huge impediment to my undergraduate studies. I became aware of class for really the first time. No one was able to

*help me find financial aid, fill out application forms, apply for scholar-
ships, etc. No one read my scholarship essays. No one took me to the
University to check it out. No one helped me to find an apartment.
Even if it had entered my parents' thoughts, no one knew how to help
me. I missed out on a huge chunk of financial aid because I missed the
relevant deadlines. Every summer for the first three years of school, I
lost 10–15 pounds for lack of food, really. I was even too stupid to
apply for food stamps."*

Another essayist talks about the influence of growing up in a Jewish
home. Though her family was "clearly working-class," most of her parents' friends were middle-class. For her, the intersection of ethnicity
and social class was somewhat positive, i.e., the influence of the Jewish
subculture offset some of the limitations of working-class subculture.
She attributes her parents' encouragement for her education to her
ethnicity. In her words, "To them, education was the most meaningful
aspect of one's life." Still, she identifies class background as an impediment to higher education:

*"In some ways my class background was an impediment to higher
education, in other ways it was not. I was not aware of many options.
My parents did not know much of the college scene and guidance
counselors at my high school were not well versed."*

The Relevance of "Social Class" as an Issue

The popular mythology in this country is that we live in a classless society
or that, since most of us are located within an amorphous middle, social
class has few consequences. The study's participants reported similar attitudes for their parents. Though 81 percent of the respondents said their
parents were aware of different class locations (most stated that their parents did not speak of *class* per se, but apparently recognized the existence
of hierarchical arrangements in society) and of their places within the
structure, nearly half said their parents saw few to no consequences for
themselves. Many reported that their parents believed that most others
were similar to themselves. The following examples are typical.

*"My parents, to this day, have absolutely no awareness of class
and the influences of class on their place in society. As far as they are*

concerned, everyone is the same as them and if you are different from them, well, there is something wrong with you."

"My parents were not significantly aware of class positions in any manner that made this clear to the children. Further, in the community we lived there were few rich people and all classes in the community participated in the same institutions (churches, schools) and lived in the same general areas. There were few families to compare one's self to and identify these as 'rich' or 'poor'."

... Given the pervasiveness of the dominant American ideology, it is no wonder that most of our respondents reported that their parents believed in the importance of individual achievement and self-motivation. Few respondents reported that their parents recognized any sort of systematic discrimination based on socioeconomic status or social class. In fact, in some cases, there was a certain kind of pride associated with belonging to the working-class. The following is a good example of this.

"... I should add that being working-class in (my hometown) carried with it no shame. You were proud to be working-class. You felt yourself to be strong and to be part of a strong breed, i.e., northern working-class. (My hometown) was built on the labor of the skilled working-class and my father was part of that class."

Weighing the Effects of Race, Gender, and Class

... The effects of racial and ethnic prejudice and discrimination cross both class and gender lines. Having the experience of racial discrimination adds an important element to the equation and modifies the experience of growing up working-class. One such modification is illustrated in the following quote from an Hispanic respondent as he explains how his father instilled suspicion of the white middle-class.

"They spoke of class only in economic terms and say the system as 'haves' versus the 'have-nots.' My dad often told me to always watch a smiling white guy because they all cheat. He saw the haves as crooked but said he would never steal as 'most whites who are rich do.' "

The effects of the intersection of gender and class are the focus of Barker's recent (1995) paper. She defines gender as carrying implied limitations within its labels (e.g., men are "naturally" smarter than women, etc.). The negative connotations associated with femininity that are present for all academics are added to the disadvantage of class background for women from working-class families. This, coupled with the expectations that women face from working-class families (i.e., that she "owes" it to her family to remain connected and supportive) generate different results for academic women from working-class backgrounds than it does for similar men. The bottom line is that these factors combine to produce a climate within which women from working-class backgrounds find it especially challenging to perform the necessary requirements to gain entry and acquire legitimacy within primarily upper middle-class, male-dominated institutions of higher learning.

The early-childhood socialization experiences of the women in our study lend support to this. The first example illustrates the implicit preference for males in working-class families:

> *"Since I was the oldest child (and only child for about nine years), I participated in ALL business and farm work: milking, field work . . . dressing turkeys, gathering and sorting and packing fruits and vegetables for sale on the routes, helping with books and often responsible for checks. . . My father often said that he had wished for a boy as his first child, but that I was [as] good as any boy would have been!"*

The following is a typical scenario for girls in working-class families:

> *"I was expected, as the oldest girl child, to baby-sit the younger children, clean house every week, do dishes, cook, help can food, mow the lawn, rake the leaves. Since I was a girl, it did not matter that I was in high school sports and held a part-time job, I was still expected to do my work around the house on top of everything else."*

In addition to the expectation that girls will take on a larger share of domestic responsibilities, there are expectations that girls will pursue particular occupational paths. Note the following example:

> *". . . I was told that my options were nurse, teacher, nun, mommy, or secretary, and since I would ultimately be 'just' a mommy anyway, any of the others would do (except nun of course!). One distant cousin was held out as an ideal to emulate; her secretarial job was with an airline, so she got to travel—it was thought that might satisfy my craving for*

something more/else. There were also strong messages to never move far away (2 hours distant was considered very far), since family, relatives, etc., were the most important thing. Two of my cousins were offered complete athletic scholarships one state (about 3 hours) away, and my aunt and uncle made them turn them down because they didn't want them to move away from home. When I finally left home to go to graduate school, I felt guilty as hell!"

The effects of gender thus intensify the difficulty for women in leaving their working-class origins. Girls in working-class families are instilled with similar levels of (limited) class culture as their male peers but with the added expectations that accompany socialization into working-class womanhood.

Conclusion: Caught in the Middle

In this paper, we have begun to explore the childhood recollections of a group of sociologists from working-class backgrounds. These individuals were socialized to assume a place within the working-class and many have experienced a particular kind of angst alongside their upward class-mobility. They have experienced a form of culture shock not unlike that experienced by travelers in a foreign land. Similar to Ryan and Sackrey's metaphor of "strangers in paradise," these respondents have described how their successes have often been accompanied by ambivalence and uncertainty. In the process of "making something" of themselves, they have moved into an ambiguous "middle," no longer working-class but not comfortably middle-class either.

By considering separately the three states of cultural capital that Bourdieu defines, the source of anxiety for academics from working-class backgrounds becomes more clear. . . . Though one has acquired the requisite institutionalized capital (i.e., the degree), not having sufficient embodied capital makes it difficult to participate fully in the consumption of objectified capital and creates a sense of status inconsistency. The insecurity that accompanies the "impostor" syndrome is common as academics from working-class backgrounds try to bridge the gap between their past and present lives.

In fact, in a myriad of subtle ways, working-class culture prepares the next generation of workers to voluntarily assume their positions in the hierarchy (Willis 1977). Culture is indeed what Wuthnow refers to as the ". . . expressive dimension of social structure. . . " (1987:13).

Culture offers meaning; it provides the process for internalizing the social structure and coming to see the status quo as natural, something that "feels right." Since a large part of the content of working-class culture is antithetical to scholarly pursuit, having grown up in an environment that assumes the "naturalness" of working-class values presents a conflict for intellectuals from such backgrounds. The conflict is, for many, deep and aching, lingering long after they have become, objectively, members of the middle-class. Socialization within a class culture is perhaps not as "determinant in the reproduction of the social structure" as Bourdieu implied (1983:253). It is possible to achieve upward mobility in this society; the lives of professional sociologists from working-class backgrounds attest to that. It is much more difficult, however, to "become" middle-class—to experience middle-class existence in a way that "feels right." It is this lingering difficulty that academics from working-class backgrounds experience as a feeling of being "caught in the middle."

REFERENCES

Barker, J. 1995. "White Working-Class Men and Women in Academia," *Race, Gender, and Class,* 3(1):65–77.

Bourdieu, P. 1984. *Taste.* (trans. by Richard Nice). Cambridge: Harvard University Press.

_____. 1986. "Forms of Capital," pp. 241–256 in John Richardson, Ed., *Handbook of Theory and Research for the Sociology of Education.* Westport, CT: Greenwood Press.

Coleman, J. S. 1988. "Social Capital in the Creation of Human Capital," *American Journal of Sociology* 94S: 95–120.

Halle, D. 1984. *America's Working Man.* Chicago: University of Chicago Press.

Kohn, M. and C. Schooler. 1983. *Work and Personality.* Norwood: Ablex.

Lareau, A. 1989. *Home Advantage: Social Class and Parental Intervention in Elementary Education.* London: Falmer Press.

Parcel, T. and E. Menaghan. 1994. *Parents' Jobs and Children's Lives.* Aldine de Gruyter.

Ryan, J. and C. Sackrey. 1984. *Strangers in Paradise: Academics from the Working Class.* Boston: South End Press.

Tokarczyk, M. and E. Fay (eds). 1993. *Working-Class Women in the Academy.* Amherst: University of Mass. Press.

Willis, P. G. 1977. *Learning to Labor.* London: Saxon House.

Wuthnow, R. 1987. *Meaning and Moral Order.* Princeton: Princeton University Press.

STUDY QUESTIONS

1. What do the authors mean by "contradictions" in this article?
2. Under what circumstances could a person escape the effects of their social class and move to another with ease? Can you think of examples where this has occurred?

Social Structure and Social Interaction

ONE OF THE ABIDING DILEMMAS OF SOCIOLOGY IS HOW to simultaneously account for and explain the macro and micro influences on human behavior. It seems that as we focus the research or theoretical lens on one, the other slips from view. Bridging this gulf between the social forces of institutions and the face-to-face world of interaction is not an easy task. One world is full of large structures like government or the economy, and the other world is rich with interpersonal contact and subtle, complex connections with persons in our immediate environments. In this topic, we examine some theory and research that help us to build a bridge across the rift in the sociological landscape and illustrate the true complexities of social life.

Social structure, most sociologists agree, is the enduring patterns in society that place people into relative positions (statuses) based on important characteristics like age, income, gender, race, or ethnicity. There is even a structure based on whether one has a disability or not. The rich are in a different social class position than the poor, women in a different social position based on gender than men, and people of color find their ethnicity and culture affecting them differently than ethnicity does for whites. New students to sociology might have one of their most difficult lessons in seeing social structure and appreciating the effects in our personal and collective lives. However, learning this lesson is the critically important dimension of a "sociological imagination." For example, knowing that your family and each classroom you attend has a structure that is set before you actually participate in them indicates that social structures exist apart from people. Parents or adults have more status (a higher position in the social structure) than children in the family; teachers a higher position than the students; and so on. Can you look at the behavior of people in your family and classroom and understand the impact of structure on behavior? Imagine the macrosocial world of ethnicity, or social class, or gender and you can glimpse the large structures that have a great impact on us, almost continuously.

Social interaction is a complex, subtle process whereby people initiate and respond to one another based on commonly understood symbols. Some of the symbols are verbal, like words, and some are nonverbal, like gestures. We learn to express ourselves, respond to others, and create continuous loops of interaction in an endless number of social situations. Because we are accustomed to the meaning of the symbols and the patterns in which they occur, we do "social interaction" without thinking about it; it seems unconscious. When sociologists study this process we discuss it as "spontaneous" and "emergent" (something that is not predetermined or set). The theory we use to study the microsocial world is "symbolic interaction," a topic covered earlier in the book. Social interaction is also an opportunity for individuals to impact social situations and affect their own and others' behavior. If social structure feels as though it impedes our ability to be creative and spontaneous, social interaction gives us some measure of autonomy as actors in social settings. Here we are, then, human actors sandwiched between the structural influences of the macrosocial world and the dynamic, creative process of social interaction in the microsocial world. Recognizing how we are affected by the world and how we affect the world certainly will enhance our understanding of human behavior and our ability to act on the world ourselves.

In Topic 5, three articles are brought to the reader as illustrations of "social structure and social interaction." First, Charles Lemert shows us how to "imagine social things, competently." Through the use of personal examples and the reviews of Durkheim and Mills, we are given several glimpses of how to look at social settings with a sociological eye. Seeing social structure will be one of our first and most important lessons in the discipline. Second, William J. Chambliss's article uses his rich qualitative study to demonstrate how social structure (social class of the boys) affects the community's perceptions, and even the boys' future life chances as they participate in two gangs, "The Saints and the Roughnecks." Finally, nothing is more personal than interactions between marriage partners, and Lillian Rubin does an excellent job of showing how gender (a structure) affects our communication (interaction) in her applied research, "The Approach-Avoidance Dance." Structure affects behavior and the behavior reinforces, but might alter, the structure of the relationship.

CHARLES LEMERT

Imagining Social Things, Competently

He was amazing to me, a miraculous boy. In school, I tried to write as he wrote (he won the prize in penmanship), talk as he talked (he always had something confident to say), and walk as he walked (he had an awkward gait but he *always* knew where he was going). This was David Bennett. In the 1940s in the less-than-classy western suburbs of Cincinnati there were few heroes. Our fathers had come back from the war bitter and broken, not at all brash and ready to build the American Century. We hardly knew the bravest generation. But David Bennett, he was something else. We never knew what became of his mother. In those days, little white boys born to merchants or professionals of modest success knew almost nothing about separation or divorce. When our lives were disrupted, we were taught to look away in silence, even to pretend that everything was just fine. I remember my grandfather's wake as the best family party ever. His face, made over to cover lines the pain of cancer had etched, rose just above the edge of the coffin around which we children played as we always had in his presence. We knew of death, of course, but in our polite and polished bourgeois world, divorce was unheard of. One of the guys said that David's mother was living in Kentucky somewhere. Why?

Then it happened that his father grew ill and died. David was left with Gramps and his grandmother. Many years later, when we were all in college, Gramps was much beloved by the boys in David's fraternity house. Such a character he was! But not the kind of parent-substitute a small boy dreams of. We could never play with David on Saturday mornings because, we were told, he was required to mop and wax the kitchen floor. And he was never, never allowed out after seven in the summers, and this is just the beginning of a long list of what we thought were harsh domestic rules—rules we could comprehend no better than divorce or separation.

But, remarkably, David seemed to know just how to master all that befell him. He accepted his losses and obeyed the demands of his upbringing. He had the best grades. The teachers loved him. In spite of this, he was our friend. He beat me out for the last spot on the school basketball team. So what? When I last heard of him, more years ago than I can remember, he was a successful doctor, living somewhere outside Chicago.

Some people are like that. They know just how to get by, often with a grace that cannot be taught. When I grew up a little more, I was surprised to learn that I too had some of that grace. Still later, when I was able to think about it even more, I realized that most people, even those who could never hope to go to medical school, had this surprisingly durable human quality that allowed David to overcome and thrive.

This quality—one might even call it a competence—turns out to be widely distributed among humans. Not only do most people enjoy the benefits of this competence, but it seems to come to the fore especially when things are as bad as they can get.

Across the world from Cincinnati where David and I dealt with the losses and pains of our otherwise secure worlds, other children of our generation faced far worse terrors. Some children, like many today who suffer the violence of poverty and dangerous streets, were exposed to the brutality of political terrors they could barely understand, even when they had to. One such child of my generation grew up to write a book about his childhood in Poland under the reign of Soviet military police during the gathering storm of the Second World War.

> Since the time of our house search, Mother does not let us take off our clothes at night. We can take off our shoes, but we have to have them beside us all the time. The coats lie on chairs, so they can be put on in the wink of an eye. In principle we are not permitted to sleep. My sister and I lie side by side, and we poke each other, shake each other, or pull each other by the hair. "Hey, you, don't sleep!" "You, too, don't sleep!" But, of course, in the midst of this struggling and shoving we both fall asleep. But Mother really does not sleep. She sits at the table and listens the whole time. The silence of our street rings in our ears. If someone's

footsteps echo in the silence, Mother grows pale. A man at this hour is an enemy. An enemy is a terrifying figure. Who else would come around at this hour? Good people are afraid; they are sitting hidden in their homes.[1]

These were Polish children in the village of Pinsk, sometime in 1939. The Soviet secret police had already deported their father. They were children just the same, able to play in the dark against a fear they understood well enough. Like them, millions of people lie awake at night, terrified that terrible men will come, sent by evil to visit fear on children when and where they are—once in Italy and Germany, then in Russia and China, then in Afghanistan and Iraq, then in Rwanda and Darfur, tomorrow who knows where. But many people facing such terrors get by, often with humor.

What is this quality of human resilience, this competence that sustains and enriches human life, even against the odds? It is, to be sure, not a simple thing. Certainly, it encompasses what is often called the "human spirit," just as it embraces "tough-mindedness," "street smarts," "grit," and other such attributes associated with the best, most determined, and most transcendent powers of human creatures. But it also includes, in significant way, something you may never have thought of, or even perhaps realized existed.

Even if the world in which they live is degraded by poverty or violence, most people get by because they are endowed with *sociological competence*. This seemingly native, highly practical, virtually ubiquitous capacity sustains us individually, but it also contributes mightily to our ability to form and keep social relations with others. Without it, social life would be impossible. Without it, every time we entered a new and different social situation, we would be forced to learn anew what to think of it and how to behave. But, most of the time, we understand what is going on and where we fit in.

Think of the number of different situations you may have encountered just in the day you are reading this book. If you happen to be a student, it is possible that earlier this day you met in a room with others with whom you are making a class. To no one's amazement you already knew just what to do. When your teacher entered, for example, it is likely that all the students, whatever their ages and backgrounds, realized it was time, gradually, to fall silent and listen. If you happen to be a mother or a father stealing a few moments to read while the children play, it is likely that already more than once today you were required to referee some fight, kiss some bruised body part, or wipe away a tear. You may not feel entirely comfortable with how you did what you did, but it is likely you did it well enough. Most parents do this kind of thing as if by second nature.

It hardly makes a difference who you are, or what you do. Nearly all of us, most hours of most days, run into social situations filled with demands and potential risks we know, as if by instinct, how to handle. Greeting strangers, entering crowded rooms, asking the time of day, finding the right subway, ordering Big Macs without fries, meeting deadlines, getting deadlines extended—all these, much more, and virtually all the little events out of which we compose the course of daily life entail sociological competence.

The sociological competence of which I speak is not, at least not initially, the trained competence of the professional sociologist. But what the professionals know and have to say depends on a competence you already possess without the benefit of special studies. Indeed, there could be, and would be, no academic discipline organized under the name "sociology" were it not the case that sociology itself is a commonly held skill of untrained people and, thus, an important feature of social life itself. This may seem a bit odd to say. The more customary attitude in our society is to think of sociology as a sometimes complicated, often jargoned, though usually interesting, field of formal study and research. It is, of course, but, before it can be this, sociology is something else.

What is this miraculously effective and possibly universal human quality? Consider again those small Polish children, or others like them elsewhere in the world. What got them through the nights was an ability to imagine the reality in which they were caught. They understood, it is clear, that they were in danger. They knew that the police had carried off their father in the night. They knew why their mother kept them dressed, why she never slept at night. Straightforward? Not quite. Remember these were children for whom the ideas of oppressive police-states, of Soviet ideology and repressions, even of bad men and enforcers, were at best illformed. Their native sociological competence, though it served them well, could not have instructed them as to the subtleties of the wider world of totalitarian regimes—regimes that in time fell away only to be replaced by more of their awful kind. What those children, like others before and after them, understood was that there was danger around, and they were able to imagine creative ways to ward off the fear, even by so touchingly gentle a way as holding each other tight in a playful game of daring, teasing, but connecting, thus imagining the only truly safe place available—a place protected by their mother's vigil, the subject of their jokes.

How human beings form relations with each other is the central mystery of any sociology. What is now reasonably well known is that children and others perform such amazing feats of courage by means of a resilient capacity to imagine—that is, by their ability to hold in mind the wider world of others, the good alongside the evil, and thus to organize what must be done. Imagination of this sort is not dreamily removed from practical things, nor is it simply a psychological endowment. On the contrary, it thrives in the practical, and it seems to be not so much an individual instinct as a common *social* sense. Frightened children have it with each other. We all have it, most of the time, in our dealings with the others we come upon.

Whenever you enter a room and "just know" you don't belong there, when you see a stranger on the subway and understand intuitively that it is safe to return his not-quite-delivered smile, when you are introduced to someone elegantly dressed in a certain way and know she is not to be called by her first name even if she offers it—these are among the evidences for the sociology in each of us. They may seem to be trivial manners by contrast to the urgency of survival through dark nights. And so they are. But, however small, they are not unimportant. They may seem inconsequential just because they come to us so naturally. But think of what life would be like if we regularly encountered people who were sociologically incompetent.

One fine evening, some time ago, I met my wife at the late train after a week away. As the station cleared, we saw a woman alone and not quite sure of where she was. It was dark and late, so we offered her a ride. She gladly jumped into the back seat. Then, in the few minutes it took to get her home, she proceeded to tell us the most intimate details of her life, including how her husband had just bilked her of millions of dollars, that Ethel Kennedy thought it was terrible, and that, by the way, "I am telling the truth." She may have been, but it was hard to believe. Though her plight may have been real, something important was missing in her dealings with us. In such situations, the normal competency rule is something like this: "Try to understand the circumstances of those to whom you tell your stories; make sure, if you can, that they want to hear what you have to say." All it would take is a few encounters like this one for most people to want to go hide, or at least to think twice about offering rides to strangers. This woman, whoever she truly was, clearly had a vivid imagination, but, it would seem, she was so upset by what had happened to her that her local sociological imagination was impaired. In those brief moments with us, she could not think of a world in which one needs an invitation before telling all to kindly strangers willing to help, but far more eager to hold each other after a week apart.

Social life, whether among passing strangers at local stations or throughout the whole of complex society, depends unforgivingly on the ability of members to understand social things competently. This competence is the key ingredient in their ability to enter imaginatively into the social realities all about. That most people can, and do, is itself a miracle of sorts. What makes this so surprising is that we all know that the competence is not something we normally think about. It is not even something we are always able to provide an account of when called upon to do so. Where exactly did you learn to avoid some strangers while welcoming others, or learn not to defer to some people while giving others full formal regard? Most of us got this competence from somewhere, and at a very young age. It is so natural that, when on those rare occasions someone asks us to discuss this skill, we are more likely to be annoyed than intrigued by the request.

Sociological competence is much like our native ability to use the language we hear as infants. All of a sudden, one day, a child begins to speak, soon in sentences, eventually without pointing, eventually in reasonably correct forms of the past and future tenses. ("Daddy, I saw some sheeps on the way home!") A child does this sometime late in the second year of life or so, and without benefit of any organized instruction in grammar. Much the same happens, though at a somewhat later age, with sociological competence. The learning may be rough, and in need of encouragement or a few gentle spankings and playground pinches or punches, but it too comes relatively easily, and quite early. Some people hate to study sociology for the same reason they hate to study grammar: "I already know this stuff. Why give it a fancy name?" This is true, of course, for a great deal of our sociological competence. Most of us know a lot already—but not *everything*.

The first accepted definition of sociology was given in 1894 by the French sociologist Emile Durkheim (1858–1917). Durkheim persuaded many who followed him that, as he put it, "social facts are things, that is, realities external to the individual."[2] *Sociology*, thereby, is the science of social things. Durkheim meant to insist, quite reasonably, that, as important as individuals are to what goes on around them, there are also certain things that are inherently, and without exception, social in nature. The status of these social things has ever since been a topic of debate among professional sociologists for the simple reason that it is obviously more difficult to define social things than it is individual ones.

When David Bennett went about being a brilliant student, a fair athlete, and a generally good guy even while being required to scrub the kitchen floor, his pals could observe what he did and how he did it. I could not tell you why he made the basketball team and I did not. But he did. His jump shot was ever so much more awkward than mine. This and many other of the uncountable little things that made him a unique individual were plainly visible. The tougher question is, What were all the features of the complex dynamic of his family life that made him the kind of kid he was? His departed mother, his dead father, his grumpy gramps, and much else, including, even, the effects of a world war on his parents' marriage or of the conventions of postwar suburban culture in the United States—all these came together in such a way as to play a part in making him the unusual person he was. These influences on his behavior as an individual are social things. Without them, David would not have been who he was, and is today—out there somewhere, presumably still alive, caring for his patients, perhaps looking in on grandchildren of his own as they come up against the different social worlds.

But, even now that I am a trained and certified professional sociologist, I could only barely begin to suggest just how to go about discovering the workings of those social things. If complicated in the case of one good white boy from the American suburbs, think how much more complicated the task is when, say, someone tries to explain just what the Soviet imperium was and why it wanted to frighten little children and their mothers. This is a social thing of a very consequential kind. It is one thing to observe the facts of the deported fathers, vigilant mothers, and terrified kids. Quite another to give a coherent account of the social thing itself, of the Soviet imperium in all its vast operations upon millions of people. Yet, it can be done. As a matter of fact, that little boy who hid at night in 1939 grew up to be a world-famous writer and journalist, able in adult life to describe in compelling terms how his feelings of terror as a boy might have been produced by the social organization of the former Soviet Union. That Ryszard Kapuściński could write *Imperium* in 1993 does not mean that all, even most, children who suffered as he did in the 1930s grew up to describe the social things that had made their lives miserable. In fact, most people are unable to describe very many of the more complex social things that affect them. They could, of course, were they to undergo the training, and many do it without much education at all. But the basic fact is that most people know, more or less well, how to get by in daily life. They are sociologically competent, even when they lack the advanced sociological training to describe their competence.

This is the problem Emile Durkheim and most professional sociologists since his day have had to face. People know a lot about social things, but they cannot talk about them very well without some help or, perhaps, without a challenge of some kind. They, therefore, are inclined, quite naturally, to mistrust the reality of social things, that is, of things just as mysterious as David Bennett's seemingly weird family arrangement, or of a totalitarian state's unusually evil methods.

The challenge Durkheim took up was that of establishing sociology as a formal, academic discipline against the commonplace prejudice that other things are much more real. Psychology, economics, history, and political science have a much easier time of it because it is relatively easier to imagine what they are about—minds (or the like), market or prices, the facts of some group or another's story, how and why people vote and govern as they do. Just why these might seem more imaginable than *social things* is itself a difficult question I will not even attempt to answer. Minds, markets, stories, and votes are hardly simple things. But, relatively speaking, they seem so to many people. By contrast, just about everyone considers *social things*—or, more familiarly, *societies*—abstract, abstruse, and fluffily vague. Most people are not wrong. Since Durkheim, and certainly before, sociologists of all kinds (including small children trying to sleep in the dark) have had to contend with this inconvenient, but most interesting, fact of social life.

Durkheim himself died before sociology became much of an organized and institutional part of the university. He died in 1917, during the First World War, when it seemed that modern Europe would collapse before the continuing inability of nations and their leaders to create a stable political environment in which their people could enjoy the benefits of the modern world.

Some years later, well after the Second World War had similarly failed to make to world a better place, another sociologist made an enduring attempt to define sociology. C. Wright Mills (1916–1962), who was born just the year before Durkheim died, defined sociology in a way that made clear what was unclear in Durkheim's definition. While Durkheim assumed that social things can be as readily imagined as other types of facts of the human condition, Mills came to the more honest, and accurate, conclusion that at least one class of social facts is normally unavailable to those not specifically trained to see them.

Imagine again those small Polish children in 1939. Too young to understand much at all about the Soviet brand of totalitarian oppression, they understood at best that something was terribly wrong, that the world somehow was filled with cruel men. Though little Ryszard grew up to understand full well who those men were and why they did what they did, as a child he could only huddle back into the trembling arms of his sister. Their attempt at a playful response, a game of a sad sort, was indeed an imaginative response to social facts they could experience but only dimly comprehend. While it seems, these children did not come to one of the more common human conclusions in the face of such odds, they might have. It is not uncommon for terrorized children to take the terror into themselves and to conclude that, in some inexplicable way, the evil visited upon them is a result of something they did. While this is just one of several self-defeating conclusions, it is a familiar one. Adult women, boys and girls, minorities, the unjustly punished, victims of family violence, children of abusers or alcoholics, even an occasional white guy of privilege are all strongly tempted to place the blame for their misery on themselves. While there are many reasons for this (most of them psychological), the sociological explanation is that, when we live in small worlds, whether as children or adults, it is usually difficult to understand the larger social forces that affect us. The more powerful social things are, the less we are equipped to comprehend them without some extra work.

This basic fact of life lay behind C. Wright Mills's now famous definition of sociology as the work of the *sociological imagination*.[3] He meant that sociology is the activity by which persons of differing degrees of training and experience often learn eventually to create imaginative reconstructions of the larger structural forces that affect their lives. Without this sociological skill, they are left with the belief that the troubles in their lives are of their own doing, or perhaps the result of some abstract fate; but, in either case, they feel that these are matters with respect to which they should, and do, feel guilty. The sociological imagination refers to the ability of some to learn—often with good luck or coaching or perhaps with formal schooling—to realize that, just as often, one's personal *troubles* are in fact public *issues*. Those children in Poland feared, and could have blamed themselves because of, a social and political system so massive in comparison to their little home in Pinsk that they could hardly be expected to comprehend the "issue" of totalitarian rule as anything other than their personal "troubles." They were, thus, no different from anyone in another situation in space and time who suffers unwittingly because of social things beyond his or her control—no different from those who fail in schools because their schools don't teach, from those unable to achieve their dreams because they are arbitrarily excluded from the places where those dreams are realized, from those unable to find the relationships they desire because they are still controlled by unconscious memories of sexual abuse they suffered in a long ago they cannot, or will not, remember—no different from children who grew up to suffer abuse in the Abu Ghraibs of the world.

It is not just the victims of society who are disadvantaged in this way. Most of us, whatever our circumstances, have need of a more vividly active sociological imagination, which we sometimes develop by the example of others, by the lessons of practical life, and, even, by courses in sociology. C. Wright Mills, though he was a professional sociologist, did not intend that the sociological imagination be a competence of only the more highly educated. On the contrary, he believed that the most important value of sociology is its potential to enrich and encourage the lives of all human beings. Mills was one of the first to insist with a defiant passion that sociology is not for the professionals alone—that the sociological imagination is every bit as important to the ordinary person, for whom it can be a matter of quite serious urgency. The passion with which he held this conviction explains why he exercised so much popular influence and why, in particular, his ideas influenced the politics of the early student movement in the 1960s. Though not alone in the conviction, Mills did more than anyone to clarify and convey the extent to which sociology is first and foremost a practical skill available to all men and women, even to boys and girls. Sociology's value as an academic field of research and instruction relies on this prior fact.

NOTES

1. Ryszard Kapuściński, *Imperium* (Random House, 1994), pp. 11–12.
2. See Emile Durkheim, *The Rules of Sociological Method* (1894; reprint, Free Press, 1982), chapter 1. The words given are Durkheim's but they are rephrased for simplicity's sake. They are nearly the same as those used in the preface to his later book, *Suicide* (1897).
3. C. Wright Mills, *The Sociological Imagination* (Oxford University Press, 1959), especially chapter 1.

STUDY QUESTIONS

1. What is Lemert's discussion of "sociological competence"? Discuss how it is used in social life and how social life is more difficult without it.
2. What important points does Lemert make through the works of Durkheim and Mills? Summarize their contributions to this discussion of "sociological competence."

WILLIAM J. CHAMBLISS

The Saints and the Roughnecks

Eight promising young men—children of good, stable, white upper-middle-class families, active in school affairs, good pre-college students—were some of the most delinquent boys at Hanibal High School. While community residents and parents knew that these boys occasionally sowed a few wild oats, they were totally unaware that sowing wild oats completely occupied the daily routine of these young men. The Saints were constantly occupied with truancy, drinking, wild driving, petty theft and vandalism. Yet not one was officially arrested for any misdeed during the two years I observed them.

This record was particularly surprising in light of my observations during the same two years of another gang of Hanibal High School students, six lower-class white boys known as the Roughnecks. The Roughnecks were constantly in trouble with police and community even though their rate of delinquency was about equal with that of the Saints. What was the cause of this disparity? the result? The following consideration of the activities, social class and community perceptions of both gangs may provide some answers.

The Saints from Monday to Friday

The Saints' principal daily concern was with getting out of school as early as possible. The boys managed to get out of school with minimum danger that they would be accused of playing hookey through an elaborate procedure for obtaining "legitimate" release from class. The most common procedure was for one boy to obtain the release of another by fabricating a meeting of some committee, program or recognized club. Charles might raise his hand in his 9:00 chemistry class and asked to be excused—a euphemism for going to the bathroom. Charles would go to Ed's math class and inform the teacher that Ed was needed for a 9:30 rehearsal of the drama club play. The math teacher would recognize Ed and Charles as "good students" involved in numerous school activities and would permit Ed to leave at 9:30. Charles would return to his class, and Ed would go to Tom's English class to obtain his release. Tom would engineer Charles' escape. The strategy would continue until as many of the Saints as possible were freed. After a stealthy trip to the car (which had been parked in a strategic spot), the boys were off for a day of fun. . . .

Having escaped from the concrete corridors the boys usually went either to a pool hall on the other (lower-class) side of town or to a cafe in the suburbs. Both places were out of the way of people the boys were likely to know (family or school officials), and both provided a source of entertainment. The pool hall entertainment was the generally rough atmosphere, the occasional hustler, the sometimes drunk proprietor and, of course, the game of pool. The cafe's entertainment was provided by the owner. The boys would "accidentally" knock a glass on the floor or spill cola on the counter—not all the time, but enough to be sporting. They would also bend spoons, put salt in sugar bowls and generally tease whoever was working in the cafe. The owner had opened the cafe recently and was dependent on the boys' business which was, in fact, substantial since between the horsing around and the teasing they bought food and drinks.

The Saints on Weekends

On weekends the automobile was even more critical than during the week, for on weekends the Saints went to Big Town—a large city with a population of over a million 25 miles from Hanibal. Every Friday and Saturday night most of the Saints would meet between 8:00 and 8:30 and would go into Big Town. Big Town activities included drinking heavily in taverns or nightclubs, driving drunkenly through the streets, and committing acts of vandalism and playing pranks.

By midnight on Fridays and Saturdays the Saints were usually thoroughly high, and one or two of them were often so drunk they had to be carried to the cars. Then the boys drove around town, calling obscenities to women and girls; occasionally trying (unsuccessfully so far as I could tell) to pick girls up; and driving recklessly through red lights and at high speeds with their lights out. Occasionally they played "chicken." One boy would climb out the back window of the car and across the roof to the driver's side of the car while the car was moving at high speed (between 40 and 50 miles an hour); then the driver would move over and the boy who had just crawled across the car roof would take the driver's seat.

Searching for "fair game" for a prank was the boys' principal activity after they left the tavern. The boys would drive alongside a foot patrolman and ask directions to some street. If the policeman leaned on the car in the course of answering the question, the driver would speed away, causing him to lose his balance. The Saints were careful to play this prank only in an area where they were not going to spend much time and where they could quickly disappear around a corner to avoid having their license plate number taken.

Construction sites and road repair areas were the special province of the Saints' mischief. A soon-to-be-repaired hole in the road inevitably invited the Saints to remove lanterns and wooden barricades and put them in the car, leaving the hole unprotected. The boys would find a safe vantage point and wait for an unsuspecting motorist to drive into the hole. Often, though not always, the boys would go up to the motorist and commiserate with him about the dreadful way the city protected its citizenry. . . .

Through all the pranks, drinking and reckless driving the boys managed miraculously to avoid being stopped by police. Only twice in two years was I aware that they had been stopped by a Big City policeman. Once was for speeding (which they did every time they drove whether they were drunk or sober), and the driver managed to convince the policeman that it was simply an error. The second time they were stopped they had just left a nightclub and were walking through an alley. . . .

The boys had a spirit of frivolity and fun about their escapades. They did not view what they were engaged in as "delinquency," though it surely was by any reasonable definition of that word. They simply viewed themselves as having a little fun and who, they would ask, was really hurt by it? The answer had to be no one, although this fact remains one of the most difficult things to explain about the gang's behavior. Unlikely though it seems, in two years of drinking, driving, carousing and vandalism no one was seriously injured as a result of the Saints' activities.

The Saints in School

The Saints were highly successful in school. The average grade for the group was "B," with two of the boys having close to a straight "A" average. Almost all of the boys were popular and many of them held offices in the school. One of the boys was vice-president of the student body one year. Six of the boys played on athletic teams.

At the end of their senior year, the student body selected ten seniors for special recognition as the "school wheels"; four of the ten were Saints. Teachers and school officials saw no problem with any of these boys and anticipated that they would all "make something of themselves."

How the boys managed to maintain this impression is surprising in view of their actual behavior while in school. Their technique for covering truancy was so successful that teachers did not even realize that the boys were absent from school much of the time. Occasionally, of course, the system would backfire and then the boy was on his own. A boy who was caught would be most contrite, would plead guilty and ask for mercy. He inevitably got the mercy he sought.

Cheating on examinations was rampant, even to the point of orally communicating answers to exams as well as looking at one another's papers. Since none of the group studied, and since they were primarily dependent on one another for help, it is surprising that grades were so high. Teachers contributed to the deception in their admitted inclination to give these boys (and presumably others like them) the benefit of the doubt. When asked how the boys did in school, and when pressed on specific examinations, teachers might admit that they were disappointed in John's performance, but would quickly add that they "knew that he was capable of doing better," so John was given a higher grade than he had actually earned. How often this happened is impossible to know. During the time that I observed the group, I never saw any of the boys take homework home. Teachers may have been "understanding" very regularly. . . .

The Police and the Saints

The local police saw the Saints as good boys who were among the leaders of the youth in the community. Rarely, the boys might be stopped in town for speeding or for running a stop sign. When this happened the boys were always polite, contrite and pled for mercy. As in school, they received the mercy they asked for. None ever received a ticket or was taken into the precinct by the local police.

The situation in Big Town, where the boys engaged in most of their delinquency, was only slightly different. The police there did not know the boys at all, although occasionally the boys were stopped by a patrolman. Once they were caught taking a lantern from a construction site. Another time they were stopped for running a stop sign, and on several occasions they were stopped for speeding. Their behavior was as before: contrite, polite and penitent. The urban police, like the local police, accepted their demeanor as sincere. More important, the urban police were convinced that these were good boys just out for a lark.

The Roughnecks

Hanibal townspeople never perceived the Saints' high level of delinquency. The Saints were good boys who just went in for an occasional prank. After all, they were well dressed, well mannered and had nice cars. The Roughnecks were a different story. Although the two gangs of boys were the same age, and both groups engaged in an equal amount of wild-oat sowing, everyone agreed that the not-so-well-dressed, not-so-well-mannered, not-so-rich boys were heading for trouble. Townspeople would say, "You can see the gang members at the drugstore, night after night, leaning against the storefront (sometimes drunk) or slouching around inside buying cokes, reading magazines, and probably stealing old Mr. Wall blind. When they are outside and girls walk by, even respectable girls, these boys make suggestive remarks. Sometimes their remarks are downright lewd."

From the community's viewpoint, the real indication that these kids were in for trouble was that they were constantly involved with the police. Some of them had been picked up for stealing, mostly small stuff, of course, "but still it's stealing small stuff that leads to big time crimes." "Too bad," people said. "Too bad that these boys couldn't behave like the other kids in town; stay out of trouble, be polite to adults, and look to their future."

The community's impression of the degree to which this group of six boys (ranging in age from 16 to 19) engaged in delinquency was somewhat distorted. In some ways the gang was more delinquent than the community thought; in other ways they were less.

The fighting activities of the group were fairly readily and accurately perceived by almost everyone. At least once a month, the boys would get into some sort of fight, although most fights were scraps between members of the group or involved only one member of the group and some peripheral hanger-on. Only three times in the period of observation did the group fight together: once against a gang from across town, once against two blacks and once against a group of boys from another school. For the first two fights the group went out "looking for trouble"—and they found it both times. The third fight followed a football game and began spontaneously with an argument on the football field between one of the Roughnecks and a member of the opposition's football team.

Jack had a particular propensity for fighting and was involved in most of the brawls. He was a prime mover of the escalation of arguments into fights.

More serious than fighting, had the community been aware of it, was theft. Although almost everyone was aware that the boys occasionally stole things, they did not realize the extent of the activity. Petty stealing was a frequent event for the Roughnecks. Sometimes they stole as a group and coordinated their efforts; other times they stole in pairs. Rarely did they steal alone.

The thefts ranged from very small things like paperback books, comics and ballpoint pens to expensive items like watches. The nature of the thefts varied from time to time. The gang would go through a period of systematically shoplifting items from automobiles or school lockers. Types of thievery varied with the whim of the gang. Some forms of thievery were more profitable than others, but all thefts were for profit, not just thrills.

Roughnecks siphoned gasoline from cars as often as they had access to an automobile, which was not very often. Unlike the Saints, who owned their own cars, the Roughnecks would have to borrow their parents' cars, an event which occurred only eight or nine times a year. The boys claimed to have stolen cars for joy rides from time to time. . . .

The Roughnecks, then, engaged mainly in three types of delinquency: theft, drinking and fighting. Although community members perceived that this gang of kids was delinquent, they mistakenly believed that their illegal activities were primarily drinking, fighting and being a nuisance to passersby. Drinking was limited among the gang members, although it did occur, and theft was much more prevalent than anyone realized. . . .

There was a high level of mutual distrust and dislike between the Roughnecks and the police. The boys felt very strongly that the police were unfair and corrupt. Some evidence existed that the boys were correct in their perception.

The main source of the boys' dislike for the police undoubtedly stemmed from the fact that the police would sporadically harass the group. From the standpoint of the boys, these acts of occasional enforcement of the law were whimsical and uncalled for. It made no sense to them, for example, that the police would come to the corner occasionally and threaten them with arrest for loitering when the night before the boys had been out siphoning gasoline from cars and the police had been nowhere in sight. To the boys, the police were stupid on the one hand, for not being where they should have been and catching the boys in a serious offense, and unfair on the other hand, for trumping up "loitering" charges against them.

From the viewpoint of the police, the situation was quite different. They knew, with all the confidence necessary to be a policeman, that these boys were engaged in criminal activities. They knew this partly from occasionally catching them, mostly from circumstantial evidence ("the boys were around when those tires were slashed"), and partly because the police shared the view of the community in general that this was a bad bunch of boys. The best the police could hope to do was to be sensitive to the fact that these boys were engaged in illegal acts and arrest them whenever there was some evidence that they had been involved. Whether or not the boys had in fact committed a particular act in a particular way was not especially important. The police had a broader view: their job was to stamp out these kids' crimes; the tactics were not as important as the end result.

Over the period that the group was under observation, each member was arrested at least once. Several of the boys were arrested a number of times and spent at least one night in jail. While most were never taken to court, two of the boys were sentenced to six months' incarceration in boys' schools.

The Roughnecks in School

The Roughnecks' behavior in school was not particularly disruptive. During school hours they did not all hang around together, but tended instead to spend most of their time with one or two other members of the gang who were their special buddies. Although every member of the gang attempted to avoid school as much as possible, they were not particularly successful and most of them attended school with surprising regularity. They considered school a burden—something to be gotten through with a minimum of conflict. If they were "bugged" by a particular teacher, it could lead to trouble. One of the boys, Al, once threatened to beat up a teacher and, according to the other boys, the teacher hid under a desk to escape him.

Teachers saw the boys the way the general community did, as heading for trouble, as being uninterested in making something of themselves. Some were also seen as being incapable of meeting the academic standards of the school. Most of the teachers expressed concern for this group of boys and were willing to pass them despite poor performance, in the belief that failing them would only aggravate the problem.

The group of boys had a grade point average just slightly above "C." No one in the group failed either grade, and no one had better than a "C" average. They were very consistent in their achievement or, at least, the teachers were consistent in their perception of the boys' achievement.

Two of the boys were good football players. Herb was acknowledged to be the best player in the school and Jack was almost as good. Both boys were criticized for their failure to abide by training rules, for refusing to come to practice as often as they should, and for not playing their best during practice. What they lacked in sportsmanship they made up for in skill, apparently, and played every game no matter how poorly they had performed in practice or how many practice sessions they had missed.

Two Questions

Why did the community, the school and the police react to the Saints as though they were good, upstanding, nondelinquent youths with bright futures but to the Roughnecks as though they were tough, young criminals who were headed for trouble? Why did the Roughnecks and the Saints in fact have quite different careers after high school—careers which, by and large, lived up to the expectations of the community?

The most obvious explanation for the differences in the community's and law enforcement agencies' reactions to the two gangs is that one group of boys was "more delinquent" than the other. Which group was more delinquent? The answer to this question will determine in part how we explain the differential responses to these groups by the members of the community and, particularly, by law enforcement and school officials.

In sheer number of illegal acts, the Saints were the more delinquent. They were truant from school for at least part of the day almost every day of the week. In addition, their drinking and vandalism occurred with surprising regularity. The Roughnecks, in contrast, engaged sporadically in delinquent episodes. While these episodes were frequent, they certainly did not occur on a daily or even a weekly basis.

The difference in frequency of offenses was probably caused by the Roughnecks' inability to obtain liquor and to manipulate legitimate excuses from school. Since the Roughnecks had less money than the Saints, and teachers carefully supervised their school activities, the Roughnecks' hearts may have been as black as the Saints', but their misdeeds were not nearly as frequent.

There are really no clear-cut criteria by which to measure qualitative differences in antisocial behavior. The most important dimension of the difference is generally referred to as the "seriousness" of the offenses.

If seriousness encompasses the relative economic costs of delinquent acts, then some assessment can be made. The Roughnecks probably stole an average of about $5.00 worth of goods a week. Some weeks the figure was considerably higher, but these times must be balanced against long periods when almost nothing was stolen.

The Saints were more continuously engaged in delinquency but their acts were not for the most part costly to property. Only their vandalism and occasional theft of gasoline would so qualify. Perhaps once or twice a month they would siphon a tankful of gas. The other costly items were street signs, construction lanterns and the like. All of these acts combined probably did not quite average $5.00 a week, partly because much of the stolen equipment was abandoned and presumably could be recovered. The difference in cost of stolen property between the two groups was trivial, but the Roughnecks probably had a slightly more expensive set of activities than did the Saints.

Another meaning of seriousness is the potential threat of physical harm to members of the community and to the boys themselves. The Roughnecks were more prone to physical violence; they not only welcomed an opportunity to fight; they went seeking it. In addition, they fought among themselves frequently. Although the fighting never included deadly weapons, it was still a menace, however minor, to the physical safety of those involved.

The Saints never fought. They avoided physical conflict both inside and outside the group. At the same time, though, the Saints frequently endangered their own and other people's lives. They did so almost every time they drove a car, especially if they had been drinking. Sober, their driving was risky; under the influence of alcohol it was horrendous. In addition, the Saints endangered the lives of others with their pranks. Street excavations left unmarked were a very serious hazard.

Evaluating the relative seriousness of the two gangs' activities is difficult. The community reacted as though the behavior of the Roughnecks was a problem, and they reacted as though the behavior of the Saints was not. But the members of the community were ignorant of the array of delinquent acts that characterized the Saints' behavior. Although concerned citizens were unaware of much of the Roughnecks' behavior as well, they were much better informed about the Roughnecks' involvement in delinquency than they were about the Saints'.

Visibility

Differential treatment of the two gangs resulted in part because one gang was infinitely more visible than the other. This differential visibility was a direct function of the economic standing of the families. The Saints had access to automobiles and were able to remove themselves from the sight of the community. In as routine a decision as to where to go to have a milkshake after school, the Saints stayed away from the mainstream of community life. Lacking transportation, the Roughnecks could not make it to the edge of town. The center of town was the only practical place for them to meet since their homes were scattered throughout the town and any noncentral meeting place put an undue hardship on some members. Through necessity the Roughnecks congregated in a crowded area where everyone in the community passed frequently, including teachers and law enforcement officers. They could easily see the Roughnecks hanging around the drugstore.

The Roughnecks, of course, made themselves even more visible by making remarks to passersby and by occasionally getting into fights on the corner. Meanwhile, just as regularly, the Saints were either at the cafe on one edge of town or in the pool hall at the other edge of town. Without any particular realization that they were making themselves inconspicuous, the Saints were able to hide their time-wasting. Not only were they removed from the mainstream of traffic, but they were almost always inside a building.

On their escapades the Saints were also relatively invisible, since they left Hanibal and travelled to Big Town. Here, too, they were mobile, roaming the city, rarely going to the same area twice.

Demeanor

To the notion of visibility must be added the difference in the responses of group members to outside intervention with their activities. If one of the Saints was confronted with an accusing policeman, even if he felt he was truly innocent of a wrongdoing, his demeanor was apologetic and penitent. A Roughneck's attitude was almost the polar opposite. When confronted with a threatening adult authority, even one who tried to be pleasant, the Roughneck's hostility and disdain were clearly observable. Sometimes he might attempt to put up a veneer of respect, but it was thin and was not accepted as sincere by the authority.

School was no different from the community at large. The Saints could manipulate the system by feigning compliance with the school norms. The availability of cars at school meant that once free from the immediate sight of the teacher, the boys could disappear rapidly. And this escape was well enough planned that no administrator or teacher was nearby when the boys left. A Roughneck who wished to escape for a few hours was in a bind. If it were possible to get free from class, downtown was still a mile away, and even if he arrived there, he was still very visible. Truancy for the Roughnecks meant almost certain detection, while the Saints enjoyed almost complete immunity from sanctions.

Bias

Community members were not aware of the transgressions of the Saints. Even if the Saints had been less discreet, their favorite delinquencies would have been perceived as less serious than those of the Roughnecks.

In the eyes of the police and school officials, a boy who drinks in an alley and stands intoxicated on the street corner is committing a more serious offense than is a boy who drinks to inebriation in a nightclub or a tavern and drives around afterwards in a car. Similarly, a boy who steals a wallet from a store will be viewed as having committed a more serious offense than a boy who steals a lantern from a construction site.

Perceptual bias also operates with respect to the demeanor of the boys in the two groups when they are confronted by adults. It is not simply that adults dislike the posture affected by boys of the Roughneck ilk; more important is the conviction that the posture adopted by the Roughnecks is an indication of their devotion and commitment to deviance as a way of life. The posture becomes a cue, just as the type of the offense is a cue, to the degree to which the known transgressions are indicators of the youths' potential for other problems.

Visibility, demeanor and bias are surface variables which explain the day-to-day operations of the police. Why do these surface variables operate as they do? Why did the police choose to disregard the Saints' delinquencies while breathing down the backs of the Roughnecks?

The answer lies in the class structure of American society and the control of legal institutions by those at the top of the class structure. Obviously, no representative of the upper class drew up the operational chart for the police which led them to look in the ghettoes and on street corners—which led them to see the demeanor of lower-class youth as troublesome and that of upper-middle-class youth as tolerable. Rather, the procedures simply developed from experience—experience with irate and influential upper-middle-class parents insisting that their son's vandalism was simply a prank and his drunkenness only a momentary "sowing of wild oats"—experience with cooperative or indifferent, powerless, lower-class parents who acquiesced to the laws' definition of their son's behavior.

Adult Careers of the Saints and the Roughnecks

The community's confidence in the potential of the Saints and the Roughnecks apparently was justified. If anything, the community members underestimated the degree to which these youngsters would turn out "good" or "bad."

Seven of the eight members of the Saints went on to college immediately after high school. Five of the boys graduated from college in four years. The sixth one finished college after two years in the army, and the seventh spent four years in the air force before returning to college and receiving a B.A. degree. Of these seven college graduates, three went on for advanced degrees. One finished law school and is now active in state politics, one finished medical school and is practicing near Hanibal, and one boy is now working for a Ph.D. The other four college graduates entered submanagerial, managerial or executive training positions with larger firms.

The only Saint who did not complete college was Jerry. Jerry had failed to graduate from high school with the other Saints. During his second senior year, after the other Saints had gone on to college, Jerry began to hang around with what several teachers described as a "rough crowd"—the gang that was heir apparent to the Roughnecks. At the end of his second senior year, when he did graduate from high school, Jerry took a job as a used-car salesman, got married and quickly had a child. Although he made several abortive attempts to go to college by attending night school, when I last saw him (ten years after high school) Jerry was unemployed and had been living on unemployment for almost a year. His wife worked as a waitress.

Some of the Roughnecks have lived up to community expectations. A number of them were headed for trouble. A few were not.

Jack and Herb were the athletes among the Roughnecks and their athletic prowess paid off handsomely. Both boys received unsolicited athletic scholarships to college. After Herb received his scholarship (near the end of his senior year), he apparently did an about-face. His demeanor became very similar to that of the Saints. Although he remained a member in good standing of the Roughnecks, he stopped participating in most activities and did not hang on the corner as often.

Jack did not change. If anything, he became more prone to fighting. He even made excuses for accepting the scholarship. He told the other gang members that the school had guaranteed him a "C" average if he would come to play football—an idea that seems far-fetched, even in this day of highly competitive recruiting.

During the summer after graduation from high school, Jack attempted suicide by jumping from a tall building. The jump would certainly have killed most people trying it, but Jack survived. He entered college in the fall and played four years of football. He and Herb graduated in four years, and both are teaching and coaching in high schools. They are married and have stable families. If anything, Jack appears to have a more prestigious position in the community than does Herb, though both are well respected and secure in their positions.

Two of the boys never finished high school. Tommy left at the end of his junior year and went to another state. That summer he was arrested and placed on probation on a manslaughter charge. Three years later he was arrested for murder; he pleaded guilty to second degree murder and is serving a 30-year sentence in the state penitentiary.

Al, the other boy who did not finish high school, also left the state in his senior year. He is serving a life sentence in a state penitentiary for first degree murder.

Wes is a small-time gambler. He finished high school and "bummed around." After several years he made contact with a bookmaker who employed him as a runner. Later he acquired his own area and has been working it ever since. His position among the bookmakers is almost identical to the position he had in the gang; he is always around but no one is really aware of him. He makes no trouble and he does not get into any. Steady, reliable, capable of keeping his mouth closed, he plays the game by the rules, even though the game is an illegal one.

That leaves only Ron. Some of his former friends reported that they had heard he was "driving a truck up north," but no one could provide any concrete information.

Reinforcement

The community responded to the Roughnecks as boys in trouble, and the boys agreed with that perception. Their pattern of deviancy was reinforced, and breaking away from it became increasingly unlikely. Once the boys acquired an image of themselves as deviants, they selected new friends who affirmed that self-image. As that self-conception became more firmly entrenched, they also became willing to try new and more extreme deviances. With their growing alienation came freer expression of disrespect and hostility for representatives of the legitimate society. This disrespect increased the community's negativism, perpetuating the entire process of commitment to deviance. Lack of a commitment to deviance works the same way. In either case, the process will perpetuate itself unless some event (like a scholarship to college or a sudden failure) external to the established relationship intervenes. For two of the

Roughnecks (Herb and Jack), receiving college athletic scholarships created new relations and culminated in a break with the established pattern of deviance. In the case of one of the Saints (Jerry), his parents' divorce and his failing to graduate from high school changed some of his other relations. Being held back in school for a year and losing his place among the Saints had sufficient impact on Jerry to alter his self-image and virtually to assure that he would not go on to college as his peers did. Although the experiments of life can rarely be reversed, it seems likely in view of the behavior of the other boys who did not enjoy this special treatment by the school that Jerry, too, would have "become something" had he graduated as anticipated. For Herb and Jack outside intervention worked to their advantage; for Jerry it was his undoing.

Selective perception and labelling—finding, processing and punishing some kinds of criminality and not others—means that visible, poor, nonmobile, outspoken, undiplomatic "tough" kids will be noticed, whether their actions are seriously delinquent or not. Other kids, who have established a reputation for being bright (even though underachieving), disciplined and involved in respectable activities, who are mobile and monied, will be invisible when they deviate from sanctioned activities. They'll sow their wild oats—perhaps even wider and thicker than their lower-class cohorts—but they won't be noticed. When it's time to leave adolescence most will follow the expected path, settling into the ways of the middle class, remembering fondly the delinquent but unnoticed fling of their youth. The Roughnecks and others like them may turn around, too. It is more likely that their noticeable deviance will have been so reinforced by police and community that their lives will be effectively channelled into careers consistent with their adolescent background.

STUDY QUESTIONS

1. Using the concepts from the article, can you illustrate the effects of social class on the community's definition of the boys?
2. How does the idea of "self-fulfilling prophesy" relate to Chambliss's research?

LILLIAN B. RUBIN

The Approach–Avoidance Dance
Men, Women, and Intimacy

For one human being to love another, that is perhaps the most difficult of all our tasks, the ultimate, the last test and proof, the work for which all other work is but preparation.

—Rainer Maria Rilke

Intimacy. We hunger for it, but we also fear it. We come close to a loved one, then we back off. A teacher I had once described this as the "go away a little closer" message. I call it the approach-avoidance dance.

The conventional wisdom says that women want intimacy, men resist it. And I have plenty of material that would *seem* to support that view. Whether in my research interviews, in my clinical hours, or in the ordinary course of my life, I hear the same story told repeatedly. "He doesn't talk to me," says a woman. "I don't know what she wants me to talk about," says a man. "I want to know what he's feeling," she tells me. "I'm not feeling anything," he insists. "Who can feel nothing?" she cries. "I can," he shouts. As the heat rises, so does the wall between them. Defensive and angry, they retreat—stalemated by their inability to understand each other.

Women complain to each other all the time about not being able to talk to their men about the things that matter most to them—about what they themselves are thinking and feeling, about what goes on in the hearts and minds of the men they're relating to. And men, less able to expose themselves and their conflicts—those within themselves or those with the women in their lives—either turn silent or take cover by holding women up to derision. It's one of the norms of male camaraderie to poke fun at women, to complain laughingly about the mystery of their minds, wonderingly about their ways. Even Freud did it when, in exasperation, he asked mockingly, "What do women want? Dear God, what do they want?"

But it's not a joke—not for the women, not for the men who like to pretend it is.

> *The whole goddamn business of what you're calling intimacy bugs the hell out of me. I never know what you women mean when you talk about it. Karen complains that I don't talk to her, but it's not talk she wants, it's some other damn thing, only I don't know what the hell it is. Feelings, she keeps asking for. So what am I supposed to do if I don't have any to give her or to talk about just because she decides it's time to talk about feelings? Tell me, will you; maybe we can get some peace around here.*

The expression of such conflicts would seem to validate the common understandings that suggest that women want and need intimacy more than men do—that the issue belongs to women alone; that, if left to themselves, men would not suffer it. But things are not always what they seem. And I wonder: "If men would renounce intimacy, what is their stake in relationships with women?"

Some would say that men need women to tend to their daily needs—to prepare their meals, clean their houses, wash their clothes, rear their children—so that they can be free to attend to life's larger problems. And, given the traditional structure of roles in the family, it has certainly worked that way most of the time. But, if that were all men seek, why is it that, even when they're not relating to women, so much of their lives is spent in search of a relationship with another, so much agony experienced when it's not available?

These are difficult issues to talk about—even to think about—because the subject of intimacy isn't just complicated, it's slippery as well. Ask yourself: What is intimacy? What words come to mind, what thoughts?

It's an idea that excites our imagination, a word that seems larger than life to most of us. It lures us, beckoning us with a power we're unable to resist. And, just because it's so seductive, it frightens us as well—seeming sometimes to be some mysterious force from outside ourselves that, if we let it, could sweep us away.

But what is it we fear?

Asked what intimacy is, most of us—men and women—struggle to say something sensible, something that we can connect with the real experience of our lives. "Intimacy is knowing there's someone who cares about the children as much as you do." "Intimacy is a history of shared experience." "It's sitting there having a cup of coffee together and watching the eleven-o'clock news." "It's knowing you care about the same things." "It's knowing she'll always understand." "It's him sitting in the hospital for hours at a time when I was sick." "It's knowing he cares when I'm hurting." "It's standing by me when I was out of work." "It's seeing each other at our worst." "It's sitting across the breakfast table." "It's talking when you're in the bathroom." "It's knowing we'll begin and end each day together."

These seem the obvious things—the things we expect when we commit our lives to one another in a marriage, when we decide to have children together. And they're not to be dismissed as inconsequential. They make up the daily experience of our lives together, setting the tone for a relationship in important and powerful ways. It's sharing such commonplace, everyday events that determines the temper and the texture of life, that keeps us living together even when other aspects of the relationship seem less than perfect. Knowing someone is there, is constant, and can be counted on in just the ways these thoughts express provides the background of emotional security and stability we look for when we enter a marriage. Certainly a marriage and the people in it will be tested and judged quite differently in an unusual situation or in a crisis. But how often does life present us with circumstances and events that are so out of the range of ordinary experience?

These ways in which a relationship feels intimate on a daily basis are only one part of what we mean by intimacy, however—the part that's most obvious, the part that doesn't awaken our fears. At a lecture where I spoke of these issues recently, one man commented also, "Intimacy is putting aside the masks we wear in the rest of our lives." A murmur of assent ran through the audience of a hundred or so. Intuitively we say "yes." Yet this is the very issue that also complicates our intimate relationships.

On the one hand, it's reassuring to be able to put away the public persona—to believe we can be loved for who we *really* are, that we can show our shadow side without fear, that our vulnerabilities will not be counted against us. "The most important thing is to feel I'm accepted just the way I am," people will say.

But there's another side. For, when we show ourselves thus without the masks, we also become anxious and fearful. "Is it possible that someone could love the *real* me?" we're likely to ask. Not the most promising question for the further development of intimacy, since it suggests that, whatever else another might do or feel, it's we who have trouble loving ourselves. Unfortunately, such misgivings are not usually experienced consciously. We're aware only that our discomfort has risen, that we feel a need to get away. For the person who has seen the "real me" is also the one who reflects back to us an image that's usually not wholly to our liking. We get angry at that, first at ourselves for not living up to our own expectations, then at the other, who becomes for us the mirror of our self-doubts—a displacement of hostility that serves intimacy poorly.

There's yet another level—one that's further below the surface of consciousness, therefore, one that's much more difficult for us to grasp, let alone to talk about. I'm referring to the differences in the ways in which women and men deal with their inner emotional lives— differences that create barriers between us that can be high indeed. It's here that we see how those early childhood experiences of separation and individuation—the psychological tasks that were required of us in order to separate from mother, to distinguish ourselves as autonomous persons, to internalize a firm sense of gender identity—take their toll on our intimate relationships.

Stop a woman in mid-sentence with the question, "What are you feeling right now?" and you might have to wait a bit while she reruns the mental tape to capture the moment just passed. But, more than likely, she'll be able to do it successfully. More than likely, she'll think for a while and come up with an answer.

The same is not true of a man. For him, a similar question usually will bring a sense of wonderment that one would even ask it, followed quickly by an uncomprehending and puzzled response. "What do you mean?" he'll ask. "I was just talking," he'll say.

I've seen it most clearly in the clinical setting where the task is to get to the feeling level—or, as one of my male patients said when he came into therapy, to "hook up the head and the gut." Repeatedly when therapy begins, I find myself having to teach a man how to monitor his internal states—how to attend to his thoughts and feelings, how to bring them into consciousness. In the early stages of our work, it's a common experience to say to a man, "How does that feel?", and to see a blank look come over his face. Over and over, I find myself listening as a man speaks with calm reason about a situation which I know must be fraught with pain. "How do you feel about that?" I'll ask. "I've just been telling you," he's likely to reply. "No," I'll say, "you've told me what happened, not how you *feel* about it." Frustrated, he might well respond, "You sound just like my wife."

It would be easy to write off such dialogues as the problems of men in therapy, of those who happen to be having some particular emotional difficulties. But it's not so, as any woman who has lived with a man will attest. Time and again women complain: "I can't get him to verbalize his feelings." "He talks, but it's always intellectualizing." "He's so closed off from what he's feeling, I don't know how he lives that way." "If there's one thing that will eventually ruin this marriage, it's the fact that he can't talk about what's going on inside him." "I have to work like hell to get anything out of him that resembles a feeling that's something besides anger. That I get plenty of—me and the kids, we all get his anger. Anything else is damn hard to come by with him." One woman talked eloquently about her husband's anguish over his inability to get problems in his work life resolved. When I asked how she knew about his pain, she answered:

> I pull for it, I pull hard, and sometimes I can get something from him. But it'll be late at night in the dark—you know, when we're in bed and I can't look at him while he's talking and he doesn't have to look at me. Otherwise, he's just defensive and puts on what I call his bear act, where he makes his warning, go-away faces, and he can't be reached or penetrated at all.

To a woman, the world men live in seems a lonely one—a world in which their fears of exposing their sadness and pain, their anxiety about allowing their vulnerability to show, even to a woman they love, is so deeply rooted inside them that, most often, they can only allow it to happen "late at night in the dark."

Yet, if we listen to what men say, we will hear their insistence that they *do* speak of what's inside them, *do* share their thoughts and feelings with the women they love. "I tell her, but she's never satisfied," they complain. "No matter how much I say, it's never enough," they grumble.

From both sides, the complaints have merit. The problem lies not in what men don't say, however, but in what's not there—in what, quite simply, happens so far out of consciousness that it's not within their reach. For men have integrated all too well the lessons of their childhood—the experiences that taught them to repress and deny their inner thoughts, wishes, needs, and fears; indeed, not even to notice them. It's real, therefore, that the kind of inner thoughts and feelings that are readily accessible to a woman generally are unavailable to a man. When he says, "I don't know what I'm feeling," he isn't necessarily being intransigent and withholding. More than likely, he speaks the truth.

Partly that's a result of the ways in which boys are trained to camouflage their feelings under cover of an exterior of calm, strength, and rationality. Fears are not manly. Fantasies are not rational. Emotions, above all, are not for the strong, the sane, the adult. Women suffer them, not men—women, who are more like children with what seems like their never-ending preoccupation with their emotional life. But the training takes so well because of their early childhood experience when, as very young boys, they had to shift their identification from mother to father and sever themselves from their earliest emotional connection. Put the two together and it does seem like suffering to men to have to experience that emotional side of themselves, to have to give it voice.

This is the single most dispiriting dilemma of relations between women and men. He complains, "She's so emotional, there's no point in talking to her." She protests, "It's him you can't talk to, he's always so darned rational." He says, "Even when I tell her nothing's the matter, she won't quit." She says, "How can I believe him when I can see with my own eyes that something's wrong?" He says, "Okay, so something's wrong! What good will it do to tell her?" She cries, "What are we married for? What do you need me for, just to wash your socks?"

These differences in the psychology of women and men are born of a complex interaction between society and the individual. At the broadest social level is the rending of thought and feeling that is such a fundamental part of Western thought. Thought, defined as the ultimate good, has been assigned to men; feeling, considered at best a problem, has fallen to women.

So firmly fixed have these ideas been that, until recently, few thought to question them. For they were built into the structure of psychological thought as if they spoke to an eternal, natural, and scientific truth. Thus, even such a great and innovative thinker as Carl Jung wrote, "The woman is increasingly aware that love alone can give her her full stature, just as the man begins to discern that spirit alone can endow his life with its highest meaning. Fundamentally, therefore, both seek a psychic relation one to the other, because love needs the spirit, and the spirit love, for their fulfillment."[1]

For a woman, "love"; for a man, "spirit"—each expected to complete the other by bringing to the relationship the missing half. In German, the word that is translated here as spirit is *Geist*. But *The New Cassell's German Dictionary* shows that another primary meaning of *Geist* is "mind, intellect, intelligence, wit, imagination, sense of reason." And, given the context of these words, it seems reasonable that *Geist* for Jung referred to a man's highest essence—his mind. There's no ambiguity about a woman's calling, however. It's love.

Intuitively, women try to heal the split that these definitions of male and female have foisted upon us.

> *I can't stand that he's so damned unemotional and expects me to be the same. He lives in his head all the time, and he acts like anything that's emotional isn't worth dealing with.*

Cognitively, even women often share the belief that the rational side, which seems to come so naturally to men, is the more mature, the more desirable.

> *I know I'm too emotional, and it causes problems between us. He can't stand it when I get emotional like that. It turns him right off.*

Her husband agrees that she's "too emotional" and complains:

> *Sometimes she's like a child who's out to test her parents. I have to be careful when she's like that not to let her rile me up because otherwise all hell would break loose. You just can't reason with her when she gets like that.*

It's the rational-man-hysterical-woman script, played out again and again by two people whose emotional repertoire is so limited that they have few real options. As the interaction between them continues, she reaches for the strongest tools she has, the mode she's most comfortable and familiar with: She becomes progressively more emotional and expressive. He falls back on his best weapons: He becomes more rational, more determinedly reasonable. She cries for him to attend to her feelings, whatever they may be. He tells her coolly, with a kind of clenched-teeth reasonableness, that it's silly for her to feel that way, that she's just being emotional. And of course she is. But that dismissive word "just" is the last straw. She gets so upset that she does, in fact, seem hysterical. He gets so bewildered by the whole interaction that his only recourse is to build the wall of reason even higher. All of which makes things measurably worse for both of them.

> *The more I try to be cool and calm her the worse it gets. I swear, I can't figure her out. I'll keep trying to tell her not to get so excited, but there's nothing I can do. Anything I say just makes it worse. So then I try to keep quiet, but . . . wow, the explosion is like crazy, just nuts.*

And by then it *is* a wild exchange that any outsider would agree was "just nuts." But it's not just her response that's off, it's his as well—their conflict resting in the fact that we equate the emotional with the nonrational.

This notion, shared by both women and men, is a product of the fact that they were born and reared in this culture. But there's also a difference between them in their capacity to apprehend the *logic* of emotions—a difference born in their early childhood experiences in the family, when boys had to repress so much of their emotional side and girls could permit theirs to flower. . . .

It should be understood: Commitment itself is not a problem for a man; he's good at that. He can spend a lifetime living in the same family, working at the same job—even one he hates. And he's not without an inner emotional life. But when a relationship requires the sustained verbal expression of that inner life and the full range of feelings that accompany it, then it becomes burdensome for him. He can act out anger and frustration inside the family, it's true. But ask him to express his sadness, his fear, his dependency—all those feelings that would expose his vulnerability to himself or to another—and he's likely to close down as if under some compulsion to protect himself.

All requests for such intimacy are difficult for a man, but they become especially complex and troublesome in relations with women. It's another of those paradoxes. For, to the degree that it's possible for him to be emotionally open with anyone, it is with a woman—a tribute to the power of the childhood experience with mother. Yet it's that same early experience and his need to repress it that raises his ambivalence and generates his resistance.

He moves close, wanting to share some part of himself with her, trying to do so, perhaps even yearning to experience again the bliss of the infant's connection with a woman. She responds, woman style—wanting to touch him just a little more deeply, to know what he's thinking, feeling, fearing, wanting. And the fear closes in—the fear of finding himself again in the grip of a powerful woman, of allowing her admittance only to be betrayed and abandoned once again, of being overwhelmed by denied desires.

So he withdraws.

It's not in consciousness that all this goes on. He knows, of course, that he's distinctly uncomfortable when pressed by a woman for more intimacy in the relationship, but he doesn't know why. And, very often, his behavior doesn't please him any more than it pleases her. But he can't seem to help it.

That's his side of the ambivalence that leads to the approach-avoidance dance we see so often in relations between men and women.

NOTE

1. Carl Gustav Jung, *Contributions to Analytical Psychology* (New York: Harcourt, Brace & Co., 1928), p. 185.

STUDY QUESTIONS

1. How does the gender structure in marriage affect communication for these married couples?
2. What is the "approach-avoidance dance" as presented by Rubin? How could we change and improve these relationships?

TOPIC 6

Social Groups

To MANY, SOCIOLOGY IS ABOUT SOCIAL GROUPS. GROUPS play an immensely important part in social life. Groups are elements embedded in larger social structures, and group membership determines much of our identity as individuals. In many ways, groups are key links between the individual and the larger society. A T-shirt slogan found around many sociology conventions reads, "Sociologists do it in groups," and this sentiment simply underscores the perceived importance of groups to sociology. The idea of "social groups" may seem simple at first, but there are many types of groups and the study of social groups will illustrate how crucial groups are to the creation and maintenance of society.

Sociology likes to typify groups based on a distinction between those that are "primary" and those that are "secondary." Primary and secondary groups rest along a continuum that distinguishes these polar opposites on several criteria. Primary groups are smaller, depend on face-to-face interaction, and have strong identification of the members with the groups. Examples of this type would include one's family or peer group. As we move along the continuum toward groups that are more secondary, these have attributes indicating they are larger, that they depend on indirect communication, and that the members identify rather weakly with the group. Examples here would include a city or a large corporation. There are other groups that have some of both primary and secondary group characteristics like a fraternity or sorority, perhaps a small church. It is important to note that even within large, complex secondary groups are small primary groups; cities are composed of neighborhoods and families, and corporations are made up of personal primary work groups or teams.

Another dimension of social groups is the formal-informal dimension. Bureaucracies are large and formal groups—they have hierarchy and rules that create the organization and channels of communication for its members. At the same time, there are lots of informal groups, like a peer group, whose activities are largely free of hierarchy and formal rules. Groups, formal or informal, provide an organizing principle in social life, and while we might believe some of them create problems for us (bureaucracies, for instance, might dehumanize us personally), they are critical to the smooth operation of large numbers of people. Many universities are prime examples of formal bureaucratic groups. In these same settings, we can find many informal activities among students and faculty that are critical to the survival of the group. Again, as we see, social life is lived along a continuum that includes diverse structures and activities, and groups point this out once more.

As the Internet emerged in the past twenty years, new "communities" or "groups" have taken shape as well. This will be discussed in more depth later, in Topic 15, but it merits discussion in our "Social Groups" topic, because people who "meet" and "chat" and support one another around a multitude of issues are performing functions much like more traditional, non-cyberspace groups. Sometimes cyber-acquaintances move on to face-to-face meetings and form relationships that may even end in marriage. Sociology will be very interested in whether cyber-groups and communities can enrich or replace social groups as we knew them before the Internet.

The three readings in this section include a work by Ronald Poulson, *et al.*, that studies college students regarding religious beliefs, alcohol, and risky sex. It is especially interesting in this study to see how gender alters the impact of the three main variables. How do you think this fits with experiences in your university or college? Second, Kraybill talks about the struggle of a religious group, the Amish, and how they have managed to maintain their members and beliefs through resisting change in a society that changes very rapidly. But, the author poses the question to us at the same time, are the Amish becoming more modern even as they resist the ways of the larger society? Finally, Fatima Mernissi, shows how a sociologist from Morocco, who is shopping for a dress in the United States, extends the concept of a harem to include the rigid expectations U.S. women face with regard to their body's size. Meeting the Western cultural expectations for being thin can be as compromising to women's freedom as a harem in the East.

RONALD L. POULSON, MARION A. EPPLER,
TAMMY N. SATTERWHITE, KARL L. WUENSCH,
AND LESSIE A. BASS

Alcohol Consumption, Strength of Religious Beliefs, and Risky Sexual Behavior in College Students

Although a strong correlation between college students' alcohol consumption and risky sexual behavior has been reported in some studies, other research findings do not agree that there is such a relationship. According to some researchers, these conflicting reports may be related to varying cultural and religious orientations associated with different regions of the country.

Given the contrasting results of the cited research, coupled with the possible effect of the region where the students live, we designed our study with two major purposes in mind. First, we wanted to estimate the incidence of risky sexual behavior at a large university in a geographic region that has been largely ignored in previous research, namely the predominantly rural, conservative agricultural area in the southeastern United States commonly referred to as the bible belt.

Our second aim was to examine how both drinking patterns and strength of religious convictions are related to risky sexual behavior. The links between religious beliefs and alcohol consumption and the relationship between alcohol consumption and risky sexual behavior in college students have been examined in many previous studies. Yet we know of no other study that has examined the relationships among all three of these variables simultaneously.

The typical sexual behavior of many college students places them at risk for contracting serious sexually transmitted diseases (STDs). Current estimates are that one in every four new cases of HIV infection occurs in people under the age of 25 years, the age group of a major percentage of undergraduate college students. Moreover, several studies have reported that high numbers of students engage in risky sexual behaviors, such as unprotected intercourse or inconsistent use of condoms.

Research findings clearly indicate that 75% or more of college students are sexually active. Caron et al. found that 86% of first-year college students were already sexually active and that 34% had experienced two or more new sexual partners since arriving at college. In a national survey, Douglas et al. found that 86.1% of college students reported that they had engaged in sexual intercourse and that 34.5% of the respondents in their study had had six or more sexual partners during their lifetimes.

A primary concern is that fewer than 25% of the students who are sexually active report consistently using condoms in every sexual encounter. To further compound the risks associated with unsafe sexual practices, college students with multiple partners were significantly less consistent in overall condom use, particularly when alcohol was involved, according to Desiderato and Crawford.

Alcohol Consumption

Alcohol consumption is one major factor that has been repeatedly linked to unsafe sexual bahavior. In a national sample of more than 17,000 college students, Wechsler et al reported that "binge" drinkers were 7 to 10 times more likely than "nonbinge" drinkers to engage in unplanned and unprotected sexual activity. Desiderato and Crawford found that in the 11 weeks before their survey of undergraduates, 90% of the respondents had consumed alcohol at least once, and alcohol had preceded the last occurrence of sexual activity for a majority of the students (66% of the men and 53% of the women). Desiderato and Crawford also found that both the frequency and quantity of alcohol consumption had a significant bearing on the number of sexual partners that students had during the previous 11 weeks. When drinking alcohol preceded sexual activity, 41% of the students said that they either did not use condoms at all or were much less likely to do so.

Not all researchers agree that alcohol is a determining factor in the incidence of unsafe sexual practices. Temple and Leigh found no significant relationship between alcohol consumption and sexual intercourse without a condom for respondents' most recent sexual encounter or their most recent encounters with new sexual partners. Leigh concluded that risky sexual behavior may be more a function of general risk taking than the simple consequence of the disinhibiting effects of alcohol. One important consideration is that, in the studies cited earlier, older adult samples were used; in other studies, higher rates of unprotected sex associated with alcohol used in adolescent and college-aged samples were found (see Temple and Leigh, 1992, for a discussion of possible age differences).

More recently, MacDonald and colleagues offered a controlled series of studies using a variety of methods (correlational and experimental, laboratory and field studies) focusing on college students. Their findings suggest that alcoholic intoxication does increase the probability of engaging in risky sexual activity, such as sex without using a condom.

Another possible explanation for the conflicting reports may be an intervening variable, such as how liberal or conservative the attitudes are in a particular geographic region. Leigh's studies were conducted in San Francisco, where participants' views regarding alcohol use and sexual behavior may be more liberal than the views of students in the rural southeastern United States. In sum, liberal attitudes may very well be related to greater risk-taking behavior. People of different geographic regions may also be more willing to disclose personal information about their sexual practices.

Religious Beliefs

Religious affiliation and the strength of religious convictions may contribute to a person's decisions about alcohol consumption. College students who reported that participating in religious activity was "not at all important" to them had a significantly higher likelihood of binge drinking than students for whom religion was somewhat important in their lives.[6] In a large sample of adolescents, Donahue and Benson found that stronger religious values were correlated with lower rates of drug and alcohol use and with a lower incidence of premarital sexual intercourse.

Hawks and Bahr compared the drinking patterns of respondents belonging to abstinence-oriented religious groups, such as the Church of Jesus Christ of Latter-day Saints (Mormons), with the drinking patterns of those belonging to less-restrictive religious groups and those with no religious affiliation. The Mormon respondents reported far less alcohol use than the other two groups. More specifically, only 31% of the Mormon group reported some alcohol use during the most recent 30-day period, compared with 63% of the respondents from other religious groups and 68% of the nonaffiliated group.

Carlucci et al. reported similar findings when they compared Protestants and Jews, who are more likely to advocate abstinence, with Catholics, who tend to hold a more permissive attitude toward alcohol consumption. These studies indicated that strong religious messages about alcohol abstinence can have a significant impact on personal rates of alcohol consumption.

In sum, reports in the literature regarding the nature of the relationship between alcohol use and unsafe sexual practices are contradictory. Because these conflicting reports may stem in part from regional differences in how conservative or liberal the value system is in a particular region, we chose to concentrate our data collection at a university located in a geographic region that has been underrepresented in past research.

Method

Participants

We drew an "accidental," or convenience, sample of 210 participants from the general student population at a large university in a rural region of the southeastern United States. Respondents in the study were college students who volunteered to participate; they received neither remuneration nor course credit for their participation.

Although this was a sample of convenience, the participants' characteristics were generally consistent with relevant demographic characteristics on this particular campus. For example, 61% ($n = 129$) of the respondents in this study were women, and 39% ($n = 79$) were men, whereas 59% of the university student body were women and 41% were men. The ethnic status of respondents represented in our study was 9% African American ($n = 20$), 86% European American ($n = 180$), and 4% other categories ($n = 8$). On this campus at the time of the survey. African American students were 12% and European Americans were 84% of the student population.

Respondents in this study ranged in age from 18 to 36 years, with a mean age of 21 years. The mean age of students at the university was 20.6 years. All selection and methodological procedures were approved by the psychology department's Human Subjects Review Committee (HSRC) and were in accord with the ethical standards and requirements set by the committee.

Materials

We collaborated with graduate and undergraduate students enrolled in psychology research methods courses to develop an extensive survey. The students assembled in small groups and collectively created a series of questions according to each group's areas of interest. The three general areas were alcohol and other drug use, sexual behavior, and religious orientation.

The 88 questions that were unanimously agreed upon by the entire class were compiled in a single questionnaire, and these questions were pilot tested under the direction of the first author. Copies of the entire questionnaire are available from the first author.

Procedure

We instructed student experimenters to solicit at least 10 participants. No student experimenter was allowed to administer more than 10 surveys. Each participant was read a summary that explained the purpose of the study, including the information that responses were anonymous and confidential. Both the researcher and the participant signed a consent form before the survey was administered. Participants were able to complete the survey in a comfortable, private setting, avoiding further discussion with the researcher or other participants.

Upon completing the questionnaire, participants were instructed to seal their surveys in envelopes provided by the experimenter, were thanked for their assistance, and were given an opportunity to ask questions or express any concerns. All sealed envelopes were given to the course instructor (first author) for processing.

Results

The vast majority of respondents (84%) reported having engaged in sexual intercourse. One third (34%) of the entire sample reported a frequency of one to three times per week, and one quarter (27%) reported a frequency of one to two times per month. Only 27% of the respondents reported they consistently used condoms, whereas more than one half (60%) reported their condom use was inconsistent.

Thirteen percent of the respondents reported that they had never engaged in any form of safer sex practice. This high rate of unprotected sex, along with the fact that almost half of the respondents (48%) reported having engaged in sexual intercourse with multiple partners during the past year, indicated that many students were placing themselves at a significant risk for contracting STDs, including HIV.

Although virtually all students reported using precautionary methods to prevent pregnancy, many tended to use mostly unreliable methods or methods that do not provide any protection from STDs (e.g., rhythm method, withdrawal, and birth control pills). It appeared that participants were more concerned with preventing pregnancy (52%) than with protecting themselves from STDs (38%). Thus, whereas most students' intentions were good, almost half (43%) stated that they did not use protective methods because they were in love and trusted their partners.

Alcohol consumption was also quite high for this sample of students. Only 25% of the respondents reported no regular use of alcohol, 46% reported typically using alcohol one to two times per week, 23% reported using alcohol three to four times per week, and 7% reported using alcohol five or more times per week, on average.

When asked how often they had been intoxicated in the past month, 24% of the respondents reported never, 23% reported being intoxicated one or two times, 17% reported three to four times, 13% reported a frequency of five to six times, and 22% reported a frequency of seven to eight times. One third (33%) reported having consumed so much alcohol that they passed out at least once during the past month.

Seventy-eight percent of the respondents reported that they had made one or more decisions while drinking that they later regretted. With regard to sexual activity, more than one third of our sample (39%) reported having used alcohol to enhance their sexual experiences, and 68% of the respondents reported that alcohol had at some time had a negative effect on their sexual behavior. Students in this study (70%) reported that they were less likely to use condoms when they consumed alcohol before engaging in sexual activity.

The strength and nature of a person's religious beliefs may also play a major role in decisions about sexual activity. We found that 60% of our respondents believed in attending church or attended church on a regular basis, 78% believed that God operated in their daily lives, and 80% believed that they would go to heaven when they died. Although at least one quarter (27%) of the participants believed that premarital sex was a sin, most of our respondents (66%) did not feel that premarital sex was a sin. Most respondents (77%) also did not believe that alcohol consumption was a sin. . . .

Risky sexual behavior was positively correlated with alcohol consumption, $r = .41$, $p < .001$, but not with religious beliefs, $r = .11$, not significant (ns). However, alcohol consumption was negatively correlated with religious beliefs, $r = 21$, $p < .004$.

The men had significantly higher rates of alcohol consumption, $M = 27.79$, $SD = 7.80$, than the women, $M = 23.45$, $SD = 7.10$, $t(191) = 3.97$, $p < .001$. The men also had higher rates of risky sexual behavior, $M = 7.92$, $SD = 1.14$, than the women, $M = 7.36$, $SD = 1.16$, $t(198) = 3.37$ $p < .001$. Men and women did not, however, differ significantly in their overall frequency of sexual activity: $M = 2.80$ for men, $M = 2.69$ for women, $SDs = 1.24$ and 1.16 respectively, $t(197) < 1$, ns. We also found no noteworthy differences for strength of religious beliefs $M = 10.21$ for men and 10.86 for women, $SD = 3.23$ for men and 2.76 for women, $t(202) = 1.53$ ns. Because there were sex differences for two of the three variables, we analyzed the correlations separately for women and men.

For the men in this sample, only one correlation was significant: Alcohol consumption was correlated with risky sexual behavior, $r = .30$, $p < .009$. Strength of religious convictions was unrelated to the other two variables, $r = .05$, for alcohol consumption and religious beliefs, and $r = .03$ for risky sexual behavior and religious beliefs.

The pattern of correlations was quite different for women; all three correlations were significant. Alcohol consumption was positively correlated with risky sexual behavior $r = .42$, $p < .001$. Strength of religious beliefs was negatively correlated with both alcohol consumption, $r = -.33$, $p < .001$, and risky sexual behavior, $r = -.22$, $p < .02$.

Discussion

We examined the relations among alcohol consumption, strength of religious convictions, and risky sexual behavior in students at a large university in a relatively conservative, rural region of the United States. Our findings supported recent research documenting the high incidence of risky sexual behavior in college students. The number of students who were sexually active in our sample (84%) was comparable to findings in previous reports (75% and 86%). The proportion of students reporting consistent use of condoms was also quite similar (27% in our study compared with 24% and 21% in other studies).

Many of our participants (48%) were engaging in sexual intercourse with multiple partners.

Our findings were consistent with reports from previous research that alcohol use is a common practice on college campuses. Many of the students were using alcohol to the point of intoxication on a regular basis (one third of our respondents reported being intoxicated more than five times in the past month).

Such excessive use of alcohol is clearly linked to impaired judgment. More than three quarters of our respondents reported they had made decisions while under the influence of alcohol that they later regretted, and two thirds reported that alcohol had at some time had a negative impact on their sexual behavior.

In particular, 70% of our respondents reported inconsistent use of condoms while under the influence of alcohol, almost twice the rate reported by Desiderato and Crawford. This high rate of inconsistent condom use may have been attributable, in part, to the fact that almost half of our respondents reported they had only one sexual partner, perhaps making them feel less vulnerable to the risks associated with unprotected sex: 43% of the respondents reported that they did not use protection because they were in love and trusted their partners. We should underscore that existing research findings suggest that many college students may not be faithful in their dating relationships.

Alcohol consumption was strongly related to risky sexual behavior for both women and men in our study. We found intriguing sex differences for the three variables and their interrelationships. Men had higher rates of alcohol consumption and higher rates of risky sexual behavior than women did, even though the overall rates of men's and women's sexual activity did not differ. Although the sex difference for religious beliefs was not significant, religion appeared to have a different effect on women than it did on men. Women with stronger religious convictions tended to consume less alcohol and were less likely to engage in risky sexual behavior, which was not true for men. This is surprising, given the relatively high degree of religious convictions expressed by both women and men in our sample.

The observed gender differences may be attributable to broader societal attitudes regarding the use of alcohol. More specifically, alcohol consumption to the point of intoxication may be viewed as permissible for men but inappropriate for women. These attitudes may be different in geographic regions where people have more or less conservative values, because conservative values often include different expectations for men's and women's behavior. Thus, a critical question stemming from our study is whether religious sanctions against the use of alcohol and premarital sex influence women and men differently. If there is a difference in the effects of religious conviction, why is this the case? Additional research is needed to address these complex issues.

Limitations of Present Study

Although our findings in this study are consistent with previous research and provide insights regarding the interrelationships among three important variables, the methods we used prevent these findings from being generalizable to other students on this campus or on other campuses. Indeed, these tentative data need to be validated by means of randomized sampling techniques.

We believe it possible that these data may be quite consistent with general drinking and sexual practices at this university. For the past 3 years (three data-collection periods), we collected pilot data ($n = 321$) regarding risky sex practices at this university. A different group of experimental psychology students, who self-selected themselves into different sections of research methods classes, collected the preliminary data. We failed to find any appreciable statistically significant differences between their pilot data and data featured in this study. Although the findings are not conclusive, they suggest that student behaviors among all those sampled seem to be quite consistent.

The second methodological concern is that our data were based on self-reports. In such reports, respondents may desire to present themselves in a more favorable light or engage in what has commonly been termed *social desirability*. Whether this means that respondents will overstate or understate their behavioral tendencies relative to alcohol consumption and risky sex is unclear. Researchers suggest that if report bias does occur, it is more likely to result from underreporting, rather than overreporting, the frequency of problematic behavior.

A third methodological issue concerns the general temptation to treat correlational results as if they were true experimental results. We are certainly aware of the possible "third variable" problem when explaining research findings on the basis of correlational data. However, our goal was not to model risky sex behavior causally, but to examine the strength of the relationships among alcohol, religious beliefs, and risky sexual behaviors in a group of college students in the rural southeastern United States.

Our preliminary data pointed to the possibility that many of our participants believed in a form of religion that is inconsistent with that taught in Christian churches in the bible belt. Our conversations with local clergy and religious leaders, for example, clearly suggested that premarital sex is a sin. Yet three quarters of our participants stated that it "should not be" and "is not" a sin.

Furthermore, drinking to excess was not considered a sin by many of our participants. In light of the reasonable percentage of participants who stated that they attended church on a regular basis, these findings appear quite intriguing. Perhaps the local clergy may want to address how students appear to go about reducing possible cognitive dissonance by modifying their thoughts rather than their behaviors. This may be particularly true for many of our male participants, whose behaviors and religious beliefs appeared to be unrelated. All too often, men are told that having sex implies "manhood" or being a "real" man. Such attitudes may lead men to believe that they are invulnerable to HIV and other STDs. Indeed, parents, educators, and administrators may want to direct even more safer-sex campaigns toward men and their behaviors.

The high incidence of unsafe sexual practices is placing college students at risk for contracting STDs, including HIV. Our preliminary findings highlight the need for more detailed examinations of the interrelationship among alcohol consumption, religious beliefs, and risky sexual behavior among students who attend universities in the bible belt. We could then compare behaviors in this and other regions of the country to see whether or not there is a link between religious value systems and the rates of alcohol consumption and safer sex practices. These kinds of studies could provide crucial data for educating college students about the consequences of their behaviors.

NOTES

1. We would like to express our sincere thanks to Jean A. Picarelli and Jennifer M. Walker for their insightful comments and help with earlier drafts of this manuscript. We would also like to thank Kelly Ransdell for her editorial comments.

2. For further information or a copy of the questionnaire, please write Ronald L. Poulson, PhD, Department of Psychology, East Carolina University, Greenville, NC 27858-4353, or PoulsonR@Mail.ECU.EDU.

REFERENCES

Robertson J, Plant M. Alcohol, sex and risks of HIV infection. *Alcohol Dependence*, 1988;22:75–78.

Doll L. Alcohol use as a cofactor for disease and high-risk behavior. Presented at the N1AAA Alcohol and AIDS network conference. Tucson, AZ: 1989.

Temple MT, Leigh BC. Alcohol consumption and unsafe sexual behavior in discrete events. *J Sex Research*, 1992;29:207–219.

Brannock JC, Schandler SL, Oncley PR. Cross-cultural and cognitive factors examined in groups of adolescent drinkers. *J Drug Issues*, 1990;20:427–442.

Carlucci K, Genova J, Rubackin F, Rubackin R, Kayson WA. Effects of sex, religion, and amount of alcohol consumption of self-reported drinking-related problem behaviors. *Psychol Rep*, 1993;72:983–987.

Wechsler H, Davenport A, Dowdall G, Moeykens B, Castillo S. Health and behavioral consequences of binge drinking in college. *JAMA*, 1994;272:1672–1677.

Bliss SK, Crown CL. Concern for appropriateness, religiosity, and gender as predictors of alcohol and marijuana use. *Social Behavior and Personality*. 1994;22:227–238.

Donahue MJ, Benson PL. Religion and the well-being of adolescents. *J Social Issues*, 1995;51:145–160.

Hawks RD, Bahr SH. Religion and drug use. *J Drug Educ*, 1992;22:1–8.

Desiderato LL, Crawford HJ. Risky sexual behavior in college students: Relationships between number of sexual partners, disclosure of previous risky behavior, and alcohol use. *J Youth and Adolescence*, 1995;24:55–68.

MacDonald TK, Zanna MP, Fong GT. Why common sense goes out the window: Effects of alcohol on intentions to use condoms. *Personality and Social Psychol Bull*, 1996;22:763–775.

Murstein BI, Chalpin MJ, Heard KV, Vyse SA. Sexual behavior, drugs, and relationship patterns on a college campus over thirteen years. *Adolescence*, 1989;24:125–139.

Caron SL, Davis CM, Halteman WA, Stickle M. Predictors of condom-related behaviors among first-year college students. *J Sex Research*, 1993;30:252–259.

Douglas KA, Collins JL, Warren C, et al. Results from the 1995 National College Health Risk Survey. *J Am Coll Health*, 1997;46:55–66.

Hansen WB, Hahn GL, Wolkenstein BH. Perceived personal immunity: Beliefs about susceptibility to AIDS. *J Sex Research*. 1990;27:622–628.

Tewksbury R, Whittier N. Safer sex practices in samples drawn from nightclub, campus, and gay bars. *Sociology and Social Research*, 1992;76:185–189.

Centers for Disease Control. *AIDS Prevention Guide: The Facts About HIV Infection and Aids*. Atlanta. GA: US Dept of Health and Human Services: 1994.

Bishop PD, Lipsitz A. Sexual behavior among college students in the AIDS era: A comparative study. *J Psychology and Human Sexuality*, 1991;4:135–148.

Whitley BE. College student contraception use: A multivariate analysis, *J Sex Research*, 1990;27:305–313.

Wechsler H, Isaac N. "Binge" drinkers at Massachusetts colleges. *JAMA*, 1992;267(21):2929–2931.

Leigh BC. The relationship of substance use during sex to high-risk sexual behavior. *J Sex Research*, 1990b;27:199–213.

Leigh BC. The relationship of sex-related alcohol expectancies to alcohol consumption and sexual behavior. *Br J Addict* 1990a;85:919–928.

Leigh BC. "Venus gets in my thinking": Drinking and female sexuality in the age of AIDS. *J Substance Abuse*, 1990c;2:129–145.

Lo CC, Globetti G. A partial analysis of the campus influence on drinking behavior: Students who enter college as nondrinkers. *J Drug Issues*. 1993;23:715–725.

Midanik LT. Validity of self-reported alcohol use: A literature review and assessment. *Br J Addict*, 1988;83:1019–1029.

Midanik LT. Perspectives on the validity of self-reported alcohol use. *Br J Addict*, 1989;84:1419–1423.

STUDY QUESTIONS

1. How do alcohol consumption and religious beliefs affect risky sexual behavior?

2. How does gender influence the relationship between the variables?

DONALD B. KRAYBILL

The Amish

Modern Amish?

Booming machine shops in some Amish settlements hold sophisticated manufacturing equipment powered by air and hydraulic pressure. Some Amish craftsmen use the latest fiberglass techniques to manufacture horse-drawn carriages. Hundreds of Amish-owned microenterprises place entrepreneurs in direct relation with the outside world on a daily basis. Successful Amish dairy farms in the more progressive settlements are efficient operations that use feed supplements, vitamins, fertilizers, insecticides, chemical preservatives, artificial insemination, and state-of-the-art veterinary practices. Professional farm consultants advise Amish farmers in some settlements about their use of pesticides, fertilizers, and seed selection. New Amish homes in the more progressive settlements tout up-to-date bathroom facilities, modern kitchens with lovely cabinets, formica, vinyl floor coverings, and the latest gas stoves and refrigerators. In spite of cherished stereotypes, some Amish are embracing certain aspects of modernity.

Modernization, however, varies considerably from settlement to settlement across North America. Among the more conservative Amish groups, refrigerators and indoor bathrooms are taboo. Cows are milked by hand and hay balers are not pulled in fields. It is reasonable to hypothesize that Amish adaptation to modern life directly varies with the population density of non-Amish who live in the same geographical area. In other words, innovative Amish behavior appears highly correlated with urbanization. Amish settlements in more isolated rural areas are, generally speaking, more resistant to modernizing influences.[1] Settlements such as the one near Lancaster, Pennsylvania, situated in the midst of a rapidly urbanizing region, are quite progressive in their use of technology and openness to the outside world.

The Amish do indeed cling to older customs in their church services, in their attitudes toward education, and in their rejection of individualism. The lack of electricity in their homes blocks the door to microwave ovens, air conditioners, toasters, doorbells, televisions, clothes dryers, and blow dryers. But does a rejection of high school education, cars, and public-utility-line electricity mean that the Amish are a premodern folk society? The unusual mixture of progress and tradition abounding in Amish society poses interesting questions about the meaning of modernization. How have the Amish responded to the pressures of modernity? What strategies have they employed to cope with modern life in the twentieth century? They have drifted along with the stream of progress in some areas of their culture but have staunchly and successfully resisted it in others. . . .

Dimensions of Modernity

To what extent have the features of modernity penetrated Amish life—their organizational structure as well as their cultural consciousness? The facets of modernity identified by social analysts are legion. The following, somewhat arbitrarily selected dimensions of modernity are not exhaustive nor do they follow a causal sequence.[2] Typically underscored by sociologists, these factors do, however, distinguish modern worlds from nonmodern ones. After a brief discussion of each dimension, we will explore the ways in which the Amish have grappled with it.

Modern societies by and large are highly *specialized*. In nonmodern societies social functions from cradle to grave—birth, work, play, education, worship, friendship, and death—revolve around the home. They often, in fact, occur in the home. In advanced societies such social activities "grow up" and leave home, and as they depart, they split into specialized spheres. These cradle-to-grave functions eventually become lodged in specialized institutions—birthing centers, fitness spas, day care centers, schools, grooming salons, factories, hospitals, golf courses, hospices, and funeral homes. It is in these sharply differentiated settings that experts deliver their highly specialized services. The automobile and mass transit enable modern folks to spend their days shuttling from site to site to both deliver and receive such services. The imprint of structural differentiation and functional specialization is thus stamped across the face of modern life.

The degree to which specialization has shaped Amish life varies of course among Amish settlements, but without exception the Amish world is clearly less differentiated than modern society. The rejection of high school and the primacy given to agriculture have minimized occupational specialization. As Amish families move from farms to microenterprises as well as into factory work in some settlements, the degree of occupational specialization will likely increase. It will undoubtedly remain low as long as high school and college remain taboo. Terminating education at eighth grade effectively deters members from pursuing professional jobs. The relatively low degree of occupational specialization has also minimized social class differences and contributed to the relative homogeneity of the Amish social structure. The rising numbers of Amish microenterprises in some settlements may over time encourage the emergence of a three-tier class structure consisting of farm owners, business entrepreneurs, and day laborers. . . .

The pluralism of modern life means that many individuals face many views of reality—a bewildering array of beliefs and opinions. The common sentiments of traditional cultures dissolve in the streams of pluralism. The wide assortment of ideas and clashing lifestyles focuses the stark relativity of modernity since "it all depends" on who you are, on where you're from, and on your point of view. The religious beliefs of individuals become especially fragile and vulnerable to change as discrepant world views collide in the public media of mass society.

At both structural and cultural levels the Amish have remained aloof from the pluralism of modern life. Their theological stance of separation from the world has in many ways insulated them from the forces of diversity afoot in the modern world. The Amish community does interact with the surrounding society, tapping the use of professional services—medicine, dentistry, and law. Moreover, they are frequently buying and selling supplies and services for personal use as well as for business purposes. The practice of endogamy, the use of the dialect, the prohibition on membership in public organizations, the taboo on political involvement, and the rejection of mass media are among many of the factors that help to preserve the cultural boundaries that separate the Amish from the winds of pluralism. All of these factors impede structural assimilation and preserve the homogeneity of Amish life.

More importantly, Amish parochial schools bridle interaction with outsiders—both peers and teachers—and restrict consciousness. Amish children do not study science or critical thinking, nor are they exposed to the relativity and diversity so pervasive in higher education today. The Amish rejection of mass media, especially television, severely limits their exposure to the smorgasbord of modern values. The tight plausibility structure embodied in the Amish community thus helps to hold the forces of pluralism at bay. . . .

In contrast to the discontinuities of modern culture, Amish societies exude continuity. Social relationships are more likely to be primary, local, enduring, and stable. The rejection of automobile ownership, bicycles, and air travel places limits on Amish mobility. To be sure, the Amish do travel in hired motor vehicles and in public busses and trains, but, all things considered, the amount of mobility is relatively low. The rejection of college and consequently of professional work enables young adults to live in their childhood communities, which increases the longevity of social ties with family, neighborhood, and place. Parents teach occupational skills to their children.

Amish schools are a supreme example of continuity. Children often walk to school, where they may have the same teacher for all eight grades. The teacher, responsible for some thirty students, may relate to only a dozen households, since many families have several children in attendance. Such continuity contrasts starkly with modern education, where children may have dozens of teachers in a few years and teachers relate to hundreds of families. . . .

The Amish commitment to a rational mentality that calculates means and ends has grown as their farming enterprises expand and as they enter the larger world of commerce via cottage industries. Although Amish entrepreneurs engage in planning to keep their businesses afloat, there is, however, decidedly less planning activity among the Amish than typically found in modern life. The absence of artificial means of family planning, career planning, and time management reflects a less rationalized approach to life—a greater willingness to yield to nature and destiny. The rejection of science and critical thinking in Amish schools, the taboo on theological training for ordained leaders, and the lack of a formal theology attenuate the level of rationality in the collective consciousness.

The tentacles of bureaucracy have barely touched Amish society. Their social architecture is remarkably decentralized, small, and informal. A central national office, with an executive director and professional staff have never developed. Church districts are organized as a loose federation in each settlement, and there is little centralized or formal coordination between settlements. The decentralized character of Amish society fosters diversity in the struggle with modernity. Different settlements and different church districts even within affiliations adapt at different paces and in different directions. The *Ordnung*, the body of policies regulating the life of the community, is generally not written down but is a fluid, dynamic set of understandings. The hierarchical, formal, rationalized structure of modern bureaucracy has simply not developed in Amish society. . . .

The . . . traits of modernity encourage *individuation*—the widely heralded triumph of modern culture. The modernizing process unhooks individuals from the confining grip of custom and encourages individualism to flourish. In traditional societies, individuals for the most part are under the tight thumb of kin, tribe, and village. Modern culture with its ideology of individual rights, liberties, privileges, and freedoms celebrates the individual as the supreme social reality. To question the rights of an individual has become a cardinal and unforgivable sin. The personal résumé is, of course, the ultimate document of individuation, and one that is missing in Amish files. Modern individuals are free to pursue careers and seek personal fulfillment, but they also carry the responsibility to succeed—"to make it"—a responsibility that entails the fear of failure.

The subordination of the individual to the community is the fundamental key that unlocks many of the riddles and puzzles of Amish life and sharply distinguishes their culture from modern ways. *Gelassenheit*, submitting and yielding to higher authorities—parents, teachers, leaders, and God—structures Amish values, symbols, personality, rituals, and social organization. Personal submission clashes with modern individualism and its concomitants of self-achievement, self-expression, and self-fulfillment. By contrast, the Amish vocabulary of obedience, simplicity, humility, and the posture of kneeling—for baptism, prayer, confession, and ordination—reflect a premodern understanding of the individual. Clothing, for instance, is used in modern life as a tool of self-expression. In Amish life, uniform dress serves as a badge of group identity and loyalty as well as a symbol of self-surrender to community priorities. The taboo on photography, publicity, jewelry, and other forms of personal adornment bridles an individualism that otherwise might foster pride and arrogance. The Amish rejection of individualism—that supremely cherished value of modern culture—reflects the heartbeat of a counterculture that has not absorbed modern ways. . . .

The Amish have made collective choices. But many of these decisions have been reactive responses to choices imposed on them by modern life. The Amish have been less likely to be proactive—deliberately initiating choices, for such initiatives parallel the modern impulse to plan, order, and control one's environment. The Amish have made collective choices not to be modern. They have rejected higher education. But in many other cases they have surely conceded to modernity by accepting the use of modern forms of technology.

Their collective decisions, however, have restricted individual choice. Individuals are not free to wear what they want, to aspire to professional occupations, to own a car, or to buy a television set. This does not necessarily mean that Amish folks are dour and unhappy. A variety of evidence suggests that they are as happy and satisfied, if not more so, than many "homeless" moderns. The range of occupational options and lifestyle choices available to the individual in Amish society is of course quite narrow. And although a restricted range of choices may suffocate the modern spirit of freedom, it also removes the burden of incessant decision making with its concomitant guilt, stress, and anxiety from the shoulders of many Amish persons.

The Great Separator

. . . The hallmark of Amish culture has been its highly integrated community where all the bits and pieces of social life, from birth to death, are gathered into a single system. To avoid the fragmentation that accompanies modernity, the Amish have separated themselves from the modern world. In order to stay whole, to preserve their community, they have separated themselves from modernity—the greatest separator of all. The Amish impulse to remain separate from the great separator has become a significant strategy in their cultural survival.

Seen in this light it is not surprising that a fundamental tenet of Amish religion is separation from the world—a belief that sprouted in the seedbed of European persecution and is legitimated today with references to the scriptures. This linkage between the fragmentation of modern life and the integration of Amish society unlocks many of the Amish riddles. For only by being a separate people are they able to preserve the integrity of their tightly knit community. Many of the seemingly odd Amish practices that often perplex outside observers are in fact social devices that shield their subculture from the divisive pressures of modernity that threaten to tear their corporate life asunder.

NOTES

1. A competing explanation to this hypothesis is the fact that some of the smaller, more rural Amish settlements are also newer. These are sometimes made up of families who want to maintain a more traditional Ordnung and have sought more rural isolated areas where they can continue in farming. Consequently a self-selection factor may complicate what otherwise appears to be an inverse relationship between urbanization and traditional Amish practices.

2. As Berger (1977) and Kraybill (1990) have shown, the various features of modernity are highly interrelated and not easily separated into discrete categories for causal analysis.

REFERENCES

Berger, Peter. 1977. *Facing Up to Modernity*. New York: Basic Books.
Kraybill, Donald B. 1990. "Modernity and Modernization," *Anabaptist-Mennonite Identities in Ferment*. Occasional papers no. 14, pp. 91–101. Elkhart, IN: Institute of Mennonite Studies.

STUDY QUESTIONS

1. What attributes distinguish the Amish as a cohesive group?
2. Based on what you have read in the Kraybill research, what would you predict for the future of the Amish? Will they prosper or slowly lose their community?

FATIMA MERNISSI

Size 6: The Western Women's Harem

It was during my unsuccessful attempt to buy a cotton skirt in an American department store that I was told my hips were too large to fit into a size 6. That distressing experience made me realize how the image of beauty in the West can hurt and humiliate a woman as much as the veil does when enforced by the state police in extremist nations such as Iran, Afghanistan, or Saudi Arabia. Yes, that day I stumbled onto one of the keys to the enigma of passive beauty in Western harem fantasies. The elegant saleslady in the American store looked at me without moving from her desk and said that she had no skirt my size. "In this whole big store, there is no skirt for me?" I said. "You are joking." I felt very suspicious and thought that she just might be too tired to help me. I could understand that. But then the saleswoman added a condescending judgment, which sounded to me like an Imam's *fatwa*. It left no room for discussion:

"You are too big!" she said.

"I am too big compared to what?" I asked, looking at her intently, because I realized that I was facing a critical cultural gap here.

"Compared to a size 6," came the saleslady's reply.

Her voice had a clear-cut edge to it that is typical of those who enforce religious laws. "Size 4 and 6 are the norm," she went on, encouraged by my bewildered look. "Deviant sized such as the one you need can be bought in special stores."

That was the first time that I had ever heard such nonsense about my size. In the Moroccan streets, men's flattering comments regarding my particularly generous hips have for decades led me to believe that the entire planet shared their convictions. It is true that with advancing age, I have been hearing fewer and fewer flattering comments when walking in the medina, and sometimes the silence around me in the bazaars is deafening. But since my face has never met with the local beauty standards, and I have often had to defend myself against remarks such as *zirafa* (giraffe), because of my long neck, I learned long ago not to rely too much on the outside world for my sense of self-worth. In fact, paradoxically, as I discovered when I went to Rabat as a student, it was the self-reliance that I had developed to protect myself against "beauty blackmail" that made me attractive to others. My male fellow students could not believe that I did not give a damn about what they thought about my body. "You know, my dear," I would say in response to one of them, "all I need to survive is bread, olives, and sardines. That you think my neck is too long is your problem, not mine."

In any case, when it comes to beauty and compliments, nothing is too serious or definite in the medina, where everything can be negotiated. But things seemed to be different in that American department store. In fact, I have to confess that I lost my usual self-confidence in that New York environment. Not that I am always sure of myself, but I don't walk around the Moroccan streets or down the university corridors wondering what people are thinking about me. Of course, when I hear a compliment, my ego expands like a cheese soufflé, but on the whole, I don't expect to hear much from others. Some mornings, I feel ugly because I am sick or tired; others, I feel wonderful because it is sunny out or I have written a good paragraph. But suddenly, in that peaceful American store that I had entered so triumphantly, as a sovereign consumer ready to spend money, I felt savagely attacked. My hips, until then the sign of a relaxed and uninhibited maturity, were suddenly being condemned as a deformity.

"And who decided the norm?" I asked the saleslady, in an attempt to regain some self-confidence by challenging the established rules. I never let others evaluate me, if only because I remember my childhood too well. In ancient Fez, which valued round-faced plump adolescents, I was repeatedly told that I was too tall, too skinny, my cheekbones were too high, my eyes were too slanted. My mother often complained that I would never find a husband and urged me to study and learn all that I could, from storytelling to embroidery, in order to survive. But I often retorted that since "Allah had created me the way I am, how could he be so wrong, Mother?" That would silence the poor woman for a while, because if she contradicted me, she would be attacking God himself. And this tactic of glorifying my strange looks as a divine gift not only helped me to survive in my stuffy city, but also caused me to start believing the story myself. I became almost self-confident. I say almost, because I realized early on that self-confidence is not a tangible and stable thing like a silver bracelet that never changes over the years. Self-confidence is like a tiny fragile light, which goes off and on. You have to replenish it constantly.

"And who says that everyone must be size 6?" I joked to the saleslady that day, deliberately neglecting to mention size 4, which is the size of my skinny twelve-year-old niece.

At that point, the saleslady suddenly gave me an anxious look. "The norm is everywhere, my dear," she said, "It's all over, in the magazines, on television, in the ads. You can't escape it. There is Calvin Klein, Ralph Lauren, Gianni Versace, Giorgio Armani, Mario Valentino, Salvatore Ferragamo, Christian Dior, Yves Saint-Laurent, Christian Lacroix, and Jean-Paul Gaultier. Big department stores go by the norm." She paused and then concluded, "If they sold size 14 or 16, which is probably what you need, they would go bankrupt."

She stopped for a minute and then stared at me, intrigued. "Where on earth do you come from? I am sorry I can't help you. Really, I am." And she looked it too. She seemed, all of a sudden, interested, and brushed off another woman who was seeking her attention with a cutting, "Get someone else to help you, I'm busy." Only then did I notice that she was probably my age, in her late fifties. But unlike me, she had the thin body of an adolescent girl. Her knee-length, navy blue, Chanel dress had a white silk collar reminiscent of the subdued elegance of aristocratic French Catholic schoolgirls at the turn of the century. A pearl-studded belt emphasized the slimness of her waist. With her meticulously styled short hair and sophisticated makeup, she looked half my age at first glance.

"I come from a country where there is no size for women's clothes," I told her. "I buy my own material and the neighborhood seamstress or craftsman makes me the silk or leather skirt I want. They just take my measurements each time I see them. Neither the seamstress nor I know exactly what size my new skirt is. We discover it together in the making. No one cares about my size in Morocco as long as I pay taxes on time. Actually, I don't know what my size is, to tell you the truth."

The saleswoman laughed merrily and said that I should advertise my country as a paradise for stressed working women. "You mean you don't watch your weight?" she inquired, with a tinge of disbelief in her voice. And then, after a brief moment of silence, she added in a lower register, as if talking to herself: "Many women working in highly paid fashion-related jobs could lose their positions if they didn't keep to a strict diet."

Her words sounded so simple, but the threat they implied was so cruel that I realized for the first time that maybe "size 6" is a more violent restriction imposed on women than is the Muslim veil. Quickly I said good-bye so as not to make any more demands on the saleslady's time or involve her in any more unwelcome, confidential exchanges about age-discriminating salary cuts. A surveillance camera was probably watching us both.

Yes, I thought as I wandered off, I have finally found the answer to my harem enigma. Unlike the Muslim man, who uses space to establish male domination by excluding women from the public arena, the Western man manipulates time and light. He declares that in order to be beautiful, a woman must look fourteen years old. If she dares to look fifty, or worse, sixty, she is beyond the pale. By putting the spotlight on the female child and framing her as the ideal of beauty, he condemns the mature woman to invisibility. In fact, the modern Western man enforces Immanuel Kant's nineteenth-century theories: To be beautiful, women have to appear childish and brainless. When a woman looks mature and self-assertive, or allows her hips to expand, she is condemned as ugly. Thus, the walls of the European harem separate youthful beauty from ugly maturity.

These Western attitudes, I thought, are even more dangerous and cunning than the Muslim ones because the weapon used against women is time. Time is less visible, more fluid than space. The Western man uses images and spotlights to freeze female beauty within an idealized childhood, and forces women to perceive aging—that normal unfolding of the years—as a shameful devaluation. "Here I am, transformed into a dinosaur," I caught myself saying aloud as I went up and down the rows of skirts in the store, hoping to prove the saleslady wrong—to no avail. This Western time-defined veil is even crazier than the space-defined one enforced by the Ayatollahs.

The violence embodied in the Western harem is less visible than in the Eastern harem because aging is not attacked directly, but rather masked as an aesthetic choice. Yes, I suddenly felt not only very ugly but also quite useless in that store, where, if you had big hips, you were simply out of the picture. You drifted into the fringes of nothingness.

By putting the spotlight on the prepubescent female, the Western man veils the older, more mature woman, wrapping her in shrouds of ugliness. This idea gives me the chills because it tattoos the invisible harem directly onto a woman's skin. Chinese foot-binding worked the same way: Men declared beautiful only those women who had small, child-like feet. Chinese men did not force women to bandage their feet to keep them from developing normally—all they did was to define the beauty ideal. In feudal China, a beautiful woman was the one who voluntarily sacrificed her right to unhindered physical movement by mutilating her own feet, and thereby proving that her main goal in life was to please men. Similarly, in the Western world, I was expected to shrink my hips into a size 6 if I wanted to find a decent skirt tailored for a beautiful woman. We Muslim women have only one month of fasting, Ramadan, but the poor Western woman who diets has to fast twelve months out of the year. "*Quelle horreur*," I kept repeating to myself, while looking around at the American women shopping. All those my age looked like youthful teenagers.

According to the writer Naomi Wolf, the ideal size for American models decreased sharply in the 1990s. "A generation ago, the average model weighed 8 percent less than the average American woman, whereas today she weighs 23 percent less. . . . The weight of Miss America plummeted, and the average weight of Playboy Playmates dropped from 11 percent below the national average in 1970 to 17 percent below it in eight years."[1] The shrinking of the ideal size, according to Wolf, is one of the primary reasons for anorexia and other health-related problems: "Eating disorders rose exponentially, and a mass of neurosis was promoted that used food and weight to strip women of . . . a sense of control."[2]

Now, at last, the mystery of my Western harem made sense. Framing youth as beauty and condemning maturity is the weapon used against women in the West just as limiting access to public space is the weapon used in the East. The objective remains identical in both cultures: to make women feel unwelcome, inadequate, and ugly.

The power of the Western man resides in dictating what women should wear and how they should look. He controls the whole fashion industry, from cosmetics to underwear. The West, I realized, was the only part of the world where women's fashion is a man's business. In places like Morocco, where you design your own clothes and discuss them with craftsmen and -women, fashion is your own business. Not so in the West. As Naomi Wolf explains in *The Beauty Myth*, men have engineered a prodigious amount of fetish-like, fashion-related para-phernalia: "Powerful industries—the $33-billion-a-year diet industry, the $20-billion cosmetic industry, the $300-million cosmetic surgery industry, and the $7-billion pornography industry—have arisen from the capital made out of unconscious anxieties, and are in turn able, through their influence on mass culture, to use, stimulate, and rein-force the hallucination in a rising economic spiral."[3]

But how does the system function? I wondered. Why do women accept it?

Of all the possible explanations, I like that of the French sociologist, Pierre Bourdieu, the best. In his latest book, *La Domination Masculine*, he proposes something he calls "*la violence symbolique*": "Symbolic vio-lence is a form of power which is hammered directly on the body, and as if by magic, without any apparent physical constraint. But this magic operates only because it activates the codes pounded in the deepest lay-ers of the body."[4] Reading Bourdieu, I had the impression that I finally understood Western man's psyche better. The cosmetic and fashion industries are only the tip of the iceberg, he states, which is why women are so ready to adhere to their dictates. Something else is going on on a far deeper level. Otherwise, why would women belittle themselves spontaneously? Why, argues Bourdieu, would women make their lives more difficult, for example, by preferring men who are taller or older than they are? "The majority of French women wish to have a husband who is older and also, which seems consistent, bigger as far as size is concerned," writes Bourdieu.[5] Caught in the enchanted submission characteristic of the symbolic violence inscribed in the mysterious lay-ers of the flesh, women relinquish what he calls "les signes ordinaires de la hiérarchie sexuelle," the ordinary signs of sexual hierarchy, such as old age and a larger body. By so doing, explains Bourdieu, women spontaneously accept the subservient position. It is this spontaneity Bourdieu describes as magic enchantment.[6]

Once I understood how this magic submission worked, I became very happy that the conservative Ayatollahs do not know about it yet. If they did, they would readily switch to its sophisticated methods, because they are so much more effective. To deprive me of food is def-initely the best way to paralyze my thinking capabilities.

Both Naomi Wolf and Pierre Bourdieu come to the conclusion that insidious "body codes" paralyze Western women's abilities to compete for power, even though access to education and professional opportuni-ties seem wide open, because the rules of the game are so different according to gender. Women enter the power game with so much of their energy deflected to their physical appearance that one hesitates to say the playing field is level. "A cultural fixation on female thinness is not an obsession about female beauty," explains Wolf. It is "an obsession about female obedience. Dieting is the most potent political sedative in women's history; a quietly mad population is a tractable one."[7] Research, she contends, "confirmed what most women know too well—that concern with weight leads to a 'virtual collapse of self-esteem and sense of effectiveness' and that . . . 'prolonged and periodic caloric restriction' resulted in a distinctive personality whose traits are passivity, anxiety, and emotionality."[8] Similarly, Bourdieu, who focuses more on how this myth hammers its inscriptions onto the flesh itself, recognizes that constantly reminding women of their physical appearance destabilizes them emotionally because it reduces them to exhibited objects. "By confining women to the status of symbolical objects to be seen and perceived by the other, masculine domination . . . puts women in a state of constant physical insecurity. . . . They have to strive ceaselessly to be engaging, attractive, and available."[9] Being frozen into the passive position of an object whose very existence depends on the eye of its beholder turns the educated modern Western woman into a harem slave.

"I thank you, Allah, for sparing me the tyranny of the 'size 6 harem,'" I repeatedly said to myself while seated on the Paris-Casablanca flight, on my way back home at last. "I am so happy that the conservative male elite does not know about it. Imagine the fundamentalists switching from the veil to forcing women to fit size 6."

How can you stage a credible political demonstration and shout in the streets that your human rights have been violated when you cannot find the right skirt?

NOTES

1. Naomi Wolf, *The Beauty Myth: How Images of Beauty Are Used Against Women* (New York: Anchor Books, Doubleday, 1992), p. 185.
2. Ibid., p. 11.
3. Ibid., p. 17.
4. Pierre Bourdieu: "La force symbolique est une forme de pouvoir qui s'exerce sur les corps, directement, et comme par magie, en dehors de toute contraine physique, mais cette magie n'opère qu'en s'appuyant sur des dispositions déposées, tel des ressorts, au plus profond des corps." In *La Domination Masculine* (Paris: Editions du Seuil, 1998), op. cit. p. 44.
   Here I would like to thank my French editor, Claire Delannoy, who kept me informed of the latest debates on women's issues in Paris by sending me Bourdieu's book and many others. Delannoy has been reading this manuscript since its inception in 1996 (a first version was published in Casablanca by Edition Le Fennec in 1998 as "Êtes-Vous Vacciné Centre le Harem").

5. *La Domination Masculine,* op. cit., p. 41.
6. Bourdieu, op. cit., p. 42.
7. Wolf, op. cit., p. 187.
8. Wolf, quoting research carried out by S. C. Woolly and O. W. Woolly, op. cit., pp. 187–188.
9. Bourdieu, *La Domination Masculine,* p. 73.

STUDY QUESTIONS

1. Women confront many different restrictions in society. How does a dress shop constitute restriction for Western women as a harem does for Eastern women?
2. Explain "symbolic violence," a concept Mernissi uses from the work of Bourdieu, as it relates to women and their bodies.

Deviance and Social Control

When sociologists examine deviance, it is understood as a cultural universal—all societies have some form of deviance. Since it is an ever-present part of social groups, there are many ways to explain it (theories) and many different examples of it (research). Norms, or rules that guide behavior, are an important reference for understanding deviance, which is a violation of societal or group norms. Upon closer examination, however, it is not just rule violation that determines deviance; it is just as important to know who made the rules and who enforces them. Social control, institutions and agencies in large societies that attempt to create order, is exercised by the police, courts, and corrections, for example. On a smaller scale, when a group has its rules (norms) violated, it can exercise informal controls on group members through disapproval or ostracism. Students of sociology are often drawn to the discipline because it provides a glimpse of life that is hidden from the view of people who live lives of greater conformity. It should be obvious, however, that the most conforming person still engages in some deviance, and the most deviant person is conforming in most circumstances.

Deviant activity in any society and the careers of deviant persons are very diverse. Of course, crime and delinquency are violations of formal norms or laws, but there are many other types of rules for behavior that don't reach the threshold of legal infractions. What about behaviors like mental illness, alcohol use/abuse, extreme facial and body disfigurations, certain eating disordered persons, non-working, homeless populations, and so on? Some would find these circumstances to be most "deviant"; others may not. Since it is left to "local standards" to determine what is pornographic, where is pornography in the list of deviant activities? Because of the diversity of such activities and the responses of different people to such activities and persons, there is no way to create a list of deviant behaviors that apply to any society at any point in time. Sometimes deviance occurs in reputable organizations like corporations, religion, and the government. Even police departments and lawyers can engage in deviance. Deviance cuts across all persons and structures in society.

Deviance is also relative—changeable. Time alone can change deviance, even a short span of time like a few years or a decade. Terrorism, a recent realization in America, was redefined in a matter of a few days. Different settings can lead to different definitions of deviance. Midtown Manhattan, New York, has activities and behaviors tolerated that would never be excused in many other towns and cities across the United States. So, rural and urban settings seem to have their relative definitions of deviance. Situations, too, redefine deviance. Taking a human life on the streets of our communities might be murder and punishable by the death of the perpetrator. If you are given a government-issue uniform and rifle and deployed to another country to fight, taking human lives in this situation would be called patriotism and the "perpetrators" might become heroes. There is enormous importance in who defines deviance for a society or group, so much so that sociology can view the definition as more important than the act itself. If we are to fully understand deviance in a society, we must know that it is "relative," and that defining and enforcing the rules and laws can tell much about social life in this culture.

The first of the three articles on the deviance topic is by DeAnn K. Gauthier and Craig J. Forsyth; their article examines the behavior of a set of "groupies," the rodeo circuit's "buckle bunnies." Women, in this case, desire the companionship of men who compete for prize money in different events. The second article is by A. Ayres Boswell and Joan Z. Spade, who look at "rape culture" as an artifact of the fraternity organization and activities on college campuses. Their research identifies some of the variables responsible for safe and unsafe environments for women. Violence is a topic that must be addressed as a masculine gender issue, of which this is one example. The third and final article is by D. L. Rosenhan, a professional psychologist, who, with some colleagues, admitted himself to a mental institution and used this personal experience to examine "sanity in insane places." This article shows how researchers can "go native" and discover how social control maintains definitions of deviance and controls the behaviors of its residents—insane or not.

DeANN K. GAUTHIER AND CRAIG J. FORSYTH

Buckle Bunnies
Groupies of the Rodeo Circuit

Introduction

The rodeo attracts many people who want to see the epitome of the Old West when roping calves and taming wild horses was part of everyday life on the ranch. Fans play an important part in the rodeo cowboy's life on the road. Among these fans are women who those around the rodeo circuit call "buckle bunnies." They are essentially cowboy groupies, who purposefully seek encounters with contestants who have proven successful in their particular rodeo event(s) (Carroll 1985; Morris 1993; Stern and Stern 1992). An easy identification system exists whereby bunnies can quickly locate their "winners" via his wearing of the winning belt buckle—hence the term "buckle bunny." These women come into contact with the cowboys at the rodeo, or in the hotels and bars where the cowboys stay. Once identified, bunnies offer the cowboys many different things, such as a ride to a rodeo, a place to sleep, a shower, or many times, just sex. There is little research on buckle bunnies, but literature does exist on rock star groupies and high profile sports groupies.

Methodology

Data for this study were gathered through interviews and observation. Subjects were identified by a key informant. Additional subjects were identified via snowball sampling, in which each subject suggests other subjects (Babbie 1998). The Internet also provided data about the rodeo. Interviews were conducted at the homes of rodeo cowboys, at rodeos, and bars and hotels. Thirty-eight interviews were conducted with individuals who currently compete on the rodeo circuit at the college, amateur, or professional levels. Seven interviews were conducted with former professional cowboys. Eight wives of rodeo cowboys were also interviewed. Twelve single women who follow the rodeo and one rodeo promoter were also interviewed. The data presented here are part of a larger occupational study of the rodeo cowboy. The intent of this article is to describe the interaction between buckle bunnies and rodeo cowboys.

Groupies

"Groupie" is a term usually used to refer to a young woman who follows rock groups around on tours. The popular San Francisco-based group of the 1960s, The Grateful Dead, attracted a large contingent of traveling fans numbering in the thousands from all over the world. These fans were given the name "Deadheads." Being a Deadhead was a master status in the eyes of the Grateful Dead. Deadheads traveled at their own expense to see the band and they invested a great deal of time and money into their traveling. . . .

The groupie subculture also surrounds professional athletics, with each sport having specific names for these women (Elson 1991). Baseball players refer to these girls as "Annies" and hockey players call them "puck bunnies." The girls who follow athletes around and wait for them at bars or hotels all want to become an "acquaintance" of the athlete. Many athletes find these women very appealing because "it is easy sex" with no expectations following the encounter. These women make themselves readily available to the athletes. . . .

Groupies who follow athletes can be innocent teenagers who just want to catch a glimpse of their favorite star (Oller 1998), but most are between the ages of 18 and 25. They are seeking money, attention, and status from being associated with high-profile athletes. These women rarely approach the athletes on the court or field. They often become acquainted with the hotels where the teams are staying or the popular after-game hang-outs. Many of the same people are seen from town to town and they are very straightforward about their intentions (Elson 1991; Oller 1998).

Buckle Bunnies

As the wife of one cowboy commented:

> *There's a lot of them [buckle bunnies] . . . at the bigger rodeos. If you were in one certain area for a while . . . you'd see a lot of the same groupies. It's just like in any sport. You have it in professional football. Girls who like athletes. [In] hockey [they] call them puck bunnies. I guess it is the ruggedness of a cowboy that they like.*

Bunnies come from a variety of backgrounds, but the majority have some family association with the rodeo. In the past, bunnies wore a distinct style of revealing Western attire. This is still true in some cases, depending on the location of the rodeo.

> *It all depends on where you go. The ones down in the circuit I was in . . . wore the tightest pants they could get in, the latest style Western shirts . . . Roper boots and a buckle. Most of the time it was a buckle from some cowboy.*

Several cowboys stated that these girls are getting away from the Western attire. As one steer wrestler stated:

> *Not a lot of people dress the rodeo part unless they're at the rodeo. A lot of the girls are doing the same thing. They're wearing Levi's, Girbaud's, Guess, something like that. They don't look the part they used to, but you can still pick them out pretty easy.*

Today, "picking them out" seems to depend in large part on the bunnies' lack of attire: "real skimpy shirts," "tank tops," "slutty," or as one interviewee put it, "They wear clothes so you can see their boobs."

Motivations behind bunny behavior seem multifaceted. One primary motivation is the atmosphere of excitement surrounding the rodeo and the cowboys. Bunnies admit to being physically attracted to cowboys in general, although looks are not the main motivation. One interviewee said:

> *I'm attracted to them, but they have to be successful in their event.*

. . . Buckle bunnies are likely to frequent the host hotel of the major rodeos. The host hotels usually send out papers so the contestants will know where to stay for these rodeos, including the Cheyenne Frontier Days, Denver, Houston, Fort Worth, and the National Finals Rodeo. The buckle bunnies usually find out the host hotel and try to get rooms there so they can be near the cowboys.

The most common place for the cowboys to encounter buckle bunnies is in a nightclub after the rodeo. This is where the majority of the buckle bunnies seek out the participants. Buckle bunnies surround the participants, waiting for them to sign an autograph, take a picture with them or to see if they can get the attention of a cowboy, each hoping she might be the favored girl of the night. As one cowboy wife notes:

> If they have a beer garden, they're there . . . a hospitality room at the hotel . . . they're there. They're everywhere the guys are socializing at.

Many times the buckle bunnies flirt with cowboys to let them know that they are interested. One cowboy told us:

> The girls kind of flirt with you, buy you a drink and they talk about rodeo. All of a sudden they pop the question on you. Who you here with? Are you going home with anybody? Do you mind if I come home with you?

Some buckle bunnies are overt and direct about their intentions:

> I've seen them ask guys if they've got a motel, or should they get one, or would they like to go back to their motel room. Some of them get off on doing guys in their campers . . . truck . . . horse trailers.

Buckle bunnies usually do not expect anything more than sex from the rodeo participants and vice versa. The majority of cowboys on the circuit are married; therefore it is even more understood by the buckle bunnies that nothing is to be expected.

> A lot of guys are married out there that they chase after . . . being with somebody who's married or just being with somebody who's going to be there for one night. They don't expect nothing from them.

A wife of a cowboy described the code of secrecy that surrounds sex with buckle bunnies on the road.

> [There is] a lot of infidelity on the road. Most of the time the guys would never let on about it. That was between them. You hope somebody would tell you if it were your husband, [but] what happens on the road stays on the road. It doesn't come back home.

Even though the cowboys enjoy the company of the buckle bunnies, many of them stated that there are negative connotations associated with them. For instance, several cowboys called these girls "whores" or "sluts." Some cowboys labeled buckle bunnies, "cut queens." . . .

As far as the sexual encounters go, these range from relatively mild flirtations to open exhibitionism. One bunny illustrates the mild form of pursuit:

> I meet cowboys at the local country bar. If I see a new bird in town I make it my business to find out who they are, buy them a drink and make them feel welcome. If they don't show an interest, I don't bother with them.

On the other hand, pursuit may be more intense, as these cowboys state:

> In Calgary, everything was different. Sex was out in the open, so to speak. The girls love cowboys and they aren't afraid to walk up to you and just ask you if you wanted to go to their hotel room or yours. They just cut to the chase and said what they wanted.

And finally, bunnies may be so enthralled with the chase that they become exhibitionists. One typical cowboy story goes as follows:

> In Fort Worth, [a bunny wanted] oral sex in the bar. She asked, I obliged her. She told everybody to turn around and put their backs to us. She dropped to her knees. They had two girls on the dance floor who watched. She did it and then went on about her business. I went home with her that night later on. Somebody do that at the bar, you think I'm gonna let her go home by herself? What you think she gonna do by herself? The guys cheered me on. They were high-fiving me.

. . . The typical cowboy perception of the buckle bunny and who she is and what she represents is stated as follows:

> A buckle bunny . . . she's been . . . rode hard and put up wet a couple times.

The cowboys recognize that bunnies want to be able to say that they had sex with a real cowboy and, as a consequence, they expect the cowboys are the nontraditional gatekeepers of sex. Traditionally, women have been recognized as sexual game players (Ronai and Ellis 2000), but the situation seems to be somewhat reversed on the rodeo circuits. Women are seeking to acquire the "best" cowboy, whose sexual "conquest" will be viewed as a form of status attainment. One cowboy points this out by saying:

> It's a status thing for the girls . . . like being with a movie star. They brag about it.

The Rating System

To determine the "best" among cowboys, there are many ways that buckle bunnies are able to rate the rodeo participants in terms of desirability. The most obvious way is through the type of event in which the cowboy participates. Several cowboys felt that many of the buckle bunnies rated them in terms of their events.

> Some of them, all they like are bull riders, some of them, all they like are steer wrestlers.

Most of the buckle bunnies stated that they prefer rough stock riders to timed event participants. The popularity of bull riders may be because of the publicity given to this particular event. This is the only rodeo event that has its own professional rodeos set aside from the Professional Rodeo Cowboys Association (PRCA). The Professional Bullriders Association (PBR) sanctions their own bull riding events. Bull riding is considered by spectators and cowboys to be the most exciting and challenging rodeo event. . . .

Image and recognizability play important roles in the ranking of cowboy desirability.

> [Bull riding's] the most challenging event. That's who [bunnies] see on TV. They know them by face and name. That's what they want. It's always been like that.

Another way the buckle bunnies rate cowboys is using the various rodeo rankings. Buckle bunnies find rodeo participants who have excelled in their events more desirable than those who have not. As one wife stated:

> Rank and standing has something to do with who the buckle bunnies choose to be with. The ones that make more money are obviously better known because they're at the top of the rankings and they're more popular. To be with a world champion or the guy who won the Salinas Rodeo or Cheyenne is a prestigious thing.

Cowboys are aware of this use of ranking by the bunnies:

> The girls inquire about your ranking or how much money you've made, but they know. They probably get the Pro Rodeo Sports News and get on the Internet to check out what's going on. Most of them keep up with the standings. They're interested in the status of a cowboy.

... Some groups of buckle bunnies have created point systems to keep track of the cowboys with whom they have been intimate. In one such system, points were given in order of prestige of the cowboy's achievements.

[One] group of girls had a point system. Sex had to be involved to get the points. If you had your PRCA card it was one point. If you made it to the finals it was two points. Won the world, it was three points. At the end of the year, whoever had the most points accumulated out of the group, it's like eight or 10 of them, the losers had to pay the one with the most points trip to the finals, plus their own way out there.

Although success in the event is important to the buckle bunnies, it seems to be more an issue of status than an issue of money. . . . Jackets are also marks of status. Rodeo participants who have been to the national finals usually wear their NFR jackets wherever they go.

They give each contestant a jacket and it has their number and their name and everything on it in Las Vegas at the national finals. The night I got there, [my husband] had won the round and they gave him a buckle, so that night afterward we were sitting down at the bar. Several girls came up to him, even while I was there and they propositioned him. They see that jacket.

I don't care who you are, if you show up at the NFR and you're not a contestant, you don't have a shot [with the bunnies]. If they can't get the jacket, they'll go after somebody else.

. . . they want the jacket. . . .

The Social Transaction

Many times, the buckle bunnies allow the cowboys to stay in their hotel rooms or at their homes so the cowboys do not have to spend another night in the truck or on the road. Cowboys often do not rent rooms of their own because they don't have enough money or because the hotel doesn't accommodate a horse trailer. Some cowboys offer to buy the women dinner if they allow them to sleep in their room and take a hot shower. If one of the guys in a group would find a woman to go home with, all of the cowboys traveling with him would follow to partake of a shower and place to sleep.

Many of the participants travel constantly and rarely go home. When they do get to stay in the same place for four or five days, they want to have fun. Buckle bunnies assist greatly in this goal.

I was at a rodeo in Oklahoma. We didn't have any place to stay, so any time one of the guys in the car would get a girl and no one else would, we would follow them to their house and that's a shower, maybe break- fast and we'd sleep. We were real young, just pro and we weren't win- ning hardly any money. Five days without a shower. We were scrungy. And, we went to their home and we were all sitting in the living room. I was kind of getting scared, there were three of us sitting down, and my buddy was with that other girl and there was two of them and she said, "Well, there's a couch right there," and I said, "I'll sleep on the floor," and she said, "No, you have a place to sleep in here with me." I ended up sleeping in the bed with her. The daughter was in the other room with my friend. The mother and daughter, she raised to be a buckle bunny. The next morning we got up and had pancakes and eggs. She handed me a paper with her number on it. . . .

Discussion and Conclusions

Several factors make the behavior of buckle bunnies deviant: having sex with married men, having sex in public, women initiating the sexual encounters, having sex with too many people, and the overt and utili- tarian rating of sexual partners. None of these are crimes, but all fall under the heading of sins or poor taste (Smith and Pollack 2000). . . .

Subcultures are, indeed, difficult for outsiders to understand. Norms of a subculture can be an antithesis to the conventional, but it is the material from which identities are constructed. The identities of the buckle bunnies emphasize a relation of unattachment, a dislocation from the confinements of work and committed relationships, and a genuine experiment with free time. It delineates the buckle bunny from others, and assists her with finding companionship with like- minded peers, enabling her to construct an identity from the symbols found in the rodeo subculture. Subculture reinforces meaningful state- ments about one's position relative to others. The subculture is com- posed of a variety of purists, those who do not quite fit in, and rebels. The attraction of the rodeo subculture is its hedonistic escape from the conventional. It offers a place to have fun and explore and expand both the traditional concepts of masculinity and femininity, but also modern roles regarding sexual pursuit. Traditional ideology maintains hege- mony; it is a male-dominated culture. But what has been negotiated is a fetished image that is a twist on traditional sex roles. The new images consist of males, still dominant in a subculture that glorifies males and masculinity, but also now in possession of a role traditionally reserved for women as a group—the gatekeepers of sex. Alternatively, women are free to pursue sexually, a role traditionally denied them as adult women in mainstream U.S. culture. If one feels like a maverick, the scripts composed in this subculture are highly attractive.

REFERENCES

Babbie, Earl. 1998. *The Practice of Social Research*. Belmont, CA: Wadsworth Publishing Company.

Carroll, E. Jean. 1985. *Female Difficulties*. New York: Bantam Books.

Elson, John. 1991. "The Dangerous World of Wannabes." *Time* 138(22) (Nov. 25):77, 80.

Morris, Michele. 1993. *The Cowboy Life*. New York: Fireside.

Ronai, Carol Rambo and Carolyn Ellis. 2000. "Turn-Ons for Money: Interactional Strategies of the Table Dancer." Pp. 407–426 in *Constructions of Deviance*, edited by Patricia A. Adler and Peter Adler. Belmont, CA: Wadsworth Publishing Company.

Smith, Alexander B. and Harriet Pollack. 2000. "Deviance As Crime, Sin, and Poor Taste." Pp. 19–28 in *Constructions of Deviance*, edited by Patricia A. Adler and Peter Adler. Belmont, CA: Wadsworth Publishing Company.

Stern, Jane and Michael Stern. 1992. "Raging Bulls." *The New Yorker* 68 (Sept. 14):90–103.

STUDY QUESTIONS

1. What are the gender patterns in the "buckle bunnies" relationships to the cowboys?
2. Why are the "buckle bunnies" considered deviant?

A. AYRES BOSWELL AND JOAN Z. SPADE

Fraternities and Collegiate Rape Culture

Date rape and acquaintance rape on college campuses are topics of concern to both researchers and college administrators. Some estimate that 60 to 80 percent of rapes are date or acquaintance rape (Koss, Dinero, Seibel, and Cox 1988). Further, 1 out of 4 college women say they were raped or experienced an attempted rape, and 1 out of 12 college men say they forced a woman to have sexual intercourse against her will (Koss, Gidycz, and Wisniewski 1985).

Although considerable attention focuses on the incidence of rape, we know relatively little about the context or the *rape culture* surrounding date and acquaintance rape. Rape culture is a set of values and beliefs that provide an environment conducive to rape (Buchwald, Fletcher, & Roth 1993; Herman 1984). The term applies to a generic culture surrounding and promoting rape, not the specific settings in which rape is likely to occur. We believe that the specific settings also are important in defining relationships between men and women.

Some have argued that fraternities are places where rape is likely to occur on college campuses (Martin and Hummer 1989; O'Sullivan 1993; Sanday 1990) and that the students most likely to accept rape myths and be more sexually aggressive are more likely to live in fraternities and sororities, consume higher doses of alcohol and drugs, and place a higher value on social life at college (Gwartney-Gibbs and Stockard 1989; Kalof and Cargill 1991). Others suggest that sexual aggression is learned in settings such as fraternities and is not part of predispositions or pre-existing attitudes (Boeringer, Shehan, and Akers 1991). To prevent further incidences of rape on college campuses, we need to understand what it is about fraternities in particular and college life in general that may contribute to the maintenance of a rape culture on college campuses.

Our approach is to identify the social contexts that link fraternities to campus rape and promote a rape culture. Instead of assuming that all fraternities provide an environment conducive to rape, we compare the interactions of men and women at fraternities identified on campus as being especially *dangerous* places for women, where the likelihood of rape is high, to those seen as *safer* places, where the perceived probability of rape occurring is lower. Prior to collecting data for our study, we found that most women students identified some fraternities as having more sexually aggressive members and a higher probability of rape. These women also considered other fraternities as relatively safe houses, where a woman could go and get drunk if she wanted to and feel secure that the fraternity men would not take advantage of her. We compared parties at houses identified as high-risk and low-risk houses as well as at two local bars frequented by college students. Our analysis provides an opportunity to examine situations and contexts that hinder or facilitate positive social relations between undergraduate men and women.

The abusive attitudes toward women that some fraternities perpetuate exist within a general culture where rape is intertwined in traditional gender scripts. Men are viewed as initiators of sex and women as either passive partners or active resisters, preventing men from touching their bodies (LaPlante, McCormick, and Brannigan 1980). Rape culture is based on the assumptions that men are aggressive and dominant whereas women are passive and acquiescent (Buchwald et al. 1993; Herman 1984). What occurs on college campuses is an extension of the portrayal of domination and aggression of men over women that exemplifies the double standard of sexual behavior in U.S. society (Barthel 1988; Kimmel 1993).

Sexually active men are positively reinforced by being referred to as "studs," whereas women who are sexually active or report enjoying sex are derogatorily labeled as "sluts" (Herman 1984; O'Sullivan 1993). These gender scripts are embodied in rape myths and stereotypes such as "She really wanted it; she just said no because she didn't want me to think she was a bad girl" (Burke, Stets, and Pirog-Good 1989; Jenkins and Dambrot 1987; Lisak and Roth 1988; Malamuth 1986; Muehlenhard and Linton 1987; Peterson and Franzese 1987). Because men's sexuality is seen as more natural, acceptable, and uncontrollable than women's sexuality, many men and women excuse acquaintance rape by affirming that men cannot control their natural urges (Miller and Marshall 1987).

Whereas some researchers explain these attitudes toward sexuality and rape using an individual or a psychological interpretation, we argue that rape has a social basis, one in which both men and women create and recreate masculine and feminine identities and relations. Based on the assumption that rape is part of the social construction of gender, we examine how men and women "do gender" on a college campus (West and Zimmerman 1987). We focus on fraternities because they have been identified as settings that encourage rape (Sanday 1990). By comparing fraternities that are viewed by women as places where there is a high risk of rape to those where women believe there is a low risk of rape as well as two local commercial bars, we seek to identify characteristics that make some social settings more likely places for the occurrence of rape.

Method

We observed social interactions between men and women at a private coeducational school in which a high percentage (49.4 percent) of students affiliate with Greek organizations. The university has an undergraduate population of approximately 4,500 students, just more than one third of whom are women; the students are primarily from upper-middle-class families. The school, which admitted only men until 1971, is highly competitive academically.

We used a variety of data collection approaches: observations of interactions between men and women at fraternity parties and bars, formal interviews, and informal conversations. The first author, a former undergraduate at this school and a graduate student at the time of the study, collected the data. She knew about the social life at the school and had established rapport and trust between herself and undergraduate students as a teaching assistant in a human sexuality course.

The process of identifying high- and low-risk fraternity houses followed Hunter's (1953) reputational approach. In our study, 40 women students identified fraternities that they considered to be high risk, or to have more sexually aggressive members and higher incidence of rape, as well as fraternities that they considered to be safe houses. The women represented all four years of undergraduate college and different living groups (sororities, residence halls, and off-campus housing). Observations focused on the four fraternities named most often by these women as high-risk houses and the four identified as low-risk houses. . . .

In addition, 50 individuals were interviewed including men from the selected fraternities, women who attended those parties, men not affiliated with fraternities, and self-identified rape victims known to the first author. The first author approached men and women by telephone or on campus and asked them to participate in interviews. The interviews included open-ended questions about gender relations on campus, attitudes about date rape, and their own experiences on campus. . . .

Results

The Settings

Fraternity Parties

We observed several differences in the quality of the interaction of men and women at parties at high-risk fraternities compared to those at low-risk houses. A typical party at a low-risk house included an equal number of women and men. The social atmosphere was friendly, with considerable interaction between women and men. Men and women danced in groups and in couples, with many of the couples kissing and displaying affection toward each other. Brothers explained that, because many of the men in these houses had girlfriends, it was normal to see couples kissing on the dance floor. Coed groups engaged in conversations at many of these houses, with women and men engaging in friendly exchanges, giving the impression that they knew each other well. Almost no cursing and yelling was observed at parties in low-risk houses; when pushing occurred, the participants apologized. Respect for women extended to the women's bathrooms, which were clean and well supplied.

At high-risk houses, parties typically had skewed gender ratios, sometimes involving more men and other times involving more women. Gender segregation also was evident at these parties, with the men on one side of a room or in the bar drinking while women gathered in another area. Men treated women differently in the high-risk houses. The women's bathrooms in the high-risk houses were filthy, including clogged toilets and vomit in the sinks. When a brother was told of the mess in the bathroom at a high-risk house, he replied, "Good, maybe some of these beer wenches will leave so there will be more beer for us."

Men attending parties at high-risk houses treated women less respectfully, engaging in jokes, conversations, and behaviors that degraded women. Men made a display of assessing women's bodies and rated them with thumbs up or thumbs down for the other men in the sight of the women. One man attending a party at a high-risk fraternity said to another, "Did you know that this week is Women's Awareness Week? I guess that means we get to abuse them more this week." Men behaved more crudely at parties at high-risk houses. At one party, a brother dropped his pants, including his underwear, while dancing in front of several women. Another brother slid across the dance floor completely naked.

The atmosphere at parties in high-risk fraternities was less friendly overall. With the exception of greetings, men and women rarely smiled or laughed and spoke to each other less often than was the case at parties in low-risk houses. The few one-on-one conversations between women and men appeared to be strictly flirtatious (lots of eye contact, touching, and very close talking). It was rare to see a group of men and women together talking. Men were openly hostile, which made the high-risk parties seem almost threatening at times. For example, there was a lot of touching, pushing, profanity, and name calling, some done by women.

Students at parties at the high-risk houses seemed self-conscious and aware of the presence of members of the opposite sex, an awareness that was sexually charged. Dancing early in the evening was usually between women. Close to midnight, the sex ratio began to balance out with the arrival of more men or more women. Couples began to dance together but in a sexual way (close dancing with lots of pelvic thrusts). Men tried to pick up women using lines such as "Want to see my fish tank?" and "Let's go upstairs so that we can talk; I can't hear what you're saying in here."

Although many of the same people who attended high-risk parties also attended low-risk parties, their behavior changed as they moved from setting to setting. Group norms differed across contexts as well. At a party that was held jointly at a low-risk house with a high-risk fraternity, the ambience was that of a party at a high-risk fraternity with heavier drinking, less dancing, and fewer conversations between women and men. The men from both high- and low-risk fraternities were very aggressive; a fight broke out, and there was pushing and shoving on the dance floor and in general.

As others have found, fraternity brothers at high-risk houses on this campus told about routinely discussing their sexual exploits at breakfast the morning after parties and sometimes at house meetings (cf. Martin and Hummer 1989; O'Sullivan 1993; Sanday 1990). During these sessions, the brothers we interviewed said that men bragged about what they did the night before with stories of sexual conquests often told by the same men, usually sophomores. The women involved in these exploits were women they did not know or knew but did not respect, or *faceless victims*. Men usually treated girlfriends with respect and did not talk about them in these storytelling sessions. Men from low-risk houses, however, did not describe similar sessions in their houses. . . .

Gender Relations

Relations between women and men are shaped by the contexts in which they meet and interact. As is the case on other college campuses, *hooking up* has replaced dating on this campus, and fraternities are places where many students hook up. Hooking up is a loosely applied term on college campuses that had different meanings for men and women on this campus.

Most men defined hooking up similarly. One man said it was something that happens

> *when you are really drunk and meet up with a woman you sort of know, or possibly don't know at all and don't care about. You go home with her with the intention of getting as much sexual, physical pleasure as she'll give you, which can range anywhere from kissing to intercourse, without any strings attached.*

The exception to this rule is when men hook up with women they admire. Men said they are less likely to press for sexual activity with someone they know and like because they want the relationship to continue and be based on respect.

Women's version of hooking up differed. Women said they hook up only with men they cared about and described hooking up as kissing and petting but not sexual intercourse. Many women said that hooking up was disappointing because they wanted longer-term relationships. First-year women students realized quickly that hook-ups were usually one-night stands with no strings attached, but many continued to hook up because they had few opportunities to develop relationships with men on campus. One first-year woman said that "70 percent of hookups never talk again and try to avoid one another, 26 percent may actually hear from them or talk to them again, and 4 percent may actually go on a date, which can lead to a relationship." Another first-year woman said, "It was fun in the beginning. You get a lot of attention and kiss a lot of boys and think this is what college is about, but it gets tiresome fast."

Whereas first-year women get tired of the hook-up scene early on, many men do not become bored with it until their junior or senior year. As one upperclassman said, "The whole game of hooking up became really meaningless and tiresome for me during my second semester of my sophomore year, but most of my friends didn't get bored with it until the following year."

In contrast to hooking up, students also described monogamous relationships with steady partners. Some type of commitment was expected, but most people did not anticipate marriage. The term *seeing each other* was applied when people were sexually involved but free to date other people. This type of relationship involved less commitment than did one of boyfriend/girlfriend but was not considered to be a hook-up. . . .

Some fraternity brothers pressure each other to limit their time with and commitment to their girlfriends. One senior man said, "The hill [fraternities] and girlfriends don't mix." A brother described a constant battle between girlfriends and brothers over who the guy is going out with for the night, with the brothers usually winning. Brothers teased men with girlfriends with remarks such as "whipped" or "where's the ball and chain?" A brother from a high-risk house said that few brothers at his house had girlfriends; some did, but it was uncommon. One man said that from the minute he was a pledge he knew he would probably never have a girlfriend on this campus because "it was just not the norm in my house. No one has girlfriends; the guys have too much fun with [each other]."

The pressure on men to limit their commitment to girlfriends, however, was not true of all fraternities or of all men on campus. Couples attended low-risk fraternity parties together, and men in the low-risk houses went out on dates more often. A man in one low-risk house said that about 70 percent of the members of his house were involved in relationships with women, including the pledges (who were sophomores).

Treatment of Women

. . . Men said that, when together in groups with other men, they sensed a pressure to be disrespectful toward women. A first-year man's perception of the treatment of women was that "they are treated with more respect to their faces, but behind closed doors, with a group of men present, respect for women is not an issue." One senior man stated, "In general, college-aged men don't treat women their age with respect because 90 percent of them think of women as merely a means to sex." Women reinforced this perception. A first-year woman stated, "Men here are more interested in hooking up and drinking beer than they are in getting to know women as real people." Another woman said, "Men here use and abuse women."

Characteristic of rape culture, a double standard of sexual behavior for men versus women was prevalent on this campus. As one Greek senior man stated, "Women who sleep around are sluts and get bad reputations; men who do are champions and get a pat on the back from their brothers." Women also supported a double standard for sexual behavior by criticizing sexually active women. A first-year woman spoke out against women who are sexually active: "I think some girls here make it difficult for the men to respect women as a whole."

One concrete example of demeaning sexually active women on this campus is the "walk of shame." Fraternity brothers come out on the porches of their houses the night after parties and heckle women walking by. It is assumed that these women spent the night at fraternity houses and that the men they were with did not care enough about them to drive them home. Although sororities now reside in former fraternity houses, this practice continues and sometimes the victims of hecklings are sorority women on their way to study in the library. . . .

Fraternity men most often mistreated women they did not know personally. Men and women alike reported incidents in which brothers observed other brothers having sex with unknown women or women they knew only casually. A sophomore woman's experience exemplifies this anonymous state: "I don't mind if 10 guys were watching or it was videotaped. That's expected on this campus. It's the fact that he didn't apologize or even offer to drive me home that really upset me." Descriptions of sexual encounters involved the satisfaction of men by nameless women. A brother in a high-risk fraternity described a similar occurrence:

> A brother of mine was hooking up upstairs with an unattractive woman who had been pursuing him all night. He told some brothers to go outside the window and watch. Well, one thing led to another and they were almost completely naked when the woman noticed the brothers outside. She was then unwilling to go any further, so the

brother went outside and yelled at the other brothers and then closed the shades. I don't know if he scored or not, because the woman was pretty upset. But he did win the award for hooking up with the ugliest chick that weekend. . . .

Discussion and Conclusion

These findings describe the physical and normative aspects of one college campus as they relate to attitudes about and relations between men and women. Our findings suggest that an explanation emphasizing rape culture also must focus on those characteristics of the social setting that play a role in defining heterosexual relationships on college campuses (Kalof and Cargill 1991). The degradation of women as portrayed in rape culture was not found in all fraternities on this campus. Both group norms and individual behavior changed as students went from one place to another. Although individual men are the ones who rape, we found that some settings are more likely places for rape than are others. Our findings suggest that rape cannot be seen only as an isolated act and blamed on individual behavior and proclivities, whether it be alcohol consumption or attitudes. We also must consider characteristics of the settings that promote the behaviors that reinforce a rape culture.

Relations between women and men at parties in low-risk fraternities varied considerably from those in high-risk houses. Peer pressure and situational norms influenced women as well as men. Although many men in high- and low-risk houses shared similar views and attitudes about the Greek system, women on this campus, and date rape, their behaviors at fraternity parties were quite different.

Women who are at highest risk of rape are women whom fraternity brothers did not know. These women are faceless victims, nameless acquaintances—not friends. Men said their responsibility to such persons and the level of guilt they feel later if the hook-ups end in sexual intercourse are much lower if they hook up with women they do not know. In high-risk houses, brothers treated women as subordinates and kept them at a distance. Men in high-risk houses actively discouraged ongoing heterosexual relationships, routinely degraded women, and participated more fully in the hook-up scene; thus, the probability that women would become faceless victims was higher in these houses. The flirtatious nature of the parties indicated that women go to these parties looking for available men, but finding boyfriends or relationships was difficult at parties in high-risk houses. However, in the low-risk houses, where more men had long-term relationships, the women were not strangers and were less likely to become faceless victims. . . .

Although this research provides some clues to gender relations on college campuses, it raises many questions. Why do men and women participate in activities that support a rape culture when they see its injustices? What would happen if alcohol were not controlled by groups of men who admit that they disrespect women when they get together? What can be done to give men and women on college campuses more opportunities to interact responsibly and get to know each other better? These questions should be studied on other campuses with a focus on the social settings in which the incidence of rape and the attitudes that support a rape culture exist. Fraternities are social contexts that may or may not foster a rape culture. . . .

REFERENCES

Barthel, D. 1988. *Putting on appearances: Gender and advertising*. Philadelphia: Temple University Press.

Boeringer, S. B., C. L. Shehan, and R. L. Akers. 1991. Social contexts and social learning in sexual coercion and aggression: Assessing the contribution of fraternity membership. *Family Relations* 40:58–64.

Buchwald, E., P. R. Fletcher, and M. Roth, eds. 1993. *Transforming a rape culture*. Minneapolis, MN: Milkweed Editions.

Burke, P., J. E. Stets, and M. A. Pirog-Good. 1989. Gender identity, self-esteem, physical abuse and sexual abuse in dating relationships. In *Violence in dating relationships: Emerging social issues*, edited by M. A. Pirog-Good and J. E. Stets. New York: Praeger.

Gwartney-Gibbs, P., and J. Stockard. 1989. Courtship aggression and mixed-sex peer groups. In *Violence in dating relationships: Emerging social issues*, edited by M. A. Pirog-Good and J. E. Stets. New York: Praeger.

Herman, D. 1984. The rape culture. In *Women: A feminist perspective*, edited by J. Freeman. Mountain View, CA: Mayfield.

Hunter, F. 1953. *Community power structure*. Chapel Hill: University of North Carolina Press.

Jenkins, M. J., and F. H. Dambrot. 1987. The attribution of date rape: Observer's attitudes and sexual experiences and the dating situation. *Journal of Applied Social Psychology* 17:875–95.

Kalof, L., and T. Cargill. 1991. Fraternity and sorority membership and gender dominance attitudes. *Sex Roles* 25:417–23.

Kimmel, M. S. 1993. Clarence, William, Iron Mike, Tailhook, Senator Packwood, Spur Posse, Magic . . . and us. In *Transforming a rape culture*, edited by E. Buchwald, P. R. Fletcher, and M. Roth. Minneapolis, MN: Milkweed Editions.

Koss, M. P., T. E. Dinero, C. A. Seibel, and S. L. Cox. 1988. Stranger and acquaintance rape: Are there differences in the victim's experience? *Psychology of Women Quarterly* 12:1–24.

Koss, M. P., C. A. Gidycz, and N. Wisniewski. 1985. The scope of rape: Incidence and prevalence of sexual aggression and victimization in a national sample of higher education students. *Journal of Consulting and Clinical Psychology* 55:162–70.

LaPlante, M. N., N. McCormick, and G. G. Brannigan. 1980. Living the sexual script: College students' views of influence in sexual encounters. *Journal of Sex Research* 16:338–55.

Lisak, D., and S. Roth. 1988. Motivational factors in nonincarcerated sexually aggressive men. *Journal of Personality and Social Psychology* 55:795–802.

Malamuth, N. 1986. Predictors of naturalistic sexual aggression. *Journal of Personality and Social Psychology* 50:953–62.

Martin, P. Y., and R. Hummer. 1989. Fraternities and rape on campus. *Gender & Society* 3:457–73.

Miller, B., and J. C. Marshall. 1987. Coercive sex on the university campus. *Journal of College Student Personnel* 28:38–47.

Muehlenhard, C. L., and M. A. Linton. 1987. Date rape and sexual aggression in dating situations: Incidence and risk factors. *Journal of Counseling Psychology* 34:186–96.

O'Sullivan, C. 1993. Fraternities and the rape culture. In *Transforming a rape culture*, edited by E. Buchwald, P. R. Fletcher, and M. Roth. Minneapolis, MN: Milkweed Editions.

Peterson, S. A., and B. Franzese. 1987. Correlates of college men's sexual abuse of women. *Journal of College Student Personnel* 28:223–28.

Sanday, P. R. 1990. *Fraternity gang rape: Sex, brotherhood, and privilege on campus.* New York: New York University Press.

West, C., and D. Zimmerman. 1987. Doing gender. *Gender & Society* 1:125–51.

STUDY QUESTIONS

1. List the characteristics of the social settings where women are at risk and where they are safe.

2. What is meant by "rape culture," and how is this "culture" supported by men?

D. L. ROSENHAN

On Being Sane in Insane Places

If sanity and insanity exist, how shall we know them?

The question is neither capricious nor itself insane. However much we may be personally convinced that we can tell the normal from the abnormal, the evidence is simply not compelling. It is commonplace, for example, to read about murder trials wherein eminent psychiatrists for the defense are contradicted by equally eminent psychiatrists for the prosecution on the matter of the defendant's sanity. More generally, there are a great deal of conflicting data on the reliability, utility, and meaning of such terms as "sanity," "insanity," "mental illness," and "schizophrenia" (1). Finally, as early as 1934, Benedict suggested that normality and abnormality are not universal (2). What is viewed as normal in one culture may be seen as quite aberrant in another. Thus, notions of normality and abnormality may not be quite as accurate as people believe they are.

To raise questions regarding normality and abnormality is in no way to question the fact that some behaviors are deviant or odd. Murder is deviant. So, too, are hallucinations. Nor does raising such questions deny the existence of the personal anguish that is often associated with "mental illness." Anxiety and depression exist. Psychological suffering exists. But normality and abnormality, sanity and insanity, and the diagnoses that flow from them may be less substantive than many believe them to be.

At its heart, the question of whether the sane can be distinguished from the insane (and whether degrees of insanity can be distinguished from each other) is a simple matter: do the salient characteristics that lead to diagnoses reside in the patients themselves or in the environments and contexts in which observers find them? From Bleuler, through Kretchmer, through the formulators of the recently revised *Diagnostic and Statistical Manual* of the American Psychiatric Association, the belief has been strong that patients present symptoms, that those symptoms can be categorized, and, implicitly, that the sane are distinguishable from the insane. More recently, however, this belief has been questioned. Based in part on theoretical and anthropological considerations, but also on philosophical, legal, and therapeutic ones, the view has grown that psychological categorization of mental illness is useless at best and downright harmful, misleading, and pejorative at worst. Psychiatric diagnoses, in this view, are in the minds of the observers and are not valid summaries of characteristics displayed by the observed (3–5).

Gains can be made in deciding which of these is more nearly accurate by getting normal people (that is, people who do not have, and have never suffered, symptoms of serious psychiatric disorders) admitted to psychiatric hospitals and then determining whether they were discovered to be sane and, if so, how. If the sanity of such pseudopatients were always detected, there would be prima facie evidence that a sane individual can be distinguished from the insane context in which he is found. Normality (and presumably abnormality) is distinct enough that it can be recognized wherever it occurs, for it is carried within the person. If, on the other hand, the sanity of the pseudopatients were never discovered, serious difficulties would arise for those who support traditional modes of psychiatric diagnosis. Given that the hospital staff was not incompetent, that the pseudopatient had been behaving as sanely as he had been outside of the hospital, and that it had never been previously suggested that he belonged in a psychiatric hospital, such an unlikely outcome would support the view that psychiatric diagnosis betrays little about the patient but much about the environment in which an observer finds him.

This article describes such an experiment. Eight sane people gained secret admission to 12 different hospitals (6). Their diagnostic experiences constitute the data of the first part of this article; the remainder is devoted to a description of their experiences in psychiatric institutions. Too few psychiatrists and psychologists, even those who have worked in such hospitals, know what the experience is like. They rarely talk about it with former patients, perhaps because they distrust information coming from the previously insane. Those who have worked in psychiatric hospitals are likely to have adapted so thoroughly to the settings that they are insensitive to the impact of that experience. And while there have been occasional reports of researchers who submitted themselves to psychiatric hospitalization (7), these researchers have commonly remained in the hospitals for short periods of time, often with the knowledge of the hospital staff. It is difficult to know the extent to which they were treated like patients or like research colleagues. Nevertheless, their reports about the inside of the psychiatric hospital have been valuable. This article extends those efforts.

Pseudopatients and Their Settings

The eight pseudopatients were a varied group. One was a psychology graduate student in his 20's. The remaining seven were older and "established." Among them were three psychologists, a pediatrician, a psychiatrist, a painter, and a housewife. Three pseudopatients were women, five were men. All of them employed pseudonyms, lest their alleged diagnoses embarrass them later. Those who were in mental health professions alleged another occupation in order to avoid the special attentions that might be accorded by staff, as a matter of courtesy or caution, to ailing colleagues (8). With the exception of myself (I was the first pseudopatient and my presence was known to the hospital administrator and chief psychologist and, so far as I can tell, to them alone), the presence of pseudopatients and the nature of the research program was not known to the hospital staffs (9).

The settings were similarly varied. In order to generalize the findings, admission into a variety of hospitals was sought. The 12 hospitals in the sample were located in five different states on the East and West coasts. Some were old and shabby, some were quite new. Some were research-oriented, others not. Some had good staff-patient ratios, others were quite understaffed. Only one was a strictly private hospital. All of the others were supported by state or federal funds or, in one instance, by university funds.

After calling the hospital for an appointment, the pseudopatient arrived at the admissions office complaining that he had been hearing voices. Asked what the voices said, he replied that they were often unclear, but as far as he could tell they said "empty," "hollow," and "thud." The voices were unfamiliar and were of the same sex as the pseudopatient. The choice of these symptoms was occasioned by their apparent similarity to existential symptoms. Such symptoms are alleged to arise from painful concerns about the perceived meaninglessness of one's life. It is as if the hallucinating person were saying,

"My life is empty and hollow." The choice of these symptoms was also determined by the *absence* of a single report of existential psychoses in the literature.

Beyond alleging the symptoms and falsifying name, vocation, and employment, no further alterations of person, history, or circumstances were made. The significant events of the pseudopatient's life history were presented as they had actually occurred. Relationships with parents and siblings, with spouse and children, with people at work and in school, consistent with the aforementioned exceptions, were described as they were or had been. Frustrations and upsets were described along with joys and satisfactions. These facts are important to remember. If anything, they strongly biased the subsequent results in favor of detecting sanity, since none of their histories or current behaviors were seriously pathological in any way.

Immediately upon admission to the psychiatric ward, the pseudopatient ceased simulating *any* symptoms of abnormality. In some cases, there was a brief period of mild nervousness and anxiety, since none of the pseudopatients really believed that they would be admitted so easily. Indeed, their shared fear was that they would be immediately exposed as frauds and greatly embarrassed. Moreover, many of them had never visited a psychiatric ward; even those who had, nevertheless had some genuine fears about what might happen to them. Their nervousness, then, was quite appropriate to the novelty of the hospital setting, and it abated rapidly.

Apart from that short-lived nervousness, the pseudopatient behaved on the ward as he "normally" behaved. The pseudopatient spoke to patients and staff as he might ordinarily. Because there is uncommonly little to do on a psychiatric ward, he attempted to engage others in conversation. When asked by staff how he was feeling, he indicated that he was fine, that he no longer experienced symptoms. He responded to instructions from attendants, to calls for medication (which was not swallowed), and to dining-hall instructions. Beyond such activities as were available to him on the admissions ward, he spent his time writing down his observations about the ward, its patients, and the staff. Initially these notes were written "secretly," but as it soon became clear that no one much cared, they were subsequently written on standard tablets of paper in such public places as the dayroom. No secret was made of these activities.

The pseudopatient, very much as a true psychiatric patient, entered a hospital with no foreknowledge of when he would be discharged.

Each was told that he would have to get out by his own devices, essentially by convincing the staff that he was sane. The psychological stresses associated with hospitalization were considerable, and all but one of the pseudopatients desired to be discharged almost immediately after being admitted. They were, therefore, motivated not only to behave sanely, but to be paragons of cooperation. That their behavior was in no way disruptive is confirmed by nursing reports, which have been obtained on most of the patients. These reports uniformly indicate that the patients were "friendly," "cooperative," and "exhibited no abnormal indications."

The Normal Are Not Detectably Sane

Despite their public "show" of sanity, the pseudopatients were never detected. Admitted, except in one case, with a diagnosis of schizophrenia (10), each was discharged with a diagnosis of schizophrenia "in remission." The label "in remission" should in no way be dismissed as a formality, for at no time during any hospitalization had any question been raised about any pseudopatient's simulation. Nor are there any indications in the hospital records that the pseudopatient's status was suspect. Rather, the evidence is strong that, once labeled schizophrenic, the pseudopatient was stuck with that label. If the pseudopatient was to be discharged, he must naturally be "in remission"; but he was not sane, nor, in the institution's view, had he ever been sane.

The uniform failure to recognize sanity cannot be attributed to the quality of the hospitals, for, although there were considerable variations among them, several are considered excellent. Nor can it be alleged that there was simply not enough time to observe the pseudopatients. Length of hospitalization ranged from 7 to 52 days, with an average of 19 days. The pseudopatients were not, in fact, carefully observed, but this failure clearly speaks more to traditions within psychiatric hospitals than to lack of opportunity.

Finally, it cannot be said that the failure to recognize the pseudopatients' sanity was due to the fact that they were not behaving sanely. While there was clearly some tension present in all of them, their daily visitors could detect no serious behavioral consequences—nor, indeed, could other patients. It was quite common for the patients to "detect" the pseudopatients' sanity. During the first three hospitalizations, when accurate counts were kept, 35 of a total of 118 patients on the admissions ward voiced their suspicions, some vigorously. "You're not crazy. You're a journalist, or a professor [referring to the continual note-taking]. You're checking up on the hospital." While most of the patients were reassured by the pseudopatient's insistence that he had been sick before he came in but was fine now, some continued to believe that the pseudopatient was sane throughout his hospitalization (11). The fact that the patients often recognized normality when staff did not raises important questions.

Failure to detect sanity during the course of hospitalization may be due to the fact that physicians operate with a strong bias toward what statisticians call the type 2 error (5). This is to say that physicians are more inclined to call a healthy person sick (a false positive, type 2) than a sick person healthy (a false negative, type 1). The reasons for this are not hard to find: it is clearly more dangerous to misdiagnose illness than health. Better to err on the side of caution, to suspect illness even among the healthy.

But what holds for medicine does not hold equally well for psychiatry. Medical illnesses, while unfortunate, are not commonly pejorative. Psychiatric diagnoses, on the contrary, carry with them personal, legal, and social stigmas (12). It was therefore important to see whether the tendency toward diagnosing the sane insane could be reversed. The following experiment was arranged at a research and teaching hospital whose staff had heard these findings but doubted that such an error could occur in their hospital. The staff was informed that at some time during the following 3 months, one or more pseudopatients would attempt to be admitted into the psychiatric hospital. Each staff member was asked to rate each patient who presented himself at admissions or on the ward according to the likelihood that the patient was a pseudopatient. A 10-point scale was used, with a 1 and 2 reflecting high confidence that the patient was a pseudopatient.

Judgments were obtained on 193 patients who were admitted for psychiatric treatment. All staff who had had sustained contact with or primary responsibility for the patient—attendants, nurses, psychiatrists, physicians, and psychologists—were asked to make judgments. Forty-one patients were alleged, with high confidence, to be pseudopatients by at least one member of the staff. Twenty-three were considered suspect by at least one psychiatrist. Nineteen were suspected by one psychiatrist *and* one other staff member. Actually, no genuine pseudopatient (at least from my group) presented himself during this period.

The experiment is instructive. It indicates that the tendency to designate sane people as insane can be reversed when the stakes (in this case, prestige and diagnostic acumen) are high. But what can be said of the 19 people who were suspected of being "sane" by one psychiatrist and another staff member? Were these people truly "sane," or was it rather the case that in the course of avoiding the type 2 error the staff tended to make more errors of the first sort—calling the crazy "sane"? There is no way of knowing. But one thing is certain: any diagnostic process that lends itself so readily to massive errors of this sort cannot be a very reliable one.

The Stickiness of Psychodiagnostic Labels

Beyond the tendency to call the healthy sick—a tendency that accounts better for diagnostic behavior on admission than it does for such behavior after a lengthy period of exposure—the data speak to the massive role of labeling in psychiatric assessment. Having once been labeled schizophrenic, there is nothing the pseudopatient can do to overcome the tag. The tag profoundly colors others' perceptions of him and his behavior.

From one viewpoint, these data are hardly surprising, for it has long been known that elements are given meaning by the context in which they occur. Gestalt psychology made this point vigorously, and Asch (13) demonstrated that there are "central" personality traits (such as "warm" versus "cold") which are so powerful that they markedly color the meaning of other information in forming an impression of a given personality (14). "Insane," "schizophrenic," "manic-depressive," and "crazy" are probably among the most powerful of such central traits. Once a person is designated abnormal, all of his other behaviors and characteristics are colored by that label. Indeed, that label is so powerful that many of the pseudopatients' normal behaviors were overlooked entirely or profoundly misinterpreted. Some examples may clarify this issue.

Earlier I indicated that there were no changes in the pseudopatients' personal history and current status beyond those of name, employment, and, where necessary, vocation. Otherwise, a veridical description of personal history and circumstances was offered. Those circumstances were not psychotic. How were they made consonant with the diagnosis of psychosis? Or were those diagnoses modified in such a way as to bring them into accord with the circumstances of the pseudopatient's life, as described by him?

As far as I can determine, diagnoses were in no way affected by the relative health of the circumstances of a pseudopatient's life. Rather, the reverse occurred: the perception of his circumstances was shaped entirely by the diagnosis. A clear example of such translation is found in the case of a pseudopatient who had had a close relationship with his mother but was rather remote from his father during his early childhood. During adolescence and beyond, however, his father became a close friend, while his relationship with his mother cooled. His present relationship with his wife was characteristically close and warm. Apart from occasional angry exchanges, friction was minimal. The children had rarely been spanked. Surely there is nothing especially pathological about such a history. Indeed, many readers may see a similar pattern in their own experiences, with no markedly deleterious consequences. Observe, however, how such a history was translated in the psychopathological context, this from the case summary prepared after the patient was discharged.

> *This white 39-year-old male . . . manifests a long history of considerable ambivalence in close relationships, which begins in early childhood. A warm relationship with his mother cools during his adolescence. A distant relationship to his father is described as becoming very intense. Affective stability is absent. His attempts to control emotionality with his wife and children are punctuated by angry outbursts and, in the case of the children, spankings. And while he says that he has several good friends, one senses considerable ambivalence embedded in those relationships also. . . .*

The facts of the case were unintentionally distorted by the staff to achieve consistency with a popular theory of the dynamics of a schizophrenic reaction (15). Nothing of an ambivalent nature had been described in relations with parents, spouse, or friends. To the extent that ambivalence could be inferred, it was probably not greater than is found in all human relationships. It is true the pseudopatient's relationships with his parents changed over time, but in the ordinary context that would hardly be remarkable—indeed, it might very well be expected. Clearly, the meaning ascribed to his verbalizations (that is, ambivalence, affective instability) was determined by the diagnosis: schizophrenia. An entirely different meaning would have been ascribed if it were known that the man was "normal."

All pseudopatients took extensive notes publicly. Under ordinary circumstances, such behavior would have raised questions in the minds of observers, as, in fact, it did among patients. Indeed, it seemed so certain that the notes would elicit suspicion that elaborate precautions were taken to remove them from the ward each day. But the precautions proved needless. The closest any staff member came to questioning these notes occurred when one pseudopatient asked his physician what kind of medication he was receiving and began to write down the response. "You needn't write it," he was told gently. "If you have trouble remembering, just ask me again."

If no questions were asked of the pseudopatients, how was their writing interpreted? Nursing records for three patients indicate that the writing was seen as an aspect of their pathological behavior. "Patient engages in writing behavior" was the daily nursing comment on one of the pseudopatients who was never questioned about his writing. Given that the patient is in the hospital, he must be psychologically disturbed. And given that he is disturbed, continuous writing must be a behavioral manifestation of that disturbance, perhaps a subset of the compulsive behaviors that are sometimes correlated with schizophrenia.

One tacit characteristic of psychiatric diagnosis is that it locates the sources of aberration within the individual and only rarely within the complex of stimuli that surrounds him. Consequently, behaviors that are stimulated by the environment are commonly misattributed to the patient's disorder. For example, one kindly nurse found a pseudopatient pacing the long hospital corridors. "Nervous, Mr. X?" she asked. "No, bored," he said.

The notes kept by pseudopatients are full of patient behaviors that were misinterpreted by well-intentioned staff. Often enough, a patient would go "berserk" because he had, wittingly or unwittingly, been mistreated by, say, an attendant. A nurse coming upon the scene would rarely inquire even cursorily into the environmental stimuli of the patient's behavior. Rather, she assumed that his upset derived from his pathology, not from his present interactions with other staff members. Occasionally, the staff might assume that the patient's family (especially when they had recently visited) or other patients had stimulated the outburst. But never were the staff found to assume that one of themselves or the structure of the hospital had anything to do with a patient's behavior. One psychiatrist pointed to a group of patients who were sitting outside the cafeteria entrance half an hour before lunchtime. To a group of young residents he indicated that such behavior was characteristic of the oral-acquisitive nature of the syndrome. It seemed not to occur to him that there were very few things to anticipate in a psychiatric hospital besides eating.

A psychiatric label has a life and an influence of its own. Once the impression has been formed that the patient is schizophrenic, the expectation is that he will continue to be schizophrenic. When a sufficient amount of time has passed, during which the patient has done nothing bizarre, he is considered to be in remission and available for discharge. But the label endures beyond discharge, with the unconfirmed expectation that he will behave as a schizophrenic again. Such labels, conferred by mental health professionals, are as influential on the patient as they are on his relatives and friends, and it should not surprise anyone that the diagnosis acts on all of them as a self-fulfilling prophecy. Eventually, the patient himself accepts the diagnosis, with all of its surplus meanings and expectations, and behaves accordingly (5).

The inferences to be made from these matters are quite simple. Much as Zigler and Phillips have demonstrated that there is enormous overlap in the symptoms presented by patients who have been variously diagnosed (16), so there is enormous overlap in the behaviors of the sane and the insane. The sane are not "sane" all of the time. We lose our tempers "for no good reason." We are occasionally depressed or anxious, again for no good reason. And we may find it difficult to get along with one or another person—again for no reason that we can specify. Similarly, the insane are not always insane. Indeed, it was the impression of the pseudopatients while living with them that they were sane for long periods of time—that the bizarre behaviors upon which their diagnoses were allegedly predicated constituted only a small fraction of their total behavior. If it makes no sense to label ourselves permanently depressed on the basis of an occasional depression, then it takes better evidence than is presently available to label all patients insane or schizophrenic on the basis of bizarre behaviors or cognitions. It seems more useful, as Mischel (17) has pointed out, to limit our discussions to *behaviors*, the stimuli that provoke them, and their correlates.

It is not known why powerful impressions of personality traits, such as "crazy" or "insane," arise. Conceivably, when the origins of and stimuli that give rise to a behavior are remote or unknown, or when the behavior strikes us as immutable, trait labels regarding the *behaver* arise. When, on the other hand, the origins and stimuli are known and available, discourse is limited to the behavior itself. Thus, I may hallucinate because

I am sleeping, or I may hallucinate because I have ingested a peculiar drug. These are termed sleep-induced hallucinations, or dreams, and drug-induced hallucinations, respectively. But when the stimuli to my hallucinations are unknown, that is called craziness, or schizophrenia—as if that inference were somehow as illuminating as the others. . . .

The Consequences of Labeling and Depersonalization

Whenever the ratio of what is known to what needs to be known approaches zero, we tend to invent "knowledge" and assume that we understand more than we actually do. We seem unable to acknowledge that we simply don't know. The needs for diagnosis and remediation of behavioral and emotional problems are enormous. But rather than acknowledge that we are just embarking on understanding, we continue to label patients "schizophrenic," "manic-depressive," and "insane," as if in those words we had captured the essence of understanding. The facts of the matter are that we have known for a long time that diagnoses are often not useful or reliable, but we have nevertheless continued to use them. We now know that we cannot distinguish insanity from sanity. It is depressing to consider how that information will be used.

Not merely depressing, but frightening. How many people, one wonders, are sane but not recognized as such in our psychiatric institutions? How many have been needlessly stripped of their privileges of citizenship, from the right to vote and drive to that of handling their own accounts? How many have feigned insanity in order to avoid the criminal consequences of their behavior, and, conversely, how many would rather stand trial than live interminably in a psychiatric hospital—but are wrongly thought to be mentally ill? How many have been stigmatized by well-intentioned, but nevertheless erroneous, diagnoses? On the last point, recall again that a "type 2 error" in psychiatric diagnosis does not have the same consequences it does in medical diagnosis. A diagnosis of cancer that has been found to be in error is cause for celebration. But psychiatric diagnoses are rarely found to be in error. The label sticks, a mark of inadequacy forever.

Finally, how many patients might be "sane" outside the psychiatric hospital but seem insane in it—not because craziness resides in them, as it were, but because they are responding to a bizarre setting, one that may be unique to institutions which harbor nether people? Goffman (4) calls the process of socialization to such institutions "mortification"— an apt metaphor that includes the processes of depersonalization that have been described here. And while it is impossible to know whether the pseudopatients' responses to these processes are characteristic of all inmates—they were, after all, not real patients—it is difficult to believe that these processes of socialization to a psychiatric hospital provide useful attitudes or habits of response for living in the "real world."

Summary and Conclusions

It is clear that we cannot distinguish the sane from the insane in psychiatric hospitals. The hospital itself imposes a special environment in which the meanings of behavior can easily be misunderstood. The consequences to patients hospitalized in such an environment—the powerlessness, depersonalization, segregation, mortification, and self-labeling—seem undoubtedly countertherapeutic. . . .

I and the other pseudopatients in the psychiatric setting had distinctly negative reactions. We do not pretend to describe the subjective experiences of true patients. Theirs may be different from ours, particularly with the passage of time and the necessary process of adaptation to one's environment. But we can and do speak to the relatively more objective indices of treatment within the hospital. It could be a mistake, and a very unfortunate one, to consider that what happened to us derived from malice or stupidity on the part of the staff. Quite the contrary, our overwhelming impression of them was of people who really cared, who were committed and who were uncommonly intelligent. Where they failed, as they sometimes did painfully, it would be more accurate to attribute those failures to the environment in which they, too, found themselves than to personal callousness. Their perceptions and behavior were controlled by the situation, rather than being motivated by a malicious disposition. In a more benign environment, one that was less attached to global diagnosis, their behaviors and judgments might have been more benign and effective.

REFERENCES AND NOTES

1. P. Ash, J. Abnorm. Soc. Psychol. 44, 272 (1949); A. T. Beck, Amer. J. Psychiat. 119, 210 (1962); A. T. Boisen, Psychiatry 2, 233 (1938); N. Kreitman, J. Ment. Sci. 107, 876 (1961); N. Kreitman, P. Sainsbury, J. Morrisey, J. Towers, J. Scrivener, ibid., p. 887; H. O. Schmitt and C. P. Fonda,

J. Abnorm. Soc. Psychol. 52, 262 (1956); W. Seaman, *J. Nerv. Ment. Dis.* 118, 541 (1953). For an analysis of these artifacts and summaries of the disputes, see J. Zubin, *Annu. Rev. Psychol.* 18, 373 (1967); L. Phillips and J. G., Draguns, *ibid.* 22, 447 (1971).

2. R. Benedict, *J. Gen. Psychol.* 10, 59 (1934).

3. See in this regard H. Becker, *Outsiders: Studies in the Sociology of Deviance* (Free Press, New York, 1963); B. M. Braginsky, D. D. Braginsky, K. Ring, *Methods of Madness: The Mental Hospital as a Last Resort* (Holt, Rinehart & Winston, New York, 1969); G. M. Crocetti and P. V. Lemkau, *Amer. Social. Rev.* 30, 577 (1965); E. Goffman, *Behavior in Public Places* (Free Press, New York, 1964); R. D. Laing, *The Divided Self: A Study of Sanity and Madness* (Quadrangle, Chicago, 1960); D. L. Phillips, *Amer. Social. Rev.* 28, 963 (1963); T. R. Sarbin, *Psychol. Today* 6, 18 (1972); E. Schur, *Amer. J. Social.* 75, 309 (l969); T. Szasz, *Law, Liberty and Psychiatry* (Macmillan, New York, 1963); *The Myth of Mental Illness: Foundations of a Theory of Mental Illness* (Hoeber-Harper, New York, 1963). For a critique of some of these views, see W. R. Gove, *Amer. Social. Rev.* 35, 873 (1970).

4. E. Goffman, *Asylums* (Doubleday, Garden City, N.Y., 1961).

5. T. J. Scheff, *Being Mentally Ill: A Sociological Theory* (Aldine, Chicago, 1966).

6. Data from a ninth pseudopatient are not incorporated in this report because, although his sanity went undetected, he falsified aspects of his personal history, including his marital status and parental relationships. His experimental behaviors therefore were not identical to those of the other pseudopatients.

7. A. Barry, *Bellevue Is a State of Mind* (Harcourt Brace Jovanovich, New York, 1971); I. Belknap, *Human Problems of a State Mental Hospital* (McGraw-Hill, New York, 1956); W. Caudill, F. C. Redlich, H. R. Gilmore, E. B. Brody, *Amer. J. Orthopsychiat.* 22, 314 (1952); A. R. Goldman, R. H. Bohr, T. A. Steinberg, *Prof. Psychol.* 1, 427 (1970); unauthored, *Roche Report* 1 (No. 13), 8 (1971).

8. Beyond the personal difficulties that the pseudopatient is likely to experience in the hospital, there are legal and social ones that, combined, require considerable attention before entry. For example, once admitted to a psychiatric institution, it is difficult, if not impossible, to be discharged on short notice, state law to the contrary notwithstanding. I was not sensitive to these difficulties at the outset of the project, nor to the personal and situational emergencies that can arise, but later a writ of habeas corpus was prepared for each of the entering pseudopatients and an attorney was kept "on call" during every hospitalization. I am grateful to John Kaplan and Robert Bartels for legal advice and assistance in these matters.

9. However distasteful such concealment is, it was a necessary first step to examining these questions. Without concealment, there would have been no way to know how valid these experiences were; nor was there any way of knowing whether whatever detections occurred were a tribute to the diagnostic acumen of the staff or to the hospial's rumor network. Obviously, since my concerns are general ones that cut across individual hospitals and staffs, I have respected their anonymity and have eliminated clues that might lead to their identification.

10. Interestingly, of the 12 admissions, 11 were diagnosed as schizophrenic and one, with an identical symptomatology, as manic-depressive psychosis. This diagnosis has a more favorable prognosis, and it was given by the only private hospital in our sample. On the relations between social class and psychiatric diagnosis, see A. deB. Hollingshead and F. C. Redlich, *Social Class and Mental Illness: A Community Study* (Wiley, New York, 1958).

11. It is possible, of course, that patients have quite broad latitudes in diagnosis and therefore are inclined to call many people sane, even those whose behavior is patently aberrant. However, although we have no hard data on this matter, it was our distinct impression that this was not the case. In many instances, patients not only singled us out for attention, but came to imitate our behaviors and styles.

12. J. Cumming and E. Cumming, *Community Ment. Health* 1, 135 (1965); A. Farina and K. Ring. *J. Abnorm. Psychol.* 70, 47 (1965); H. E. Freeman and O. G. Simmons, *The Mental Patient Comes Home* (Wiley, New York, 1963); W. J. Johannsen, *Ment. Hygiene* 53, 218 (1969); A. S. Linsky, *Soc. Psychiat.* 5, 166 (1970).

13. S. E. Asch, *J. Abnorm. Soc. Psychol.* 41, 258 (1946); *Social Psychology* (Prentice-Hall, New York, 1952).

14. See also I. N. Mensh and J. Wishner, *J. Personality* 16, 188 (1947); J. Wishner, *Psychol. Rev.* 67, 96 (1960); J. S. Bruner and R. Tagiuri, in *Handbook of Social Psychology*, G. Lindzey. Ed.

(Addison-Wesley, Cambridge, Mass., 1954), vol. 2, pp. 634–654; J. S. Bruner, D. Shapiro, R. Tagiuri, in *Person Perception and Interpersonal Behavior*, R. Tagiuri and L. Petrullo, Eds. (Stanford Univ. Press, Stanford, Calif., 1958), pp. 277–288.

15. For an example of a similar self-fulfilling prophecy, in this instance dealing with the "central" trait of intelligence, see R. Rosenthal and L. Jacobson, *Pygmalion in the Classroom* (Holt, Rinehart & Winston, New York, 1968).

16. E. Zigler and L. Phillips, *J. Abnorm. Soc. Psychol.* 63, 69 (1961). See also R. K. Freudenberg and J. P. Robertson, *A.M.A. Arch. Neurol. Psychiatr.* 76, 14 (1956).

17. W. Mischel, *Personality and Assessment* (Wiley, New York, 1968).

STUDY QUESTIONS

1. Rosenhan and his colleagues faked their way into a mental institution with symptoms. Why was this so easy?

2. If a person really was mistakenly sent to a mental hospital, what processes discussed in the article would keep them from getting out?

PART THREE

Social Inequalities

TOPIC 8

Social Class

SOCIAL STRATIFICATION SYSTEMS CREATE "LAYERS" OF people in society based on the unequal distribution of scarce rewards. Social classes are the relative position of people based on such things as income, education, and occupation. Less tangible, but no less important, is the role of prestige or how people rank the relative importance of others. This is often based on occupation, and a person who owns a garbage truck and collects trash may make more money than a college professor, but the professor has more prestige. Complex measures of class tell us about the juxtaposition of persons and groups of persons based on these criteria. People who share the same position in the social stratification system comprise a social class. Social class determines a great deal about our lives; such as where we live, where we shop, the sort of car we drive, political values, and even the colleges we attend. From the super rich to the very poor, life chances are dramatically affected by the economic and social resources available to us.

The economic dimension of American life is undergoing some fascinating changes. First, it is abundantly clear that "the rich are getting richer, and the poor are getting poorer." More wealth and more income are being concentrated in fewer and fewer people at the very top of the class system. There is evidence that this is occurring throughout the world as well. From the middle-class downward in the class system, where the majority of the people are, income and assets are becoming scarcer. At the same time, large corporations are receiving benefits from local, state, and federal governments in the forms of tax breaks that some call "corporate welfare." Second, the structure of labor markets in the United States is changing as well. In the post-industrial age, there are fewer skilled labor jobs with higher wages and many more service jobs with lower wages. An $8.00 per hour job, worked for 40 hours per week and 50 weeks, would return $16,000 in wages for the year—just about the poverty line for a family of four in the United States. As we know, many people work for less than that. Hence, the standard of living of many in the United States is being affected by the transformation of labor markets in our own country.

A persistent problem in America, as well as the world, is poverty. Nearly one in six Americans live in economic conditions that directly affect diet, health, education, personal development, crime victimization, and so on. When we look at children, these percentages move toward one in four. Being raised in poverty, living in substandard housing, and missing needed medical care mean that life is burdened by inequalities. The economics of poverty "costs" more than the poor, as America creates and funds programs to relieve the circumstances of lower-class lifestyles. The poor and the near-poor struggle with everyday events (hunger, no personal transportation, illness), which the rest of the class structure rarely notice. Indeed, it may seem as though we do live in "separate worlds."

The three readings in this topic are designed to look at sociological observations on poverty, the upper class, and blue-collar life. The first reading is by Stephan J. Goetz and Hema Swaminathan, who researched the impact of placing a Wal-Mart store in a community, showing how employers who pay low wages and provide minimal health benefits actually increase the poverty rate in counties. Wal-Mart, as a universal symbol for U.S. prosperity and consumption, when brought under sociological investigation, can actually have a negative impact on regional economics. The second reading, by Stephen Haseler, takes us to the other end of the social class spectrum and discusses the wealth and lifestyle of the world's billionaires. This is a fascinating look at a small group of the world's wealthiest who are living in ways that give them more power than entire, sovereign nations. Finally, a university president, John R. Coleman, takes a sabbatical and enters blue-collar life—quite a change in status and activity. Here, another professional uses biographical experience to produce an ethnography of the working class and let us know about the contradictions in upper-middle and blue-collar work.

STEPHAN J. GOETZ AND HEMA SWAMINATHAN

Wal-Mart and County-Wide Poverty

Local leaders and academic researchers are increasingly interested in the community-level effects of "big box" retailers and discount department stores. Wal-Mart, in particular, has received considerable and mostly negative public media and congressional attention, in addition to spawning a number of hostile websites.[1] The interest in Wal-Mart is not surprising as it has no equal among big box retailers. With total revenues of $256 billion in 2003, Wal-Mart Stores Inc. is the largest corporation in the world. The chain employs 1.3 million workers worldwide and operates 4,750 stores (3,600 in the United States). Because of its size, purchasing power, and technological sophistication, the chain is revolutionizing not only the industrial organization of local retail trade, but also the entire wholesale, transportation, and logistics sector. *Business Week* recently described the "Wal-Mart effect" in a cover story,[2] referring to the corporation's cost efficiency that has contributed to economy-wide productivity gains and reduced the annual rate of inflation by about one percentage point. On the other hand, Wal-Mart has been blamed for the loss of U.S. manufacturing jobs and the demise of mom-and-pop-type retailers.

This study examines the impact of Wal-Mart stores on county-level family-poverty rates in the United States. The analysis is relevant to local policymakers as they debate the pros and cons of having Wal-Mart and other "big box" retailers locate in their communities. The attraction of such retailers has been viewed as a strategy for stimulating local economic growth (e.g., Ketchum and Hughes, 1997). However, retail stores have a much smaller net economic impact on local economies than do manufacturing firms, for example. In particular, retail stores are usually part of what economists call the nonbasic sector, which exists solely to serve the so-called *basic* sector. The basic sector commonly includes agriculture, mining, and manufacturing, and it is responsible for exporting goods and services that bring "new money" into a community. As this new money is spent and respent in the community, economic growth occurs. Although important (because it supports the basic sector), the nonbasic sector does not play this role of bringing in new money and it therefore makes a much smaller contribution to local economic growth over time than does the basic sector.

Wal-Mart and Poverty

There are a number of possible reasons why the presence of a Wal-Mart store may exert an independent effect on poverty rates in a community, that is, exert a residual effect after other determinants of poverty have been taken into account. The first and perhaps most direct effect is the demise of existing mom-and-pop-type operations that is caused by the arrival of Wal-Mart in a community. We hypothesize that this in turn may have a number of consequences.

Poverty rates will rise if retail workers displaced from existing mom-and-pop-type operations work for Wal-Mart at lower wages because they have no alternatives (this assertion has been contested in the literature), all else equal. Although Wal-Mart is estimated to employ no more than 2 percent of the average county's workforce, there is at least anecdotal evidence that the arrival of the chain also forces other local retailers to reduce wages in order to remain competitive. Also, the share of Wal-Mart's employment in total county retail jobs is substantially greater than only 2 percent. In addition, the Wal-Mart jobs may be part time as opposed to full time, leading to lower family incomes, all else equal.

A perhaps more profound effect, and one that has not been discussed in the literature, is that the demise of mom-and-pop stores leads to the closing of local businesses that previously supplied those stores: wholesalers, transporters, logistics providers, accountants, lawyers, and others. Many of these are higher-paying jobs. Wal-Mart handles all or most of these service functions through its headquarters in Bentonville, Arkansas, providing tremendous labor-saving scale economies. This consolidation and rationalization of the local retail supply chain potentially devastates local labor markets in smaller communities. As a reviewer pointed out, it is unlikely that the incomes of lawyers, bankers, and accountants who provided services to the local stores fall below the poverty line after the chain store's arrival. However, it is likely that these more highly-educated individuals depart from the rural community in pursuit of better opportunities elsewhere, contributing to the rural-to-urban exodus over the last decade, leaving behind those with fewer opportunities and raising the poverty rate by reducing the number of nonpoor households in the denominator.

It may not be desirable or even possible to stop these trends, but it is important to be aware of and understand them. In the future, with the introduction of radio frequency identification (RFID) tags, Wal-Mart is poised to become even more efficient in deploying workers in the stores themselves.[3] A reduced demand for workers in specific communities translates into lower wages (with minimum wages serving as a floor) if the supply of workers remains constant.

Even though Wal-Mart presents itself as a "good local citizen" and engaged in local philanthropy though the Sam Walton Foundation in the amount of $106.9 million in 2003 alone,[4] this type of philanthropy may not be as extensive or effective as that which the displaced mom-and-pop-type stores would have provided. A perhaps more subtle effect may be that by destroying the local class of entrepreneurs, the Wal-Mart chain also destroys local leadership capacity. Rural sociologists and others have pointed to this as one outcome of the increasing concentration of nonlocal bank ownership and the resulting branch plant economy that is believed to have destroyed the pool of local leadership talent.

The destruction of small, locally owned businesses may also reduce social capital levels, as argued, for example, by Cornell University's T. Lyson (Personal Communication, 2002). Social capital, or civic capacity, is an essential ingredient for economic growth to occur, according to Harvard University's Robert Putnam and, more recently, Skinner and Staiger (2005), who show that this variable is even more important than certain economic factors in explaining why some regions lag behind others. This elimination of local leaders as a key group of entrepreneurs may be the single most important and far-reaching impact of Wal-Mart Corp.

In summary, detractors have consistently argued that because Wal-Mart jobs are low paying, and the hours worked are often less than 40 per week, these jobs do not help families transition out of poverty. *BusinessWeek* reports that the average wage for an "associate" in 2001 was $8.23 per hour, for an annual income of $13,861, which was below the federal poverty line for a family of three at that time. Although individual workers have the option of working or not working for Wal-Mart, a public policy issue arises if the chain creates externalities that raise poverty levels in the community. In that case, both the demand for and eligibility to participate in welfare programs increase, leading not only to new claims on tax dollars but also a dis-utility for those who are concerned about poor people living in their community. The Wal-Mart phenomenon is such that the chain seeks to minimize its workers' pay, while the rents captured by the Walton heirs place them among the 10 wealthiest Americans.[5]

Two important issues arise here. First, even if Wal-Mart raises poverty rates, it also lowers prices to consumers (at least in the short run), thereby in effect lowering the real poverty threshold. It should be noted, however, that the poverty rate is inflation adjusted, so this beneficial effect of the chain is already reflected in the poverty rate measured at any point in time. If the winners can compensate the losers, then the presence of a Wal-Mart store is still Pareto optimal. We are not able to address this question in the present study. Second, the increased cost to taxpayers resulting from the increased eligibility for welfare payments (caused by Wal-Mart) needs to be added to any other subsidies that the chain may receive in exchange for opening a store, such as infrastructure improvements. These subsidies are dollar-for-dollar transfers to the corporation's bottom line.

The Impact of Wal-Mart: Previous Literature

Popular press articles on Wal-Mart focus on the company's nonunionization policy and the provision of part-time jobs with low wages and few benefits, along with impacts on the environment, congestion, and crime rate (see footnote 1). In the academic literature, considerable attention has also been paid to retail restructuring caused by the chain (e.g., Artz and McConnon, 2001; Stone 1997; Franklin, 2001; Huang et al., 2002), usually focusing on loss of retail employment, decreases in the number of establishments, and decline of downtown shopping areas. However, with some exceptions (e.g., Vias, in press), these articles are based on case studies for specific states or on anecdotal evidence. There are no academic studies that examine the impact of Wal-Mart on county-wide family-poverty rates, or contemporaneous changes in those rates over time. Likewise, we were unable to locate any econometric study of Wal-Mart's location strategy at the level of all U.S. counties (Graff, 1998 describes Wal-Mart Supercenter locations relative to locations of distribution centers and county populations).

Basker's path-breaking study examines the effect of Wal-Mart expansions on retail employment in 1,749 counties over a 23-year period and concludes (2002:19) "that Wal-Mart entry has a small positive effect on retail employment at the county level while reducing the number of small retail establishments in the county." Basker also finds small reductions in wholesale employment and no effect in those sectors in which the chain does not sell goods or services (specifically, restaurants and motor vehicle sales and services). On balance, she concludes that a decade after a Wal-Mart store's entry into a community (2002:17), "the estimated effect on total [county] employment . . . is statistically zero." Basker's work has two potential shortcomings, however: the use of a limited set of counties (truncated at employment levels above 1,500 in 1964, which may have eliminated some of the most interesting counties), and the choice only of employment as an impact measure (albeit an important one). Given the data with which she was working, Basker also was unable to distinguish between full- and part-time employment.

Hicks and Wilburn (2001) evaluate the effect of Wal-Mart stores on the retail trade sector in both the county in which the store is located and in adjacent counties in southern West Virginia using spatial analysis. They control for potential reverse causation (endogeneity) between population growth and entrance of Wal-Mart, but this raises the question of whether population growth is even a factor in Wal-Mart's location strategy (see also Franklin, 2001). Hicks and Wilburn cite the work of Vance and Scott (1992), who argued that the costs of a Wal-Mart were not as high as the benefits. Hicks and Wilburn conclude (2001:312) that there "is clearly a net benefit to employment and wages in having a Wal-Mart locate in a county." Furthermore, they note (2001:313) that "the criticisms leveled against Wal-Mart are a familiar refrain . . . [and that] local monopolies may have a great deal to lose from entrance by firms that enjoy, and exploit, economies of scale." As already noted, these conclusions are based on results from a specific region in a single state.

Ketchum and Hughes (1997) studied Wal-Mart's effects on employment and wages in Maine and failed to find support for the claim made by Wal-Mart's opponents that the entry of the firm harms local economic growth because of a negative effect on wages, employment levels, or the number of retail establishments. In their subsequent study of 19 communities in Maine that received a Wal-Mart between 1992 and 1995, Artz and McConnon (2001:24) find that the introduction of a Wal-Mart store leads to "significant changes in retail market structure" both in the town hosting the store and in adjacent communities. In his study of rural Iowa counties, Stone (1997) concludes that no single recent phenomenon has had a larger adverse impact on rural Iowa communities than mass discount merchandisers (i.e., Wal-Mart). As noted, all these studies are limited in that they focus on data from only a few counties or individual states. None focuses on county-wide poverty rates.

Estimation Strategy, Hypotheses, and Data

Our estimation strategy is simple and yet provides a relatively powerful test of the independent effect of Wal-Mart on changes in poverty rates in a community. The strategy is also innovative in that we correct for likely simultaneity (reverse causation) in the phenomenon of which we are trying to measure the impact—that is, the new Wal-Mart stores—using a common two-stage procedure that is based on instrumental variables (IV) estimation. In other words, it could be that Wal-Mart locates in communities that are poor because poverty is a widely claimed characteristic of their shoppers, or the communities are poor because Wal-Mart is located in them. . . .

In terms of the variables included in the store location, we hypothesize that Wal-Mart locates its stores in counties with a high retail pull factor, interstate highway access, more female-headed households and female labor force participation (to have a larger pool of workers), longer commuting times to work (which increase the opportunity cost of time spent shopping), more purchasing power as reflected in earnings and educational attainment, and that it avoids communities with existing Wal-Mart stores. By including the initial poverty rate, we also are able to test empirically whether Wal-Mart is drawn into communities with higher poverty rates.

In addition, we hypothesize that communities with higher levels of social capital, greater political competition, and more self-employed workers are better able to organize to prevent Wal-Mart stores from locating in their communities. Wal-Mart avoids counties with higher population density (at least until recently) in part because of higher land costs in these counties, and while the chain has traditionally located in rural communities, it also avoids sparsely populated, more remote places. We include state fixed effects to, among other factors, capture differences in state policy and population growth rates that may affect Wal-Mart's location strategy. . . .

Results: Discussion

The retail pull factor, existing Wal-Mart stores, adults with a college degree, social capital stocks, self-employment, interstate highway access, commuting time, and earnings power each have the expected signs and are statistically significant at below 1 percent level. The effect of population density is negative, all else equal and as expected.

In terms of state fixed effects, the following states had more new Wal-Mart stores (relative to Wyoming): Arizona, California, Florida, Indiana, Iowa, Maine, Massachusetts, Michigan, Minnesota, New Hampshire, North Carolina, Ohio, Oregon, Pennsylvania, Utah, West Virginia, and Wisconsin. Especially noteworthy is the absence of Nevada from this list, despite the fact that no state experienced more rapid population growth in relative terms over the period studied. In contrast, Pennsylvania is one of the slowest-growing states in the nation, and yet it attracted a number of stores. From this we conclude that rapid population growth may not be a prerequisite for the Wal-Mart Corporation to locate new stores.

We next turn to our . . . primary interest, the change in the poverty rate.[6] Holding constant the initial (1989) poverty rate, the results show that counties with more Wal-Mart stores (in 1987) had a higher poverty rate in 1999 (or a smaller reduction in the rate) than did counties with fewer or no Wal-Mart stores in 1987. Equally important, counties in which new Wal-Mart stores were built between 1987 and 1998 also experienced higher poverty rates, ceteris paribus. The marginal effect of another Wal-Mart store on the average poverty rate was 0.204, while that of each existing store was 0.099 percentage points.

These results have potentially profound implications for public policy related to big box operations. In particular, the chain is not the engine of local economic growth that the company's spokespersons and public relations materials suggest. It is of no small consequence that, after controlling for other determinants of changes in poverty rates, residual variation remains in the dependent variable that can be accounted for by the presence of Wal-Mart stores, and this at a statistically significant level. . . .

The public costs that the chain imposes by raising the poverty rate suggest that public infrastructure subsidies may not be warranted or, as a minimum, that these two types of costs need to be added together to assess the overall cost of the chain to a community. The question remains for future research of how these effects on poverty operate through one or all of the six factors identified above. Our analysis does not allow us to determine the relative importance of these factors in explaining the results. Even so, we believe that both in terms of substance and policy relevance, a focus in future work on the effect of big boxes on local social capital and civic capacity has the potential to generate the largest payoffs. . . . diversity, less political competition, smaller self-employment rates, and lower levels of social capital each were associated with smaller reductions in poverty rates over the decade, as hypothesized. . . .

Finally, we discuss shortcomings of our work as suggestions for areas of improvement in future endeavors. As noted by a reviewer, our study involves only two points in time (although our data represent events and processes that occurred over an entire decade); we do not measure the size of the Wal-Mart store (e.g., there are differences between Supercenters and regular stores); and we are forced to concentrate on only a single chain—Wal-Mart—rather than examining the effects of all big boxes. To the extent that Wal-Mart is the industry pacesetter, however, this appears to be reasonable. As noted above, and this is one innovation of our work, we do control for the effect of stores on neighboring counties using spatial econometric methods.

Summary and Conclusion

After carefully and comprehensively accounting for other local determinants of changes in poverty, we find that the presence of Wal-Mart was unequivocally associated with smaller reductions in family-poverty rates in U.S. counties during the 1990s relative to places that had no stores. This was true not only in terms of existing stores in a county in 1987, but also an independent outcome of new stores built between 1987 and 1998. The question of whether the cost of relatively higher poverty in a county is offset by the benefits of lower prices and wider choices available to consumers associated with a Wal-Mart store cannot be answered here.

However, if Wal-Mart does contribute to a higher poverty rate, then it is not bearing the full economic and social costs of its business practices. Instead, Wal-Mart transfers income from the working poor and from taxpayers, though welfare programs directed at the poor, to stockholders and the heirs of the Wal-Mart fortune, as well as to consumers. These transfers are in addition to the public infrastructure subsidies often provided by local communities. Regardless of the distributional effects, the empirical evidence shows that the Wal-Mart business model extracts cumulative rents that exceed those earned by owners of other corporations, including Microsoft and Home Depot.

In conclusion, the costs to communities in terms of labor displacement and higher poverty need to be weighed against the benefits of lower prices and greater shopping convenience. Similarly, once local businesses have been driven out, the possibility of monopolies or oligopolies emerging in retailing (both on the input and the output side) needs to be considered carefully by public policymakers.[7]

NOTES

1. A prominent example is (www.walmartwatch.com); bumper stickers include "SprawlMart sucks the life out of downtown businesses." Other negative coverage includes a recent report that the chain was fined $3.1 million by the EPA for violating for the second time the Clean Water Act by failing to control runoff from its construction sites (*Salt Lake Tribune* online, May 13, 2004). Anecdotal evidence suggests that Wal-Mart stores increase crime rates or at least the cost of dealing with crime (see "Crime Linked to Wal-Mart Overwhelms Small-Town Police," *Daily News, Huntingdon, PA,* May 25, 2004, p.7), and a recent report by the advocacy group Good Jobs First suggests that the chain benefits from substantial public subsidies (Mattera and Purinton, 2004). See Miller (2004) for the congressional report.

2. See the October 6, 2003 issue.

3. For example, with this technology a single worker can potentially keep track of 10 check-out lines because a cart containing purchases can be scanned in a matter of seconds without items even being removed from the shopping cart.

4. See (http://www.wffhome.com/Grant%20Awards.htm), accessed May 8, 2004. This amount represents about one-tenth of 1 percent of the estimated wealth of the Wal-Mart heirs.

5. As reported in *Forbes* magazine (2003 Special Issue on the 400 Richest People in America), widow Helen R. Walton and heirs S. Robson, John T., Jim C., and Alice L. Walton each had a wealth of $20.5 billion in 2003. Alternatively, at a combined total of $102.5 billion, the Walton wealth is twice that controlled by Microsoft Chairman William H. Gates. Only three individuals had greater wealth in 2003: William H. Gates with $46 billion, Warren Buffett with $36 billion, and Paul Allen (also of Microsoft), $22 billion. As a comparison to the annual earnings of an associate worker of approximately $14,000, assuming a conservative annual rate of return on the Wal-Mart wealth of 1 percent in 2003, each of the five heirs would have earned an income of $205 million in 2003.

6. The mean of the dependent variable is negative (average poverty rates dropped nationwide during the 1990s); therefore, a positive coefficient estimate. . . indicates that a higher value of the exogenous variable (repressor) caused a *smaller* reduction than average in the poverty rate (the variable essentially contributed to a higher ending period poverty rate), while a negative coefficient estimate implies that the independent variable contributed to greater reductions in poverty.

7. One dimension of this is the vast amount of information held by Wal-Mart on consumer purchasing decisions. According to some estimates, the amount of information stored on Wal-Mart computers is twice that available on the entire World Wide Web.

REFERENCES

Artz, G. M., and J. C. McConnon, Jr. 2001. "The Impact of Wal-Mart on Host Towns and Surrounding Communities in Maine." Paper presented at the NAREA Meeting. Bar Harbor, ME.

Basker, E. 2002. "Job Creation or Destruction? Labor Market Effects of Wal-Mart Expansion." Ch. 1 in *Essays on Local Labor Markets* (Ph.D. Dissertation). Cambridge, MA: Massachusetts Institute of Technology, Department of Economics.

Franklin, A. W. 2001. "The Impact of Wal-Mart Supercenters on Supermarket Concentration in U.S. Metropolitan Areas." *Agribusiness* 17(1): 105–14.

Graff, T. O. 1998. "The Locations of Wal-Mart and Kmart Supercenters: Contrasting Corporate Strategies." *Professional Geographer* 50(1):46–57.

Hicks, M. J., and K. L. Wilburn. 2001. "The Regional Impact of Wal-Mart Entrance: A Panel Study of the Retail Trade Sector in West Virginia." *Review of Regional Studies* 31(3):305–13.

Huang, C. L., J. E. Epperson, B. J. Cude, and B. J. Woo. 2002. "Walmart Supercenter: The New Low-Price Food Retailer in Town." *Choices* 6(9):40–41.

Ketchum, B. A., and J. W. Hughes. 1997. "Walmart and Maine: The Effect on Employment and Wages." *Maine Business Indicators* 42(2):6. Available at ⟨http://www.usm.maine.edu/cber/mbi/summer97/hughes.htm⟩.

Mattera, Philip, and Anna Purinton. 2004. *Shopping for Subsidies: How Wal-Mart Uses Taxpayer Money to Finance Its Never-Ending Growth.* Washington, DC: Good Jobs First.

Miller, George. 2004. *Everyday Low Wages: The Hidden Price We All Pay for Wal-Mart.* Report by the Democratic Staff of the Committee on Education and the Workforce, U.S. House of Representatives. Available at ⟨http://edworkforce.house.gov/democrats/WALMARTREPORT.pdf⟩.

Skinner, J., and D. Staiger. 2005. *Technology Adoption from Hybrid Corn to Beta Blockers.* National Bureau of Economic Research, Working Paper No. 11251. Available at ⟨http://www.nber.org/papers/W11251⟩.

Stone, K. E. 1997. "Impact of the Wal-Mart Phenomenon on Rural Communities." Pp. 189–200 in *Increasing Understanding of Public Problems and Policies*, Oak Brook, IL: Farm Foundation.

Vias, A. C. In press. "Bigger Stores, More Stores, or No Stores: Paths of Retail Restructuring in Rural America." *Journal of Rural Studies.* Available at ⟨http://www.sciencedirect.com/science/journal/07430167⟩.

STUDY QUESTIONS

1. Please reiterate the authors' findings regarding how a Wal-Mart store increases poverty in an area.

2. Where do you stand on the value of Wal-Mart to the U.S. economy? How would you vote if Wal-Mart wanted to move a store into your area and citizens were asked to decide?

STEPHEN HASELER

The Super-Rich

The Super-Rich

The end of the forty years of Cold War was more than the political triumph of the West over the Soviet Union. It was also more than the victory of freedom and pluralism over command communism. When the Berlin Wall cracked open and the iron curtain fell a new form of capitalism came into its own—global capitalism—and with it new global elite, a new class.

This new class already commands wealth beyond the imagination of ordinary working citizens. It is potentially wealthier than any super-rich class in history (including the robber barons, those 'malefactors of great wealth' criticised by Teddy Roosevelt, and the nineteenth-century capitalists who inspired the opposition of a century of Marxists). The new class of super-rich are also assuming the proportions of overlordship, of an overclass—as powerful, majestic and antidemocratic as the awesome, uncompromising imperial governing classes at the height of the European empires.

The awesome new dimension of today's super-rich—one which separates them sharply from earlier super-rich—is that they owe no loyalty to community or nation. The wealthy used to be bounded within their nations and societies—a constraint that kept aggregations of wealth within reason and the rich socially responsible. Now, though, the rich are free: free to move their money around the world. In the new global economy super-rich wealth (capital) can now move their capital to the most productive (or high profit, low cost) haven, and with the end of the Cold War—and the entry into global economy of China, Russia, Eastern Europe and India—these opportunities have multiplied.

The super-rich are also free to move themselves. Although still less mobile than their money, they too are becoming less rooted, moving easily between many different locations.

Millionaires

Mobility is made possible by the lack of a need to work—a 'lifestyle' normally fixed in one nation or location for many years at a time. It is this escape from the world of work which effectively defines the super-rich. The lowest-ranking dollar *millionaire* household can, depending upon the interest and inflation rate, secure an *unearned* annual income of, say, $60,000 per year, which is almost double that of the median annual income of American families and four times that of the median income of British households.[1]

These millionaires are by no means lavishly well-off, particularly if they are in three- or four-people families or households. However, they are financially independent—as one commentary put it, they can 'maintain their lifestyle for years and years without earning even one month's pay'.[2] It has been estimated that in 1996 there were as many as six million dollar millionaires in the world, up from two million at the end of the Cold War.[3] Over half of these—estimates claim about 3.5—are to be found in the United States.[4]

Multimillionaires

However, these dollar millionaires find themselves at the *very* lower reaches of the world of the super-rich. Their homes and pensions are included in the calculations that make them millionaires, they often work—if not for a living, then for extras—and their lifestyles are often not particularly extravagant or sumptuous. They are, in fact, poor cousins in comparison with the more seriously rich families and individuals who are now emerging in the global economy. Official US statistics report that around a million US households—the top 1 per cent of total US households—possess a *minimum* net worth of over $2.4 million each and an average of $7 million each. In Britain the top 1 per cent have an average of around $1.4 million each.

The top half a per cent of US households, about half a million people, are staggeringly rich. This group has a *minimum* net worth of $4.7 million and an *average* of over $10 million each, which could produce an unearned annual income of over $600,000. In Britain the top half a per cent, around 48,000 households, have on average something like $2 million each—a fortune that can produce, again depending on interest and inflation rates, an unearned annual income of around $120,000 before tax and without working.[5]

These households are the truly super-rich, whose net worth, much of it inherited, is the source of considerable economic power and produces an income (mainly unlinked to work) that allows, even by affluent Western standards, extraordinarily sumptuous lifestyles. Estimates vary about the world-wide number of such super-rich families and individuals, but over two million in the plus $2.5 million category and over one million in the over $4.7 million (average $10 million) category would seem reasonable.[6]

Although huge amounts of the money of these multimillionaires are held outside the United States, in Europe, Asia and Latin America, this tells us nothing about the nationality of the holders.[7] In a sense these super-rich multimillionaires are the world's true global citizens—owing loyalty to themselves, their families and their money, rather than to communities and territorial boundaries—but reasonable estimates suggest that over half of them are American, and that most of the rest are European, with—certainly until the 1998 crash in Asia—a growing contingent from Asia.[8]

Their money is highly mobile, and so are they themselves, moving between their various homes around the world—in London, Paris and New York; large houses in the Hamptons in the United States, in the English and French countryside, and in gated communities in sun-belt America, particularly Florida, southern California and Arizona, and for the global super-rich the literal mobility of yachts in tropical paradises not scarred by local poverty.

Mega-Rich and Billionaires

Amongst multimillionaires there is a sharpish distinction to be made between those at the lower end—say the $20 million net worth households—and those at the higher end—say the $500 million plus households. The distinction is one of power, not lifestyle. From most perspectives the income from $20 million (say $1 million)—about 70,000 US households in 1994—can, at least on the face of it, produce the same kind of lifestyle as income from the net worth of the more serious multimillionaires (there is arguably a limit to the number of homes, yachts and cars that can be enjoyed and consumed in a lifetime).[9] $50 million in net worth, however, simply does not command as much economic power—over employment, over small businesses—than do the resources of the big time multimillionaires, much of whose money is tied up in big transnational corporations.

At the very top of this mega-rich world are the dollar billionaires, those who command over $1000 million in net worth, a fortune that can secure an unearned annual income, depending on inflation and interest rates, of $50 million a year before tax—staggeringly well over 1000 times more than the average US income. In 1997, estimates of the number of these ultra-super-rich individuals varied from 358 to 447 world-wide, and the number is growing fast, virtually doubling during the few years of the post Cold War era.[10]

Who Are the Billionaires?

The 400 or so billionaires in the world are a varied lot. In one sense they are like the rest of us (and like those who will read this book). They are overwhelmingly Western, primarily American or European, and male, but they represent no single ethnic group, no single social background, and certainly possess no single business or financial secret for acquiring these awesome fortunes.

Many of the billionaires, though, would not be in the mega-rich category without an inheritance—which remains the most well-trodden route to great multimillion dollar wealth. Of the top 400 wealthiest people in the United States, 39 made the list through inheritance alone and many of the others had some inheritance to help get them started.[11] The British queen, Elizabeth Windsor, is perhaps the most famous example of such massive unearned wealth. In 1997 Phillip Beresford (*The Sunday Times*' 'Rich List', (*Sunday Times* 6 April 1997) put her net worth at a staggering $10.4 thousand million in 1992 (double the 1997 figure for top-listed Joseph Lewis). However, after she took a rival 'rich list' to the Press Complaints Commission over its valuation of her assets, *The Sunday Times*' Wealth Register excluded from its calculations the royal art collection, which, had it been included, would have given her a $16 billion figure, making her the world's wealthiest woman and the second wealthiest person in the world, with half the net worth of the Sultan of Brunei but more than the Walton family.[12]

In contrast to the inheritors, there are some 400 'self-made' mega-rich men (there are no women). Yet even these men of merit have not necessarily made their inordinate fortunes through extraordinary amounts of work and talent—certainly not its continuous application. Many of the self-made mega-rich are certainly talented and creative (and often ruthless), but many of them have become mega-rich through one-off bursts of insight or risk or luck.

William (Bill) Gates is seen as 'self-made', very much the American entrepreneurial hero. His vast resources—*Newsweek* calls him 'the Croesus of our age'—have been built upon the meritorious image of having run a successful company which provides a real service, a real addition to human understanding and communication. His huge net worth—he was listed in 1997 by *Forbes* magazine as the richest American at $36.4 billion—is based upon the value of his shares in his company Microsoft. It was Gates' original burst of imagination that created his fortune—the initial stock offering in 1986 of 100 Microsoft shares cost $2100 but by the first trading day in August 1997 this had risen to 3600 shares at $138.50 each! Gates' personal share of the company rose from $234 million to $37.8 billion in the same period.[13] Certainly Gates has managed the company and taken many crucial decisions. Yet as Microsoft grew he needed the more 'routine' skills of thousands of major company directors—such as managerial aptitude and the ability to stave off competition. As with all established businesses, less and less risk and less and less creativity was needed (and a junior hospital doctor probably put in more hours).

Paul Raymond is a different type of self-made billionaire. Described by academic John Hills as Britain's richest man—in 1995 he placed him ahead of Joseph Lewis—Raymond's fortune is thought to be well over £1.65 billion. Having founded Raymond's revue bar in the Soho district of London, with topless dancers, he made his money by investing in soft pornography and property.[14] Like Gates he had the talent to spot a coming market—albeit one that was less elevating and educational. And also like Gates, and the other mega-rich, once the original burst of inventiveness (perhaps amounting only to the one great insight) was over the rest of his working life has consisted of simply managing his empire and watching his money grow. . . .

Comparisons

This group of late twentieth-century billionaires not only dwarf their 'ordinary' super-rich contemporaries but also the earlier race of mega-rich 'robber barons' who were so identified with the burgeoning capitalism of the early twentieth-century. In terms of resources at their personal command, in 1997 William Gates was three times richer than John D. Rockefeller (Standard Oil) was in 1918, Warren Buffet was over ten times richer than Andrew Carnegie (Steel) was in 1918, and it was estimated that in 1992 the British queen was ten times richer than Henry Ford (automobiles) was in 1918, although some of these early-twentieth-century super-rich probably commanded a greater percentage of their nations' resources.[15]

The resources at the disposal of these super-rich families—a huge pool of the globe's wealth—are truly astounding, beyond the wildest imaginings of most of the affluent Western middle classes. These high net worth individuals (HNWI's, as they are depicted in the financial services sector that serves them) accounted for almost $17 trillion in assets in 1996.

The power—that is, command over resources—of the world's super-rich is normally expressed in raw monetary figures, but the sheer, egregious extent of these private accumulations of wealth can also be given some meaning by making comparisons. . . . Eighty four of the world's richest people have a combined worth greater than that of China.[16] So the wealth of just one of these super-rich individuals is equal to that of about 12.5 million of his fellow humans.

Just as awe-inspiring is the fact that the total wealth of the world's few hundred billionaires equals the combined income of 45 per cent of the planet's population.[17] It is also somewhat sobering to realise that the *individual* wealth of the world's billionaires can exceed the gross national product of whole nations.[18] The world's ten richest billionaires all individually possess more in wealth than the GNP of many nation-states. The world's richest individual, the Sultan of Brunei, weighing in at over $45 billion, commands more resources than the combined GNP of 40 nation-states. To give his wealth some form of reality, it is larger than the GNP of the Czech republic (population 10.3 million); while William Gates commands more resources than the GNP of Africa's oil-rich giant, Nigeria (with a population of 111.3 million); the Walton family commands over $27.6 billion, more than the GNP of Vietnam (peopled by 73.5 million); Paul Sacher and the Hoffmann family command over $13 billion, more than the GNP of Bulgaria (population 8.4 million); Karl and Theo Albrecht command over $8 billion, more than the GNP of Panama (with its 2.6 million inhabitants); Joseph Lewis, the highest ranking mega-rich British citizen, commands just under $5 billion, which gives him more control over resources than his country of residence, the Bahamas.[19]

Another way of grasping the huge personal agglomerations of wealth in the modern global economy is to compare income levels. On 1997 interest-rate figures, and assuming that all assets are not income producing, the Sultan of Brunei could easily receive from his assets something in the region of $3 billion a year as income—compared with an average of $430 per person in the 49 lowest-income nation-states, $2030 per person in the 40 middle-income nation-states, $4260 in the 16 upper-middle income states and $24,930 in the 25 highest income economies. . . .

Get the world's top three mega-rich (dollar billionaire) people into one room and you would have assembled command over more resources than the GNP of Israel; the top four and you would tie with Poland, the top ten and you would beat Norway and South Africa. Europe's richest 20 families command around $113 billion, a little more than the whole Polish economy; America's richest 10 ($158 billion) and Britain's richest 1000 families ($156 billion) together command more resources than the GNP of the entire Russian Federation.[20]

If the top 200 or so billionaires could ever be assembled together then the command over assets, in that one room, would outrank the GNP of each of Australia, the Netherlands, Belgium, possibly even Brazil; and with 400 or so billionaires the one gathering would outrank Britain and almost overtake France!

It is these kinds of statistics that bring into sharp focus the economic power limitations of elected presidents and prime ministers (and other public sector officials)—who also have to share their economic power with cabinets and parliaments—compared with the economic power of the unelected mega-rich, whose only accountability is to the market. Such economic power was on display when the American media billionaire Ted Turner decided to donate $1 billion to the United Nations and 'to put on notice . . . every rich person in the world . . . that they're going to be hearing from me about giving money'.[21] For a Western politician to move a billion dollars in the direction of the UN would have involved months and months of negotiating and a bruising campaign.

All of our four categories of the world's super-rich (the 'ordinary' millionaires with up to $2.5 million, those with $2.5-5 million, those with $5-1000 million, and the billionaires with over $1000 million) have a combined net worth of $17 trillion, more than double the GNP of the United States.[22]

Just as awe-inspiring is the proportion of national wealth of the Western nations held by their own passport-holding super-rich.[23]

In 1995 in the US the amount of wealth (total net worth) held by 90 per cent of American households—everyone under the top 10 per cent—came to only 31.5 per cent, whereas the top 10 per cent of American households own 69.5 per cent of the US. More striking still, the top 1 per cent of Americans hold 35.1 per cent of US wealth, and the top half a per cent of households (500,000 households), those with a minimum net worth of $4.7 million, own 27.5 per cent of the US.

In Britain too the super-rich also own a huge proportion of the net worth of their country.[24] In 1992 the top 10 per cent of Britons owned half of the country's marketable wealth (for the top US 10 per cent the 1995 figure was a whopping 69.5 per cent). The wealthiest 5 per cent of Britons owned around 37 per cent of Britain's marketable wealth. The top 1000 super-rich families in Britain own about $160 billion worth of wealth, about the same average (0.16 billion each) as the top half a per cent in the US; Britain's top 100 command $89 billion, its top 50 own $69 billion and the top 20 own $42 billion.[25]

Among the 1997 British 'top twenty' Joseph Lewis (finance) was estimated to have a net worth of $4.8 thousand million; Hans Rausing (food packaging) came just behind with $4.72 thousand million; David Sainsbury (retailing) and Garfield Weston and family (food production) third with $4 thousand million each; Richard Branson (airline, retailing and entertainment), Sir Adrian and John Swire (shipping and aviation) and the Duke of Westminster (landownership) all joint fifth with $2.72 thousand million each; Lakshimi and Usha Mittal (steel) eighth with $2.4 thousand million; and Joe and Sir Anthony Bamford (construction equipment) and Viscount Rothermere (newspapers) joint ninth with $1.92 thousand million.

A particular feature of the British super-rich scene is the concentration in very few hands of land ownership. Britain—or rather the land area known as the United Kingdom—is, quite literally, owned by a very small caste; as is the capital city, London. It remains a poignant commentary on wealth concentration that large tracts of London are owned by just a few individuals. The Duke of Westminster, through the Grosvenor Estate, owns around 200 acres of Belgravia and 100 acres of Mayfair—a dynastic inheritance created by the seventeen-century marriage of Cheshire baronet Thomas Grosvenor to Mary Davies, the '12 year old heiress to a London manor that at the time included 200 acres of Pimlico'. Viscount Portman owns 110 acres north of Oxford Street. Lord Howard de Walden's four daughters, through a holding company, own 90 acres of Marylebone. Elizabeth Windsor, the queen, remains the 'official' owner of 150 acres of 'crown estates' in central London, as the eight crown estates commissioners address their annual report to her. Andrew Lycett has argued that although 'millions of pounds are exchanged every week in leasehold property deals ... London still has no sizable new landowners' with the exception of the Sultan of Brunei and Paul Raymond.[26]

Richer Still, Yet Richer

And the super rich are getting richer. The former vice chairman of the US Federal Reserve Board said in 1997 that 'I think when historians look back at the last quarter of the twentieth century the shift from labour to capital, the almost unprecedented shift of money and power up the income pyramid, is going to be their number one focus.'[27] The figures are indeed dramatic. In the US the top half a per cent rose from 23 per cent to 27.5 per cent between 1989 and 1995. The next half a per cent rose from 7.3 per cent to 7.6 per cent in same period. However, the next 9 per cent fell from 37.1 per cent 33.2 per cent, while the lowest 90 per cent fell from 32.5 per cent to 31.5 per cent. As the most reliable and scholarly analysis put it, the evidence shows 'a statistically significant increase in the share of household net worth held by the wealthiest half a per cent of [US] households from 1992 to 1995'.[28]

There are no figures available for the British top half a per cent, but tax authority figures—which do not include the considerable amounts of offshore money held by the British-passport-holding rich—suggest that whereas the top 1 per cent of the population were losing ground between 1950 and 1980, during the Thatcherite, globalising 1980s and 1990s their share of the wealth of Britain stabilised.[29]

And the assets held by the world-wide super-rich (the HNWIs) are expected to continue to grow. One assessment portrays them as more than doubling (from $7.2 trillion in 1986 to $15.1 trillion in 1995), and they are projected to grow from the 1996 level of $17 trillion to $25 trillion (up by more than 50 per cent) by the new millennium. . . .

An Overclass?

If the new global super-rich do not amount to an old-style ruling class, they are certainly becoming an overclass: the mirror image of the more publicised urban underclass—separated from the rest of us, with distinct interests that differ from those of the mass of the peoples of Western societies.

In a very real sense the new super-rich are becoming removed from their societies. This is happening physically. The higher levels of the super-rich have always lived apart: within their walled estates or in wealthy ghettos in the centre of Manhattan, London and other cities. They have always owned possessions that have singled them out. Today, of course, mere diamonds, helicopters and expensive cars no longer signify the apex of great wealth. Now it is the luxury yacht (normally personally designed by John Banneman), the personal aeroplane—the Sultan of Brunei has a Boeing 747—(normally supplied by Grumanns), and one or two of the highest valued paintings that signify someone has reached the top. . . .

Of course one test of loyalty to a society is a willingness to pay its taxes, particularly if they are not onerous. Yet increasingly the super-rich are dodging the taxes of their countries of origin. In 1997 the *New York Times* reported that

> *nearly 2,400 of the Americans with the highest incomes paid no federal taxes in 1993, up from just 85 individuals and couples in 1977. While the number of Americans who make $200,000 or more grew more than 15 fold from 1977 to 1993, the number of people in that category who paid no income taxes grew 28 fold or nearly twice as fast, according to a quarterly statistical bulletin issued by the IRS.[30]*

So difficult was it for the US authorities to collect taxes from the super-rich that Congress introduced a new tax altogether—the Alternative Minimum Tax—to catch them.[31] With the American 'middle classes'— the middle income groups—paying a larger percentage of their earnings in taxes (including sales taxes, property taxes and social security payroll taxes), tax evasion and avoidance is becoming a growing cause of economic inequality and social fracture. . . .

'The World Is in the Hands of These Guys'

The emergence of this global overclass not only raises the question of equality—or inequality—but also of power. Supporters of this new 'free market' global capitalism tend to celebrate it as a force for pluralism and freedom; yet so far these egregious aggregations of assets and money have placed in very few hands enormous power and influence over the lives of others. Through this accumulation of assets and money the super-rich control or heavily influence companies and their economic policies, consumer fashions, media mores, political parties and candidates, culture and art.

What is more the resources at the disposal of many of these super-rich individuals and families represent power over resources unattained by even the most influential of the big time state politicians and officials—'the panjamdrums of the corporate state' who populated the earlier, more social democratic era, and who became targets of the new capitalist right's criticism of the abuse of political power.

In the new capitalist dispensation it is the global super-rich who are 'lords of humankind', or 'lords of the Earth' like Sherman McCoy in Tom Wolfe's all too apt social satire on Wall Street, Bonfire of the Vanities, wielding power like old-fashioned imperial pro-consuls. The new global super-rich have now got themselves into a position where they not only have a 'free market' at their disposal, and not only is this market now global, but they can also command the support of the world's major governments. . . .

Onward and Upward

The new super-rich global overclass seems to be possessed of one crucial attribute: a sense of ultimate triumph. As globalisation has proceeded all the bulwarks of social democracy that stood in their way, the cultures that acted as a balancing force and succeeded in civilising, and to some extent domesticating, raw capitalism have fallen. The primary casualty has been the nation-state and its associated public sector and regulated markets. The global economy has also helped to remove that other crucial balancing power available in the Western world—trade unions—which for the most part acted to check unbridled business power and ensure some basic rights to employees, often at the expense of rises in short-term money incomes.

Finally, the end of the Cold War was a seminal moment and played a fateful role as midwife. At one fell swoop the end of command communism (in Eastern Europe, in Russia and, in the economic field, in China) made footloose capital both possible and highly attractive by adding a large number of low-cost production and service centres and new markets to the economy. It also removed the need for the Western super-rich to be 'patriotic' (or pro-Western). It also made redundant the instinct of social appeasement held by many Western capitalists and induced by the need, in the age of Soviet communism, to keep Western publics from flirting with an alternative economic model.

The stark truth is that not one of these obstacles—not the public sector, not the trade unions, not an alternative economic and social model—is ever likely to be reerected. In the short to medium term, without a change in the political climate of the Western world there is nothing to stop further globalisation, higher and higher profits, more and more millionaires. For the new overclass it is onward and upward.

NOTES

1. The median income of US families was about $37,000 in 1993. US Census Bureau, Income and Poverty, CD-ROM, table 3F (1993). The median income of UK households was about $16,500 (The exchange rate used here is $1.6 to the pound) in 1990 at 1993 prices. See John Hills, *Income and Wealth*, vol. 2 (Joseph Rowntree Foundation, Feb. 1995).

2. Thomas J. Stanley and William D. Danko, *The Millionaire Next Door* (Atlanta, GA: 1997). Some scholars have suggested defining 'the rich' not in terms of millions but rather as those with a family income over nine times the poverty line—in US terms about $95,000 a year in 1987. See S. Danziger, P. Gottschalk and E. Smolensky, 'How The Rich Have Fared, 1973-87', *American Economic Review*, vol. 72, no. 2 (May, 1989), p. 312.

3. The US Finance House Merrill Lynch in conjunction with Gemini Consulting, 'World Wealth Report 1997' (London: Merrill Lynch, 1997).

4. Stanley and Danko, *The Millionaire Next Door*, op. cit., p. 12.

5. US figures for 1995 from Arthur B. Kennickell (board of governors of the Federal Reserve System) and R. Louise Woodburn, 'Consistent Weight Design for the 1989, 1992 and 1995 SCF's and the Distribution of Wealth', revised July, 1997 unpublished. The UK figures are for 1993-4. For the UK figures, which include pensions, see Hills, *Income and Wealth*, op. cit., ch. 7.

6. Merrill Lynch, 'World Wealth Report, 1997', op. cit.

7. The 'World Wealth Report, 1997' (Merrill Lynch, op. cit.) projected, before the late 1997 Asian economic decline, that in 2000 the division of high net worth assets by source region would be Europe 7.1, North America 5.8, Asia 6.1, Latin America 3.8, Middle East 1.2 and Africa 0.4.

8. Of these multimillionaire Americans, families of British (that is English, Scottish, Welsh and Irish) and German descent account for 41.3 per cent of the total.

9. *Newsweek*, 4 Aug. 1997 (source IRS).

10. The UN *Human Development Report* (1996) put the figure at 358, and *Forbes* magazine's 1997 wealth list put the figure at 447, up from 274 in 1991.

11. *Newsweek* 4 Aug. 1997 (source *Forbes*, op. cit.)

12. See also, Phillip Hall, *Royal Fortune: Tax, Money and The Monarchy* (London: 1992) for a systematic account of the mysteries of the royal finances. One fact about the Queen's money remains: since 1998 she has remained above the law as far as taxation is concerned as she is not treated in exactly the same way—with all tax laws applying to her—as every other British person.

13. See *Newsweek*, 'The New Rich', 4 Aug. 1997.

14. Hills, *Income and Wealth*, op. cit., p. 9. Hills suggests that 'If Britain's richest man, Soho millionaire Paul Raymond, receives a modest 3 per cent net real return on his reported £1.65 billion fortune' his income would be £1 million a week.

15. Figures from *Newsweek*, 4 Aug. 1997, reporting *Forbes* in June 1997. The figures for the Queen were for 1992 (as published in *The Sunday Times'* 'Rich List', 1997), and were subsequently revised downwards following a complaint to the Press Complaints Commission.

16. John Gray, 'Bill Rules the World—And I Don't Mean Clinton', *Daily Express;* 11 Sep. 1998.

17. UN, *Human Development Report*, (1966). Comparing wealth with income is highly problematic, but nonetheless serves to display the enormity of the comparison. These comparisons—between asset net worth and gross national product (GNP) are not of course comparing like with like, but are used in order to show the extent of the egregious financial and economic power of the high net worth individuals. The most reasonable method of comparison would be to compare the net worth of super-rich individuals and groups of super-rich individuals with the total net worth of each country (that is, each individual/family in the country). These figures are not available for more than a handful of countries.

18. 'Billion' here and throughout the book is used in the US sense that is, nine noughts.

19. Wealth figures from *The Sunday Times*', 1997 'Rich List', op. cit., population figures for 1995 from *World Development Report* (Washington, DC: World Bank, 1997).

20. The US figure is from *Forbes*, June 1977, and the European and British from *The Sunday Times*, 6 April, 1977. For GNP figures see World Bank, *The World Atlas*, op. cit.

21. *Guardian*, 23 Sep. 1997.

22. These estimates are based upon the net worth estimates cited in *Forbes* magazine, June 1977, and in 'The Wealth Register', compiled by Dr Richard Beresford for *The Sunday Times* (extracts published in *The Sunday Times*, 6 April, 1997), who also cites *Forbes* magazine. *The World Atlas*, op. cit.

23. As I argue throughout this book, the super-rich are in reality global; but they all need a passport, and we are talking here about US passport holders.

24. The percentage of net worth of the total marketable net worth of all British passport holders.

25. *The Sunday Times*, 6 April, 1997. This is the British billion, that is, 12 noughts as opposed to the US nine noughts.

26. Andrew Lycett, 'Who Really Owns London?', *The Times*, 17 Sep. 1997.

27. Alan Blinder, former vice chairman of the US Federal Reserve, quoted in *Newsweek*, 23 June 1997.

28. Figures from 'Consistent Weight Design for the 1989, 1992 and 1995 SCF's and the Distribution of Wealth' by Arthur Kennickell (Federal Reserve System) and R. Louise Woodburn (Ernst and Young), revised July 1997 (unpublished). Figures derived from the Survey of Consumer Finances sponsored by the US Federal Reserve System and the Statistics of Income Division of the IRS.

29. See Charles Feinstein, 'The Equalising of Wealth In Britain Since The Second World War', *Oxford Review of Economic Policy*, vol. 12, no. 1 (Spring 1996), p. 96 ff. In British estimates distinctions tend to be made between marketable wealth and total wealth—marketable wealth excludes state pensions, occupational pensions and tenancy rights.

30. *New York Times*, 18 April, 1997.

31. The US Alternative Minimum Tax is levied on those who have substantial incomes but, because of their use of tax shelters and exemptions, submit a zero tax return.

STUDY QUESTIONS

1. The "super-rich" may be reshaping the global economy. What power do they have and how might they exercise it?

2. What social theory would you use to explain why the "super-rich" have come into existence? Use some sociological concepts to show how this happened.

JOHN R. COLEMAN

Blue-Collar Journal
A College President's Sabbatical

In the spring of 1973, I took a leave from my job as a college president. There were no strings attached. I could do whatever I chose for months on end. I had secretly known what I wanted to do if ever such a chance came along; now I had to discover whether I was serious about it.

What I wanted to do was to try my hand at manual work, for reasons more complex than I pretend to understand. I only know that, every time in recent years when I looked ahead to some time out, my thoughts turned to seeking and holding blue-collar jobs. The idea of breaking out of what I normally do and of taking up different roles for a while was so compelling that I would have felt cheated had I done anything less.

This is a record of what I did once I pulled out of the driveway of my house. The journal covers eight weeks. It omits the first week when I worked with friends of thirty years' standing, Pat and Russell Best, on their dairy farm in Ontario. That week conditioned me for physical work; thirteen hours a day in a milk shed, cow barns, and the woods have that effect. It omits the last weeks of my leave when I fulfilled a quite different dream by spending a week in Florence and a night each at Vienna's Staatsoper and at Milan's La Scala.

From the start I realized how fortunate I was in being able to get away at all, and in being able to leave without telling anyone where I was going or what I planned to do. I am divorced. I consider my children old enough and independent enough—and they consider me so—that I can disappear for some time without their having to worry

about me. The college board of trustees and my administrative colleagues were trusting enough not to push me with questions about
how I proposed to use the time out. And I had a paycheck going into
the bank each month to meet the tuition, insurance, utility, and tax bills
that found their way to the house, however far away I might be.

I did not tell anyone about what I planned to do with my sabbatical
because I was afraid the response would be what part of me also said:
"Jack, that's crazy." No reply to that charge would sound convincing,
and I felt that my orthodoxy and my quest for respectability would take
over at that point. I would probably end up using my leave to do some
sort of survey of recent developments in liberal arts education, and it
would no doubt be published somewhere through the help of friends
in editorial posts. But it wouldn't be worth much because I'm not an
original thinker on that subject. All in all, I thought, it was better to keep
to myself the urge to reenter the blue-collar world for the first time
since 1945. Let me see if I am willing to go where I want to go. And then
let me see if I can explain it afterward. . . .

Friday, February 16, 1973   *Atlanta, Georgia*

The drive from Philadelphia to Atlanta seemed long, no matter how
good the road was. I hadn't counted on Georgia's being so far from
home. I was keyed up, and the miles went by as slowly as they did for
my children years ago on our vacations, when, one hour after we
started the all-day drive to Maine, they asked, "Are we almost there?"

The sky was still dark when I pulled out of the driveway of my campus home this morning. Even in dim light, the big old house looked
inviting. I knew that I would miss its comfort and space—the books
and records in the library downstairs, the paintings in the living room,
the kitchen where it is fun both to cook and to talk, and the big clut-
tered desk in the study upstairs.

In addition to the car, I brought two hundred dollars in travelers
checks with me and a gasoline credit card. The checks were to tide me
over until I got a paycheck. The credit card was to let me get home even
if I ran out of money for food and lodging. I had a duffel bag full of
clothes, a few kitchen supplies, a box of books, a portable radio, and my
camera. I also brought my social security card—I had already decided
to use my own name—but nothing else. The rest of my past had to stay
home. I would invent an earlier work history as I went along.

The strongest feeling today was one of freedom. Just how much
freedom there was became clear as soon as I reached the main road

running past the campus. I could head in any direction I chose. I stayed with my original plan and headed south, but I felt freed just in knowing that I could have changed my mind on the spot. . . .

It was 6:00 in the evening when I got into Atlanta, and time to eat. I passed up the restaurants I would ordinarily have sought out and headed for a diner on the outskirts of the downtown area. There was a copy of the morning's *Atlanta Journal* still on sale. I skipped the front pages and turned to the classified ads. The Help Wanted columns didn't look as promising as they had last month, particularly for outdoor work.

The only choices appeared to be yardman, construction worker, or general laborer. Yardman was a risky job; the weather was cold for Atlanta (18°) and work could be spotty. Just a few days of bad weather and I'd have trouble supporting myself on my earnings. Most building construction ads called for experience; I thought it would probably be better if I toughened up elsewhere before I tried to make out in that league. That left the simple classification of "laborer."

Four ads were similar. Someone was paying a lot to get clean water into, and dirty water out of, the Atlanta area. This one stood out:

> *"Laborers. Sewer and water line construction. Transportation furnished. Call MU 2-0736 after 7 p.m."*

It was those words "after 7 p.m." that caught my eye. I had expected to use the night to build up my courage to start making calls at dawn. But here was a chance to get hired right now. Seven o'clock was drawing near; it was time to act.

I finished my hamburger and went to the telephone booth outside. I walked up and down with a dime in my hand for some time. In part, I was nervous about the work; in part, I wanted to avoid seeming too anxious by calling too soon. It was 7:05 when I dialed.

A male voice answered.

"Hello. My name is John Coleman. I'm calling about your ad for sewer laborers. Could you tell me about the job?"

"I start them at two-seventy-five an hour."

That was that. Obviously I needed more questions.

"What's the work like?"

"At this time of year it's dirty, and sloppy, and wet, and cold. It's a lousy job any way you look at it. Are you interested?"

"Yes. I'd like to try."

"What kind of work have you been doin'?"

"I've just come here from Pennsylvania. I used to be in sales. [That was true for a college president by a small stretch of the imagination.] But I got tired of it. [That would surely be true if the first statement were literally true.] So I've been working as a laborer for a while. [Completely false, except for that warm-up week on the dairy farm.]"

"Well, like I say, I start you at two-seventy-five. If you're any good, I'll move you ahead. Some of my men get three-and-a-half. Some get four."

"Do you want to meet me before you hire me?"

"No. Just come ready for work. Dress warmly. We'll supply boots when you get wet work."

"Is it a hard-hat job?"

"It's supposed to be. But I've stopped givin' them out. The men won't wear them, even though it's for their own good."

He gave me detailed instructions on how to find the job site and told me to be ready for work at 7:30 on Monday. I asked if I could start tomorrow.

"All right, if you need the money."

"I'll be there at seven-thirty. What's your name?"

"Gus Reed. R-E-E-D."

"Thank you, Mr. Reed."

That was all. I felt relieved at being hired on my first try—and without even being asked my age.

Saturday, February 17

I didn't sleep very well—partly from excitement, partly from doubts about whether I could do the day's work at 51. . . .

It was 5:45 this morning when I came down to check out at the motel desk. . . .

"Going to work?" he asked. I decided I had passed the appearance test.

"Yes."

"What do you do?"

"I'm starting today with a sewer company."

"On a cold morning like this?"

"Yes."

"You poor shit!"

It occurred to me that he could be right. . . .

There were orders to each man to start on a specified task. It was 7:50 before Gus turned to me. "Get a shovel out of the trailer and get in that ditch. Just follow the backhoe along and throw all the shit that it misses up on the bank." . . .

Gus was rather easy on me. He pointed to where the jackhammers had ripped up a road which the sewer line was to cross. The curbs on both sides of the road were left intact.

"John, take your time but shovel out that shit from under the curbs. Tunnel through from both sides so that we save the curbs."

No problem, I thought. But the six-foot-thick walls of clay there were packed hard. Sometimes I shoveled from a stooped position. Sometimes I had to kneel in the mud to get further under the curb. Either way the shovel hit the same unyielding clay with a thud. Only a small amount of dirt fell away with each try. . . .

With the tunnels under the curb done, the long ditch stretched out before me. It might not have seemed so long from the street level, and certainly wouldn't be long to anyone whizzing by in a car, but the view from the trench was of banks of mud that stretched on and on. The backhoe had moved rapidly while I was digging away at the packed clay. How many thousand shovel loads of loose dirt had it left behind for me? And would I ever catch up to that machine again?

In the work I do as college president, there are only two tasks that require doing the same thing over and over again for any sustained period of time. One is shaking hands at commencement and parents' day (a happy task); the other is signing thank-you notes to alumni contributors (a very happy task). But both the lines of people waiting to be greeted and the pile of notes waiting to be signed have definite ending points: I know when I'll be done with them. The ditch today didn't seem to have an end. As fast as I cleaned up one foot of it, the backhoe made at least one more foot of it ahead. . . .

It was 6:00 when Gus called it a day.

"John, go in that truck with all that equipment. You might as well learn where all that shit goes at night."

Everything had a neat place in the trailer. There was no way of making a mistake in stowing it for the night.

Gus and Stanley were talking down the road at some length. Or rather Gus was talking. Only the four-letter words and the strong gestures carried as far as the trailer.

At last Gus came to me. "See you Monday. This wasn't our usual work. We don't often lay lines along the highway. Usually we're over in the swampy stuff. Someday soon you'll be up to your ass in mud. Seven-thirty Monday."

I took off my coveralls before I got in my car. They were muddy enough for one clean day. . . .

I had no zest for looking for a place for the night. I had read rooming-house ads in yesterday's paper, but they were all downtown. I'm lazy enough to prefer living near the job; more than five years of stepping out of the door of a fine old home and crossing two small fields beneath the trees on the way to my office have spoiled me for commuting. I had no idea tonight where rooms could be found in the suburbs, and I was too weary to try to find out.

I remembered passing a motel this morning that advertised rooms for "$8 a day." Compared with the prices I usually paid, that seemed a steal. It was only after I registered that I realized eight dollars represented almost three hours of labor today. But at least I could now have a bath, eat, and get into bed. . . .

Sunday, April 15

These days are done. I suppose I should have unmixed emotions about going home, but I don't. No matter how restless I am to get back to my desk, I know too that some day I'll want to do again just what I've done this spring—or perhaps move to fulfill some other half-formed dream. Whatever comes, I expect to do a better job at home because I got away.

The Hasidic rabbi Zusia said, "When I shall face the celestial tribunal, I shall not be asked why I was not Abraham, Jacob, or Moses. I shall be asked why I was not Zusia."

Once, I thought I was leaving my identity behind when I set out on this leave. Now I think I may even have found some part of it along the way.

STUDY QUESTIONS

1. Coleman has some major adjustments to make to his new blue-collar status. What were his most difficult accommodations?
2. Which would be easier, the downward mobility of Coleman or the upward mobility of "working-class" sociologists? Give some specific reasons for your answer.

TOPIC 9
Race and Ethnicity

It is projected that the combined population of American minority groups will outnumber whites in the next fifty years. Many rural and urban environments are already finding diversity in similar proportions. As a nation of immigrants, except for a small proportion of Native Americans, we will soon find whites, officially "white, non-Hispanics," in the numerical minority. America is very diverse, and diversity issues abound in both the structural and personal senses. How many of us understand the effects of institutionalized racism? How many of us possess the "cultural competence" to feel at ease with persons of different racial and ethnic groups?

American history is filled with examples of racial and ethnic discrimination—slavery, "separate but equal" as an educational plan struck down by *Brown vs. Topeka*, legal discrimination against members of minority groups, underemployment and underpayment of ethnic group members, the use of illegal aliens to work crops in the American southwest, and many others. The ill-treatment of groups based on race or ethnicity is prevented by law in this country and yet it persists. The formal and informal aspects of social discrimination cannot be overcome by law or in a short period of time. Persons of color have made great strides once the legal barriers were removed, but there are many more marches and many more battles to fight before full equality is achieved. Poverty, unemployment, health, and education are not equally available to all persons in America, and "equal" appears to be as much an ideal as a reality for minorities.

Prejudice (an attitude) and discrimination (a behavior) exist on the world stage as well as in America. Anti-Semitism directed against the Jews in Eastern Europe during the Third Reich in Germany accounted for six million deaths in concentration camps. More recently we have seen "ethnic cleansing" as an outgrowth of conflicts in several parts of the world. Genocide, the extermination of an entire race or group, may seem impossible in the twenty-first century, but history would suggest otherwise. America, Yugoslavia, and Rwanda remind us of these possibilities. Some are quite recent.

Segregation of minorities is part of America's past and present. While we know that contact between different racial groups decreases prejudice, separation of these groups from one another and from white society persists. Busing began in the 1960s but has not solved the problem. Our communities and neighborhoods are defined by homogeneous groupings and represent both ethnic and class lines of distinction. Churches and business and services are often tied to racial and ethnic groups with few who will cross the lines. Will we welcome different groups to our schools and our neighborhoods? Will we lead the way to cross the color lines and create dialogue between distant groups? It is easy to deny the reality of racism and discrimination when our own lives do not intersect with those who suffer the indignities each day.

The articles in Topic 9: Race and Ethnicity are presented to capture some of the diversity of American life. First, Cornel West shows a most worrisome picture of race in the current American scene. Foment rests just beneath the surface and manifests in violent and predictable ways. Indeed, "race matters" in America. Second, Pierrette Hondagneu-Sotelo gives us a microsocial view of domestic labor in Los Angeles, California. Through many interviews and excerpts, the reader is treated to the complex fabric of Latina women who work inside homes where the wealthy have ways of distancing themselves from the "maids". Finally, the article by Erika Vora and Jay Vora enlists the help of a black church to work with students from a college as a way to create contact and reduce prejudice. This experiential approach actively teaches a lesson to all concerned and reminds us of the importance of personal connections in building bridges toward a future of cross-race understanding.

CORNEL WEST

Race Matters

What happened in Los Angeles in April of 1992 was neither a race riot nor a class rebellion. Rather, this monumental upheaval was a multiracial, trans-class, and largely male display of justified social rage. For all its ugly, xenophobic resentment, its air of adolescent carnival, and its downright barbaric behavior, it signified the sense of powerlessness in American society. Glib attempts to reduce its meaning to the pathologies of the black underclass, the criminal actions of hoodlums, or the political revolt of the oppressed urban masses miss the mark. Of those arrested, only 36 percent were black, more than a third had full-time jobs, and most claimed to shun political affiliation. What we witnessed in Los Angeles was the consequence of a lethal linkage of economic decline, cultural decay, and political lethargy in American life. Race was the visible catalyst, not the underlying cause.

The meaning of the earthshaking events in Los Angeles is difficult to grasp because most of us remain trapped in the narrow framework of the dominant liberal and conservative views of race in America, which with its worn-out vocabulary leaves us intellectually debilitated, morally disempowered, and personally depressed. The astonishing disappearance of the event from public dialogue is testimony to just how painful and distressing a serious engagement with race is. Our truncated public discussions of race suppress the best of who and what we are as a people because they fail to confront the complexity of the issue in a candid and critical manner. The predictable pitting of liberals against conservatives, Great Society Democrats against self-help Republicans, reinforces intellectual parochialism and political paralysis.

The liberal notion that more government programs can solve racial problems is simplistic—precisely because it focuses *solely* on the economic dimension. And the conservative idea that what is needed is a change in the moral behavior of poor black urban dwellers (especially poor black men, who, they say, should stay married, support their children, and stop committing so much crime) highlights immoral actions while ignoring public responsibility for the immoral circumstances that haunt our fellow citizens.

The common denominator of these views of race is that each still sees black people as a "problem people," in the words of Dorothy I. Height, president of the National Council of Negro Women, rather than as fellow American citizens with problems. Her words echo the poignant "unasked question" of W. E. B. Du Bois, who, in *The Souls of Black Folk* (1903), wrote:

> *They approach me in a half-hesitant sort of way, eye me curiously or compassionately, and then instead of saying directly, How does it feel to be a problem? they say, I know an excellent colored man in my town. . . . Do not these Southern outrages make your blood boil? At these I smile, or am interested, or reduce the boiling to a simmer, as the occasion may require. To the real question, How does it feel to be a problem? I answer seldom a word.*

Nearly a century later, we confine discussions about race in America to the "problems" black people pose for whites rather than consider what this way of viewing black people reveals about us as a nation.

This paralyzing framework encourages liberals to relieve their guilty consciences by supporting public funds directed at "the problems"; but at the same time, reluctant to exercise principled criticism of black people, liberals deny them the freedom to err. Similarly, conservatives blame the "problems" on black people themselves—and thereby render black social misery invisible or unworthy of public attention.

Hence, for liberals, black people are to be "included" and "integrated" into "our" society and culture, while for conservatives they are to be "well behaved" and "worthy of acceptance" by "our" way of life. Both fail to see that the presence and predicaments of black people are neither additions to nor defections from American life, but rather *constitutive elements of that life.*

To engage in a serious discussion of race in America, we must begin not with the problems of black people but with the flaws of American society—flaws rooted in historic inequalities and longstanding cultural stereotypes. How we set up the terms for discussing racial issues shapes our perception and response to these issues. As long as black people are viewed as a "them," the burden falls on blacks to do all the "cultural" and "moral" work necessary for healthy race relations. The implication is that only certain Americans can define what it means to be American—and the rest must simply "fit in."

The emergence of strong black-nationalist sentiments among blacks, especially among young people, is a revolt against this sense of having to "fit in." The variety of black-nationalist ideologies, from the moderate views of Supreme Court Justice Clarence Thomas in his youth to those of Louis Farrakhan today, rest upon a fundamental truth: white America has been historically weak-willed in ensuring racial justice and has continued to resist fully accepting the humanity of blacks. As long as double standards and differential treatment abound—as long as the rap performer Ice-T is harshly condemned while former Los Angeles Police Chief Daryl F. Gates's antiblack comments are received in polite silence, as long as Dr. Leonard Jeffries's anti-Semitic statements are met with vitriolic outrage while presidential candidate Patrick J. Buchanan's anti-Semitism receives a genteel response—black nationalisms will thrive.

Afrocentrism, a contemporary species of black nationalism, is a gallant yet misguided attempt to define an African identity in a white society perceived to be hostile. It is gallant because it puts black doings and sufferings, not white anxieties and fears, at the center of discussion. It is misguided because—out of fear of cultural hybridization and through silence on the issue of class, retrograde views on black women, gay men, and lesbians, and a reluctance to link race to the common good—it reinforces the narrow discussions about race.

To establish a new framework, we need to begin with a frank acknowledgment of the basic humanness and Americanness of each of us. And we must acknowledge that as a people—*E Pluribus Unum*—we are on a slippery slope toward economic strife, social turmoil, and cultural chaos. If we go down, we go down together. The Los Angeles upheaval forced us to see not only that we are not connected in ways we would like to be but also, in a more profound sense, that this failure to connect binds us even more tightly together. The paradox of race in America is that our common destiny is more pronounced and imperiled precisely when our divisions are deeper. The Civil War and its legacy speak loudly here. And our divisions are growing deeper. Today, eighty-six percent of white suburban Americans live in neighborhoods that are less than 1 percent black, meaning that the prospects for the country depend largely on how its cities fare in the hands of a suburban electorate. There is no escape from our interracial interdependence, yet enforced racial hierarchy dooms us as a nation to collective paranoia and hysteria—the unmaking of any democratic order.

The verdict in the Rodney King case which sparked the incidents in Los Angeles was perceived to be wrong by the vast majority of Americans. But whites have often failed to acknowledge the widespread mistreatment of black people, especially black men, by law enforcement agencies, which helped ignite the spark. The verdict was merely the occasion for deep-seated rage to come to the surface. This rage is fed by the "silent" depression ravaging the country—in which real weekly wages of all American workers since 1973 have declined nearly 20 percent, while at the same time wealth has been upwardly distributed.

The exodus of stable industrial jobs from urban centers to cheaper labor markets here and abroad, housing policies that have created "chocolate cities and vanilla suburbs" (to use the popular musical artist George Clinton's memorable phrase), white fear of black crime, and the urban influx of poor Spanish-speaking and Asian immigrants—all have helped erode the tax base of American cities just as the federal government has cut its supports and programs. The result is unemployment, hunger, homelessness, and sickness for millions.

And a pervasive spiritual impoverishment grows. The collapse of meaning in life—the eclipse of hope and absence of love of self and others, the breakdown of family and neighborhood bonds—leads to the social deracination and cultural denudement of urban dwellers, especially children. We have created rootless, dangling people with little link to the supportive networks—family, friends, school—that sustain some sense of purpose in life. We have witnessed the collapse of the spiritual communities that in the past helped Americans face despair, disease, and death and that transmit through the generations dignity and decency, excellence and elegance.

The result is lives of what we might call "random nows," of fortuitous and fleeting moments preoccupied with "getting over"—with acquiring pleasure, property, and power by any means necessary. (This is not what Malcolm X meant by this famous phrase.) Post-modern culture is more and more a market culture dominated by gangster mentalities and self-destructive wantonness. This culture engulfs all of us—yet its impact on the disadvantaged is devastating, resulting in extreme violence in everyday life. Sexual violence against women and homicidal assaults by young black men on one another are only the most obvious signs of this empty quest for pleasure, property, and power.

Last, this rage is fueled by a political atmosphere in which images, not ideas, dominate, where politicians spend more time raising money than debating issues. The functions of parties have been displaced by public polls, and politicians behave less as thermostats that determine the climate of opinion than as thermometers registering the public mood. American politics has been rocked by an unleashing of greed among opportunistic public officials—who have followed the lead of their counterparts in the private sphere, where, as of 1989, 1 percent of the population owned 37 percent of the wealth and 10 percent of the population owned 86 percent of the wealth—leading to a profound cynicism and pessimism among the citizenry.

And given the way in which the Republican Party since 1968 has appealed to popular xenophobic images—playing the black, female, and homophobic cards to realign the electorate along race, sex, and sexual-orientation lines—it is no surprise that the notion that we are all part of one garment of destiny is discredited. Appeals to special interests rather than to public interests reinforce this polarization. The Los Angeles upheaval was an expression of utter fragmentation by a powerless citizenry that includes not just the poor but all of us.

What is to be done? How do we capture a new spirit and vision to meet the challenges of the post-industrial city, post-modern culture, and post-party politics?

First, we must admit that the most valuable sources for help, hope, and power consist of ourselves and our common history. As in the ages of Lincoln, Roosevelt, and King, we must look to new frameworks and languages to understand our multilayered crisis and overcome our deep malaise.

Second, we must focus our attention on the public square—the common good that undergirds our national and global destinies. The vitality of any public square ultimately depends on how much we *care* about the quality of our lives together. The neglect of our public infrastructure, for example—our water and sewage systems, bridges, tunnels, highways, subways, and streets—reflects not only our myopic economic policies, which impede productivity, but also the low priority we place on our common life.

The tragic plight of our children clearly reveals our deep disregard for public well-being. About one out of every five children in this country lives in poverty, including one out of every two black children and two out of every five Hispanic children. Most of our children—neglected by overburdened parents and bombarded by the market values of profit-hungry corporations—are ill-equipped to live lives of spiritual and cultural quality. Faced with these facts, how do we expect ever to constitute a vibrant society?

One essential step is some form of large-scale public intervention to ensure access to basic social goods—housing, food, health care, education, child care, and jobs. We must invigorate the common good with a mixture of government, business, and labor that does not follow any existing blueprint. After a period in which the private sphere has been sacralized and the public square gutted, the temptation is to make a fetish of the public square. We need to resist such dogmatic swings.

Last, the major challenge is to meet the need to generate new leadership. The paucity of courageous leaders—so apparent in the response to the events in Los Angeles—requires that we look beyond the same elites and voices that recycle the older frameworks. We need leaders—neither saints nor sparkling television personalities—who can situate themselves within a larger historical narrative of this country and our world, who can grasp the complex dynamics of our peoplehood and imagine a future grounded in the best of our past, yet who are attuned to the frightening obstacles that now perplex us. Our ideals of freedom, democracy, and equality must be invoked to invigorate all of us, especially the landless, propertyless, and luckless. Only a visionary leadership that can motivate "the better angels of our nature," as Lincoln said, and activate possibilities for a freer, more efficient, and stable America—only that leadership deserves cultivation and support.

This new leadership must be grounded in grass-roots organizing that highlights democratic accountability. Whoever *our* leaders will be as we approach the twenty-first century, their challenge will be to help Americans determine whether a genuine multiracial democracy can be created and sustained in an era of global economy and a moment of xenophobic frenzy.

Let us hope and pray that the vast intelligence, imagination, humor, and courage of Americans will not fail us. Either we learn a new language of empathy and compassion, or the fire this time will consume us all.

STUDY QUESTIONS

1. There is a threatening tone to this discussion of race. What is your assessment of "race matters" in the United States today? Do you agree with West?
2. As the economic infrastructure of U.S. cities has eroded, what impact has this had on the racial groups who reside there?

PIERRETTE HONDAGNEU-SOTELO

Maid in L.A.

The title of this chapter was inspired by Mary Romero's 1992 book, *Maid in the U.S.A.*, but I am also talking the pun to heart: most Latina immigrant women who do paid domestic work in Los Angeles had no prior experience working as domestics in their countries of origin. Of the 153 Latina domestic workers that I surveyed at bus stops, in ESL classes, and in parks, fewer than 10 percent reported having worked in other people's homes, or taking in laundry for pay, in their countries of origin. This finding is perhaps not surprising, as we know from immigration research that the poorest of the poor rarely migrate to the United States; they simply cannot afford to do so. . . .

For Maribel Centeno, newly arrived from Guatemala City in 1989 at age twenty-two and without supportive family and friends with whom to stay, taking a live-in job made a lot of sense. She knew that she wouldn't have to spend money on room and board, and that she could soon begin saving to pay off her debts. Getting a live-in job through an agency was easy. The *señora*, in her rudimentary Spanish, only asked where she was from, and if she had a husband and children. Chuckling, Maribel recalled her initial misunderstanding when the *señora*, using her index finger, had drawn an imaginary "2" and "3" in the palm of her hand. "I thought to myself, well, she must have two or three bedrooms, so I said, fine. 'No,' she said. 'Really, really big.' She started counting, 'One, two, three, four . . . two-three rooms.' It was twenty-three rooms! I thought, *huy*! On a piece of paper, she wrote '$80 a week,' and she said, 'You, child, and entire house.' So I thought, well, I have to do what I have to do, and I happily said, 'Yes.'"

"I arrived on Monday at dawn," she recalled, "and I went to the job on Wednesday evening." When the *señora* and the child spoke to her, Maribel remembered "just laughing and feeling useless. I couldn't understand anything." On that first evening, the *señora* put on classical music, which Maribel quickly identified. "I said, 'Beethoven.' She said, 'Yeah,' and began asking me in English, 'You like it?' I said 'Yes,' or perhaps I said, '*Sí*,' and she began playing other cassettes, CDs. They had Richard Clayderman and I recognized it, and when I said that, she stopped in her tracks, her jaw fell open, and she just stared at me. She must haven been thinking, 'No schooling, no preparation, no English, how does she know this music?'" But the *señora*, perhaps because of the language difficulty, or perhaps because she felt upstaged by her live-in's knowledge of classical music, never did ask. Maribel desperately wanted the *señora* to respect her, to recognize that she was smart, educated, and cultivated in the arts. In spite of her best status-signaling efforts, "They treated me," she said, "the same as any other girl from the countryside." She never got the verbal recognition that she desired from the *señora*.

Maribel summed up her experiences with her first live-in job this way: "The pay was bad. The treatment was, how shall I say? It was cordial, a little, uh, not racist, but with very little consideration, very little respect." She liked caring for the little seven-year-old boy, but keeping after the cleaning of the twenty-three-room house, filled with marble floors and glass tables, proved physically impossible. She eventually quit not because of the polishing and scrubbing, but because being ignored devastated her socially.

Compared to many other Latina immigrants' first live-in jobs, Maribel Centeno's was relatively good. She was not on call during all her waking hours and throughout the night, the parents were engaged with the child, and she was not required to sleep in a child's bedroom or on a cot tucked away in the laundry room. But having a private room filled with amenities did not mean she had privacy or the ability to do simple things one might take for granted. "I had my own room, with my own television, VCR, my private bath, and closet, and a kind of sitting room—but everything in miniature, Thumbelina style," she said. "I had privacy in that respect. But I couldn't do many things. If I wanted to walk around in a T-shirt, or just feel like I was home, I couldn't do that. If I was hungry in the evening, I wouldn't come out to grab a banana because I'd have to walk through the family room, and then everybody's watching and having to smell the banana. I could never feel at home, never. Never, never, never! There's always something invisible that tells you this is not your house, you just work here."

It is the rare California home that offers separate maid's quarters, but that doesn't stop families from hiring live-ins; nor does it stop newly arrived Latina migrant workers from taking jobs they urgently need. When live-ins cannot even retreat to their own rooms, work seeps into their sleep and their dreams. There is no time off from the job, and they say they feel confined, trapped, imprisoned.

"I lose a lot of sleep," said Margarita Gutiérrez, a twenty-four-year-old Mexicana who worked as a live-in nanny/housekeeper. At her job in a modest-sized condominium in Pasadena, she slept in a corner of a three-year-old child's bedroom. Consequently, she found herself on call day and night with the child, who sometimes went several days without seeing her mother because of the latter's schedule at an insurance company. Margarita was obliged to be on her job twenty-four hours a day; and like other live-in nanny/housekeepers I interviewed, she claimed that she could scarcely find time to shower or brush her teeth. "I go to bed fine," she reported, "and then I wake up at two or three in the morning with the girl asking for water, or food." After the child went back to sleep, Margarita would lie awake, thinking about how to leave her job but finding it hard to even walk out into the kitchen. Live-in employees like Margarita literally have no space and no time they can claim as their own.

Working in a larger home or staying in plush, private quarters is no guarantee of privacy or refuge from the job. Forty-four-year-old Elvia Lucero worked as a live-in at a sprawling, canyon-side residence, where she was in charge of looking after twins, two five-year-old girls. On numerous occasions when I visited her there, I saw that she occupied her own bedroom, a beautifully decorated one outfitted with delicate antiques, plush white carpet, and a stenciled border of pink roses painstakingly painted on the wall by the employer. It looked serene and inviting, but it was only three steps away from the twins' room. Every night one of the twins crawled into bed with Elvia. Elvia disliked this, but said she couldn't break the girl of the habit. And the parents' room lay tucked away at the opposite end of the large (more than 3,000 square feet), L-shaped house.

Regardless of the size of the home and the splendor of the accommodations, the boundaries that we might normally take for granted disappear in live-in jobs. They have, as Evelyn Nakano Glenn has noted, "no clear line between work and non-work time," and the line between job space and private space is similarly blurred.[1] Live-in nanny/housekeepers are at once socially isolated and surrounded by other people's territory; during the hours they remain on the employers' premises, their space, like their time, belongs to another. The sensation of being among others while remaining invisible, unknown and apart, of never being able to leave the margins, makes many live-in employees sad, lonely, and depressed. Melancholy sets in and doesn't necessarily lift on the weekends.

Rules and regulations may extend around the clock. Some employers restrict the ability of their live-in employees to receive telephone calls, entertain friends, attend evening ESL classes, or see boyfriends during the workweek. Other employers do not impose these sorts of restrictions, but because their homes are located on remote hillsides, in suburban enclaves, or in gated communities, their live-in nanny/housekeepers are effectively kept away from anything resembling social life or public culture. A Spanish-language radio station, or maybe a *telenovela,* may serve as their only link to the outside world.

Food—the way some employers hoard it, waste it, deny it, or just simply do not even have any of it in their kitchens—is a frequent topic of discussion among Latina live-in nanny/housekeepers. These women are talking not about counting calories but about the social meaning of food on the job. Almost no one works with a written contract, but anyone taking a live-in job that includes "room and board" would assume that adequate meals will be included. But what constitutes an adequate meal? Everyone has a different idea, and using the subject like a secret handshake, Latina domestic workers often greet one another by talking about the problems of managing food and meals on the job. Inevitably, food enters their conversations.

No one feels the indignities of food more deeply than do live-in employees, who may not leave the job for up to six days at a time. For them, the workplace necessarily becomes the place of daily sustenance. In some of the homes where they work, the employers are out all day. When these adults return home, they may only snack, keeping on hand little besides hot dogs, packets of macaroni and cheese, cereal, and peanut butter for the children. Such foods are considered neither nutritious nor appetizing by Latina immigrants, many of whom are accustomed to sitting down to meals prepared with fresh vegetables, rice, beans, and meat. In some employers' homes, the cupboards are literally bare. Gladys Villedas recalled that at one of her live-in jobs, the *señora* had graciously said, "'Go ahead, help yourself to anything in the kitchen.' But at times," she recalled, "there was nothing, nothing in the refrigerator! There was nothing to eat!" Even in lavish kitchens outfitted with Subzero refrigerators and imported cabinetry, food may be scarce. A celebrity photographer of luxury homes that appear in posh magazines described to a reporter what he sees when he opens the doors of some of Beverly Hills' refrigerators: "Rows of cans of Diet Coke, and maybe a few remains of pizza."[2]

Further down the class ladder, some employers go to great lengths to economize on food bills. Margarita Gutiérrez claimed that at her live-in job, the husband did the weekly grocery shopping, but he bought things in small quantities—say, two potatoes that would be served in half portions, or a quarter of a watermelon to last a household of five all week. He rationed out the bottled water and warned her that milk would make her fat. Lately, she said, he was taking both her and the children to an upscale grocery market where they gave free samples of gourmet cheeses, breads, and dips, urging them all to fill up on the freebies. "I never thought," exclaimed Margarita, formerly a secretary in Mexico City, "that I would come to this country to experience hunger!"

Many women who work as live-ins are keenly aware of how food and meals underline the boundaries between them and the families for whom they work. "I never ate with them," recalled Maribel Centeno of her first live-in job. "First of all, she never said, 'Come and join us,' and secondly, I just avoided being around when they were about to eat." Why did she avoid mealtime? "I didn't feel I was part of that family. I knew they liked me, but only because of the good work I did, and because of the affection I showered on the boy; but apart from that, I was just like the gardener, like the pool man, just one more of their staff." Sitting down to share a meal symbolizes membership in a family, and Latina employees, for the most part, know they are not just like one of the family.

Food scarcity is not endemic to all of the households where these women work. In some homes, ample quantities of fresh fruits, cheeses, and chicken stock the kitchens. Some employer families readily share all of their food, but in other households, certain higher-quality, expensive food items may remain off-limits to the live-in employees, who are instructed to eat hot dogs with the children. One Latina live-in nanny/housekeeper told me that in her employers' substantial pantry, little "DO NOT TOUCH" signs signaled which food items were not available to her; and another said that her employer was always defrosting freezer-burned leftovers for her to eat, some of it dating back nearly a decade.

Other women felt subtle pressure to remain unobtrusive, humble, and self-effacing, so they held back from eating even when they were hungry. They talked a lot about how these unspoken rules apply to fruit. "Look, if they [the employers] buy fruit, they buy three bananas, two apples, two pears. So if I eat one, who took it? It's me," one woman said, "they'll know it's me." Another nanny/housekeeper recalled: "They would bring home fruit, but without them having to say it, you just knew these were not intended for you. You understand this right away, you get it." Or as another put it, "*Los Americanas* have their apples counted out, one for each day of the week." Even fruits growing in the garden are sometimes contested. In Southern California's agriculture-friendly climate, many a residential home boasts fruit trees that hang heavy with oranges, plums, and peaches, and when the Latina women who work in these homes pick the fruit, they sometimes get in trouble.[3] Eventually, many of the women solve the food problem by buying and bringing in their own food; early on Monday mornings, you see them walking with their plastic grocery bags, carting, say, a sack of apples, some chicken, and maybe some prepared food in plastic containers.

The issue of food captures the essence of how Latina live-in domestic workers feel about their jobs. It symbolizes the extent to which the families they work for draw the boundaries of exclusion or inclusion, and it marks the degree to which those families recognize the live-in nanny/housekeepers as human beings who have basic human needs. When they first take their jobs, most live-in nanny/housekeepers do not anticipate spending any of their meager wages on food to eat while on the job, but in the end, most do—and sometimes the food they buy is eaten by members of the family for whom they work.

Although there is a wide range of pay, many Latina domestic workers in live-in jobs earn less than minimum wage for marathon hours: 93 percent of the live-in workers I surveyed in the mid-1990s were earning less than $5 an hour (79 percent of them below minimum wage, which was then $4.25), and they reported working an average of sixty-four hours a week.[4] Some of the most astoundingly low rates were paid for live-in jobs in the households of other working-class Latino immigrants, which provide some women their first job when they arrive in Los Angeles. Carmen Vasquez, for example, had spent several years working as a live-in for two Mexican families, earning only $50 a week. By comparison, her current salary of $170 a week, which she was earning as a live-in nanny/housekeeper in the hillside home of an attorney and a teacher, seemed a princely sum.

Many people assume that the rich pay more than do families of modest means, but working as a live-in in an exclusive, wealthy neighborhood, or in a twenty-three-room house, provides no guarantee of a high salary. Early one Monday morning in the fall of 1995, I was standing with a group of live-in nanny/housekeepers on a corner across the street from the Beverly Hills Hotel. As they were waiting to be picked up by their employers, a large Mercedes sedan with two women (a daughter and mother or mother-in-law?) approached, rolled down the windows, and asked if anyone was interested in a $150-a-week live-in job. A few women jotted down the phone number, and no one was shocked by the offer. Gore Vidal once commented that no one is allowed to fail within a two-mile radius of the Beverly Hills Hotel, but it turns out that plenty of women in that vicinity are failing in the salary department. In some of the most affluent Westside areas of Los Angeles—in Malibu, Pacific Palisades, and Bel Air—there are live-in nanny/housekeepers earning $150 a week. And in 1999, the *Los Angeles Times* Sunday classified ads still listed live-in nanny/housekeeper jobs with pay as low as $100 and $125.[5] Salaries for live-in jobs, however, do go considerably higher. The best-paid live-in employee whom I interviewed was Patricia Paredes, a Mexicana who spoke impeccable English and who had legal status, substantial experience, and references. She told me that she currently earned $450 a week at her live-in job. She had been promised a raise to $550, after a room remodel was finished, when she would assume weekend housecleaning in that same home. With such a relatively high weekly salary she felt compelled to stay in a live-in job during the week, away from her husband and three young daughters who remained on the east side of Los Angeles. The salary level required that sacrifice.

But once they experience it, most women are repelled by live-in jobs. The lack of privacy, the mandated separation from family and friends, the round-the-clock hours, the food issues, the low pay, and especially the constant loneliness prompt most Latina immigrants to seek other job arrangements. Some young, single women who learn to speak English fluently try to move up the ranks into higher-paying live-in jobs. As soon as they can, however, the majority attempt to leave live-in work altogether. Most live-in nanny/housekeepers have been in the United States for five years or less; among the live-in nanny/housekeepers I interviewed, only two (Carmen Vasquez and the relatively high-earning Patricia Paredes) had been in the United States for longer than that. Like African American women earlier in the century, who tired of what the historian Elizabeth Clark-Lewis has called "the soul-destroying hollowness of live-in domestic work,"[6] most Latina immigrants try to find other options.

Until the early 1900s, live-in jobs were the most common form of paid domestic work in the United States, but through the first half of the twentieth century they were gradually supplanted by domestic "day work."[7] Live-in work never completely disappeared, however, and in the last decades of the twentieth century, it revived with vigor, given new life by the needs of American families with working parents and young children—and, as we have seen, by the needs of newly arrived Latina immigrants, many of them unmarried and unattached to families. When these women try to move up from live-in domestic work, they see few job alternatives.

NOTES

1. Glenn 1986:141.
2. Lacher 1997:E1.
3. One nanny/housekeeper told me that a *señora* had admonished her for picking a bag of fruit, and wanted to charge her for it; another claimed that her employer had said she would rather watch the fruit fall off the branches and rot than see her eat it.
4. Many Latina domestic workers do not know the amount of their hourly wages; and because the lines between their work and nonwork tend to blur, live-in nanny/housekeepers have particular difficulty calculating them. In the survey questionnaire I asked live-in nanny/housekeepers how many days a week they worked, what time they began their job, and what time they ended, and I asked them to estimate how many hours off they had during an average workday (39 percent said they had no time off, but 32 percent said they had a break of between one and three hours). Forty-seven percent of the women said they began their workday at 7 A.M. or earlier, with 62 percent ending their workday at 7 P.M. or later. With the majority of them (71 percent) working five days a week, their average workweek was sixty-four hours. This estimate may at first glance appear inflated; but consider a prototypical live-in nanny/housekeeper who works, say, five days a week, from 7 A.M. until 9 P.M., with one and a half hours off during the children's nap time (when she might take a break to lie down or watch television). Her on-duty work hours would total sixty-four and a half hours per week. The weekly pay of live-in nanny/housekeepers surveyed ranged from $130 to $400, averaging $242. Dividing this figure by sixty-four yields an hourly wage of $3.80. None of the live-in nanny/housekeepers were charged for room and board—and, as we will see in chapter 8, this practice is regulated by law—but 86 percent said they brought food with them to their jobs. The majority reported being paid in cash.
5. See, e.g., Employment Classified Section 2, *Los Angeles Times*, June 6, 1999, G9.
6. Clark-Lewis 1994:123. "After an average of seven years," she notes in her analysis of African American women who had migrated from the South to Washington, D.C., in the early twentieth century, "all of the migrant women grew to dread their live-in situation. They saw their occupation as harming all aspects of their life" (124). Nearly all of these women transitioned into day work in private homes. This pattern is being repeated by Latina immigrants in Los Angeles today, and it reflects local labor market opportunities and constraints. In Houston, Texas, where many Mayan Guatemalan immigrant women today work as live-ins, research by Jacqueline Maria Hagan (1998) points to the tremendous obstacles they face in leaving live-in

work. In Houston, housecleaning is dominated by better-established immigrant women, by Chicanas and, more recently, by the commercial cleaning companies—so it is hard for the Maya to secure those jobs. Moreover, Hagan finds that over time, the Mayan women who take live-in jobs see their own social networks contract, further reducing their internal job mobility.

7. As noted in chapter 1, several factors explain the shift to day work, including urbanization, interurban transportation systems, and smaller private residences. Historians have also credited the job preferences of African American domestic workers, who rejected the constraints of live-in work and chose to live with their own families and communities, with helping to promote this shift in the urban North after 1900 (Katzman 1981; Clark-Lewis 1994: 129–35). In many urban regions of the United States, the shift to day work accelerated during World War I, so that live-out arrangements eventually became more prevalent (Katzman 1981; Palmer 1989). Elsewhere, and for different groups of domestic workers, these transitions happened later in the twentieth century. Evelyn Nakano Glenn (1986:143) notes that Japanese immigrant and Japanese American women employed in domestic work in the San Francisco Bay Area moved out of live-in jobs and into modernized day work in the years after World War II.

STUDY QUESTIONS

1. What boundary issues were confronted by the live-in maids in this study?

2. As newly arriving immigrants, are these Latina able to move into different and higher paying jobs?

ERIKA VORA AND JAY A. VORA

Undoing Racism in America
Help from a Black Church

Can a Black community help reduce racism? The answer is an unequiv-
ocal yes! Our study showed that a Black church community that is
supportive of and committed to helping young White college students
positively changed their attitudes and behaviors toward African
Americans. The purpose of this study was to investigate whether a
well-planned engagement of White students with members of a Black
community, in a welcoming environment, would help reduce racism
and prejudice.

Racism and ethnic prejudice are major problems in our society. They
are indeed our most troubling and potentially catastrophic national
dilemma requiring persistent critical inquiry (Janzen, 2000; Van Dijk,
1987). Both blatant and very subtle forms of racism permeate organizational and personal levels of our society, from governmental, business,
and educational institutions to our everyday interactions (Gonzalez,
Houston, & Chen, 1998; Jackson, 1992; Jamieson & O'Mara, 1992; Seelye,
1993; Tjosvold, 1991). "Without the Afrocentric perspective the imposi-
tion of the European line as universal hinders cultural understanding
and demeans humanity" (Asante, 1987, p 10). All of us have a responsibility to be change agents toward facilitating nonracist ways of thinking
and acting. To undo racism now and for future generations, we need to
be involved in this process so that our attitudes and communications
will change toward racial self-acceptance without any feelings of ethnic
superiority. We need to open our eyes to see the incredible potential
that diversity offers, and we need to recognize the deep pain and the

enormous waste of human talent that occur in everyday life where racial antagonism persists. We are challenged to create learning experiences and programs that help us recognize that our associations with diverse others enrich us and that respecting one another's racial backgrounds and ethnic groups is the key to solving our most pressing national and global problem. We need to directly confront racism by engaging our students and ourselves in self-examination of our attitudes and behaviors concerning racial diversity.

As educators, it is our quest to make our students aware of their "personal baggage" (Beane, 1990), to help them look at their personal filters, and to gently remove their ethnocentric blinders. Our educational goal for this project was to provide new opportunities for our students to understand and respond effectively to our culturally diverse nation and pluralistic world. This is not an easy task because the overwhelming majority of our students come from relatively small, homogeneous European American communities in central Minnesota. They have had very little exposure to culturally diverse individuals, especially to those of African heritage. This lack of personal intercultural experience is supplemented by media images that are relatively negative (Davis, 1992). Rather than merely learning about a culture through the usual academic classroom endeavors, we challenged our students to get involved with an African American church community and to "walk the talk."

In this article, we would like to share an approach we adopted toward engaging students directly in culture learning by offering them an opportunity to actively participate in the activities of a culture different from their own. Because the emotional wall between Black and White folks is so huge in this country, we were especially interested in undoing racism and prejudice of European Americans toward African Americans. Therefore, our specific purpose for this experiential learning was to provide an opportunity to change the attitudes, knowledge, and behavior of our White students toward African Americans and to study the impact of this intercultural engagement to effect such a change.

Help from a Black Church

Located in a highly homogeneous, White, small Midwestern town, we searched for a variety of ways to engage our students face-to-face in a culturally diverse community and found it 75 miles away in a warm and inviting African American church. We asked the dynamic leader of this church if we could bring our White students to participate in her Sunday services. She was delighted and welcomed us graciously with open arms. Committed to making the students feel at home, she encouraged the community members to greet our students as they entered the church and to interact with them after the service. During the service, each student was recognized by name (with the help of name cards). The preacher thanked them for coming, prayed for them, and encouraged them to come back soon. During the spirited service, the preacher was leading the congregation to "come forward and hug each other." Thus, each student was hugged not only by the preacher but also by the members of the congregation. This warm and sincere embrace made a big impact on the students, for it was the first time for them to ever be hugged by a Black person. The preacher, a caring and dynamic church leader, also organized lunch events at the nearby community center and encouraged all community members to come and interact with the students and to make them feel at home. She also asked her creative choir director and good friend to teach the students a hymn or two, which they could sing together with the community members. Before leaving for their 75-mile journey home, the preacher prayed for the students' safe trip home and encouraged them again to come back soon. The members of the congregation not only greeted the students warmly and truly made all of them feel welcome, but they also waved good-bye as the students' cars were leaving for home. We could think of no better way for our students to engage with and learn about African Americans.

This open church community and our intercultural communication classes have been partners in learning, and what a rewarding and uplifting experience it has been. Our students are always welcome with open arms in this church, always encouraged to come and participate in the events that unfold during and after the services. The climate in this community is incredibly inviting, supportive, and congenial. The community knows that we are not traveling some 70 miles for religious reasons but for building human bridges of understanding and sharing across our racial divide. Over the years, the community members have built the most heartwarming and effective bridges imaginable. We sing and pray together. After the church services, we walk together to the nearby community center where we have lunch together, and thanks to the creative choir director, we learn a new song or two and sing together, swaying and making a joyful noise.

Method of Study

In this study, 510 undergraduate students participated in the activities of an African American church community and were actively engaged in creating meaningful dialogue with members of the community. The data were collected from the students enrolled in our intercultural communication classes over a period of 5 years.

Before participating in this daylong field trip to the African American church community, the students studied and discussed such concepts as cultural anxiety, functions of prejudice, stereotyping, African spirituality (Richards, 1985), and Afrocentrism (Asante, 1987). In an open and supportive classroom environment, the students were encouraged to explore the underlying reasons for their own prejudices and what each of us could do to decrease our prejudices (Vora, 1998). This was followed by an orientation to the homiletics of the Black church (Hamlet, 1998; Richards, 1985; Stewart, 1984) and an orientation to this specific church and community.

The students drove their own cars or carpooled 75 miles to this community, leaving at 10:00 A.M. and returning about 5:00–6:00 P.M. on a Sunday. They attended the church services and actively engaged in dialogue with the members of the community at the nearby community center.

After returning home, each student was asked to anonymously respond to a 7-point Likert-type scale questionnaire seeking data on the student's changes in attitude, knowledge, and behavior toward African Americans as a result of participating in this event. In addition, the students were asked to write a brief paper describing how this intercultural field trip affected their attitudes toward African Americans, their feelings of ethnocentrism, and their intended behavioral change toward African Americans in the future.

To ensure that each student expressed his or her feelings freely, without any concern of what might be considered an expected or desirable answer, no grade was given for the written report of the experience. Every student received the same number of points for merely participating in this field trip, regardless of the content of their written papers.

The demographics of the 510 participants were 283 females and 227 males. They were all Caucasian. Four hundred forty-nine participants were between 21 and 24 years of age, and 61 participants were between 25 and 35 years of age.

Analysis and Results

Changes in Attitude

The students reported that, as a result of their participation in this experiential learning, their anxiety about interacting with African Americans in an African American community was greatly reduced, as indicated by the mean (2.06) and mode (1.00) scores on this question. They also viewed African Americans in a more positive light than they did before the field trip, as reflected by the mean (1.91) and mode (1.00) scores; their attitudes toward African Americans in general had become more positive and inclusive with mean (1.74) and mode (1.00) scores. The mode of 1.00 on each question indicated that the majority of the participants strongly agreed that their attitudes had changed positively toward African Americans. These changes in attitude had occurred relatively fast because 91% of the participants reported this to be their first time to have ever been in an African American community.

The qualitative data of the students' responses reinforced the findings of the above quantitative data. The following quotations were representative of the students' comments: . . .

I strongly believe that people can talk about this until their tongues fall off. It is not until a person experiences other cultures that they can truly say they understand that culture a little better. Man, and did I learn today, just from being in that community. My whole predisposition toward African Americans has changed from anxiety and avoidance to awareness that if I am open, and let others in, I will be the richer for it. Today I am truly rich!

To tell you the truth, I really did have a "phobia" about Black people. Now that I was there, I feel that Black people have been given an unfair chance in society. The oppression they have gone through has certainly not been done by people who have gotten to know them and knew what they were doing, but by those who, like me, have a phobia toward people they don't know. I now would question those people on how they got their stereotypes and prejudices, whether they know if they are correct, and whether they have experienced the culture and people toward which they were being racist. My own ignorance has continued too long, and I am so happy that it was not too late to bring it to an end. Thank you so much for this opportunity.

Both the quantitative and qualitative data support that the attitudes of the White students toward African Americans were favorably and significantly affected by their participation in this experiential learning. Their anxiety to interact with African Americans was reduced after this field trip. The students overwhelmingly reported that they viewed African Americans in a more positive light and that they were ashamed of their previous stereotypes and prejudices. The students reported that their attitude toward African Americans had definitely become more positive and inclusive. Occasionally, a student remarked how much there is to learn from African Americans, especially from the courage, strength, and love of the people he or she met in this community.

Change in Ethnocentrism

The all-day engagement of the White students with members in this African American community was found to have a significant but balanced effect on the students' ethnocentric views. In relation to the statement, "My ways of living and interacting with others are the best," the mean was 4.60, with a mode of 4.00 and a standard deviation of 1.36, indicating that they disagreed with the statement. Similarly, in relation to the statement, "African American ways of living and interacting with others are the best," the mean was 4.57, with a standard deviation of 1.29 and a mode of 4.00. The students' active participation in the African American community led them to believe that neither their own ways nor African American ways of living and interacting are the best. The students reported that both cultures have their own appropriateness and value.

The qualitative data supported these quantitative findings as reflected in the following quotations:

> *This whole experience made me ashamed of all the superior "hoopla" that I unnecessarily went through, because of my Euro-centric way in which I was raised. This fieldtrip informed me and enlightened me. In my mind, all the way home, I began to count all of my classmates that I had in high school. Then it struck me so sad to realize that out of those 89 students, I may be the only one who will have ever experienced what I had that day. That is probably so because of the small town that I had come from, none of them have ever taken a step, such as this one, and will ever realize the difference and greatness of African American ways. This saddens me, for I have changed my views so much.*

This experience has definitely shown me that my culture is not better than the Black culture we visited. As a matter of fact, there were many aspects that I enjoyed more about the African American culture, like music, and the free spirited expression, specially [sic] the drums, the highly animated preacher, the call and the response. That's just great! But my way of expression is fine for me too, even though now it seems boring. As they say, "to each his own."

I learned that the "us" can become "they" and the "they" can become "us." It all depends how we look at things. If you don't get to know another way, you will always think your own way is better. That is what I have done in relation to religion and I believed that you must pray quietly in a church. Well, today I learned that you can "make a joyful noise" and still praise the Lord, and that He probably does not care how you do it, as long as you are sincere. . . .

Discussion

The experiential activity in this study was designed to give White American students, who had very little contact with African Americans, the opportunity to get to know their African American neighbors better, and to do so in a supportive environment. The field trip was carefully designed with appropriate orientation, organized activities, and debriefing reports so that White students from highly homogeneous small towns would take the first step toward engaging in meaningful interactions with and gain respect for African Americans. It was also designed to change the students' attitudes and anxieties toward African Americans and establish a level of trust in a warm and supportive environment. The many efforts of the truly warm and inviting church leader to engage the students with the community members and to make them feel welcome and at home played a significant role in the overwhelming success of this field trip. The various engagements with members of the African American church community greatly helped the White students to recognize that they had many prejudices toward a people that they had never even met. The day's events and the active engagements of the White students with members of this truly welcoming Black community helped immensely in building a bridge toward understanding and sharing. Hence, this experiential learning adventure was a success.

The empirical evidence of this study supported the notion that a positive experience in another culture does positively impact the attitudes, understanding, and behavior of the participants. The positive experiences of the White students in this Black church community led to their positive attitudes toward African Americans. The insight gained from these findings was that, even at age 25 and beyond, a person with negative attitudes toward another culture can change these attitudes after an intensive and positive experience in that culture. This promises to be a very hopeful sign for developing intercultural understanding and mutual respect, and it gives us hope that we can indeed undo racism between Black and White folks in the United States.

The findings of this study seem to suggest that positive attitudes toward people from other cultures are also related to, and may be followed by, two other outcomes: tempering of ethnocentrism and increasing interactive behavior with individuals from other cultures. After actively participating in the Black community and engaging with its members, a large majority of the participants in this study rejected the notion that their Eurocentric ways were the best. They recognized that Afrocentric ways are equally appropriate. On the behavioral side, many of the participants indicated that they intend to interact, or already have increased their interactions, with African Americans. The experience had an uplifting effect on the participating students and shed a lot of their preconceived notions. In the words of one of the students, "It offered hope for change in many of us." Black and White folks praying together, singing, making a joyful noise together, eating, and creating meaningful dialogue created community and goodwill between them and brought them closer together. The students thoroughly enjoyed this positive experience and were thankful for the opportunity to engage in a meaningful way with members of this remarkable community. Many students reported shedding their inhibitions and desired to seek more contact with African Americans in the future.

The partnership and engagement between a predominantly White Midwestern university and a welcoming and warm African American community proved extremely successful toward helping reduce the students' intercultural anxiety, prejudice, and even racism. This unique partnership between a Black church and a White student body has turned the students' intercultural anxiety and fear into enthusiasm and excitement. Help toward undoing racism and opening cultural blinders came generously from a Black church community, and with open arms.

The implications for educators are that the traditional teacher-centered model needs to shift to a student-centered learning model, especially in relation to culture learning that involves both the cognitive and the affective domains. Positive interactions between Black folks and White folks result in positive attitudes toward one another, reduce ethnocentrism, and increase effective intercultural interactions. Furthermore, if future interactions remain positive, there would be deeper understanding of and mutual respect for one another. Because this study was designed with a careful orientation to relevant cultural concepts for a positive intercultural experience, no conclusions can be drawn about the effect of negative experiences on intercultural understanding, attitudes, and behavior.

REFERENCES

Asante, M. K. (1987). *The Afrocentric idea*. Philadelphia: Temple University Press.

Beane, J. (1990). *Affect in the curriculum: Toward democracy, dignity and diversity*. New York: Teachers College Press.

Davis, N. (1992). Teaching about inequality: Student resistance, paralysis, and rage. *Teaching Sociology, 20*, 232–238.

Gonzalez, A., Houston, M., & Chen, V. (Eds.). (1998). *Our voices: Essays in culture, ethnicity, and communication*. Los Angeles: Roxbury.

Hamlet, J. (1998). The reason why we sing. In A. Gonzalez et al. (Eds.), *Our voices: Essays in culture, ethnicity, and communication* (pp. 92–97). Los Angeles: Roxbury.

Jackson, S. E. (1992). *Diversity in the workplace*. New York: The Guilford Press.

Jamieson, D., & O'Mara, J. (1992). *Managing workplace 2000: Gaining the diversity advantage*. San Francisco: Jossey-Bass.

Janzen, R. (1999). Five paradigms of ethnic relations. In L. Samovar & R. Porter (Eds.), *Intercultural communication: A reader* (9th ed.) (pp. 52–59). Belmont, CA: Wadsworth.

Richards, D. (1985). The implications of African American spirituality. In M. K. Asante & K. W. Asante (Eds.), *African culture: The rhythms of unity* (pp. 209–214). Trenton, NJ: Africa World.

Seelye, H. N. (1993). *Teaching culture: Strategies for intercultural communication*. Lincolnwood, IL: National Textbook Company.

Stewart, W. H., Sr. (1984). *Interpreting God's word in Black preaching*. Valley Forge, PA: Judson.

Tjosvold, D. (1991). *The conflict-positive organization: Stimulate diversity and create unity*. Reading, MA: Addison-Wesley.

Van Dijk, T. A. (1987). *Communicating racism: Ethnic prejudice in thought and talk*. Newbury Park, CA: Sage.

Vora, E. (1998). *Managing conflict across cultures*. Paper presented at the annual conference for public administrators. Port Elizabeth, South Africa.

STUDY QUESTIONS

1. How much of an impact did the visits to the Black church have on the students? Report the data.
2. Why were these experiences so "inspiring" for the students?

Gender

GENDER IS A BASIC, FUNDAMENTAL QUALITY OF SOCIAL LIFE. Each of us has been affected through socialization into gender roles and each of us has a component of gender in our identity. More recently, sociology has decided to examine gender as a social structure—something that is part of all the institutions in society. We notice strong gender patterns in the family, the economy, religion, education, the law, politics, medicine, and even in our marriages and peer groups. Everywhere we look gender is present—in every social structure and organization, in every person. Something so elemental in society must certainly be important to understanding how society is structured and how boys and girls and men and women experience social life.

Sociology and the area of women's studies have shown that men and women do not have the same opportunities in society. The distribution of power in society, when it is based on gender, finds a disproportionate amount going to males. Males are privileged and females become a minority group that suffers through discrimination in nearly every area of life. Patriarchal structures, those that advantage men and disadvantage women, are typical of society. In general, men make more money in the economy, men have more power in families, marriages, religious settings, politics, and are benefited more than women at every turn in life. Gender stratification in society has become a heated and much studied issue as women's roles in America have begun to change so dramatically in the past 100 years and even more dramatically in the past 50 years.

While it is not true that "men are from Mars and women are from Venus," television and magazines and popular culture stress the extreme differences between the sexes. Science, in general, and sociology, specifically, does not believe that men and women are opposites. Rather, it is understood that boys and girls and men and women adapt to gender roles in social settings (structures) in ways that affirm gender differences and give men an advantage at the expense of women. Women in America do two or three times as much home labor as men and may carry as much as 90 percent of the child care responsibilities. The family, then, is a place that can be seen as oppressing women while giving men the benefits of family life with little of the labor. These same patterns of dominance and submission are enacted in every structure in society. What is to be learned from a sociological look at gender? Is equal pay and equal power something that we can expect, or is it just another ideal pursued by a minority of people who cannot affect the social structures that maintain the differences?

Men are a more recent topic in the sociology of gender. While women comprise the minority group, men are not without their gender issues in America. Violence, in its many obvious and not-so-obvious forms, is part of the masculine legacy of dominance. The agreed-upon cultural imperative for men to be "real men" or "traditional men" is called hegemonic masculinity. Hegemony for men carries with it problems of violence, poor health, elevated criminal activity, increased physical risk, and shorter lives—by nearly seven years compared to women. Is it really "a man's world"?

First, the piece from Judith Lorber analyzes gender as a social structure and illuminates how the "paradox of gender" brings contrary influences to society and our lives. This seminal theoretical piece has been the standard of recent discussions about gender as "social construction" and gender as "structure." Second, in a quantitative study of advertisements by Simon Davis, we learn that gender typing occurs for both men and women. A novel use of "personal ads" points to the reciprocal gender biases that allow men and women to be viewed as objects. Third, Beth Quinn looks at the process of "girl watching" in organizations where people work and interact. She notices that men have difficulty seeing their behaviors as sexually harassing in this very applied and interesting study.

JUDITH LORBER

"Night to His Day"
The Social Construction of Gender

Talking about gender for most people is the equivalent of fish talking about water. Gender is so much the routine ground of everyday activities that questioning its taken-for-granted assumptions and presuppositions is like thinking about whether the sun will come up.[1] Gender is so pervasive that in our society we assume it is bred into our genes. Most people find it hard to believe that gender is constantly created and re-created out of human interaction, out of social life, and is the texture and order of that social life. Yet gender, like culture, is a human production that depends on everyone constantly "doing gender" (West and Zimmerman 1987).

And everyone "does gender" without thinking about it. Today, on the subway, I saw a well-dressed man with a year-old child in a stroller. Yesterday, on a bus, I saw a man with a tiny baby in a carrier on his chest. Seeing men taking care of small children in public is increasingly common—at least in New York City. But both men were quite obviously stared at—and smiled at, approvingly. Everyone was doing gender—the men who were changing the role of fathers and the other passengers, who were applauding them silently. But there was more gendering going on that probably fewer people noticed. The baby was wearing a white crocheted cap and white clothes. You couldn't tell if it was a boy or a girl. The child in the stroller was wearing a dark blue T-shirt and dark print pants. As they started to leave the train, the father put a Yankee baseball cap on the child's head. Ah, a boy, I thought. Then I noticed the gleam of tiny earrings in the child's ears, and as they got off, I saw the little flowered sneakers and lace-trimmed socks. Not a boy after all. Gender done.

Gender is such a familiar part of daily life that it usually takes a deliberate disruption of our expectations of how women and men are supposed to act to pay attention to how it is produced. Gender signs and signals are so ubiquitous that we usually fail to note them—unless they are missing or ambiguous. Then we are uncomfortable until we have successfully placed the other person in a gender status; otherwise, we feel socially dislocated. In our society, in addition to man and woman, the status can be *transvestite* (a person who dresses in opposite-gender clothes) and *transsexual* (a person who has had sex-change surgery). Transvestites and transsexuals carefully construct their gender status by dressing, speaking, walking, gesturing in the ways prescribed for women or men—whichever they want to be taken for—and so does any "normal" person.

For the individual, gender construction starts with assignment to a sex category on the basis of what the genitalia look like at birth.[2] Then babies are dressed or adorned in a way that displays the category because parents don't want to be constantly asked whether their baby is a girl or a boy. A sex category becomes a gender status through naming, dress, and the use of other gender markers. Once a child's gender is evident, others treat those in one gender differently from those in the other, and the children respond to the different treatment by feeling different and behaving differently. As soon as they can talk, they start to refer to themselves as members of their gender. Sex doesn't come into play again until puberty, but by that time, sexual feelings and desires and practices have been shaped by gendered norms and expectations. Adolescent boys and girls approach and avoid each other in an elaborately scripted and gendered mating dance. Parenting is gendered, with different expectations for mothers and for fathers, and people of different genders work at different kinds of jobs. The work adults do as mothers and fathers and as low-level workers and high-level bosses, shapes women's and men's life experiences, and these experiences produce different feelings, consciousness, relationships, skills—ways of being that we call feminine or masculine.[3] All of these processes constitute the social construction of gender.

Gendered roles change—today fathers are taking care of little children, girls and boys are wearing unisex clothing and getting the same education, women and men are working at the same jobs. Although many traditional social groups are quite strict about maintaining gender differences, in other social groups they seem to be blurring. Then why the one-year-old's earrings? Why is it still so important to mark a child as a girl or a boy, to make sure she is not taken for a boy or he for a girl? What would happen if they were? They would, quite literally, have changed places in their social world.

To explain why gendering is done from birth, constantly and by everyone, we have to look not only at the way individuals experience gender but at gender as a social institution. As a social institution, gender is one of the major ways that human beings organize their lives. Human society depends on a predictable division of labor, a designated allocation of scarce goods, assigned responsibility for children and others who cannot care for themselves, common values and their systematic transmission to new members, legitimate leadership, music, art, stories, games, and other symbolic productions. One way of choosing people for the different tasks of society is on the basis of their talents, motivations, and competence—their demonstrated achievements. The other way is on the basis of gender, race, ethnicity—ascribed membership in a category of people. Although societies vary in the extent to which they use one or the other of these ways of allocating people to work and to carry out other responsibilities, every society uses gender and age grades. Every society classifies people as "girl and boy children," "girls and boys ready to be married," and "fully adult women and men," constructs similarities among them and differences between them, and assigns them to different roles and responsibilities. Personality characteristics, feelings, motivations, and ambitions flow from these different life experiences so that the members of these different groups become different kinds of people. The process of gendering and its outcome are legitimated by religion, law, science, and the society's entire set of values. . . .

Western society's values legitimate gendering by claiming that it all comes from physiology—female and male procreative differences. But gender and sex are not equivalent, and gender as a social construction does not flow automatically from genitalia and reproductive organs, the main physiological differences of females and males. In the construction of ascribed social statuses, physiological differences such as sex, stage of development, color of skin, and size are crude markers. They are not the source of the social statuses of gender, age grade, and race. Social statuses are carefully constructed through prescribed processes of teaching, learning, emulation, and enforcement. Whatever genes, hormones, and biological evolution contribute to human social institutions is materially as well as qualitatively transformed by social practices. Every social institution has a material base, but culture and social practices transform that base into something with qualitatively different patterns and constraints. The economy is much more than producing food and goods and distributing them to eaters and users; family and kinship are not the equivalent of having sex and procreating; morals and religions cannot be equated with the fears and ecstasies of the brain; language goes far beyond the sounds produced by tongue and larynx. No one eats "money" or "credit"; the concepts of "god" and "angels" are the subjects of theological disquisitions; not only words but objects, such as their flag, "speak" to the citizens of a country.

Similarly, gender cannot be equated with biological and physiological differences between human females and males. The building blocks of gender are *socially constructed statuses*. Western societies have only two genders, "man" and "woman." Some societies have three genders—men, women, and *berdaches* or *hijras* or *xaniths*. Berdaches, hijras, and xaniths are biological males who behave, dress, work, and are treated in most respects as social women; they are therefore not men, nor are they female women; they are, in our language, "male women."[4] There are African and American Indian societies that have a gender status called *manly hearted women*—biological females who work, marry, and parent as men; their social status is "female men" (Amadiume 1987; Blackwood 1984). They do not have to behave or dress as men to have the social responsibilities and prerogatives of husbands and fathers; what makes them men is enough wealth to buy a wife.

Modern Western societies' *transsexuals* and *transvestites* are the nearest equivalent of these crossover genders, but they are not institutionalized as third genders (Bolin 1987). Transsexuals are biological males and females who have sex-change operations to alter their genitalia. They do so in order to bring their physical anatomy in congruence with the way they want to live and with their own sense of gender identity. They do not become a third gender; they change genders. Transvestites are males who live as women and females who live as men but do not intend to have sex-change surgery. Their dress, appearance, and mannerisms fall within the range of what is expected from members of the opposite gender, so that they "pass." They also change genders, sometimes temporarily, some for most of their lives. Transvestite women have fought in wars as men soldiers as recently as the nineteenth century; some married women, and others went back to being women and married men once the war was over.[5] Some were discovered when their wounds were treated; others not until they died. In order to work as a jazz musician, a man's occupation, Billy Tipton, a woman, lived most of her life as a man. She died recently at seventy-four, leaving a wife and three adopted sons for whom she was husband and father, and musicians with whom she had played and traveled, for whom she was "one of the boys" (*New York Times* 1989).[6] There have been many other such occurrences of women passing as men to do more prestigious or lucrative men's work (Matthaei 1982, 192–93).[7]

Genders, therefore, are not attached to a biological substratum. Gender boundaries are breachable, and individual and socially organized shifts from one gender to another call attention to "cultural, social, or aesthetic dissonances" (Garber 1992, 16). These odd or deviant or third genders show us what we ordinarily take for granted—that people have to learn to be women and men. . . .

For Individuals, Gender Means Sameness

Although the possible combinations of genitalia, body shapes, clothing, mannerisms, sexuality, and roles could produce infinite varieties in human beings, the social institution of gender depends on the production and maintenance of a limited number of gender statuses and of making the members of these statuses similar to each other. Individuals are born sexed but not gendered, and they have to be taught to be masculine or feminine.[8] As Simone de Beauvoir said: "One is not born, but rather becomes, a woman . . . ; it is civilization as a whole that produces this creature . . . which is described as feminine" (1952, 267).

Children learn to walk, talk, and gesture the way their social group says girls and boys should. Ray Birdwhistell, in his analysis of body motion as human communication, calls these learned gender displays *tertiary* sex characteristics and argues that they are needed to distinguish genders because humans are a weakly dimorphic species—their only sex markers are genitalia (1970, 39–46). Clothing, paradoxically, often hides the sex but displays the gender.

In early childhood, humans develop gendered personality structures and sexual orientations through their interactions with parents of the same and opposite gender. As adolescents, they conduct their sexual behavior according to gendered scripts. Schools, parents, peers, and the mass media guide young people into gendered work and family roles. As adults, they take on a gendered social status in their society's stratification system. Gender is thus both ascribed and achieved (West and Zimmerman 1987). . . .

Gender norms are inscribed in the way people move, gesture, and even eat. In one African society, men were supposed to eat with their "whole mouth, wholeheartedly, and not, like women, just with the lips, that is halfheartedly, with reservation and restraint" (Bourdieu [1980] 1990, 70). Men and women in this society learned to walk in ways that proclaimed their different positions in the society:

> *The manly man . . . stands up straight into the face of the person he approaches, or wishes to welcome. Ever on the alert, because ever threatened, he misses nothing of what happens around him. . . . Conversely, a well brought-up woman . . . is expected to walk with a slight stoop, avoiding every misplaced movement of her body, her head or her arms, looking down, keeping her eyes on the spot where she will next put her foot, especially if she happens to have to walk past the men's assembly. (70)*

. . . For human beings there is no essential femaleness or maleness, femininity or masculinity, womanhood or manhood, but once gender is ascribed, the social order constructs and holds individuals to strongly gendered norms and expectations. Individuals may vary on many of the components of gender and may shift genders temporarily or permanently, but they must fit into the limited number of gender statuses their society recognizes. In the process, they re-create their society's version of women and men: "If we do gender appropriately, we simultaneously sustain, reproduce, and render legitimate the institutional arrangements. . . . If we fail to do gender appropriately, we as individuals—not the institutional arrangements—may be called to account (for our character, motives, and predispositions)" (West and Zimmerman 1987, 146).

The gendered practices of everyday life reproduce a society's view of how women and men should act (Bourdieu [1980] 1990). Gendered social arrangements are justified by religion and cultural productions and backed by law, but the most powerful means of sustaining the moral hegemony of the dominant gender ideology is that the process is made invisible; any possible alternatives are virtually unthinkable (Foucault 1972; Gramsci 1971).[9]

For Society, Gender Means Difference

The pervasiveness of gender as a way of structuring social life demands that gender statuses be clearly differentiated. Varied talents, sexual preferences, identities, personalities, interests, and ways of interacting fragment the individual's bodily and social experiences. Nonetheless, these are organized in Western cultures into two and only two socially and legally recognized gender statuses, "man" and "woman."[10] In the social construction of gender, it does not matter what men and women actually do; it does not even matter if they do exactly the same thing. The social institution of gender insists only that what they do is *perceived* as different.

If men and women are doing the same tasks, they are usually spatially segregated to maintain gender separation, and often the tasks are given different job titles as well, such as executive secretary and administrative assistant (Reskin 1988). If the differences between women and men begin to blur, society's "sameness taboo" goes into action (G. Rubin 1975, 178). At a rock and roll dance at West Point in 1976, the year women were admitted to the prestigious military academy for the first time, the school's administrators "were reportedly perturbed by the sight of mirror-image couples dancing in short hair and dress gray trousers," and a rule was established that women cadets could dance at these events only if they wore skirts (Barkalow and Raab 1990, 53).[11] Women recruits in the U.S. Marine Corps are required to wear makeup—at a minimum, lipstick and eye shadow—and they have to take classes in makeup, hair care, poise, and etiquette. This feminization is part of a deliberate policy of making them clearly distinguishable from men Marines. Christine Williams quotes a twenty-five-year-old woman drill instructor as saying: "A lot of the recruits who come here don't wear makeup; they're tomboyish or athletic. A lot of them have the preconceived idea that going into the military means they can still be a tomboy. They don't realize that you are a *Woman Marine*" (1989, 76–77).[12]

If gender differences were genetic, physiological, or hormonal, gender bending and gender ambiguity would occur only in hermaphrodites, who are born with chromosomes and genitalia that are not clearly female or male. Since gender differences are socially constructed, all men and all women can enact the behavior of the other, because they know the other's social script: "'Man' and 'woman' are at once empty and overflowing categories. Empty because they have no ultimate, transcendental meaning. Overflowing because even when they appear to be fixed, they still contain within them alternative, denied, or suppressed definitions" (J. W. Scott 1988a, 49). . . .

Gender Ranking

For one transsexual man-to-woman, however, the experience of living as a woman changed his/her whole personality. As James, Morris had been a soldier, foreign correspondent, and mountain climber; as Jan, Morris is a successful travel writer. But socially, James was far superior to Jan, and so Jan developed the "learned helplessness" that is supposed to characterize women in Western society:

> We are told that the social gap between the sexes is narrowing, but I can only report that having, in the second half of the twentieth century, experienced life in both roles, there seems to me no aspect of existence, no moment of the day, no contact, no arrangement, no response, which is not different for men and for women. The very tone of voice in which I was now addressed, the very posture of the person next in the queue, the very feel in the air when I entered a room or sat at a restaurant table, constantly emphasized my change of status.
>
> And if other's responses shifted, so did my own. The more I was treated as [a] woman, the more woman I became. I adapted willy-nilly. If I was assumed to be incompetent at reversing cars, or opening bottles, oddly incompetent I found myself becoming. If a case was thought too heavy for me, inexplicably I found it so myself. . . . Women treated me with a frankness which, while it was one of the happiest discoveries of my metamorphosis, did imply membership of a camp, a faction, or at least a school of thought; so I found myself gravitating always towards the female, whether in sharing a railway compartment or supporting a political cause. Men treated me more and more as junior, . . . and so, addressed every day of my life as an inferior, involuntarily, month by month I accepted the condition. I discovered that even now men prefer women to be less informed, less able, less talkative, and certainly less self-centered than they are themselves; so I generally obliged them (1975, 165–66). . . . [13]

Gender as Process, Stratification, and Structure

As a social institution, gender is a process of creating distinguishable social statuses for the assignment of rights and responsibilities. As part of a stratification system that ranks these statuses unequally, gender is a major building block in the social structures built on these unequal statuses.

As a *process*, gender creates the social differences that define "woman" and "man." In social interaction throughout their lives, individuals learn what is expected, see what is expected, act and react in expected ways, and thus simultaneously construct and maintain the gender order: "The very injunction to be a given gender takes place through discursive routes: to be a good mother, to be a heterosexually desirable object, to be a fit worker, in sum, to signify a multiplicity of guarantees in response to a variety of different demands all at once" (J. Butler 1990, 145). Members of a social group neither make up gender as they go along nor exactly replicate in rote fashion what was done before. In almost every encounter, human beings produce gender, behaving in the ways they learned were appropriate for their gender status, or resisting or rebelling against these norms. Resistance and rebellion have altered gender norms, but so far they have rarely eroded the statuses.

Gendered patterns of interaction acquire additional layers of gendered sexuality, parenting, and work behaviors in childhood, adolescence, and adulthood. Gendered norms and expectations are enforced through informal sanctions of gender-inappropriate behavior by peers and by formal punishment or threat of punishment by those in authority should behavior deviate too far from socially imposed standards for women and men. . . .

As part of a *stratification* system, gender ranks men above women of the same race and class. Women and men could be different but equal. In practice, the process of creating difference depends to a great extent on differential evaluation. As Nancy Jay (1981) says: "That which is defined, separated out, isolated from all else is A and pure. Not-A is necessarily impure, a random catchall, to which nothing is external except A and the principle of order that separates it from Not-A" (45). From the individual's point of view, whichever gender is A, the other is Not-A; gender boundaries tell the individual who is like him or her, and all the rest are unlike. From society's point of view, however, one gender is usually the touchstone, the normal, the dominant, and the other is different, deviant, and subordinate. In Western society, "man" is A, "wo-man" is Not-A. (Consider what a society would be like where woman was A and man Not-A.)

The further dichotomization by race and class constructs the gradations of a heterogeneous society's stratification scheme. Thus, in the United States, white is A, African American is Not-A; middle class is A, working class is Not-A, and "African-American women occupy a position whereby the inferior half of a series of these dichotomies converge"

(P. H. Collins 1990, 70). The dominant categories are the hegemonic ideals, taken so for granted as the way things should be that white is not ordinarily thought of as a race, middle class as a class, or men as a gender. The characteristics of these categories define the Other as that which lacks the valuable qualities the dominants exhibit.

In a gender-stratified society, what men do is usually valued more highly than what women do because men do it, even when their activities are very similar or the same. In different regions of southern India, for example, harvesting rice is men's work, shared work, or women's work: "Wherever a task is done by women it is considered easy, and where it is done by [men] it is considered difficult" (Mencher 1988, 104). A gathering and hunting society's survival usually depends on the nuts, grubs, and small animals brought in by the women's foraging trips, but when the men's hunt is successful, it is the occasion for a celebration. Conversely, because they are the superior group, white men do not have to do the "dirty work," such as housework; the most inferior group does it, usually poor women of color (Palmer 1989). . . .

Societies vary in the extent of the inequality in social status of their women and men members, but where there is inequality, the status "woman" (and its attendant behavior and role allocations) is usually held in lesser esteem than the status "man." Since gender is also intertwined with a society's other constructed statuses of differential evaluation—race, religion, occupation, class, country of origin, and so on—men and women members of the favored groups command more power, more prestige, and more property than the members of the disfavored groups. Within many social groups, however, men are advantaged over women. The more economic resources, such as education and job opportunities, are available to a group, the more they tend to be monopolized by men. In poorer groups that have few resources (such as working-class African Americans in the United States), women and men are more nearly equal, and the women may even outstrip the men in education and occupational status (Almquist 1987).

As a *structure*, gender divides work in the home and in economic production, legitimates those in authority, and organizes sexuality and emotional life (Connell 1987, 91–142). As primary parents, women significantly influence children's psychological development and emotional attachments, in the process reproducing gender. Emergent sexuality is shaped by heterosexual, homosexual, bisexual, and sadomasochistic patterns that are gendered—different for girls and boys, and for women and men—so that sexual statuses reflect gender statuses.

When gender is a major component of structured inequality, the devalued genders have less power, prestige, and economic rewards than the valued genders. In countries that discourage gender discrimination, many major roles are still gendered; women still do most of the domestic labor and child rearing, even while doing full-time paid work; women and men are segregated on the job and each does work considered "appropriate"; women's work is usually paid less than men's work. Men dominate the positions of authority and leadership in government, the military, and the law; cultural productions, religions, and sports reflect men's interests.

In societies that create the greatest gender difference, such as Saudi Arabia, women are kept out of sight behind walls or veils, have no civil rights, and often create a cultural and emotional world of their own (Bernard 1981). But even in societies with less rigid gender boundaries, women and men spend much of their time with people of their own gender because of the way work and family are organized. This spatial separation of women and men reinforces gendered differentness, identity, and ways of thinking and behaving (Coser 1986).

Gender inequality—the devaluation of "women" and the social domination of "men"—has social functions and a social history. It is not the result of sex, procreation, physiology, anatomy, hormones, or genetic predispositions. It is produced and maintained by identifiable social processes and built into the general social structure and individual identities deliberately and purposefully. The social order as we know it in Western societies is organized around racial ethnic, class, and gender inequality. I contend, therefore, that the continuing purpose of gender as a modern social institution is to construct women as a group to be the subordinates of men as a group. The life of everyone placed in the status "woman" is "night to his day—that has forever been the fantasy. Black to his white. Shut out of his system's space, she is the repressed that ensures the system's functioning" (Cixous and Clément [1975] 1986, 67).

NOTES

1. Gender is, in Erving Goffman's words, an aspect of *Felicity's Condition:* "any arrangement which leads us to judge an individual's . . . acts not to be a manifestation of strangeness. Behind Felicity's Condition is our sense of what it is to be sane" (1983, 27). Also see Bern 1993; Frye 1983, 17–40; Goffman 1977.
2. In cases of ambiguity in countries with modern medicine, surgery is usually performed to make the genitalia more clearly male or female.
3. See J. Butler 1990 for an analysis of how doing gender *is* gender identity.
4. On the hijras of India, see Nanda 1990; on the xaniths of Oman, Wikan 1982, 168–86; on the American Indian berdaches, W. L. Williams 1986. Other societies that have similar institutionalized third-gender men are the Koniag of Alaska, the Tanala of Madagascar, the Mesakin of Nuba, and the Chukchee of Siberia (Wikan 1982, 170).

5. Durova 1989; Freeman and Bond 1992; Wheelwright 1989.
6. Gender segregation of work in popular music still has not changed very much, according to Groce and Cooper 1989, despite considerable androgyny in some very popular figures. See Garber 1992 on the androgyny. She discusses Tipton on pp. 67–70.
7. In the nineteenth century, not only did these women get men's wages, but they also "had male privileges and could do all manner of things other women could not: open a bank account, write checks, own property, go anywhere unaccompanied, vote in elections" (Faderman 1991, 44).
8. For an account of how a potential man-to-woman transsexual learned to be feminine, see Garfinkel 1967, 116–85, 285–88. For a gloss on this account that points out how, throughout his encounters with Agnes, Garfinkel failed to see how he himself was constructing his own masculinity, see Rogers 1992.
9. The concepts of moral hegemony, the effects of everyday activities (praxis) on thought and personality, and the necessity of consciousness of these processes before political change can occur are all based on Marx's analysis of class relations.
10. Other societies recognize more than two categories, but usually no more than three or four (Jacobs and Roberts 1989).
11. Carol Barkalow's book has a photograph of eleven first-year West Pointers in a math class, who are dressed in regulation pants, shirts, and sweaters, with short haircuts. The caption challenges the reader to locate the only woman in the room.
12. The taboo on males and females looking alike reflects the U.S. military's homophobia (Bérubé 1989). If you can't tell those with a penis from those with a vagina, how are you going to determine whether their sexual interest is heterosexual or homosexual unless you watch them having sexual relations?
13. See Bolin 1988, 149–50, for transsexual men-to-women's discovery of the dangers of rape and sexual harassment. Devor's "gender blenders" went in the opposite direction. Because they found that it was an advantage to be taken for men, they did not deliberately cross-dress, but they did not feminize themselves either (1989, 126–40).

REFERENCES

Almquist, Elizabeth M. 1987. Labor market gendered inequality in minority groups. *Gender & Society* 1:400–14.

Amadiume, Ifi. 1987. *Male daughters, female husbands: Gender and sex in an African society*. London: Zed Books.

Barkalow, Carol, with Andrea Raab. 1990. *In the men's house*. New York: Poseidon Press.

Bem, Sandra Lipsitz. 1993. *The lenses of gender: Transforming the debate on sexual inequality*. New Haven: Yale University Press.

Bernard, Jessie. 1981. *The female world*. New York: Free Press.

Bérubé, Allan. 1989. Marching to a different drummer: Gay and lesbian GIs in World War II. In Duberman, Vicinus, and Chauncey.

Birdwhistell, Ray L. 1970. *Kinesics and context: Essays on body motion communication*. Philadelphia: University of Pennsylvania Press.

Blackwood, Evelyn. 1984, Sexuality and gender in certain Native American tribes: The case of cross-gender females. *Signs* 10:27–42.

Bolin, Anne. 1987. Transsexualism and the limits of traditional analysis. *American Behavioral Scientist* 31:41–65.

———. 1988. *In search of Eve: Transsexual rites of passage*. South Hadley, Mass.: Bergin & Garvey.

Bourdieu, Pierre. [1980] 1990. *The logic of practice*. Stanford, Calif.: Stanford University Press.

Butler, Judith. 1990. *Gender trouble: Feminism and the subversion of identity*. New York and London: Routledge.

Cixous, Hélène, and Catherine Clément. [1975] 1986. *The newly born woman*, translated by Betsy Wing. Minneapolis: University of Minnesota Press.

Collins, Patricia Hill. 1989. The social construction of Black feminist thought. *Signs* 14:745–73.

Connell, R.[Robert] W. 1987. *Gender and power: Society, the person, and sexual politics*. Stanford, Calif.: Stanford University Press.

Coser, Rose Laub. 1986. Cognitive structure and the use of social space. *Sociological Forum* 1:1–26.

De Beauvoir, Simone. 1953. *The second sex*, translated by H. M. Parshley, New York: Knopf.

Devor, Holly. 1989. *Gender blending: Confronting the limits of duality*. Bloomington: Indiana University Press.

Durova, Nadezhda. 1989. *The cavalry maiden: Journals of a Russian officer in the Napoleonic Wars*, translated by Mary Fleming Zirin. Bloomington: Indiana University Press.

Faderman, Lillian. 1991. *Odd girls and twilight lovers: A history of lesbian life in twentieth-century America*. New York: Columbia Univeristy Press.

Foucault, Michel. 1972. *The archeology of knowledge and the discourse on language*, translated by A. M. Sheridan Smith. New York: Pantheon.

Freeman, Lucy, and Alma Halbert Bond. 1992. *America's first woman warrior: The courage of Deborah Sampson*. New York: Paragon.

Frye, Marilyn. 1983. *The politics of reality: Essays in feminist theory*. Trumansburg, N.Y.: Crossing Press.

Garber, Marjorie. 1992. *Vested interests: Cross-dressing and cultural anxiety*. New York and London: Routledge.

Garfinkel, Harold. 1967. *Studies in ethnomethodology*. Englewood Cliffs, N.J.: Prentice-Hall.

Goffman, Erving. 1977. The arrangement between the sexes. *Thoery and Society* 4:301–33.

Gramsci, Antonio. 1971. *Selections from the prison notebooks*, translated and edited by Quintin Hoare and Geoffrey Nowell Smith. New York: International Publishers.

Jacobs, Sue-Ellen, and Christine Roberts. 1989. Sex, sexuality, gender, and gender variance. In *Gender and anthropology*, edited by Sandra Morgen. Washington, D.C.: American Anthropological Association.

Jay, Nancy. 1981. Gender and dichotomy. *Feminist Studies* 7:38–56.

Matthaei, Julie A. 1982. *An economic history of women's work in America*. New York: Schocken.

Mencher, Joan. 1988. Women's work and poverty: Women's contribution to household maintenance. In Dwyer and Bruce.

Morris, Jan. 1975. *Conundrum*. New York: Signet.

Nanda, Serena. 1990. *Neither man nor woman: The hijiras of India*. Belmont, Calif.: Wadsworth.

New York Times. 1989a. Musician's death at 74 reveals he was a woman. 2 February.

Palmer, Phyllis. 1989. *Domesticity and dirt: Housewives and domestic servants in the United States, 1920–1945*. Philadelphia: Temple University Press.

Reskin, Barbara F. 1988. Bringing the men back in: Sex differentiation and the devaluation of women's work. *Gender & Society* 2:58–81.

Rogers, Mary F. 1992. They were all passing: Agnes, Garfinkel, and company. *Gender & Society* 6:169–91.

Rubin, Gayle. 1975. The traffic in women: Notes on the political economy of sex. In *Toward an anthropology of women*, edited by Rayna R[app] Reiter. New York: Monthly Review Press.

Scott, Joan Wallach. 1988a. *Gender and the politics of history*. New York: Columbia University Press.

West, Candace, and Don Zimmerman. 1987. Doing gender. *Gender & Society* 1:125–51.

Wheelwright, Julie. 1989. *Amazons and military maids: Women who cross-dressed in pursuit of life, liberty and happiness*. London: Pandora Press.

Wikan, Unni. 1982. *Behind the veil in Arabia: Women in Oman*. Baltimore, Md.: Johns Hopkins University Press.

Williams, Christine L. 1989. *Gender differences at work: Women and men in nontraditional occupations*. Berkeley: University of California Press.

Williams, Walter L. 1986. *The spirit and the flesh: Sexual diversity in American Indian culture*. Boston: Beacon Press.

STUDY QUESTIONS

1. What does it mean when Lorber writes "night to his day"? What are the sociological implications of this metaphor?

2. After reading this selection, which includes a great deal of sociological theory, how different do you think men and women really are? List the differences and similarities.

SIMON DAVIS

Men as Success Objects and Women as Sex Objects
A Study of Personal Advertisements

Previous research has indicated that, to a large extent, selection of opposite-sex partners is dictated by traditional sex stereotypes (Urberg, 1979). More specifically, it has been found that men tend to emphasize sexuality and physical attractiveness in a mate to a greater extent than women (e.g., Harrison & Saeed, 1977; Deaux & Hanna, 1984; Nevid, 1984); this distinction has been found across cultures, as in the study by Stiles and colleagues (1987) of American and Icelandic adolescents.

The relatively greater preoccupation with casual sexual encounters demonstrated by men (Hite, 1987, p. 184) may be accounted for by the greater emotional investment that women place in sex; Basow (1986, p. 80) suggests that the "gender differences in this area (different meaning attached to sex) may turn out to be the strongest of all gender differences."

Women, conversely, may tend to emphasize psychological and personality characteristics (Curry & Hock, 1981; Deaux & Hanna, 1984), and to seek longevity and commitment in a relationship to a greater extent (Basow, 1986, p. 213).

Women may also seek financial security more so than men (Harrison & Saeed, 1977). Regarding this last point, Farrell (1986, p. 25) suggests that the tendency to treat men as success objects is reflected in the media, particularly in advertisements in women's magazines. On the other hand, men themselves may reinforce this stereotype in that a number of men still apparently prefer the traditional marriage with working husband and unemployed wife (Basow, 1986, p. 210).

Men have traditionally been more dominant in intellectual matters, and this may be reinforced in the courting process: Braito (1981) found in his study that female coeds feigned intellectual inferiority with their dates on a number of occasions. In the same vein, Hite, in her 1981 survey, found that men were less likely to seek intellectual prowess in their mate (p. 108).

The mate selection process has been characterized in at least two ways. Harrison and Saeed (1977) found evidence for a matching process, where individuals seeking particular characteristics in a partner were more likely to offer those characteristics in themselves. This is consistent with the observation that "like attracts like" and that husbands and wives tend to resemble one another in various ways (Thiessen & Gregg, 1980). Additionally, an exchange process may be in operation, wherein a trade-off is made with women offering "domestic work and sex for financial support" (Basow, 1986, p. 213).

With respect to sex stereotypes and mate selection, the trend has been for "both sexes to believe that the other sex expects them to live up to the gender stereotype" (Basow, 1986, p. 209).

Theoretical explanations of sex stereotypes in mate selection range from the sociobiological (Symons, 1987) to radical political views (Smith, 1973). Of interest in recent years has been demographic influences, that is, the lesser availability of men because of population shifts and marital patterns (Shaevitz, 1987, p. 40). Age may differentially affect women, particularly when children are desired; this, combined with women's generally lower economic status [particularly when unmarried (Halas, 1981, p. 124)], may mean that the need to "settle down" into a secure, committed relationship becomes relatively more crucial for women.

The present study looks at differential mate selection by men and women as reflected in newspaper companion ads. Using such a forum for the exploration of sex stereotypes is not new; for instance, in the study by Harrison and Saeed (1977) cited earlier, the authors found that in such ads women were more likely to seek financial security and men to seek attractiveness; a later study by Deaux and Hanna (1984) had similar results, along with the finding that women were more likely to seek psychological characteristics, specific personality traits, and to emphasize the quality and longevity of the relationship. The present study may be seen as a follow-up of this earlier research, although on this occasion using a Canadian setting. Of particular interest was the following: Were traditional stereotypes still in operation, that is, women being viewed as sex objects and men as success objects (the latter defined as financial and intellectual accomplishments)?

Method

Personal advertisements were taken from the *Vancouver Sun*, which is the major daily newspaper serving Vancouver, British Columbia. The *Sun* is generally perceived as a conservative, respectable journal— hence it was assumed that people advertising in it represented the "mainstream." It should be noted that people placing the ads must do so in person. For the sake of this study, gay ads were not included. A typical ad would run about 50 words, and included a brief description of the person placing it and a list of the attributes desired in the other party. Only the parts pertaining to the attributes desired in the partner were included for analysis. Attributes that pertained to hobbies or recreations were not included for the purpose of this study.

The ads were sampled as follows: Only Saturday ads were used, since in the *Sun* the convention was for Saturday to be the main day for personal ads, with 40–60 ads per edition—compared to only 2–4 ads per edition on weekdays. Within any one edition *all* the ads were included for analysis. Six editions were randomly sampled, covering the period of September 30, 1988, to September 30, 1989. The attempt to sample through the calendar year was made in an effort to avoid any unspecified seasonal effect. The size of the sample (six editions) was large enough to meet goodness-of-fit requirements for statistical tests.

The attributes listed in the ads were coded as follows:

1. *Attractive:* specified that a partner should be, for example, "pretty" or "handsome."
2. *Physique:* similar to 1; however, this focused not on the face but rather on whether the partner was "fit and trim," "muscular," or had "a good figure." If it was not clear if body or face was being emphasized, this fell into variable (1) by default.
3. *Sex:* specified that the partner should have, for instance, "high sex drive," or should be "sensuous" or "erotic," or if there was a clear message that this was an arrangement for sexual purposes ("lunchtime liaisons—discretion required").
4. *Picture:* specified that the partner should include a photo in his/her reply.
5. *Profession:* specified that the partner should be a professional.
6. *Employed:* specified that the partner should be employed, e.g., "must hold steady job" or "must have steady income."

7. *Financial:* specified that the partner should be, for instance, "financially secure" or "financially independent."
8. *Education:* specified that the partner should be, for instance, "well educated" or "well read," or should be a "college grad."
9. *Intelligence:* specified that the partner should be "intelligent," "intellectual," or "bright."
10. *Honest:* specified, for instance, that the partner should be "honest" or have "integrity."
11. *Humor:* specified "sense of humor" or "cheerfulness."
12. *Commitment:* specified that the relationship was to be "long term" or "lead to marriage," or some other indication of stability and longevity.
13. *Emotion:* specified that the partner should be "warm," "romantic," "emotionally supportive," "emotionally expressive," "sensitive," "loving," "responsive," or similar terms indicating an opposition to being cold and aloof.

In addition to the 13 attribute variables, two other pieces of information were collected: The length of the ad (in lines) and the age of the person placing the ad. Only if age was exactly specified was it included; if age was vague (e.g., "late 40s") this was not counted.

Variables were measured in the following way: Any ad requesting one of the 13 attributes was scored once for that attribute. If not explicitly mentioned, it was not scored. The scoring was thus "all or nothing," e.g., no matter how many times a person in a particular ad stressed that looks were important it was only counted as a single score in the "attractive" column; thus, each single score represented one person. Conceivably, an individual ad could mention all, some, or none of the variables. Comparisons were then made between the sexes on the basis of the variables, using percentages and chi-squares. Chi-square values were derived by cross-tabulating gender (male/female) with attribute (asked for/not asked for). Degrees of freedom in all cases equaled one. Finally, several of the individual variables were collapsed to get an overall sense of the relative importance of (a) physical factors, (b) employment factors, and (c) intellectual factors.

Results

A total of 329 personal ads were contained in the six newspaper editions studied. One ad was discarded in that it specified a gay relationship, leaving a total sample of 328. Of this number, 215 of the ads were placed by men (65.5%) and 113 by women (34.5%).

The mean age of people placing ads was 40.4. One hundred and twenty seven cases (38.7%) counted as missing data in that the age was not specified or was vague. The mean age for the two sexes was similar: 39.4 for women (with 50.4% of cases missing) and 40.7% for men (with 32.6% of cases missing).

Sex differences in desired companion attributes are summarized in Table I. It will be seen that for 10 of the 13 variables a statistically significant difference was detected. The three largest differences were found for attractiveness, professional and financial status. To summarize the table: in the case of attractiveness, physique, sex, and picture (physical attributes) the men were more likely than the women to seek these. In the case of professional status, employment status, financial status, intelligence, commitment, and emotion (nonphysical attributes) the women were more likely to seek these. The women were also more likely to specify education, honesty and humor, however not at a statistically significant level.

The data were explored further by collapsing several of the categories: the first 4 variables were collapsed into a "physical" category, Variables 5–7 were collapsed into an "employment" category, and Variables 8 and 9 were collapsed into an "intellectual" category. The assumption was that the collapsed categories were sufficiently similar

TABLE I   Gender Comparison for Attributes Desired in Partner

	Gender		
Variable	Desired by men (n = 215)	Desired by women (n = 113)	Chi-square
1. Attractive	76 (35.3%)	20 (17.7%)	11.13[a]
2. Physique	81 (37.7%)	27 (23.9%)	6.37[a]
3. Sex	25 (11.6%)	4 (3.5%)	6.03[a]
4. Picture	74 (34.4%)	24 (21.2%)	6.18[a]
5. Profession	6 (2.8%)	19 (16.8%)	20.74[a]
6. Employed	8 (3.7%)	12 (10.6%)	6.12[a]
7. Financial	7 (3.2%)	22 (19.5%)	24.26[a]
8. Education	8 (3.7%)	8 (7.1%)	1.79 (ns)
9. Intelligence	22 (10.2%)	24 (21.2%)	7.46[a]
10. Honest	20 (9.3%)	17 (15.0%)	2.44 (ns)
11. Humor	36 (16.7%)	26 (23.0%)	1.89 (ns)
12. Commitment	38 (17.6%)	31 (27.4%)	4.25[a]
13. Emotion	44 (20.5%)	35 (31.0%)	4.36[a]

[a]*Significant at the .05 level.*

(within the three new categories) to make the new larger categories conceptually meaningful; conversely, it was felt the remaining variables (10–13) could not be meaningfully collapsed any further.

Sex differences for the three collapsed categories are summarized in Table II. Note that the Table II figures were not derived simply by adding the numbers in the Table I categories: recall that for Variables 1–4 a subject could specify all, one, or none; hence simply adding the Table I figures would be biased by those individuals who were more effusive in specifying various physical traits. Instead, the Table II categories are (like Table I) all or nothing: whether a subject specified one or all four of the physical attributes it would only count once. Thus, each score represented one person.

In brief, Table II gives similar, although more exaggerated results to Table I. (The exaggeration is the result of only one item of several being needed to score within a collapsed category.) The men were more likely than the women to specify some physical attribute. The women were considerably more likely to specify that the companion be employed, or have a profession, or be in good financial shape. And the women were more likely to emphasize the intellectual abilities of their mate.

One can, incidentally, also note from this table an overall indication of attribute importance by collapsing across sexes, i.e., it is apparent that physical characteristics are the most desired regardless of sex.

TABLE II Gender Comparison for Physical, Employment, and Intellectual Attributes Desired in Partner

| | Gender | | |
| | Desired by men ($n = 215$) | Desired by women ($n = 113$) | |
Variable			Chi-square
Physical (collapsing Variables 1–4)	143 (66.5%)	50 (44.2%)	15.13[a]
Employment (collapsing Variables 5–7)	17 (7.9%)	47 (41.6%)	51.36[a]
Intellectual (collapsing 8 and 9)	29 (13.5%)	31 (27.4%)	9.65[a]

[a]Significant at the .05 level.

Discussion

Sex Differences

This study found that the attitudes of the subjects, in terms of desired companion attributes, were consistent with traditional sex role stereotypes. The men were more likely to emphasize stereotypically desirable feminine traits (appearance) and deemphasize the nonfeminine traits (financial, employment, and intellectual status). One inconsistency was that emotional expressiveness is a feminine trait but was emphasized relatively less by the men. Women, on the other hand, were more likely to emphasize masculine traits such as financial, employment, and intellectual status, and valued commitment in a relationship more highly. One inconsistency detected for the women concerned the fact that although emotional expressiveness is not a masculine trait, the women in this sample asked for it, relatively more than the men, anyway. Regarding this last point, it may be relevant to refer to Basow's (1986, p. 210) conclusion that "women prefer relatively androgynous men, but men, especially traditional ones, prefer relatively sex-typed women."

These findings are similar to results from earlier studies, e.g., Deaux and Hanna (1984), and indicate that at this point in time and in this setting sex role stereotyping is still in operation.

One secondary finding that was of some interest to the author was that considerably more men than women placed personal ads—almost a 2:1 ratio. One can only speculate as to why this was so; however, there are probably at least two (related) contributing factors. One is that social convention dictates that women should be less outgoing in the initiation of relationships: Green and Sandos (1983) found that women who initiated dates were viewed less positively than their male counterparts. Another factor is that whoever places the ad is in a "power position" in that they can check out the other person's letter and photo, and then make a choice, all in anonymity; one could speculate that this need to be in control might be more an issue for the men.

Methodological Issues

Content analysis of newspaper ads has its strengths and weaknesses. By virtue of being an unobtrusive study of variables with face validity, it was felt some reliable measure of gender-related attitudes was being achieved. That the mean age of the men and women placing the ads was similar was taken as support for the assumption that the two sexes in this sample were demographically similar. Further, sex differences in desired companion attributes could not be attributed to differential verbal ability in that it was found that length of ad was similar for both sexes.

On the other hand, there were some limitations. It could be argued that people placing personal ads are not representative of the public in general. For instance, with respect to this study, it was found that the subjects were a somewhat older group—mean age of 40—than might be found in other courting situations. This raises the possibility of age being a confounding variable. Older singles may emphasize certain aspects of a relationship, regardless of sex. On the other hand, there is the possibility that age differentially affects women in the mate selection process, particularly when children are desired. The strategy of controlling for age in the analysis was felt problematic in that the numbers for analysis were fairly small, especially given the missing data, and further, that one cannot assume the missing cases were not systematically different (i.e., older) from those present.

REFERENCES

Basow, S. (1986). *Gender stereotypes: Traditions and alternatives.* Brooks/Cole Publishing Co.

Braito, R. (1981). The inferiority game: Perceptions and behavior. *Sex Roles, 7,* 65–72.

Curry, T., & Hock, R. (1981). Sex differences in sex role ideals in early adolescence. *Adolescence, 16,* 779–789.

Deaux, K., & Hanna, R. (1984). Courtship in the personals column: The influence of gender and sexual orientation. *Sex Roles, 11,* 363–375.

Farrell, W. (1986). *Why men are the way they are.* New York: Berkley Books.

Green, S., & Sandos, P. (1983). Perceptions of male and female initiators of relationship. *Sex Roles, 9,* 849–852.

Halas, C. (1981). *Why can't a woman be more like a man?* New York: Macmillan Publishing Co.

Harrison, A., & Saeed, L. (1977). Let's make a deal: An analysis of revelations and stipulations in lonely hearts advertisements. *Journal of Personality and Social Psychology, 35,* 257–264.

Hite, S. (1981). *The Hite report on male sexuality.* New York: Alfred A. Knopf.

Hite, S. (1987). *Women and love: A cultural revolution in progress.* New York: Alfred A. Knopf.

Nevid, J. (1984). Sex differences in factors of romantic attraction. *Sex Roles, 11,* 401–411.

Shaevitz, M. (1987). *Sexual static.* Boston: Little, Brown & Co.

Smith, D. (1973). Women, the family and corporate capitalism. In M. Stephenson (Ed.), *Women in Canada.* Toronto: New Press.

Stiles, D., Gibbon, J., Hardardottir, S., & Schnellmann, J. (1987). The ideal man or woman as described by young adolescents in Iceland and the United States. *Sex Roles, 17,* 313–320.

Symons, D. (1987). An evolutionary approach. In J. Geer & W. O'Donohue (Eds.), *Theories of human sexuality.* New York: Plenum Press.

Thiessen, D., & Gregg, B. (1980). Human assortive mating and genetic equilibrium: An evolutionary perspective. *Ethology and Sociobiology, 1,* 111–140.

Urberg, K. (1979). Sex role conceptualization in adolescents and adults. *Developmental Psychology, 15,* 90–92.

STUDY QUESTIONS

1. What does it mean when Davis concludes that men and women are "objectified" by personal ads? Give an example of how you have objectified someone of the other gender and an example of how you have been objectified, too.
2. What conclusions does Davis draw from the two tables printed in the article?

BETH A. QUINN

Sexual Harassment and Masculinity

The Power and Meaning of "Girl Watching"

Confronted with complaints about sexual harassment or accounts in the media, some men claim that women are too sensitive or that they too often misinterpret men's intentions (Bernstein 1994; Buckwald 1993). In contrast, some women note with frustration that men just "don't get it" and lament the seeming inadequacy of sexual harassment policies (Conley 1991; Guccione 1992). Indeed, this ambiguity in defining acts of sexual harassment might be, as Cleveland and Kerst (1993) suggested, the most robust finding in sexual harassment research.

Using in-depth interviews with 43 employed men and women, this article examines a particular social practice—"girl watching"—as a means to understanding one way that these gender differences are produced. This analysis does not address the size or prevalence of these differences, nor does it present a direct comparison of men and women; this information is essential but well covered in the literature.[1] Instead, I follow Cleveland and Kerst's (1993) and Wood's (1998) suggestion that the question may best be unraveled by exploring how the "subject(ivities) of perpetrators, victims, and resistors of sexual harassment" are "discursively produced, reproduced, and altered" (Wood 1998, 28).

This article focuses on the subjectivities of the perpetrators of a disputable form of sexual harassment, "girl watching." The term refers to the act of men's sexually evaluating women, often in the company of other men. It may take the form of a verbal or gestural message of "check it out," boasts of sexual prowess, or explicit comments about a woman's body or imagined sexual acts. The target may be an individual woman or group of women or simply a photograph or other representation. The woman may be a stranger, coworker, supervisor, employee, or client. For the present analysis, girl watching within the workplace is centered.

The analysis is grounded in the work of masculinity scholars such as Connell (1987, 1995) in that it attempts to explain the subject positions of the interviewed men—not the abstract and genderless subjects of patriarchy but the gendered and privileged subjects embedded in this system. Since I am attempting to delineate the gendered worldviews of the interviewed men, I employ the term "girl watching," a phrase that reflects their language ("they watch girls").

I have chosen to center the analysis on girl watching within the workplace for two reasons. First, it appears to be fairly prevalent. For example, a survey of federal civil employees (U.S. Merit Systems Protection Board 1988) found that in the previous 24 months, 28 percent of the women surveyed had experienced "unwanted sexual looks or gestures," and 35 percent had experienced "unwanted sexual teasing, jokes, remarks, or questions." Second, girl watching is still often normalized and trivialized as only play, or "boys will be boys." A man watching girls—even in his workplace—is frequently accepted as a natural and commonplace activity, especially if he is in the presence of other men.[2] Indeed, it may be required (Hearn 1985). Thus, girl watching sits on the blurry edge between fun and harm, joking and harassment. An understanding of the process of identifying behavior as sexual harassment, or of rejecting this label, may be built on this ambiguity. . . .

Previous Research

The question of how behavior is or is not labeled as sexual harassment has been studied primarily through experimental vignettes and surveys.[3] In both methods, participants evaluate either hypothetical scenarios or lists of behaviors, considering whether, for example, the behavior constitutes sexual harassment, which party is most at fault, and what consequences the act might engender. Researchers manipulate factors such as the level of "welcomeness" the target exhibits and the relationship of the actors (supervisor-employee, coworker-coworker).

Both methods consistently show that women are willing to define more acts as sexual harassment (Gutek, Morasch, and Cohen 1983; Padgitt and Padgitt 1986; Powell 1986; York 1989; but see Stockdale and Vaux 1993) and are more likely to see situations as coercive (Garcia, Milano, and Quijano 1989). When asked who is more to blame in a particular scenario, men are more likely to blame, and less likely to empathize with, the victim (Jensen and Gutek 1982; Kenig and Ryan 1986). In terms of actual behaviors like girl watching, the U.S. Merit Systems Protection Board (1988) survey found that 81 percent of the women surveyed considered "uninvited sexually suggestive looks or gestures" from a supervisor to be sexual harassment. While the majority of men (68 percent) also defined it as such, significantly more men were willing to dismiss such behavior. Similarly, while 40 percent of the men would not consider the same behavior from a coworker to be harassing, more than three-quarters of the women would.

The most common explanation offered for these differences is gender role socialization. This conclusion is supported by the consistent finding that the more men and women adhere to traditional gender roles, the more likely they are to deny the harm in sexual harassment and to consider the behavior acceptable or at least normal (Gutek and Koss 1993; Malovich and Stake 1990; Murrell and Dietz-Uhler 1993; Popovich et al. 1992; Pryor 1987; Tagri and Hayes 1997). Men who hold predatory ideas about sexuality, who are more likely to believe rape myths, and who are more likely to self-report that they would rape under certain circumstances are less likely to see behaviors as harassing (Murrell and Dietz-Uhler 1993; Pryor 1987; Reilly et al. 1992). . . .

Method

I conducted 43 semistructured interviews with currently employed men and women between June 1994 and March 1995. . . . The interviews ranged in length from one to three hours. With one exception, interviews were audiotaped and transcribed in full. . . .

The interviews began with general questions about friendships and work relationships and progressed to specific questions about gender relations, sexual harassment, and the policies that seek to address it.[4] Since the main aim of the project was to explore how workplace events are framed as sexual harassment (and as legally bounded or not), the term "sexual harassment" was not introduced by the interviewer until late in the interview. . . .

Several related themes emerged and are discussed in the subsequent analysis. First, girl watching appears to function as a form of gendered play among men. This play is productive of masculine identities and premised on a studied lack of empathy with the feminine other. Second, men understand the targeted woman to be an object rather than a player in the game, and she is most often not the intended audience. This obfuscation of a woman's subjectivity, and men's refusal to consider the effects of their behavior, means men are likely to be confused when a woman complains. Thus, the production of masculinity though girl watching, and its compulsory disempathy, may be one factor in gender differences in the labeling of harassment.

Findings: Girl Watching as "Hommo-Sexuality"

[They] had a button on the computer that you pushed if there was a girl who came to the front counter. . . . It was a code and it said "BAFC"—Babe at Front Counter. . . . If the guy in the back looked up and saw a cute girl come in the station, he would hit this button for the other dispatcher to [come] see the cute girl.

—Paula, *police officer*

In its most serious form, girl watching operates as a targeted tactic of power. The men seem to want everyone—the targeted woman as well as coworkers, clients, and superiors—to know they are looking. The gaze demonstrates their right, as men, to sexually evaluate women. Through the gaze, the targeted woman is reduced to a sexual object, contradicting her other identities, such as that of competent worker or leader. . . .

But when they ogle, gawk, whistle and point, are men always so directly motivated to disempower their women colleagues? Is the target of the gaze also the intended audience? Consider, for example, this account told by Ed, a white, 29-year-old instrument technician.

When a group of guys goes to a bar or a nightclub and they try to be manly. . . . A few of us always found [it] funny [when] a woman would walk by and a guy would be like, "I can have her." [pause] "Yeah. OK, we want to see it!" [laugh]

In his account—a fairly common one in men's discussions—the passing woman is simply a visual cue for their play. It seems clear that it is a

game played by men for men; the woman's participation and awareness of her role seem fairly unimportant.

As Thorne (1993) reminded us, we should not be too quick to dismiss games as "only play." In her study of gender relations in elementary schools, Thorne found play to be a powerful form of gendered
social action. One of its "clusters of meaning" most relevant here is that
of "dramatic performance." In this, play functions as both a source of
fun and a mechanism by which gendered identities, group boundaries,
and power relations are (re)produced. . . .

Producing Masculinity

I suggest that girl watching in this form functions simultaneously as a
form of play and as a potentially powerful site of gendered social
action. Its social significance lies in its power to form identities and
relationships based on these common practices for, as Cockburn (1983,
123) has noted, "patriarchy is as much about relations between man
and man as it is about relations between men and women." Girl watching works similarly to the sexual joking that Johnson (1988) suggested
is a common way for heterosexual men to establish intimacy among
themselves.

In particular, girl watching works as a dramatic performance played
to other men, a means by which a certain type of masculinity is produced and heterosexual desire displayed. It is a means by which men
assert a masculine identity to other men, in an ironic "hommo-sexual"
practice of heterosexuality (Butler 1990).[5] As Connell (1995) and others
(Butler 1990; West and Zimmerman 1987) have aptly noted, masculinity
is not a static identity but rather one that must constantly be reclaimed.
The content of any performance—and there are multiple forms—is
influenced by a hegemonic notion of masculinity. When asked what
"being a man" entailed, many of the men and women I interviewed
triangulated toward notions of strength (if not in muscle, then in
character and job performance), dominance, and a marked sexuality,
overflowing and uncontrollable to some degree and natural to the
male "species." Heterosexuality is required, for just as the label "girl"
questions a man's claim to masculine power, so does the label "fag"
(Hopkins 1992; Pronger 1992). I asked Karl, for example, if he would
consider his sons "good men" if they were gay. His response was laced
with ambivalence; he noted only that the question was "a tough one."

The practice of girl watching is just that—a practice—one
rehearsed and performed in everyday settings. This aspect of rehearsal

was evident in my interview with Mike, a self-employed house painter who used to work construction. In locating himself as a born-again Christian, Mike recounted the girl watching of his fellow construction workers with contempt. Mike was particularly disturbed by a man who brought his young son to the job site one day. The boy was explicitly taught to catcall, a practice that included identifying the proper targets: women and effeminate men.

Girl watching, however, can be somewhat tenuous as a masculine practice. In their acknowledgment (to other men) of their supposed desire lies the possibility that in being too interested in women the players will be seen as mere schoolboys giggling in the playground. Taken too far, the practice undermines rather than supports a masculine performance. In Karl's discussion of girl watching, for example, he continually came back to the problem of men's not being careful about getting caught. He referred to a particular group of men who, though "their wives are [pause] very attractive—very much so," still "gawk like schoolboys." Likewise, Stephan explained that men who are obvious, who "undress [women] with their eyes" probably do so "because they don't get enough women in their lives. Supposedly." A man must be interested in women, but not too interested; they must show their (hetero)sexual interest, but not overly so, for this would be to admit that women have power over them. . . .

The Problem with Getting Caught

But are women really the untroubled objects that girl watching— viewed through the eyes of men—suggests? Obviously not; the game may be premised on a denial of a woman's subjectivity, but an actual erasure is beyond men's power! It is in this multiplicity of subjectivities, as Butler (1990, ix) noted, where "trouble" lurks, provoked by "the unanticipated agency of a female 'object' who inexplicably returns the glance, reverses the gaze, and contests the place and authority of the masculine position." To face a returned gaze is to get caught, an act that has the power to undermine the logic of girl watching as simply a game among men. Karl, for example, noted that when caught, men are often flustered, a reaction suggesting that the boundaries of usual play have been disturbed.[6]

When a woman looks back, when she asks, "What are you looking at?" she speaks as a subject, and her status as mere object is disturbed. When the game is played as a form of hommo-sexuality, the confronted man may be baffled by her response. When she catches them looking, when she complains, the targeted woman speaks as a subject. The men, however, understand her primarily as an object, and objects do not object. . . .

Reactions to Anti-Sexual Harassment Training Programs

The role that objectification and disempathy play in men's girl watching has important implications for sexual harassment training. Consider the following account of a sexual harassment training session given in Cindy's workplace. Cindy, an Italian American woman in her early 20s, worked as a recruiter for a small telemarketing company in Southern California.

> [The trainer] just really laid down the ground rules, um, she had some scenarios. Saying, "OK, would you consider this sexual harassment?" "Would you . . . " this, this, this? "What level?" Da-da-da. So, um, they just gave us some real numbers as to lawsuits and cases. Just that "you guys better be careful" type of a thing.

From Cindy's description, this training is fairly typical in that it focuses on teaching participants definitions of sexual harassment and the legal ramifications of accusations. The trainer used the common strategy of presenting videos of potentially harassing situations and asking the participants how they would judge them. Cindy's description of the men's responses to these videos reveals the limitation of this approach.

> We were watching [the TV] and it was [like] a studio audience. And [men] were getting up in the studio audience making comments like "Oh well, look at her! I wouldn't want to do that to her either!" "Well, you're darn straight, look at her!"

Interestingly, the men successfully used the training session videos as an opportunity for girl watching through their public sexual evaluations of the women depicted. In this, the intent of the training session was doubly subverted. The men interpreted scenarios that Cindy found plainly harassing into mere instances of girl watching and sexual (dis)interest. . . .

Conclusions

In this analysis, I have sought to unravel the social logic of girl watching and its relationship to the question of gender differences in the interpretation of sexual harassment. In the form analyzed here, girl watching functions simultaneously as only play and as a potent site where power is played. Through the objectification on which it is premised and in the nonempathetic masculinity it supports, this form of girl watching simultaneously produces both the harassment and the barriers to men's acknowledgment of its potential harm.

The implications these findings have for anti-sexual harassment training are profound. If we understand harassment to be the result of a simple lack of knowledge (of ignorance), then straightforward informational sexual harassment training may be effective. The present analysis suggests, however, that the etiology of some harassment lies elsewhere. While they might have quarreled with it, most of the men I interviewed had fairly good abstract understandings of the behaviors their companies' sexual harassment policies prohibited. At the same time, in relating stories of social relations in their workplaces, most failed to identify specific behaviors as sexual harassment when they matched the abstract definition. As I have argued, the source of this contradiction lies not so much in ignorance but in acts of ignoring. Traditional sexual harassment training programs address the former rather than the later. As such, their effectiveness against sexually harassing behaviors born out of social practices of masculinity like girl watching is questionable.

Ultimately, the project of challenging sexual harassment will be frustrated and our understanding distorted unless we interrogate hegemonic, patriarchal forms of masculinity and the practices by which they are (re)produced. We must continue to research the processes by which sexual harassment is produced and the gendered identities and subjectivities on which it poaches (Wood 1998). My study provides a first step toward a more process-oriented understanding of sexual harassment, the ways the social meanings of harassment are constructed, and ultimately, the potential success of antiharassment training programs.

NOTES

1. See Welsh (1999) for a review of this literature.
2. For example, Maria, an administrative assistant I interviewed, simultaneously echoed and critiqued this understanding when she complained about her boss's girl watching in her presence: "If he wants to do that in front of other men . . . you know, that's what men do."
3. Recently, more researchers have turned to qualitative studies as a means to understand the process of labeling behavior as harassment. Of note are Collinson and Collinson (1996), Giuffre and Williams (1994), Quinn (2000), and Rogers and Henson (1997).
4. Acme employees were interviewed at work in an office off the main lobby. Students and referred participants were interviewed at sites convenient to them (e.g., an office, the library).
5. "Hommo" is a play on the French word for man, homme.

6. Men are not always concerned with getting caught, as the behavior of catcalling construction workers amply illustrates; that a woman hears is part of the thrill (Gardner 1995). The difference between the workplace and the street is the level of anonymity the men have vis-à-vis the woman and the complexity of social rules and the diversity of power sources an individual has at his or her disposal.

REFERENCES

Bernstein, R. 1994. Guilty if charged. *New York Review of Books*, 13 January.

Buckwald, A. 1993. Compliment a woman, go to court. *Los Angeles Times*, 28 October.

Butler, J. 1990. *Gender trouble: Feminism and the subversion of identity*. New York: Routledge.

Cleveland, J. N., and M. E. Kerst. 1993. Sexual harassment and perceptions of power: An under-articulated relationship. *Journal of Vocational Behavior* 42 (1): 49–67.

Cockburn, C. 1983. *Brothers: Male dominance and technological change*. London: Pluto Press.

Conley, F. K. 1991. Why I'm leaving Stanford: I wanted my dignity back. *Los Angeles Times*, 9 June.

Connell, R. W. 1987. *Gender and power*. Stanford, CA: Stanford University Press.

———. 1995. *Masculinities*. Berkeley: University of California Press.

Garcia, L., L. Milano, and A. Quijano. 1989. Perceptions of coercive sexual behavior by males and females. *Sex Roles* 21 (9/10): 569–77.

Gardner, C. B. 1995. *Passing by: Gender and public harassment*. Berkeley: University of California Press.

Giuffre, P., and C. Williams. 1994. Boundary lines: Labeling sexual harassment in restaurants. *Gender & Society* 8:378–401.

Guccione, J. 1992. Women judges still fighting harassment. *Daily Journal*, 13 October, 1.

Gutek, B. A., and M. P. Koss. 1993. Changed women and changed organizations: Consequences of and coping with sexual harassment. *Journal of Vocational Behavior* 42 (1): 28–48.

Gutek, B. A., B. Morasch, and A. G. Cohen. 1983. Interpreting social-sexual behavior in a work setting. *Journal of Vocational Behavior* 22 (1): 30–48.

Hearn, J. 1985. Men's sexuality at work. In *The sexuality of men*, edited by A. Metcalf and M. Humphries. London: Pluto Press.

Hopkins, P. 1992. Gender treachery: Homophobia, masculinity, and threatened identities. In *Rethinking masculinity: Philosophical explorations in light of feminism*, edited by L. May and R. Strikwerda. Lanham, MD: Littlefield, Adams.

Jensen, I. W., and B. A. Gutek. 1982. Attributions and assignment of responsibility in sexual harassment. *Journal of Social Issues* 38 (4): 121–36.

Johnson, M. 1988. *Strong mothers, weak wives*. Berkeley: University of California Press.

Kenig, S., and J. Ryan. 1986. Sex differences in levels of tolerance and attribution of blame for sexual harassment on a university campus. *Sex Roles* 15 (9/10): 535–49.

Malovich, N. J., and J. E. Stake. 1990. Sexual harassment on campus: Individual differences in attitudes and beliefs. *Psychology of Women Quarterly* 14 (1): 63–81.

Murrell, A. J., and B. L. Dietz-Uhler. 1993. Gender identity and adversarial sexual beliefs as predictors of attitudes toward sexual harassment. *Psychology of Women Quarterly* 17 (2): 169–75.

Padgitt, S. C., and J. S. Padgitt. 1986. Cognitive structure of sexual harassment: Implications for university policy. *Journal of College Student Personnel* 27:34–39.

Popovich, P. M., D. N. Gehlauf, J. A. Jolton, J. M. Somers, and R. M. Godinho. 1992. Perceptions of sexual harassment as a function of sex of rater and incident form and consequent. *Sex Roles* 27 (11/12): 609–25.

Powell, G. N. 1986. Effects of sex-role identity and sex on definitions of sexual harassment. *Sex Roles* 14:9–19.

Pronger, B. 1992. Gay jocks: A phenomenology of gay men in athletics. In *Rethinking masculinity: Philosophical explorations in light of feminism*, edited by L. May and R. Strikwerda. Lanham, MD: Littlefield Adams.

Pryor, J. B. 1987. Sexual harassment proclivities in men. *Sex Roles* 17 (5/6): 269–90.

Quinn, B. A. 2000. The paradox of complaining: Law, humor, and harassment in the everyday work world. *Law and Social Inquiry* 25 (4): 1151–83.

Reilly, M. E., B. Lott, D. Caldwell, and L. DeLuca. 1992. Tolerance for sexual harassment related to self-reported sexual victimization. *Gender & Society* 6:122–38.

Rogers. J. K., and K. D. Henson. 1997. "Hey, why don't you wear a shorter skirt?" Structural vulnerability and the organization of sexual harassment in temporary clerical employment. *Gender & Society* 11:215–38.

Stockdale, M. S., and A. Vaux. 1993. What sexual harassment experiences lead respondents to acknowledge being sexually harassed? A secondary analysis of a university survey. *Journal of Vocational Behavior* 43 (2): 221–34.

Tagri, S., and S. M. Hayes. 1997. Theories of sexual harassment. In *Sexual harassment: Theory, research and treatment*, edited by W. O'Donohue. New York: Allyn & Bacon.

Thorne, B. 1993. *Gender play: Girls and boys in school*. Buckingham, UK: Open University Press.

U.S. Merit Systems Protection Board. 1988. *Sexual harassment in the federal government: An update*. Washington, DC: Government Printing Office.

Welsh, S. 1999. Gender and sexual harassment. *Annual Review of Sociology*: 169–90.

West, C., and D. H. Zimmerman. 1987. Doing gender. *Gender & Society* 1:125–51.

Wood, J. T. 1998. Saying makes it so: The discursive construction of sexual harassment. In *Conceptualizing sexual harassment as discursive practice*, edited by S. G. Bingham. Westport, CT: Praeger.

York, K. M. 1989. Defining sexual harassment in workplaces: A policy-capturing approach. *Academy of Management Journal* 32:830–50.

STUDY QUESTIONS

1. What methods were used in this research and why were they chosen for this topic?

2. What ways do men and women define "girl watching" differently? Is it harmless fun or sexual harassment?

PART FOUR

Social Institutions

TOPIC 11

Family

ONE OF THE MOST POPULAR SUBJECTS IN SOCIOLOGY IS THE study of family. The family is a common experience for nearly every person in society. We might idealize the family to be something that nurtures us and out of which we are launched into life, a source of affection and encouragement. It is also true that the family is a place of violence and pain for many people. Families, as a part of society, have many different roles to play in the lives of people who inhabit them. There is an economic role the family plays, an emotional role, and a role to socialize and parent children, and it is also a place where couples play out their relational lives. Family is central to our existence as social beings. Family is an institutional pattern, a social structure that focuses social life into a home where busy lives of work and school and activities must be integrated into some semblance of order. This organizing principle of the family is fraught with pitfalls and potential problems. It is not easy for all these goals to be met, and it is not easy for all persons involved to feel as though they receive what is due them as members of families.

People fall in love, may marry, and often have children. These children will grow up and fall in love and likely marry and have children of their own. These generational patterns create any number of subjects for sociology to study. Dating, courtship, marriage, parenting styles, divorce, dual-earner and dual-career families, grandparents, and many more areas of study arise out of the family. Many of us who study sociology find our own lives represented in these "sociological snapshots" of family life, and we can become interested in how it is that people select a partner or what class and ethnicity differences there are in child rearing. We could wonder how the divorce our own parents might have experienced will affect choices we make about marrying and whether their divorce will affect our own chances for divorce. These and many other topics enliven the pages of sociology texts and research journals.

The intimate relationships that occur inside families are among the most important in our lives. The love and support of a partner, as well as the close connection we experience between parents and children and between siblings, will last for decades and bring us a sense of importance and belonging. Alternately, intimate family relationships are full of a history, which can be negative. Negative history in family relations burdens them with "baggage" and resentments where we might find ourselves struggling to grow through the problems we inherit as a result of family life. Positive and negative, families are crucibles of intense feelings and strong allegiances. Learning about the family allows us to bring closure on much of our own childhood while understanding that we are caught in and creating patterns for the next generation as well.

Families, the bedrock of any society, are changing. As society changes, families must adapt to the new structures and processes resulting from this change. Families are the nexus of activities that include gender and employment and parenting and leisure. As the roles of American women have changed through increased employment and the emancipation from household labor, this has put additional pressures on the family to adapt to dual-earner households, higher divorce rates, and the need for childcare. In the personal lives of many, these changes have become significant political and economic issues.

Article selections in Topic 11: Family focus on cohabitation, "peer marriages," and how the family contributes to the relative success of siblings once they become adults. First, Susan L. Brown gives us a look at relationship quality among cohabiting couples. Cohabiting is one of the fastest growing trends in American families, and understanding the variables that affect the outcomes of cohabitating is the insight in this quantitative research. Second, Pepper Schwartz takes us inside the marriages of people who are more friends than lovers. Peer marriages illustrate equity and equality, but they have their own, unique problems as well. Third, an except from an award-wining book by Dalton Conley calls into question some of the most "tried and true" notions about social class and success, at least as tied to the family. Conley mounts a persuasive argument showing that most of our relative success in adulthood starts with the way we are treated by our family, and sibling differences in this regard are tied to which ones get the most resources as we grow up.

SUSAN L. BROWN

Relationship Quality Dynamics of Cohabiting Unions

Cohabitation is now a common feature in the life course. In 1970, there were 500,000 cohabiting couples, whereas today more than 4.2 million couples cohabit (U.S. Bureau of the Census, 1999). A majority of marriages today are preceded by cohabitation (Bumpass & Sweet, 1989). Most of the decline in the first marriage rate and all of the decline in the remarriage rate are offset by corresponding increases in cohabitation (Bumpass, Sweet, & Cherlin, 1991). The rapid increase in cohabitation has led researchers to explore its linkages to other important life events, such as divorce (Bennett, Blanc, & Bloom, 1988; Booth & Johnson, 1988; DeMaris & MacDonald, 1993; DeMaris & Rao, 1992; Lillard, Brien, & Waite, 1995; Schoen, 1992) and nonmarital childbearing (Bachrach, 1987; Landale & Fennelly, 1992; Loomis & Landale, 1994; Manning, 1993, 1995; Manning & Landale, 1996). Essentially, researchers have treated cohabitation as a measure of a premarital event that may influence the likelihood of subsequent events.

But is this how cohabitation ought to be conceptualized? Researchers continue to debate the answer to this question. Cohabiting unions are typically so short (averaging less than 2 years in duration) that we often think of them as transitory in nature. Indeed, research indicates that for most groups, cohabitation serves largely as a stepping-stone to marriage (e.g., Manning, 1993, 1995). For some segments of the population, however, cohabitation appears to be a long-term substitute for marriage (e.g., Puerto Rican women; Landale & Fennelly, 1992). Some researchers have argued that cohabitation is similar to being single

(Rindfuss & VandenHeuvel, 1990), whereas others have maintained that cohabitation is very much like marriage (Brown & Booth, 1996) and ought to be treated as a family status (Bumpass et al., 1991).

To resolve this debate, we need to move beyond research whose interest in cohabitation lies solely in its relationship to other life events (e.g., childbearing and divorce) and begin to explore the nature of the cohabiting relationship itself. In fact, understanding the nature of cohabiting relationships will help us to decipher those links between cohabitation and other important life events.

Relationship Quality among Cohabitors

Cross-sectional studies demonstrate that on average, cohabitors are involved in unions that are of poorer quality than marriages (Brown & Booth, 1996; Nock, 1995). Cohabitors report more frequent disagreements, less fairness and happiness, and greater instability than their married counterparts. However, a comparison of marrieds to cohabitors who plan to marry their partner (75% of cohabitors plan to formalize their union) reveals that the relationship quality of the two groups does not differ. Cohabitors without plans to marry their partner have especially poor relationship quality and are also in unions of longer duration than their counterparts with marriage plans, suggesting that duration and relationship quality are negatively related. Indeed, relationship duration has a greater negative effect on the relationship quality of cohabitors than of marrieds (Brown & Booth, 1996).

Marriage improves some aspects of cohabitors' relationship quality. For instance, cohabitors are less likely to use violence to solve relationship disputes after they marry (Brown, in press). Marriage also increases cohabiting women's happiness with their relationship. And marriage seems to ameliorate the negative consequences long unions have on perceptions of relationship fairness and happiness. Nevertheless, the strongest predictor of relationship quality at a later point in time is relationship quality at an earlier point in time; cohabitors' relationship quality appears stable. . . .

Taken together, studies of cohabitors' relationship quality and the literature on marital quality suggest potential similarities in union quality patterns for the two groups. For both marrieds and cohabitors, duration is negatively associated with relationship quality, yet relationship quality remains stable over time (Brown & Booth, 1996; Johnson et al., 1992). Consequently, it can be expected that relationship duration will have similar effects on the relationship quality of both cohabitors and marrieds. The present analysis evaluates whether the dynamics of cohabitors' relationship quality exhibit a pattern analogous to that found for marital quality. . . .

Data and Measures

Data come from the fast wave of the NSFH. The NSFH is a multistage probability sample of 13,007 persons who were interviewed during 1987 to 1988. These data are arguably the best available for studying the cohabiting population because cohabitors were oversampled ($N = 678$), and extensive information was gathered about the quality of their unions. More than 6,800 respondents were married at first interview. Fewer than 5% of cohabiting unions last more than 10 years (Bumpass & Sweet, 1989). To maximize comparability with marriages, analyses are restricted to those respondents in cohabiting or marital unions of no more than 10 years' duration.[1] This strategy has been employed in other research on NSFH cohabitors (Brown, 2000; DeMaris & MacDonald, 1993; Nock, 1995; Thomson & Colella, 1992). Also, only Blacks and Whites are examined here due to the small numbers of Hispanic, Asian, and other race cohabitors. These restrictions result in 646 cohabitors and 3,086 marrieds for analysis.[2]

Dependent Variables

Three measures of relationship quality are examined. The relationship happiness variable refers to the respondent's response to the question "Taking all things together, how happy are you with your relationship?" Responses range from 1 = *very unhappy* to 7 = *very happy*. Relationship interaction, a six-category variable, measures the amount of time the respondent spent alone with his or her partner during the past month. . . . Finally, the relationship instability variable gauges the respondent's estimation (on a 5-point scale) of the chance that the relationship will dissolve.

Independent Variables

Relationship duration is measured in months in the NSFH, but for ease of interpretation, this measure has been multiplied by 12 to yield a measure in which the unit is 1 year. The presence of children in the household, prior marital experience, and prior cohabiting experience are all indicator variables. Plans to marry among cohabitors is also a dichotomous measure; it is coded 1 if the respondent either reports definite plans to marry or thinks that she or he eventually will marry the current cohabiting partner, and 0 otherwise.

Control Variables

Variables associated with cohabitation and relationship quality are included as control variables. A control for race is included in all models because prior research (e.g., Adelmann et al., 1996) demonstrates that Blacks report poorer marital quality than Whites and because there are considerable racial differences in union formation rates (Raley, 1996). Gender, coded 1 for female, is included as a control variable both because women and men typically report unique views of marital quality (Thompson & Walker, 1989) and because cohabitation is more common among women (Bumpass & Sweet, 1989; Thornton, 1988). Both education and age are associated with cohabitation and relationship quality (Brown & Booth, 1996; Bumpass & Sweet, 1989; Glenn, 1990; Nock, 1995) and thus are included as controls. Education measures the number of years of school completed. Age is coded in years. . . .

Results

Table 1, which shows the means and standard deviations of all variables used in the analyses, reveals that although cohabitors report significantly more interaction with their partners than do marrieds, cohabitors are also significantly less happy with their relationships and believe their relationships are more unstable than do their married counterparts. The average duration of a cohabiting relationship is slightly less than 3 years, whereas among marrieds, average marital duration is a little more than 5 years. Marrieds are significantly more likely to have children than are cohabitors (66% vs. 41%, respectively). Although cohabitors are more likely to have prior marital experience, they are less likely to have prior cohabiting experience than marrieds, perhaps because a majority of cohabitors quickly transform their unions into marriages (Bumpass & Sweet, 1989). And as expected, about 72% of cohabitors report plans to marry their current partners. . . .

Cohabitors' happiness with their relationships, patterns of interaction, and perceived instability are all duration dependent. . . . Figure 1 graphically depicts [the] regression results. . . . With the passage of

TABLE 1 **Weighted Means and Standard Deviations of Variables Used in the Analyses**

Variable	Cohabiting M (SD)		Married M (SD)	
Dependent variables				
Relationship interaction	5.09	(1.29)	4.78	(1.44)
Relationship happiness	5.77	(1.33)	5.95	(1.32)
Relationship instability	2.00	(1.06)	1.46	(0.79)
Independent variables				
Duration	2.80	(2.24)	5.16	(2.78)
Children	0.41	(0.50)	0.66	(0.48)
Previously married	0.44	(0.50)	0.32	(0.47)
Previously cohabited	0.22	(0.42)	0.46	(0.50)
Plans to marry	0.72	(0.45)		
Control variables				
Black	0.18	(0.39)	0.10	(0.33)
Female	0.50	(0.50)	0.50	(0.50)
Education	12.36	(2.70)	13.23	(2.71)
Age	30.49	(9.45)	32.97	(10.22)

Source: National Survey of Families and Households.
Note: Mean values on all variables—except female—significantly differ for cohabitators and marrieds at the $p = .001$ level.

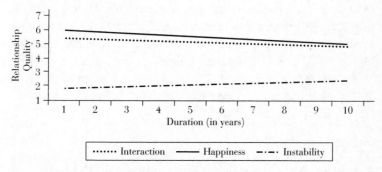

FIGURE 1 **Cohabitors' Predicted Relationship Quality**

time, happiness and interaction decrease, whereas instability increases. Similar to Glenn's (1998) analysis of marital quality, these results demonstrate that cohabitors also experience a linear decline in relationship quality during the first decade. . . .

In Figure 2, the pattern of interaction across duration is essentially the same for cohabitors and marrieds. Average levels of happiness appear slightly higher among marrieds than cohabitors, but happiness

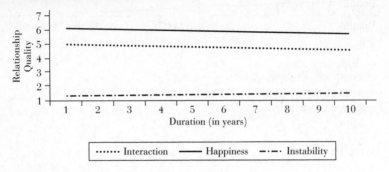

FIGURE 2   Marrieds' Predicted Relationship Quality

declines linearly with the passage of time for both groups. Instability exhibits unique patterns for marrieds and cohabitors. Although cohabitors experience a steady increase in relationship instability over time, marrieds' levels of instability are not related to duration. Rather, marital instability appears static across the first decade of marriage. These findings support the assertion by Johnson et al. (1992) that positive dimensions of marital quality tend to decline with time, whereas negative dimensions, such as instability, remain stable. Among marrieds, race is significantly associated with marital interaction, happiness, and instability. Blacks report lower levels of interaction and happiness and higher levels of instability than Whites, confirming findings from recent research (Adelmann et al., 1996) on racial differences in marital quality. Note that there are no significant racial differences in relationship quality among cohabitors.

Children

The presence of children tends to worsen cohabitors' relationship quality but does not explain the negative association between duration and relationship quality. Children decrease interaction and relationship happiness among cohabitors but do not alter perceptions of the stability of the relationship. Similar effects are observed for marrieds. Additional analyses (results not shown) reveal that differentiating stepchildren from biological children does not alter the pattern of effects. Also, the presence of adult children (i.e., children who are at least 18 years of age) has no significant effects on the three dimensions of relationship quality. Among cohabitors, children and duration negatively interact in their effects on relationship interaction and happiness (results not shown). In long cohabiting unions, children are associated with especially low levels of interaction and happiness, perhaps because nearly half of these unions involve children from prior unions. Among marrieds, children do not modify the effect of duration on marital quality. Children have similar effects on relationship happiness and instability for both cohabitors and marrieds, but the negative effect of children on interaction is somewhat weaker for cohabitors than for marrieds (results not shown).

Prior Union Experience

Prior union experience has significant consequences for the relationship quality of cohabitors and marrieds, but these effects are independent of duration. Among cohabitors, prior cohabitation experience decreases partner interaction and happiness with the current relationship and increases perceived instability. Among marrieds, prior cohabitation experience decreases relationship interaction and happiness and increases instability. There are no significant effects of prior marital unions. Union type does not modify the effects of prior cohabitation experience on relationship quality, nor does duration (results not shown), meaning that the adverse effects of earlier cohabiting unions persist throughout the duration of the current union.

Plans to Marry

Cohabitors with plans to marry their partner report higher relationship quality, on average, than those without such plans. . . . The plans-to-marry variable modifies the effect of duration on instability such that among those in unions of relatively short duration, plans to marry is associated with lower levels of relationship instability; whereas among those in relatively long unions, the plans-to-marry variable is actually associated with higher levels of instability (results not shown). This finding implies that cohabitors with marriage plans expect that their unions will be transformed quickly into marriages. When these expectations are not met, cohabitors perceive greater instability. In contrast, couples who do not desire marriage gain confidence over time that their relationship will remain intact. Hence, the effect of duration on relationship instability is conditioned by the cohabitor's marital intentions. . . .

Discussion

Cohabiting unions are experienced by a majority of young people today (Bumpass & Sweet, 1989). Although researchers (e.g., Brown & Booth, 1996; Nock, 1995) have compared the relationship quality of cohabitors and marrieds, little attention has been paid to the dynamics of cohabitors' relationship quality. Does the quality of cohabiting unions vary according to union duration? If so, how similar is the pattern for cohabiting unions to that observed for marriages?

The present study examines the duration dependence of relationship quality for cohabitors and marrieds and evaluates whether the presence of children or prior union experience account for or moderate the effect of duration. Cohabitors and marrieds experience similar declines in interaction with their partners during the first decade of their unions. Both groups also experience lower levels of happiness across time, although happiness is consistently higher among marrieds than cohabitors. Relationship instability increases considerably with the passage of time among cohabitors, but remains stable among marrieds. For cohabitors, long union duration has particularly devastating consequences for levels of happiness and instability. Both the presence of children and prior cohabitation experience are significantly associated with lower levels of relationship quality. The effect of duration on cohabitors' relationship quality is modified by the presence of children. Cohabitors in long unions with children report especially low levels of relationship interaction and happiness, possibly because nearly one half of such unions involve children from previous cohabitations or marriages.

There are important differences among cohabitors in the effects of duration on relationship quality. Among cohabitors without marriage plans, duration has no significant effect on the three dimensions of relationship quality. Among cohabitors with plans to marry, the effects of duration are similar to those observed for marrieds. For both groups, longer unions are associated with poorer relationship quality (except that marrieds experience no significant duration-related changes in instability).

Cohabiting unions are of relatively short duration, yet the dynamics of relationship quality parallel that of marriages in many regards. An important difference in the duration/relationship quality association for cohabitations and marriages is that the instability of cohabiting unions increases over time, whereas among marriages, reported instability does not vary with duration. This difference is probably due to the role of cohabitation in the life course. For most cohabitors, cohabitation is a transitory stage, typically a step in the courtship process. Most people enter cohabitation not expecting a long-term union but rather a short-term substitute for marriage. Not surprisingly, half of all cohabiting unions are formalized through marriage or dissolve within 2 years, and more than 90% end within 5 years (Bumpass & Sweet, 1989). Hence, the longer a cohabiting union persists, the greater the perceived instability, because cohabiting unions that are not formalized through marriage are likely to soon end in separation. Less than 10% of cohabiting unions are maintained for an extended (i.e., 5 or more years) period of time.

The present study demonstrates that despite their short length, the quality of cohabiting unions varies with time. Cohabitors experience declines in relationship interaction and happiness that are similar to those experienced by marrieds. But unlike marriages, the stability of cohabiting unions is related to duration. This unique effect is indicative of the meaning of cohabitation as well as its role in the family life course. The higher levels of instability characterizing long cohabitations probably result from unrealized marital intentions. Most cohabitors expect to marry their partners, and provided that they do so within a few years of initiating the cohabiting union, perceived instability remains low. Instability levels are extremely high for cohabitors in relatively long unions who intend to marry their partner. The longer cohabitors' intentions remain unmet, the less confident they are that the relationship will remain intact. Factors hindering marriage entry may include relationship stressors such as children or prior union experience, but ultimately, at least one partner is hesitant to marry. Without a commitment to marriage, the union is likely to fail. Thus, these analyses suggest that cohabitations serving as a prelude to marriage are characterized by low levels of instability, whereas cohabitations that are not readily transformed into marriages are hindered not only by high levels of instability but also especially low levels of relationship interaction and happiness.

NOTES

1. There is the potential for bias in the estimates of duration effects using cross-sectional models, but this potential is minimized by restricting the analyses to individuals in unions of no more than 10 years' duration.
2. A very small number of cases have missing data on some variables. For respondents with missing data on independent and control variables, the overall mean was substituted.

However, for respondents with missing data on the dependent variables (i.e., the three dimensions of relationship quality), mean substitutions were not made. Consequently, the sample sizes used in each of the relationship quality models vary slightly.

REFERENCES

Adelmann, P. K., Chadwick, K., & Baerger, D. R. (1996). Marital quality of Black and White adults over the life course. *Journal of Social and Personal Relationships, 13,* 361–384.

Bachrach, C. (1987). Cohabitation and reproductive behavior in the U.S. *Demography, 24,* 623–647.

Bennett, N. G., Blanc, A. K., & Bloom, D. E. (1988). Commitment and the modern union: Assessing the link between premarital cohabitation and subsequent marital stability. *American Sociological Review, 53,* 127–138.

Booth, A., & Johnson, D. R. (1988). Premarital cohabitation and marital success. *Journal of Family Issues, 9,* 255–272.

Brown, S. L. (in press). Moving from cohabitation to marriage. Effects on relationship quality. *Social Science Research.*

Brown, S. L. (2000). The effect of union type on psychological well-being: Depression among cohabitors versus marrieds. *Journal of Health and Social Behavior, 41,* 241–255.

Brown, S. L., & Booth, A. (1996). Cohabitation versus marriage: A comparison of relationship quality. *Journal of Marriage and the Family, 58,* 668–678.

Bumpass, L. L., & Sweet, J. A. (1989). National estimates of cohabitation. *Demography, 26,* 615–625.

Bumpass, L. L., Sweet, J. A., & Cherlin, A. J. (1991). The role of cohabitation in declining rates of marriage. *Journal of Marriage and the Family, 53,* 913–927.

DeMaris, A., & MacDonald, W. (1993). Premarital cohabitation and marital instability: A test of the unconventionality hypothesis. *Journal of Marriage and the Family, 55,* 399–407.

DeMaris, A., & Rao, K. V. (1992). Premarital cohabitation and subsequent marital stability in the United States: A reassessment. *Journal of Marriage and the Family, 54,* 178–190.

Glenn, N. D. (1990). Quantitative research on marital quality in the 1980s. *Journal of Marriage and the Family, 52,* 818–831.

Glenn, N. D. (1998). The course of marital success and failure in five American ten-year marriage cohorts. *Journal of Marriage and the Family, 60,* 569–576.

Johnson, D. R., Amoloza, T. O., & Booth, A. (1992). Stability and developmental change in marital quality: A three-wave panel analysis. *Journal of Marriage and the Family, 54,* 582–594.

Landale, N. S., & Fennelly, K. (1992). Informal unions among mainland Puerto Ricans: Cohabitation or an alternative to legal marriage? *Journal of Marriage and the Family, 54,* 269–280.

Lillard, L. A., Brien, M., & Waite, L. J. (1995). Premarital cohabitation and subsequent marital dissolution: Is it self-selection? *Demography, 32,* 437–458.

Loomis. L. S., & Landale, N. S. (1994). Nonmarital cohabitation and childbearing among Black and White American women. *Journal of Marriage and the Family, 56,* 949–962.

Manning, W. D. (1993). Marriage and cohabitation following premarital conception. *Journal of Marriage and the Family, 55,* 839–850.

Manning, W. D. (1995). Cohabitation, marriage, and entry into motherhood. *Journal of Marriage and the Family, 57,* 191–200.

Manning, W. D., & Landale, N. S. (1996). Racial and ethnic differences in the role of cohabitation in premarital childbearing. *Journal of Marriage and the Family, 58,* 63–77.

Nock, S. L. (1995). A comparison of marriages and cohabiting relationships. *Journal of Family Issues, 16,* 53–76.

Raley, R. K. (1996). A shortage of marriageable men? A note on the role of cohabitation in Black-White differences in marriage rates. *American Sociological Review, 61,* 973–983.

Rindfuss, R. R., & VandenHeuvel, A. (1990). Cohabitation: A precursor to marriage or an alternative to being single? *Population and Development Review, 16,* 703–726.

Schoen, R. (1992). First unions and the stability of first marriages. *Journal of Marriage and the Family, 54,* 281–284.

Thompson, L., & Walker, A. J. (1989). Gender in families: Women and men in marriage, work, and parenthood. *Journal of Marriage and the Family, 51,* 845–871.

Thomson, E., & Colella, U. (1992). Cohabitation and marital stability: Quality or commitment? *Journal of Marriage and the Family, 54,* 259–267.

Thornton, A. (1988). Cohabitation and marriage in the 1980s. *Demography, 25,* 497–508.

U.S. Bureau of the Census. (1999). *Unmarried-couple households, by presence of children: 1960 to present,* AD-2. Retrieved June 13, 2000, from http://www.census.gov/population/socdemo/ms-la/tabad-2.txt

STUDY QUESTIONS

1. What are the differences between cohabiting and married couples as the author discusses them?

2. What are the main variables, as presented in Brown's study, that affect the quality of the cohabiting union?

PEPPER SCHWARTZ

Peer Marriage
How Love Between Equals Really Works

In 1983 Philip Blumstein and I published the results of a large study on the nature of American relationships; it was called *American Couples*. The study, which received an enormous amount of notice from the press and the public, was composed of over 12,000 questionnaires and 600 interviews from married, cohabiting, lesbian, and gay members of couples.[1] During the course of what turned out to be a decade-long effort, I noticed that there were many same-sex couples with an egalitarian relationship but very few such heterosexual couples. Because the homosexual couples did not have to surmount the traditions of sex differences, they more often worked out relationships that both partners felt were fair and supportive to each other. My curiosity about their success at this aspect of their relationship, plus my admiration for the few egalitarian heterosexual couples in the study, made me want to know more about how married couples could get past traditions of gender and construct a relationship built on equality. Previous sociological studies on marriage made chances for egalitarian marriage seem grim, but since my own marriage was successfully egalitarian, I had both scientific and personal motivation to see why some couples reconstructed gender roles and others did not. To that end, I reexamined some of the egalitarian marriages in the *American Couples* study, used them as an archetype, and then sought more of these couples to talk to and learn from.

The couples, I discovered, based their marriages on a mix of equity (each person gives in proportion to what he or she receives) and equality (each person has equal status and is equally responsible for emotional, economic, and household duties). But these couples were distinguished by more than their dedication to fairness and collaboration; the most happy and durable among them also had refocused their relationship on *intense companionship*. To be sure, they shared child raising, chores, and decision making more or less equally and almost always equitably, but for most of them, this was just part of a plan for a true companionship marriage. The point of the marriage was not to share everything fifty-fifty. Rather, the shared decisions, responsibility, and household labor were in the service of an intimate and deeply collaborative marriage. I call this kind of marriage peer marriage; it is a marriage of equal companions, a collaboration of love and labor in order to produce profound intimacy and mutual respect.

The people in peer marriage for the most part are not ideologues. They construct and maintain a peer marriage because they find it rewarding. If they are without the means to hire the services of a homemaker, they seek work that allows both spouses to share child care and housework. These couples do not strike acquaintances as odd; they look just like their friends and co-workers, except that they have vigilantly preserved their commitment to equality. Additionally, they see peer marriage as salvation from instability. Many of them have witnessed the deterioration of their own previous marriage, or that of friends, and they believe that the only way to maintain a lifetime together is to create an irreplaceable, and interdependent, union of equals. . . .

In general, four characteristics of peer couples emerged. First, the partners did not generally have more than a sixty-forty traditional split of household duties and child raising. (An exception was made for the early periods of infancy, and even then, there had to be significant paternal involvement.) Second, each partner believed that each person in the couple had equal influence over important and disputed decisions. Third, partners felt that they had equal control over the family economy and reasonably equal access to discretionary funds. Most research has indicated that money confers power and relative income influences decision making.[2] These couples either had to earn similar amounts, or share power over family resources (such as having similar ability to undertake nonmonitored private spending). Fourth, each person's work was given equal weight in the couple's life plans. The person with the less glamorous and remunerative job could not always be the person with the most housework or child care. The requirement of sharing money, influence, decision making, child care and homemaking applied even for couples in which one person had a salaried job and the other stayed home. Among older couples, a history of traditional role division that no longer existed was allowable as long as it had not been true for the previous three years. The point was not to define these characteristics as the only way to reach a just, rewarding, and durable relationship but to use them to define the new, and spreading, phenomenon of marriages in which traditional roles were absent and there was no hidden hierarchy. . . .

My snowball sample (the term sociologists use for a sample whereby one person recommends the next) makes any statistical conclusions about peer couples seriously suspect. Nonetheless, certain attributes appeared again and again and are at least worth mentioning, if only as a guide for future research. These couples tended to be dual income; only three couples contained women who did not work at all. They were in their late twenties to mid-forties. There was only one much older couple (in their mid-sixties) and only a few in their mid-fifties. The age similarity was partially an artifact of the snowball sample but also probably a cohort effect. It was the baby boom generation who came of age at a time when feminist ideology was having its rebirth. This generation, born between 1945 and 1957, and its younger followers had to evaluate whether to embrace the new tenets and criticisms of marriage, or opt for the traditional model. The baby boom and post-baby boom women who endorsed feminist philosophy—or at least wanted to shuck old gender roles and constraints—have had to consider consciously the role of marriage in determining their life. Some had to think about *if* they wanted to be married, and all have examined *how* they wanted to be married. More of these women might be expected to want a relationship that gives them equal standing in marriage. Oddly, younger women among this group sometimes assumed a certain amount of equality and equity and thereby unconsciously settled for less.

This cohort explanation may also explain why almost half of these marriages contain a previously divorced partner. People in this age group have a higher divorce rate than the cohorts ahead of them. Also, the older women of the baby boom generation were more likely to have started marriage under one set of norms and reexamined it under a new, more feminist consciousness. Most of these women who were previously divorced said they left their first marriage because of inequitable treatment. Peer men were far more likely to recite a great number of reasons for the breakup of their marriage but were also likely to say it was either the end of their marriage or the difficult period after the marriage was over, a devastating period of fighting over property and support, that made them seek a peer relationship. Accusations of betrayal or continued emotional and financial dependence of the ex-spouse made these men much more interested in a different kind of marriage the next time: an independent, working spouse who could hold her own in a partnership.

The last, and rather unexpected, commonality among the peer couples was that they tended to be more middle class than working or upper middle class. As we shall see, egalitarian couples seem more likely when male income is not so grand that it encourages a nonworking wife or makes the wife's income unimportant. When a peer marriage had a high-earning male, it was likely there was also a high-earning female (or, as in a couple of cases, a female with a prestigious job such as an elected politician or a successful artist). But generally, most male occupations were *not* high pressure and high profile. It seems to be easier to create an egalitarian relationship if the man has a job (or creates one) that has some flexibility and controllable hours, and if both partners make similar amounts of money (for example, if both partners are teachers). Still, these kinds of background data do not provide the answers to the most intriguing commonalities of all: How did these people come to be in an egalitarian marriage? Why did they want to be peers?. . . .

Why Peer Marriage?

To any woman who was or is part of the women's movement, the answer to this question is clear. Women in the recent history of the United States, Canada, and most of Western European have experienced a rise in personal freedom that can be expected to extend to their family and personal life. This is particularly true for the women of the baby boom generation who grew up indulged by a kind economy and relatively permissive parents and who, along with the males in their cohort, rebelled against traditional social expectations: what it meant to be a woman, a man, a partner, a spouse.

Their critique of traditional marriage included the perception that it was unacceptably anti-individualistic. Traditionally, marriage is a corporate entity in which the self is supposed to be transformed to fulfill, depending on one's gender, the demands of supporter and provider, or father and mother. Both men and women, but especially a number of women, defied that loss of individuality and rigid description of duties. Women, for example, decided, either rationally or de facto, that virginity was no longer required in order to be a desirable spouse or a good wife. The institutionalization of premarital sex was just part of the questioning of gender requirements. Young people proclaimed that individual happiness was more important than familial duty. There was a general rejection of capitulation to traditional expectations. A number of women wrote about new ways to be female. Theories of male oppression and patriarchal culture flourished. And although the number of women who directly participated in these forums may have been statistically small, the reach of their thoughts and feelings was deep and broad. Women left marriage—or were left—in extraordinary numbers; the divorce rate has more than doubled since the early 1960s. Both women who stayed in marriages and women who left them learned a new language of anger and inequity. The appetite for equality and equity grew nationally and internationally, and even those who held onto traditional values about roles and relationships found themselves more aware and critical of some of the bargains of male and female relations. . . .

Of course, even if we wanted to, we could not erase all the differences between men and women that make them attracted and attached to each other, emotionally, erotically, and pragmatically. But now that we offer a real possibility of equality, many people get cold feet. They do not seek true equality because they are scared that all they will get is trouble for their effort. In some ways, the most dangerous impact of well-meaning books like *The Second Shift* is that they confirm readers' worst fears about the changing nature of male and female roles: that liberated women will only be liberated for more work, less love, less protection, and more exploitation. Men and women are worried about who they will have to be if they give up their traditional gender territories and remap their personal and family life. They are worried as well that the opening up of roles to personal choice rather than by sex will obliterate sexual differences and the interdependence of the sexes. Men and women know how to enjoy gender and marriage by the old ways, they feel lost when it comes to egalitarian marriage, have trouble believing the rewards of peer marriage would be worth the sacrifice it takes to get there, and they feel they are good enough where they are, having made significant strides from their parents' marriages and moving as close to egalitarian as they will ever get. They don't believe they can take the next step, so they stop short of it. They have a false sense of how far they have come and how far it is possible to go; they do not realize that the path they are on is not actually leading them to the place they want to go.

Then why peer marriage? Why have some couples moved through this considerable gauntlet to create an egalitarian partnership? Most simply, it is because they want to love each other as much as possible. They want a marriage that has intensity and partnership and does not create the distance between men and women that is inevitable between people of unequal status and power. These men and women looked at the lack of intimacy, and even at the anger and resentment between their parents or in previous relationships of their own, and wanted to avoid replication. Women who were consciously feminist did not want to be angry about inequity; men in love did not want to have an accusatory and resentful partner. Men and women who began as friends became deeply committed to maintaining that friendship, and took steps to preserve the relationship from the impact of traditional marriage. The common theme among these peer couples is the preservation of intimacy, the desire to be neither oppressor nor oppressed, the commitment to a relationship that creates a shared universe rather than parallel lives. When they designed their relationship to ensure those goals, the rewards of peer marriage became self-reinforcing.

But Who Would Be a Peer Man?

The common perception is that men do not want a peer marriage. Why should they give up all the privileges conferred by traditional marriage? And even if we can imagine that a man would like to share the burden of supporting a family or would like a career woman with whom to share his life, we know that most men have been loath to take on the burdens that women carry. It is hard to imagine as well that men who have the opportunity for high earnings and a prestigious job would sacrifice either for a more participatory family life. Because of these and similar observations, many women feel that peer men are born, not made, and so few of them exist that they are not worth looking for.

That is a misconception. Peer men often *are* made, *not* born. Many men came to peer values after they tried a fairly traditional relationship and found it didn't work for them. They enjoyed having service, support and household management from a traditional wife or a girlfriend—up to a point. Then they reported being either bored or overwhelmed with responsibility. Some fell in love with a "new woman"—an independent peer who was exactly the sort of woman they avoided or felt insecure around when they were younger. Many of the first wives of these men were furious at losing husbands after they had fulfilled the contract they both had signed. And when these women dated or remarried, they no longer presented themselves as they had as younger, more traditional women.

Others of these men had had traditional relationships that they liked just the way they were, until they went sour for a variety of reasons. It was the aftermath of the separation, divorce, custody, and alimony battles that changed their mind about what they wanted in their next relationship. Many of these men were very attached to their children and vowed never again to be the minor parent. Others had ex-wives who were lost without them, and the responsibility and guilt of that situation made them look for someone stronger.

Nevertheless, some of these men *were* "born peer." They came from homes where they got along with and respected an impressive mother or sister. Some had grown up doing their fair share of chores and babysitting. Quite a few of them were men who never felt comfortable with macho standards of masculinity. They liked female company; they liked to talk; they liked being in a family environment. One common distinguishing factor is that they liked children, looked forward to having their own, and wanted to be involved in the day-to-day upbringing of their family.

Some of these men were ambitious in their work; others were clear from the beginning that their work would come second to their marriage and family. But what they usually shared in common was the idea that they wanted an in-depth personal relationship that would not be sacrificed to work. They wanted a best friend.

It was this goal of deeper friendship that helped to "make" peer men. Much of what evolved between these men and women happened because of their strong desire to stay emotionally connected to one another. They saw each other as individuals rather than as roles and wanted the same things for each other that they sought for themselves. More often than not, the women in these relationships were good communicators and were clear about how they wanted and needed to be treated; they had a strong sense of what was a fair deal. The men had the ability to understand and support their partner's wishes. Most of these couples had to negotiate early in the relationship—and keep negotiating throughout it—to keep it a partnership rather than watching it slip into more traditional roles. One of the interesting things about peer men, is that they too had an investment in keeping that from happening. They were looking for an equal, a partner and a friend. They didn't want to lose that person to pressures to live a more conventional relationship. . . .

Rewards of Peer Marriage

Primacy of the Relationship

Egalitarian couples give priority to their relationship over their work and over all other relationships—with friends, extended family, even their children. Their mutual friendship is the most satisfying part of their lives. The point of equality and equity in these relationships is to create a marriage that makes each partner feel secure in the other person's regard and support.

Intimacy

Peer couples experience much more of each other's lives than do traditional or near peers. Because they share housework, children, and economic responsibility, they empathize as well as sympathize. They experience the world in a more similar way, understand the other partner's personality more accurately, and communicate better because they know each other and each other's world better and because equal power in the relationship changes interaction style. They negotiate more than other couples, they share conversational time, and they are less often high-handed, dismissive, or disrespectful than other couples. They choose to spend a lot of time together.

Commitment

These couples are more likely than traditional couples to find each other irreplaceable. They are likely to describe their relationship as "unique." Their interdependence becomes so deep (unlike near-peer dual-career couples) and so utterly customized that the costs of splitting up become prohibitive.

Costs of Peer Marriage

So if the rewards are so great, how come there are near peers? Why would anyone who believed in equality back off? The following problems will be discussed throughout the chapters.

Treason Against Tradition

One of the costs of defining gender and marriage differently is that many people feel that the nature and purpose of marriage and sex roles have been betrayed. Far from enabling a man to stay home with his children or a woman to take her role as equally responsible breadwinner seriously, co-workers and managers and friends will often question the couple's philosophy and deny modifications of work or schedules that could help the couple share family life more easily. Parents of the man may feel he has been emasculated; parents of the woman may feel she is setting herself up for a fall. Validation and support are rare and have to be consciously sought.

Career Costs

Peer couples need jobs that allow them to coparent. Sometimes they wait long enough to get enough clout in their careers to be able to modify their schedules so that they can share parenting. But more often they have to be lucky enough to be in jobs that naturally support child raising (for example, both working at home work stations), or they have to modify their career ambitions in favor of their family aspirations. This means avoiding or changing jobs that require extensive travel, changing venues in quick succession, and jobs that are all consuming (for example, a high-powered litigator in lengthy trials). Many couples have experienced one or both partners' having to forgo career opportunities. Sometimes it is painful to watch others who have dedicated themselves more singlemindedly to careers do financially better or achieve more prestigious positions.

Identity Costs

By downplaying work and emphasizing family, peer couples go against the prevailing standards of male and female role success. Marriages have traditionally defined themselves as a success if the man made money and created a good life-style for the family and the wife created good children and a satisfied husband. Peer couples have to define success differently. Except for "power couples" who can afford the help that allows them to have high-voltage careers and family time, economic success may have to be modified. Neither sex can assess their success according to traditional roles. It is hard to know how to evaluate oneself.

Sexual Dynamism

Peer partners get so close that some complain that an "incest taboo" sets in. They are each other's best friends, and if they aren't careful, that is exactly what they will start acting like in bed. Many find ways to get around this overfamiliarization problem, but the fact is that their absolute integration in each other's lives has to be leavened with some artifice to put romance back into the relationship.

Exclusion of Others

These couples become each other's best friend, and that can make everyone else feel a bit excluded. Kin and close friends stop getting the kind of attention they used to have and may be resentful. Although these couples tend to be child centered and have in fact organized their lives so that they can parent better, they are also dedicated to their adult relationship. This means they have to be careful not to make their own children feel excluded.

Calibrating the Right Mix of Equity and Equality

It is not always clear how to maintain a peer relationship. Sometimes it requires *equality*, with both partners supporting each other in the home and with the children. This prevents the relationship from being divided into low and high prestige worlds, and undermining deep friendship. But other times the best answer is *equity*. Each partner can and should give in different coin, and that is the best way to be loving and collaborative and supportive to the marriage. Figuring out the right thing to do all the time is tiring and inexact. Sometimes couples just want to retreat to doing the "boy thing" and the "girl thing"—not because it works—but because it is much clearer what each person should do to do his or her part for the relationship.

The Balance of Costs and Rewards

In spite of the costs, the peer couples described in this book believe that they have created an extremely rewarding marriage and family. Many of the costs I have outlined are not costs they feel they have suffered—or if they have, they feel those costs are a manageable part of an otherwise terrific arrangement. Many of them have varied and effective coping strategies that they believe solve or minimize these issues in their relationship.

NOTES

1. Philip Blumstein and Pepper Schwartz, *American Couples* (New York: William Morrow, 1983).
2. Philip Blumstein and Pepper Schwartz, *American Couples*. See also Philip Blumstein and Pepper Schwartz, "Money and Ideology: Their Impact on Power and the Division of Household Labor," and Judith Treas, "The Common Pot or Separate Purses? A Transactional Analysis," both in Rae Lesser Blumber, Ed., *Gender, Family and Economy* (Newbury Park, Calif.: Sage, 1991).

STUDY QUESTIONS

1. What are the positive and negative attributes of peer marriages? Would you ever want to be in this sort of marriage? Why or why not?
2. Please answer the question raised in the article, "But who would be a peer man?" If a man becomes a "peer," what does he give up?

DALTON CONLEY

Inequality Starts at Home
An Introduction to the Pecking Order

Let me start with a story.

Once upon a time a future president was born. William Jefferson Blythe IV entered the world one month premature but at a healthy six pounds and eight ounces. At twenty-three, his mother, Virginia, was young by today's standards, but perhaps a touch old for Arkansas in the 1940s. She was a widow, so times were tight during Bill's early years. In fact, times would be tough during all of Bill's childhood. Nonetheless, he seemed destined for great things. According to family lore, in second grade Bill's teacher "predicted that he would be President someday."[1]

His mother eventually married Roger Clinton, but that didn't make life any easier for Bill. Roger was a bitterly jealous alcoholic who often became physically abusive to his wife. Bill cites the day that he stood up to his stepfather as the most important marker in his transition to adulthood and perhaps in his entire life. In 1962, when Bill was sixteen, Virginia finally divorced Roger, but by then there was another Roger Clinton in the family, Bill's younger half brother.

Though Bill despised his stepfather, he still went to the Garland County courthouse and changed his last name to Clinton after his mother's divorce from the man—not for the old man's sake, but so that he would have the same last name as the younger brother he cherished. Though they were separated by ten years, were only half siblings, and ran in very different circles, the brothers were close. The younger Roger probably hated his father more than Bill did, but he nonetheless started to manifest many of the same traits as he came of age. He was a fabulous salesman: at age thirteen, he sold twice as many magazines as any of his classmates for a school project, winning a Polaroid camera and a turkey for his superior effort. He also had an affinity for substance abuse: by eighteen, he was heavily into marijuana. During Bill's first (unsuccessful) congressional campaign in 1974, Roger spent much of his time stenciling signs while smoking joints in the basement of campaign headquarters.

As Bill's political fortunes rose, Roger's prospects first stagnated and then sank. He tried his hand at a musical career, worked odd jobs, and eventually got into dealing drugs. And it was not just pot; in 1984, then-governor Bill Clinton was informed that his brother was a cocaine dealer under investigation by the Arkansas state police. The governor did not stand in the way of a sting operation, and Roger was caught on tape boasting how untouchable he was as the brother of the state's chief executive. Then the axe fell. After his arrest, Roger was beside himself in tears, threatening suicide for the shame he had brought upon his family—in particular, his famous brother. Upon hearing this threat Bill shook Roger violently. (He, in truth, felt responsible for his brother's slide.)

The next January, Roger was sentenced to a two-year prison term in a federal corrections facility in Fort Worth, Texas. Bill describes the whole ordeal as the most difficult episode of his life. David Maraniss—the author of *First in His Class*, the most comprehensive biography of Clinton to date—summarizes the family situation as follows:

> How could two brothers be so different: the governor and the coke dealer, the Rhodes scholar and the college dropout, one who tried to read three hundred books in three months and another who at his most addicted snorted cocaine sixteen times a day, one who could spend hours explaining economic theories and another whose economic interests centered on getting a new Porsche? In the case of the Clinton brothers, the contrasts become more understandable when considered within the context of their family history and environment. They grew up in a town of contrast and hypocrisy, in a family of duality and conflict. Bill and Roger were not so much opposites as two sides of the same coin.[2]

If asked to explain why Bill succeeded where Roger failed, most people will immediately point to genetic differences. After all, they were only half siblings to begin with. Others will pin it on birth order, claiming that firstborns are more driven and successful. But both of these accounts rely on individual explanations—ones particular to the unique biology or psychology of Bill and Roger—and both are incomplete. Was Bill more favored and more driven because he was a firstborn? My research shows that in families with two kids, birth order does not really matter that much. In fact, just under one-fourth of U.S. presidents were firstborns—about what we would expect from chance. The fact is that birth position only comes into play in larger families. But what about genes: was Bill simply luckier in the family gene pool? That may be so, but it still does not explain why sibling disparities are much more common in poor families and broken homes than they are in rich, intact families. In fact, when families have limited resources, the success of one sibling often generates a negative backlash among the others.

Sure, if one kid is born a mathematical genius and the other with no talents whatsoever, their respective dice may be cast at birth. But for most of us, how genes matter depends on the social circumstances around us. A child in one family may be born with innate athletic talent that is never nurtured because the parents in that family value reading ability over all else. Yet in another family, the fit between the individual talents of a particular child—say spatial reasoning—and the values of the parents may be perfect, and those abilities are realized. Finally, what kind of rewards talent brings depends entirely on the socioeconomic structure of the time. Fifty years ago, musical talent might have led to a decent living. Today—in an economy that rewards the most popular musicians handsomely at the expense of everyone else—innate musical ability is more often a route to financial struggle.

In Bill Clinton's case, he obviously had good genes—which contributed to his sharp mind, quick wit, tall stature, and verbal charisma—but there was not much advantage to being the firstborn. What really made a difference in his life was the good fit between his particular talents, the aspirations of those around him, and the political opportunities in a small state like Arkansas. This good fit combined with his family's lack of economic resources to generate an enormous sibling difference in success. However, had Virginia had money, she might not have had to put all her eggs—all her hopes and dreams—in Bill's basket. She might have been able to actively compensate for Bill's success by giving Roger extra financial and nonfinancial support—sending him, for example, to an elite private school when he started to veer off track. Instead, Bill's success seemed to come at the expense of Roger's—particularly when it led Roger to a false sense of invincibility.

On the surface, it may seem that the case of the Clintons is atypical. And, of course, a pair of brothers who are, respectively, the president and an ex-con is a bit extreme. But the basic phenomenon of sibling differences in success that the Clintons represent is not all that unusual. In fact, in explaining economic inequality in America, sibling differences represent about *three-quarters* of all the differences between individuals. Put another way, only one-quarter of all income inequality is between families. The remaining 75 percent is *within* families.[3] Sibling differences in accumulated wealth (i.e., net worth) are even greater, reaching 90-plus percent.[4] What this means is that if we lined everyone in America up in rank order of how much money they have— from the poorest homeless person to Bill Gates himself—and tried to predict where any particular individual might fall on that long line, then knowing about what family they came from would narrow down our uncertainty by about 25 percent (in the case of income). In other words, the dice are weighted by which family you come from, but you and your siblings still have to roll them. For example, if you come from a family that ranks in the bottom 5 percent of the income hierarchy, then you have a 40 percent chance of finding yourself in the lowest 10 percent, a 21 percent chance of making it to somewhere between the 30th and 70th percentile, and only a one in a thousand chance of making it to the top 10 percent. If you come from the richest 5 percent of families in America, then your odds are flipped. And if you start at the dead middle of the American income ladder, then you are about 63 percent likely to end up somewhere in that 30th- to 70th-percentile range, with a 4 percent chance of ending up either in the top or the bottom 10 percent.[5] A similar pattern holds for educational differences. For example, if you attended college there is almost a 50 percent chance that one of your siblings did not (and vice versa).[6]

What do sibling disparities as large as these indicate? They imply an American landscape where class identity is ever changing and not necessarily shared between brothers and sisters. Taken as a whole, the above statistics present a starkly darker portrait of American family life than we are used to. We want to think that the home is a haven in a heartless world. The truth is that inequality starts at home. These statistics also pose problems for those concerned with what seems to be a marked erosion of the idealized nuclear family. In fact, they hint at a trade-off between economic opportunity and stable, cohesive families.

While it may be surprising to realize how common sibling inequality is on the whole, my analysis of national data shows that Americans are quite aware of sibling disparities within their own families. For instance, when given a choice of fourteen categories of kin ranging from parents to grandparents to spouses to uncles, a whopping 34 percent of respondents claimed that a sibling was their most economically successful relative. When the question is flipped, 46 percent of respondents report a sibling being their least successful relative. Both these figures dwarf those for any other category.[7] When respondents were asked to elaborate about why their most successful relative got that way, their most common answer was a good work ethic (24.5 percent); when we add in other, related categories like "responsible, disciplined," "perseverance, motivation," or "set goals, had a plan," the total is well over half of all responses. Contrast that with the 22.6 percent that covers all categories of what might be called socioeconomic influences, such as "inheritance," "coming from a family with money," "marrying money," and so on. When accounting for the success of our kin, individual characterological explanations win out.

The pattern becomes even more striking when we flip the question to ask about the misfortune of the *least* successful relative. Only 9.6 percent of respondents cite social forces like poverty, lack of opportunity, or the pitfalls of a particular field as an explanation. Meanwhile, a whopping 82.4 percent cite individualistic reasons—having a "bad attitude" or "poor emotional or mental health." The single largest category was "lack of determination."[8]

That shows us how harsh we are on our brothers and sisters. Are we fair when we pass this kind of judgment, or terribly biased? I think the latter. In this book I challenge the perceived split between individual personality-based explanations for success and failure, and sociological ones. I argue that in each American family there exists a pecking order between siblings—a status hierarchy, if you will. This hierarchy emerges over the course of childhood and both reflects and determines the siblings' positions in the overall status ordering in society. It is not just the will of the parents or the "natural" abilities of the children themselves that determines who is on top in the family pecking order; the pecking order is conditioned by the swirling winds of society, which envelop the family. Gender expectations, the economic cost of schooling in America, a rising divorce rate, geographic mobility, religious and sexual orientations—all of these societal issues weigh in heavily on the pecking order between siblings. In other words, in order to truly understand the pecking orders within American families, you cannot view them in isolation from the larger economy and social structures in which we live. The family is, in short, no shelter from the cold winds of capitalism; rather it is part and parcel of that system. What I hope you end up with is a nuanced understanding of how social sorting works—in America writ large, and in your family writ small. And just maybe—along the way—we will all have a little more sympathy for our less fortunate brothers and sisters.

Who Gets Ahead?

Books about siblings debate why children raised by the same parents in the same house under the same circumstances turn out differently— sometimes very differently. They offer genetic explanations, or focus on birth order or the quality of parenting. *The Pecking Order* takes all these issues into account, but, based on years of research with three separate studies, it now moves us beyond those factors. Why is there a pecking order in American families, and how does it work? The reasons go way beyond relationships between family members. Americans like to think that their behavior and their destiny are solely in their own hands. But the pecking order, like other aspects of the social fabric, ends up being shaped by how society works.

In fact, siblings serve merely as a tool by which I hope to shed light on why some of us are rich and others poor; on why some are famous and others in America are anonymous. However, in figuring this all out, we do not gain much traction by comparing Bill Clinton with Joe Q. Public, Bill Gates with the average reader of this book, or any pair of randomly associated people. Some books tell you that the best way to understand why one person succeeds and another does not is to examine big amorphous categories like class or economics or race. I say the best way to do it is to examine differences within families, specifically to compare siblings with one another. Only by focusing in on the variety of outcomes that arise within a given family can we gain a real understanding of the underlying forces, of the invisible hands of the marketplace, that push each of us onto our chosen (or assigned) path in life. Siblings provide a natural experiment of sorts. They share much of their genetic endowment.[9] They also share much of the same environment. So it's logical to ask: how and why is it that some siblings end up in radically different positions in life? If we find an answer to that question, I think we will understand something very fundamental to American life.

NOTES

1. David Maraniss, *First in His Class: The Biography of Bill Clinton* (New York: Simon and Schuster, 1995), p. 424.
2. Ibid.
3. This is represented by $1 - R^2_s$ (where R^2 is the square of the sibling correlation coefficient in log-income). Mary Corcoran, Roger Gordon, Deborah Laren, and Gary Solon estimate a brother-brother correlation in *permanent* income of .45 using data from the Panel Study of Income Dynamics. See page 364 of their "Effects of Family and Community Background on Economic Status," *American Economic Review* 80 (1990): 362–66. Their estimates for women's sibling correlations in family income is .276 and .534 for men's log-earnings. (Gary Solon, Mary Corcoran, Roger Gordon, and Deborah Laren, "A Longitudinal Analysis of Sibling Correlation in Economic Status," *Journal of Human Resources* 26 [1992]: 509–34.) Sibling resemblance for other outcomes like welfare usage, education, and occupation follow similar patterns and are sensitive to the specification deployed—particularly for nonlinear measures. For example, if a woman's sister has received welfare, she is over three times more likely to use it herself (.66 versus .20 probability in their PSID sample). Differences for "persistent participation" in welfare programs by sibling welfare status are even greater. When I reanalyze more recent waves of PSID data—in which the siblings are on average older and more stable economically—I find that the sibling correlation has not changed much overall, but notably for sisters (see Dalton Conley, "Sibling Correlations in Socio-Economic Status: Results on Education, Occupation, Income and Wealth," working paper, Center for Advanced Social Science Research, New York University, 2003). The sibling correlation is .449 for the natural logarithm of brothers' income-to-needs ratio (slightly lower for log-income); for sisters the correlation in log-income-to-needs is .555. (It is .517 for all siblings.) For sisters the total (logged) family income correlation (as contrasted to the logged income-to-needs ratio) is .508, significantly higher than the figure of .276 reported by Solon, Corcoran, Gordon, and Laren in their "A Longitudinal Analysis."
4. For the natural logarithm of total net worth (i.e., accumulated wealth minus debts), sibling correlations are .224 for all siblings, .239 for brothers, and .271 for sisters (Conley, "Sibling Correlations"). In this analysis, those with negative or zero net worth are set to zero on the log scale. This approach yields the *highest* sibling correlation between randomly selected adult siblings in the 2001 wave of the PSID. Correlations are not much different for other recent waves.
5. These probabilities come from table 4 in Solon, Corcoran, Gordon, and Laren, "A Longitudinal Analysis," 526.
6. The actual figure is a .48 probability that a randomly selected sibling of an individual who graduated from a four-year college will not have graduated. This result comes from analysis of the 2001 wave of the Panel of Income Dynamics (see Conley, "Sibling Correlations"). Daphne Kuo and Robert Hauser analyze the Occupational Changes in a Generation (OCG) survey data and find that for education, sibling differences (within-family variance components) for various age groups of black and white brothers range between 38 percent and 52 percent. (See Kuo and Hauser, "Trends in the Family Effects on the Education of Black and White Brothers," *Sociology of Education* 68 [1995]: 136–60.) In the PSID, I find a lower degree of sibling resemblance in education level (measured as a continuous variable from 1 to 17 years of schooling). The correlation coefficient for siblings in the 2001 wave is .429. For brothers it is .529, and for sisters it is .400. These correlations, when squared, imply a less robust within-family component than found by Kuo and Hauser. Likewise, one-quarter of sibling pairs in the Study of American Families diverge substantially in terms of the prestige of their jobs. ("Substantial" means the difference between a professional such as a lawyer or businessman, on the one hand, and a salesclerk or blue-collar worker on the other.) In the PSID, the sibling correlation in 2001 occupational prestige is only .225 for sisters, .302 for brothers, and .233 for all siblings (Conley, "Sibling Correlations").

7. These results come from analysis of the Study of American Families.
8. These data come from the GSS-SAF survey. People may be more likely to explain others' relative success with outside social factors than individual attributes in order to lessen the taste of the sour grapes.
9. It is generally said that siblings (other than identical twins) share 50 percent of their genes (the same degree of similarly as with their respective parents); however, this is only true if parents were randomly assigned to mate with each other. The reality is that there is a process called assortative mating where reproductive mates select each other based on traits that have some sort of genetic basis. This assortative mating can result in a lower than 50 percent genetic similarity among OSC than 50 percent similarity since parents are positively matched on attributes and thus are contributing some of the "same" genes to OSC their children (and themselves). These issues will be discussed in greater detail in the sections that follow.

STUDY QUESTIONS

1. How does the family pecking order influence adult success when comparing siblings?
2. According to Conley, which is a larger determinant of adult success: the family or the social class of the family?

Education
and Religion

ALONG WITH THE FAMILY, TWO OF THE MOST IMPORTANT institutions in society are education and religion. For many, formal education in schools is a focal point of early life, and the formal and informal aspects of education continue for many years into adulthood. Often we are educated and trained on the job. Clearly, much of our life is encompassed by the educational institution. Religion is a central part of American life, and often a significant part of individual and family life. America is a very religious country as measured by the proportion of believers and attendees. Who can doubt the impact of religion in the unfolding of American history—from the Puritans to the followers of Sun Myung Moon or Krishna Consciousness? Even the politics of American life is laced with religious reference, often to the point that sociologists talk of a "civil religion." Education and religion reach into everyone's life, sometimes personally and sometimes in more distant ways. As social institutions, education and religion house much of our lives and create focal points that may last a lifetime.

The educational institution in society is seen as being coercive. Just like prisons, schools often control and indoctrinate and they do so in bell-ringing, punctual ways. As young persons, we are often forced to be there by law until the age of 16, and too many absences may result in referral to juvenile court. Some sociologists question whether schools are the optimal way to educate the populace, but schools are a critical part of learning, credentialing, and success in society. Who among us will forget the social cultures in middle and high schools? Remember the intense feelings associated with belonging, or not belonging? Remember how important relationships could become? Remember how a single day or a single hour might hold the greatest joy and greatest pain of our young lives? Understanding schools, and the behavior of children in them, has become a national priority, as has improving achievement at all levels.

Religion is a social institution with the responsibility for creating connections between people, a sense of community and social integration, and responsibility for answering sacred questions about life, death, faith, and catastrophes. As a part of social life, believing in something that transcends everyday experiences, religion is able to create understanding and acceptance where science, or other explanations, might fail. How would parents explain the death of their child, or how would a victim explain a rape or the onset of a terminal disease? The history of religion, and indeed the history of the world, is dominated by secularization or the increasing importance of everyday (profane) life and the decreasing importance of religion (sacred). Even religious organizations have secularized their activities and might spend more time and money on new buildings than on the spiritual life of members. In the Western world, particularly, we have seen the separation of church and state. Even early in the twenty-first century, this debate rages daily in the press and courts as it is decided when and where we pray, about the placement of the Ten Commandments in public buildings, and whether it is a good idea for political leaders to invoke support from gods and prophets.

The three selections for Topic 12: Education and Religion examine some of the more questionable aspects of social institutions. This representation reminds us that even social institutions are "dysfunctional" at times, and that the personal and structural effects of these social patterns are not always positive. Don E. Merten examines the "meanness" of a group of high-status, popular girls. Violence in our schools has brought sociology and the entire nation to focus on more in-depth understanding of the dynamics that are precursors to such violence. Girls are not strangers to this type of "violence" in junior high schools. Mary Crow Dog and Richard Erdoes autobiographically recount the historical practice of taking Native American children from their families and raising them in boarding schools on the reservation as a way to "civilize" them. This separation from the family and culture, and the mistreatment in the schools, would have a lasting impact on the lives of the children. Theresa Krebs uses a structural analysis to bring understanding to scandals within the Catholic Church. This research teaches us a valuable lesson about how the culture of religious organizations can go awry, just as they can in businesses and governments.

DON E. MERTEN

The Meaning of Meanness
Popularity, Competition, and Conflict among Junior High School Girls

The sociocultural construction of meanness among a clique of popular girls in junior high school is the focal point of this article. The term *sociocultural* is used here to designate the interplay of social and cultural phenomena in the construction of meanness (Berger and Luckmann 1967; Geertz 1973; Searle 1995). In the context of the research presented here, the construction was explored primarily by examining how the social relationships, and their meanings, of junior high school girls were shaped by the broader contours of mainstream American culture. Therefore, it considered how meanness acquired meaning through (1) its relationship to other related concepts, such as "niceness"; (2) the meaning of competition and conflict for girls; and (3) the tension between hierarchy and equality. Thus, the construction of meanness involved both social interaction and cultural meaning—the latter often tacit.

For the clique of popular girls whose actions are the focus of this article, meanness became an essential feature of their competition for, and conflict over, popularity. The relationship among competition, conflict, and meanness was far from simple. Sometimes, meanness was a byproduct of competition and conflict, but at other times, girls used meanness instrumentally to gain a competitive advantage in pursuit or protection of popularity. Yet it was not obvious why being mean seemed reasonable to these girls—much less why they took meanness to the point of being considered the meanest girls in school. . . .

Method and Context

The data for this article are from a three-year longitudinal study of junior high school students. The first year was spent observing and interviewing students in the junior high school. Data from the initial observations and interviews (precohort) were used to orient research for the study of the student cohort that entered junior high school the following year. All students who wanted to participate and who had signed informed-consent letters (270 students, 127 boys and 143 girls, 80 percent of the eligible students) formed the study cohort. During the seventh and eighth grades, two school ethnographers observed and interviewed the cohort students at school. A third ethnographer interviewed the parents and adults in the community. . . .

The community in which the junior high school was located was a middle- to upper-middle-class suburb that was overwhelmingly White but was ethnically relatively diverse. It was a community with a heavy emphasis on mobility, both geographic and economic. The adults in the community were also aware that it was not getting any easier to succeed and that children would have to work hard to do as well as their parents—much less surpass them. Community and family resources were expended to create an educational and activity environment that provided students with opportunities that prepared them for future success. The local high school sent many graduates to college, and both the adults and students perceived the two years in junior high school as an important stop in this educational journey. . . .

The Clique: Popular and Mean

Our first encounter with members of the clique came when the community ethnographer spent a day with each of the sixth-grade classes that sent cohort students to the junior high school. Because the elementary school from which the clique came had four sixth-grade classrooms, the ethnographer spent four days there and recorded the following in her notes:

> *A clique of 8 to 10 girls dominate the 6th grade, as opposed to Edison [another elementary school] where the dominant group was boys. These*

girls are considered "cool," "popular," and "mean." They are a combination of cute, talented, affluent, conceited, and powerful. Their presence as a group is much more obvious during noon hour than when they are separated in classrooms.

The core membership of the clique (Megan, Gretchen, Sara, Brenda, Melissa, Sherry, Beth, Gloria, and Alice) came together in sixth grade. In addition, a number of other girls were, from time to time, included and excluded; the clique usually had 10 to 12 members.

Brenda characterized the clique in terms similar to those noted by the ethnographer: "Well, everybody liked us. Everybody thought highly of everyone in the group. A lot of kids were scared of us. Scared that we were going to beat them up or that we wouldn't be friends with them." Even though the clique's members did not physically attack other girls, they intimidated peers with threats to do so. The clique's reputation as being mean and powerful meant that they were able to get their way without resorting to physical violence. Yet as Brenda noted, the clique was highly regarded and popular. Many girls tried desperately to become members and to share the other girls' popularity.

Popularity and Its Management

In junior high school, popularity had two different but interrelated referents. When a girl said someone was popular, she meant first, that the student was widely *known or recognized* by classmates and second, that he or she was *sought after* as a friend. In the best of all worlds, a student enjoyed widespread recognition *and* was sought out by many peers. Two well-traveled routes to popularity were to attract the interest of high-status boys (those who were especially athletic or handsome) by being physically attractive and/or participating in high-prestige activities. For example, cheerleading placed girls in front of their peers by performing at school sports events, and cheerleaders were able to wear their uniforms in class on days they performed, which further enhanced their recognition. Even though attractiveness to boys is important in elementary school (Adler et al. 1992), it became an especially prominent source of popularity during this transition from childhood to adolescence, since dating is a quintessential feature of adolescence. Because cheerleading positions and high-status boys were scarce, acquiring popularity via these routes was a highly competitive undertaking. Whereas being widely recognized enhanced a girl's chances to be sought after as a friend, it also helped if she was friendly or nice. . . .

The clique's popularity made it attractive, and many girls sought to associate with the members, but the members only allowed certain girls to do so. Girls with the potential to be popular or those who were especially nice were sometimes allowed in. However, inclusion in the clique, as Melissa pointed out, sometimes transformed nice girls:

> Once she got into the group she started getting real stuck-up and like she was the big one and the hot shot and everything. And she started going out with boys that they [the members] liked, and they started getting jealous. They would tell her that she was acting real hot and they didn't like the way she was acting. Then she would get upset.

The exhilaration of popularity was not easy for some girls to contain as they tried to take advantage of their high status. However, the established members of the clique were not looking for competitors. They were willing to accept girls who were grateful for the opportunity to associate with them, but did not hesitate to be aggressive in putting them in their place if they overreached their acceptance.

An often unrealized ideal was that popular girls would also be nice. Being nice, however, carried more weight in interpersonal interaction than with regard to schoolwide recognition. Nevertheless, niceness remained an important interpersonal ideal and was part of female gender construction that emphasizes nurturance and giving (Beauvior, 1957). Junior high school girls used the terms *nice* and *mean* as general evaluative characterizations for peers and their actions. Sherry described what it meant to be nice: "Someone who cares about people's feelings and is real nice to them. Nice to everybody and treats everybody equal and stuff like that. Talk to them, comfort them, ask them to be your partner and stuff like that." Treating peers as equals and caring about their feelings reduced the social distance between individuals and made interaction more comfortable.

Sara also emphasized "caring" for people as an aspect of niceness when she talked about her nonclique friend Missy. She described what made Missy "nicer" than her friends in the clique:

> 'Cause she is better than even they [the clique members] are. She treats me better. Not that they treat me bad, but she is always there when I need her. She is always understanding. She always knows what to say. She is never off with someone else when you need to talk to her. That is why she is nicer.

Junior High School

The transition to junior high school brought about two, somewhat countervailing, changes. On the one hand, as seventh graders, the clique was at the bottom of the school hierarchy; eighth graders were on top. On the other hand, the junior high school had many more organized activities than did the elementary school from which they came (Merten 1996). In keeping with Eder, Evans and Parker's (1995) observation that extracurricular activities may contribute to the preoccupation with popularity found in American schools, these activities were resources of variable prestige value (Adler and Adler 1994). For girls, the two most valuable activities were cheerleading and pom-pom (the performance of choreographed routines set to music while shaking pom-poms). Compared to these activities, any other was a distant third in popularity. All eight of the seventh-grade cheerleaders were members of the clique, and two other members were on the pom-pom squad. Thus, the activity structure of junior high school enhanced and, more important, publicly validated, the clique's popularity. In other words, the clique's success in *monopolizing* the most prestigious activity in junior high school allowed the members to consolidate and enact their popularity publicly in ways that had not been possible in elementary school.

With their entry into junior high school, the clique's members acknowledged their previous meanness, but saw themselves now as less mean. As Megan observed: "We thought we were really hot. I have cooled down a little this year because of the eighth graders. We just thought that we were the greatest." Megan associated the clique's decreased meanness with their diminished social status now that they were *below* the eighth graders. However, the clique did not "cool" down as much as Megan suggested, nor did their meanness subside much; it simply turned inward. The reality was that the clique had "cornered" most of the popularity available in the seventh grade. This fact, along with the constraining effect that the eighth graders' dominance had on the clique, contributed to the clique's members becoming mean toward each other.

Self-Promotion and Paybacks

As the members directed their meanness toward each other, Sherry became the target of intense meanness. Because her account is not always easy to follow, it is helpful to start with an excerpt from the notes of a fieldworker whom Sherry and her (nonclique) friend Wellsley stopped in the hall:

> Sherry was absolutely in tears. It was like she was starting to hyper-
> ventilate; she could not talk through her tears. I asked what was the
> matter, and Sherry looked at Wellsley and [said] "You tell her; I can't
> talk." Wellsley, in her real quiet little voice, started to tell me that Rick
> Castleton has broken up with Missy and that everybody in that group
> [clique] is blaming Sherry for the breakup.

The fieldworker interviewed Sherry several days later. Sherry began by talking about how she was invited into the clique, "a really mean group," as she described them, in the sixth grade. Then she described the foregoing incident:

> Gretchen was starting to get really mad at me. I talked to her about it
> and I asked her what was wrong. She just said, "Oh, I heard something
> that you said about me." But I didn't say anything about her. Sara was
> mad at me, I don't know why. She started being mad at me and then
> she started making up things that [she said] I said. Sara told Brenda
> and Gretchen so that they would get mad at me, too. So now I guess
> Gretchen has made up something and told Wellsley. They are all mad
> at me and laughing and everything.

. . . Because most of the meanness occurred outside the classroom (in the hall, the library, and the lunchroom), teachers seldom observed it. The social organization of junior high school—moving from class-room to classroom and teacher to teacher—provided opportunities for surreptitious meanness. Furthermore, some teachers found it difficult to believe that girls who were good students and otherwise popular could be so mean to a friend. Other teachers thought this situation was the sort of peer conflict that students had to learn to handle them-selves; for example, one teacher walked away from Sherry and refused to listen as she tried to explain her plight. Sherry's father told of how the principal said he would do whatever he could to make the situation better, *but* if Sherry retaliated, she, too, would be punished. Even more frustrating to Sherry's father were his conversations with the parents of the other girls in the clique. Regarding one mother, he had the following to say:

> One mother's attitude that we talked to is "girls are going to be girls."
> She said that this type of behavior in preadolescent girls is typical, and
> it is nothing to be worried about. It is a phase that girls go through,

and it will pass. "You are making a mountain out of a molehill. What are you getting so upset about?"

Parents' and teachers' responses were shaped by their interpretation of girls' conflicts as developmental and therefore "natural." First, by considering meanness developmentally "normal," they minimized its seriousness. Second, the school philosophy, which emphasized the need for students to be more independent and self-reliant, dictated that these girls should take care of such conflicts without adult intervention. Thus, a junior high school with a social organization that diffused adult responsibility and with an ideology that demanded students to be self-reliant facilitated meanness. . . .

Contested Status Change

At the beginning of junior high school, popularity was dynamic, and the increased popularity of some of the clique's middle-level members threatened to surpass the popularity of those at the top. Moreover, popularity, and the status it helped determine, was often experienced as schismogenic (Bateson 1958); that is, as the popularity of one girl increased, the popularity of another decreased. Since those at the top of the clique had the most to lose, they were concerned with the other members' successes. Megan, the least physically attractive of the top clique members, was especially vulnerable as attractiveness to boys became an increasingly important source of popularity. Melissa, a seventh-grade cheerleader, found herself more and more attractive to high-status boys; yet her popularity threatened to be short-lived. She described her situation as follows:

> *At the beginning of the year when I got into cheerleading, everything was fun. But after Christmas vacation, people started thinking that I was stuck-up. . . . They started writing on the walls, "Melissa Martin is stuck-up." That got me pretty upset.*

Melissa never learned who had written these messages, but her friendships in the clique were not going well:

> *I thought that my friends were the people in my class like Sara and Megan. After Christmas vacation, they started not to like me. They thought I was stuck-up, too. . . . After Christmas, Megan had a party, and I couldn't go to it because Brenda and I already had skiing arrangements. So I guess that is the time they all got mad at me.*

Melissa viewed her situation as one in which her increased popularity was followed by being characterized as stuck-up, and then her closest friends stopped liking her. . . .

Melissa's concern with her friends' meanness toward her extended to such things as family vacations because absence from interaction with the clique often resulted in meanness toward the absent member. Melissa described her predicament as follows:

I was so afraid that when I came back to school that all of them wouldn't like me. I didn't want to go at first. We were going to go on spring vacation [but] I was afraid my friends wouldn't like me. That is like when they were getting mad at me all of the time. That was after Christmas vacation when they thought they had a whole lot of power over me. And they were just getting mad at me all of the time for all dumb reasons. They were trying to make me look real bad. Like I would come home from the games and be really upset.

Melissa was so desirous of remaining in the clique that even though she knew the reasons offered for being mad at her, what she called "dumb reasons," were not the real ones, she was in no position to complain. Making her look bad in cheerleading was another way to undermine her popularity. . . .

Because most of the clique's meanness was directed toward its own members, most outsiders continued to think of the members as individuals with whom it would be nice to have a relationship. Thus, the internal focus of meanness generally had the effect of protecting the clique's popularity within the wider social system. . . .

Discussion

Competition-conflict to gain or preserve popularity was an ever-present undercurrent in the interpersonal relationships of the clique and thereby constituted an important condition for meanness. Yet to understand the meaning of meanness, it is necessary to go beyond the competition-conflict with which meanness was often associated. Because competition-conflict between females is frequently mediated in other contexts, one has to ask why competition-conflict around popularity vitiated the norm of mediation. In other words, was there an advantage to being mean when one was trying to be or to remain popular? . . .

Hierarchy and Meanness

... To gain a greater understanding of the relationship between hierarchy and meanness, it is necessary to consider how hierarchy was viewed in this community. Hierarchy was perceived as being significantly *truncated*; that is, rather than perceiving many gradations of status, students thought of their own status as essentially dichotomous— either high or low, winners or losers (Merten, 1994). Thus, minor losses in relative popularity were frequently experienced as significant losses in status. ...

One's position in the clique was important, because it both symbolized one's popularity and was salient in protecting it. That is, hierarchical position was an essential factor for the successful use of meanness in the sense that a girl's effectiveness in being mean depended on her status in the clique. Melissa observed that those members who had more status than she could be mean to her, but she could not effectively be mean to them because they simply became angry and mobilized *her* friends against her. The other side of the hierarchical meaning of meanness was that high status protected girls from the meanness of members with less social status and thus demonstrated their superiority. ...

The Cultural Logic of Meanness

The larger question, What led these girls to express their concerns with popularity and hierarchy in terms of meanness? requires an examination of the cultural logic by which doing so made sense. To understand how meanness was constructed and what it meant in the context of this junior high school, it is necessary to consider what other possibilities existed. Perhaps the one thing that popular girls dreaded most was losing their popularity by being labeled stuck-up. Loss of popularity in this manner was especially disconcerting in that being labeled stuck-up used the "force" (to use a judo metaphor) of a girl's popularity against her to invert her status. Therefore, it was precisely when a girl enjoyed popularity (as a cheerleader, for example) that she was most vulnerable to being labeled stuck-up. The problem was how to express and enjoy popularity and still manage to keep it. Expressing one's sense of one's own popularity could be as little as projecting a self-confident demeanor or as much as refusing to acknowledge or to associate with anyone who was less popular. Any action that suggested that a girl considered herself popular, however, *could* be taken as an indication that she thought she was superior and hence was stuck-up. Yet to be popular and be unable to express it, and thereby not enjoy it, was less than satisfying. Thus, these girls faced a cultural dilemma that is common for women: They were being implicitly asked to encompass both aspects of a cultural dichotomy—to seek popularity, but when they were successful, to pretend they were not popular. This dilemma is similar to girls being called on, in another context, to be "seductive virgins" (Schwartz and Merten 1980). . . .

To put this rather complex relationship between popularity and meanness another way: Both meanness and popularity had hierarchical aspects and implications. Popularity was an expression and a source of hierarchical position. Furthermore, popularity could be transformed into power, which was also hierarchical. Like popularity, meanness could also be transformed into power. Hence, power was a common denominator between popularity and meanness. In this respect, meanness could be expressed in terms of popularity, and popularity could be expressed in terms of meanness, with power mediating the transition from one to the other. Just as "the language of social inequality is one of vertical imagery" (Schwartz 1981:125), so was the language of meanness. Thus, meanness was, in a fundamental sense, discourse about hierarchical position, popularity, and invulnerability (Gergen 1984).

Conclusion

Why a clique of girls that was popular and socially sophisticated was also renowned for its meanness was the question with which this article began. Yet in this junior high school, where acting like everyone else was important and acting superior to peers was discouraged, popularity was as problematic as it was desired. When something highly valued cannot be openly expressed, alternative forms of expression are often invoked. At this level, it can be said that meanness resulted from the failure of the culture to allow hierarchy to be explicitly celebrated (Merten 1996). That is, the cultural logic that allowed meanness to make sense to these junior high school girls was grounded in broader cultural tensions between hierarchy and equality. As Shweder (1991:108) noted about American society, "We do not know how to justify status obligations and hierarchical relationships, but we live them." Thus, meanness, in a context in which equality was a paramount value and myth, was an action that awkwardly attempted to express and preserve popularity, despite its hierarchical implications.

For women in mainstream American culture, the tension between hierarchy and equality is further exacerbated by the taboo on *open* competition—especially among friends (Tracy 1991). If well-educated, successful women find it difficult to mediate the opposition between solidarity with friends and competition for individual success (Keller and Moglen 1987), then it is little wonder that junior high school girls found it difficult to do so.

REFERENCES

Adler, Patricia and Peter Adler. 1994. "Social Reproduction and the Corporate Other: Institutionalization of Afterschool Activities." *Sociological Quarterly* 35:309–28.

Adler, Patricia, Steven Kless, and Peter Adler. 1992. "Socialization to Gender Roles: Popularity among Elementary School Boys and Girls." *Sociology of Education* 65:169–87.

Beauvoir, Simone de. 1957. *The Second Sex.* New York: Alfred A. Knopf.

Berger, Peter and Thomas Luckmann. 1967. *The Social Construction of Reality: A Treatise in the Sociology of Knowledge.* Garden City, NY: Doubleday Anchor Books.

Eder, Donna with Catherine Collins Evans and Stephen Parker. 1995. *School Talk: Gender and Adolescent Culture.* New Brunswick, NJ: Rutgers University Press.

Geertz, Clifford. 1973. *The Interpretation of Cultures.* New York: Basic Books.

Gergen, Kenneth. 1984. "Aggression as Discourse." Pp. 51–68 in *Social Psychology of Aggression: From Individual Behavior to Social Interaction,* edited by Amelie Mummendey. New York: Springer-Verlag.

Keller, Evelyn and Helene Moglen. 1987. "Competition: A Problem for Academic Women." Pp. 21–37 in *Competition: A Feminist Taboo?* edited by Valerie Miner and Helen E. Longino. New York: Feminist Press.

Merten, Don E. 1994. "The Cultural Context of Aggression: The Transition to Junior High School." *Anthropology and Education Quarterly* 25:29–43.

———. 1996. "Burnout as Cheerleader: The Cultural Basis for Prestige and Privilege in Junior High School." *Anthropology and Education Quarterly,* 27:51–70.

Schwartz, Barry. 1981. *Vertical Classification: A Study in Structuralism and the Sociology of Knowledge.* Chicago: University of Chicago Press.

Schwartz, Gary and Don Merten. 1980. *Love and Commitment.* Beverly Hills, CA: Sage.

Searle, John. 1995. *The Construction of Social Reality.* New York: Free Press.

Shweder, Richard. 1991. "Cultural Psychology: What Is It?" Pp. 73–110 in *Thinking Through Cultures: Expeditions in Cultural Psychology.* Cambridge, MA: Harvard University Press.

Tracy, Laura. 1991. *The Secret Between Us: Competition Among Women.* Boston: Little, Brown.

STUDY QUESTIONS

1. Very popular girls are "mean" to one another. What social value comes from being mean?
2. Popularity is a very tricky issue among these girls. How would you explain this issue and "being popular" to one of your friends?

MARY CROW DOG AND RICHARD ERDOES

Civilize Them with a Stick

. . . Gathered from the cabin, the wickiup, and the tepee,
partly by cajolery and partly by threats;
partly by bribery and partly by force,
they are induced to leave their kindred
to enter these schools and take upon themselves
the outward appearance of civilized life.
— Annual report of the Department of Interior, 1901

It is almost impossible to explain to a sympathetic white person what a typical old Indian boarding school was like; how it affected the Indian child suddenly dumped into it like a small creature from another world, helpless, defenseless, bewildered, trying desperately and instinctively to survive and sometimes not surviving at all. I think such children were like the victims of Nazi concentration camps trying to tell average, middle-class Americans what their experience had been like. Even now, when these schools are much improved, when the buildings are new, all gleaming steel and glass, the food tolerable, the teachers well trained and well-intentioned, even trained in child psychology—unfortunately the psychology of white children, which is different from ours—the shock to the child upon arrival is still tremendous. Some just seem to shrivel up, don't speak for days on end, and have an empty look in their eyes. I know of an eleven-year-old on another reservation who hanged herself, and in our school, while I was there, a girl jumped out of the window, trying to kill herself to escape an unbearable situation. That first shock is always there.

Although the old tiyospaye has been destroyed, in the traditional Sioux families, especially in those where there is no drinking, the child is never left alone. It is always surrounded by relatives, carried around, enveloped in warmth. It is treated with the respect due to any human being, even a small one. It is seldom forced to do anything against its will, seldom screamed at, and never beaten. That much, at least, is left of the old family group among full-bloods. And then suddenly a bus or car arrives, full of strangers, usually white strangers, who yank the child out of the arms of those who love it, taking it screaming to the boarding school. The only word I can think of for what is done to these children is kidnapping.

Even now, in a good school, there is impersonality instead of close human contact; a sterile, cold atmosphere, an unfamiliar routine, language problems, and above all the maza-skan-skan, that damn clock—white man's time as opposed to Indian time, which is natural time. Like eating when you are hungry and sleeping when you are tired, not when that damn clock says you must. But I was not taken to one of the better, modern schools. I was taken to the old-fashioned mission school at St. Francis, run by the nuns and Catholic fathers, built sometime around the turn of the century and not improved a bit when I arrived, not improved as far as the buildings, the food, the teachers, or their methods were concerned.

In the old days, nature was our people's only school and they needed no other. Girls had their toy tipis and dolls, boys their toy bows and arrows. Both rode and swam and played the rough Indian games together. Kids watched their peers and elders and naturally grew from children into adults. Life in the tipi circle was harmonious—until the whiskey peddlers arrived with their wagons and barrels of "Injun whiskey." I often wished I could have grown up in the old, before-whiskey days.

Oddly enough, we owed our unspeakable boarding schools to the do-gooders, the white Indian-lovers. The schools were intended as an alternative to the outright extermination seriously advocated by generals Sherman and Sheridan, as well as by most settlers and prospectors overrunning our land. "You don't have to kill those poor benighted heathen," the do-gooders said, "in order to solve the Indian Problem. Just give us a chance to turn them into useful farmhands, laborers, and chambermaids who will break their backs for you at low wages." In that way the boarding schools were born. The kids were taken away from their villages and pueblos, in their blankets and moccasins, kept completely isolated from their families—sometimes for as long as ten years—suddenly coming back, their short hair slick with pomade, their necks raw from stiff, high collars, their thick jackets always short in the sleeves and pinching under the arms, their tight patent leather shoes giving them corns, the girls in starched white blouses and clumsy, high-buttoned boots—caricatures of white people. When they found out—and they found out quickly—that they were neither wanted by whites nor by Indians, they got good and drunk, many of them staying drunk for the rest of their lives. I still have a poster I found among my grandfather's stuff, given to him by the missionaries to tack up on his wall. It reads:

1. Let Jesus save you.
2. Come out of your blanket, cut your hair, and dress like a white man.
3. Have a Christian family with one wife for life only.
4. Live in a house like your white brother. Work hard and wash often.
5. Learn the value of a hard-earned dollar. Do not waste your money on giveaways. Be punctual.
6. Believe that property and wealth are signs of divine approval.
7. Keep away from saloons and strong spirits.
8. Speak the language of your white brother. Send your children to school to do likewise.
9. Go to church often and regularly.
10. Do not go to Indian dances or to the medicine men.

The people who were stuck upon "solving the Indian Problem" by making us into whites retreated from this position only step by step in the wake of Indian protests.

The mission school at St. Francis was a curse for our family for generations. My grandmother went there, then my mother, then my sisters and I. At one time or other every one of us tried to run away. Grandma told me once about the bad times she had experienced at St. Francis. In those days they let students go home only for one week every year. Two days were used up for transportation, which meant spending just five days out of three hundred and sixty-five with her family. And that was an improvement. Before grandma's time, on many reservations they did not let the students go home at all until they had finished school. Anybody who disobeyed the nuns was severely punished. The building in which my grandmother stayed had three floors, for girls only. Way up in the attic were little cells, about five by five by ten feet. One time she was in church and instead of praying she was playing jacks. As punishment they took her to one of those little cubicles where she stayed in darkness because the windows had been boarded up. They left her there for a whole week with only bread and water for nourishment. After she came out she promptly ran away, together with three other girls. They were found and brought back. The nuns stripped them

naked and whipped them. They used a horse buggy whip on my grandmother. Then she was put back into the attic—for two weeks.

My mother had much the same experiences but never wanted to talk
about them, and then there I was, in the same place. The school is now
run by the BIA—the Bureau of Indian Affairs—but only since about fifteen years ago. When I was there, during the 1960s, it was still run by the
Church. The Jesuit fathers ran the boys' wing and the Sisters of the
Sacred Heart ran us—with the help of the strap. Nothing had changed
since my grandmother's days. I have been told recently that even in the
'70s they were still beating children at that school. All I got out of school
was being taught how to pray. I learned quickly that I would be beaten if
I failed in my devotions or, God forbid, prayed the wrong way, especially
prayed in Indian to Wakan Tanka, the Indian Creator.

The girls' wing was built like an F and was run like a penal institution. Every morning at five o'clock the sisters would come into our
large dormitory to wake us up, and immediately we had to kneel down
at the sides of our beds and recite the prayers. At six o'clock we were
herded into the church for more of the same. I did not take kindly to
the discipline and to marching by the clock, left-right, left-right. I was
never one to like being forced to do something. I do something
because I feel like doing it. I felt this way always, as far as I can remember, and my sister Barbara felt the same way. An old medicine man
once told me: "Us Lakotas are not like dogs who can be trained, who
can be beaten and keep on wagging their tails, licking the hand that
whipped them. We are like cats, little cats, big cats, wildcats, bobcats,
mountain lions. It doesn't matter what kind, but cats who can't be
tamed, who scratch if you step on their tails." But I was only a kitten and
my claws were still small.

Barbara was still in the school when I arrived and during my first
year or two she could still protect me a little bit. When Barb was a seventh-
grader she ran away together with five other girls, early in the morning
before sunrise. They brought them back in the evening. The girls had to
wait for two hours in front of the mother superior's office. They were
hungry and cold, frozen through. It was wintertime and they had been
running the whole day without food, trying to make good their escape.
The mother superior asked each girl, "Would you do this again?" She
told them that as punishment they would not be allowed to visit home
for a month and that she'd keep them busy on work details until the
skin on their knees and elbows had worn off. At the end of her speech
she told each girl, "Get up from this chair and lean over it." She then

lifted the girls' skirts and pulled down their underpants. Not little girls either, but teenagers. She had a leather strap about a foot long and four inches wide fastened to a stick, and beat the girls, one after another, until they cried. Barb did not give her that satisfaction but just clenched her teeth. There was one girl, Barb told me, the nun kept on beating and beating until her arm got tired.

I did not escape my share of the strap. Once, when I was thirteen years old, I refused to go to Mass. I did not want to go to church because I did not feel well. A nun grabbed me by the hair, dragged me upstairs, made me stoop over, pulled my dress up (we were not allowed at the time to wear jeans), pulled my panties down, and gave me what they called "swats"—twenty-five swats with a board around which Scotch tape had been wound. She hurt me badly.

My classroom was right next to the principal's office and almost every day I could hear him swatting the boys. Beating was the common punishment for not doing one's homework, or for being late to school. It had such a bad effect upon me that I hated and mistrusted every white person on sight, because I met only one kind. It was not until much later that I met sincere white people I could relate to and be friends with. Racism breeds racism in reverse.

The routine at St. Francis was dreary. Six A.M., kneeling in church for an hour or so; seven o'clock, breakfast; eight o'clock, scrub the floor, peel spuds, make classes. We had to mop the dining room twice every day and scrub the tables. If you were caught taking a rest, doodling on the bench with a fingernail or knife, or just rapping, the nun would come up with a dish towel and just slap it across your face, saying, "You're not supposed to be talking, you're supposed to be working!" Monday mornings we had cornmeal mush, Tuesday oatmeal, Wednesday rice and raisins, Thursday cornflakes, and Friday all the leftovers mixed together or sometimes fish. Frequently the food had bugs or rocks in it. We were eating hot dogs that were weeks old, while the nuns were dining on ham, whipped potatoes, sweet peas, and cranberry sauce. In winter our dorm was icy cold while the nuns' rooms were always warm.

I have seen little girls arrive at the school, first-graders, just fresh from home and totally unprepared for what awaited them, little girls with pretty braids, and the first thing the nuns did was chop their hair off and tie up what was left behind their ears. Next they would dump the children into tubs of alcohol, a sort of rubbing alcohol, "to get the germs off." Many of the nuns were German immigrants, some from Bavaria, so that we sometimes speculated whether Bavaria was some sort of Dracula country inhabited by monsters. For the sake of objectivity I ought to mention that two of the German fathers were great linguists and that the only Lakota-English dictionaries and grammars which are worth anything were put together by them.

At night some of the girls would huddle in bed together for comfort and reassurance. Then the nun in charge of the dorm would come in and say, "What are the two of you doing in bed together? I smell evil in this room. You girls are evil incarnate. You are sinning. You are going to hell and burn forever. You can act that way in the devil's frying pan." She would get them out of bed in the middle of the night, making them kneel and pray until morning. We had not the slightest idea what it was all about. At home we slept two and three in a bed for animal warmth and a feeling of security.

The nuns and the girls in the two top grades were constantly battling it out physically with fists, nails, and hair-pulling. I myself was growing from a kitten into an undersized cat. My claws were getting bigger and were itching for action. About 1969 or 1970 a strange young white girl appeared on the reservation. She looked about eighteen or twenty years old. She was pretty and had long, blond hair down to her waist, patched jeans, boots, and a backpack. She was different from any other white person we had met before. I think her name was Wise. I do not know how she managed to overcome our reluctance and distrust, getting us into a corner, making us listen to her, asking us how we were treated. She told us that she was from New York. She was the first real hippie or Yippie we had come across. She told us of people called the Black Panthers, Young Lords, and Weathermen. She said, "Black people are getting it on. Indians are getting it on in St. Paul and California. How about you?" She also said, "Why don't you put out an underground paper, mimeograph it. It's easy. Tell it like it is. Let it all hang out." She spoke a strange lingo but we caught on fast.

Charlene Left Hand Bull and Gina One Star were two full-blood girls I used to hang out with. We did everything together. They were willing to join me in a Sioux uprising. We put together a newspaper which we called the *Red Panther*. In it we wrote how bad the school was, what kind of slop we had to eat—slimy, rotten, blackened potatoes for two weeks—the way we were beaten. I think I was the one who wrote the worst article about our principal of the moment, Father Keeler. I put all my anger and venom into it. I called him a goddam wasičun son of a bitch. I wrote that he knew nothing about Indians and should go back to where he came from, teaching white children whom he could relate to.

I wrote that we knew which priests slept with which nuns and that all they ever could think about was filling their bellies and buying a new car. It was the kind of writing which foamed at the mouth, but which also lifted a great deal of weight from one's soul.

On Saint Patrick's Day, when everybody was at the big powwow, we distributed our newspapers. We put them on windshields and bulletin boards, in desks and pews, in dorms and toilets. But someone saw us and snitched on us. The shit hit the fan. The three of us were taken before a board meeting. Our parents, in my case my mother, had to come. They were told that ours was a most serious matter, the worst thing that had ever happened in the school's long history. One of the nuns told my mother, "Your daughter really needs to be talked to." "What's wrong with my daughter?" my mother asked. She was given one of our *Red Panther* newspapers. The nun pointed out its name to her and then my piece, waiting for mom's reaction. After a while she asked, "Well, what have you got to say to this? What do you think?"

My mother said, "Well, when I went to school here, some years back, I was treated a lot worse than these kids are. I really can't see how they can have any complaints, because we was treated a lot stricter. We could not even wear skirts halfway up our knees. These girls have it made. But you should forgive them because they are young. And it's supposed to be a free country, free speech and all that. I don't believe what they done is wrong." So all I got out of it was scrubbing six flights of stairs on my hands and knees, every day. And no boy-side privileges.

The boys and girls were still pretty much separated. The only time one could meet a member of the opposite sex was during free time, between four and five-thirty, in the study hall or on benches or the volleyball court outside, and that was strictly supervised. One day Charlene and I went over to the boys' side. We were on the ball team and they had to let us practice. We played three extra minutes, only three minutes more than we were supposed to. Here was the nuns' opportunity for revenge. We got twenty-five swats. I told Charlene, "We are getting too old to have our bare asses whipped that way. We are old enough to have babies. Enough of this shit. Next time we fight back." Charlene only said, "Hoka-hay!"

We had to take showers every evening. One little girl did not want to take her panties off and one of the nuns told her, "You take those underpants off—or else!" But the child was ashamed to do it. The nun was getting her swat to threaten the girl. I went up to the sister, pushed her veil off, and knocked her down. I told her that if she wanted to hit a little girl she should pick on me, pick one her own size. She got herself transferred out of the dorm a week later.

In a school like this there is always a lot of favoritism. At St. Francis it was strongly tinged with racism. Girls who were near-white, who came from what the nuns called "nice families," got preferential treatment. They waited on the faculty and got to eat ham or eggs and bacon in the morning. They got the easy jobs while the skins, who did not have the right kind of background—myself among them—always wound up in the laundry room sorting out ten bushel baskets of dirty boys' socks every day. Or we wound up scrubbing the floors and doing all the dishes. The school therefore fostered fights and antagonism between whites and breeds, and between breeds and skins. At one time Charlene and I had to iron all the robes and vestments the priests wore when saying Mass. We had to fold them up and put them into a chest in the back of the church. In a corner, looking over our shoulders, was a statue of the crucified Savior, all bloody and beaten up. Charlene looked up and said, "Look at that poor Indian. The pigs sure worked him over." That was the closest I ever came to seeing Jesus.

I was held up as a bad example and didn't mind. I was old enough to have a boyfriend and promptly got one. At the school we had an hour and a half for ourselves. Between the boys' and the girls' wings were some benches where one could sit. My boyfriend and I used to go there just to hold hands and talk. The nuns were very uptight about any boy-girl stuff. They had an exaggerated fear of anything having even the faintest connection with sex. One day in religion class, an all-girl class, Sister Bernard singled me out for some remarks, pointing me out as a bad example, an example that should be shown. She said that I was too free with my body. That I was holding hands which meant that I was not a good example to follow. She also said that I wore unchaste dresses, skirts which were too short, too suggestive, shorter than regulations permitted, and for that I would be punished. She dressed me down before the whole class, carrying on and on about my unchastity.

I stood up and told her, "You shouldn't say any of those things, miss. You people are a lot worse than us Indians. I know all about you, because my grandmother and my aunt told me about you. Maybe twelve, thirteen years ago you had a water stoppage here in St. Francis. No water could get through the pipes. There are water lines right under the mission, underground tunnels and passages where in my grandmother's time only the nuns and priests could go, which were off-limits to everybody else. When the water backed up they had to go through all the water lines and clean them out. And in those huge pipes they found the bodies of newborn babies. And they were white babies. They weren't Indian babies. At least when our girls have babies, they don't do away with them that way, like flushing them down the toilet, almost.

"And that priest they sent here from Holy Rosary in Pine Ridge because he molested a little girl. You couldn't think of anything better than dump him on us. All he does is watch young women and girls with that funny smile on his face. Why don't you point him out for an example?"

Charlene and I worked on the school newspaper. After all we had some practice. Every day we went down to Publications. One of the priests acted as the photographer, doing the enlarging and developing. He smelled of chemicals which had stained his hands yellow. One day he invited Charlene into the darkroom. He was going to teach her developing. She was developed already. She was a big girl compared to him, taller too. Charlene was nicely built, not fat, just rounded. No sharp edges anywhere. All of a sudden she rushed out of the darkroom, yelling to me, "Let's get out of here! He's trying to feel me up. That priest is nasty." So there was this too to contend with—sexual harassment. We complained to the student body. The nuns said we just had a dirty mind.

We got a new priest in English. During one of his first classes he asked one of the boys a certain question. The boy was shy. He spoke poor English, but he had the right answer. The priest told him, "You did not say it right. Correct yourself. Say it over again." The boy got flustered and stammered. He could hardly get out a word. But the priest kept after him: "Didn't you hear? I told you to do the whole thing over. Get it right this time." He kept on and on.

I stood up and said, "Father, don't be doing that. If you go into an Indian's home and try to talk Indian, they might laugh at you and say, 'Do it over correctly. Get it right this time!' "

He shouted at me, "Mary, you stay after class. Sit down right now!"

I stayed after class, until after the bell. He told me, "Get over here!" He grabbed me by the arm, pushing me against the blackboard, shouting, "Why are you always mocking us? You have no reason to do this."

I said, "Sure I do. You were making fun of him. You embarrassed him. He needs strengthening, not weakening. You hurt him. I did not hurt you."

He twisted my arm and pushed real hard. I turned around and hit him in the face, giving him a bloody nose. After that I ran out of the room, slamming the door behind me. He and I went to Sister Bernard's office. I told her, "Today I quit school. I'm not taking any more of this, none of this shit anymore. None of this treatment. Better give me my diploma. I can't waste any more time on you people."

Sister Bernard looked at me for a long, long time. She said, "All right, Mary Ellen, go home today. Come back in a few days and get your diploma." And that was that. Oddly enough, that priest turned out okay. He taught a class in grammar, orthography, composition, things like that. I think he wanted more respect in class. He was still young and unsure of himself. But I was in there too long. I didn't feel like hearing it. Later he became a good friend of the Indians, a personal friend of myself and my husband. He stood up for us during Wounded Knee and after. He stood up to his superiors, stuck his neck way out, became a real people's priest. He even learned our language. He died prematurely of cancer. It is not only the good Indians who die young, but the good whites, too. It is the timid ones who know how to take care of themselves who grow old. I am still grateful to that priest for what he did for us later and for the quarrel he picked with me—or did I pick it with him?—because it ended a situation which had become unendurable for me. The day of my fight with him was my last day in school.

STUDY QUESTIONS

1. Mary Crow Dog was mistreated, along with many other generations of Native American children, in reservation schools. What was the theory or explanation that allowed this to happen, and what social effects did it have?

2. What did Mary have to do to be released from the school? Is there a lesson in this for us regarding conformity and rebellion?

THERESA KREBS

When the Clergy Goes Astray
Pedophilia in the Catholic Church

In 1993 the highest governing official in the Roman Catholic Church revealed his position regarding the sexual abuse of children by clergy and religious in the North American Catholic Church. As reported in the *Edmonton Journal* on June 24, under the headline "Permissive Society to Blame for Abusive Priests—Vatican," the chief Vatican spokesman, Joaquin Navarro-Valls, identified pedophilic clergy in the Roman Catholic Church as a uniquely North American phenomenon: "One would have to ask if the real culprit is not a society that is irresponsibly permissive, hyperinflated with sexuality [that is] capable of creating circumstances that induce even people who have received a solid moral formation to commit grave moral acts."[1]

Navarro-Valls extended the blame to the media for sensationalizing cases of pedophilia when the number of priests implicated in North America amounts to about four hundred, little more than 1 percent. In a further move that denied institutional responsibility for priestly pedophilia, Navarro-Valls pointed out that the percentage of priests involved in pedophilic acts may be less than in other sectors of the general population (see, e.g., Bishop's Administrative Committee 1989, 394). The Vatican's statement demonstrates the Church's protective stance toward pedophilic clergy in its ranks. By continuing to look beyond itself for possible causes, the Church avoids examining how its structure may facilitate pedophilia among some of its personnel.

I argue that pedophilia among Catholic clergy is possible because both longstanding and newly erected structures within the institutional

Church facilitate it. The Church's international nature, its organizational hierarchy, and its internal polity allow pedophiles to remain anonymous to all but a few within the Church hierarchy and secular society. It maintains this anonymity through a complex network of archdioceses, dioceses, provinces, and parishes that absorb and protect perpetrators across geographically disparate regions. By acknowledging instances of such behavior and not removing priests from the priesthood (or reporting them to secular officials), the Church hierarchy accords pedophilia a place within its organization.[2]. . .

The Overall Picture

To analyze pedophilia in longstanding structures in the institutional Catholic Church, I build on Anson Shupe's structural conflict model of clergy malfeasance in North American religious organizations. Shupe argues that new structures adopted by the Catholic Church, such as official policies, are positive responses toward effecting change. I, however, offer an alternative interpretation of the Church's remedial response: While no longer denying pedophilia among its ranks, the Church nevertheless continues to deflect institutional responsibility for it. I come to this conclusion with international examples interpreted through Jean-Guy Vaillancourt's study of Vatican control over lay Catholic elites.

Shupe defines clergy malfeasance as "the exploitation and abuse of a religious group's believers by the elites of that religion in whom the former trust" (Shupe 1995, 15). Pedophilia is a subgroup of sexual malfeasance, and it takes place in what he calls hierarchical denominations. A crucial point in understanding a structural relationship between pedophilia and its occurrence in a hierarchical religious group (such as the Catholic Church) is that the local authority of individual clergy is an extension of a bureaucratic authority that legitimizes it (Shupe 1993, 19).

Hierarchical religious organizations exhibit five characteristics of power inequalities that conceptually facilitate pedophilia. First, institutional religion is based on systems of power inequalities termed "hierarchies of unequal power" (Shupe 1993, 10; 1994, 4; 1995, 27–28). The unequal power is spread across several dimensions, such as elites' claims to possess disproportionate spiritual wisdom, experience, or charisma of office as well as their organizational knowledge and insights.

Second, persons occupying elite positions retain a significant capacity for moral persuasion, and in some instances the "theological authority to deny access to privileges of membership, including ultimate spiritual statuses such as salvation," through excommunication or shunning and other forms of ostracization.

Third, unlike their secular counterparts, religious organizations such as the Catholic Church represent what Shupe calls "trusted hierarchies." Individuals in positions of authority explicitly encourage and admonish individuals in lower statuses to trust in their honorable intentions and unselfish motives. More specifically, leaders encourage parents or guardians to socialize children into honoring the intentions and motives of priests by advocating respect and obedience without question.

Fourth, because of their special status as trusted hierarchies, churches provide unique "opportunity structures" or "protected places" that allow leaders to engage in deviance. At a power disadvantage, organization members who do not hold positions of authority are more susceptible to exploitation, abuse, and manipulation.

Finally, in a social structural sense, clergy malfeasance (the elite exploitation of lay members) occurs in trusted hierarchies because they systematically provide opportunities for such behaviors and allow them to continue. Shupe argues that deviance/malfeasance, when occasional, is "normal" to religious hierarchies rather than "the result of psychological pathologies or moral lapses" (Shupe 1995, 31).

An essential dimension of Shupe's typology, and crucial for understanding how established Roman Catholic Church structures facilitate pedophilia, is lay members' ability to gain access to officials in a hierarchically structured religious organization when making claims against pedophilic clergy. He characterizes the locus of control of religious polities by their degree of *permeability*. How receptive is the official hierarchy to complainants' allegations against its administration or its personnel? Traditional authority in hierarchical religious polities is least responsive to complaints against personnel and slowest to implement resolution and remedies.

One reason for this unresponsiveness is that hierarchical religious organizations consciously employ strategies of "neutralization" to protect their personnel or the Church community (Shupe 1995, 80). Moreover, engaging in these neutralization strategies perpetuates the good reputation of the organization and diffuses public perception and awareness of malfeasance. The institutional Catholic Church's neutralizing allegations of pedophilia against its personnel gives perpetrators tacit approval from their superiors to continue engaging in such behavior.

Although Shupe (1995, 81) proposes that hierarchical religious groups "are more likely to develop policies addressing clergy malfeasance" than are local autonomous congregational groups, new structures such as official policies and parish study groups often appear to be responses to public pressure or legal proceedings—in fact, the Church sometimes ignores them. Documented evidence shows that even with sensitive, well-formulated policies in place, as well as uniform plans of action for responding to allegations of pedophilia, some members of the Catholic Church hierarchy continue to neutralize complainants by offering monetary settlements on condition of secrecy.

Yet, the dynamics of secrecy within Catholicism reveal how the Church continues to deflect institutional responsibility for the pedophilic crimes of some of its personnel. In his study of Vatican control over Catholic elites, Vaillancourt (1980, 286) indicates that one of the most ironic aspects of secrecy is that officials "often hide themselves behind an ideology of dialogue, communication, and participation. The leadership remains bureaucratic and secretive, while it veils its manipulation behind a screen of words." Interestingly, the majority of members do not leave the Church when knowledge about pedophilic clergy becomes public. In some respects, membership is even strengthened, because the hierarchy actively solicits lay involvement under the guise of implementing organizational reform while retaining the right to make final decisions.

According to Vaillancourt, therefore, clerical appeals for official policies and open discussion further neutralize critics. Engaging public awareness of policy and encouraging parishioner participation in study groups and workshops are evidence of further neutralization strategies on the Church's part. Combining the observations of both Shupe and Vaillancourt, I argue that newly erected structures further facilitate opportunities for pedophilia for some Catholic priests and religious.

Longstanding Structures That Facilitate Pedophilia

Within the Roman Catholic Church, three longstanding structures facilitate pedophilia among some clergy: the international institution itself, its hierarchical organization, and its government or polity.

The International Roman Catholic Church

The North American Roman Catholic Church engaged in an institutional cover-up of clerical pedophilia for decades. Indeed, the magnitude of the scandal facing the Church today demonstrates its international dimensions. At the same time that Church officials denied that clergy or lay religious leaders engaged in sexual activities with children, they privately assured complainants that the "problem" would be investigated and resolved immediately. In actuality, the Church began to transfer perpetrators either to active ministry in other parishes or to church-affiliated treatment centers. The international scope of the Catholic Church allowed the official hierarchy to relocate offending individuals to distant geographical locations (Isely and Isely 1990, 92–93). For Church officials, such moves solved the problem.

For example, the diocese of Northampton, England, transferred British priest Anton Mowat to Atlanta, Georgia, without informing the Archdiocese of Atlanta about Mowat's "known predilection for young boys." When Georgia police investigated allegations against Mowat of child sexual abuse in 1990, he fled the United States for a monastery in Turin, Italy. Although U.S. authorities repeatedly appealed to his home diocese in Northampton for information regarding Mowat's whereabouts, Church officials denied having any knowledge (Burkett and Bruni 1993, 33). Indeed, if Mowat's home diocese knew where he was, by denying that knowledge it tacitly approved his actions. Moreover, the Church in three separate countries (England, the United States, and Italy) played host to Mowat. By refusing to disclose his hiding place to authorities and by transferring him to another country, the international Church facilitated Mowat's inclination to pedophilic activity.

Earlier, during the 1960s, dozens of priests accused of pedophilia were on assignment in the United States from England, Mexico, Ireland, Sri Lanka, and Italy (Burkett and Bruni 1993, 41). These assignments had already concerned John Salazar, a consulting psychologist for the Servants of the Paraclete treatment facility in New Mexico. In February 1967, Salazar met with the archbishop of Santa Fe, Robert Sanchez, to explain the dangers in allowing pedophilic priests and lay religious "brought from all over the world" to return to working with children at their former, or any, parishes (Burkett and Bruni 1993, 168). Archbishop Sanchez, however, was less than proactive on the issue, perhaps because (as it became known) he himself maintained sexual relationships with young women—as many as five during the 1980s and others before then (Shupe 1995, 3). Sanchez eventually resigned the priesthood in disgrace.[3]

An alternative to transferring alleged pedophilic clergy to distant parishes is transferring them to treatment centers in other countries. Father Canice Connor, former executive director of Southdown Treatment Centre for clergy and religious near Toronto, Ontario, is president and chief executive officer of St. Luke's Institute in Suitland, Maryland. (In 1990, priest and psychiatrist Michael Peterson founded St. Luke's to treat the psychiatric problems of clergy, which include the suffering caused by depression, alcoholism, and other addictions.) In 1983, St. Luke's broadened its treatment to include priests who sexually abuse children. Connor told the *Washington Post* that St. Luke's patient lists include Roman Catholic priests from South Africa and Australia (Miller 1993). On July 16, 1994, Mary Jane Boland reported in the *New Zealand Herald* under the headline "Church Unveils Its Shame" that before that year, the New Zealand Catholic Church responded to allegations of priestly pedophilia by sending priests to treatment centers "overseas"—facilities probably in the United States. (Before it closed, House of Affirmation in Missouri described itself on its letterhead as the "International Therapeutic Center for Clergy and Religious.")[4]. . .

Hierarchical Organization of the Church

The bishop holds the highest authority in an archdiocese or diocese, and is answerable only to the Supreme Pontiff. His hierarchical roles include teacher of doctrine, priest of worship, and minister of government. As the highest governing official in a diocese, a bishop has executive power to apply the universal laws of the Church, to exercise legislative and judicial power, and to enforce civil law in a diocese. The bishop himself is subject to canon law and, as a citizen, to the civil and criminal laws of the country in which he serves. According to Church and civil laws, the bishop's power, therefore, is limited and not arbitrary. Answerable within the Church only to the pope, bishops nevertheless also possess the potential for considerable power in their dioceses (Archdiocesan Commission of Enquiry [ACE] 1990, 1:69–70).

Former Archbishop Alphonsus Penney's management of pedophilic clergy in Newfoundland is a particularly telling example of the Church hierarchy's ability to manipulate public perception while denying claimants' allegations. Evidence from as early as 1979 suggests that when Penney assumed the bishopric in the archdiocese in St. John's, he knew that priests and Christian Brothers in Newfoundland were committing pedophilic acts with young members of the Church and wards of the Mount Cashel Orphanage. As the representative official of the Archdiocese of St. John's, Newfoundland, and according to Church law, he was responsible for all juridic affairs, including allegations of pedophilic crimes against Church personnel (Paulson 1988, 103). Therefore, by both canon and civil law, Penney ought to have acted on his knowledge and reported the crimes to Church and civil authorities.

A sex scandal of enormous proportions swirled around Penney's mitre while he followed a tragic course of denial, covering his inaction by transferring or counseling perpetrators rather than indicting them under canon and civil criminal law. Moreover, secular authorities investigating suspected and named abusers met with little cooperation from Church and affiliated institutional officials.

As the highest governing official in a diocese, a bishop is responsible for the physical and spiritual well-being of all Church personnel. Alphonsus Penney reportedly advised priests struggling with their sexual predilections to avail themselves of professional counseling services that he retained for their use. One year after he assumed the office of bishop in the Archdiocese of St. John's, Alphonsus Penney established the Ministry to Priests Program (MPP) to address problems of morale associated with restrictions and requirements of the priesthood, another indication that he knew some clergy were engaged in sexual activities proscribed by their vows of celibacy.

The program, however, served another purpose than that intended. Former members testified that its greatest value lay in the opportunity for socializing with peers. Most clergy, however, avoided associating with the group within the MPP known to have a homosexual orientation. The majority of allegations against and convictions of pedophilic priests were of members belonging to that segment of the MPP (ACE 1990, 1:96–99).

The MPP represents one example of the way the Church hierarchy facilitates pedophilia by following a course of denial and diffusion rather than by reporting offenses to appropriate secular authorities. As pastor to the priests in his archdiocese, Penney did take steps to address the problem of pedophilia among them. He ignored his obligations to civil law, however, by providing a forum that facilitated rather than eliminated their illegal sexual practices. . . .

Jason Berry, author of *Lead Us Not into Temptation*, followed the pedophilic priest scandal in the U.S. Catholic Church from Louisiana to

Washington, seat of the U.S. papal nunciature, investigating Father Gilbert Gauthe, from the Diocese of Lafayette in Louisiana, who managed to commit pedophilic crimes for many years, apparently undetected. Berry blames the complicity between Church personnel and the official Church hierarchy for perpetuating the problem. "The crisis in the Catholic Church lies not with the fraction of priests who molest youngsters but in an ecclesiastical power structure that harbors pedophiles, conceals other sexual behavior patterns among its clerics, and uses strategies of duplicity and counterattack against the victims" (Berry 1992, xx). . . .

Internal Polity

Shupe characterizes the internal polities of religious organizations by the extent of their permeability and of their neutralization. He measures permeability by the extent to which administrators and leaders in the hierarchy, first, are authentically open to receiving complaints against the organization by lay members and, second, act to eliminate a problem from recurring (Shupe 1995, 118–119). Shupe assesses organizational neutralization by the degree to which administrators and leaders in the hierarchy blame victims, dismiss grievances, or intimidate, bribe, or threaten to ensure the silence and secrecy of complainants. Taking any neutralizing action means that the problem can recur.

The internal polity of the Catholic Church employs numerous methods to neutralize attempts to require accountability or restitution from the Church. Unfortunately, the relationship between parishioners and the Church hierarchy does not encourage, or even allow, demands for institutional accountability. The hierarchy camouflages abuse and abusers against public perception. Relying on their perceived authority, Church officials intimidate claimants, downplay the effects of the acts, or ensure silence from victims by stating that what occurred is an isolated incident. The hierarchy treats each set of allegations in confidence, rather than collaborating and compiling records on named abusers in order to explore behavior patterns. Bishops speak to victims privately, victimizing them further by planting doubts in their minds about possibly having encouraged the attention of the sexual deviant, having enjoyed the attention, and so forth. Bishops also neglect to inform law enforcement officials of sexual abuse. By insulating perpetrators from outside authorities, internal polities of the Catholic Church also promote aspects of pedophilia. . . .

Almost invariably, the Church's internal polity insists that officials maintain secrecy regarding claimants' allegations of sexual abuse against priests or other religious leaders. Often secrecy can be negotiated. In Gauthe's case, mentioned earlier, the Church paid an average of $450,000 to each of nine families. Those settlements, however, came with conditions: Accepting payment required signing an agreement of no liability on the part of the Church. Furthermore, the Gauthe case remains sealed, which decreases the Church's risk of media and public exposure (Berry 1992, 6–25).

In the Gauthe case, as in others researched, the hierarchy sought to protect itself and its priests from public exposure by neutralizing claims. Neutralizing claims, however, ultimately deferred scandals only for a short time (Burkett and Bruni, 1993: 60–62). Documented accounts demonstrate that the pedophiles continued to accumulate victims.

NOTES

1. Former Benedictine monk A. W. Richard Sipe estimates that approximately 2 percent of North American priests are sexually fixated on young children and that an additional 4 percent find older youths sexually appealing. Church officials challenge these figures, but Fr. Thomas Doyle, canon lawyer and former advisor to North American bishops regarding sexual abuse by clergy, estimates that three thousand American priests "may be so inclined" (which supports Sipe's estimates). Jason Berry calls disputes over percentage estimates further examples of "concealment strategies" by which Church officials attempt to deny or diffuse the problem of pedophilia among their personnel. The logic runs, "If there are no numbers, [then] it cannot be true" (cited in Berry 1992: xx–xxi).

2. Part of the reason the Church continues to harbor perpetrators rather than dismiss them may be the aging and declining clerical population in North America caused, in part, by resignations and fewer ordinations. The complex canonical process involved in laicizing clergy also may help to explain why the Church excuses pedophilic clergy within its ranks. See, for example, Gilmour 1992, B6; Schoenherr and Young 1990, 463–481; Schoenherr, Young, and Vilarino 1988, 499–523.

3. Perhaps not so ironically, Archbishop Robert Sanchez's March 19, 1993, letter to the Pope requested permission to resign from his position. CBS-TV's *60 Minutes* segment "The Archbishop," aired March 21, 1993, investigated the New Mexico archdiocese where Sanchez faced accusations of "sexual improprieties." The program suggested that as a result of his own sexual proclivities Sanchez was lenient toward other priests who engaged in sexual activity with children. See Sanchez 1993, 722–724.

4. Private correspondence from House of Affirmation, in possession of the author.

REFERENCES

Archdiocesan Commission of Enquiry into the Sexual Abuse of Children by Members of the Clergy [ACE]. 1990. *The Report of the Archdiocesan Commission of Enquiry into the Sexual Abuse of Children by Members of the Clergy.* 2 vols. St. John's, Newfoundland: Archdiocese of St. John's.

Berry, Jason. 1992. *Lead Us Not into Temptation: Catholic Priests and the Sexual Abuse of Children.* New York: Doubleday.

Burkett, Elinor, and Frank Bruni. 1993. *A Gospel of Shame: Children, Sexual Abuse, and the Catholic Church.* New York: Viking.

Isely, Paul J., and Peter Isley. 1990. "The Sexual Abuse of Male Children by Church Personnel: Intervention and Prevention." *Pastoral Psychology* 39 (2): 85–99.

Miller, Jeanne. 1993. "Update." *Missing Link* (newsletter of The Linkup, Inc.) 1 (4): 2.

Paulson, Jerome E., 1988. "The Clinical and Canonical Considerations in Cases of Pedophilia: The Bishop's Role." *Studia Canonica* 22 (1): 77–124.

Shupe, Anson. 1995. *In the Name of All That's Holy: A Theory of Clergy Malfeasance.* Westport, Conn.: Praeger.

———. 1994. "Authenticity Lost: When Victims of Clergy Abuse Confront Betrayed Trust." Paper presented at the annual meeting of the Association for the Sociology of Religion, Los Angeles.

———. 1993. "Opportunity Structures, Trusted Hierarchies, and Religious Deviance: A Conflict Theory Approach." Paper presented at the annual meeting of the Society for the Scientific Study of Religion, Raleigh, North Carolina.

Vaillancourt, Jean-Guy. 1980. *Papal Power: A Study of Vatican Control over Lay Catholic Elites.* Berkeley: University of California Press.

STUDY QUESTIONS

1. What are the organizational structures that permitted the protection of priests when they victimized the children?

2. What similarities does the Catholic Church, as an organization, have with big businesses like Enron and Wall Street brokerage firms?

Politics and the Economy

THE TWO REMAINING INSTITUTIONS TO DISCUSS IN "PART 4: Social Institutions" are politics and the economy. The sociological view of these two institutions is that they are closely connected, and any of us can recognize the reciprocal impact of the economy and politics. How does politics respond to the demands of big business, the wealthy, political action committees, or lobbies like the National Rifle Association? How is the economy affected by political action in the form of tax refunds, changing interest rates, prosecution of business and investment companies, or tax breaks to corporations (corporate welfare)? Politics creates and oversees the rule of law in society, and as some have said, is really about "who gets what." The economy affects each family and person in society. Having a job, or not, puts people in dramatically different circumstances. In American society where capitalism reigns, the economy regularly moves through "boom and bust" cycles. Full employment and a growing economy make for good times personally and politically. High unemployment and a weak economy have the opposite effect. Many of us have felt the impact of such a changeable economy.

Politics, more than any other institution, is about power and authority. These two ideas illuminate the difference between getting your way through force and coercion (power), and legitimately exercising power such that the decisions made are supported by those who are affected (authority). Inside of politics there is a broad range of views, from the most reactionary to the most radical. Reactionaries wish that there was a way to return to the "good old days" where government did influence everyday life and people could settle their problems the old-fashioned way. Reactionaries, like militia groups, might resort to violence to make their views known. Radicals, who want to change society and social institutions in dramatic ways, may also have violence as part of their political approach. In either case, most Americans reject such extremes and see themselves as "conservative" or "liberal." These are the more moderate positions on the political continuum, and rarely do we experience decades like the sixties when radicals pushed social unrest, or the eighties when reactionaries were making their views felt with violence. Having a political consciousness, an understanding of the micro and macro influences of governmental decisions, is very much a part of the sociological imagination.

The economic institution in society is often the most mysterious. While many of us have our lives and livelihood driven by the economy, we may be least able to see it and understand its impact. Somehow this lumbering giant of activity, from the most personal pay raise or promotion to the nation's gross national product, escapes our notice. Different societies have different economies; capitalism and socialism are two examples. Along with the economics of socialism, where prices and wages are monitored so that economic change is more controlled, there comes less possibility for rapid expansion and longer periods of a "languishing" economy. In capitalism, where a free market economy and competition drive the dynamics, there is the possibility of making great sums of money (profit), with the likelihood that soon there will be a "bust" in the cycle and many people out of work. In the margins between such economic systems, issues like healthcare make interesting political issues like who should bear the cost of health services for the poor or the elderly. Many of us will have careers of more than forty years and understanding the dynamics of this enormous event in our lives will certainly make it more pleasant.

The first article is by C. Wright Mills and we are given a theoretical examination of "the power elite" in American politics. Here business, government, and the military are seen in their collective impact on both politics and the economy. In the second article, the loss of jobs, "corporate downsizing," is qualitatively researched by Charles Koeber. What is the process by which persons who have been the victims of economic downturns make sense of and cope with their experiences? Finally, Robert W. Fuller brings a new concept of "rankism" to bear on one of the oldest sociological issues: abuse of power. Using power to harm, dominate, manipulate, and humiliate others is the most common of daily occurrences. Has Fuller identified a new form of domination based on abuse of power? Is this like racism, classism, and sexism?

C. WRIGHT MILLS

The Power Elite

Except for the unsuccessful Civil War, changes in the power system of the United States have not involved important challenges to its basic legitimations. Even when they have been decisive enough to be called 'revolutions,' they have not involved the 'resort to the guns of a cruiser, the dispersal of an elected assembly by bayonets, or the mechanisms of a police state.'[1] Nor have they involved, in any decisive way, any ideological struggle to control masses. Changes in the American structure of power have generally come about by institutional shifts in the relative positions of the political, the economic, and the military orders. From this point of view, and broadly speaking, the American power elite has gone through four epochs, and is now well into a fifth. . . .

. . . We study history, it has been said, to rid ourselves of it, and the history of the power elite is a clear case for which this maxim is correct. Like the tempo of American life in general, the long-term trends of the power structure have been greatly speeded up since World War II, and certain newer trends within and between the dominant institutions have also set the shape of the power elite. . . .

I. In so far as the structural clue to the power elite today lies in the political order, that clue is the decline of politics as genuine and public debate of alternative decisions—with nationally responsible and policy-coherent parties and with autonomous organizations connecting the lower and middle levels of power with the top levels of decision. America is now in considerable part more a formal political democracy than a democratic social structure, and even the formal political mechanics are weak.

The long-time tendency of business and government to become more intricately and deeply involved with each other has, in the fifth epoch, reached a new point of explicitness. The two cannot now be seen clearly as two distinct worlds. It is in terms of the executive agencies of the state that the rapprochement has proceeded most decisively. The growth of the executive branch of the government, with its agencies that patrol the complex economy, does not mean merely the 'enlargement of government' as some sort of autonomous bureaucracy: it has meant the ascendancy of the corporation's man as a political eminence. . . .

II. In so far as the structural clue to the power elite today lies in the enlarged and military state, that clue becomes evident in the military ascendancy. The warlords have gained decisive political relevance, and the military structure of America is now in considerable part a political structure. The seemingly permanent military threat places a premium on the military and upon their control of men, materiel, money, and power; virtually all political and economic actions are now judged in terms of military definitions of reality: the higher warlords have ascended to a firm position within the power elite of the fifth epoch. . . .

III. In so far as the structural clue to the power elite today lies in the economic order, that clue is the fact that the economy is at once a permanent-war economy and a private-corporation economy. American capitalism is now in considerable part a military capitalism, and the most important relation of the big corporation to the state rests on the coincidence of interests between military and corporate needs, as defined by warlords and corporate rich. Within the elite as a whole, this coincidence of interest between the high military and the corporate chieftains strengthens both of them and further subordinates the role of the merely political men. Not politicians, but corporate executives, sit with the military and plan the organization of war effort. . . .

The power elite is composed of political, economic, and military men, but this instituted elite is frequently in some tension: it comes together only on certain coinciding points and only on certain occasions of 'crisis.' In the long peace of the nineteenth century, the military were not in the high councils of state, not of the political directorate, and neither were the economic men—they made raids upon the state but they did not join its directorate. During the 'thirties, the political man was ascendant. Now the military and the corporate men are in top positions.

Of the three types of circle that compose the power elite today, it is the military that has benefited the most in its enhanced power, although the corporate circles have also become more explicitly intrenched in the more public decision-making circles. It is the professional politician that has lost the most, so much that in examining the events and decisions, one is tempted to speak of a political vacuum in which the corporate rich and the high warlord, in their coinciding interests, rule.

It should not be said that the three 'take turns' in carrying the initiative, for the mechanics of the power elite are not often as deliberate as that would imply. At times, of course, it is—as when political men, thinking they can borrow the prestige of generals, find that they must pay for it, or, as when during big slumps, economic men feel the need of a politician at once safe and possessing vote appeal. Today all three are involved in virtually all widely ramifying decisions. Which of the three types seems to lead depends upon 'the tasks of the period' as they, the elite, define them. Just now, these tasks center upon 'defense' and international affairs. Accordingly, as we have seen, the military are ascendant in two senses: as personnel and as justifying ideology. That is why, just now, we can most easily specify the unity and the shape of the power elite in terms of the military ascendancy.

But we must always be historically specific and open to complexities. The simple Marxian view makes the big economic man the *real* holder of power; the simple liberal view makes the big political man the chief of the power system; and there are some who would view the warlords as virtual dictators. Each of these is an oversimplified view. It is to avoid them that we use the term 'power elite' rather than, for example, 'ruling class.'

In so far as the power elite has come to wide public attention, it has done so in terms of the 'military clique.' The power elite does, in fact, take its current shape from the decisive entrance into it of the military. Their presence and their ideology are its major legitimations, whenever the power elite feels the need to provide any. But what is called the 'Washington military clique' is not composed merely of military men, and it does not prevail merely in Washington. Its members exist all over the country, and it is a coalition of generals in the roles of corporation executives, of politicians masquerading as admirals, of corporation executives acting like politicians, of civil servants who become majors, of vice-admirals who are also the assistants to a cabinet officer, who is himself, by the way, really a member of the managerial elite.

Neither the idea of a 'ruling class' nor of a simple monolithic rise of 'bureaucratic politicians' nor of a 'military clique' is adequate. The power elite today involves the often uneasy coincidence of economic, military, and political power. . . .

Despite their social similarity and psychological affinities, the members of the power elite do not constitute a club having a permanent membership with fixed and formal boundaries. It is of the nature of the power elite that within it there is a good deal of shifting about, and that it thus does not consist of one small set of the same men in the same positions in the same hierarchies. Because men know each other personally does not mean that among them there is a unity of policy; and because they do not know each other personally does not mean that among them there is a disunity. The conception of the power elite does not rest, as I have repeatedly said, primarily upon personal friendship.

As the requirements of the top places in each of the major hierarchies become similar, the types of men occupying these roles at the top—by selection and by training in the jobs—become similar. This is no mere deduction from structure to personnel. That it is a fact is revealed by the heavy traffic that has been going on between the three structures, often in very intricate patterns. The chief executives, the warlords, and selected politicians came into contact with one another in an intimate, working way during World War II; after that war ended, they continued their associations, out of common beliefs, social congeniality, and coinciding interests. Noticeable proportions of top men from the military, the economic, and the political worlds have during the last fifteen years occupied positions in one or both of the other worlds: between these higher circles there is an interchangeability of position, based formally upon the supposed transferability of 'executive ability,' based in substance upon the co-optation by cliques of insiders. As members of a power elite, many of those busy in this traffic have come to look upon 'the government' as an umbrella under whose authority they do their work.

As the business between the big three increases in volume and importance, so does the traffic in personnel. The very criteria for selecting men who will rise come to embody this fact. The corporate commissar, dealing with the state and its military, is wiser to choose a young man who has experienced the state and its military than one who has not. The political director, often dependent for his own political success upon corporate decisions and corporations, is also wiser to choose a man with corporate experience. Thus, by virtue of the very criterion of success, the interchange of personnel and the unity of the power elite is increased.

Given the formal similarity of the three hierarchies in which the several members of the elite spend their working lives, given the ramifications of the decisions made in each upon the others, given the coincidence of interest that prevails among them at many points, and given the administrative vacuum of the American civilian state along with its enlargement of tasks—given these trends of structure, and adding to them the psychological affinities we have noted—we should indeed be surprised were we to find that men said to be skilled in administrative contacts and full of organizing ability would fail to do more than get in touch with one another. They have, of course, done much more than that: increasingly, they assume positions in one another's domains.

The unity revealed by the interchangeability of top roles rests upon the parallel development of the top jobs in each of the big three domains. The interchange occurs most frequently at the points of their coinciding interest, as between regulatory agency and the regulated industry; contracting agency and contractor. And, as we shall see, it leads to co-ordinations that are more explicit, and even formal.

The inner core of the power elite consists, first, of those who interchange commanding roles at the top of one dominant institutional order with those in another: the admiral who is also a banker and a lawyer and who heads up an important federal commission; the corporation executive whose company was one of the two or three leading war materiel producers who is now the Secretary of Defense; the wartime general who dons civilian clothes to sit on the political directorate and then becomes a member of the board of directors of a leading economic corporation.

Although the executive who becomes a general, the general who becomes a statesman, the statesman who becomes a banker, see much more than ordinary men in their ordinary environments, still the perspectives of even such men often remain tied to their dominant locales. In their very career, however, they interchange roles within the big three and thus readily transcend the particularity of interest in any one of these institutional milieux. By their very careers and activities, they lace the three types of milieux together. They are, accordingly, the core members of the power elite.

These men are not necessarily familiar with every major arena of power. We refer to one man who moves in and between perhaps two circles—say the industrial and the military—and to another man who moves in the military and the political, and to a third who moves in the political as well as among opinion-makers. These in-between types most closely display our image of the power elite's structure and operation, even of behind-the-scenes operations. To the extent that there is any 'invisible elite,' these advisory and liaison types are its core. Even if—as I believe to be very likely—many of them are, at least in the first part of their careers, 'agents' of the various elites rather than themselves elite, it is they who are most active in organizing the several top milieux into a structure of power and maintaining it. . . .

The outermost fringes of the power elite—which change more than its core—consist of 'those who count' even though they may not be 'in' on given decisions of consequence nor in their career move between the hierarchies. Each member of the power elite need not be a man who personally decides every decision that is to be ascribed to the power elite. Each member, in the decisions that he does make, takes the others seriously into account. They not only make decisions in the several major areas of war and peace; they are the men who, in decisions in which they take no direct part, are taken into decisive account by those who are directly in charge.

On the fringes and below them, somewhat to the side of the lower echelons, the power elite fades off into the middle levels of power, into the rank and file of the Congress, the pressure groups that are not vested in the power elite itself, as well as a multiplicity of regional and state and local interests. If all the men on the middle levels are not among those who count, they sometimes must be taken into account, handled, cajoled, broken or raised to higher circles. . . .

The conception of the power elite and of its unity rests upon the corresponding developments and the coincidence of interests among economic, political, and military organizations. It also rests upon the similarity of origin and outlook, and the social and personal intermingling of the top circles from each of these dominant hierarchies. This conjunction of institutional and psychological forces, in turn, is revealed by the heavy personnel traffic within and between the big three institutional orders, as well as by the rise of go-betweens as in the high-level lobbying. The conception of the power elite, accordingly, does *not* rest upon the assumption that American history since the origins of World War II must be understood as a secret plot, or as a great and co-ordinated conspiracy of the members of this elite. The conception rests upon quite impersonal grounds.

There is, however, little doubt that the American power elite—which contains, we are told, some of 'the greatest organizers in the world'—has also planned and has plotted. The rise of the elite, as we have already made clear, was not and could not have been caused by a plot; and the tenability of the conception does not rest upon the existence of any secret or any publicly known organization. But, once the conjunction of structural trend and of the personal will to utilize it gave rise to the power elite, then plans and programs did occur to its members and indeed it is not possible to interpret many events and official policies of the fifth epoch without reference to the power elite. 'There is a great difference,' Richard Hofstadter has remarked, 'between locating conspiracies *in* history and saying that history *is*, in effect, a conspiracy. . .' [2]

The structural trends of institutions become defined as opportunities by those who occupy their command posts. Once such opportunities are recognized, men may avail themselves of them. Certain types of men from each of the dominant institutional areas, more far-sighted than others, have actively promoted the liaison before it took its truly modern shape. They have often done so for reasons not shared by their partners, although not objected to by them either; and often the outcome of their liaison has had consequences which none of them foresaw, much less shaped, and which only later in the course of development came under explicit control. Only after it was well under way did most of its members find themselves part of it and become gladdened, although sometimes also worried, by this fact. But once the co-ordination is a going concern, new men come readily into it and assume its existence without question.

So far as explicit organization—conspiratorial or not—is concerned, the power elite, by its very nature, is more likely to use existing organizations, working within and between them, than to set up explicit organizations whose membership is strictly limited to its own members. But if there is no machinery in existence to ensure, for example, that military and political factors will be balanced in decisions made, they will invent such machinery and use it, as with the National Security Council. Moreover, in a formally democratic polity, the aims and the powers of the various elements of this elite are further supported by an aspect of the permanent war economy: the assumption that the security of the nation supposedly rests upon great secrecy of plan and intent. Many higher events that would reveal the working of the power elite can be withheld from public knowledge under the guise of secrecy. With the wide secrecy covering their operations and decisions, the power elite can mask their intentions, operations, and further consolidation. Any secrecy that is imposed upon those in positions to observe high decision-makers clearly works for and not against the operations of the power elite.

There is accordingly reason to suspect—but by the nature of the case, no proof—that the power elite is not altogether 'surfaced.' There is nothing hidden about it, although its activities are not publicized. As an elite, it is not organized, although its members often know one another, seem quite naturally to work together and share many organizations in common. There is nothing conspiratorial about it, although its decisions are often publicly unknown and its mode of operation manipulative rather than explicit. . . .

The idea of the power elite rests upon and enables us to make sense of (1) the decisive institutional trends that characterize the structure of our epoch, in particular, the military ascendancy in a privately incorporated economy, and more broadly, the several coincidences of objective interests between economic, military and political institutions; (2) the social similarities and the psychological affinities of the men who occupy the command posts of these structures, in particular the increased interchangeability of the top positions in each of them and the increased traffic between these orders in the careers of men of power; (3) the ramifications to the point of virtual totality, of the kind of decisions that are made at the top, and the rise to power of a set of men who, by training and bent, are professional organizers of considerable force and who are unrestrained by democratic party training.

Negatively, the formation of the power elite rests upon (1) the relegation of the professional party politician to the middle levels of power, (2) the semi-organized stalemate of the interests of sovereign localities into which the legislative function has fallen, (3) the virtually complete absence of a civil service that constitutes a politically neutral, but politically relevant, depository of brainpower and executive skill, and (4) the increased official secrecy behind which great decisions are made without benefit of public or even Congressional debate.

As a result, the political directorate, the corporate rich, and the ascendant military have come together as the power elite, and the expanded and centralized hierarchies which they head have encroached upon the old balances and have now relegated them to the middle levels of power. Now the balancing society is a conception that pertains accurately to the middle levels, and on that level the balance has become more often an affair of intrenched provincial and nationally irresponsible forces and demands than a center of power and national decision.

NOTES

1. Cf. Elmer Davis, *But We Were Born Free* (Indianapolis: Bobbs-Merrill, 1953), p. 187.
2. Richard Hofstadter, *The Age of Reform* (New York: Knopf, 1955), pp. 71–2.

STUDY QUESTIONS

1. What parts of society make up the "power elite" discussed by Mills? What practices allow this concentration of power?
2. Is the "power elite" an accident or a conspiracy? Defend your answer with information from the article.

CHARLES KOEBER

Corporate Restructuring, Downsizing, and the Middle Class

The Process and Meaning of Worker Displacement in the "New" Economy

Introduction

The term "downsizing" refers to the large-scale and systematic displacement of workers by typically corporate employers. Although the term is arguably a euphemism, its recent and common usage indicates the pervasiveness of the corporate job-cutting trend. This trend has not only resulted in mass job loss, but has contributed to the transformation of the post-World War II model of employment (Rubin 1996), altered the prevailing structure of labor markets (Osterman 1999), and significantly affected the American class structure (Perrucci and Wysong 1999).

During the 1970s and 1980s, plant closings and displacement of manufacturing workers were largely *reactive* measures that occurred as a response to economic recessions, drops in product demand, and the failure of U.S. companies to compete globally (Bluestone and Harrison 1982). However, during the 1990s, the downsizing of not only manufacturing workers, but also service, managerial, and professional workers became a *proactive* measure, a management strategy that companies in a variety of industries used in attempts to be more competitive and profitable or to increase their stock market value (Downs 1995). Downsizing thus became a defining feature of the new capitalism under which *all* types and classes of workers were at risk of losing their jobs (Smith 2001; Budros 1998; Sennett 1998).[1]

Paradoxically, the job cuts of the mid and late 1990s were not accompanied by or did not result in high levels of national unemployment. Unlike previous waves of layoffs in the twentieth century during periods of economic contraction, these layoffs occurred during an economic recovery and expansion in which many new jobs were created and unemployment rates hovered at or near record lows. Thus, two seemingly contradictory realities characterized part of the U.S. economic environment at the end of the twentieth century: high numbers of job cuts and low unemployment.

The dual reality of high numbers of job cuts alongside low rates of unemployment suggests that studies of worker displacement should focus not merely on aggregate job losses or job loss as an event. Rather, it appears that for many Americans, work has increasingly become a *transitional and transformational process* of "serial employment." Due in part to corporate restructuring and downsizing that occur in the context of a rapidly changing global economy, many workers lose their jobs (Baldoz et al. 2001). When employment levels are sufficiently high, most displaced workers find new jobs and experience an accompanying change in the conditions and relations of their work. This perspective suggests that research concerning downsizing and worker displacement should focus on the complex relationship between the changing work experiences and mobility of displaced workers and changes in the structure of the economy, organizations, and labor markets (Kraft 1999).

Research Methods

The project employed qualitative case study methods as the basis for collecting and analyzing information. The methods of this study yield at least three main advantages. First, the case study approach helps to break down the larger research population of displaced workers into manageable units (White 1992, p. 83), enabling an account of the complex experiences of a specific group of displaced workers. Second, case study techniques provide the subjects with the opportunity to have a "voice" and to tell their "story" (Ragin and Becker 1992, p. 43). The third and most important advantage is that case study procedures encourage and facilitate the development of "grounded theory" (Glaser and Strauss 1967; Strauss and Corbin 1990). In this study I develop grounded theoretical concepts related to work and employment change of displaced workers.

The study draws upon thirty interviews with workers. It is difficult to sample displaced workers, as firms do not publicize the names of workers they displace and often provide limited information about workforce reductions to the public. Since it was not possible to develop a complete sampling frame of displaced workers, I relied on a variation of "snowball" sampling. This sampling procedure is appropriate when studying hard-to-access populations (Babbie 2001). Initial contacts occurred through personal acquaintances I sought out as a resident of the Binghamton area. These contacts provided me with telephone numbers of additional respondents who in turn provided me with further references. . . .

The occupational composition of the sample fell into mostly white-collar and professional positions and included eight engineers, seven administrative workers, four managers, three programmers, three designers, two technicians, one salesperson, one materials handler and one training instructor. All but one of the respondents were employed full time in the jobs that they lost. In terms of demographic characteristics, all respondents were white. Twenty-one were males and nine, females. The mean age of respondents was 46, but the males in the sample were older than the females. The mean job tenure of respondents in the lost job was 20 years. . . .

I used retrospective interviews to order events and occurrences. According to Schutt, retrospective interviewing is appropriate when longitudinal data are not available and the researcher believes respondents can provide reliable information about their histories (1996, p. 131). The interviews allowed for analysis of work histories and comparison of objective characteristics of respondents' work and employment—such as wages, hours, types of tasks, and types of work relations—before and after job loss. The interviews also explored displaced workers' subjective experiences with downsizing, displacement, and employment change.

Although most of the data for the study came from interviews with displaced workers, I used data from the Department of Labor to examine work and employment conditions in the Binghamton metropolitan statistical area (MSA). This information was useful in approximating the quantity of workforce reductions at IBM and Link and for describing the structural context of the job search and labor market encounters of respondents. The combination of multiple methods and sources of information (or triangulation) in this study is consistent with suggestions in the literature concerning use of multiple research techniques to enhance social science findings (Chen 1998).

The Process of Displacement

The subjects of this study underwent a process by which they experienced work and employment change and by which they became separated and detached from prior conditions, relations, and meanings of work. As noted earlier, I conceptualize this pattern of experiences as the "displacement process." Interviews with workers suggest this process occurred in three main stages, which are summarized in Table 1. The first *stage* of the displacement process began before job loss and occurred in two distinct *phases*. In phase 1A workers experienced a transformation of work relations as the firms began reorganizing and reducing their workforces. During phase 1B, participants lost their jobs. The second stage occurred following job loss, when respondents faced difficulty in the labor market; it was comprised of three phases. Phase 2A consisted of making work-related decisions about the future. Phase 2B involved re-education and/or retraining for most of the subjects. Phase 2C entailed a job search. Stage three of the displacement process covers the re-employment experience. This stage consisted of two phases. Phase 3A involved a period of transitional employment and/or "job hopping" during which time respondents worked in jobs mainly as a means to support themselves while looking or waiting for more favorable work. Phase 3B involved employment resettlement. . . .

TABLE 1   Stages and Phases of the Displacement Process

Stage 1 Employment and job loss		Stage 2 Unemployment			Stage 3 Re-employment	
Phase 1A	*Phase 1B*	*Phase 2A*	*Phase 2B*	*Phase 2C*	*Phase 3A*	*Phase 3B*
Working in a downsizing firm	Losing or leaving one's job	Decision making	Additional education or training	Job searching	Job hopping in transitional employment	Resettling into new employment

Description of Stage One: Employment and Job Loss

Restructuring and downsizing had several related, overlapping and often contradictory effects on the work environments at IBM and Link. Workers' experiences and comments suggested these effects could be divided into four related outcomes: 1) fear of job loss; 2) decline of work effort and enthusiasm; 3) workplace conflict; and 4) diminished work expectations. . . .

Not surprisingly, many workers reacted emotionally to their job loss. They expressed feelings of shock, anger, fear, and unpleasant surprise. These emotions were expressed not only as a reaction to job loss per se, but as a reaction to the abandonment of longstanding familial relations and the job security that had previously characterized the two companies. The following IBM worker articulates a common sentiment found among the sample:

> [It was] very discouraging and depressing. You felt a sense of betrayal. It was almost like your wife divorcing you, because you had a strong sense of family. In fact, that was one of IBM's big things, a big happy family. And they did at least try to propagate that feeling through their employees. . . So I felt betrayed, basically. I trusted the organization and it betrayed me. I was doing the best that I knew how to do what I was supposed to be doing. Then they slap you around saying you're worthless and then they show you the door, or you show yourself the door before they do (26).

More surprisingly, some workers did express favorable reactions to their displacement, describing feelings of happiness and relief. While job loss was an unfortunate occurrence, as the following two respondents indicated, it also represented an exit from unsatisfactory conditions and relations of work or a sense of closure to the open-ended possibility of job loss:

> I had a real problem—this is like when I sat down with my second-level manager and we started talking about (early) retirement—I had a real hard time keeping a grin off my face and shaking his hand and saying, "Thank you!" Because the pressure was off; I didn't have to worry any longer what was gonna happen (18).
>
> As I was walking down, a guy says, "What happened to you? You look like you are happier than hell." [I said], "I'm laid off!" A couple guys said, "I'll trade you." That was the atmosphere: people were looking to get out of there (16).

Description of Stage Two: Unemployment

As noted by the model, stage two of the displacement process involved a period of unemployment consisting of three phases. The first, phase 2A, entailed making difficult decisions about one's work and employment. A major issue in this phase concerned workers' decisions regarding physical relocation options and choices related to job opportunities. Respondents in this sample chose to remain in the Binghamton area. Although some respondents indicated that they chose to remain because they did not think they would be able to sell their homes (and/or sell them at a reasonable price), the most often cited reason for staying among the sample was the preference to remain near family:

> My family's here. I'm an only child. His [her husband] family's here and he is very important in his family. His father is passed away, so he's [her husband] looked upon [sic]. We weren't gonna leave (9).

Following relocation decisions, workers were confronted with the issue of whether to obtain additional education or training (phase 2B). The benefits of education and training for respondents were limited. Although respondents indicated that additional education and training helped them to secure a job, education or training did not necessarily result in higher earnings. There was little difference in the amount of earnings or earnings loss for those in the sample who received re-education/retraining versus those who did not. The mean annual gross earnings of both groups were similar before job loss (approximately $40,000) and after job loss (approximately $30,000) with both groups losing approximately $10,000 per year.

Additionally, having more education in general did not immunize respondents from earnings loss. Although those who possessed education beyond high school did not experience as much earnings loss as those with only a high school diploma, the categories of those with either a high school diploma, an associate's degree, or a bachelor's degree all experienced in subsequent employment yearly gross earnings losses that ranged from an average of $9,000 to $12,000 approximately.

For most workers, the re-education/retraining experience led to a difficult job search. The difficulties were compounded if the participants were searching for employment with pay and benefit levels comparable to their former jobs. In phase 2C participants searched extensively— looking for openings in the newspaper and on the Internet, networking, sending out dozens of resumes—taking many steps in their attempts to secure a job. For these respondents the consequences of corporate downsizing included not only the loss of their jobs, but also difficulties of finding new ones in the Binghamton area. Even professional jobs that one might expect to be in high demand were seemingly in scarce supply in Binghamton. As two respondents commented:

> It was kind of a rude awakening. I honestly thought that there would be no problem, you know, getting back into industry in the engineering field. So I started filling out resumes and mailed 'em out to a few places around town, and nothing. No response. It kind of shocked me a little (13).
>
> With IBM downsizing, Link downsizing, it didn't leave a lot of opportunity to find corporations that would be hiring finance people. The number of jobs were few and the number of people looking for jobs was many (23).

Description of Stage Three: Re-employment

For most workers in the study, re-employment occurred in two distinct phases. Workers first experienced a transition in their employment, moving from one job to another, attempting to find satisfactory work (phase 3A). After averaging twenty years of tenure in their prior jobs, at the time of the study respondents had been separated from IBM or Link for an average of four years, during which time they had an average of more than two jobs.

Sometimes transitional employment entailed nonstandard job experiences in which respondents were employed as "contingent" or "alternative/indirect" workers. Some even returned as contingent workers to the same sites from which they were displaced. For instance, as part of an arrangement in which IBM outsourced its customer service functions, an IBM contractor leased a vacant portion of the IBM facility. Several displaced IBM respondents worked part time for the contractor as telephone customer service representatives, troubleshooting problems with clients' IBM products. Other respondents at both IBM and Link were called back to perform the same jobs from which they were displaced, albeit on a temporary basis. And, in a few cases, some returned to their old workplaces as temporary employees to perform jobs they occupied earlier in their careers. One respondent tersely summed up the main source of discontent that he experienced under this arrangement: "I'm doing the same job I did five years ago for probably a quarter—not even a quarter—of the pay!" (15).

Job hopping also occurred for respondents outside of the Link and IBM organizational context. Some worked for temporary help agencies, bouncing from job to job. Others experimented with various types of sales jobs, working for commission. In the absence of full-time employment opportunities, some respondents worked part-time in service and retail jobs, in restaurants and department stores, as waitresses and clerks.

While nearly half the sample continued to encounter employment transition at the time of interview, the other half indicated that they had entered phase 3B, resettling in a job in which they planned to remain. Re-employment outcomes in this sample corresponded with differences in gender and age. Men under age 50 more often settled in comparable positions whereas women and those age 50 and over were more likely to continue to job hop or to settle in lower paying jobs. The differences between these three gender/age groups were evident in not only the comparison of annual earnings change but also in occupational change and change in the number of hours worked per week. . . .

Younger men, while experiencing formidable challenges of a competitive labor market, were not subject to the same disadvantages that confronted women and older men. Several of these men—mainly engineers and programmers—eventually secured employment at other large high-tech firms in the region. However, even for this group, the process of displacement was arduous. For some, losing a job was particularly hard on their self-esteem, given self-perceptions as breadwinners in the prime of their lives. Some lost income in transition; many worked contingent/alternative jobs before finding comparable work. One relocated and left his family for a year before returning to find work in the Binghamton area. Another commuted an hour each way to and from work. Over half of the respondents in this group reported they were less satisfied with their present employment than with their job at IBM or Link. As a former Link worker explains, the displacement process typically involved drawbacks, even for those who eventually found comparable paying jobs:

> Well, obviously the decrease in salary was one of the things. I had to tighten my belt somewhat until I had gone through the training period because I was on a fixed amount of money, which was $9,000 less than I was making before. So obviously I had to cut some corners for probably a good six to eight months. So that was an impact. Getting into the type of [job] situation where my time really wasn't my time, it was my

client's time. Obviously to be successful in this type of business you have to pay a price, you have to sacrifice something else to be successful. . . . A lot of times I don't get out of here until 5:30 or 6:00 and I may have an appointment with somebody (later in the evening) so this job's the sacrifice. Now my style of managing my time is important, more so now than it was then. It was regimented there. Now I have to manage it. And because of that managing I have to try to reduce the time away from the family as much as I can. I don't have as much time. So I try to structure my day in such a way that is less impacted to the family life because that is obviously just as important or more important than your work life. So it's more of a juggling act now. That can have stress on a marriage. . . . To be successful in anything you have to pay a price and in some cases that price will be your family. So going into this business I knew I'd have to give up something. It wasn't going to be all hunky-dory. If I wanted to succeed in this business I would have to pay a price, a price I didn't have to pay over there (22).

Conclusion

Given recent developments in national and global economic and employment trends, some researchers have called for more social science research on work and employment issues in this "era of flexibility." In a recent review essay, Smith notes: "We need a deeper understanding of personal experience, subjective interests, and of how aspirations are sustained or crushed as the opportunity structure undergoes changes that appear to be permanent and radical" (1997, p. 335). This study is an example of one approach to the issue raised by Smith and others. By addressing the ramifications of corporate downsizing in the 1990s, it provides insights into how workers, especially those of a roughly middle-class character, experience this abstract concept.

The experiences of workers before, during, and after job loss suggest that we need to expand the conventional meaning of worker displacement. They also highlight a number of work and employment problems, issues, and new questions concerning the downsizing phenomenon. To be displaced means to be separated or detached. Participants in this study became separated or detached in many ways, and not merely because they lost their jobs. The displacement model illustrates how this patterned process occurred for many workers. As we saw, the meanings of displacement were shaped by workers' prior history of paternalistic work relations at IBM and Link as well as by subsequent restructuring and workforce reductions. Following job loss, the meaning of displacement continued to be shaped by changes at IBM and Link, as workforce reductions transformed the structure of the labor market from one characteristic of a thriving company town to one characteristic of a de-industrialized area. For half the sample, displacement led to contingent employment. This finding raises several interesting questions about the relationship between downsizing and contingent work that may be addressed by future research. For many participants, re-employment was marked by a continuation of severance from more favorable work conditions and relations as they lost careers and became downwardly mobile. Finally, we saw that outcomes of the displacement process varied by age and gender. This suggests a need for more research of the causal mechanisms of gender and age differences among displaced workers and their experiences with downsizing, displacement and employment change.

The generalizability of this case study of displaced workers in the Binghamton, New York area is limited. However, national-level data indicate that the phenomenon of corporate downsizing has been far from limited to Binghamton, New York. Thus, it is likely that hundreds of thousands or even millions of workers have experienced or will experience the displacement process in terms similar to the model presented in this study.

Politically, popular solutions to employment problems of displaced workers, such as education or retraining, imply that workers must adapt to new and inexorable economic realities. As we have seen, this adaptation may involve moving through stages and phases in an arduous process. In one scenario, the displaced worker experiences little in the way of material hardship, but nonetheless suffers a temporary disruption in her or his working life and is forced to redefine expectations and attitudes about work and working. Another less attractive but frequent outcome is that the process of displacement leads many workers through experiences of job instability, downward mobility, and the permanent loss of previously favorable conditions, relations, and meanings of work. The evidence in this study as well as in some larger studies indicates that many workers do not fare well. As we saw, this is not only the case for displaced blue-collar workers; many white-collar and middle-class workers lose their jobs and become downwardly mobile (Newman 1988; Rubin 1994). Even those who do appear to overcome job losses on favorable terms have no guarantee they will not again be displaced. No matter how adaptable the worker, no job is secure. As we move deeper into the twenty-first century, this emerging reality confronts the American workforce and raises issues that will require attention by workers, policy makers, academics, and all interested citizens.

NOTES

1. At the end of the twentieth century, many business organizations made frequent and large numbers of job cuts. According to Challenger, Gray and Christmas, a consulting firm that tracks corporate workforce reductions, 1998 was a record-setting year for the number of job cut announcements (677,795), breaking the previous record set in 1993 (615,186) by ten percent (Laabs 1999, p. 21). Near record-high numbers of job cut announcements (675,123) were present in 1999 (*The Detroit News* 2000, p. M1). As I write in October of 2001, layoffs and layoff announcements have substantially increased following the events of September 11th and as the economy has slowed down.

REFERENCES

Babbie, E. (2001). *The practice of social research, ninth edition.* Belmont, CA: Wadsworth/Thomson Learning.

Baldoz, R., Koeber C., & Kraft, P. (2001). *The critical study of work: Labor, technology, and global production.* Philadelphia: Temple University Press.

Bluestone, B., & Harrison, B. (1982). *The deindustrialization of America: Plant closings, community abandonment, and the dismantling of basic industry.* New York: Basic Books.

Budros, A. (1998). The new capitalism and organizational rationality: The adoption of downsizing programs, 1979–1994. *Social Forces,* 76, 229–250.

Chen, S. (1998). *Mastering research: A guide to the methods of social and behavioral science.* Chicago: Nelson-Hall Publishers.

Downs, A. (1995). *Corporate executions: The ugly truth about layoffs—how corporate greed is shattering lives, companies, and communities.* New York: American Management Association.

Glaser, B. G., & Strauss, A. A. (1967). *The discovery of grounded theory.* Chicago: Aldine.

Kraft, P. (1999). To control and inspire: U.S. management in the age of computer information systems and global production. In M. Wardell, T. L. Steiger, & P. Meiksins (Eds.), *Rethinking the labor process.* Albany: State University of New York Press.

Newman, K. S. (1988). *Falling from grace.* New York: Free Press.

Osterman, P. (1999). *Securing prosperity: The American labor market: How has it changed and what to do about it.* Princeton: Princeton University Press.

Perrucci, R., & Wysong, E. (1999). *The new class society.* Lanham, MD: Rowman and Littlefield.

Ragin, C. C., & Becker, H. S. (1992). *What is a case: Exploring the foundations of social inquiry.* New York: Vintage Books.

Rubin, B. A. (1996). *Shifts in the social contract: Understanding change in American society.* Thousand Oaks, CA: Pine Forge Press.

Rubin, L. (1994). *Families on the fault line: America's working class speaks about the family, the economy, race and ethnicity.* New York: Harper Perennial.

Schutt, R. K. (1996). *Investigating the social world: The process and practice of research.* Thousand Oaks, CA: Pine Forge Press.

Sennett, R. (1998). *The corrosion of character: The personal consequences of work in the new capitalism.* New York: W. W. Norton & Company.

Smith, V. (1997). New forms of work organization. In J. Hagan & K. S. Cook (Eds.), *Annual review of sociology* (pp. 315–339). Palo Alto: Annual Reviews Inc.

Smith, V. (2001). *Crossing the great divide: Worker risk and opportunity in the new economy.* Ithaca: ILR Press.

Strauss, A., & Corbin, J. (1990). *Basics of qualitative research: Grounded theory procedures and techniques.* Newbury Park, CA: Sage.

White, H. (1992). Cases are for identity, for explanation or for control. In C. Ragin & H. Becker (Eds.), *What is a case: Exploring the foundations of social inquiry* (pp. 83–104). New York: Cambridge University Press.

STUDY QUESTIONS

1. What are the stages in the process of adjustment to losing one's job? How would you feel if this happened to you?
2. Many of these "displaced workers" had college degrees and advanced training. Was it easier or more difficult for them to get jobs because of this?

ROBERT W. FULLER

Somebodies and Nobodies
The Abuse of Rank

As a student at Oberlin College during the 1950s, I was taught to be proud of its early advocacy of equal opportunity for women and blacks. But by the late 1960s, Oberlin students, like their counterparts across America, were in rebellion. The few dozen black students on campus were protesting their paltry numbers. Women students were criticizing the status of women in the college and the country. And many students who were upset over national policy on Vietnam turned their ire on whatever college policies impinged on their rights as young adults.

When Oberlin's Board of Trustees appointed me president of the college in 1970, the choice was clear: either embrace the changes "blowing in the wind" or be blown away. Within a few years, Oberlin, like most other colleges, added many African-Americans to its student body, faculty, and staff. Simultaneously, a feminist revolution transformed the College in a thousand subtle ways, and student pressure brought overdue reforms to social and educational policies.

The simultaneous activities of the black, women's, and student movements made me realize that there was something deeper going on. Something beyond differences in color, gender, and educational credentials underpinned the racism, sexism, and disenfranchisement of students that lay claim to our immediate attention. I sensed that the familiar "isms" were all manifestations of a more fundamental cause of discrimination, but I couldn't put my finger on it. It was not until I had left the presidency and had become a target of this kind of discrimination myself that I was able to identify it.

412

Lacking the protection of title and status in the years after Oberlin, I experienced what it's like to be taken for a "nobody." I found myself comparing the somebody-nobody divide with the white-black polarity of racism, the male-female opposition of sexism, and the teacher-student dichotomy in schools. There were differences, but there were similarities as well, the most important ones being (1) indignity and humiliation feel pretty much the same to a nobody, a black, a woman, or a student, and (2) no matter the excuse for abuse, it persists only in the presence of an underlying difference of rank signifying power. No one would dare to insult Queen Elizabeth I or General Colin Powell.

In the US, perhaps twenty percent of us have suffered directly from racism, and about fifty percent from sexism. But virtually all of us suffer from rank-based abuse—which I shall be calling "rankism"—in one context or another, at one time or another. Sooner or later, everyone gets taken for a nobody. Sooner or later, most of us treat someone else as a nobody. It always hurts to be "dissed," no matter what your status. Yet if it weren't for the fact that most everyone has known the sting of rankism, would there ever have been empathy for victims of racism and sexism?

At first I thought that rankism was just another ism, one more in the litany of isms with which we were growing weary, and I resisted the notion. Then it dawned on me that the familiar isms could be seen as subspecies of rankism. Racism, sexism, anti-Semitism, ageism and other isms all depend for their existence on differences of social rank that in turn reflect underlying power differences, so they are forms of rankism. Overcoming rankism would therefore undermine racism, sexism, and other isms that have been fought under those names but ultimately derive their force from power differences woven into the social fabric.

Gradually, I realized that the gains would go much further. For example, the reason so many students—regardless of color—withhold their hearts and minds from learning can be traced to the fact that their top priority and constant concern is to shield themselves from the rankism that permeates education from kindergarten to graduate school.

Rankism erodes the will to learn, distorts personal relationships, taxes economic productivity, and stokes ethnic hatred. It is the cause of dysfunctionality, and sometimes even violence, in families, schools, and the workplace. Like racism and sexism, rankism must be named and identified and then negotiated out of all our social institutions.

How could a scourge like rankism have gone thus far unremarked? Well, of course, it has not. We've been traumatized and battered by one or another of its manifestations for centuries, and many of these have long been recognized and acquired individual names. The situation is analogous to the era in medicine when malignancies peculiar to different organs were seen as disparate diseases. In time they were all recognized to be various forms of one disease—cancer.

Regardless of surface distinctions such as ethnicity, religion, color, or gender, persistent abuse and discrimination is predicated on power differences inherent in rank. Race-based discrimination is called racism, gender-based discrimination is called sexism. By analogy, rank-based discrimination can be called rankism.

Rankism is the "cancer" that underlies many of the seemingly disparate maladies that afflict the body politic. Unnamed, it will continue to debilitate, damage, and destroy; named, we can begin to unravel its pathology and take steps to protect ourselves. Attacking the familiar isms singly, one at a time, is like developing a different chemotherapy for each kind of cancer. To go after rankism directly is to seek to eliminate a whole class of malignancies.

Once you have a name for it, you see it everywhere. The outrage over self-serving corrupt executives is indignation over rankism. Sexual abuse by clergy is rankism. Elder abuse in life care facilities is rankism. Scientists taking credit for their assistants' research is rankism. More generally, rank-based discrimination is an ever-present reality in society at large, where it takes its greatest toll on those lacking the protections of social rank—the working poor. In her book *Nickel and Dimed: On (Not) Getting By in America*, Barbara Ehrenreich argues that the working poor are unacknowledged benefactors whose labor effectively subsidizes everyone else. The "living wage" movement is a harbinger of a "dignitarian" movement against social rankism.

The casualties of pell-mell globalization—economic and environmental—are attributable to rankism. International terrorism has complex origins and multiple causes, but one of them—and one within our control—is rankism, both inadvertent and intentional, between nations. There is no fury like that borne of chronic humiliation.

The effects of rankism on its targets are the same as those of racism and sexism on minorities and women. But unlike these familiar isms, rankism knows no limits and plays no favorites. It afflicts people of every race, gender, age, and class.

It is crucial to get one thing straight from the start: power differences, in themselves, are not the culprit. To bemoan power differences is like bemoaning the fact that the sun is brighter than the moon. And rank differences merely reflect power differences, so rank differences are not the problem either, any more than color or gender differences are innately a problem. Difficulties arise only when these differences are used as an excuse to abuse, humiliate, exploit, and subjugate. So it is with power and rank. Power differences are a fact of life. Making it okay to discuss the uses of power with those holding positions of authority, with an eye towards distinguishing between appropriate and inappropriate uses of their power, is what this book is about.

Typically, the abuse of the power vested in rank-holders takes the form of disrespect, inequity, discrimination, and exploitation. Since hierarchies are pyramids of power, rankism is a malady to which hierarchies of all types are susceptible.

Let's begin with a simple example of interpersonal rankism:

> An executive pulls up to valet parking at a restaurant, late to a business lunch, and finds no one to take his car keys. Anxious and fuming, he spots a teenager running toward him in the rearview mirror and yells, "Where the hell were you? I haven't got all day."
>
> He tosses the keys at the kid's feet. Bending to pick them up, the boy says, "Sorry, sir. About how long do you expect to be?"
>
> The executive hollers over his shoulder, "You'll know when you see me, won't you?" The valet winces, but holds his tongue. Postscript: he goes home and bullies his kid brother.

Further examples leap to mind: a boss harassing an employee, a cook or a customer demeaning a server, a coach bullying a player, a doctor disparaging a nurse, a school principal insulting a teacher, a professor exploiting a teaching assistant, a teacher humiliating a student, students ostracizing other students, a parent belittling a child, an officer abusing a suspect, a caretaker mistreating an invalid.

Again, it's not that rank itself is illegitimate. When rank has been earned and signifies excellence, then it's generally accepted, and rightfully so. But the power of rank can be and often is abused, as in the examples above. Power begets power, authority becomes entrenched, and rank-holders become self-aggrandizing, capricious, and overbearing. Most of us have tasted rankism; for many, it's a dietary staple.

Rankism insults the dignity of subordinates by treating them as invisible, as nobodies. Nobody is another n-word and, like the original, it is used to justify denigration and inequity. Nobodies are insulted, disrespected, exploited, ignored. In contrast, somebodies are sought after, given preference, lionized.

You may be thinking that rankism is just a new name for bullying. While bullying is indeed archetypal rankism, the old word has limited range. The term rankism is more inclusive, grouping disparate actions by their common underlying cause and affording us a fresh look at behaviors we now put up with, sometimes collude in and, on occasion, indulge in ourselves.

Rankism—Mother of "Isms"

It might be supposed that if one overcame tendencies to racism, sexism, ageism and other narrowly defined forms of discrimination, one would be purged of rankism as well. But rankism is not just another ism. It subsumes the familiar dishonorable isms. It's the mother of them all.

What makes is possible for one group to discriminate against another? For example, whites segregating blacks, Gentiles imposing quotas on Jews, or straights harassing gays? Color, religion, gender, and sexual orientation are simply pretexts for constructing and exploiting social stratifications; they are not the actual cause of ongoing injustice. Such discrimination is predicated on social dominance that depends on established, constructed power differences, fortified by customs and laws. As the power gap closes through the breakdown of customs and the repeal of prejudicial legislation, systemic abuse becomes harder and harder to sustain.

Like other predators, human beings select as prey those they perceive as weak. It's a safer bet; there's less chance of retaliation. Distinguishing traits such as color, gender, or sexual orientation only signify weakness if there is a social consensus in place that handicaps those bearing the trait. A social consensus such as Jim Crow, the feminine mystique, or homophobia functions to keep an entire group of people weak and usable by the dominant group (whites, males, or straights, in these cases).

Power matters. In fact, it's more or less all that matters, and it is important for those who temporarily lack it to realize this so they can set about building a countervailing power. It is only as those subordinated by a particular consensus organize and gain power commensurate with that of their oppressors that the prevailing consensus unravels and the pretext for exploitation is disallowed.

Although rank-based discrimination *feels* the same to its targets as the more familiar kinds, there are some important differences in the way it works. Unlike race or gender, rank is mutable. You can be taken for a nobody one day and for a somebody the next. You can be a nobody at home and a somebody at work, or vice versa. The mutability of rank means that most of us have been both victims and perpetrators of rankism, in different contexts.

Rankism, like racism, is a source of social injustice as well as personal indignity. As we'll see, a great deal of what's labeled social pathology has its origins in rankism. But unlike racists and sexists, who are now on notice, rankists still go largely unchallenged. The indignity suffered by those who've been "nobodied" festers. It builds to indignation and sometimes erupts in violence. When a person or a people is nobodied, it not only does them an injustice, but also plants a time bomb in our midst.

The consequences range from school shootings to revanchism, even to genocide. The twentieth century has seen many demagogues who have promised to restore the pride and dignity of a people that felt nobodied. Hitler enjoyed the support of Germans humiliated by punitive reparations in the aftermath of World War I. The national impotence imposed on the German nation (the Fatherland) by the victors reverberated through every German family, as well. In opting for Hitler, many Germans were not only voting to restore rank to the Fatherland, but also to overcome the sense of inadequacy they'd experienced as the heads of German families. Similarly, President Milosevic of Yugoslavia traded on the wounded pride of the Serbs in the 1990s. Once war begins, people will become apologists for crimes they would otherwise condemn to get even with those they believe have nobodied them.

Globally, there are few counterparts to the democratic institutions that mitigate the most flagrant displays of rankism within nations. However, nowhere are rankism's effects more acute than in the still largely extra-legal realm of international relations; weaker states are often compelled to do the bidding of stronger ones.

In the distinction between rank and rankism lies the difference between dignity and indignity—for persons, for peoples, for nations. A truly great power, to be worthy of the name, distinguishes itself from a "mere" superpower through its sensitivity to this difference in its dealings with weaker states.

Attacking the familiar isms, one at a time, is like lopping heads off the Hydra of discrimination and oppression; going after rankism aims to drive a stake through the Hydra's heart.

Equal in Dignity

Dignity is not negotiable.

—Vartan Gregorian, American writer, university president, and
foundation executive (1934–   )

Though most of us have experienced rankism, we do not routinely protest it, at least not to the perpetrators. We limit our complaints to those who share our station. Uncle Tom's policy of "to get along, go along" recommends itself to almost everyone when it comes to confronting rankism. As a short-term solution this is understandable because the power difference upon which rankism is predicated makes resisting it dangerous. But in the long run, appeasement fails. Uncle Tom ended up being whipped to death.

Despite the fact that we may acquiesce to unequal treatment or even collude in self-abnegation, most of us sense that there is something about human beings that is universal, absolute, and, yes, equal.

Equal? We are obviously unequal in skill, talent, beauty, strength, health, or wealth—in any measurable trait for that matter.

What then? For millennia, there have been people of every faith, often in opposition to their own religious leaders, who have sensed that all human beings are of equal dignity. Though this spiritual insight is routinely violated, it is grounded in (and represents an intuitive grasp of) more pragmatic reasons for opposing rankist abuses of power, reasons that we'll explore in the chapters to follow.

Rankism is invariably an assault on dignity. If people are fundamentally equal in dignity, then discrimination on the basis of power differences—experienced as an insult to dignity—has no legitimacy and must be disallowed. The notion of rankism links ethics and politics through dignity.

All ranks, like all races, are worthy of equal dignity. Deviations from equal dignity set in motion a dynamic that draws attention away from whatever we're doing—working, learning, or healing. When energy is diverted to defending one's dignity against insults in the workplace, productivity suffers. In schools, students sacrifice their learning to defend their dignity. Today, it is not so much racial prejudice as misuse of rank that functions to keep students of all colors from committing themselves to education. It is rankism that creates the specious divide between winners and losers at an early age and extinguishes ambition in many before they reach third grade.

More than other peoples, Americans seem to believe that if you fail, it's your own fault. Yet we all know of many instances where power, position, and privilege—not merit—have predetermined an outcome. The rich, the powerful, and the famous enjoy unearned perks in all walks of life. Celebrities go to the head of the line; their transgressions are forgiven. We hope to be treated evenhandedly, but are not surprised when we're not.

Over the centuries, the democratization of our civic institutions has curtailed the most blatant kinds of governmental rankism. But rising voter apathy now signals that the issues that matter most—education, health policy, and working conditions—are perceived as lying beyond the effective reach of government. The challenge is to find a way to bring the core principle of democracy—the idea of mutual accountability and non-rankist service—to all our social institutions.

The Myth of Meritocracy

America sees itself as a meritocracy, in contrast to aristocratic Europe. But while opportunity is more equal here than it was in aristocracies, it is still far from merit-based. The last half-century has seen an assault on race, gender, sexual orientation, and age-based barriers to equal opportunity, but the surface upon which we compete for recognition is still a steep hill, not a level playing field.

Paradoxically, it is rank itself that now poses the greatest obstacle to basing rewards on merit. This is because rank acquired in one realm often confers advantages in other, unrelated ones. Why should rank shield perpetrators from the consequences of rule-breaking, misdeeds, or incompetence? Why should it be harder for those of low rank to improve their station than for those of high rank to retain theirs? If rank is based on merit, high rank today should not be a guarantor of high rank tomorrow. Nor should low rank carry the stigma of perpetual loser. Discrimination based on rank differences is as inconsistent with actual meritocracy as is discrimination based on color or gender differences.

In a true meritocracy, rank would have to be precisely defined, and rewards would reflect current rank within a large and growing number of narrowly defined niches. High rank in one specialty, as determined on one occasion, would not signify merit in general or indefinitely. Because individuals' talents, abilities, and skills vary markedly from niche to niche, composite, overall rankings that ignore variations from specialty to specialty yield spurious results. We don't simply declare the winner of the mile the best runner, because that would overlook the fact that there are sprinters and marathoners who, in their events, can outdo the fastest miler. Merit has no significance, and therefore should carry no weight, beyond the precise realm wherein it is assessed. From this perspective, IQ measures not the broad amorphous trait "intelligence"—now recognized to assume a myriad of specialized forms—but rather the ability to do well on a particular kind of test. Similarly, ranking schools by their students' average test scores is a measure of how a selected group of students did on a particular test, not the schools' intrinsic educational merit.

Achievers of high rank often use their position to disadvantage those who would challenge them, or to hang on to rewards they may once have earned but have since ceased to merit. An aura of social rank—a vestige of aristocratic class—envelops winners (who are seen as somebodies), and is denied to runners-up (who are seen as nobodies). Parents pay premiums to elite universities in the belief that the prestige of these famous schools will rub off on their offspring and bring them advantages after graduation.

Although most new organizations start out with the intention of doing good and providing a service, once rankism gains a foothold, like a parasitical disease, it subverts that purpose to the narrower goal of advancing the well-being of high-ranking members. The discriminatory, morale-sapping effects of rankism can be seen in hierarchies of all kinds: schools and universities; firms, corporations, and businesses; labor unions; medical, religious and nonprofit organizations; the guardian professions and the military; bureaucracies and governments.

Meritocracy is a myth in the presence of rankism, just as it was in the presence of racism and sexism. Until there are effective procedures that curtail rank-based discrimination in all of our social institutions, American meritocracy is unworthy of the name.

Democracy's Next Step

During the two centuries since the American and French Revolutions, and despite woeful lapses and delays, the franchise in modern democracies has gradually widened to include virtually all adults.

But although we've made significant inroads against racism and sexism, diminishing returns seem to be setting in. At this stage an all-inclusive approach might do more to advance the causes of minorities, women, and other identity groups than the splintering, sometimes divisive, group-based politics of recent years. A practical way to further justice at this point, including the rights of specific groups, is to attack the universal underlying cause of indignity, regardless of who is targeted. That cause is rankism.

Unequal opportunity and unfairness are incompatible with democratic ideals. The indignities of rankism, no less than those of racism and sexism, are inefficient, cruel, and self-defeating. They have no place in democracy's future.

In the 1960s, America faced a moral crisis that threatened to tear the country apart. Once we understood that there was no way to end the crisis without dismantling racism, we took steps to do so. As we enter the twenty-first century, a moral crisis looms that could become equally grave. Our political and economic institutions, both national international, are rife with rankism.

Democracy is a work in progress. Its essence is its capacity for self-correction. Overcoming rankism—in the family, the schools, the workplace, and the boardroom, and in domestic and international politics—is now at the top of democracy's agenda. The purpose of this book is to shine a spotlight on rank-based abuse, to learn to recognize its various faces, assess its costs, and conceive a world without it.

Like racism and sexism, rankism can't be eradicated overnight, but its perpetrators can be put on notice. Authority can be democratized without being undermined. Democracies, which succeeded in circumscribing rank in national government, led the world in the last century. The nations that are most successful in removing rankism from business, education, and their international relations will lead in the next.

STUDY QUESTIONS

1. In the author's way of thinking, what makes "rankism" the "mother of all isms"?
2. How would a world without rankism be different from today? Would you like to be part of that world?

PART FIVE

Social Change in a Modern World

Population
and Ecology

THE FUTURE OF THE PLANET AND OUR LIVES ARE TIED
to the macrosocial effects of population and the distribution of population in emerging and developed nations. The social and environmental
ecology of urban areas brings focus to the sociological forces that will
write the future of entire continents and ultimately the world. While it
is true that the dramatic world population growth of the 1960s and
1970s has slowed, what will 12 billion living persons mean to urban
areas already impossibly choked by poor living conditions, widespread
illness, and environmental pollution? Urbanization is now just as
important as population alone, with its own tremendous impact on the
environment.

The population of the world passed 6 billion living inhabitants a few
years ago. Even with a slowing growth rate, it is estimated that somewhere in the next century we will almost double the population again.
As developed nations reach zero-population growth or have negative
growth rates, will the demand for certain types of labor and requirements in their economies mean greater immigration from growing,
developing nations where the economies cannot find jobs for residents?
Examples of these events can be found in Europe and North America
already. Such events may result in even greater diversity in receiving
countries and help to ease the crises in poorer nations. As Malthus's
"dismal thesis" regarding the population's ability to outstrip subsistence
(food and resources) fades into insignificance, how will the enormous
economic disparity between the world's countries influence the future?

Cities, regions, entire nations, and even the world must contend with changes in the environment. Ecological disaster can come from social, economic, and natural phenomena and thereby change life for small and large numbers of people. Contaminated water supplies from agricultural "runoff" might mean serious health problems for an area. Deforestation in the rain forests could result in worldwide changes in the climate. Global warming, as evidence mounts for its existence, may change the water level in the oceans, just as acid rain from upwind polluters destroys natural habitat for more circumscribed populations. The world has been made "smaller" with the dynamics of transportation, communication, and globalization. We begin to realize that oceans and mountains and international borders are less important than in the past, and all of us live in a vast web of interconnections often determined by macrolevel events, which have examples in our own backyards.

Population and ecology are part and parcel of a key future determinant of life—the politics of consumption. In the world of nations, there are a few very rich, a few in the middle, and many at the bottom of the global stratification system. How will we decide who is to give, who is to support, who is to repay, and who is to have autonomy? Are we on the verge of a "new world order"? Because of the extreme inequalities, where people in many countries live on less than $200 a year and a few countries have per capita incomes 100 times that much, the political processes in the near future must address population, world government, consumption, and economic inequality for the entire planet. This is a monumental task when individual nations can rarely find the ability to do such things for themselves.

The three selections in Topic 14: Population and Ecology present, first, an analysis of how Hurricane Katrina set the stage for secondary storms of "wilding" from the nation's capital to local neighborhoods; second, a micro look at the social ecology of an urban skid row; and, third, a clear explanation of how human population and its effects are bringing catastrophic pollution to a complex and intricate eco-system. In "Katrina: The Perfect Wilding Storm," Charles Derber shows how social breakdown occurs in the aftermath of a hurricane and releases people from controls that are hidden by conformity. John Bardo, Jeff Riemer, Ron Matson, and Bob Knapp elaborate our understanding of "social ecology" as they map the interrelated dimensions of skid row. Milton Saier, in "Pollution," has us confront the impending dangers brought on by overpopulation and what this might mean for the future of humankind.

CHARLES DERBER

Katrina: The Perfect Wilding Storm

As we move into the new century, the crises of greed and violence that motivated my desire to write this book have deepened. The most sensational news stories of the 1990s were about individual wilding by O. J. Simpson and Tonya Harding. But the most dramatic stories in the first few years of the twenty-first century have been about Enron, the Catholic Church scandal, the political "culture of corruption," terrorism and torture, and America's war in Iraq. Greed and violence remain epidemic among individuals, but it is wilding by giant institutions in the economy, the government, and civil society that is now making headlines.

On September 29, 2005, the New Orleans Police Department announced that it was investigating 12 of its officers for looting during Hurricane Katrina. Osman Khan owns the hotel where several officers were staying during the storm. "They'd leave nine or 10 at night and come back 4:30 in the morning," said Kahn of the officers. They were carrying "everything from Adidas shoes to Rolex watches." A hotel staff member, Perry Emery, brought towels into the officers' rooms and saw "Jewelry, generators, fans." Kahn said he saw police take one generator from Tulane University Hospital, which was trying to save dying patients. Emery saw other booty: "One time they came back with a bunch of weapons."[1]

Erlaine McLaurin told CNN that she and her father saw two officers walk from their car into an apartment building on their block and then come out loaded with stolen goods. "They done fill up the white car, the police car," she said. "He got a four pack of soda, a microwave, CD player. . . . I know everybody that lives here. Ain't no cops live here." Another resident saw police kick in a door of a Garden District home in a different area of the city. "They got police escorts coming in here, breaking in houses and taking the stuff."[2] A *Times-Picayune* journalist was one of several witnesses who saw police steal items off the shelves of a Lower Garden District Wal-Mart that they were supposed to be guarding.[3]

When police openly loot homes or stores they are sworn to protect, it suggests a collapse of civil society. Hurricane Katrina, a massive hurricane that smashed the Gulf Coast on August 29, 2005, is called a "natural disaster," but the term is misleading when viewed from a sociological perspective. Yes, it was one of the worst weather storms to hit the United States. But Katrina, sociologically speaking, was a perfect storm of wilding. It concentrated all the types of wilding in a single epic event. Political wilders failed to prevent the flooding in the first place. Corporate wilders made a killing off the mayhem following the storm. Individual wilders—from police to ordinary citizens—used the tragedy to get some additional pocket change and conveniences.

Katrina opened a window that had long been shut, one that allowed ordinary Americans to see the core of societal wilding rotting the fabric of our nation. Fortunately, it also has pointed the way to how we might move in a new direction and curb the wilding epidemic. In this chapter, we reflect on Katrina as a tragic monument to the different varieties of wilding in America and how Katrina reflects the old Sicilian adage "A fish rots from the head first."

Individual Wilding

Stories of personal wilding rocked America from the first day of flooding in New Orleans. We heard of snipers shooting at medevac helicopters as they tried to rescue critically ill patients from hospitals. We saw footage of looters breaking into stores and carrying out television sets and cartons of liquor. We heard shocking reports of rape, child molestation, torture, and murder inside the New Orleans Superdome, as thousands of abandoned residents tried to survive in barbaric conditions.

A month after the storm, new reports suggested that many of these stories were false. A new picture, of a large majority of the abandoned poor coming together to help and often save each other, began to emerge. All this, as I show later, suggests that the original reports of wilding on the streets reflected mainly media wilding and the national ingrained habit of "blaming the victim."

Nonetheless, some residents did exploit the chaotic, desperate situation to cherry-pick DVDs, televisions, computers, and other items from deserted stores or offices. A major target was a New Orleans Wal-Mart, where police joined residents in a frenzy of looting, carting off not only essential food and water but also computers and DVD players. The gun section of the Wal-Mart was cleaned out. There were also credible reports of a nursing home bus being carjacked, of liquor stores being broken into, and of car batteries and stereos being stolen.[4]

Some credible eyewitness reports of wilding in the Superdome came from vacationing British students who took shelter there. Jamie Trout, 22, kept a diary, writing, "It was something like Lord of the Flies—one minute everything calm, the next it descends into chaos." In one entry, he reports that "a man has been arrested for raping a seven year old in the toilet, this place is hell, I feel sick." Seeing guns, crack cocaine, and threats of violence, the students became so terrified that they formed a cordon with the young women inside and the young men on the outside, using chairs as a protective ring. Zoe Smith, 21, said, "We were absolutely terrified, the situation has descended into chaos."[5]

A month after Katrina, Judy Benetiz, director of the Louisiana Foundation against Sexual Assault, reported that individual women, who had been too afraid earlier, were coming to medical centers to report being raped. At this writing, the numbers and details have not been officially confirmed, and tales of the rapes of two young girls in the Superdome's women's restroom have been officially repudiated. But Benetiz says that individual women are slowly coming forward to report being raped or seeing rapes. Other witnesses filed reports with the police and media. Charmaine Neville, a New Orleans singer and songwriter, told WAFB-TV that she had reported to New Orleans police that "a lot of us women had been raped down there by guys who had come . . . into the neighborhood where we were."[6]

Regarding snipers, one man, Wendell Bailey, 20, was indicted on October 8 by a federal grand jury on the charge of firing out of his New Orleans apartment window at a military rescue helicopter during the storm. Police found two revolvers and a box of ammunition under his bed. No motive for the sniping was established; it was apparently a form of expressive wilding for pleasure or revenge.[7] . . .

Corporate Wilding

On September 27, 2005, New Jersey became the first state to sue oil companies for price gouging in the wake of Katrina. A few weeks earlier, New Jersey drivers had reported sudden spikes of oil prices up to $3.16 a gallon, the highest ever in the state. New Jersey sued Hess, Sunoco, and Motiva Shell, as well as several gas stations, with violating its motor fuels and consumer fraud laws. New Jersey attorney general Peter C. Harvey said the oil companies were involved in "artificial inflation and economic exploitation." He added that there were other "unconscionable practices" that involved charging consumers' credit cards for more gas than they had received and filling tanks with low-octane gas while charging high-octane prices, but the price gouging was the corporate wilding that captured consumers' attention.[8]

All over the country, thousands of motorists called better business bureaus and special government hotlines to report price gouging, often in emergency situations just after the storm. In Alabama alone, a special hotline for price gouging got 890 calls in the few days immediately following the storm, complaining of unjustified price spikes. The Mississippi attorney general's office received more than 7,000 such calls on its own hotline. This led to attorney generals from more than 30 states conferring on September 1 to coordinate a national antigouging effort.[9]

Tennessee was among the first of several states to file suits against gas station owners, such as Tip Top Mart of Chattanooga, which had allegedly charged more than $5 a gallon after the storm. These practices understandably led many consumers to see gas station owners as the main culprits. But investigators in states such as Florida believe that it was the oil companies and suppliers that artificially had hiked the prices, leaving many stations no choice but to raise their own prices at the pump.[10]

New Mexico governor Bill Richardson called a special session of his state legislature after the storm to deal with price gouging by the oil companies. In an interview with Richardson, journalist Juan Gonzales noted that, right after the storm hit, Shell had put a notice on its Web site warning consumers of price gouging and asking them to report any stations that they suspected of doing it. But Shell, as Gonzales noted, with the highest profits of any corporation in the world, raised its prices to wholesalers six times in the 10 days following the hurricane. In the third quarter of 2005, following the storm,

Exxon, the biggest U.S. oil company, reported one of the highest corporate quarterly profits in American history of $10 billion, representing a per-minute profit of $74,789 during the quarter. Royal Dutch Shell reported its own record profit of almost $9 billion, and all S&P 500 U.S. oil and gas companies reported an astonishing 62 percent rise in quarterly profits totaling $25.9 billion, leading a corporate-friendly Republican Congress to summon the heads of the five largest oil giants and interrogate them about oil profiteering.[11] Richardson, a former energy secretary in the Clinton administration, noted that "there's an unexplained trend between the price of gasoline at the pump and the price of crude. In other words, wholesale prices have nearly tripled. So the increase in prices at the pump and gasoline, what consumers are paying, is disproportionately high." He said that the "increase is so high" that he and other governors were asking for a more formal investigation by the president and Congress into corporate oil price gouging.[12]

While the oil companies were major wilders, there were wilding plums for a huge range of other giant companies, especially those involved in reconstruction efforts and with useful political connections. Within a month of the storm, the *New York Times* found that 80 percent of the $1.5 billion in relief and rebuilding contracts had been awarded in no-bid or very limited bidding arrangements, mainly to huge, politically connected corporations such as Halliburton and Bechtel. . . .

Political Wilding

Political wilding literally created the New Orleans disaster, with former and current administrations failing to fund reconstruction of the levees that would have prevented flooding by a massive hurricane, as well as creating crony appointments incapable of responding to the disaster that they knew was coming. Political wilding after the storm delayed and bungled the governmental response, leading to the tragic loss of life and property that beset millions of mainly black and poor residents. The wilding of an emerging system of "disaster capitalism" allowed the government and its corporate allies to eliminate worker and environmental protections and make astounding profits, all in the name of compassionate conservatism and rebuilding America. The sordid actions of government, to enrich politicians and corporations at the expense of needy citizens, highlights American wilding as an epidemic starting at the top leadership of the nation, in the White House and on Capitol Hill.

On September 1, 2005, President Bush said on *Good Morning America*, "I don't think anyone anticipated breach of the levees." But a FEMA report before September 11, 2001, explicitly named a hurricane disaster in New Orleans as one of the three most likely catastrophes in the United States, along with a San Francisco earthquake and a terrorist attack on New York City. In 2002, FEMA director Joe Allbaugh, a close Bush confidant, ordered a simulation of a New Orleans hurricane that envisioned "that some part of the levee would fail. . . . The water will flow through the city." Local emergency officials did their own studies. Emergency coordinator Walter Maestri in Jefferson Parish, in New Orleans, announced in September 2002 that a widely publicized simulation of a massive storm led them to "change the name of that storm from Delaney to K-Y-A-G-B—kiss your ass goodbye—because anybody who was here as that category five storm came across was gone."[13]

Federal and local officials have known at least since 1995, when a hard rain flooded New Orleans and killed six people, that the levees had to be strengthened. In 1995, Congress funded the Southeast Louisiana Urban Flood Control Project (SELA) to help rebuild the levees, and it allocated $430 million over the next decade to the project. As early as October 2001, though, the New Orleans *Times-Picayune* reported that "federal officials are postponing new projects . . . of SELA," endangering the city. Modest spending on the program continued until 2003, when the Bush administration cut off most of its funding. In June 2004, with the levees dangerously weakening, the Army Corps of Engineers project manager, Al Naomi, pleaded for $2 million more from Washington, telling the *Times-Picayune* that "the levees are sinking. Everything is sinking, and if we don't get the money fast enough to raise them," he said prophetically, disaster loomed. "The problem that we have isn't that the levee is low but that the federal funds have dried up so that we can't raise them."[14] The Army Corps of Engineers, responsible for a multiyear project to fix the levees, saw its budget cut for the New Orleans Hurricane project repeatedly by the Bush administration:

Fiscal year 2004: Army Corps request: $11 million; Bush budget: $3 million

Fiscal year 2005: Army Corps request: $22.5 million; Bush budget: $3.5 million[15]

For fiscal year 2006, Bush proposed $3 million, a precipitous cut after the intense Florida hurricane season and when the Corps of Engineers, New Orleans officials, and others were clamoring for funding for a $15-million project for Lake Pontchartrain, the Corps of Engineers was seeking $35 million for new levee construction, and further studies were recommending how to rebuild the levees to protect against the worst hurricanes. A study released eight weeks after the storm by three different teams of independent engineers revealed that design failures by the Corps of Engineers—with the concrete pilings not dug deep enough to withstand even a Category 3 storm surge—were responsible for major levee breaches during Katrina. The catastrophe in New Orleans, that the local New Orleans media and citizens had warned about so many times, would have been prevented had the design flaws been fixed.[16]...

What CNN called "The Big Disconnect"—between what the government was saying and what was happening on the ground—illustrated political wilding of disinformation, incompetence, and abandonment. [Michael] Brown said, "I have just learned today ... that we are in the process of evacuating hospitals, that those are going very well," while CNN's medical correspondent, Dr. Sanjay Gupta, was saying, "It's gruesome ... when patients die in the hospital, there is no place to put them, so they're in the stairwells. It is one of the most unbelievable situations I've seen as a doctor, certainly as a journalist as well. There is no electricity. There is no water. There's over 200 patients still here remaining."[17]...

Societal Wilding

A picture is worth a thousand words. And the pictures that we Americans kept viewing on our TV screens during the Katrina crisis seared our brains: desperate people walking down the interstate from New Orleans like refugees from a third world country with only their shirts on their backs; dead bodies floating in the toxic water of the flooded city; armed bands roaming and looting deserted streets; people begging for police protection at the Superdome and crying out for food and water at the Convention Center.

The faces were black and poor. We had not seen these faces—featured on national TV—for years. The shame of black, urban poverty is a harsh truth of big-city life all over the United States. But most

Americans had forgotten about the urban poor, something that is not an accident, but a design of the politicians and the media.

Katrina exposed that the emperor had no clothes. After years of discussion of the magic of the free market—how it lifts all boats—Katrina woke Americans up to the wilding at the center of our society. We remain a society segregated by race and class, with 40 million poor people and millions more teetering on the edge. The problem has intensified by virtue of deliberate policies carried out by ruling elites who had promised an SUV in every garage and a return to traditional moral values.

Senator Barack Obama of Illinois (D) observed, "I hope we realize that the people of New Orleans weren't just abandoned during the hurricane. They were abandoned long ago—to murder and mayhem in the streets, to substandard schools, to dilapidated housing, to inadequate health care, to a pervasive sense of hopelessness."[18]

What Obama didn't say was that both political parties had abandoned the poor over the last several decades in order to serve their corporate patrons—and that this abandoment is the dominant systemic wilding of our current order. During the New Deal, Franklin Roosevelt challenged the failed corporate regime of the 1920s, mobilizing workers, family farmers, and the poor to recapture government from corporations and helping to create jobs and social welfare for all. But by 1980, in the name of compassionate conservatism, the New Right elected President Reagan with the intent of dismantling the New Deal and restoring government to corporate ownership.[19]

The new corporate regime systemically set about smashing unions, weakening environmental rules, cutting social spending, ending welfare, and siphoning off billions of dollars to "corporate welfare," while dramatically cutting the taxes of the rich. This deliberate "reverse Robin Hood" policy has had predictable effects nakedly exposed in Katrina. Poverty in America is now increasing. The gap between rich and poor is skyrocketing. The plight of urban African-Americans is worsening. All of this was happening before Katrina but went largely unseen, as Americans became more geographically and economically separated by race and class.[20]

The promise of Katrina is that it opened, at least for a short period, a new window to see through the blinders that have been carefully constructed by ruling elites. The immediacy of the tragedy, the tortured faces of the urban poor, the abandonment and destruction of "the least among us" have the potential to dramatically change the conversation in America. It is no longer as easy to deny the terror of poverty or America's current segregation by race and class, a new American apartheid. As *Newsweek's* Jonathan Alter writes, Katrina created a change: "For the moment at least, Americans are ready to fix their restless gaze on enduring problems of poverty, race and class that have escaped their attention. . . this disaster may offer a chance to start a skirmish, or at least make Washington think harder why part of the richest country on earth looks like the Third World." Sociologist Andrew Cherlin said of Katrina that "this was a case where the poor were clearly not at fault. It was a reminder that we have a moral obligation to provide every American with a decent life."[21]

But we still lack political leaders and media analysts capable of explaining why this systemic wilding has occurred and how it can change. The Bush administration and Republican congressional leaders have added insult to injury by using the storm to push through the punitive "disaster capitalism" that will intensify the problems of the poor and perhaps ethnically cleanse New Orleans. Indeed, one of the most chilling forms of wilding during the reconstruction was the decision by Congress to pay for rebuilding by dramatically cutting social programs— in the Gulf Coast and around the nation. We were left with the absurdity of cutting antipoverty programs—for education, health care, and social welfare—in the name of helping the poor.

Even white, affluent residents are feeling abandoned, wondering angrily whether any kind of viable city will be rebuilt. On the day before Thanksgiving, November 23, 2005, 12 weeks after the storm, John Biguenet, a novelist and New Orleans resident, wrote that that he does not have much to feel thankful about. "On my way every day to where we used to live," he laments,

> *I drive through a city I love that lies in ruins. The park that lines one of the boulevards I follow home is now a solid wall of debris 20 feet high. On the other side of the street, desolate houses destroyed by the flood gape back with shattered windows, open doors and ragged holes in rooftops kicked out by families trapped in their attics when the water rose . . . everything is covered in a pall of gray dust, as if all the color of this once vibrant city has been leached out.*

Biguenet added that only "fifteen percent or so of residents have returned. Most people can't come home . . . half the houses in New Orleans are still not reconnected to the city sewer system and as many still lack natural gas for heating and cooking, 40% have no electricity and a quarter of the city is without drinkable water." Beyond the wilding of corporate reconstruction lies the wilding of complete abandonment of New Orleans, and it is still unclear which will triumph.[22]

Only new social movements will bring sane analysis and solutions to the wilding epidemic. Memories of Katrina may yet catalyze them and build support among the public. The role of sociologists is to help build awareness of race and class wilding systems, and to condemn them in forthright terms while offering a new direction.

Katrina's Lessons

While Katrina was a perfect wilding storm, it also demonstrated why there is hope. It showed that while wilding has taken over Washington and our nation's elites, it has not yet swallowed up the rest of our society. Remember first, that much of the looting and other personal wilding originally reported by the media during the storm proved to be false. While it is true that many residents broke into grocery stories, Wal-Marts, or pharmacies, the majority did it to get the food, water, and medicine to help their families and neighbors survive. Rather than participating in a wilding frenzy, most residents exhibited remarkable solidarity, risking their own homes and lives to help others survive.

NOTES

1. CNN.com. 2005. "New Orleans Police Face Looting Probe." *CNN.com*, September 29. Retrieved from www.cnn.com/2005/US/09/29/nopd.looting/ndex.html on January 2006.
2. Ibid.
3. Nossiter, Adam, 2005. "New Orleans Police under Investigation in Looting Probe." *Boston Globe*, September 30, p. A5.
4. CBS News, 2006. "New Orleans Fights to Stop Looting." August 31. Retrieved from www.cbsnews.com/stories/2005/08/31/katrina/printable808193 on January 2006.
5. Perry, Ryan. "Brits' Hell Inside the Terror Dome." *Mirror.co.uk*, September 2, 2005. Retrieved from www.mirror.co.uk/printable_version.cfm?objectid+1592236&siteid=94762 on January 2006.
6. Lauer, Nancy Cook, 2005. "Efforts to Track Rape Emerge between Hurricanes." September 23. Retrieved from www.womensenews.org/article.cfm/dyn/aid/2460 on January 2006.
7. Associated Press, 2005. "Man Charged with Firing Gun at Rescue Helicopter Arrested." October 9. Retrieved from www.wwltv.com/topstories/stories/WWL100905rescue.d9c6b807.html on January 2006.
8. AP wire report, MSNBC, September 27, 2005. Retrieved from www.msnbc.msn.com/id/9501181/ on January 2006.
9. Kelley, Rob, 2005. "Thousands of Gouging Complaints Filed." CNN/*Money*, September 7. Retrieved from http://money.cnn.com/2005/09/07/news/gouging_reactions/index.htm on January 31, 2006.
10. Retrieved from www.cbsnews.com/stories/2005/09/12/earlyshow/main835066.shtml on January 2006.

11. Ball, Jeffery, John Fialka and Russell Gold, 2005. "Backlash Spreads as Oil Companies' Profits Surge." *Wall Street Journal* and post-gazette.com, October 28. Retrieved from www.post-gazette.com/pg/05301/596812.stm on January 2006; Isodore, Chris, 2005. "Oil Executives in Hot Seat," November 8. Retrieved from www.money.cnn.com/2005/11/07/news/economy/oil_hearing/?cnn=yes on January 2006.
12. Goodman, Amy. "Democracy Now." September 22. Retrieved from www.democracynow.org/article.pl?sid=05/09/22/1334217 on January 2006.
13. Barge, Matthew, 2005. "Is Bush to Blame for New Orleans Flooding?" *Fact Check*, September 2. Retrieved from www.factcheck.org/article344.html on January 2006.
14. *Times-Picayune*, June 18, 2004; Chatterjee, Pratap, 2005. "Big, Easy Iraqi-style Contracts Flood New Orleans." *CorpWatch*, September 20. Retrieved from http://corpwatch.org/print-article.php?id=12647 on January 2006.
15. Figures for both 2004 and 2005 cited in Barge, "Is Bush to Blame?"
16. Warrick, Joby, and Michael Grimwald, 2005. "Investigators Posit Levee Design Flaws." *Boston Globe*, October 26, p. A3.
17. CNN.com. 2005. "The Big Disconnect on New Orleans." *CNN.com*, September 2. Retrieved from www.sent.cnn.com/2005/US/09/02/katrina.response/ on January 2006.
18. Alter, Jonathan, 2005. "The Other America." *Newsweek*, September 19.
19. Derber, Charles, 2005. *Hidden Power*. San Francisco: Berrett-Koebber, chaps 1–2.
20. Ibid., chap. 2.
21. Alter, "The Other America."
22. Biguenet, John, 2005. "Turkey with a Dash of Bitterness." *New York Times*, November 23, p. A29.

STUDY QUESTIONS

1. Explain what is meant by the concept of "wilding."
2. Based on our experience with Hurricane Katrina, where does "wilding" occur in the social environment?

JOHN W. BARDO, JEFFREY W. RIEMER,
RONALD R. MATSON AND ROBERT K. KNAPP

The Social Ecology
of Skid Row

Introduction

Since the early days of the Chicago School, human ecologists, urban sociologists, and deviance specialists have emphasized social structures and life-styles of inhabitants in the "zone in transition," or "moral zone" located near U.S. central business districts. Classic studies such as Zorbaugh's *Gold Coast and the Slum* (1929), Reckless' "Distribution of Commercialized Vice in Chicago" (1926), Thrasher's *The Gang* (1929), Anderson's *The Hobo* (1923), and Cressey's *The Taxi Dancehall* (1932) all portray the deviant aspects of life in the run-down central city slums. More recent studies, such as Suttles' *Social Order of the Slum* (1967), Rainwater's *Behind Ghetto Walls* (1970), Gans' *The Urban Villagers* (1962), and Liebow's *Tally's Corner* (1967), have stressed the significance of slum life as an adaptation to social structural conditions. The poor and other inhabitants of central city slums are seen not within a perjorative, deviance framework but more in relation to their adaptations to such situations as economic and social marginality, discrimination, and harassment by legal authorities such as the justice system or urban renewal.

This paper reports the results of an application of a sociological-ecological approach to a study of an urban skid row area. Specifically a sociocultural ecological model is applied to the problem of possibly relocating homeless men who inhabit a blighted area immediately adjacent to a midwestern city's central business district.

Defining Skid Row

Sociological studies have generally employed one of two orientations in defining the concept of skid row: it is seen either as a natural area, in the ecological sense, or as a style of life, without geographic boundaries, typical of certain deviant groups.

Ecologically, skid row areas have been typically portrayed as bounded neighborhoods that provide needed institutional services and facilities to inhabitants. Bahr (1973) suggests that cheap hotels and lodging houses, gospel missions, and bars are three necessary elements that "when they appear in close proximity, indelibly mark a neighborhood as a skid row" (p. 123). Other supplementary institutions mentioned by Bahr include the following:

> restaurants, liquor stores, secondhand stores and thrift shops, pawn-shops, junk yards, public parks, barber colleges, all night movies, public libraries, banks . . . hospitals, . . . and small grocery stores. (p. 148)

When agents of social control concern themselves with a skid row area they typically focus on these facilities and their run-down condition. Wiseman (1970) offers a listing of common terms used by professionals to describe the condition of these facilities: "below code," "deteriorated property," "dilapidated structures," "blighted zone," "detrimental land use," and "firetraps" (p. 5).

These unattractive physical conditions are easily linked to the essential character of the inhabitants. According to Wiseman (1970),

> studies that speak of stench, degrading social conditions, and urban blight also describe . . . the residents as depressed, down and out, apathetic, mentally and physically ill, the dregs of society, having a dependency problem, lacking in religious belief, needing counseling and psychic support, needing rehabilitation, requiring institutional care, discouraged and frustrated. (p. 6)

Culturally, skid row has been portrayed as a unique urban subcommunity. Wallace (1965) defines skid row as "an isolated and deviant subcultural community expressing the features of a distinct and recognizable way of life" (p. 96). The proponents of the approach suggest that skid row members are trapped in their life-style by virtue of being stigmatized by outsiders (and themselves) as undesirable. To use Goffman's (1963) term they are a "discredited" community.

Blumberg, Shipley, and Moor (1971) suggest that urban areas not referred to as skid row also harbor persons with the same social characteristics. They suggest that skid row is really a human condition and not a place. Similarly, Spradley (1970) argues that "the institutions which seek to control and punish these men for living as urban nomads actually draw them into this world and keep them there" (p. 253). Bahr (1973) also argues this way when he suggests that

> the primary problem of the skid row man is not alcoholism. Nor is it advanced age, physical disability and moral inferiority. Instead, the primary problem is that the combined weight of stigmatization which accompanies many different kinds of human defectiveness is focused upon a few men in a distinctive neighborhood. (p. 287)

In both of these definitions it is clear that the residents of skid row are considered deviant. In the former skid row is a locale; in the latter it is a way of life. In this study skid row is defined as the nexus of these two traditional positions: a geographical area, a natural area where the residents exhibit a life-style that is defined as deviant by the dominant society. What is highlighted in the literature on skid row renewal is a perception of skid row members as objectionable persons who need to be rehabilitated (Vander Kooi, 1973).

Methods

This research was conducted in a middle-sized midwestern city, with a population of approximately 250,000. Skid row in this city is located immediately east of the downtown along a three-block section of the major east-west thoroughfare. The city's urban renewal agency and the local downtown development corporation had decided to rehabilitate this section by upgrading the businesses and buildings on the north side of the street and constructing a park, a convention center, and major hotel on the south side. In addition, an old hotel, which at the time housed transients, was to be upgraded as a support facility for the convention center. (At the time these data were collected only the park had been constructed, and a building previously used by the Salvation Army had been acquired.)

A team of sociologists was hired by the urban renewal agency to determine (1) the nature of the population on skid row, (2) where skid row members might be relocated, (3) probable areas to which skid row residents would gravitate in the event of nonrelocation, and (4) ways in which this relocation could be implemented. The research design used to determine probable outcomes of renovation of this area included both fieldwork and ecological analyses.

Life-style data were generated using standard field research techniques including informal semistructured interviews and observation. Interview schedules were devised and committed to memory by field interviewers. Respondents interviewed included a number of transients, Salvation Army employees, residents, shopkeepers, and police, as well as public and private social service workers. Field notes were not usually taken during the interview in an effort to minimize expected difficulties in obtaining responses but were completed immediately following each interview period. Observations were conducted in and around the skid row area to determine space utilization and locational structure and to obtain a feel for the geist (spirit) of the area. Observational data were also noted immediately following observation periods.

Observations and interviews centered on the following:

1. the life patterns of the various groups living around the skid row area;
2. the services needed by and the services provided to these groups;
3. the locational needs of the individuals based on their own life-styles;
4. the responses of these persons to dislocation;
5. the likely ways in which successful relocation of the target population might be conducted; and
6. an estimation of the size of the target population in the skid row area.

Most observations were made in the early spring, and it is therefore probable that perceptions of the size of the population may have been affected by the recency of the winter months. Additionally, it had been a hard winter so movement of the population may have been suppressed.

As a means of testing the validity of the field research design several teams of researchers collected data independently. On completion of the fieldwork, each team was debriefed and their conclusions compared for consistency. Results obtained revealed no major inconsistencies or issues of conflict, so results were accepted as valid.

The ecological analysis portion of this research involved close examination of land use patterns (Firey, 1937; Jonassen, 1949; Michelson, 1976; Seeley, 1956; Jacobs, 1961; Young and Willmott, 1957; Gans, 1962, 1967) in the central area of the city; this area covered approximately 20 square miles.

Individual plot maps were obtained for the targeted area and were analyzed for specific land use patterns and location relative to significant ecological structures typifying the skid row area. All locations not possessing ecological characteristics similar to the skid row area were eliminated; remaining locations were retained for further analysis as potential sites for skid row relocation.

Using the plot maps of the skid row area, the ecological territory of the local transient group was mapped according to location of significant institutions. Remaining areas were then compared by apparent structure, by plot, and by site visit to determine possible alternative locations. Finally, areas were analyzed according to sociodemographic and ecological structure-specific variables to ensure comparability.

Findings

Data generated during field research revealed that skid row is the habitat for many significant groups and organizations, and each group plays a significant role in skid row's functioning. The most important of these identifiable clusters of people and organizations are merchants, police, service organizations, and the skid row residents.

Merchants

Merchants (operators of pawnshops, taverns, liquor stores, clothing stores, restaurants, hotels, etc.) on skid row do a limited business with persons in the skid row population. The liquor store, secondhand clothing stores, and taverns in the area do the most business. In general, the merchants expressed a tolerant acceptance of the members of the local population saying that "they don't cause much trouble." Any trouble is easily handled by a call to the police.

Merchants' estimations of the skid row population's size range from 10 to 200. Most merchants believed renewal of the area would encourage the local population to stay and increase the likelihood that more like them would come to the city. One merchant, when asked if the transients were leaving the area, responded, "Why should they? Urban renewal came in and built them nice benches to lie on. They built a beautiful park for them to sleep in."

Merchants in the area were also concerned about the new, period, old-fashioned street lamps, which provide far less light than the modern, high-intensity ones that they replaced. One merchant had his front window broken and merchandise stolen the first night the new lights were used.

In general, the merchants were tolerant of the skid row residents, were skeptical of the consequences urban renewal would have on the area, and did not think that the skid row members would relocate or that their numbers would decline.

Police

The police officers who worked the skid row area were tolerant of the local population. Police tended to view the members more as an eyesore than a real problem. Keeping the peace rather than enforcing the law appeared to be their approach (see Bittner, 1967).

The police gave estimates of the total population on the street (about 100) similar to those given by the merchants. They also thought it unlikely that the skid row residents would move and thought that they needed very little to survive on the street. The police were not aware of any movement by residents to other parts of the city because of changes in the area.

All the officers contended that young people are more of a problem in the area than the residents. (Teenagers tend to use this area for their local weekend "dragging" and drinking sprees.) The police expect that as the area becomes renovated there will be more trouble and more calls to make. Calls in the area made by the police were usually of the nuisance type or involved only minor problems. One officer thought that any attempt to improve the area would achieve only cosmetic results and not involve any real change in social structure.

Service Organizations

The main organizations in the skid row area that provide some service to transients include the mission, the detoxification center, and a day labor personnel recruitment office.

The mission does not cater to the hard-core problem drinkers. Rather it provides clothing, food, shelter, and religious education to persons passing through the city and to a few poor men in need of food at the end of each month who have overextended their social security or other pension checks. On average, about 15 persons sleep in the mission each night.

The detoxification center provides food and shelter for problem drinkers, and it is the major service facility for the hard-core members of the skid row area. The center handles between 18 and 25 persons a night with highest attendance during the last two weeks of the month.

The personnel office offers temporary work opportunities to the residents. Day labor provides an opportunity for residents to quickly obtain a small amount of money; current policy allows a worker to draw $8 at the end of the day against his paycheck thus allowing some money for a drink, a little food, and possibly a room. Hard-core skid row residents rarely use the personnel office; it is mainly used by transients who also make their homes on skid row for the short period they are in town.

In general, the various service organizations in the skid row area believed that the skid row population was not going to relocate because of urban renewal efforts and portrayed the residents as a collection of various diverse subgroups.

A Taxonomy of the Skid Row Population

Our research suggests that the population of this skid row area is composed of two major groupings: locals and true transients. The local group, however, can be divided into several significant subcategories.

Locals

The locals were the more stable members of the area. The size of the total group varied with the time of year, available work, and the extent of their individual life problems. This group is best understood by focusing on the four major subgroups making up the larger group.

Young Locals

The young locals numbered approximately 70–100 persons at any one time. They ranged in age from 20 to 40 years, typically had drinking problems, worked intermittently, lived in cheap housing in the area, and would, given prevailing circumstances, either become more or less a part of the skid row subculture. Their age gave them some flexibility to control their fate. However, it is this group that would eventually become the hard-core local group.

Old Hard-Core Locals

This was the focal group in the skid row area. Many of the members had lived in this area for most of their lives and some had relatives in the city or nearby towns. They numbered only 10–15 persons but were highly visible because they lived on the street. All had serious drinking problems. In addition, they were ill, extremely poor, and old. Most were older than 60, and some were in their 70s.

Intermittent Older Locals

This group strayed in and out of the core local population. Although older, some members were still mobile and traveled around the country usually by riding freight trains or hitch hiking. They still considered this skid row area their home territory and had strong friendships with the hard-core locals. (Some even wrote letters in care of general delivery when traveling.) This subgroup numbered from 15 to 20 persons. They were characterized by serious drinking problems and poor health. These men received some money from social security and pensions, and they became highly visible through living on the street when in town.

Intermittent Locals

This group fell in between the local and transient. They spent more than a few days in the city, and some would try to set down roots. Numbering from 20 to 40, they usually had drinking problems, lived in cheap housing, were poor and relatively young, but were also relatively mobile.

Transients

This group lived only a short time in the city; they were just "passing through." They would avail themselves of the local facilities for a short period and then leave. This group often included families (husband and wife with children). Transients were usually poor but also included some of the middle-class youth who were hitchhiking and backpacking across the country. This was the least stable of the groups in skid row.

Salvation Army Resident Center

Although the Salvation Army had been relocated to an area several miles away on the northern edge of the city it had played an important role in skid row life. At the time of the study the center provided long-term housing and meals for persons who conformed to the program. To fit into the program was to stay sober and typically to work for the Salvation Army in some capacity. A common job was to work on the trucks or on the material docks. The level of group solidarity was quite high, and the residents clearly distinguished between themselves and the derelicts, as well as between themselves and transients. Transients were persons in transit, whose stay at the center was usually very brief.

The SA bus took residents to their job sites each morning and returned them to the center in time for the evening meal. The returning bus might also bring transients to the center. The number of such transients fluctuated, peaking during bad weather, with minor peaks occurring on weekends. During midweek in good weather, only one transient might be among the returning residents; on a chilly Friday, as many as 15 transients might come to the center. Clearly, the transient group (an entity distinct from the skid row derelicts) represented a minority among center residents, a group as large as 50 persons. The center was not highly regimented, so no one seemed to know exactly how many beds were occupied at any given time. There was also an outflow from the center, again depending on weather, job availability, and idiosyncratic factors.

In sum, the center met the needs of a fairly large and diverse group of persons for whom it was home. There was a certain pride in being a member of the center family. This pride stemmed in part from the resident's awareness of fitting the program. (To get drunk was to risk expulsion from the program.) There were complaints expressed by some, but no one problem was severe enough to produce flight from the center. These persons might have disaffiliated from contemporary society, but most had clearly (and somewhat contentedly) affiliated with the Salvation Army program. So, although previous relationship to skid row was altered by urban renewal, the Salvation Army program relocated its constituent population and maintained its major functions.

Ecological Structure of Skid Row

The primary territory inhabited by the skid row residents spanned a six-block area adjacent to the central business district and along a major east-west thoroughfare. The most significant characteristics of this area included (1) a liquor store on a corner of the main street, (2) a detoxification center on the northern edge of the area, (3) alleys honeycombing the area, (4) a "drinking tree" at a railroad overpass and main street, and (5) an alley on the south side of the main street and a large hotel.

Locals spent most of their time near the main street in the alleys, on the park benches, and by the drinking tree. Those people, many of whom did not have rooms, slept in doorways, alleys, behind buildings, under loading docks, or in abandoned warehouses. The remainder of the territory was traversed to reach the detoxification center and a local food store.

For the locals, skid row was a relatively compact area encompassing only a few square blocks. It provided shelter, liquor, access to food, and, the very important factor, easy access to downtown. For the transients who inhabited the skid row area, its territory was not so circumscribed. Transients found skid row a convenient place to find cheap lodging, and it also provided easy access to day labor in the center city. Ecologically, it was the caliber of the hotels in the area and the nearness to the center city that were significant. Use of space other than hotels and center city did not appear as consistent for transients as for locals. This resulted from two conditions: (1) transients' life-styles did not permit them to be as committed to a particular area and (2) location in skid row was more a matter of convenience than design. Because transients resided in the city for only a short time they did not establish the ties to the skid row manifested by locals. Transients sought out skid row because its location provided them with access to the center city, which supported their life-style, and low-cost lodging.

Discussion

The data presented above suggest that life-style diversity and differences in territoriality among skid row residents would result in several diverse movements of people if urban renewal were to occur as planned. First, upgrading or demolition of cheap accommodations in skid row would probably remove most transients from the area. They would either leave the city or seek lodging in another location. (Other transients moving through the city after renewal would also have to seek lodging elsewhere in low-cost accommodation.) Locals, conversely, because of their ties to the locale and because of their use of specific facilities in skid row (e.g. the liquor store, a specific food market, detoxification center, the drinking tree, the park benches, and the railroad overpass) were found to more likely hold on to the skid row locale.

We find that a socioculture ecological model can provide important insights into the probable effects of urban renewal of a skid row area. Applying this model to a particular skid row has shown a possible explanation for apparently conflicting findings in previous research on skid row renewal. Vander Kooi (1973) argues that skid row renewal results in the dispersion of the population; Bloomberg and co-workers (1978) show that it is possible for skid row to relocate. What this current study suggests is that the probable outcomes of skid row renewal depend on several factors including (1) the nature of the renewal project, (2) its location relative to the territory defined and used by skid row residents, (3) the types of people who inhabit skid row and the diversity of their life-styles and territorial definitions, and (4) the availability of areas likely to become skid rows in other parts of the city.

It would be expected, for instance, that if most skid row residents consisted of a diverse and amorphous grouping of transients with little affinity for the specific territory they occupied, renewal would result in their dispersion to other low-rent areas. On the other hand, local populations who are tied to the skid row neighborhood would probably not relocate or would move only a short distance depending upon the degree to which urban renewal disrupted their territory. Only if their entire territory were renewed and no new skid row areas existed, would it be likely for locals to scatter rather than relocate. Because their use of space can be seen as being governed both by the location of institutions and sentimental attachment to a local area and certain people, dispersion would not be a likely outcome.

REFERENCES

Anderson, Nels
  1923 The Hobo. Chicago: University of Chicago Press.
Bahr, Howard M.
  1973 Skid Row. New York: Oxford University Press.
Bittner, Egon
  1967 "The police on skid row: A study of peace keeping." American Sociological Review 32 (October):699–715.
Blumberg, Leonard U., Thomas Shipley, Jr., and Joseph Moor, Jr.
  1971 "The skid row man and the skid row status community." Quarterly Journal of Studies on Alcohol 32 (December):909–929.
Blumberg, Leonard U., Thomas E. Shipley, Jr., and Stephen F. Barsky
  1978 Liquor and Poverty: Skid Row as a Human Condition. New Brunswick, N.J.: Rutgers Center of Alcohol Studies.
Cressey, Paul G.
  1932 The Taxi Dancehall. Chicago: University of Chicago Press.
Firey, Walter
  1937 Land Use in Central Boston. Cambridge, Mass.: Harvard University Press.
Gans, Herbert
  1962 The Urban Villagers. New York: Free Press.
  1967 The Levittowners. New York: Pantheon Books.
Goffman, Erving
  1963 Stigma. Englewood Cliffs, N.J.: Prentice-Hall.
Jacobs, Jane
  1961 The Life and Death of Great American Cities. New York: Random House.

Jonassen, Christen T.

  1949 "Cultural variables in the ecology of an ethnic group." American Sociological Review 14:32–41.

Liebow, Elliot

  1967 Tally's Corner. Boston: Little, Brown and Company.

Michelson, William

  1976 Man and His Urban Environment. Reading, MA: Addison Wesley.

Rainwater, Lee

  1970 Behind Ghetto Walls. Chicago: Aldine.

Reckless, Walter C.

  1926 "The distribution of commercialized vice in Chicago." Publications of the American Sociological Society 20:164–176.

Seeley, John, Alexander Sim, and E. W. Loosley

  1956 Crestwood Heights. New York: Basic Books.

Spradley, James P.

  1970 You Owe Yourself a Drunk. Boston: Little, Brown and Company.

Suttles, Gerald

  1967 The Social Order of the Slum. Chicago: University of Chicago Press.

Thrasher, Frederick

  1929 The Gang. Chicago: University of Chicago Press.

Vander Kooi, Ronald

  1973 "The main stem: Skid row revisited." Society 10:64–71.

Wallace, Samuel E.

  1965 Skid Row as a Way of Life. New York: Harper & Row.

Wiseman, Jacqueline

  1970 Stations of the Lost: The Treatment of Skid Row Alcoholics. Englewood Cliffs, N.J.: Prentice-Hall.

Young, Michael, and Peter Willmott

  1957 Family and Kinship in East London. Baltimore: Penguin.

Zorbaugh, Harvey

  1929 Gold Coast and the Slum. Chicago: University of Chicago Press.

STUDY QUESTIONS

1. What do the authors mean by "social ecology"? List some of the parts of this ecology.

2. What types of residents live on skid row? Is transience a social problem? Why or why not?

MILTON SAIER

Pollution

Crops flourish in a silent season,
and pelican mothers weep noiselessly,
waiting at the bus stop with raw throats—they weep
for dodo birds and progeny lost
as we, a prolific species, sit down to the
neverending feast.

Pollutants are harmful chemical or physical substances released into the atmosphere, a water source, the soil or a component of the biosphere. When a new chemical compound is developed and produced in large amounts for commercial or medical purposes, immediate benefits to mankind often result. However, side effects that may not be evident for years or even decades after their introduction may be unfortunate consequences. These side effects may alter human behavior or physiology, but more often their adverse effects are first detected by disruption of a component in the ecosystem. One species will be primarily affected, and this will have a domino effect on many others, up and down the food chain. As a result, massive death of many organismal types, from microorganisms to large plants and animals will occur. In this essay I cite a few well-documented examples out of thousands of similar cases where pollution has had a dramatic effect on our lives and our planet.

Particle Pollutants

"They're so small you can't see 'em,
But when you wheeze and sneeze, it may be 'em."

The results of a recent UCLA–USC-based study, published in the journal, *Environmental Health Perspectives*, showed that microscopic airborne particles disrupt cellular processes, harming the human body. These particles are normally present in dust and smoke, but they are most prevalent in the exhaust that results from the burning of fossil fuels. They are so small, that over 10,000 can fit on the head of a pin! Because of their inert nature, they can bypass the body's normal defense mechanisms.

These particles not only penetrate the lungs and bloodstream, they are also found deep inside the cellular organelles of our body tissues, causing oxidative stress and damage, for example, to the powerhouse of the cell, the mitochondrion. The presence of these particles shortens life span and leads to common pathologies such as cancer and heart failure. In less dramatic cases, they reduced lung function. Their presence is believed to be responsible for cases of asthma in hundreds of thousands of people in the LA area alone.

Associated respiratory problems have led to school absences and hospital admissions. In fact, the Los Angeles basin proved to be one of the worst places in the nation for particle pollution. However, throughout U.S. urban communities where traffic and industry are prevalent, the consequences of particle pollution have been documented. It seems clear that a major fraction of the U.S. population suffers some adverse consequence of particle pollution.

Toxins

"Lacewings and ladybirds, mind where you roam,
The plants are all poisoned that once were your home.
They've spliced in a toxin to kill off the pests.
Now friendly bug-eaters will die like the rest."

The bodies of Americans carry an array of toxins derived from plastics, cosmetics, food additives, and even pesticides banned decades ago. Importantly, fetuses, infants and young children contain much higher levels than do adults. Researchers believe that these pollutants can permanently alter a child's intelligence, memory, motor skills, behavior, and immune system. Organophosphate pesticides, for example, present in bug bombs and lawn sprays, have been shown to cause abnormal brain development, and many of these compounds are present in children's brains at more than twice the levels found in adults! Since children eat, drink and breathe three times as much as adults on a weight basis, these statistics are not entirely unexpected.

Although DDT was banned for use as a pesticide back in the 1970s, it can still be found in the bodies of American children. This long-lasting compound remains unaltered for decades in the soil, from which it can be accumulated by plants, and then concentrated by grazing animals. Since DDT and other poisons have been found to increase the incidence of cancer in adults, the danger to young children may be of major concern.

The problem of chemical pollution has recently been elevated to a new level of concern as a result of genetic engineering. Genetically modified plant crops are already being used to provide food for the burgeoning human population, currently increasing at the incredible rate of 250,000 people per day. To counteract the costly effects of pests on crops, genes encoding pesticides have been introduced. At a recent meeting of entomologists, it was noted that some genetically engineered crops exude 10–20 times the amounts of toxins contained in conventional bug sprays. These chemicals kill beneficial insects such as bees and ladybugs and inhibit the growth of beneficial soil microorganisms, such as those that provide natural nitrogen fertilizer by fixing nitrogen in root nodules of alfalfa, peas and beans. Finally, these toxic agents harm the insect-eating birds that were the traditional sources of pest control before mankind decided to "improve" upon Nature.

Some environmental chemicals have been shown to mimic the normal hormonal responses of the human body, causing suppressed immunity, inhibited brain development and feminization of boys. Comparable effects have been documented in wild animal populations. It seems likely that such chemicals will prove to affect a major part of the biosphere upon which we depend. The prospects are ominous to say the least.

DDT and the California Pelican

"A wondrous bird is the pelican,
His beak holds more than his belican.
He can take in his beak,
Enough food for a week!
I'll be damned if I know how the helican!"

—Dixon L. Merritt

I remember as a boy watching the spectacular California pelicans dive for fish, marveling at their remarkable eyesight and skill. In fact, these pelicans provided our family with endless amusement as we watched the ever-changing show they would put on for us. Then in the early 1970s, these remarkable birds disappeared. For years not a single pelican was sighted in the Monterey Bay. At first, we had no idea why.

The brown pelican breeds in large colonies in a few choice locations on the Channel Islands in Southern California, along the Baja peninsula and in the Gulf of California, Mexico. During the summer months, they fly northward from their breeding grounds as far as Vancouver, Canada. These impressive birds, with silvery coloration, massive bills and unparalleled throat pouches, are the only species of pelican that dives frequently for its prey. Its primary source of nutrition is small surface schooling fish such as anchovies and sardines.

Because the species nests in large colonies on small-island breeding sites called rookeries, the brown pelican has in the past been the target of egg hunters who raided the rookeries by boat. They were also hunted throughout the 19th and 20th centuries for their feathers. Still worse, fishermen who erroneously thought them to be competitors for commercially valuable fish slaughtered thousands. As a result, by 1970, brown pelican populations along the coast had been reduced to less than 20% of their normal numbers.

Losses due to exploitation were dwarfed by the dramatic tragedy that befell these birds during the early 1970s when they essentially disappeared from the California coast. Pesticides such as DDT and endrin were then used to kill mosquitoes and other insects, and unknown to those of us who used DDT, it interferes with the process of calcium deposition, necessary for the formation of eggshells. Pelican eggs became too thin and brittle to allow the parents to successfully incubate their clutch.

The disappearance of the California pelican was researched, revealing that DDT runoff into streams that emptied into the oceans was responsible. Pesticide "biomagnification" resulted because non-lethal doses are ingested and concentrated by the fish that the pelicans consume. Many birds died due to the accumulation of lethal doses, but the problem of eggshell thinning resulted in almost complete reproductive failure. On Anacapa Island off the California coast, in one year, only a single fledgling survived out of 552 nesting pairs. The number of pairs at this site had exceeded 10,000 prior to human exploitation and the use of DDT.

In 1972, the cause of the tremendous reduction in the pelican population became recognized, and DDT as well as other related pesticides were banned by the U.S. Environmental Protection Agency. Gradually the brown pelican, which had remained viable off the Baja coast, returned to California. Since then, numbers have significantly increased, and with the help of naturalists, old breeding and nesting sites have been recovered. In 1997, about 4,000 breeding pairs on West Anacapa Island were identified. The crisis induced by DDT was over for the pelican, but the full extent of damage to these and many other species will never be fully comprehended.

Atrazine and Frogs

"Frog, he goes a wooin',
But she says: no cooin', nothing doin'."

Atrazine is a stable chemical herbicide used in countries that produce corn. In the U.S., atrazine is the most widely used weed killer. The production and sale of this one compound results in multibillion-dollar profits for the herbicide industry. This compound has been detected in the oceans and fresh waters of countries distant from those that use it, showing that it is stable enough to circle the globe. It exerts measurable effects on wildlife virtually everywhere on Earth.

Recent studies conducted in the laboratory of Tyrone Hayes at the University of California, Berkeley, linked the presence of very low levels of atrazine to developmental abnormalities in both experimental and wild populations of frogs. Specifically, Hayes' studies showed that the compound turns nearly half of the exposed male frogs into transsexual hermaphrodites. Some male frogs develop multiple sex organs, while others have both ovaries and testes, a characteristic of the hermaphrodite. A majority of exposed frogs also showed shrunken larynxes, a crippling handicap for a frog wishing to call to and then mate a female. It is probable that these effects are at least in part responsible for the huge decline in amphibian populations worldwide.

History tells us that research conducted by scientists who are paid to get a specific answer is not likely to be reliable. For example, the tobacco industry conducted research "proving" that smoking cigarettes is not harmful to human health. As we all know, however, extensive research conducted by impartial workers has revealed that it is *so* harmful that it cuts an average of 20 years off a person's life! Thus, although Hayes' conclusions have been challenged in studies funded by the major producer of atrazine, Syngenta, the results of Hayes' challengers can probably be discounted.

The amounts of atrazine that cause measurable effects on frog sexuality proved to be more than 30-fold *lower* than the "safe level" amount set by the Environmental Protection Agency for our drinking water. Could the compound also affect humans? Possible effects on human sexuality and fertility should be considered. Dramatic decreases in human male fertility in the U.S. over the past few decades are well documented. Moreover, puzzling rises in premature human birth over the past 20 years is also documented. Is there a connection with atrazine? One study revealed that male workers at a Louisiana plant where atrazine is made exhibited incidents of prostate cancer nearly 10 times that observed for the average male Louisianan.

In light of these findings and possibilities, one might assume that the use of this herbicide would be strictly prohibited. In fact, this is the case in most European countries. However, in the U.S. and most third world countries, no such regulation is in effect. The levels of atrazine worldwide continue to increase at an alarming rate.

Agriculture and Coral

"A fish who seeks a reef,
In brief, is in for grief."

Coral reefs are the major breeding grounds for innumerable species of fish and shellfish. As the human population has grown, first with the advent of agriculture, and later with the industrial revolution, the balance of nature in the oceans has been upset and then largely destroyed. At the end of the 20th century, it was conservatively estimated that one-third of the world's coral reefs are dead, over one-third are sick and dying, and less than one-third remain healthy. This fact accounts only in part for declines in commercially important marine fish populations, which have been reduced to only a few percent of their pre-exploitation levels. One-third of all still surviving fish species worldwide are endangered. This is the largest percentage for any one type of animal.

Many studies have focused on the destruction of our coral reefs, leading to the conclusion that there are multiple causes. First, rising temperatures lead to "bleaching" which can result in coral death. Second, increasing concentrations of atmospheric CO_2 make the carbonate chemistry of the oceans less favorable for calcification, an essential process for coral development. Third, bacterial and viral pathogens have been identified as primary causes of coral polyp death, but susceptibility to these microbial diseases may result secondarily from severe weakening of the organisms' defenses.

Recent studies have shown that a fourth major source of coral instability is related to agricultural practices that have been developed and expanded over the past couple of centuries. This conclusion does not target a specific pesticide or fertilizer, although these may contribute to the demise of the coral building polyps. Instead, it appears that increased sedimentation of particulate matter from continental material is a primary cause. Extensive use of agriculture accompanied by alternating periods of drought and heavy rainfall promote erosion that results in the periodic transportation of vast amounts of soil to the oceans. This sediment poses a hazard to reef building corals, first by decreasing access to light and second by interfering with normal feeding practices.

To document the importance of agriculture sedimentation, McCulloch and his coworkers developed methods for measuring the history of sedimentation on Australia's Great Barrier Reef. The results showed that sedimentation increased dramatically following European settlement and agricultural expansion in northeastern Australia.

Coral preserve the history of terrestrial sediment delivery as they build their skeletons of calcium and carbonate because they accidentally incorporate traces of other elements, depending on availability. Suspended sediments from river water, for example, contain barium, a calcium analogue. This gets incorporated into the long lasting coral skeleton in proportion to its concentration in the seawater. Since the skeletons grow at a rate of less than one inch per year, conditions over the ages can be determined and dated for the coral skeletal matter, just as the contents of the rings of a redwood tree can be used to estimate events that took place in its environment over the duration of its long life. Happily, however, a large mass of coral need not be destroyed in order to conduct the experiment.

Detailed studies have allowed quantitation of the amounts and types of sedimentation from 1750 to the present. Sediment levels increased dramatically, about 10-fold, after 1870, shortly following European settlement when both average and maximal barium levels increased. Domestic grazing and land clearance were considered to be the main culprits, increasing erosion. The use of independent research methods allowed confirmation of these conclusions.

The results of these long-term studies in Australia's Great Barrier Reef have been generalized to many other parts of the world. For example, in East Africa, the study of marine corals revealed a similar story of erosion prompted by colonial agricultural practices during the early 20th century. We therefore know that sedimentation has influenced the health and distribution of coral species worldwide.

Global warming is believed to increase the erratic nature of seasonal climate change. This means that erosion, marine sedimentation, and the consequent loss of healthy coral polyp life are likely to increase as human-produced greenhouse gases accumulate. The tragedy of man-promoted coral destruction thus provides one more example of how we are inadvertently disturbing the balance of nature through seemingly harmless activities meant only to sustain the human population.

Taken together we see that almost every aspect of man's activities, our agricultural practices, the burning of fossil fuels, destruction of the forests and wetlands, hunting and fishing, the use of chemicals that alter the balance of nature, the use of medicines that alleviate suffering and prolong life, all add to the global levels of pollution, endangering our delicate biosphere and altering the physiology and behavior of our own species. To me, it seems clear that none of these problems can be truly solved until we have dealt with the primary cause: a tremendously excessive human population. If we can find a rational solution to this problem, then the human race has a chance for long-term survival. If not, we will undoubtedly learn the hard way: through suffering, death and devastation.

REFERENCES

Baldridge, A.: 1973, 'The status of the brown pelican in the Monterey region of California: Past and present,' *Western Birds* 4, 93–100.

Calle, E.E., Frumkin, H., Henley, S.J., Savitz, D.A., and Thun, M.J.: 2002, 'Organochlorines and breast cancer risk,' *CA Cancer J. Clin.* 52, 301–309.

Cole, J.: 2003, 'Dishing the dirt on coral reefs', *Nature* 421, 705–706.

Elliott, A.: 1992, Family *Pelecanidae* (Pelicans) in del Hoyo, J., Elliott, A., and Sargatal. J. (eds.) *Handbook of the Birds of the World, Volume 1*, Lynx Edicions, Barcelona.

Frumkin, H.: 2001, 'Beyond toxicity: Human health and the natural environment,' *Am. J. Prev. Med.* 20, 234–240.

Frumkin, H. and Thun, M.J.: 2001, 'Arsenic,' *CA Cancer J. Clin.* 51, 254–262.

Frumkin, H.: 2002, 'Urban sprawl and public health.' *Public Health Rep.* 117, 201–217.

Hayes, T., Haston, K., Tsui, M., Hoang, A., Haeffele, C., and Vonk, A.: 2002, 'Feminization of male frogs in the wild.' *Nature* 419, 895–896.

Li, N., Sioutas, C., Cho. A., Schmitz, D., Misra, C., Sempf, J., Wang, M., Oberley. T., Froines, J., and Nel, A.: 2003, 'Ultra-fine particulate pollutants induce oxidative stress and mitochondrial damage.' *Eviron. Health Perspect.* 111, 445–460.

McCulloch, M., Fallon, S., Wyndham, T., Hendy, E., Lough, J., and Barnes, D.: 2003, 'Coral record of increased sediment flux to the inner Great Barrier Reef since European settlement,' *Nature* 421, 727–728.

Renner, R.: 2002, 'Conflict brewing over herbicide's link to frog deformities,' *Science* 298, 938–939.

Royte, E.: 2003, 'Transsexual frogs,' *Discover*, February, 46–53.

STUDY QUESTIONS

1. What is the most important cause of the breakdown in our ecosystem at the human level?
2. What happens to our ecosystems as we lose species and polar ice caps?

TOPIC 15

Technology and Globalization

Much of what we in sociology understand about social change and the future is tied to such things as "technology" and "globalization." Some would argue that we live in the technological age, that we are experiencing a "biological revolution." Others would mention the effect of the microchip on the world as we swim in a sea of "information" and the "communication revolution" brought on by wireless technology and the Internet. The personal and structural aspects of all these changes remind humans that we are often led by technology into social arrangements with which we have not yet learned to cope. It is true; culture "lags" behind technology. The success of the Genome Project has brought about the prospect of human engineering and cloning. The advent of the computer a short half-century ago brings us to the brink of e-mail, e-commerce, and e-communities. Much of the world perches on our visual and intellectual doorstep as a computer monitor. A new reality waits nanoseconds away. How has and how will social life be affected by such rapid change?

Toffler's "future shock" theory warned us that the future is rushing toward us at an ever-increasing pace. If this is true, the mandate for social and personal adaptation seems more real than ever. Perhaps the "post-modern" world is more about pretense than substance, more about TV shows than human relationships and substantive issues. Will technology and computers and movies and electronic games become reality? If this is so, the shift toward virtual reality will soon affect all our definitions of what is important and meaningful, and social life will have passed into another level that can no longer be understood using the traditional tools of science. Technology, by itself, is neither good nor bad. The Internet is a place of great, expanding possibilities for commerce and learning and, simultaneously, is a place of gross pornography that victimizes women and children while feeding lewd interests among the masses. Will society, indeed humanity, rise to meet such challenges?

Globalization is the worldwide adoption of similar social and economic patterns. When the entire world watches American TV, the news and shows of the day will be defined, in part, by the filtered content on the screen. This content, in turn, affects individual perceptions and collective cultural values. Social life is leveled to a plane that has more similarity than diversity, and the world proceeds with a "globalized" sense of what is right and just and true. Is this something that rests in the immediate future? Will America's version of capitalism be exported across the globe and become the standard by which many societies measure themselves? Will democracy become the political preference for many nations? To be sure, McDonald's has arrived on the world scene and most are rejoicing. Even the standardization of computer software, which more and more of us use through much of the day, creates culturally imposed patterns and globalized restrictions on creativity.

In Topic 15: Technology and Globalization, three articles outline some of the important issues raised by this introduction. First, George Ritzer's "The McDonaldization of Society" illustrates the underlying rationality of production done to preserve profit at the least expense. With thousands of stores worldwide, and success of storybook proportions, other businesses will adopt the McDonald's approach to hiring, creating, and selling a product. Second, the Internet is useful in identifying and attracting persons who are susceptible to recruitment by the Nazi Skinhead organizations in the United States. Once identified, the contact of these young people and their recruitment into the organization make for an interesting glimpse into marginal lives and extremist groups. Finally, Austin T. Turk takes us into a sociological examination of terrorism. Over the past few years, the world has changed and all of us feel the risk of possible harm in ways we would never have imagined. How do we deal with terrorism in the United States and around the globe while "enemies without an address" threaten our domestic calm? Indeed, the future of our lives may depend on a clearer understanding of terrorism.

GEORGE RITZER

The McDonaldization of Society

Ray Kroc, the genius behind the franchising of McDonald's restaurants, was a man with big ideas and grand ambitions. But even Kroc could not have anticipated the astounding impact of his creation. McDonald's is one of the most influential developments in twentieth-century America. Its reverberations extend far beyond the confines of the United States and the fast-food business. It has influenced a wide range of undertakings, indeed the way of life, of a significant portion of the world. And that impact is likely to expand at an accelerating rate.[1]

However, this is *not* a book about McDonald's, or even the fast-food business, although both will be discussed frequently throughout these pages. Rather, McDonald's serves here as the major example, the "paradigm," of a wide-ranging process I call *McDonaldization*, that is,

> *the process by which the principles of the fast-food restaurant are coming to dominate more and more sectors of American society as well as of the rest of the world.*

As you will see, McDonaldization affects not only the restaurant business, but also education, work, health care, travel, leisure, dieting, politics, the family, and virtually every other aspect of society. McDonaldization has shown every sign of being an inexorable process by sweeping through seemingly impervious institutions and parts of the world.

McDonald's success is apparent: in 1993 its total sales reached $23.6 billion with profits of almost $1.1 billion.[2] The average U.S. outlet has total sales of approximately $1.6 million in a year.[3] Many entrepreneurs envy such sales and profits and seek to emulate McDonald's success. McDonald's, which first began franchising in 1955, opened its 12,000th outlet on March 22, 1991. By the end of 1993, McDonald's had almost 14,000 restaurants worldwide.

The impact of McDonaldization, which McDonald's has played a central role in spawning, has been manifested in many ways:

- The McDonald's model has been adopted not only by other budget-minded hamburger franchises such as Burger King and Wendy's, but also by a wide array of other low-priced fast-food businesses. Subway, begun in 1965 and now with nearly 10,000 outlets, is considered the fastest-growing of these businesses, which include Pizza Hut, Sbarro's, Taco Bell, Popeye's, and Charley Chan's. Sales in so-called "quick service" restaurants in the United States rose to $81 billion by the end of 1993, almost a third of total sales for the entire food-service industry.[4] In 1994, for the first time, sales in fast-food restaurants exceeded those in traditional full-service restaurants, and the gap between them is projected to grow.[5]
- The McDonald's model has also been extended to "casual dining," that is, more "upscale," higher-priced restaurants with fuller menus. For example, Outback Steakhouse and Sizzler sell steaks, Fuddrucker's offers "gourmet" burgers, Chi-Chi's and Chili's sell Mexican food, The Olive Garden proffers Italian food, and Red Lobster purveys . . . you guessed it.
- McDonald's is making increasing inroads around the world.[6] In 1991, for the first time, McDonald's opened more restaurants abroad than in the United States.[7] As we move toward the next century, McDonald's expects to build twice as many restaurants each year overseas than it does in the United States. By the end of 1993, over one-third of McDonald's restaurants were overseas; at the beginning of 1995, about half of McDonald's profits came from its overseas operations. McDonald's has even recently opened a restaurant in Mecca, Saudi Arabia. . . .[8]
- Almost 10% of America's stores are franchises, which currently account for 40% of the nation's retail sales. It is estimated that by the turn of the century, about 25% of the stores in the United States will be chains, by then accounting for a whopping two-thirds of retail businesses.[9] About 80% of McDonald's restaurants are franchises.[10]

McDonald's as "Americana"

McDonald's and its many clones have become ubiquitous and immediately recognizable symbols throughout the United States as well as much of the rest of the world. For example, when plans were afoot to raze Ray Kroc's first McDonald's restaurant, hundreds of letters poured into McDonald's headquarters, including the following:

> Please don't tear it down! . . . Your company's name is a household word, not only in the United States of America, but all over the world. To destroy this major artifact of contemporary culture would, indeed, destroy part of the faith the people of the world have in your company.[11]

In the end, the restaurant was not only saved, but turned into a museum! A McDonald's executive explained the move: "McDonald's . . . is really a part of Americana." Similarly, when Pizza Hut opened in Moscow in 1990, a Russian student said, "It's a piece of America."[12] Reflecting on the growth of fast-food restaurants in Brazil, the president of Pepsico (of which Pizza Hut is part) of Brazil said that his nation "is experiencing a passion for things American."[13]

McDonald's truly has come to occupy a central place in popular culture.[14] It can be a big event when a new McDonald's opens in a small town. Said one Maryland high-school student at such an event, "Nothing this exciting ever happens in Dale City."[15] Newspapers avidly cover developments in the fast-food business. Fast-food restaurants also play symbolic roles on television programs and in the movies. A skit on the television show *Saturday Night Live* satirized specialty chains by detailing the hardships of a franchise that sells nothing but Scotch tape. In the movie *Coming to America*, Eddie Murphy plays an African prince whose introduction to America includes a job at "McDowell's," a thinly disguised McDonald's. Michael Douglas, in *Falling Down*, vents his rage against the modern world in a fast-food restaurant dominated by mindless rules designed to frustrate customers. *Moscow on the Hudson* has Robin Williams, newly arrived from Russia, obtain a job at McDonald's. H. G. Wells, a central character in the movie *Time After Time*, finds himself transported to the modern world of a McDonald's, where he tries to order the tea he was accustomed to drinking in Victorian England. In *Sleeper*, Woody Allen awakens in the future only to encounter a McDonald's. Finally, *Tin Men* ends with the heroes driving off into a future represented by a huge golden arch looming in the distance.

Many people identify strongly with McDonald's; in fact to some it has become a sacred institution.[16] At the opening of the McDonald's in Moscow, one journalist described the franchise as the "ultimate icon of Americana," while a worker spoke of it "as if it were the Cathedral in

Chartres . . . a place to experience 'celestial joy.' "[17] Kowinski argues that shopping malls, which almost always encompass fast-food restaurants, are the modern "cathedrals of consumption" to which people go to practice their "consumer religion."[18] Similarly, a visit to another central element of McDonaldized society, Walt Disney World,[19] has been described as "the middle-class hajj, the compulsory visit to the sun-baked holy city."[20]

McDonald's has achieved its exalted position because virtually all Americans, and many others, have passed through its golden arches on innumerable occasions. Furthermore, most of us have been bombarded by commercials extolling McDonald's virtues, commercials that are tailored to different audiences. Some play to young children watching Saturday-morning cartoons. Others solicit young adults watching prime-time programs. Still others coax grandparents to take their grandchildren to McDonald's. In addition, these commercials change as the chain introduces new foods (such as breakfast burritos), creates new contests, and ties its products to things such as new motion pictures. These ever-present commercials, combined with the fact that people cannot drive very far without having a McDonald's pop into view, have served to embed McDonald's deep in popular consciousness. A poll of school-age children showed that 96% of them could identify Ronald McDonald, second only to Santa Claus in name recognition.[21]

Over the years, McDonald's has appealed to people in many ways. The restaurants themselves are depicted as spick-and-span, the food is said to be fresh and nutritious, the employees are shown to be young and eager, the managers appear gentle and caring, and the dining experience itself seems fun-filled. People are even led to believe that they contribute, at least indirectly, to charities such as the Ronald McDonald Houses for sick children.

The Long Arm of McDonaldization

McDonald's has strived to continually extend its reach within American society and beyond. As the company's chairman said, "Our goal: to totally dominate the quick service restaurant industry worldwide. . . . I want McDonald's to be more than a leader. I want McDonald's to dominate."[22]

McDonald's began as a phenomenon of suburbs and medium sized towns, but in recent years it has moved into big cities and smaller towns,[23] in the United States and beyond, that supposedly could not support such a restaurant. You can now find fast-food outlets in New York's Times Square as well as on the Champs Elysees in Paris. Soon after it opened in 1992, the McDonald's in Moscow sold almost 30,000 hamburgers a day and employed a staff of 1,200 young people working two to a cash register.[24] McDonald's plans to open many more restaurants in the former Soviet Union and in the vast new territory in Eastern Europe that has now been laid bare to the invasion of fast-food restaurants. In early 1992, Beijing witnessed the opening of the world's largest McDonald's, with 700 seats, 29 cash registers, and nearly 1,000 employees. On its first day of business, it set a new one-day record for McDonald's by serving about 40,000 customers.[25]

Small satellite, express, or remote outlets, opened in areas that cannot support full-scale fast-food restaurants, are expanding rapidly. They have begun to appear in small store fronts in large cities and in nontraditional settings such as department stores, service stations, and even schools. These satellites typically offer only limited menus and may rely on larger outlets for food storage and preparation.[26] McDonald's is considering opening express outlets in museums, office buildings, and corporate cafeterias.

No longer content to dominate the strips that surround many college campuses, fast-food restaurants have moved onto many of those campuses. The first fast-food restaurant opened at the University of Cincinnati in 1973. Today, college cafeterias often look like shopping-mall food courts. In conjunction with a variety of "branded partners" (for example, Pizza Hut and Subway), Marriott now supplies food to almost 500 colleges and universities.[27] The apparent approval of college administrations puts fast-food restaurants in a position to further influence the younger generation.

More recently, another expansion has occurred: People no longer need to leave the highway to obtain fast food quickly and easily. Fast food is now available at convenient rest stops along the highway. After "refueling," we can proceed with our trip, which is likely to end in another community that has about the same density and mix of fast-food restaurants as the locale we left behind. Fast food is also increasingly available in service stations,[28] hotels,[29] railway stations, airports, and even on the trays for in-flight meals. The following advertisement appeared in the *Washington Post* and the *New York Times* a few years ago: "Where else at 35,000 feet can you get a McDonald's meal like this for your kids? Only on United's Orlando flights." Now, McDonald's so-called "Friendly Skies Meals" are generally available to children on

Delta flights. Similarly, in December 1994, Delta began to offer Blimpie sandwiches on its North American flights,[30] and Continental now offers Subway sandwiches. How much longer before McDonaldized meals will be available on all flights everywhere by every carrier? In fact, on an increasing number of flights, prepackaged "snacks" have already replaced hot main courses. . . .

As powerful as it is, McDonald's has not been alone in pressing the fast-food model on American society and the rest of the world. Other fast-food giants, such as Burger King and Kentucky Fried Chicken, have played a key role, as have innumerable other businesses built on the principles of the fast-food restaurant.

Even the derivatives of McDonald's and the fast-food industry in turn exert their own influence. For example, the success of *USA TODAY* has led many newspapers across the nation to adopt, for example, shorter stories and color weather maps. As one *USA TODAY* editor put it, "The same newspaper editors who call us McPaper have been stealing our McNuggets."[31] The influence of *USA TODAY* is blatantly manifested in *The Boca Raton News*, a Knight-Ridder newspaper. This newspaper is described as "a sort of smorgasbord of snippets, a newspaper that slices and dices the news into even smaller portions than does *USA TODAY*, spicing it with color graphics and fun facts and cute features like 'Today's Hero' and 'Critter Watch'.[32] As in *USA TODAY*, stories in *The Boca Raton News* usually do not jump from one page to another; they start and finish on the same page. To meet this need, long, complex stories often have to be reduced to a few paragraphs. Much of a story's context, and much of what the principals have to say, is severely cut back or omitted entirely. With its emphasis on light news and color graphics, the main function of the newspaper seems to be entertainment. Even the *New York Times* has undergone changes (for example, the use of color) as a result of the success of *USA TODAY*.

The expansion deep into the newspaper business suggests that McDonaldization may be inexorable and may therefore come to insinuate itself into every aspect of society and people's private lives. In the movie *Sleeper*, Woody Allen not only created a futuristic world in which McDonald's was an important and highly visible element, but he also envisioned a society in which even sex underwent the process of McDonaldization. The denizens of his future world were able to enter a machine called an "orgasmatron," which allowed them to experience an orgasm without going through the muss and fuss of sexual intercourse.

Sex actually has, like virtually every other sector of society, under-gone a process of McDonaldization. "Dial-a-porn" allows people to have intimate, sexually explicit, even obscene conversations with people they have never met and probably never will meet.[33] There is great specialization here: Dialing numbers such as 555-FOXX will lead to a very different phone message than dialing 555-SEXY. Those who answer the phones mindlessly and repetitively follow "scripts" that have them say such things as, "Sorry, tiger, but your Dream Girl has to go . . . Call right back and ask for me."[34] Escort services advertise a wide range of available sex partners. People can see highly specialized pornographic movies (heterosexual, homosexual, sex with children, and sex with ani-mals) at urban multiplexes and can rent them from local video stores for viewing in the comfort of their living rooms. Various technologies (vibrators, for example) enhance the ability of people to have sex on their own without the bother of having to deal with a human partner. In New York City, an official called a three-story pornographic center "the McDonald's of sex" because of its "cookie-cutter cleanliness and compliance with the law."[35] These examples suggest that no aspect of people's lives is immune to McDonaldization.

The Dimensions of McDonaldization

Why has the McDonald's model proven so irresistible? Four alluring dimensions lie at the heart of the success of this model and, more gen-erally, of McDonaldization. In short, McDonald's has succeeded because it offers consumers, workers, and managers efficiency, calcula-bility, predictability, and control.[36]

First, McDonald's offers *efficiency*, or the optimum method for get-ting from one point to another. For consumers, this means that McDonald's offers the best available way to get from being hungry to being full. (Similarly, Woody Allen's orgasmatron offered an efficient method for getting people from quiescence to sexual gratification.) Other institutions, fashioned on the McDonald's model, offer similar efficiency in losing weight, lubricating cars, getting new glasses or con-tacts, or completing income-tax forms. In a society where both parents are likely to work, or where there may be only a single parent, efficiently satisfying the hunger and many other needs of people is very attractive. In a society where people rush, usually by car, from one spot to another, the efficiency of a fast-food meal, perhaps even without leaving their cars by wending their way along the drive-through lane, often proves impossible to resist. The fast-food model offers people, or at least appears to offer them, an efficient method for satisfying many needs.

Like their customers, workers in McDonaldized systems function efficiently. They are trained to work this way by managers, who watch over them closely to make sure they do. Organizational rules and regulations also help ensure highly efficient work.

Second, McDonald's offers *calculability*, or an emphasis on the quantitative aspects of products sold (portion size, cost) and service offered (the time it takes to get the product). Quantity has become equivalent to quality; a lot of something, or the quick delivery of it, means it must be good. As two observers of contemporary American culture put it, "As a culture, we tend to believe deeply that in general 'bigger is better.' "[37] Thus, people order the *Quarter Pounder*, the *Big Mac*, the *large* fries. More recently, there is the lure of the "double this" (for instance, Burger King's "Double Whopper With Cheese") and the "triple that." People can quantify these things and feel that they are getting a lot of food for what appears to be a nominal sum of money. This calculation does not take into account an important point: the extraordinary profitability of fast-food outlets and other chains, which indicates that the owners, not the consumers, get the best deal.

People also tend to calculate how much time it will take to drive to McDonald's, be served the food, eat it, and return home; then, they compare that interval to the time required to prepare food at home. They often conclude, rightly or wrongly, that a trip to the fast-food restaurant will take less time than eating at home. This sort of calculation particularly supports home-delivery franchises such as Domino's, as well as other chains that emphasize time saving. A notable example of time saving in another sort of chain is Lens Crafters, which promises people, "Glasses fast, glasses in one hour."

Some McDonaldized institutions combine the emphases on time and money. Domino's promises pizza delivery in half an hour, or the pizza is free. Pizza Hut will serve a personal pan pizza in five minutes, or it, too, will be free.

Workers at McDonaldized systems also tend to emphasize the quantitative rather than the qualitative aspects of their work. Since the quality of the work is allowed to vary little, workers focus on such things as how quickly tasks can be accomplished. In a situation analogous to that of the customer, workers are expected to do a lot of work, very quickly, for low pay.

Third, McDonald's offers *predictability*, the assurance that their products and services will be the same over time and in all locales. The Egg McMuffin in New York will be, for all intents and purposes, identical to those in Chicago and Los Angeles. Also, those eaten next week or next year will be identical to those eaten today. There is great comfort in knowing that McDonald's offers no surprises. People know that the next Egg McMuffin they eat will taste about the same as the others they have eaten; it will not be awful, but it will not be exceptionally delicious, either. The success of the McDonald's model suggests that many people have come to prefer a world in which there are few surprises.

The workers in McDonaldized systems also behave in predictable ways. They follow corporate rules as well as the dictates of their managers. In many cases, not only what they do, but also what they say, is highly predictable. McDonaldized organizations often have scripts that employees are supposed to memorize and follow whenever the occasion arises.[38] This scripted behavior helps create highly predictable interactions between workers and customers. While customers do not follow scripts, they tend to develop simple recipes for dealing with the employees of McDonaldized systems.[39] As Robin Leidner argues,

> McDonald's pioneered the routinization of interactive service work and remains an exemplar of extreme standardization. Innovation is not discouraged . . . at least among managers and franchisees. Ironically, though, 'the object is to look for new, innovative ways to create an experience that is exactly the same no matter what McDonald's you walk into, no matter where it is in the world.'[40]

Fourth, *control*, especially through the *substitution of nonhuman for human technology*, is exerted over the people who enter the world of McDonald's. A *human technology* (a screwdriver, for example) is controlled by people; a *nonhuman technology* (the assembly line, for instance) controls people. The people who eat in fast-food restaurants are controlled, albeit (usually) subtly. Lines, limited menus, few options, and uncomfortable seats all lead diners to do what management wishes them to do—eat quickly and leave. Further, the drive-through (in some cases walk-through) window leads diners to leave before they eat. In the Domino's model, customers never come in the first place.

The people who work in McDonaldized organizations are also controlled to a high degree, usually more blatantly and directly than customers. They are trained to do a limited number of things in precisely the way they are told to do them. The technologies used and the way the organization is set up reinforce this control. Managers and inspectors make sure that workers toe the line.

McDonald's also controls employees by threatening to use, and ultimately using, nonhuman technology to replace human workers. No matter how well they are programmed and controlled, workers can foul up the system's operation. A slow worker can make the preparation and delivery of a Big Mac inefficient. A worker who refuses to follow the rules might leave the pickles or special sauce off a hamburger, thereby making for unpredictability. And a distracted worker can put too few fries in the box, making an order of large fries seem skimpy. For these and other reasons, McDonald's has felt compelled to steadily replace human beings with nonhuman technologies, such as the soft-drink dispenser that shuts itself off when the glass is full, the french-fry machine that rings and lifts itself out of the oil when the fries are crisp, the preprogrammed cash register that eliminates the need for the cashier to calculate prices and amounts and, perhaps at some future time, the robot capable of making hamburgers.[41] This technology increases the corporation's control over workers. Thus, McDonald's can assure customers that their employees and service will be consistent.

The Advantages of McDonaldization

This discussion of four of the fundamental characteristics of McDonaldization makes it clear that there are good, solid reasons why McDonald's has succeeded so phenomenally and why the process of McDonaldization is moving ahead so dramatically. As a result, people such as the economic columnist, Robert Samuelson, strongly support McDonald's. Samuelson confesses to "openly worship McDonald's," and he thinks of it as "the greatest restaurant chain in history." However, even Samuelson recognizes that there are those who "can't stand the food and regard McDonald's as the embodiment of all that is vulgar in American mass culture."[42]

McDonaldization has undoubtedly led to positive changes.[43] Here are a few specific examples:

- There is a far greater availability of goods and services than before; their availability depends less on time or geographic location.
- This wider range of goods and services is available to a much larger portion of the population.
- People are able to get what they want or need almost instantaneously.

- It is far more convenient to get what they want or need.
- Goods and services are of a far more uniform quality; at least some people get even better goods and services than before McDonaldization.
- Far more economical alternatives to high-priced, customized goods and services are widely available; therefore, people can afford things they could not previously afford.
- Fast, efficient goods and services are available to a population that is working longer hours and has fewer hours to spare. . . .

More specifically, McDonald's itself offers many praiseworthy programs, such as its Ronald McDonald Houses, which permit parents to stay with children undergoing treatment for serious medical problems; job-training programs for teenagers; programs to help keep its employees in school; efforts to hire and train the handicapped; the McMasters program, aimed at hiring senior citizens; and an enviable record of hiring and promoting minorities.[44]

A Critique of McDonaldization: The Irrationality of Rationality

Though McDonaldization offers powerful advantages, it has a downside. Efficiency, predictability, calculability, and control through nonhuman technology can be thought of as the basic components of a *rational* system.[45] However, rational systems inevitably spawn irrationalities. The downside of McDonaldization will be dealt with most systematically under the heading of the *irrationality of rationality*; in fact, paradoxically, the irrationality of rationality can be thought of as the fifth dimension of McDonaldization. The basic idea here is that rational systems inevitably spawn irrational consequences. Another way of saying this is that rational systems serve to deny human reason; rational systems are often unreasonable.

For example, McDonaldization has produced a wide array of adverse effects on the environment. Take just one example: the need to grow uniform potatoes to create those predictable french fries that people have come to expect from fast-food restaurants. It turns out that the need to grow such potatoes has adversely affected the ecology of the Pacific Northwest. The huge farms that now produce such potatoes rely on the extensive use of chemicals. The need to produce a perfect fry means that much of the potato is wasted, with the remnants either fed to cattle or used for fertilizer. However, the underground water supply is now showing high levels of nitrates that may be traceable to the fertilizer and animal wastes.[46] There are, of course, many other ecological problems associated with the McDonaldization of society—the forests felled to produce paper, the damage caused by polystyrene and other materials, the enormous amount of food needed to produce feed cattle, and so on.

Another unreasonable effect of the fast-food restaurant is that it is often a dehumanizing setting in which to eat or work. Customers lining up for a burger or waiting in the drive-through line and workers preparing the food often feel as though they are part of an assembly line. Hardly amenable to eating, assembly lines have been shown to be inhuman settings in which to work.

Of course, the criticisms of the irrationality of the fast-food restaurant will be extended to all facets of the McDonaldizing world. For example, at the opening of Euro Disney, a French politician said that it will "bombard France with uprooted creations that are to culture what fast food is to gastronomy."[47] This clearly indicates an abhorrence of McDonaldization, whatever guise it may take.

As you have seen, there *are* great gains to be made from McDonaldization. However, this book [The McDonaldization of Society] will focus on the great costs and enormous risks of McDonaldization. McDonald's and the other purveyors of the fast-food model spend billions of dollars each year outlining the benefits of their system. However, the critics of the system have few outlets for their ideas. There are, for example, no commercials between Saturday-morning cartoons warning children of the dangers associated with fast-food restaurants.

A legitimate question may be raised about this critique of McDonaldization: Is it animated by a romanticization of the past and an impossible desire to return to a world that no longer exists? Some critics do base their critiques on the idea that there was a time when life was slower and less efficient, and offered more surprises; when people were freer; and when one was more likely to deal with a human being than a robot or a computer.[48] Although they have a point, these critics have undoubtedly exaggerated the positive aspects of a world without McDonald's, and they have certainly tended to forget the liabilities associated with such a world. As an example of the latter, take the following case of a visit to a pizzeria in Havana, Cuba:

The pizza's not much to rave about—they scrimp on tomato sauce, and the dough is mushy.

It was about 7:30 P.M., and as usual the place was standing-room-only, with people two deep jostling for a stool to come open and a waiting line spilling out onto the sidewalk.

The menu is similarly Spartan. . . . To drink, there is tap water. That's it—no toppings, no soda, no beer, no coffee, no salt, no pepper. And no special orders.

A very few people are eating. Most are waiting. . . . Fingers are drumming, flies are buzzing, the clock is ticking. The waiter wears a watch around his belt loop, but he hardly needs it; time is evidently not his chief concern. After a while, tempers begin to fray.

But right now, it's 8:45 P.M. at the pizzeria, I've been waiting an hour and a quarter for two small pies.[49]

Few would prefer such irrational systems to the rationalized elements of society. More important, critics who revere the past do not seem to realize that we are not returning to such a world. In fact, fast-food restaurants have begun to appear in Havana.[50] The increase in the number of people, the acceleration of technological change, the increasing pace of life—all this and more make it impossible to go back to the nonrationalized world, if it ever existed, of home-cooked meals, traditional restaurant dinners, high-quality foods, meals loaded with surprises, and restaurants populated only by chefs free to fully express their creativity.

While one basis for a critique of McDonaldization is the past, another is the future.[51] The future in this sense is defined as human potential, unfettered by the constraints of McDonaldized systems. This critique holds that people have the potential to be far more thoughtful, skillful, creative, and well-rounded than they are now. If the world were less McDonaldized, people would be better able to live up to their human potential. This critique is based not on what people were like in the past, but on what they could be like in the future, if only the constraints of McDonaldized systems were eliminated, or at least eased substantially.

NOTES

1. For a similar but narrower viewpoint to the one expressed here, see Benjamin R. Barber. "Jihad Vs. McWorld." *The Atlantic Monthly*, March 1992, pp. 53–63.
2. These and other data on McDonald's come from its most recent (1993) annual report, *The Annual*.
3. Cynthia Rigg. "McDonald's Lean Units Beef up NY Presence." *Crain's New York Business*, October 31, 1994, p. 1.

4. The source for this information is Pepsico, Inc.'s 1993 Annual Report, p. 18.
5. Mark Albright. "INSIDE JOB: Fast-Food Chains Serve a Captive Audience." *St. Petersburg Times*, January 15, 1995, p. 1H.
6. Bill McDowall. "The Global Market Challenge." *Restaurants & Institutions*, vol. 104, no. 26, November 1, 1994, pp. 52ff.
7. Eben Shapiro in "Overseas Sizzle for McDonald's." *New York Times*, April 17, 1992, pp. D1, D4.
8. "Investors with Taste for Growth Looking to Golden Arches." *Tampa Tribune*, January 11, 1995, Business and Finance, p. 7.
9. Paul Gruchow. "Unchaining America: Communities Are Finding Ways to Keep Independent Entrepreneurs in Business." *Utne Reader*, January–February 1995, pp. 17–18.
10. McDonald's Corporation Customer and Community Relations.
11. E. R. Shipp. "The McBurger Stand That Started It All." *New York Times*, February 27, 1985, section 3, p. 3.
12. "Wedge of Americana: In Moscow, Pizza Hut Opens 2 Restaurants." *Washington Post*, September 12, 1990, p. B10.
13. Jeb Blount. "Frying Down to Rio." *Washington Post/Business*, May 18, 1994, pp. F1, F5.
14. Marshall Fishwick, Ed. *Ronald Revisited. The World of Ronald McDonald*. Bowling Green, OH: Bowling Green University Press, 1983.
15. John F Harris. "McMilestone Restaurant Opens Doors in Dale City." *Washington Post*, April 7, 1988, p. DI.
16. Conrad Kottak. "Rituals at McDonald's," in Marshall Fishwick (ed.). *Ronald Revisited: The World of Ronald McDonald*. Bowling Green, OH: Bowling Green University Press, 1983, pp. 52–58.
17. Bill Keller. "Of Famous Arches, Beeg Meks and Rubles." *New York Times*, January 28, 1990, section 1, pp. 1, 12.
18. William Severini Kowinski. *The Malling of America: An Inside Look at the Great Consumer Paradise*. New York: William Morrow, 1985, p. 218.
19. Stephen M. Fjellman. *Vinyl Leaves: Walt Disney World and America*. Boulder, CO: Westview Press, 1992. In another example of other countries creating their own McDonaldized systems and exporting them, Japan's Sega Enterprises is planning to open the first Segaworld indoor urban theme park in London in 1996; see "A Sega Theme Park for Piccadilly Circus." *New York Times*, February 14, 1995, p. D5.
20. Bob Garfield. "How I Spent (and Spent and Spent) My Disney Vacation." *Washington Post*, July 7, 1991, p. B5. See also Margaret J. King. "Empires of Popular Culture: McDonald's and Disney," in Marshall Fishwick (ed.). *Ronald Revisited: The World of Ronald McDonald*. Bowling Green, OH: Bowling Green University Press, 1983, pp. 106–119.
21. Steven Greenhouse. "The Rise and Rise of McDonald's." *New York Times*, June 8, 1986, section 3, p. 1.
22. Richard L. Papiernik. "Mac Attack?" *Financial World*, April 12, 1994, p. 30.
23. Laura Shapiro. "Ready for McCatfish?" *Newsweek*, October 15, 1990, pp. 76–77; N. R. Kleinfeld. "Fast Food's Changing Landscape." *New York Times*, April 14, 1985, section 3, pp. 1, 6.
24. Louis Uchitelle. "That's Funny, Those Pickles Don't Look Russian." *New York Times*, February 27, 1992, p. A4.
25. Nicholas D. Kristof. "'Billions Served' (and That Was Without China)." *New York Times*, April 24, 1992, p. A4.
26. Cynthia Rigg. "McDonald's Lean Units Beef up NY Presence." *Crain's New York Business*, October 31, 1994, p. 1.
27. Carole Sugarman. "Dining Out on Campus." *Washington Post/Health*, February 14, 1995, p. 20.
28. Gilbert Chan. "Fast Food Chains Pump Profits at Gas Stations." *Fresno Bee*, October 10, 1994, p. F4.
29. Edwin McDowell. "Fast Food Fills Menu for Many Hotel Chains." *New York Times*, January 9, 1992, pp. D1, D6.
30. "Fast-Food Flights." *Phoenix Gazette*, November 25, 1994, p. D1.
31. Peter Prichard. *The Making of McPaper: The Inside Story of USA TODAY*. Kansas City, MO: Andrews, McMeel and Parker, 1987, pp. 232–233.
32. Howard Kurtz. "Slicing, Dicing News to Attract the Young." *Washington Post*, January 6, 1991, p. AI.
33. Nicholas D. Kristof. "Court Test Is Likely on Dial-a-Porn Service Game." *New York Times*, October 15, 1986, section 1, p. 16.

34. Cited in Robin Leidner. *Fast Food, Fast Talk: Service Work and the Routinization of Everyday Life.* Berkeley: University of California Press, 1993, p. 9.
35. Martin Gottlieb. "Pornography's Plight Hits Times Square." *New York Times,* October 5, 1986, section 3, p. 6.
36. Max Weber. *Economy and Society.* Totowa, NJ: Bedminster Press, 1921/1968; Stephen Kalberg. "Max Weber's Types of Rationality: Cornerstones for the Analysis of Rationalization Processes in History." *American Journal of Sociology 85*(1980): 1145–1179.
37. Ian Mitroff and Warren Bennis. *The Unreality Industry: The Deliberate Manufacturing of Falsehood and What It Is Doing to Our Lives.* New York: Birch Lane Press, 1989, p. 142.
38. Robin Leidner has developed the idea of scripts in her book, *Fast Food, Fast Talk: Service Work and the Routinization of Everyday Life.* Berkeley: University of California Press, 1993.
39. The idea of recipes comes from the work of Alfred Schutz. See, for example, *The Phenomenology of the Social World.* Evanston, IL: Northwestern University Press, 1932/1967.
40. Robin Leidner. *Fast Food, Fast Talk: Service Work and the Routinization of Everyday Life.* Berkeley: University of California Press, 1993, p. 82.
41. Experimental robots of this type already exist.
42. Robert J. Samuelson. "In Praise of McDonald's." *Washington Post,* November 1, 1989, p. A25.
43. I would like to thank my colleague, Stan Presser, for suggesting that I enumerate the kinds of advantages listed on these pages.
44. Edwin M. Reingold. "America's Hamburger Helper." *Time,* June 29, 1992, pp. 66–67.
45. It should be pointed out that the words *rational, rationality,* and *rationalization* are being used differently here and throughout the book than they are ordinarily employed. For one thing, people usually think of these terms as being largely positive; something that is rational is usually considered to be good. However, they are used here in a generally negative way. The positive term in this analysis is genuinely human "reason" (for example, the ability to act and work creatively), which is seen as being denied by inhuman, rational systems such as the fast-food restaurant. For another, the term *rationalization* is usually associated with Freudian theory as a way of explaining away some behavior, but here it describes the increasing pervasiveness of rationality throughout society. Thus, in reading this book, you must be careful to interpret the terms in these ways rather than in the ways they are conventionally employed.
46. Timothy Egan. "In Land of French Fry, Study Finds Problems." *New York Times,* February 7, 1994, p. A10.
47. Alan Riding. "Only the French Elite Scorn Mickey's Debut." *New York Times,* April 13, 1992, p. A 13.
48. George Stauth and Bryan S. Turner. "Nostalgia, Postmodernism and the Critique of Mass Culture." *Theory, Culture and Society 5*(1988):509–526; Bryan S. Turner. "A Note on Nostalgia." *Theory, Culture and Society 4*(1987):147–156.
49. Lee Hockstader. "No Service, No Smile, Little Sauce." *Washington Post,* August 5, 1991, p. A12.
50. Douglas Farah. "Cuban Fast Food Joints Are Quick Way for Government to Rally Economy." *Washington Post,* January 24, 1995, p. A14.
51. In this sense, this resembles Marx's critique of capitalism. Marx was not animated by a romanticization of precapitalist society, but rather by the desire to produce a truly human (communist) society on the base provided by capitalism. Despite this specific affinity to Marxist theory, this book is, as you will see, premised far more on the theories of Max Weber.

STUDY QUESTIONS

1. What is the meaning of McDonaldization? How is this related to "globalization"?

2. List other businesses that have become like the McDonald's restaurant. Can you look at places where you go that have become like McDonald's? What similarities do they have with McDonald's?

RANDY BLAZAK

White Boys to Terrorist Men
Target Recruitment of Nazi Skinheads

There is an important distinction between hate crimes and hate group activity. Although reported hate crimes appear to be declining, there is evidence that hate group activity is increasing. This includes hate group consolidation, the increase in hate Web sites, and more sophisticated recruitment of youth. This research explores how hate groups, specifically racist skinheads, target specific youth populations for recruitment. Using a layman's interpretation of Durkheim's "anomie," skinheads look for youth who live in a world of change. Based on ethnographic research and guided interviews, this research finds that older Nazi skinheads manipulate anomic teens and indoctrinate them into a world of terror.

Skinheads in Denver murder a police officer and a Black man waiting for a bus, critically injuring a White woman who tried to help the victim. A Black Texan is dragged to his death behind a truck driven by three members of the Aryan Brotherhood. A member of the World Church of the Creator goes on a shooting spree in Illinois and Indiana, killing two minorities and wounding nine others. The late 1990s saw its share of violence committed by members of hate groups.

According to the Southern Poverty Law Center's (SPLC) (2000a) *Intelligence Report*, the number of hate groups may be on the decline, but their activity is not. "Official" data on hate crimes are becoming more reliable since the implementation of the 1990 Hate Crimes Statistics Acts, but there are still problems. Many police departments are not trained to identify hate crimes or, for various reasons, may choose not to report acts as hate crimes. Several states have no hate crime laws, and those that do have varying definitions of who should be included in the laws' "protected class." Should women, homosexuals, the disabled, and others be protected by hate crime laws? And, of course, there is a great reluctance by many to report hate crimes.

According to the Federal Bureau of Investigation (FBI) data that we do have, most hate crimes are committed by young people. In their research, Levin and McDevitt (1993) classified 60% of hate criminals as "youthful thrill seekers." Some of these youth are members of hate groups; most are not. That hate crimes tend to be more vicious and injurious than normal violent crimes only adds to the destructive impact they have on the community. As with other forms of crime, most youthful hate criminals will "age out" of their criminality. But, some will be brought into the fray of terrorist hate groups. These groups may perpetrate or encourage other hate crimes, but more importantly, they create a climate where bias-motivated crime is justified. To groups such as the Aryan Nations, the Ku Klux Klan (KKK, Klan), and the World Church of the Creator, the hate criminal is a hero, doing God's work to save the White race from extinction.

The process by which young people are brought into the shadowy world of White supremacy must be researched for two primary reasons. First, we must be able to identify the macro-level social dynamics that create environments conducive to hate. Hate group membership ebbs and flows. Although some of this may be due to law enforcement policing and the courtroom challenges of legal groups such as the SPLC, it must also be related to shifts in social dynamics, including the economy, immigration, and changes in gender roles. Second, by understanding the root explanations behind hate group recruitment, strategies can be developed to combat youth involvement in adult terrorist groups. Prevention programs on the local level (education, mentoring, etc.) as well as the global level (multicultural curriculums, youth employment, etc.) can feed from the findings of sociological research.

The distinction between hate crimes and hate group activity is an important one. Although official data reflect increases and decreases in their activity, hate groups continue to operate. The SPLC (2000b) reports that in 1998, there were 537 identifiable active hate groups, but in 1999, there were only 457, 80 fewer. Understanding this trend is crucial because a significant part of change is related to the development of more sophisticated recruitment tactics. The reduction in the number of hate groups relates to five key trends:

1. Consolidation: Like corporations in merger frenzy, small hate groups are being swallowed up by larger ones. A Michigan chapter of the neo-Nazi group the American Nationalist Party joined the National Alliance. The New Jersey Confederate Knights merged with the Alabama-based America's Empire of the KKK. Even skinheads who have been fiercely defensive of their autonomy are being brought back into adult racist groups. Most notable is the Hammerskin Nation, which has moved beyond its Texas home to recruit skinheads from Oregon to Russia. According to the SPLC, the group increased in size by 70% in 1999. According to the Center's *Intelligence Report* director, Joseph Roy, the situation is deeply troubling: "Many of the less active groups have joined forces with much more serious players. There is strong evidence that far more people are now in really hard-lined groups like the National Alliance and the Hammerskin Nation" (Southern Poverty Law Center, 2000b, p. 7).

2. Web sites: More than 300 hate sites on the Web allow hate groups to spread their messages to those who might not ever travel to a rally or clandestine meeting. But, Web sites also allow individuals not associated with groups to spread their ideologies. The SPLC reports that 47% of hate sites are not affiliated with active hate groups. But, these sites may be gateways into established hate groups because most provide links to them; just a click away.

3. Leaderless resistance: On October 23, 1992, Christian Identity leader Pete Peters launched the idea of the leaderless resistance into the extreme right. At a meeting of White supremacists who desired to respond to the siege at Ruby Ridge, Idaho, earlier that year, Peters argued that the Klan, militias, and others should move away from the hierarchical organizations of the past because of their tendency to be infiltrated by law enforcement agents. Small cells of terrorists who shared an ideology and agenda (as laid out in *The Turner Diaries*, a fictional manual for starting a race war) would avoid government policing. Timothy McVeigh and Terry Nichols, the 1995 Oklahoma City bombers, represent Peters's concept. As some right-wing extremists consolidate into larger hate groups, others (perhaps more) join no groups, only the vague leaderless resistance. This includes skinheads. Whereas some merge into the Hammerskin Nation, others claim no affiliation, making it hard for law enforcement and community groups to monitor nameless, small groups of skinheads.

4. Mainstream politics: It should be acknowledged that many right-wing extremists may have found homes in mainstream right-wing politics. Encouraged by the election to the Louisiana State legislature as a Republican of David Duke, the leader of the National Association for the

Advancement of White People, others have taken off their Klan hoods and played the mainstream game. Successful campaigns against affirmative action in California, Washington, and Texas, the power of the gun lobby and the antihomosexual lobby, and sizable campaigns to preserve the Confederate battle flag's place in Southern society give right-wingers legitimate opportunities to advance their causes.

5. Recruitment: Like gangs and cults, hate groups have a high turnover rate. Research shows that most members stay in hate groups only as long as the groups meet their personal needs (Ezekial, 1995). Hate groups play the role of subcultural "problem solver" (Cohen, 1955). When they no longer appear to be solving the problem, members move on. Although many hate groups may find new members from the mainstream right-wing community, this research focuses on how skinhead groups specifically target young, "anomic" people. Both skinhead and nonskinhead groups are increasingly skilled in identifying "strained" populations that have gone through some type of ascribed status crisis ranging from factory layoffs to interracial schoolyard fights. Instead of the general recruitment of Whites in the past, skinheads and similar groups now target specific populations from which they are most likely to successfully recruit new members.

These five trends create a three-level environment conducive to right-wing terrorism: (a) stronger, consolidated hate groups with chapters in many states and even nations; (b) an unknown number of leaderless cells that share much of the hate groups' philosophy along with a mandate that supports violence against representatives of the government, abortion, and multiculturalism; and (c) a populace in which bigoted, antigovernment agendas are reinforced and supported. . . .

Skinheads as Terrorists

Skinheads have been affiliated with hate groups in America for more than 15 years. Their roots as a subculture go back to the mid-1960s, when they emerged in London as a working-class response to the hippie phenomenon. Not initially racists (in fact, skinhead style draws heavily from Black "rude boys," Jamaican immigrants), skinheads were reactionary, resenting social forces representing social change (Hebdige, 1979). Skinheads first appeared as a reactionary element of the American punk rock scene, but it was not until the mid-1980s that they began to be recruited by more established racist groups (Blazak, 1995).

As groups such as the Klan, the White Aryan Resistance (WAR), and the New Order (a Nazi group) increased their recruitment of skinheads, skinhead violence also rose. Hundreds of acts of violence and destruction in the last 1980s were attributed to skinhead groups. One of the better known cases was the murder of Mulugeta Seraw in Portland, Oregon, in 1988. The day after an airing of an episode of *Geraldo* that featured skinheads and Nazis violently rioting on TV, Seraw was killed by three skinheads. The skinheads claimed membership in a Portland hate group known as East Side White Pride. In a 1990 civil trial, SPLC founder Morris Dees successfully proved that East Side White Pride members had been recruited by the California-based WAR to become foot soldiers in a violent race war. The trial ended with a $12.5 million judgment against WAR leader Tom Metzger and his son John, head of the Aryan Youth Movement.

Although the judgment may have temporarily sidelined WAR from recruiting skinheads (Metzger's Web site, http://www.resist.com, is now one of the most popular sources of hate propaganda on the Web), skinhead violence continued well into the 1990s. Some of the most violent acts made headlines. In 1990, two Houston, Texas, skinheads killed a Vietnamese teenager whose dying words were "Please stop. I'm sorry I ever came to your country. God forgive me!" (SPLC, 2000a, p. 11). In 1992, three skinheads recruited by Bill Riccio's Aryan National Front stabbed to death a homeless Black man. Two Aryan Nations skinheads killed their parents and brother in 1995 in Allentown, Pennsylvania. Their motivation was that their parents were Jehovah's Witnesses. In 1996, a dozen Nazi skinheads stabbed to death a youth who had ejected them from a party. Denver, Colorado, saw a wave of skinhead violence in 1997 that included two murders. There have also been numerous synagogue and church attacks, random bombings, and malicious harassment cases that police attribute to skinhead groups.

Although the number of skinhead groups may have peaked in 1991, when the SPLC counted 144 groups, they may be more active now in consolidated groups such as the Hammerskins or in unaffiliated small cells. Many racist skinheads share a belief in an inevitable race war in America. Although this race war will lead to an "autonomous Aryan homeland in the Northwest" (as a Volksfront newsletter describes it), the ultimate goal is an America that has been ethnically cleansed of all enemies, including White race traitors. This civil war may require some "sparking," as described in *The Turner Diaries* (which was written by National Alliance leader William Pierce). Act of violence and terror by skinheads are viewed within the movements as important in speeding the polarization of the public into racial "tribes."

The relatively infrequent attacks by racist skinheads (compared with economically or interpersonally motivated crimes) should not distract observers from the increase in hate group activity. Effective policing on the federal and local levels as well as the willingness of prosecutors to test new hate crime laws may have discouraged some violence. But, recruitment and consolidation, along with the spread of unaffiliated cells, are part of racists' vision of forming armies in preparation for the prophesied racial civil war. This "drawing up of sides" is reflected in a recent statement on the Hammerskin Nation Web site:

Skinheads are meant to be a visible opposition on the street, but when you're out there, try to earn respect rather than contempt. Even those of us who aren't so visible anymore matter, because people still know who we are. Only with people's respect will we ever gain any public sympathy, which will lead us toward our goals. It takes the few brave souls to lead before the "sheep" will follow. I am reminded of some of the "outlaw" motorcycle clubs who calls themselves "1 percenters" because they are the few who have the courage to "live on the edge" and defy the law. I say Hammerskins are like 1 percenters, except that we are forced to the edge. We are sane people in an insane world. Let us bring that edge inward until our values, morals, honor and glory are the only law and we have won back the minds, hearts and souls of our people! (Hyde, 2000)

Strain Theory and Hate Group Recruitment

From Durkheim and Merton to Passas and Agnew (1997), it has been argued that the effect of macro-level anomie can manifest on the micro level as criminal behavior. Existing as a sense of "normlessness" or as a disjunction between aspirations and expectations, this stage is reflected in a form of psychological distress or strain. Whether it is Agnew's (1992) general strain theory or Messner and Rosenfeld's (1994) institutional anomie theory, the human face of strain is the same: frustration, anger, and a need to resolve some perceived inequity.

Much has been written about how strained boys and men end up in gangs as a way to address their blocked goal attainment (Cohen, 1955, Cloward & Ohlin, 1960). Not as evident are data that suggest that strained youth are actually targeted for recruitment by delinquent subcultures. This article explores research on racist skinhead groups and their recruitment targets. Although the criminal activity of skinheads is often seen as a phenomenon separate from street gangs (Blazak, 1998; Hamm, 1993; Levin & McDevitt, 1993), criminologists have referred to skinhead groups as "White gangs." Increasingly, local police departments are including skinheads in their gang-monitoring activities.

Strain as a Red Flag

What does strain look like? How can one tell if someone is experiencing anomie? Agnew (1985) discussed the presentation of "life hassles" coming from the presentation of negative stimuli and the removal of positively valued stimuli as well as blocked opportunities. This "negative affect" generates anger and frustration, and crime becomes a corrective action. Cohen (1955) researched how strained individuals search out subcultural solutions (i.e., gangs) to resolve their strain but not how gangs search out strained individuals to recruit. On the street, strain can manifest in the values seen in Cohen's delinquent boys: nonutilitarianism, maliciousness, and negativism.

This "reaction formation" to dominant conforming values can appear as antisocial behavior (e.g., fighting or vandalism) before the strained individual finds his or her collective solution in either a nonutilitarian gang or, if he or she has the opportunity, in a more goal-oriented gang (Cloward & Ohlin, 1960). Regardless of the path, the individual is exhibiting behavior reflective of his or her psychic stress. Researchers have found evidence of this desire for a group to relieve individual alienation. In Wooden and Blazak's (2000) work on skinheads, graffiti taggers, and skaters, the authors identify anomie as a motivating factor for joining deviant groups.

Although the musical tastes and styles of dress differ from group to group, these adolescents share one commonality: They are experiencing what sociologists refer to as anomie, a sense of rootlessness or normlessness. In part, to combat this state, they join groups and assume identities that, for many, become all encompassing, a form of a "master status," the core way of defining themselves. And, embracing or identifying with a specific group—whether a "metaler" clique, a stoner gang, or a tagger crew—provides these "tearaway" teenagers with a way of reducing their anxiety and alienation (Wooden & Blazak, 2000, p. 12).

The logic of anomie theory is that the individual experiences strain, which then leads him or her to group delinquency. Much of the research focuses on the group delinquency (Cloward & Ohlin, 1960) or the presence of strain from noxious stimuli (Agnew, 1985) but not necessarily on the precriminal expressions of strain. There is an assumption that the anomic person is flailing around, frustrated, angry, and inching toward the "criminal solution." High school counselors are skilled at identifying these "at-risk" youth. They exhibit certain characteristics of alienation including maliciousness, rebellious dress, and antisocial attitudes, all of which are red flags.

Other red flags can be the social–structural conditions that create anomie. The disjunction between goals and legitimate opportunities or between aspirations and expectations can take the form of economic blockage, as described in the classic strain theory of Cohen (1955); in more micro-level problems, as described in Agnew's general strain theory (1985); or in the institutional over-emphasis on economic success, as described in Messner and Rosenfeld's (1994) institutional anomie theory. In each of these instances, the individual wants something—a car, popularity, wealth—and society has not regulated the means to attain these positively valued goals. There is also evidence that cultural status (Blazak, 1995) and masculinity (Messerchmidt, 1993) may represent goals that when blocked lead to criminal activity. Gangs, for example, may use the lack of opportunity for material wealth and legitimate performances of masculinity in poor urban areas to offer a group solution for those strained boys who need to "be a man and make money."

With regard to the racist skinheads, the negative stimuli can be represented in the presence of threats to class and ascribed status. Skinhead belief is based on the traditional cultural superiority of heterosexual, White men; therefore, anything that could undermine that group's dominance represents a threat. Antiracism, gay rights, feminism, and multiculturalism are all perceived as enemies of the status quo. Therefore, in places where these concepts are a part of the dominant discourse, it can be assumed that a certain segment of heterosexual White men will feel a great deal of strain as their traditional picture of the world and their place in it is threatened.

I theorize that both identifiers of strain are used by skinheads to target recruits. The presence of structural conditions that represent threats to ascribed status first attract the attention of the group to a specific population. . . .

I hypothesize that racist skinhead groups use these red flags of strain to guide their recruiting activity. Threats to the traditional status quo or "cultural anomie" attract the groups, which then seek out strained individuals. The threats exist in four categories:

1. Threats to ethnic or racial status
   - growth in the minority student population
   - minority student organizations or events
   - shifts to multicultural curricula
   - racial conflict in which the institutions appear to support the minority group

2. Threats to gender status
   - conflict over female participation in male activities
   - feminist activist groups
   - antisexual violence events or programs

3. Threats to heterosexual status
   - sexual minority organizations
   - gay pride events
   - inclusiveness movements or sponsored dialogue

4. Threats to economic status
   - factory layoffs
   - large employer downsizing
   - high competition for manual labor or service sector jobs

The most common scenario involves the transition in secondary schools from Eurocentric curricula to inclusive, multicultural curricula. Here, the representations of ethnic Whites as the "heroes" of civilization (where every month is "White History Month") are replaced with a more balanced picture of social history that presents non-White perspectives that may be seen as vilifying White participation in society. Especially when reluctantly presented by "old-school" White teachers, this new curriculum may be portrayed as attempting to create "White guilt" over issues such as slavery, colonialism, and segregation. A 15-year-old boy, born in the 1980s, without the benefit of firsthand experience of his country's overtly racist past, may wonder why he has been pegged as the bad guy in history. He notices Black, Hispanic, and Asian student groups flourishing, yet he is branded a racist if he asks why there is no White student group. He is in the middle of cultural change without the tools to navigate it. This condition of anomie is exactly what racist groups are looking for.

Method

The data to support the theory that culturally strained youth end up in skinhead groups were collected in a 7-year ethnographic study (Blazak, 1995) in which it was found that members of skinhead groups had experienced threats to economic status (usually, their parents had experienced downward mobility), racial status (through the increased integration of White suburbs), gender status (represented in the perceived end of the ability to be "real men" because of feminism), and heterosexual status (fostered by the idea that the gay rights movement was destroying the traditional family). Data on the recruiting goals of the skinheads were retrieved more through guided conversations and anecdotal experiences. . . .

Based on the 65 formal interviews, approximately 200 informal interviews from the ethnographic study, the interview with three skinhead recruiters through Oregon Spotlight, and the additional data from approximately 200 Oregon secondary school students, a theory can be inductively reasoned. Ultimately, future research will test the hypotheses that (a) schools that publicly experience a threat to culturally valued status are targeted for recruitment and (b) individuals expressing the negative affect of strain are targeted for recruitment.

Findings

Of the 65 intensively interviewed skinheads, roughly half admitted being involved in some form of recruitment activities. Usually, these involved getting flyers into high schools or rock clubs. The flyers contained contact addresses or phone numbers for those who were interested. An informal youth network was also used to find out about specific individuals who might be easily recruited. The three skinheads in the Oregon Spotlight research were all active recruiters in the Portland and Eugene areas. All three have also served prison terms for various hate crimes, and one is currently incarcerated for a parole violation.

The Selection of Anomic Populations

Members of organizations such as Youth Corps (the youth wing of the KKK), the Aryan Youth Movement (the youth wing of WAR), and Volksfront (an Oregon Nazi skinhead group) often discussed strategy meetings in which core members would discuss target populations where recruitment activities would have the greatest results. Leafleting was the most common strategy, but members might also stage a violent confrontation with an "enemy" to raise visibility and awareness. There was a manipulation of the power of rumor and the knowledge that young people will quickly spread forbidden information. Trey, a 22-year-old Portland skinhead, said,

> There was this fight at [Walker] High School between a Black kid and a White kid and everyone was supporting the Black kid who had been picking on this White forever. Typical bullshit, right? But we knew that there were Whites there who were sick and tired of being called "racists" just for sticking up for themselves. So we went down there one day, right, when school was letting out and beat the shit out of some gangster-looking nigger. The next day everyone at Milwaukee was talking about, "Oh man, did you hear that the skinheads kicked some nigger's ass?" It was the talk of the school so we went back a week later and put up a bunch of flyers and got a bunch of calls from kids wanting to know what they could do.

... Over 15 years, I have heard these stories over and over again: Skinheads leafleting neighborhoods where automobile or textile workers have been laid off, blaming affirmative action and "Jewish capitalism." Skinheads coming to the "rescue" of White youth who have been victimized by minority gangs. Skinheads who present a viable model of masculinity to boys confronted with the "homofication" (a skinhead term) of American culture. But, perhaps the newest recruitment technique is to target schools that are experiencing a curriculum shift toward multiculturalism. As history and social science books are retooled to be more inclusive, the voice that is diminishing is the hegemonic, straight, White male perspective. Without the proper context, this shift can seem to be a conspiracy to write White contributions out of the standard educational curriculum. Several high schools in Oregon have been targeted for recruitment using the backlash against multiculturalism as a way in. ...

Discussion

I found that the skinhead recruiters interviewed were aware of the experience of normlessness among certain youth populations. These populations were targeted because of their desire for structure, a subcultural solution to their anomie, as well as their need for consistent models of authority and masculinity. They were easily manipulated and brought into the fray of right-wing hate groups.

The violent solution that these groups offer (becoming a soldier in a race war) will appeal to a large percentage of anomic young men because of its simplistic reality. Wars are won. Evil conspirators are banished. The mythical past of unchallenged, straight, White male hegemony is restored. For a generation weaned on video games and violent media, the world of Aryan terrorists can be intoxicating.

Sociological research is crucial in unlocking this attraction that makes recruiting so easy. The recruiting process is similar to that used by cults. Young skinheads may also end up in more serious right-wing groups such as Aryan Nations and even militia groups. Additionally, the readiness of the coming youth generation to look for extremist, subcultural solutions must be discussed. Finally, intervention strategies are proposed that will prevent young people from entering the world of racist terror. . . .

Generation Why?

Despite the success of multicultural curriculums in reducing bias among youth, no cohort may be more ripe for recruitment than the current teenage generation. Unlike the culture-shaping baby boomers and the relatively small Generation X, youth born after 1981 face numerous sources of anomie and thus have been dubbed "Generation Why?" (Wooden & Blazak, 2000).

The youth of Generation Why? were born after the experience of overt racism (busing, segregation, etc.) and have always known Black History Month. But, they are also a more racially diverse generation. Thirty-three percent of the high school class of 2000 were members of minority groups. Only 28% of Americans, in general, are minorities (Foster, 1999). The potential for racial unity exists as more youth define themselves as "multiracial," but there is also a potential for conflict as schools and communities become "less White," inciting fears among racists. The 2000 census is expected to reveal that California is the first state where Whites are a minority.

This has been described as a generation in crisis. They are less likely to spend time with their parents or to be known by name to their teachers. Nanette Davis (1999), in her book *Youth Crisis: Growing Up in the High-Risk Society*, points out that all the institutions involved in helping youth make a safe transition from childhood to adulthood are in a state of crisis. These include the family, schools, religion, the juvenile justice system, and the occupational structure. Davis outlines seven of the manifestations of cultural "crisis":

1. Modern life is uncertain.
2. Politicians opt for short-term solutions, ignoring long-term consequences.

3. The emphasis on consumerism.
4. Race, class, age, and ethnic divisions discourage youth from believing in social institutions.
5. There is a lack of adequate child care.
6. Risk reduction attempts do not target the most vulnerable.
7. There is a "cult of individualism." (pp. 14–15) . . .

Prevention Strategies

Considering the proclivity of hate groups to bring young people into their dark world of conspiracy and violence through the skinhead subculture, strategies must be developed to protect youth. Although the life of the terrorist might seem romantic or heroic, the reality is far different. Death in police shoot-outs or from unexpectedly exploding pipe bombs is normative in adult hate groups such as The Order. More likely are long prison terms due to stricter policing by the FBI, the Bureau of Alcohol, Tobacco, and Firearms, and local police, and enhanced sentences mandated by new hate crime laws. The fact that the largest skinhead group, the Aryan Brotherhood, is essentially a prison gang reflects this.

Reducing Cultural Anomie

Reducing cultural anomie on the macro level is no easy task. As long as society values correcting the power imbalances that have given certain categories privilege, straight, White men will feel threatened. No one likes to lose the privileges of power. Riane Eisler advocates the development of institutions based on partnerships (Eisler, Love, & Loye, 1998). The current dichotomous power model (male-female, straight-gay, White-Black) dictates that one group be dominant and the other group subordinate. Here, the advances of the subordinate group are seen as losses by the dominant party in a zero-sum game format. Erasing those boundaries allows all to share in the advancement of any member of society. The gains of women and ethnic and sexual minorities are not seen as threats to men, Whites, and heterosexuals in the partnership model.

Shifting society out of the dominant-subordinate paradigm may be plausible, but I argue here that an achievable macro-level solution is to reduce threats to economic status. The policies of deregulation under Ronald Reagan and the North American Free Trade Agreement under Bill Clinton have propelled the deindustrialization of the American workforce. The Dow Jones industrial average topping 10,000 and the creation of millions of low-wage, service-sector jobs in the 1990s have not prevented a significant portion of Americans from feeling that they have lost out on the American dream. As has been done in other countries, legislation can be passed that protects factory workers from layoffs and white-collar workers from downsizing. Currently, few politicians advocate for the working class, leaving racists free reign in their interpretations.

REFERENCES

Agnew, R. (1985). A revised strain theory of delinquency. *Social Forces, 64*, 151–167.

Agnew, R. (1992). Foundations for a general strain theory of crime and delinquency. *Criminology, 30*, 47–87.

Blazak, R. (1995). *The suburbanization of hate: An ethnographic study of the skinhead subculture.* Unpublished doctoral dissertation, Emory University.

Blazak, R. (1998). Hate in the suburbs: The rise of the skinhead counterculture. In L. J. McIntyre (Ed.), *The practical skeptic: Readings in sociology.* Mountain View, CA: Mayfield.

Cloward, R. A., & Ohlin, L. E. (1960). *Delinquency and opportunity.* New York: Free Press.

Cohen, A. (1955). *Delinquent boys.* New York: Free Press.

Davis, N. J. (1999). *Youth crisis: Growing up in the high-risk society.* Westport, CT: Praeger.

Eisler, R., Love, D., & Loye, D. (1998). *The partnership way: New tools for living and learning.* New York: Holistic Education Press.

Ezekial, R. S. (1995). *The racist mind: Portraits of American neo-Nazis and Klansmen.* New York: Penguin.

Foster, D. (1999, September 12). Y2K generation forced to grow up fast. *Desert Sun,* p. A-3.

Hamm, M. S. (1993). *American skinheads: The criminology and control of hate crime.* Cincinnati, OH: Anderson.

Hebdige, D. (1979). *Subculture: The meaning of style.* London: Methuen.

Hyde, H.F.F.H.F. (2000). Retrieved from the World Wide Web: http://www.hammerskins.com/press/whatmakes.html

Levin, J., & McDevitt, J. (1993). *Hate crimes: The rising tide of bigotry and bloodshed.* New York: Plenum.

Messerschmidt, J. (1993). *Masculinities and crime.* Lanahm, MD: Rowman and Littlefield.

Messner, S. F., & Rosenfeld, R. (1994). *Crime and the American dream.* Belmont, CA: Wadsworth.

Passas, N., & Agnew, R. (1997). *The future of anomie theory.* Boston: Northeastern University.

Southern Poverty Law Center. (2000a, Winter). Bombs, bullets, bodies: The decade in review. *Intelligence Report, 97.*

Southern Poverty Law Center. (2000b, Winter). The year in hate. *Intelligence Report, 97.*

Wooden, W., & Blazak, R. (2000). *Renegade kids, suburban outlaws.* Belmont, CA: Wadsworth.

STUDY QUESTIONS

1. Which persons are most susceptible to becoming skinheads?
2. What techniques are employed to recruit and turn out these terrorists?

AUSTIN T. TURK

Sociology of Terrorism

Introduction

Sociologists had until September 11, 2001, shown little interest in terrorism. Although conflict analysis, in one form or another, is a long established approach in the field, researchers have focused mostly on class and labor struggles, race relations, criminalization and other deviance-labeling, and the collective violence of riots and revolutions. Nonetheless, sociological concepts and methods have been fruitfully applied (albeit mostly by nonsociologists) in efforts to understand and counter terrorism. The aim of this review is to note what has been learned in order to suggest agendas for future research on the dynamics through which terrorism becomes a social phenomenon.

The Social Construction of Terrorism

Probably the most significant contribution of sociological thinking to our understanding of terrorism is the realization that it is a social construction (Ben-Yehuda 1993, Turk 2002a). Contrary to the impression fostered by official incidence counts and media reports, terrorism is not a given in the real world but is instead an interpretation of events and their presumed causes. And these interpretations are not unbiased attempts to depict truth but rather conscious efforts to manipulate perceptions to promote certain interests at the expense of others. When people and events come to be regularly described in public as terrorists and terrorism, some governmental or other entity is succeeding in a war of words in which the opponent is promoting alternative designations such as "martyr" and "liberation struggle." . . .

The United States has a long history of violence associated with political, labor, racial, religious, and other social and cultural conflicts (Gurr 1989). Assassinations, bombings, massacres, and other secretive deadly attacks have caused many thousands of casualties. Yet, few incidents have been defined as terrorism or the perpetrators as terrorists. Instead, authorities have typically ignored or downplayed the political significance of such violence, opting to portray and treat the violence as apolitical criminal acts by deranged or evil individuals, outlaws or gangsters, or "imported" agitators such as the radical Molly Maguires of Pennsylvania's coal miners' struggles. Although violent acts believed to be politically motivated are assigned the highest investigative priority, those accused are rarely charged with terrorism (Smith 1994, p. 7). In official public usage, terrorism is far more likely to refer to incidents associated with agents and supporters of presumably foreign-based terrorist organizations such as al Qaeda than with the violence of home-grown militants acting in the name of such groups as the Animal Liberation Front, Earth First!, or the American Coalition for Life Activists (one of whose founders, Paul Hill, was executed in Florida on September 3, 2003, for murder, not terrorism).

In sum, to study terrorism presupposes investigating the ways in which parties in conflict are trying to stigmatize one another. The construction and selective application of definitions of terrorism are embedded in the dynamics of political conflicts, where ideological warfare to cast the enemy as an evildoer is a dimension of the struggle to win support for one's own cause.

Terrorism as Political Violence

Differing sociological perspectives encourage contrasting views of political violence. Insofar as functionalism assumes that order and peace are normal, violence is an aberration, a presumably temporary deviation from the normal state of human social life. Even archaic versions of functionalism (e.g., Germanic "combat theories") arguing that war is necessary to sustain national identity and strength do not imply acceptance of nongovernmental violence, especially assaults on public order and authority, as other than deviant behavior. More liberal and critical theories tend to posit that violence is an understandable response to oppression and exploitation, the last resort of the deprived and desperate. Whether reflecting anarchist objections to regimentation, communist or socialist critiques of capitalism, or simply liberal objections to excessive "possessive individualism," critical theories presume that political and/or economic inequalities are the sources of collective violence.

While acknowledging that social inequities may be causally involved, particularly in originating conflicts, analytical or "structural" conflict theories (Collins 1975) attend more to the possibility that violence may be a product of strategic and tactical decisions in a process of ongoing conflict. That interests or values may not be reconcilable is accepted, as is the proposition that various forms of violent action may be political options within the perceptual range of parties in conflict.

It is increasingly clear that terrorism is most usefully defined, for empirical research purposes, as the deliberate targeting of more or less randomly selected victims whose deaths and injuries are expected to weaken the opponent's will to persist in a political conflict (Turk 2002b). Terrorist acts are political, rarely involving psychopathology or material deprivation. Indeed, the evidence is mounting that terrorism is associated with relative affluence and social advantage rather than poverty, lack of education, or other indicators of deprivation. The typical terrorist comes from a relatively well-off part of the world, and appears to be motivated by political-ideological resentments rather than economic distress. Suicide bombers, for instance, appear increasingly likely to be respected individuals from advantaged classes, with stable family and community ties. Although their violent deaths may surprise relatives and friends, they are far more likely to be honored than to be condemned or stigmatized as somehow deviant. . . .

Traditional notions about violence are misleading insofar as they lead terrorism researchers to focus on psychopathologies (see, for example, Robins & Post 1997) or material disadvantage instead of the political contexts in which terrorist acts occur. A priority for research is to connect the emergence of terrorism to the political histories of the settings in which people come to see it as an option in their struggles over who will have what life chances. Recognizing that terrorism is the product of a blending of demographic, economic, and political determinants, a panel of the National Research Council (Smelser & Mitchell 2002) observed that regions most likely to generate terrorist threats have a history of colonialist exploitation by Western interests, and more recently of postcolonial economic and cultural penetration. These facts have facilitated identification of the West as the source of global economic and political disadvantage, military weakness, and cultural malaise, which provides a credible focus for resentment and moral outrage in the recruitment of terrorists and the mobilization of supporters and sympathizers.

Terrorism as Communication

The considerable and growing literature on the role of the media in framing images of criminality readily extends to terrorism (Jenkins 2003). Since the nineteenth century caricatures of anarchists in newspapers (deranged, bearded bombers), the established media have encouraged the belief that political violence in opposition to authority is both criminal and crazy. Assassins are widely portrayed as lone disturbed persons whose murderous acts are attributable to their individual pathologies, the consequences of loveless lives and frustrated ambitions (see Turk 2002a). Suicidal attacks are similarly pictured as the irrational or obviously misguided acts of uninformed people driven by despair or fanaticism.

Even when some recognition is given to the possibility that grievances may arise from real injustices, reportage in mainstream outlets tends to accentuate the theme that grievances never justify violence. The consistent message is that violence expresses hate, which only leads to reciprocal violence in destructive escalations of hostilities. Who is blamed for ongoing terrorist violence depends on which media one examines. For example, Western, especially American, media reports generally blame Palestinians and their supporters for the ongoing violence between Arabs and Israelis, whereas non-Western media reports in outlets such as al Jazeera generally blame Israel and supporters—especially the United States.

Certainly alternative views are more often expressed in outlets independent of the politics and economics of mainstream, especially Western, media competition. Sympathetic comments accepting terrorism as an understandable, perhaps even legitimate, form of defense and protest against oppression and threat are more likely to appear in radical, underground, or non-Western communications.

Whether alternative descriptions and interpretations of terrorists and terrorism should be disseminated is a major issue in debates over counterterrorism policies. Reminiscent of the idea that collective violence (food riots, strikes, ethnic and racial clashes, etc.) signals authorities that something is amiss, terrorism has been analyzed as a communication through violence that problems exist (Schmid & de Graaf 1982). The usual assumption is that peaceful methods of seeking the redress of grievances have failed, so that violence is left as the only way in which to force attention to the aggrieved.

Governmental and other organizational authorities are predisposed to minimize the risks of either public sympathy for terrorists or public fear of terrorism. Accordingly, the inclination in counterterrorism policymaking is to deny legitimacy to oppositional violence and to discourage the media from granting too public a voice to those who resort to or sympathize with terrorism. A complicating factor is that a satiation effect has been noted as a contributor to terrorism, in that acts of terrorism must be ever more horrendous in order to overcome the tendency for newsmakers and their publics to become inured to "ordinary" violence. . . .

Organizing Terrorism

Most of what is known about terrorist organizations is now outdated. Even distinctions such as "international" and "domestic" terrorism are decreasingly meaningful because technological advances (electronic communications, transportation networks) and corporate globalization facilitate more complex and flexible ways to organize terrorist activities, frequently involving cooperation among various "international" and "domestic" parties.

The classic model of the terrorist organization is a tightly organized hierarchy comprised of small, isolated cells whose members have little if any knowledge of planning and organization above and outside their cell. They are disciplined by a blend of social isolation from all outsiders (especially family and former friends), blackmail after crimes demonstrating their commitment, physical threat, and indoctrination without access to other sources of ideas and information. The aims of such organizations have historically been relatively simple: to overthrow an oppressive regime or system or to drive an alien force from their land. The financial resources needed to sustain terrorist organizations were obtained from donations by sympathizers and sometimes supplemented by criminal acts (e.g., kidnapping for ransom, bank robbery, or protection racketeering).

As the last century ran its course, the motives and organization of terrorism became less simple and local. Nationalist and material concerns receded (though still significant in particular times and places, as in the Balkan conflicts ignited by Serbian ethnic cleansing), while ideological, especially religious, and wider geopolitical concerns were in the ascendant (e.g., the India-Pakistan conflict over Kashmir). Most recently, religious fundamentalism (Juergensmeyer 2000) has propelled the recruitment and organization of multitudes into loose networks of terrorist groups acting more or less on their own with encouragement and logistical assistance from facilitators with resources (on the global level most notably Osama bin Laden and Al Qaeda, along with various Middle Eastern entities). Funds are increasingly provided by a wide range of legitimate business operations and donations to "independent" charitable organizations, and channeled through legitimate financial institutions. . . .

Because terrorism is increasingly organized in networks, and in some places committed by lone individuals, conventional organizational analysis offers little promise; models developed through network analyses are obviously needed. Most such work has so far been operational, with little produced beyond descriptive accounts focused on the identification of connections among persons and institutions believed by governmental agencies to be committing or facilitating terrorism, and on the frequency and distribution of terrorist incidents. Explaining as well as tracking the financial and logistical support for terrorism appears to be the most promising focus for social network researchers. Whatever approach is used, to make a contribution sociologists must get past operational to analytical (more clearly generalizable and explanatory) models of the nature and dynamics of the organizing of terrorism.

Socializing Terrorists

High on the research agenda is understanding why and how individuals become terrorists. Although some earlier commentators argued that political criminals were either deranged or lacking proper "moral socialization," it is now well established that opposition to authority or a particular social order is more likely to stem from a reasoned position than from pathology or deficient socialization. As indicated above, reasoning in cosmological, religious terms is increasingly characteristic of the rationales by which terrorists justify their acts to themselves and others.

People learn to accept terrorism as a political option when their experiences lead them to see truth in messages that defending their way and kind cannot be accomplished by nonviolent means. In democratic societies political radicals usually come from relatively advantaged sectors and go through a sequence beginning with conventional political activism (Turk 1982, pp. 81–108). The more educated and affluent their backgrounds, the more impatient they are likely to be with the inevitable disappointments of political life—where one rarely gets all that is envisioned. Socialized to be knowledgeable about the gaps between ideals and realities and to see themselves as significant participants in political struggles, higher class young people (especially from liberal or otherwise contrarian families and communities) are more likely than their less advantaged counterparts to become involved in a process of radicalization moving toward violence. Although social banditry and peasant uprisings may challenge social orders, organized terrorism is by far most likely to originate in the alienation and analytics of higher status younger people. Whether the Weather Underground of Vietnam-era America or the Al Qaeda network of today, initiating and committing terrorist acts is nearly always the work of radicalized younger persons with the intellectual and financial resources, and the ideological drive, to justify (at least to themselves) and enable adopting the violence option.

However, although liberal family and educational backgrounds may encourage an openness to violence as a political option, few even of the most militant radicals become terrorists. Those who do appear to have undergone something of a conversion experience in making the transition from a willingness to "trash" public property and fight riot police, to a readiness to murder specific politically significant persons (e.g., governmental or corporate leaders, police officers, or soldiers), and then to the random targeting of populations including noncombatants as well as combatants.

Exposure to ideologies justifying terrorism appears to be a crucial ingredient in the mix of personal and vicarious learning experiences leading to a commitment to terrorism. Before bombing the Murrah federal office building in Oklahoma City (killing 168 men, women, and children), Timothy McVeigh immersed himself in the writings of William Pierce (author of *Hunter* and *The Turner Diaries*). Pierce detailed his vision of how brave heroes resist the imminent threat to the white race and America posed by Jews, blacks, and other minorities. McVeigh, encouraged by his coterrorist Terry McNichols and probably others, was so impressed that he visited Elohim City, a white supremacist bastion, and sold or gave away copies of *The Turner Diaries* at gun shows (Hamm 1997). McVeigh's military background, including distinguished service in the Gulf War, undoubtedly played a role in his self-definition as a soldier who had merely inflicted "collateral damage" in performing his duty.

One may hypothesize that self-education to terrorism is less likely in societies where personal mobility and access to intellectual resources are more limited. Islamist fundamentalism, in particular, seems to depend on radicalization through formal education consisting mostly of religious indoctrination. In madrassas throughout the world, potential recruits to organized terorism are drilled in the most extreme interpretations of Sunni theology, emphasizing the duty to engage in holy war (jihad) against all enemies of the true Islam. The most spectacular product of the madrassas so far is the Taliban ("students of religion") of Afghanistan, who until overthrown by the United States and allied troops in 2001 provided a base for al Qaeda, and who still threaten all who do not accept their archaic and rigid version of an Islamic society (Kushner 2003, pp. 357–59).

Once underway, campaigns of terrorism and related political violence tend to gain momentum. Inspired by the ideological messages, the charisma of leaders, the potential for material or status gains, or whatever else attracts them, others are likely to join. Particularly in nondemocratic societies, conflicts are likely to proceed along fault lines reflecting class, ethnic, racial, or religious divisions. If such conflicts persist, years of reciprocal violence tend to result in its institutionalization, so that individuals caught up in the conflict may have no real comprehension of why they go on attacking one another—the classic feud. The bloody years-long slaughter of whole villages of "conservatives" by "liberals," and vice versa, in Colombia's *la violencia* is a chilling historic example (Fals Borda 1969). In such contexts, explaining why people become terrorists is relatively straightforward: They see themselves as having to fight for "us" against "them."

The key to explaining the socialization of terrorists is understanding how specific individuals are brought to the point where they see themselves as bearers of the responsibility for violent actions. Education, training, socialization—deliberate or not—may encourage the development of a self-concept as one who must fight against the threat to "us." However, little has been learned so far about how eventual terrorists are selected in the course of their political socialization.

It is woefully unhelpful merely to point to religious schools as "facto-ries" producing terrorists, or to assume that only the foolish or aberrant become terrorists, or to blame terrorists as evil souls or acclaim them as heroic fighters. Researchers have to be much more aware of the impact of media and political-ideological influences on the definition and characterization of terrorists if their life courses are to be understood.

Social Control of Terrorism

Efforts to understand terrorism have generally been incidental or sec-ondary to efforts to control it. By definition, the goal of operational studies is to provide authorities with information needed to prevent terrorist attacks and to neutralize terrorists. Operational research nec-essarily, then, prioritizes immediately applicable results rather than theoretical knowledge whose applicability is problematic. It follows that debates over the respective merits of counterterrorism options revolve around the weighing of legal against military options, the political risks associated with different options, the levels of threat associated with current and potential enemies, and the ability of control agencies to implement policy decisions. Regardless of specific issues and situa-tions, decisions are heavily influenced by calculations of how control actions may strengthen or weaken the chances of retaining power.

Nationally and internationally, legal systems and procedures have been developed without anticipating the contingencies involved in dealing with modern terrorism. For the first time in history, terrorists are gaining access to weapons of mass destruction. Credible threats of worldwide terrorist campaigns are now regularly documented, attacks and attempts in various countries are frequently reported, and multina-tion cooperation in countering terrorism is a growing reality. Political pressures to lessen legal restraints on police, and military responses to terrorism have resulted in the, possibly temporary, erosion in the United States and elsewhere of legal protections against intrusive and secret surveillance, arbitrary detention, and hurtful interrogation meth-ods, as well as assassination and extralegal executions.

When President George W. Bush declared a war on terrorism immediately following the catastrophic attack of September 11, 2001, not only most Americans but also governments and millions of peo-ple throughout the world agreed that international terrorism had to be stopped. But it has become obvious that "the devil is in the details." The extraordinary threat of modern terrorism has been mirrored by extraordinary counter measures. For example, the U.S. government adopted two fateful policies. The first was the decision to dilute or abrogate established legal restraints on governmental power. The second was the decision to invade Iraq without United Nations legitimation. . . .

The decision to launch an essentially unilateral invasion of Iraq was a huge departure from generally and increasingly accepted (outside the United States) international norms for reviewing interstate grievances and providing for a collective (Security Council) decision authorizing military action against a sovereign government. The long effort to subject national sovereignties to international legal restrictions (Jones 2002) has surely been set back by the globalization of terrorist and counterterrorist operations. With a war proclaimed, the military option is being emphasized over the legal option in attempting to control terrorism (Smith et al. 2002, Turk 2002c).

As the world's superpower, the United States has weighed and accepted the political costs of ignoring the United Nations, many international and American legalists, and other voices questioning the unilateral adoption of the military option. The prevailing assumption is that the threat is beyond the control capacities of established legal systems and procedures. Regard for legalities has been subordinated to concerns with assessing levels of threat and with the demonstrated shortcomings of intelligence agencies in making and responding to such assessments. Numerous other governments have joined the United States in expanding investigative and enforcement powers against terrorism, at the expense of democratic governance and declining investments in public services (Haque 2002). The politically dominant approach is to persuade the general public to accept the necessity of militarizing and delegalizing the effort to counter terrorism. Post-invasion developments in Afghanistan and Iraq, and continuing attacks in those countries and elsewhere, have led to increasingly acrimonious debates over the effectiveness of investing so disproportionately in the military option. As long as the terrorism war rages, we should expect, given the history of political conflict in wartime and periods of civil turmoil, that the military option will continue to be given priority over the legal option, and that expansion of legal powers will continue at some cost in civil liberties. The citizens of democratic societies are unlikely ever to see again the freedoms from governmental surveillance that existed in earlier times (Marx 1988, Staples 1997). . . .

Theorizing Terrorism

Developing a sociological explanation of terrorism is a politically and intellectually formidable task. Political obstacles abound: Officials are inclined to be wary of outsiders with independent agendas and resources. Policymakers and control agencies prefer operational findings clearly applicable to targeting and neutralizing defined enemies. Funding priorities are affected by rivalries within and among intelligence and enforcement agencies, as well as competition for budgetary influence among politicians, lobbyists, and other interested parties such as grant applicants, whose concerns seldom include basic research. The organizational penchant for keeping records confidential is heightened in agencies charged with controlling terrorism. Such political constraints exacerbate the intellectual problems encountered in terrorism research.

Gurr (1985) is one of the first to have explicated methodological options in studying terrorism and indicated which kinds of research questions are appropriate to each method. Theoretically significant levels of analysis are posited: global, national, group, incident, and individual. Gurr argues cogently for "question first" (i.e., theory-driven) research that treats terrorist groups and incidents, for example, as "independent" rather than "dependent" variables, focusing on their causation rather than their traits and consequences. The crucial need for relevant datasets is emphasized, as is the necessity for their availability to researchers "insulated from direct involvement in policy-making or operations" (Gurr 1985, p. 34).

Regardless of whether official or independent datasets are constructed, transforming information about terrorism into measures of conceptually meaningful variables is clearly a daunting task. . . .

The intellectually ambitious and stimulating research on terrorism from a world systems perspective (Bergesen & Lizardo 2002) begins with the premise that the passage of time makes structural analysis more applicable than participant analysis. As time passes, the appropriate level of analysis moves from (a) the individual to (b) group and social movement, (c) nation and state, (d) the present historical period, (e) a past historical analogy, and finally (f) longer historical cycles. At this ultimate level of analysis, terrorism is to be explained in terms of cyclical rhythms in which waves of terrorist activity are associated with cycles of political–economic deterioration and replacement by new forms of political order. As the previous global order breaks down, semiperipheral areas are drawn into a process of modernization characterized by conflict in the absence of a unifying hegemonic power (core). Perforce, once peripheral areas are caught up in the dynamics of political (re)organization, "the first signs of strain in the semiperipheral zones are those of terrorism and pan-religious/ethnic ideological movements" (Bergesen & Lizardo 2002, p. 17). Bergesen & Lizardo (2002) raise the question of whether the current wave of terrorism signals the beginning of a global restructuring that will end the hegemony of the United States. . . .

However one approaches the sociological study of terrorism, the distinctive objective is to develop an explanation of its causation, the dynamics of its escalation and de-escalation in relation to other forms of political violence, and its impact on the stability and change of social orders. Turk (2002d) has outlined a scheme for analyzing the social dynamics involved in the progression from coercive, to injurious, to destructive violence—the most extreme of which is terrorism. The main hypothesis is that terrorism is the culmination of a conflict process that predictably, having reached this extreme, ends in either the annihilation of one party or mutual exhaustion. Assuming that they must somehow continue to live in proximity and interdependence, survivors have to begin anew the search for a viable relationship. Whether "cosmic wars" can stop short of the extermination of one or both sides, and be ended by acceptance of the need to recognize one another's right to exist, has still to be determined.

REFERENCES

Adams J. 1986. *The Financing of Terror*. New York: Simon & Schuster.

Ben-Yehuda N. 1993. *Political Assassinations by Jews*. Albany: State Univ. New York Press.

Bergesen AJ, Lizardo OA. 2002. Terrorism and world-system theory. In *Transnational Terrorism in the World System Perspective*, ed. R Stemplowski, pp. 9–22. Warsaw: The Polish Inst. Int. Aff.

Collins R. 1975. *Conflict Sociology: Toward an Explanatory Science*. New York: Academic.

Fals Borda O. 1969. *Subversion and Social Change in Colombia*. New York: Columbia Univ. Press.

Gurr TR. 1985. *Methodologies and data for the analysis of oppositional terrorism*. Presented at the Symp. Int. Terror. Def. Intell. Coll., Dec., Washington, DC.

Gurr TR, ed. 1989. *Violence in America*, Vols. 1, 2. Newbury Park, CA: Sage.

Hamm MS. 1997. *Apocalypse in Oklahoma: Waco and Ruby Ridge Revenged*. Boston, MA: Northeastern Univ. Press.

Haque MS. 2002. Government responses to terrorism: critical views of their impacts on people and public administration. *Pub. Admin. Rev.* 62 (September):170–80.

Jenkins P. 2003. *Images of Terror: What We Can and Can't Know about Terrorism*. New York: Aldine de Gruyter.

Jones DV. 2002. *Toward a Just World: The Critical Years in the Search for International Justice*. Chicago, IL: Univ. Chicago Press.

Kushner HW. 2003. *Encyclopedia of Terrorism*. Thousand Oaks, CA: Sage.

Marx G. 1988. *Undercover: Police Surveillance in America*. Berkeley: Univ. Calif. Press.

Robins RS, Post JM. 1997. *Political Paranoia: The Psychopolitics of Hatred*. New Haven, CT: Yale Univ. Press.

Schmid A, de Graaf J. 1982. *Violence as Communication*. Beverly Hills, CA: Sage.

Smelser NJ, Mitchell F. ed. 2002. *Terrorism: Perspectives from the Behavioral and Social Sciences.* Washington, DC: The Natl. Acad. Press.

Smith B. 1994. *Terrorism in America: Pipe Bombs and Pipe Dreams.* Albany: State Univ. New York Press.

Staples WG. 1997. *The Culture of Surveillance: Discipline and Social Control in the United States.* New York: St. Martin's.

Turk AT. 1982. *Political Criminality: The Defiance and Defense of Authority.* Beverly Hills, CA: Sage.

Turk AT. 2002a. Assassination. In *Encyclopedia of Crime and Justice,* ed. J Dressler, 1:776–81. New York: Macmillan. 2nd ed.

Turk AT. 2002b. Terrorism. In *Encyclopedia of Crime and Justice,* ed. J Dressler, 4:1549–56. New York: Macmillan. 2nd ed.

STUDY QUESTIONS

1. Identify and write a brief summary of each of the seven sociological issues in terrorism.

2. What role do religion and politics play in the creation of terrorism?

503

504

West: *Different Cultures, Different Harems* by Fatema Mernissi, pp. 208–220. Copyright © 2001 by Fatema Mernissi. Reprinted with permission of Washington Square Press, a Division of Simon & Schuster, Inc.

DeAnne K. Gauthier and Craig J. Forsyth, from "Buckle Bunnies: Groupies of the Rodeo Circuit," *Deviant Behavior* 21, pp. 349–365. Copyright © 2000, reprinted by permission of Taylor & Francis, Inc., http://www.routledge-ny.com.

A. Ayres Boswell and Joan Z. Spade, "Fraternities and Collegiate Rape Culture: Why Are Some Fraternities More Dangerous Places for Women?" *Gender and Society*, 10, April, pp. 133–147. Copyright © 1996 by Sage Publications. Reprinted by permission of Sage Publications.

D. L. Rosenhan, excerpted with permission from "On Being Sane in Insane Places," *Science* 179, January, pp. 250–258. Copyright © 1973 AAAS.

Stephan J. Goetz and Hema Swaminathan, "Wal-Mart and County-Wide Poverty" from *Social Science Quarterly*, Vol. 87, No. 2, June 2006, pp. 211–225. Copyright © 2006 Southwestern Social Science Association. Reprinted by permission of Blackwell Publishing and the author.

Stephen Haseler, from *The Super-Rich*, pp. 1–26. Copyright © 2000 by Stephen Haseler. Reproduced with permission of Palgrave Macmillan.

John R. Coleman, from *Blue Collar Journal: A College President's Sabbatical* (pp. 7–31, 252). Philadelphia: Lippincott, 1974. Reprinted by permission of the author.

Cornel West, from *Race Matters*. Copyright © 1993, 2001 by Cornel West. Reprinted by permission of Beacon Press, Boston.

Pierrette Hondagneu-Sotelo, "Maid in L.A." from *Domestica: Immigrant Workers Cleaning and Caring in the Shadows of Affluence*, pp. 29–37, 252–255. Copyright © 2001 by the University of California Press. Reprinted by permission of The University of California Press and the author.

Erika Vora and Jay A. Vora, from "Undoing Racism in America: Help from a Black Church," *Journal of Black Studies*, 32(4), pp. 389–404. Copyright © 2002 by Sage Publications. Reprinted by permission of Sage Publications.

Judith Lorber, from *Paradoxes of Gender* (pp. 13–36). Copyright © 1994 by Yale University Press. Reprinted by permission.

Simon Davis, "Men as Success Objects and Women as Sex Objects: A Study of Personal Advertisements," *Sex Roles*, 23, pp. 43–50. Copyright © 1990 Plenum Publishing Corporation. Reprinted by permission of Kluwer Academic/Plenum Publishers.

Beth A. Quinn, from "Sexual Harassment and Masculinity: The Power and Meaning of 'Girl Watching,'" *Gender and Society*, 16(3), pp. 386–402. Copyright © 2002 Sage Publications. Reprinted by permission of Sage Publications.

Susan L. Brown, from "Relationship Quality Dynamics of Cohabiting Unions," *Journal of Family Issues*, 24(5), July, pp. 583–601. Copyright © 2003 by Sage Publications. Reprinted by permission of Sage Publications.

Pepper Schwartz, from *Peer Marriage: How Love Between Equals Works*. Reprinted and edited with the permission of The Free Press, a Division of Simon & Schuster Adult Publishing Group. Copyright © 1994 by Pepper Schwartz. All rights reserved.

Dalton Conley, from *The Pecking Order*. Copyright © 2004 by Dalton Conley. Used by permission of Pantheon Books, a division of Random House, Inc.

Don E. Merton, from "The Meaning of Meanness: Popularity, Competition, and Conflict among Junior High School Girls," *Sociology of Education*, 70, July 1997, pp. 175–191. Reprinted by permission of the American Sociological Association and Don E. Merton.

Mary Crow Dog and Richard Erdoes, from *Lakota Woman* (pp. 28–41). Copyright © 1990 by Mary Crow Dog and Richard Erdoes. Used by permission of Grove/Atlantic, Inc.

Theresa Krebs, from "Church Structures that Facilitate Pedophilia among Roman Catholic Clergy," in Anson Shupe (ed.), *Wolves Within the Fold: Religious Leadership and Abuses of Power* (pp. 15–32). New Brunswick, NJ: Rutgers, 1998. Reprinted by permission of Theresa Krebs.

C. Wright Mills, from *The Power Elite, New Edition*. Copyright © 1956, 2000 by Oxford University Press, Inc. Used by permission of Oxford University Press.

Charles Koeber, from "Corporate Restructuring, Downsizing, and the Middle Class: The Process and Meaning of Worker Displacement in the 'New' Economy," *Qualitative Sociology*, 25(2), pp. 217–246.

Additional Titles of Interest

Nicholas Abercrombie, Stephen Hill, and Bryan S. Turner, *The Penguin Dictionary of Sociology*, Fifth Edition

Stephanie Coontz, *Marriage, a History: From Obedience to Intimacy*

Stephanie Coontz, *Marriage, a History: How Love Conquered Marriage*

Jared Diamond, *Collapse: How Societies Choose to Fail or Succeed*

W. E. B. Du Bois, *The Souls of Black Folk*

Emile Durkheim, *On Suicide*

Karl Marx, *The Communist Manifesto*

Karl Marx, *The Portable Karl Marx*

John Stuart Mill, *On Liberty*

Friedrich Nietzsche, *A Nietzsche Reader*

Mike Rose, *Lives on the Boundries*

Jean-Jaques Rousseau, *The Social Contract*

Joni Seager, *The State of Women in the World Atlas*

Maz Weber, *The Protestant Ethic and the Spirit of Capitalism*

Gregory Howard Williams, *Life on the Color Line: The True Story of a White Boy Who Discovered He Was Black*

Juan Williams, *Eyes on the Prize*